Census of the Sioux and Cheyenne Indians
Of Pine Ridge Agency, South Dakota.
1896

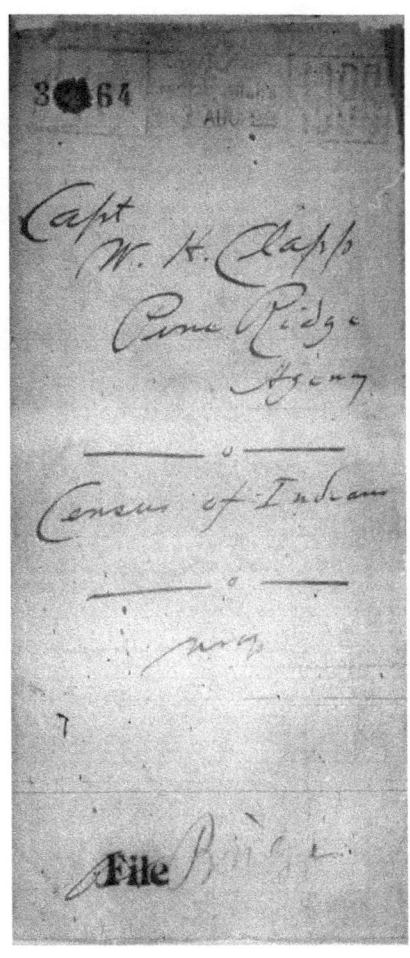

RECAPITULATION.

---oOo---

Districts.	Males.		Females.		Total.	School Age.
	Over 18	Under 18	Over 14	Under 14		
Wakpamini	270	222	353	187	1032	273
White Clay	369	275	452	214	1310	325
Porcupine	210	180	278	174	842	210
Wounded Knee	371	291	470	263	1395	459
Medicine Root	245	211	357	178	991	257
Pass Creek	230	213	285	183	911	248.
	1695	1392	2195	1199	6481	1772.

Census of the Sioux And Cheyenne Indians
Of Pine Ridge Agency, South Dakota.
June 30, 1896

Wakpamini District

Census Of The Sioux And Cheyenne Indians Of Pine Ridge Agency, South Dakota. Taken by W. H. Clapp, Captain 16th Infantry, Acting United States Indian Agent, June 30, 1896. (Wakpamini District)

Key: Number; Indian Name *(if given)*; English Name; Sex; Relation; Age

1 Jennie Whalen; F; Mother; 44
2 Rosa Whalen; F; Dau; 25
3 Julia Whalen; F; Dau; 21
4 Nellie Whalen; F; Dau; 17
5 James Whalen; M; Son; 15
6 Jennie Whalen; F; Dau; 12
7 Mary Whalen; F; Dau; 10
8 Richard Whalen; M; Son; 5

9 Winyan Sica; Bad Looking Woman; F; 83

10 E. G. Bettelyoun; M; Father; 26
11 Josephine Bettelyoun; F; Wife; 25
12 Isaac Bettelyoun; M; Son; 3-7
13 Lucy Janis; F; Niece; 13
14 Harwood Bettelyoun; M; Son; 1

15 Mato Hinsma; Hairy Bear; M; Father; 68
16 Winorcala Sica; Bad Old Woman; F; Wife 61
17 Gliyopsica; Jumps Off; M; Son; 24

18 Waslipa; Licks; M; Father; 67
19 Wiciyela Win; Yankton Woman; F; Wife; 65
20 Zintkala Wimbli; Eagle Bird; M; Son; 20
21 Winyan Tanka; Big Woman; F; Dau; 15

22 Peter Shangreau; M; Father; 36
23 Lucy Shangreau; F; Wife; 26
24 Antonio Shangreau; M; Son; 12
25 Rosa Shangreau; F; Dau; 13
26 Jessie Shangreau; F; Dau; 7
27 Sarah Shangreau; F; Dau; 4
28 Angeline Shangreau; F; Dau; 1-4

29 Akicita Najin; Standing Soldier #1; M; Father; 45
30 Akicita Najin; Katie Standing Soldier; F; Wife 46
31 Akicita Najin; Philip Standing Soldier; M; Son; 19
32 Akicita Najin; Henry Standing Soldier; M; Son; 14
33 Akicita Najin; Mary Standing Soldier; F; Dau; 12
34 Akicita Najin; Dinah Standing Soldier; F; Dau; 9
35 Akicita Najin; Victoria S. Standing Soldier; F; Dau; 3-6

36 James D. Janis; M; Father 39
37 Mollie Janis; F; Wife; 41
38 Minnie Janis; F; Dau; 7
39 Louise Janis; F; Dau; 4-6
40 Julia Janie; F; Dau; 0-6

41 Wankal Iyanka; Runs Above; M; Father; 49
42 Marpiya Hinapa; Cloud Come Out; F; Wife; 49
43 Caje Wanica; No Name; M; Son; 13
44 Nakipa; Runs Away; M; Son; 13
45 Tok Kute; Shoots Enemy; M; F. in L. 69

46 Rapya Mani; Noisy Walks; M; Father; 34
47 Petaga; Fire; F; Wife; 26
48 Okicize Tawa; Owns The Fight; M; Son; 8
49 Ptesan Hoksila; White Cow Boy; M; Son; 5
50 Rapya Mani, Lena Noisy Walk; F; Dau; 0-8

51 Tasunke Maza; Iron Horse; M; Father; 46
52 Nata; The Head; F; Wife; 34
53 Wicegna Glicu; Comes From Amongst; F; Dau; 15

5

Census Of The Sioux And Cheyenne Indians Of Pine Ridge Agency, South Dakota. Taken by W. H. Clapp, Captain 16th Infantry, Acting United States Indian Agent, June 30, 1896. (Wakpamini District)

Key: Number; Indian Name *(if given)*; English Name; Sex; Relation; Age

54 Nakpogi; Brown Ears; F; Dau; 12
55 Ehake Gli; Comes Last; F; Dau; 4-6
56 Taninyan Mani; Walks In Sight; F; Dau; 0-6
57 Sungmanitu Ska; White Wolf; M; Father; 51
58 Sungmanitu Ska; WM. White Wolf; M; Son; 24
59 Wamniomni; Whirlwind; F; Dau; 14
60 Pankeska Win; Shell Woman; F; Dau; 8
61 Sungmanitu Ska; Georgianna W. Wolf; F; Dau; 6
62 Oye Luta; Red Track; F; 78
63 Nacaka; Chief #1; M; Father; 33
64 Nacaka; Susie Chief; F; Wife; 34
65 Marpiya Isnala; Lone Cloud; M; Son; 14
66 Sunkitacan Agli; Brings Chief Horse; F; Dau; 7
67 Sunkgliyoki; Comes After Horses; M; Son; 2-6
68 Nacaka; Mollie Chief; F; Dau; 0-4
69 Miwakan Yula; George Sword; M; Father; 49
70 Miwakan Yula; Lucy Sword; F; Wife; 30
71 Jessie Sword; F; Dau; 8
72 Archie White; M; Nephew; 21
73 Mastincala Ska; White Rabbit; M; Father; 59
74 Witko Winla; Crazy Woman; F; Wife; 48
75 Hinrota; Roan; M; Son; 24
76 Anpo Wicakte; Kills In Morning; F; Dau; 23
77 Mastincala Ska; Julia White Rabbit; F; Dau; 18
78 Mastincala Ska; Annie White Rabbit; F; Dau; 15
79 Kutepi; Shoots At Him; M; Son; 13
80 Peji Rota Win; Grey Grass Woman; F; Dau; 3-4
81 Mato Kokipapi; Afraid Of Bear; M; Father; 54
82 Mato Kokipapi; Robert Afraid Of Bear; M; Son; 19
83 Mato Kokipapi; Lucy Afraid Of Bear; F; Dau; 13
84 Tucuhu; Ribs; M; Father; 38
85 Ipiyaka Cola; No Belt; F; Wife; 39
86 Oksantan Kte; Kills Around; M; Son; 11
87 Cetan, Hawk; M; Son; 7
88 Kiyela; Close; M; S.Son; 21
89 Tasunke Luzahan; Fast Horse; M; Father; 45
90 Wamniomni; Whirlwind; F; Wife; 42
91 Tasunke Luzahan; Julia Fast Horse; F; Dau; 13
92 Kicopi; Calls Them; F; Dau; 11
93 Tok Kute; Shoots Enemy; M; Son; 8
94 Yuha; Keeps; M; Son; 1-1
95 Gertie Janis; F; Mother; 38
96 Susie Janis; F; Dau; 4-6
97 Alice; F; Dau; 0-4
98 Charles Janis; M; Father; 44
99 Lives Well; F; Wife; 22
100 Susanna Janis; F; Dau; 18
101 Louis Janis; M; G.Son; 6
102 Henry Janis; M; G.Son; 2-4

Census Of The Sioux And Cheyenne Indians Of Pine Ridge Agency, South Dakota. Taken by W. H. Clapp, Captain 16th Infantry, Acting United States Indian Agent, June 30, 1896. (Wakpamini District)

Key: Number; Indian Name *(if given)*; English Name; Sex; Relation; Age

103 Getan Oranko; Quick Hawk; M; Father; 34
104 Maeto Hinopa; Bear Comes Out; F; Wife; 22
105 Nagwaka; Kicks; F; M. in L.; 54
106 Hiyohipi; Comes After Him; M; Son; 1-1
107 Sunka Ska; White Dog; M; 62

108 Mary Deon #1; F; Mother; 63
109 Sam Deon; M; Son; 24
110 William Deon; M; Son; 23
111 Cecilia Deon; F; Dau; 20
112 Sophia Deon; F; Dau; 19

113 Sungmanitu Ska; John White Wolf; M; Father; 25
114 Sungmanitu Ska; Alice White Wolf; F; Wife; 23
115 Ptesan Luta; Red White Cow; F; Dau; 1-10

116 Wambli Rota; Roan Eagle; M; Father; 33
117 Rapya Mani; Noisy Walk; F; Wife; 25
118 Wanopa Gli; Comes Wounded; M; Son; 12
119 Anpo Wakuwa; Charges In Morning; M; Son; 2-4
120 Zintkala Hinsma; Mrs. Hairy Bird #2; F; Mother; 59

121 Tiglake; Traveler; F; Mother; 40
122 Cecilia Armstrong; F; Dau; 13
123 Wambli Nopa; Julia Two Elk; F; Dau; 0-4

124 Louise Allman; F; Mother; 39
125 Charles Allman; M; Son; 14
126 Sam Allman; M; Son; 11
127 Nora Allman; F; Dau; 9
128 Lily Allman; F; Dau; 16
129 Lydia Allman; F; dau; 5
130 Lorina Allman; F; Dau; 3

131 Alice Allman; F; Dau; 0-2

132 Julia Richard; F; 70

133 Pawiyakpa; Makes Shine; M; Father; 28
134 Anpetu Hinapa; Day Comes Out; F; Wife; 28
135 Tonweya; Scout; M; Son; 7
136 Ciyeku; Oldest Brother; M; Son; 4
137 Isna Wakuwa; Chase Alone; M; Son; 1-6

138 Zintkala Hinsma; Chas Bird; M; Father; 30
139 Jennie; F; Wife; 22
140 Rosa; F; Dau; 3-6
141 Paneska Win; Shell Woman; F; Mother; 58
142 Eugene; M; Brother; 16

143 Sunkgleska Win; Spotted Horse Woman; F; 67

144 Tasunke Wambli; Eagle Horse; M; Father; 41
145 Onpau Win; Elk Woman; F; Wife; 33
146 Sinte Sapa; Black Tail; M; Son; 16
147 Seven Up; M; Son; 10
148 Wasicu Wayankapi; Looks White; F; Dau; 5
149 Tasunke; Her Horse; F; Dau; 1-6
150 Itonkasan Kte; Kills White Weasel; M; Bro; 31
151 Anpo Watakpe; Charge In Morning; M; Bro; 23
152 David; M; Bro; 9

153 Sahunwinla Tanka; Big Cheyenne Woman; F; Mother; 65

Census Of The Sioux And Cheyenne Indians Of Pine Ridge Agency, South Dakota. Taken by W. H. Clapp, Captain 16th Infantry, Acting United States Indian Agent, June 30, 1896. (Wakpamini District)

Key: Number; Indian Name *(if given)*; English Name; Sex; Relation; Age

154	Wakan Wacipi; Medicine Dance; M; Son; 21
155	Pankeska Win; Shell Woman; F; G.Dau; 7
156	Cekpa; Twin; F; G.Dau; 7
157	Alice Pallardy; F; 49
158	Jennie Pugh; F; Mother; 26
159	Stanley R Pugh; M; Son; 6
160	William G Pugh; M; Son; 4
161	Victoria Adams; F; Mother; 76
162	Sunkowa; Painted Horse; M; Son; 48
163	Mato Lowan; Singing Bear; M; Father; 54
164	Wambli Sun; Eagle Feather; F; Wife; 64
165	Sunkhinsa Yuha; Red Horse Owner; M; Son; 6
166	Ptesan; White Cow; F; G.Dau; 9
167	Taopi Ota; Moses Plenty Wounds; M; Husb; 42
168	Hin Waste Win; Good Haired Woman; F; Wife; 29
169	Ska Agli; Brings White; F; Mother; 27
170	Wanaron; Hears; F; Dau; 5
171	Sunkska Win; White Horse Woman; F; 56
172	Joseph Mouseau; M; Father; 29
173	Nellie Mouseau; F; Wife; 27
174	Ellen Mouseau; F; Dau; 7
175	Maglor'd Mouseau; M; Son; 4-7
176	Joseph Mouseau, Jr; M; Son; 0-1-15[sic]
177	Sungmanitu Gi; Yellow Wolf; M; 66
178	Kangi Tanka; Big Crow; M; Father; 59
179	Mato Sina Ksupi; Bears Beaded Blanket; F; Wife; 57
180	Kangi Tanka; Ida Big Crow; F; Dau; 25
181	Kangi Tanka; Susie Big Crow; F; Dau; 23
182	Kangi Tanka; Mary Big Crow; F; Dau; 21
183	Kangi Tanka; Lucy Big Crow; F; Dau; 19
184	Takoleaku; Many Friends; M; G.Son; 3
185	Kansu; Kittie Card; F; 74
186	Sunkhinto; Blue Horse; M; Father; 75
187	Peta Omniciye; Council Fire; F; Wife; 66
188	Sunkhinto; Jennie Blue Horse; F; Dau; 25
189	Sunkhinto; Lizzie Blue Horse; F; G.Dau; 0-3
190	Takola Win; Sophia Fox; F; 48
191	Mary Janis; F; G.Mo; 57
192	Louis Matthews; M; G.Son; 25
193	Maggie Janis; F; G.Dau; 15
194	Hankepi Wicakte; Kills At Night; F; G.Mo; 84
195	Kiyela Opi; Shot Close; M; G.Son; 10
196	Mato Luta; Red Bear; M; Father; 54
197	Wambli Koyaka; Wears The Eagle; F; Wife; 39
198	Tonweya Gli; Comes From Scout; M; Son; 22
199	Nata Witko; Bald Head; M; Son; 19

Census Of The Sioux And Cheyenne Indians Of Pine Ridge Agency, South Dakota. Taken by W. H. Clapp, Captain 16th Infantry, Acting United States Indian Agent, June 30, 1896. (Wakpamini District)

Key: Number; Indian Name *(if given)*; English Name; Sex; Relation; Age

200 Mato Luta; Dick Red Bear; M; Son; 11
201 Zuya Ciqala; Little Warrior; M; Son; 5
202 Cokula; Flesh; M; Father; 55
203 Winyan Wakan; Holy Woman; F; Wife; 45
204 Akicita Ota; Plenty Soldier; M; Son; 5-6
205 Tok Kute; Shoots The Enemy; M; Son; 3
206 Maka Win; Earth Woman; F; Niece; 18

207; Zintkala Oranko; Swift Bird; M; Father; 63
208 Zintkala Oranko; Marion Swift Bird; F; Dau; 20
209 Zintkala Wakan; Holy Bird; M; G.Son; 1-4

210 Inyan Wicasa; Rock Man; M; Husb; 33
211 Oye Sapa; Black Tracks; F; Wife; 36

212 Mato Hinapa; Bear Comes Out; F; 39

213 Maka Cega; Dirt Kettle; M; 48

214 Wambli Kokipapi; Afraid Of Eagle; M; Husb; 54
215 Tipi Tanka; Big Lodge; F; Wife; 65
216 Tanyan Hinapa; Comes Out Good; F; G.Dau; 9

217 Marpiya Luta; Red Cloud; M; Husb; 73
218 Marpiya Luta; Mary Red Cloud; F; Wife; 65
219 Hektakiya Gli; Comes Back; M; G.Son

220 Mato Hunkesni; Luke Slow Bear; M; G.Son; 13
221 Sunkhinsa; Lucie Red Horse; F; Sister; 32
222 Caje Wanica; No Name; F; Sister; 44
223 Gleska Agli; Brings Spotted; F; G.Mo; 84
224 Sunkhinsa; George Red Horse; M; Nephew; 12
225 Sunkhinsa; Louise Red Horse; F; Niece; 10

226 Sina Rota; Gray Blanket; M; Father; 35
227 Pankeska; Shell; F; Wife; 40
228 James Galligo; M; Son; 12
229 Winyan Ciqala; Little Woman; F; Dau; 12
230 Wambli Waste; Good Eagle; F; Dau; 5
231 Sophia Somorrow; F; S. in L.; 17
232 Lilly Somorrow; F; S. in L.; 20
233 Sina Rota; Lucy Grey[sic] Blanket; F; Dau; 11-6

234 Wiite[sic]; Woman Face; F; Sister; 33
235 Wicarpi Wanjila; One Star; M; Bro; 25

236 Capa Ska; White Beaver; F; 70

237 Sungmanitu Nakpa; Wolf Ears; M; Father; 62
238 Itonkasan; Weasel; F; Wife; 57
239 Wawokiya; Helper; M; Son; 14

240 Frank McMahon; M; Husb; 32
241 Julia McMahon; F; Wife; 33
242 Wanita; F; S. In L.; 18
243 Hoksila Waste; Frank Good Boy; M; B. in L.; 25

Census Of The Sioux And Cheyenne Indians Of Pine Ridge Agency, South Dakota. Taken by W. H. Clapp, Captain 16th Infantry, Acting United States Indian Agent, June 30, 1896. (Wakpamini District)

Key: Number; Indian Name *(if given)*; English Name; Sex; Relation; Age

244	William Janis; M; Father; 26
245	Mabel Janis; F; Wife; 27
246	Wilson Janis; M; Son; 2-8
247	Thomas Janis; M; Son; 0-4
248	Tasunke Hinzi; Yellow Horse; M; Father; 36
249	Aiyapi; Talks About; F; Wife; 32
250	Wayankapi; Comes To See Her; F; Dau; 14
251	Tonweya Gli; Comes From Scout; M; Son; 7
252	Tasunke Hinzi; Lillian Yellow Horse; F; Dau; 2-2
253	Zintkala Wakan; Holy Bird; M; Father; 23
254	Tipi Luta; Red Lodge; F; Wife; 25
255	Sunkhiyohipi; Comes After Horses; F; Dau; 4-6
256	Zintkala Wakan; Julia Holy Bird; F; Dau; 1-8
257	Anpetu Luta; Red Day; F; Dau; 0-5
258	Howaste Win; Good Voice Woman; F; Mother; 58
259	Niyanke Kte; Kills Alive; F; Dau; 25
260	Sallie; F; G.Dau; 13
261	Tawa Kte; Kills Her Own; F; G.Dau; 2-5
262	John Nelson; M; Father; 26
263	Lizzie Nelson; F; Wife; 27
264	William Nelson; M; Son; 8
265	Samuel Nelson; M; Son; 6
266	Reuben Nelson; M; Son; 2-10
267	Julia Nelson; F; Sister; 21
268	Annie Nelson; F; Dau; 0-4
269	Wambli Win; Eagle Woman; F; Mother; 33
270	Wahacanka; Shield; M; Son; 7
271	Wapsakapi; Cut From Rope; F; Dau; 4
272	Cetan Wakuwa; Chasing Hawk; M; Father; 65
273	Hunska Tanka Narco; Big Leggins Down; F; 64
274	Naca Agli; Brings The Chief; M; Husb; 23
275	Mato Sapa; Mary Black Bear; F; Wife; 20
276	Iyawasaka; Strong Talk; M; Father; 33
277	Tatiyopa; Her Door; F; Wife; 24
278	Wicarpi Luta; Red Star; F; Dau; 5
279	Heraka Luta; Red Elk; F; Dau; 3-5
280	Hinzi Agli; Brings Yellow; M; Nephew; 23
281	Tipi Ikceya; Lodge; F; Mother; 57
282	Watayeya; Good Shot; M; Son; 12
283	Tasunke Iyanka; Chas. Running Horse; M; Son; 19
284	Mata; Mata; F; 76
285	Hektakiya Ekte; Kills Back; M; Father; 30
286	Kpazo; Shows; F; Wife; 28
287	Mato Hoksila; Bear Boy; M; Son; 4-6
288	Wahacanka Warpiya; Cloud Shield; M; Father 55
289	Pehin; Hair; F; Wife; 40
290	Tasunke Hinzi; Yellow Hair; F; Dau; 17
291	Hihan Wakan; Holy Owl; M; Son; 10

Census Of The Sioux And Cheyenne Indians Of Pine Ridge Agency, South Dakota. Taken by W. H. Clapp, Captain 16th Infantry, Acting United States Indian Agent, June 30, 1896. (Wakpamini District)

Key: Number; Indian Name *(if given)*; English Name; Sex; Relation; Age

292	Sunk Tacanku; Horse Road; M; Son; 7	314	Capa Maza; Iron Beaver; M; Husb; 35
293	Wahacanka Marpiya; Thomas Cloud Shield; M; Son; 4-6	315	Tawanbli; Her Eagle; F; Wife 28
294	Maza Ciqala; Little Iron; M; Husb; 37	316	Nuwmpi; Swimmer; M; Father; 63
295	Ptesan; White Cow; F; Wife; 37	317	Winyan Tanka; Big Woman; F; Wife 59
296	Nata Witko; Fool Head; M; Father; 28	318	Sunk Icu; Takes The Horse; F; Dau; 12
297	Canku Maza; Iron Road; F; Wife; 20	319	Alexander Salvis; M; Father; 40
		320	Mollie Salvis; F; Wife; 38
298	Mni Hinapa; Water Comes Out; F; Dau; 1-10	321	Oliver Salvis; M; Son; 20
		322	Alice Salvis; F; Dau; 17
299	Nata Witko; Annie Fool Head; F; Dau; 0-4	323	Charles Salvis; M; Son; 16
		324	Willie Salvis; M; Son; 13
		325	Julia Salvis; F; Dau; 11
300	Sunkska; White Horse; M; Father; 49	326	Alexander Salvis, Jr; M; Son; 7
		327	Stacy Salvis; M; Son; 6
301	Ite Owakita; Looks In Face; F; Wife; 51	328	Frank Salvis; M; Son; 4-6
		329	Lucy Salvis; F; Dau; 0-9
302	Ehake Gli; Comes Last; M; Son; 21		
		330	Thomas Mills; M; Father; 33
		331	Nellie Mills; F; Wife; 27
303	Hintani; Old Hair; M; Father; 33	332	Richard Mills; M; Son; 6
304	Zintkala To; Blue Bird; F; Wife; 30	333	Annie Mills; F; Dau; 1-5
305	Pahin; Porcupine; M; Son; 9	334	Benjamin Mills; M; Father; 25
306;	Wapaha Luta; Red War Bonnet; F; Dau; 7	335	Jessie Mills; F; Wife; 22
		336	Thomas Mills; M; Son; 1
307	Tasunke Opi; Wounded Horse; M; Son; 3-8	337	Zintkala Zi; Yellow Bird; M; Father; 38
308	Agli Ti; Comes And Camps; F; Dau; 1-5	338	Zintkala Zi; Annie Yellow Bird; F; Wife; 37
309	Toka Opi; Makes Enemy; M; Father; 38	339	Zintkala Zi; David Yellow Bird; M; Son; 18
310	Tacanupa; Her Pipe; F; Wife; 36	340	Zintkala Zi; Lizzie Yellow Bird; F; Dau; 14
311	Petaga; Coal Of Fire; F; G.Mo; 63	341	Zintkala Zi; Josephine Yellow Bird; F; Dau; 12
312	Akicize; Fight Over; M; G.Son; 21	342	Zintkala Zi; Harry Yellow Bird; M; Son; 9
313	Zintkaela Maza; Iron Bird; M; G.Son; 12	343	Zintkala Zi; Eddie Yellow Bird; M; Son; 6

Census Of The Sioux And Cheyenne Indians Of Pine Ridge Agency, South Dakota. Taken by W. H. Clapp, Captain 16th Infantry, Acting United States Indian Agent, June 30, 1896. (Wakpamini District)

Key: Number; Indian Name *(if given)*; English Name; Sex; Relation; Age

344 Zintkala Zi; Alex Yellow Bird; M; Son; 1-8
345 Okute; Shoots In; M; Father; 27
346 Sina Win; Her Blanket; F; Wife; 26
347 Mazaska Ole; After Money; F; Dau; 2-10

348 Maka Okawinr Mani; Country Traveler; M; Husb; 53
349 Sahunwanla; Cheyenne Woman; F; Wife; 58
350 Maka Okawinr Mani; Benj. Traveler; M; G.Son; 18

351 Mato Najin; Standing Bear; M; Father; 45
352 Tasina Wanbli; Hattie Eagle Shawl; F; Dau; 19
353 Zintkala; Bird; M; Son; 11

354 Ptesan Sapa; Black Cow; F; 38

355 Kimimila Ska; White Butter Fly; M; Father; 31
356 Zintkala Waste; Pretty Bird; F; Wife; 27
357 Kimimila Ska; Annie White Butterfly; F; Dau; 11

358 Mato Ska; Wm White Bear; M; Father; 23
359 Mato Ska; Jennie White Bear; F; Wife; 24
360 Mato Ska; Alice White Bear; F; Dau; 1-2

361 Tatanka Wankatuya; High Bull; M; Father; 38
362 Sina; Shawl; F; Wife; 39
363 Cangleska Wanbli; Eagle Hoop; M; Son; 14
364 Pejuta Win; Medicine Woman; F; Dau; 7

365 Tasunke Inyanka; Running Horse; M; Father; 36
366 Howaste Win; Good Voiced Woman; F; Wife; 33
367 Itonkasan Luta; Red Weasel; M; Son; 11
368 Naronpi; Hears Him; M; Son; 9;
369 Cante Waste; Good Hearted; F; Dau; 2-8

370 Wahacanka To; Blue Shield; M Father; 55
371 Taanpetu; Her Day; F; Wife; 55
372 Ehaka Win; Last Woman; F; Dau; 11
373 Orlaka Kaotinzapi; Fills The Hole; M; Son; 16

374 Ho Naron; Hears A Voice; F; Aunt; 44
375 William; M; Nephew; 26
376 Winyan Waste; Good Woman; F; Niece; 22

377 Tarca Win; Antelope Woman; F; Mother; 25
378 Hektakiya Gli; Comes Back; M; Son; 5

379 Frank Goings; M; Father; 24
380 Can Wanjila; Lone Tree; F; Wife; 18
381 Earl Goings; M; Son; 2-2
382 Garnett Goings; M; Son; 0-8

383 Tainyan Wakuwa; Chase In Sight; M; Father; 30
384 Wayank Najin; Stands And Looks; M; Son; 3-6
385 Cetan Waste Win; Good Hawk Woman; F; Mother; 62
386 Ptesan Hinapa Win; White Cow Comes Out; F; Dau; 0-6

387 Ptesan Luta; Red White Cow; F; Mother; 39

Census Of The Sioux And Cheyenne Indians Of Pine Ridge Agency, South Dakota. Taken by W. H. Clapp, Captain 16th Infantry, Acting United States Indian Agent, June 30, 1896. (Wakpamini District)

Key: Number; Indian Name *(if given)*; English Name; Sex; Relation; Age

388 Eagle Feather; F; Dau; 14
389 Ayutapi; Looks At Him; F; Dau; 6
390 Mary Dun; F; 78
391 Wasicu Waza; Iron White Man; M; Father; 27
392 Tokeya Win; Leading Woman; F; Wife; 30
393 Cante Waste; Good Heart; F; Dau; 11
394 Canupa Qupi; Gives Pipe; M; Son; 6
395 Tainyan Najin; Stands In Sight; M; Son; 0-10

396 Wakan Hinapa; Comes Out Holy; M; Husb; 30
397 Sunk Sapa; Black Horse; F; Wife; 38
398 Ahu; Brings; M; Bro; 24

399 Hanpa Nasica; Bad Moccosin[sic]; M; Father; 60
400 Wanbli Luta; Red Eagle; F; Wife; 49
401 Zintkala Mato; Bear Bird; M; Son; 24
402 Ninglicu; Comes Alive; F; Dau; 22
403 Sunkhinsa; Red Horse; F; Dau; 16
404 Agliti; Comes And Camps; F; Niece; 11

405 Ahpo Wakuwa; Chase In Morning; M; Father; 25
406 Tatanka Wicoti; Bull Village; F; Wife; 28
407 Nakipa; Runs Away from[sic] Him; M; Son; 14
408 Najinyapi; Surrounded; M; Son; 8
409 Sunkicu; Takes Horses; F; Dau; 5

410 Piya Icaga; Lives Again; M; Son; 0-3

411 Wambli Sun; Eagle Feather; F; Mother; 47
412 Wambli Sun; Jane Eagle Feather; F; Dau; 30

413 Maskablaska; Flat Iron; M; Father; 67
414 Maza Sna Win; Rattling Iron; F; Wife; 60
415 Tacanku Waste; Her Good Road; F; Dau; 17
416 Tokeya Kte; Kills Leader; M; G.Son; 11

417 Toka Kte; Kills Enemy; M; Husb; 33
418 Okogna Iyanka; Runs Between; F; Wife; 31
419 Catherine; F; Dau; 3 das

420 Wanbli Takeya; Eagle Louse; M; Husb; 27
421 Kangi Tasagye; Crow Cane; F; Wife; 42

422 Tarca Ska; White Deer; M; Father; 37
423 Winyan Luta; Red Woman; F; Wife; 39
424 Cangleska Waste; Good Ring; M; Son; 8
425 Tonwan; Sight; M; Son; 4
426 Najin; Lizzie Stands; F; Dau; 27

427 Sungmanitu Tanka; Big Wolf; M; Father; 72
428 Caje Wanica; No Name; F; Wife; 71
429 Mato Istima; John Sleeping Bear; M; G.Son; 20

430 Mato Ehakela; Last Bear; M; Husb; 57

Census Of The Sioux And Cheyenne Indians Of Pine Ridge Agency, South Dakota. Taken by W. H. Clapp, Captain 16th Infantry, Acting United States Indian Agent, June 30, 1896. (Wakpamini District)

Key: Number; Indian Name *(if given)*; English Name; Sex; Relation; Age

431 Cekpa; Twin; F; Wife; 47
432 Wicarpi; Edward Star; M; Husb; 27
433 Wicarpi; Anna Star; F; Wife; 24
434 Pejuta Win; Medicine Woman; F; Dau; 0-6
435 Onayan; Runs Prairie; M; Father; 31
436 Ptesan Hinapa; White Cow Out; F; Wife; 31
437 Wanbli Isnala; Lone Eagle; M; Son; 2-9
438 Wamniomni; Whirlwind; M; 70
439 Wanbli Wicarca; Old Eagle; M; Husb; 74
440 Pte Waste; Good Cow; F; Wife; 72
441 Cetan Ciqala; Little Hawk; M; Father; 61
442 Tipi Ska; White House; F; Wife; 61
443 Mazasu Ota; Many Cartridges; M; Son; 23
444 Cetan Ciqala; Wm Little Hawk; M; G.Son; 14
445 Tasunke Iyanka; Running Horse; M; Father; 34
446 Wicarpi Wanbli; Eagle Star; M; Bro; 25
447 Ptesan; White Cow; F; Wife; 33
448 Zintkala Luta; Red Bird; F; Dau; 12
449 Tasunke Iyanka; Lizzie Running Horse; F; Dau; 7
450 Toka Kokipapi; Afraid Of Enemy; M; Son; 4
451 Oye Luta; Red Track; F; 75
452 Mato Sapa; Black Bear; M; Father; 70
453 Wiciyela Win; Yankton Woman; F; Wife; 47
454 Wiciyela; Edward Yankton; M; Son; 26
455 Pekin Ji; Yellow Hair; F; Dau; 10
456 Tayan Hinapa; Comes Out Right; F; G.Dau; 2-6
457 Itazipa Kicun; Uses Bow; M; Husb; 37
458 Cante Win; Heart; F; Wife; 27
459 Ota Hinapa; Comes Out Plenty; F; Niece; 9
460 Mato; John Bear; M; Father; 58
461 Anpo Wakita; Looks At Daylight; F; Wife; 45
462 Mato; Louise Bear; F; Dau; 16
463 Sallie Hunter; F; Aunt; 37
464 John Hunter; M; Nephew; 12
465 Kakab Ekte; Kills Ahead; M; Father; 48
466 Heraka Sapa; Black Elk; F; Wife; 48
467 John Ladeaux; M; Son; 22
468 John Brooks; M; Son; 19
469 Yuha; Keeps; M; Son; 12
470 Sunkmani; Steals Horses; M; Son; 9
471 Tok Huwa; Charging Enemy; M; Father; 55
472 Ista Gi; Yellow Eyes; F; Sister; 62
473 Sunkgleska Yuha; Has Spotted Horses; M; Son; 20
474 Mato Ciqala; Bob Little Bear; M; Father; 46
475 Mato Ciqala; Zuzella Little Bear; F; Wife; 37

Census Of The Sioux And Cheyenne Indians Of Pine Ridge Agency, South Dakota. Taken by W. H. Clapp, Captain 16th Infantry, Acting United States Indian Agent, June 30, 1896. (Wakpamini District)

Key: Number; Indian Name *(if given)*; English Name; Sex; Relation; Age

476	Mato Ciqala; Henry Little Bear; M; Son; 21		499	Oliver Marrisette; M; Son; 21
477	Mato Ciqala; James Little Bear; M; Son; 14		500	Joseph Marrisette; M; Son; 15
478	Mato Ciqala; Alice Little Bear; F; Dau; 0-9		501	Wahuwapa Sica; Bad Cob; M; Father; 42
479	Wosla Najin; Stands Up; M; Father; 53		502	Mni Sni; Cold Water; F; Wife; 32
480	Akiyanpi; Flies Over Her; F; Wife; 48		503	Wawakpansni; Rustler; M; Son; 6
481	Iyuha Kawicapa; Beats All; F; Dau; 12		504	Wiyakasa; Red Feather; M; B. in L.; 29
482	Canupa Waci Hoksila; Pipe Dance Boy; M; Son; 2-11		505	Tatanka Ciqala; Edward Little Bull; M; Nephew; 20
483	Wizipan; Frank Baggage; M; Son; 24		506	Tasunke Kinyela; Flying Horse; M; Father; 24
484	Peggie; F; Mother; 50		507	Gleska Agli; Brings Spotted; F; Wife; 21
485	James Richard; M; Bro; 21		508	Wiyaka Waste; Good Feather; F; Dau; 0-5
486	Winyan Cuwignaka; Mary Womans Dress; F; Sister; 34		509	Cetan Tanka; Big Hawk; M; Father; 33
487	Susie; F; Niece; 1-3		510	Tarca Cincala; Mary Young Deer; F; Wife; 34
488	Sunka Isna; Lone Dog; M; Father; 45		511	James Galligo; M; Son; 17
489	Winyan Suta; Hard Woman; F; Wife; 39		512	Alice Galligo; F; Dau; 15
490	Tatanka Ptesela; Short Bull; M; Son; 13		513	Ella Galligo; F; Dau; 8
491	Pehinsa; Red Hair; F; Dau; 0-1		514	Zonie Galligo; F; Dau; 6
			515	Pejuta Win; Medicine Woman; F; Dau; 4
492	Heraka Waste; Good Elk; F; 74		516	Charles Merrivall; M; Father; 25
			517	Maggie Merrivall; F; Wife; 25
493	Cetan Luta; Chas Red Hawk; M; Father; 23		518	Laura Merrivall; F; Dau; 2-7
494	Sungmanitu Hanska; Hannah Long Wolf; F; Wife; 20		519	Wakan Iyotaka; Sitting Medicine; M; Father; 50
495	Heraka Win; Elk Woman; F; Mother; 58		520	Huste Win; Lame Woman; F; Wife; 40
496	Cante Suta; George Hard Heart; M; Bro; 17		521	Tayan Kte; Kills Well; M; Son; 15
497	Cetan Luta; Thomas Red Hawk; M; Son; 5		522	Winyan Waste; Good Woman; F; Dau; 12
498	Rosa Marrisette; F; Mother; 53		523	Wakan Iyotoka[sic]; Jessie Sitting Medicine; F; Dau; 8

Census Of The Sioux And Cheyenne Indians Of Pine Ridge Agency, South Dakota. Taken by W. H. Clapp, Captain 16th Infantry, Acting United States Indian Agent, June 30, 1896. (Wakpamini District)

Key: Number; Indian Name *(if given)*; English Name; Sex; Relation; Age

524 Enakiya; Quite; F; 52

525 Kangi Bloka; He Crow; M; Father; 59
526 Sunkagli; Brings Horses; F; Wife; 60
527 Canicipawega Waste; Good Cross; M; Son; 19

528 Kutepi; Mack Kutepi; M; 35

529 Maka Luta; Red Earth; F; Aunt; 66
530 Topa Waci Canupa; Four Pipe Dance; F; Niece; 44
531 Psica Oyate; Jumping Nation; F; G.Dau; 16
532 Mato; Bear; M; G.Dau[sic]; 13

533 Mato Catka; Left Hand Bear; M; Father; 34
534 Oye Wanbli; Eagle Track; F; Wife; 44
535 Hoksila Ska; White Boy; M; Son; 10
536 Wircincala; Girl; F; Dau; 4-6
537 Kokob Najin; Stands In Front; M; Son; 14

538 Wisake; Finger Nail Woman; F; Mother; 43
539 Toha Oyuspa; Catches Enemy; M; Son; 10
540 Wasicu Wakan; Doctor; F; Dau; 6

541 Waypezi Win; Yellow Feet Woman; F; Mother; 54
542 Sunkole; Hunts Horses; M; Son; 20

543 Akicita Najin; Standing Soldier #2; M; Father; 68
544 Wanbli Win; Eagle Woman; F; Wife; 59

545 Hi Kapsun; Breaks Teeth; M; Son; 23
546 Mato Win; Bear Woman; F; Dau; 15
547 Tikanyela Iyanka; Runs Close To Lodge; M; G.Son; 7
548 Kakija; Sufferer; F; Dau; 18
549 Zuyayesa; Warrior; F; G.Dau; 0-8

550 Nape; Marshall Hand; M; Father; 28
551 Kangi Ciqala; Mary Little Crow; F; Wife; 28
552 Nape; Joseph Hand; M; Son; 0-6

553 Cetan Ska; White Hawk; M; Husb; 78
554 Mama; F; Wife; 54
555 Agli; Brings In; M; G.Son; 0-3

556 Najinyapi; Surrounded; F; Mother; 44
557 Tokeya Win; Leading Woman; F; Dau; 19

558 Zintkala Wanbli; Bird Eagle; M; Father; 39
559 Blewakan; Holy Lake; F; Wife; 33
560 Toka Kte; Kills Enemy; F; Dau; 8
561 Tiapa Wicakte; Kills The Village; M; Son; 7
562 Taku Kte; Kills Something; M; Son; 4-6

563 Hoksila Zi; Grover Yellow Boy; M; Father; 26
564 Hoksila Zi; Kittie Yellow Boy; F; Wife; 25
565 Hoksila Zi; Jessie Yellow Boy; F; Dau; 6
566 Hoksila Zi; Lucy Yellow Boy; F; Dau; 4-3

Census Of The Sioux And Cheyenne Indians Of Pine Ridge Agency, South Dakota. Taken by W. H. Clapp, Captain 16th Infantry, Acting United States Indian Agent, June 30, 1896. (Wakpamini District)

Key: Number; Indian Name *(if given)*; English Name; Sex; Relation; Age

567 Hoksila Zi; George Yellow Boy; M; Son; 2-5
568 Hoksila Zi; Thomas Yellow Boy; M; Son; 0-6
569 Janjanyela; Clear; M; Father; 39
570 Tatesna Win; Ringing Wind; F; Wife; 34
571 Tatesna; Lucy; F; Dau; 14
572 Janjanyela; Thomas Clear; m; Son; 12

573 Ohitika Win; Brave Woman #1; F; Mother; 44
574 Rosa Morrison; F; Dau; 16
575 Brother Morrison; M; Son; 6
576 Charles Morrison; M; Son; 4

577 Cetan Win; Hawk Woman; F; Mother; 32

578 Tapankeska; Her Shell; F; Mother; 64
579 Wakan Gli; Comes Medicine; F; Dau; 20

580 Hoksila Zi; Yellow Boy; M; Father; 30
581 Winyan Topa; Four Woman; F; Wife #1; 39
582 Iyakuwin; Comes Talking; F; Wife #2; 21
583 Hoksila Zi; Mamie Yellow Boy; F; Dau; 16
584 Hoksila Zi; Cahrles[sic] Yellow Boy; M; Son; 13
585 Tainyan Yanka; Sits In Sight; F; Dau; 11
586 Skagli; Comes White; F; Dau; 4-4
587 Raute Rlo; Growing Cedar; F; Dau; 1-8
588 Hoksila Zi; Mary Yellow Boy; F; Dau; 0-9

589 Winyan Hanska; Tall Woman #1; F; 68

590 Heraka Ciqala; Paul Little Elk; M; Father; 42
591 Taanpetu; Her Day; F; Wife; 26
592 Maka Mahel Mani; Made In The Earth; F; Dau; 6
593 Wicincala; Girl; F; Dau 3-3

594 Winyan Hanska; Tall Woman #2; F; 52

595 Toka Kte; Kills Enemy; M; Son; 22
596 James; M; Cousin; 20
597 Hinhan Luta; Red Owl; F; Mother; 67

598 Onasola; Pacer; M; Father; 31
599 Ptesan; White Cow; F; Wife; 30
600 Sina Icu; Takes Blanket; F; Dau; 14
601 Wakan Gli; Comes Holy; F; Dau; 8
602 Inyan Cante; Stone Heart; F; Dau; 4
603 Pahin Luta; Red Porcupine; F; Dau; 0-4

604 Mazakan Icu; Takes The Gun; F; G.Mo; 76
605 Anpetu Waste; Good Day; M; G.Son; 23

606 Mato Wankatuya; High Bear; M; Husb; 35
607 Tasina Wakan; Her Holy Blanket; F; Wife; 45

608 Zintkala Wanbli; Bird Eagle; F; Mother; 60
609 Winyan Tanka; Big Woman; F; Dau; 25
610 Tasunke Ota; Many Horses; F; Dau; 8

Census Of The Sioux And Cheyenne Indians Of Pine Ridge Agency, South Dakota. Taken by W. H. Clapp, Captain 16th Infantry, Acting United States Indian Agent, June 30, 1896. (Wakpamini District)

Key: Number; Indian Name *(if given)*; English Name; Sex; Relation; Age

611 Taspan; Apple; M; Father; 49
612 Caje Wanica; No Name; F; Wife; 38
613 Taspan; John Apple; M; Son; 23
614 Taspan; Dora Apple; F; Dau; 18
615 Taspan; George Apple; M; Son; 17
616 Taspan; Jennie Apple; F; Dau; 9
617 Blaska; Flat; M; Son; 7
618 Ite Tanka; Big Face; M; Son; 3-5
619 Inyan Winyan; Rock Woman; F; Niece; 17
620 Hoksila Tanka; Big Boy; M; G.Son; 16
621 Naca Ota; Plenty Chief; M; Son; 1

622 Pehin Luta; Red Hair; M; Father; 57
623 Caje Oglaka; Tells Her Name; F; Wife; 43
624 Can Wiyumni; Twisted Wood; M; Son; 24
625 Kangi Wanbli; Crow Eagle; M; Son; 22
626 Rante Hoksila; Cedar Boy; M; Son; 22
627 Ataya Wakan; All Holy; F; Dau; 18
628 Wagmu; Pumpkin; F; Dau; 10
629 Ite Nopa; Two Face; M; Son; 8
630 Otacan; Leader; M; Son; 7

631 Ista Gi; Brown Eyes; F; Mother; 42
632 Cokab Iyaya; Goes In Center; F; Dau; 14
633 Thomas; M; Son; 7
634 Wiyaka Nupa; Two Feathers; M; Son; 4

635 Wanbli Gleska; Spotted Eagle; M; Bro; 64

636 Tatanka; Bull; M; Bro; 52
637 Kangi Ciqala; Little Crow; M; Father; 66
638 Ake; Again; F; Wife; 54
639 Ota Kute; Shoots Plenty; M; Son; 16

640 Lizzie Graham; F; Mother; 32
641 Howard Graham; M; Son; 8
642 Alfred Graham; M; Son; 6
643 Ollie Graham; F; Dau; 1-10
644 Henry Moore; M; Bro; 22

645 Mary Sierro; F; Mother; 34
646 Cemona Sierro; F; Dau; 16
647 Seberino Sierro; M; Son; 13
648 Susie Sierro; F; Dau; 11
649 Bennett Sierro; M; Son; 7
650 Antonia Sierro; F; Dau; 4
651 Santac Sierro; M; Son; 2-8
652 Joseph Sierro; M; Son; 0-4

653 Wanbli Luta; Red Eagle; M; Father; 54
654 Parmi; Crooked Nose; F; Wife; 41
655 Hi Maza; Iron Teeth; F; Dau; 21
656 Pejuta; Medicine; M; Son; 20
657 Abe Summers; M; Nephew; 29
658 Tasunl; Plenty Horses; F; Niece; 23

659 Ogle Sa; Red Shirt; M; Father; 49
660 Tainyan; In Sight; F; Wife; 42
661 Ogle Sa; Mary Red Shirt; F; Dau; 19
662 Ogle Sa; Anna Red Shirt; F; Dau 17
663 Hoksila Waste; Good Boy; M; Son; 15
664 Eliza; F; Dau; 13
665 Kolayapi; Friendly; M; Son; 12

Census Of The Sioux And Cheyenne Indians Of Pine Ridge Agency, South Dakota. Taken by W. H. Clapp, Captain 16th Infantry, Acting United States Indian Agent, June 30, 1896. (Wakpamini District)

Key: Number; Indian Name *(if given)*; English Name; Sex; Relation; Age

666 Wawokiya; Helps; M; Father; 55
667 Wawokiya; Lucy Helps; F; Dau; 26
668 Wawokiya; Jennie Helps; F; Dau; 21
669 Blo Wanicla; Lone Ridge; M; Son; 16
670 Maniku; Comes Walking; M; Son; 13
671 Ptesan Wayanka; Sees White Cow; F; Dau; 12
672 Otakuye; No Relation; F; Dau; 11

673 Can Zi; Yellow Wood; M; Father; 34
674 Tahalo; Hide; F; Wife; 39
675 Wakan Win; Medicine Woman; F; Dau; 7
676 Ite Ogna Opi; Ida Shot In The Face; F; Niece; 21

677 Tinopa; Door; F; Mother; 47
678 Wicincala; Girl; F; Dau; 5

679 Spayo; Mexican; M; Husb; 37
680 Winyan Wasaka; Strong Woman; F; Wife; 35

681 Nancy Bissonette; F; Mother; 57
682 Millie Bissonette; F; Dau; 23
683 Lulu Bissonette; F; Dau; 22
684 Tatanka Hanska; Nellie Long Bull; F; G.Dau; 1-3

685 Mato Waste; Good Bear; F; Mother; 34
686 Inyan Sa; Red Rock; F; Dau; 12
687 Tasunke; Her Horses; F; Dau; 7
688 Wicokanyan; Midday; M; Son; 3

689 Ista Ska; Addie White Eyes; F; 19

690 Piya Icaga; Lives Again; F; G.Mo; 69
691 Can Ptecela; Short Wood; M; G.Son; 18
692 Sunkhinto; Jennie Blue Horse; F; G.Dau; 15

693 Mni; Water; M; Father; 30
694 Paha Wakan; Holy Hill; F; Wife; 29
695 Icapsipsicala; Swallow; F; Dau; 14
696 Toka Wicaku; Gives Enemy; M; Son; 6
697 Kuwa Wicakte; Kills Charging; F; Dau; 3-6
698 Heraka Wakan; Thunder Elk; M; Son; 1-5

699 Wakinyan Peta; George Fire Thunder; M; Father; 39
700 Wakinyan Peta; Mary Fire Thunder; F; Wife; 29
701 Wakinyan Peta; Bessie Fire Thunder; F; Dau; 5
702 Wakinyan Peta; George Fire Thunder, Jr; M; Son; 3-1
703 Wakinyan Peta; Annie Fire Thunder; F; Dau; 1-5

704 Termuga; Fly; M; Father; 52
705 Tasunke; Her Horse; F; Wife; 43
706 Opo; Fog; M; Son; 24
707 Gli Najin; Comes And Stands; F; Dau; 15
708 Termuga; Peter Fly; M; Son; 4-6
709 Termuga; Susie Fly; F; Dau; 0-7

710 Hoyekiya; Throws Her Voice; F; G.Mo; 76
711 Winyan Isnala; Lone Woman; F; G.Dau; 25
712 Hiyokipi; Comes After Him; M; G.Son; 13

Census Of The Sioux And Cheyenne Indians Of Pine Ridge Agency, South Dakota. Taken by W. H. Clapp, Captain 16th Infantry, Acting United States Indian Agent, June 30, 1896. (Wakpamini District)

Key: Number; Indian Name *(if given)*; English Name; Sex; Relation; Age

713 Awean; M; Father; 34
714 Canku Maza; Iron Road; F; Wife; 29
715 John Awean; M; Son; 1

716 Akicipa Ciqala; Little Soldier; M; Father; 34
717 Canku Waste; Good Road; F; Wife; 48
718 Wanju; Arrow Quiver; M; Son; 18
719 Ptesan; White Cow; F; dau; 11

720 Tasunke Ciqala; Little Horse; M; Father; 39
721 Sunsunla Sapa; Black Mule; F; Wife; 39
722 Kimnila; Butterfly; M; Son; 14

723 Onpan Hinske; Elk Tooth; F; G.Mo; 74
724 Ehake Gli; Comes Last; M; G.Son; 15

725 Sunkhinto; Baldwin Blue Horse; M; Father; 40
726 Marpiya Wakan; Stephen Medicine Cloud; M; Son; 21

727 Catka; Left Hand; M; Husb; 65
728 Winorcala Sica; Bad Old Woman; F; Wife; 59

729 Husa Luta; Red Leg; M; Father; 70
730 Tarca Sa; Red Deer; F; Wife; 47
731 Sunkska Yuha; Owns White Horse; M; Son; 18

732 Tacupa; Marrow Bone; M; Father; 42
733 Winyan Hunkesni; Slow Woman; F; Wife; 49
734 Tacupa; Joshua Marrow Bone; M; Son; 19

735 Wanbli Heton; Eagle Horn; M; Son; 9
736 Wakinyan Omani; Thunder Traveler; M; Son; 7
737 Wanbli Win; Eagle Woman; F; Dau; 13
738 Zintkala Maza; Iron Bird; M; Son; 5
739 Wasicu Winyan Waste; Good White Woman; F; Dau; 2-1

740 Ohitika Win; Brave Woman #1; F; 70

741 Heraka Iyotaka; Sitting Elk; M; Father; 41
742 Ptesan Yuha; Owns White Cow; F; Wife; 37
743 Heraka Iyotaka; Julia Sitting Elk; F; Dau; 12

744 Mary Armijo; F; G.Mo; 48
745 Lamott Armijo; M; G. Son; 18

746 Manirupa; Calico; M; Father; 53
747 Sunka Waste; Good Dog; F; Wife; 55
748 Mato Witko; Crazy Bear; M; Son; 17
749 Hogan Wanbli; Eagle Fish; M; Son; 8

750 Ate Ciqala; Little Feather; M; Father; 52
751 Mani; Walking; F; Wife; 56
752 Kipanpi; Calls Him; M; Son; 23
753 Wahukeza Win; Lance Woman; F; Dau; 14

754 Ojuha Sa; Red Sack; M; Father; 57
755 Winorcala Wakan; Holy Old Woman; F; Wife; 53
756 Ojuha Sa; Sallie Red Sack; F; Dau; 21

Census Of The Sioux And Cheyenne Indians Of Pine Ridge Agency, South Dakota. Taken by W. H. Clapp, Captain 16th Infantry, Acting United States Indian Agent, June 30, 1896. (Wakpamini District)

Key: Number; Indian Name *(if given)*; English Name; Sex; Relation; Age

757 Sunkhinsa; Red Horse; F; Dau; 13	781 Ite Ska Yuha; White Face Owner; F; Aunt; 56
758 Tacanku; His Road; M; Son; 8	782 Taopi Ota; Many Wounds; M; Nephew; 18
759 Wicasa Ptecela; Short Man; M; Husb; 36	783 Mato Nupa; Two Bears; M; Father; 61
760 Tasina Ota; Plenty Shawl; F; Wife; 34	784 Joseph; M; Son; 14
761 James Buckman; M; Father; 38	785 Mato Hakikto; Bear Looks Back; M; Husb; 51
762 Susie Buckman; F; Wife; 28	786 Wanbli; Eagle; F; Wife; 44
763 Gives Up On Him; F; Dau; 11	
764 Millie Buckman; F; Dau; 6	787 Anpetu Hinapa; Day Comes Out; F; 64
765 George Buckman; M; Son; 4-6	
766 Benjamin Buckman; M; Son; 0-2	
767 Yuse; Dripping; M; Father; 64	788 Mato Ha Sina; Paul Bear Robe; M; Father; 27
768 Sasa; Reddy; F; Wife; 34	789 Ptesan Rla Win; Rattling White Cow; F; Wife; 21
759[sic] Witko Kte; Kills A Fool; M; Son; 12	790 Tatanka Iyotaka; Sitting Bull; M; Son; 4
770 Sina Wakan; Medicine Sheet; M; Son; 5	791 Winyan Waste; Good Woman; F; Dau; 1-7
771 Tatanka Wajin; Standing Bull; M; Nephew; 60	
772 Wasicau Wicakte; Kills White Man; M; Uncle; 64	792 Antonia Janis; M; Father; 37
	793 Fannie Janis; F; Wife; 33
	794 Lucy Janis; F; Dau; 14
773 Zintkala Ska; White Bird; M; Husb; 54	795 Bessy Janis; F; Dau; 12
	796 Herbert Janis; M; Son; 6
774 Tasunke Wayankapi; Sees Her Horse; F; Wife; 44	797 Peter Janis; M; Son; 2-3
	798 Fanny Janis; F; Dau; 0-3
	799 Julia Good Win; F; S. in L.; 22
775 Zintkala Ska; Leon White Bird; M; Father; 23	
776 Ptesan Winyan; White Cow Woman; F; Wife; 24	800 Mary Colhoff; F; Mother; 33
	801 John R. Colhoff; M; Son; 16
777 Tasunke Wanbli; Eagle Horse; M; Son; 2-10	802 Elizabeth Colhoff; F; Dau; 14
	803 George Colhoff; M; Son; 12
	804 Anna Colhoff; F; Dau; 10
778 Tacanku Waste; Her Good Road; F; Mother; 21	805 William Colhoff; M; Son; 6
779 Taopi; Wounded; M; Son; 2-3	806 Rlawin; Rattler; F; 44
780 Can Nup Yuha; John Two Sticks; M; Son; 10 da	807 S. Tanka Ciqala; Little Grey Wolf; M; Father; 41

Census Of The Sioux And Cheyenne Indians Of Pine Ridge Agency, South Dakota. Taken by W. H. Clapp, Captain 16th Infantry, Acting United States Indian Agent, June 30, 1896. (Wakpamini District)

Key: Number; Indian Name *(if given)*; English Name; Sex; Relation; Age

808	Ranhi; Slow; F; Wife; 42
809	Winyan Nupa; Two Woman[sic]; F; Dau; 9
810	Tonweya; Scout; M; Son; 4
811	Canowicakte; Kills In Timber; F; Mother; 32
812	Pankeska; Shell Woman; F; Dau; 10
813	Wanbli; Eagle; F; Dau; 6
814	Oyate Wicakte; Kills Tribe; M; Son; 2-2
815	Wanbli Nupa; Two Eagle; M; Husb; 34
816	Louis Martin; M; Bro; 27
817	Berry Martin; M; Bro; 21
818	Santa Rosa Martin; M; Bro; 18
819	Zintkala Gleska; Spotted Bird; M; Father; 40
820	Winyan Isnala; Lone Woman; F; Wife; 37
821	Palani Kte; Kills Bee; M; Son; 17
822	Taopi Ota; Plenty Wounds; M; Son; 6
823	Wanbli Wicasa; Eagle Man; M; Son; 3-6
824	John Lee; M; Father; 31
825	Sophia Lee; F; Wife; 26
826	Emma Lee; F; Dau; 9
827	James Lee; M; Son; 7
828	Anna Lee; F; Dau; 2-1
829	Mary Merrivall; F; Mother; 61
830	Deaf And Dumb; M; Son; 22
831	Emma Merrivall; F; Dau; 20
832	Jennie Merrivall; F; Dau; 19
833	Rosa Lee White; F; G.Dau; 15
834	S. Nakpa Hoksila; Young Wolf Ears; M; Father; 31
835	Pejuta Win; Medicine Woman; F; Wife; 35
836	Tawa Agli; Bring Her Own; F; Dau; 2-5
837	Heraka Wakan; Holy Elk; M; Father; 40
838	Ho Waste; Good Voice; F; Wife; 35
839	Tezi; Belly; M; Son; 17
840	Tiwicakte; Kills A Man; M; Son; 15
841	Cetan Ho; Hawk Voice; M; Son; 5
842	Wamniomni Ska; White Whirlwind; M; Father; 38
843	Ataye Waste; All Good; F; Wife; 42
844	Asapi; Shouts At; M; Son; 21
845	Onyan Iyayapi; Leaves Him; M; Son; 10
846	Tonweya Kte; Kills Scout; M; Son; 8
847	Wicegna; Among; M; Son; 7
848	Tasunke Ota; Her Plenty Horses; F; Dau; 3-1
849	Charles Giroux; M; Father; 34
850	Rosa Giroux; F; Wife; 38
851	Mary Giroux; F; Dau; 11
852	Lottie Giroux; F; Dau; 8
853	Lizzie Giroux; F; Dau; 6
854	Charles Giroux, Jr; M; Son; 0-1
855	Sungmanitu Ota; Plenty Wolf; M; Father; 45
856	Icaga; Grows; F; Wife; 34
857	Wapaha Nupa; Two Bonnet; M; Son; 22
858	Rante Sa; Red Cedar; F; Dau; 18
859	Tipi Yuha; Own House; M; Son; 10
860	Oye Wanbli; Eagle Track; F; Dau; 2-10
861	Sungmanitu Ota; Sam Plenty Wolf; M; Son; 0-8

Census Of The Sioux And Cheyenne Indians Of Pine Ridge Agency, South Dakota. Taken by W. H. Clapp, Captain 16th Infantry, Acting United States Indian Agent, June 30, 1896. (Wakpamini District)

Key: Number; Indian Name *(if given)*; English Name; Sex; Relation; Age

862 Rupahu Ska; White Wing; F; G.Mo; 57	889 John Cottier, Jr; M; Son; 8
863 Benjamin; M; G.Son; 22	890 Esther Cottier; F; dau; 2-8
	891 Eddie Cottier; M; Son; 1-2
864 Lizzie Means; F; Mother; 31	892 Nick S. Janis; M; Father; 35
865 Eugene Means; M; S.Son; 22	893 Emma Janis; F; Wife; 37
866 Robert B Means; M; S.Son; 18	894 Susie Garnett; F; Dau; 17
867 William Burgen; M; S.Son; 16	895 Berthia Janis; F; Dau; 12
868 Minnie Vlandry; F; Dau; 11	896 John Janis; M; Son; 9
869 Bert Means; M; Son; 3-10	897 Vinna Janis; F; Dau; 6
870 Frank Means; M; Son; 9	898 Joseph Janis; M; Son; 5
871 John Means; M; Son; 1	899 Lizzie Janis; F; Dau; 1-1
	900 Julia Menard; F; S. in L.; 20
872 Wankpahi; Picks Arrows; M; Husb; 26	901 Ptesan Yatapi; Chief White Cow; F; 38
873 Sagye Win; Vane Woman; F; Wife; 28	
	902 Rante Win; Cedar Woman; F; Mother; 44
874 Huhu Napin; Bone Necklace #2; M; Son; 28	903 Wanbli Ciqala; Small Eagle; M; Son; 23
875 Ptesan Wayankapi; Looks At White Cow; F; Mother; 60	904 Rante Win; Susie Cedar Woman; F; Dau; 10
876 Ramania Jansen; F; Mother; 18	
877 Minnie Jansen; F; Dau; 1-1	905 Emma Stirk; F; Mother; 36
	906 Tony Stirk; M; Son; 16
878 Sunksapa; Charles Black Horse; M; Father; 33	907 James Stirk; M; Son; 14
	908 Prudy Stirk; F; Dau; 11
879 Winyan Luta; Red Woman; F; Wife; 30	909 Ellen Stirk; F; Dau; 9
880 John Lamott; M; Son; 6	910 Richard Stirk; M; Son; 7
881 Mato Yamni; Thomas Three Bears; M; Bro; 42	911 Louise Stirk; F; Dau; 5
	912 George Stirk; M; Son; 3-2
	913 Nellie Stirk; F; Dau; 0-10
882 Heraka Wanbli; Eagle Elk; M; Father; 44	914 Ella Irving; F; Mother; 30
	915 Benjamin Irving; M; Son; 16
883 Sagye Luta; Red Cane; F; Wife; 36	916 William Irving; M; Son; 13
	917 Elizabeth Irving; F; Dau; 11
884 Honaronpi; Hears His Voice; M; Son; 3-4	918 Julia Irving; F; Dau; 0-2
885 Heraka Wanbli; Joe Eagle Elk; M; Son; 0-5	919 Heraka Gi; Brown Elk; M; Father; 30
	920 Heraka Gi; George Elk; M; Son; 4
886 John Cottier; M; Father; 31	
887 Susie Cottier; F; Wife; 33	
888 Lucy Cottier; F; Dau; 7	921 Raymond Smith; M; Bro; 26

Census Of The Sioux And Cheyenne Indians Of Pine Ridge Agency, South Dakota. Taken by W. H. Clapp, Captain 16th Infantry, Acting United States Indian Agent, June 30, 1896. (Wakpamini District)

Key: Number; Indian Name *(if given)*; English Name; Sex; Relation; Age

922 Josephine Smith; F; Sister; 21

923 Nettie Goings; F; Mother; 41
924 Louis Goings; M; Son; 22
925 Blanche Goings; F; Dau; 20
926 James Goings; M; Son; 14
927 Baby Goings; F; Dau; 12

928 Kisun Sni; Unbraided; M; Father; 24
929 Snawin; Ringing; F; Dau; 3

930 Louis Deon; M; Father; 26
931 Mary Deon; F; Wife; 25
932 Maria Johns; F; Dau; 6-6
933 Ward Deon; M; Son; 1-4

934 Alexander Merrivall; M; Father; 28
935 Susie Merrivall; F; Wife; 25
936 Kira Merrivall; F; Dau; 1-10
937 Herman Merrivall; M; Son; 0-2

938 Pejuta Win; Medicine Woman; F; Mother; 44
939 Wagmeza Ape; Corn Leaf; F; Dau; 24
940 Kokob Iyanka; Runs Ahead; M; Son; 17

941 Mary Rando; F; Mother; 49
942 William Bullock; M; Son; 31
943 Julia; F; Dau; 24
944 Susia[sic]; F; Dau; 22
945 William Rando; M; Son; 9
946 Sylvester Rando; M; Son; 8
947 Josephine Rando; F; Dau; 4
948 Heraka Win; Elk Woman; F; Mother; 88

949 Tolo Kaksa; Cut Flesh; M; Father; 43
950 Osun Soka; Thick Braid; F; Wife; 57
951 Tasunke Yukan; Owns Horse; M; Son; 11

952 Pte Tacanku; Buffalo Road; F; Mother; 70
953 Wakan Iyotaka; Sits Holy; M; Son; 21

954 Zintkala Zi; Herbert J Zintkala zi; M; 8

955 Tasunke Ehakela; Fannie Last Horse; F; 11

956 Lucy Matthews; F; 27

957 Tatanka Nupa; Two Bulls; M; 45

958 Lucy Chamberlain; F; 41

959 Iglonica; Resist; F; Mother; 41
960 Kici Iyanka; Runs With; M; Son; 17
961 Sunk Ska; White Horse; M; Son; 12

962 Taha Saka; Hard Robe; M; Father; 34
963 Winyan Ota Najin; Standing Plenty Woman; F; Wife; 35
964 Sis; F; Dau; 16
965 Mastincala; Rabbit; F; Dau; 14
966 Marpatanka; Black Bird; M; Son; 9
967 Hektakiya Ekte; Kills Back; F; Dau; 5

968 Tarca Win; Antelope Woman; F; Mother; 29
969 Ptesan; White Cow; F; Niece; 11
970 Wakan Hinapa; Comes Out Holy; F; Dau; 4

971 Lizzie Hill; F; Sister; 22
972 Robert Hill; M; Bro; 19
973 Susie Hill; F; Sister; 16

974 Nape Ruwimna; Stinking Hand; M; Husb; 47

Census Of The Sioux And Cheyenne Indians Of Pine Ridge Agency, South Dakota.
Taken by W. H. Clapp, Captain 16th Infantry, Acting United States Indian Agent,
June 30, 1896. (Wakpamini District)

Key: Number; Indian Name *(if given)*; English Name; Sex; Relation; Age

975	Wickte; Kills; F; Wife; 36	997	Tasunke Luzahan; Charles Fast Horse; M; Son; 10
976	Louise Henderson; F; Mother; 26	998	Tasunke Luzahan; Cecilia Fast Horse; F; Dau; 1-4
977	Stella L. Henderson; F; Dau; 0-9	999	Wanbli Sun Koyaka; Wear Eagle Feather; F; 43
978	Frank Young; M; Father; 35		
979	Maggie Young; F; Wife; 23		
980	Walter Young; M; Son; 4	1000	Cetan Ciqala; Luke Little Hawk; M; Father; 25
981	Louisa Young; F; Dau; 1-10	1001	Wowapi Yuka; Carry Flag; F; Wife; 22
982	Ista Gonga; Blind Man; M; Father; 45	1002	Tasunke Opi; Wounded Horse; M; Son; 1-9
983	Wamniomni To; Blue Whirlwind; F; Wife; 49		
984	Mahel Cuwignaka; Dress Inside; M; Son; 11	1003	Kicopi; Calls Her; F; Mother; 35
		1004	Jennie; F; Dau; 2-4
985	Taopi Ciqala; Little Wound; M; Son; 9	1005	Tasunke Wayankapi; Looks At Her Horses; F; Dau; 0-2
986	Huhu Napin; Bone Necklace #1; M; 74	1006	Baptiste Garnier; M; Father; 49
		1007	Julia Garnier; F; Wife; 32
		1008	John Garnier; M; Son; 15
987	Wanbli Wicarca; Henry Old Eagle; M; Husb; 25	1009	Lizzie Garnier; F; Dau; 14
		1010	Lucy Garnier; F; Dau; 13
988	Kici Yanka; Sits With Her; F; Wife; 18	1011	Ellen Garnier; F; Dau; 12
		1012	Emma Garnier; F; Dau; 8
		1013	Sophia Garnier; F; Dau; 7
989	Sunkakan; Robert Horse; M; Father; 23	1014	Sallie Garnier; F; Dau; 6
		1015	Baptiste Garnier, Jr; M; Son; 1-6
990	Wanbli; Maggie Old Eagle; F; Wife; 24		
		1016	Wicegna Hiyu; Harry C.A. Them; M; Husb; 25
991	Sunkakan; Annie Horse; F; Dau; 0-3	1017	Niyan; Breathing; F; Wife; 19
992	Tasunke Luzahan; Joseph Fast Horse; M; Father; 50	1018	Naca; James Chief; M; Husb; 20
		1019	Hakikta; Looks Back; F; Wife; 16
993	Tasunke Luzahan; Jennie Fast Horse; F; Wife; 41		
994	Tasunke Luzahan; Thomas Fast Horse; M; Son; 12	1020	John Galligo; M; Father; 19
		1021	Toka Kte; Kills Enemy; F; Wife; 29
995	Tasunke Luzahan; Alice Fast Horse; F; Dau; 11	1022	John Galligo, Jr; M; Son; 0-1
996	Tasunke Luzahan; Amos Fast Horse; M; Son; 11	1023	Tatanka Wanagi; Ghost Bull; M; 39

Census Of The Sioux And Cheyenne Indians Of Pine Ridge Agency, South Dakota.
Taken by W. H. Clapp, Captain 16th Infantry, Acting United States Indian Agent,
June 30, 1896. (Wakpamini District)

Key: Number; Indian Name *(if given)*; English Name; Sex; Relation; Age

1024 Heraka Nupa; Richard Two Elk; M; Husb; 41
1025 Wanbli Conica; Eagle Flesh; F; Wife; 22

1026 Ohitika; Clayton Brave; M; Husb; 32
1027 Ituhu Suta; Holy Forehead; F; Wife; 38
1028 Ohitika; Charles Brave; M; Father; 24
1029 Tasunke Kpazo; Shows Her Horse; F; Wife; 40
1030 Zintkala Nopin; Frank Bird Necklace; M; S.Son; 20

1031 Hanhepi Wicakte; Kills At Night; F; G.Mo; 84
1032 Kiyela Opi; Shot Close; M; G.Son; 10

Census of the Sioux And Cheyenne Indians
Of Pine Ridge Agency, South Dakota.
June 30, 1896

Porcupine District

Census Of The Sioux And Cheyenne Indians Of Pine Ridge Agency, South Dakota. Taken by W. H. Clapp, Captain 16th Infantry, Acting United States Indian Agent, June 30, 1896. (Porcupine District)

Key: Number; Indian Name *(if given)*; English Name; Sex; Relation; Age

1033 Miyogli; Whetstone; M; Father; 59
1034 Mato Bloka; He Bear; M; Son; 5
1035 William Twiss; M; Husb; 34
1036 Lizzie Cuny; F; Wife; 31
1037 Maggie Twiss; F; Niece; 11
1038 James Twiss; M; Father; 38
1039 Rosella Twiss; F; Wife; 40
1040 Fannie Twiss; F; Dau; 18
1041 Thomas Twiss; M; Son; 7
1042 Frank Twiss; M; Son; 3-6
1043 Hoksila Waste; Good Boy; M; Son; 0-9

1044 Julia Kocer; F; Mother; 51
1045 Ruth Kocer; F; Dau; 15
1046 Rena Kocer; F; Dau; 10
1047 Frank Kocer; M; Son; 13
1048 Hobart Kocer; M; Son; 12
1049 Joanna Kocer; F; Dau; 2-5

1050 Wanbli Sun; William Eagle Feather; M; 33

1051 John Conroy; M; Father; 35
1052 Lucy Conroy; F; Wife; 27
1053 Maggie Conroy; F; Dau; 14
1054 Benjamin Conroy; M; Son; 10
1055 Annie Conroy; F; Dau; 8
1056 Millie Conroy; F; Dau; 5
1057 Taylor Conroy; M; Son; 3-3
1058 Lena Conroy; F; Dau; 0-8

1059 Ella Russell; F; Mother; 34
1060 Louisa Russell; F; Dau; 14
1061 Amilia[sic] Russell; F; Dau; 17
1062 Ruth Russell; F; Dau; 3-1
1063 Nellie Russell; F; Dau; 0-7

1064 Mato Gi; James Yellow Bear; M; 22

1065 William D. McGaa; M; Father; 37

1066 Anna Clifford McGaa; F; Wife; 23
1067 Etta McGaa; F; Dau; 11
1068 William McGaa; M; Son; 12
1069 Charlotte McGaa; F; Dau; 9
1070 Albert McGaa; M; Son; 8
1071 Agnes McGaa; F; Dau; 6
1072 George Leroy McGaa; M; Son; 3-7

1073 Wasu Isnala; Lone Hail; F; 74

1074 Pa on Waapa; Strikes With Nose; M; Father; 49
1075 Tacanku Waste Win; Her Good Road; F; Wife; 57
1076 Warpa Tanka; Cora Black Bird; F; Dau; 23
1077 Warpa Tanka; Louis Black Bird; M; G.Son; 2-6

1078 Hinhan Tanka; Big Owl; M; Father; 39
1079 Hinhan Tanka; Lucy Big Owl; F; Wife; 28
1080 Hinhan Tanka; Edward Big Owl; M; Son; 15
1081 Hinhan Tanka; Thomas Big Owl; M; Son; 6
1082 Hinhan Tanka; George W. Big Owl; M; Son; 4
1083 Hinhan Tanka; John Big Owl; M; Son; 1-7

1084 Pankeska Hoksila; Shell Boy; M; Father; 39
1085 Heraka Win; Elk Woman; F; Wife; 49
1086 Pankeska Hoksila; Ida Shell Boy; F; Dau; 12
1087 Heraka Ciqala; Little Elk; M; Father; 63
1088 Peji Rota; Sage Bush; F; Wife; 50

Census Of The Sioux And Cheyenne Indians Of Pine Ridge Agency, South Dakota. Taken by W. H. Clapp, Captain 16th Infantry, Acting United States Indian Agent, June 30, 1896. (Porcupine District)

Key: Number; Indian Name *(if given)*; English Name; Sex; Relation; Age

1089 Heraka Ciqala; John Little Elk; M; Son; 15
1090 Nica; Has None; F; Dau; 9
1091 Iglakesa; Paul Moves; M; Husb; 23
1092 Pehan Catka; Grace Left Heron; F; Wife; 20
1093 Hektakiya Ekte; John Kills Back; M; 32
1094 Inyan; Samuel Rock; M; Father; 35
1095 Zintkala Luta; Red Bird; F; Wife; 37
1096 Inyan; Charles Rock; M; Son; 10
1097 Inyan; John Rock; M; Son; 8
1098 Inyan; Bessie Rock; F; Dau; 5
1099 Palani Sica; Bad Ree; M; Husb; 71
1100 Tipi; House; F; Wife; 68
1101 Huhu Yuha; Keeps The Bone; F; Father; 68
1102 Kutepi; Charles Shot At; M; Son; 28
1103 Mato Bloka; He Bear; M; Father; 50
1104 Winyan Hanska; Tall Woman; F; Wife; 31
1105 Mato Bloka; Mary He Bear; F; Dau; 13
1106 Mato Bloka; George He Bear; M; Son; 9
1107 Tokeya Inyanka; Runs First; F; Dau; 6
1108 Tokala Wanbli; Eagle Fox; M; Father; 24
1109 Pispiza; Mary Prairie Dog; F; Wife; 20
1110 Wohitika; Has Courage; F; Dau; 0-4
1111 Tatanka Ktepi; Kills The Bull; M; Father; 66
1112 Pankeska Luta; Red Shell; F; Wife; 55
1113 Tatanka Ktepi; Ellen Kills The Bull; F; Dau; 12
1114 Annaie[sic]; F; Dau,Gr.; 6
1115 Tasunke T. Najin; Horse Stands In Sight; M; Father; 35
1116 Tarca Ha; Buckskin; F; Wife; 38
1117 Yawa; Count; M; Son; 6
1118 Taninyan Najin; Robert Stands I. Sight; M; Son; 0-5
1119 Wayartaka; Bite; M; G.Father; 73
1120 Orau Waste; Good Action; F; Wife; 74
1121 Najinyapi; Surrounded; F; G.Dau; 15
1122 Ninglica; Comes Alive; F; G.Dau; 12
1123 Itohu Suta; Frank Hard Forehead; M; Father; 26
1124 Iothu[sic] Suta; Louisa Hard Forehead; F; Wife; 25
1125 Itohu Suta; Thomas Hard Forehead; M; Son; 2-10
1126 Heraka Waste; Pretty Elk; M; Father; 37
1127 Tasunke Waste; Good Horse; F; Wife; 34
1128 Anpo; Ethon[sic] Daylight; M; S.Son; 22
1129 Heraka Waste; Robert Pretty Elk; M; Son; 13
1130 Heraka Waste; Jessie Pretty Elk; F; Dau; 11
1131 Heraka Waste; Lillie Pretty Elk; F; Dau; 9

Census Of The Sioux And Cheyenne Indians Of Pine Ridge Agency, South Dakota. Taken by W. H. Clapp, Captain 16th Infantry, Acting United States Indian Agent, June 30, 1896. (Porcupine District)

Key: Number; Indian Name *(if given)*; English Name; Sex; Relation; Age

1132 Heraka Waste; Maggie Pretty Elk; F; Dau; 5
1133 Heraka Waste; Lizzie Pretty Elk; F; Dau; 2-5
1134 Tatanka Sinte; Bull Tail; M; Father; 27
1135 Tatanka Site[sic]; Sarah Bull Tail; F; Wife; 23
1136 Wayank Najin; Stands And Looks; F; Dau; 6
1137 Sungmanu; Steals Horses; M; Father; 38
1138 Tawawbli; Her Eagle; F; Wife; 42
1139 Itonkasan Luta; Red Weasel; F; Dau; 1-1
1140 Mato Wakuwa; Emma Charging Bear; F; S.Dau; 17
1141 Tatanka Ciqala; Little Bull; M; Husb; 53
1142 Zuya Ehake; Late Warrior; F; Wife; 49
1143 Hinapapi Sica; Goes Out Bad; M; Husb; 68
1144 Huncase; Garter; F; Wife; 64
1145 Maku Yublu; Julia Breaks Land; F; Mother; 46
1146 Emma; F; Dau; 18
1147 Oscar; M; Son; 15
1148 Mollie; F; Dau; 13
1149 Wahacanka Wicarca; Old Shield; M; G.Father; 68
1150 Nazunspe Tanka; Big Ax; F; Wife; 63
1151 Toka Oyuspa; Lucy Catches Enemy; F; G.Dau; 12
1152 Hotain; Voice In Sight; M; G.Son; 9
1153 Wahacauka Wicarca; George Old Shield; M; G.Son; 4
1154 Wahacauka Wicarca; Julia O.S. Woodruff; F; Wife; 30
1155 Tatanka Ska; White Bull; M; Father; 39
1156 Tarca; Deer; F; Wife; 38
1157 Tatanka Ska; Helena White Bull; F; Dau; 12
1158 Winyan Wakau; Holy Woman; F; Dau; 6
1159 Tasunke; Wounded Horse; M; Son; 4
1160 Mato Hauska; Long Bear; M; Son; 1-2
1161 Tatanka Ska; Richard White Bull; M; Husb; 17
1162 Wazi Zintakla; Ella Pine Bird; F; Wife; 19
1163 Aglagla Iyanka; Peter Runs Along T. Edge; M; Father; 30
1164 Tasunke Luta; Her Red Horse; F; Wife; 24
1165 Ptesan Najin; Standing White Cow; F; Dau; 5
1166 Mato Wanjila; Lone Bear #2; M; G.Fa; 67
1167 Palani Win; Ree Woman; F; Cousine[sic]; 74
1168 Tezi Ska; Frank White Belly; M; G.Son; 20
1169 Kici Kiciza; Jacob Fights With; M; G.Son; 12
1170 Mato Yatapi; Chief Bear; M; Father; 29
1171 Mato Yatapi; Susie Chief Bear; F; Wife; 26
1172 Hoksila Waste; Good Boy; M; Son; 1-5
1173 Hanomani; Night Walker; F; 65

Census Of The Sioux And Cheyenne Indians Of Pine Ridge Agency, South Dakota. Taken by W. H. Clapp, Captain 16th Infantry, Acting United States Indian Agent, June 30, 1896. (Porcupine District)

Key: Number; Indian Name *(if given)*; English Name; Sex; Relation; Age

1174 Bkaska Rpaya; Lays On His Belly; M; Father; 61
1175 Tiglake; Moves; F; Wife; 54
1176 Canupa Agli; Brings Pipe; F; Dau; 22
1177 Cante Witko; Fool Heart; F; G.Dau; 0-7
1178 Heraka Sica; Julia Bad Elk; F; Mother; 22
1179 Heraka Sica; Susie Bad Elk; F; Dau; 0-7
1180 Kangi; Thomas Crow; M; Father; 33
1181 Kangi; Alice Crow; F; Wife; 33
1182 Kangi; Lucy Crow; F; Dau; 6
1183 Kangi; James Crow; M; Son; 3-8
1184 Kangi; Anna Crow; F; Dau; 1day
1185 Mato Tatanka; Bull Bear; M; 79
1186 Wakte Gli; Comes Killing; M; Son; 19
1187 Canku Wakan; Holy Road; M; Mother; 50
1188 Wanbli Situpi; Eagle Tail Feather; M; Father; 42
1189 Tainyan Najin; Standing In Sight; F; Wife; 28
1190 Pejuta Waste; Good Medicine; F; Dau; 1-5
1191 Marpiya To; David Arapahoe; M; Father; 21
1192 Sinte Nopa; Ada Two Tails; F; Wife; 20
1193 Karoliyeyapi; Throws Him; M; Son; 0-7
1194 Marpiya Tucuhu; Cloud Ribs; F; Mother; 47
1195 Marpiya To; William Arapahoe; M; Son; 11
1196 Marpiya To; Jennie Arapahoe; F; Dau; 6
1197 Marpiya To; Girl Arapahoe; F; Dau; 3-6
1198 Cetan; Florence Hawk; F; Niece; 24
1199 Cetan; Lizzie Hawk; F; 19
1200 Tiokte; Kills In Lodge; M; Son; 28
1201 Winorcala; Old Woman; F; Mother; 64
1202 Angeline Yates; F; Niece; 24
1203 Wica Ktercin; Wants To Be A Man; F; Mother; 56
1204 Lucy; F; Dau; 23
1205 Wahacanka Wicarcala; Isaac Old Shield; M; Father; 25
1206 Winyan Waste; Pretty Woman; F; Wife; 26
1207 Canwegna; Among Timber; F; M. in L.; 63
1208 Kiyan Win; Flying Woman; F; S.Dau; 7
1209 Wahacanka Wicarcal[sic]; Susie Old Shield; F; Dau; 0-7
1210 Tokeya Najin; Stands First; M; Father; 45
1211 Tokeya Najin; Nancy Stands First; F; Wife; 40
1212 Tokeya Najin; Alexander Stands First; M; Son; 21
1213 Hoksila Waste; Good Boy; M; Son; 5
1214 Tokeya Najin; Ella Stands First; F; Dau; 1-8
1215 Wanopi; Geo. Wounded Arrows; M; Husb; 22
1216 Pankeska Win; Shield Woman; F; Wife; 20

Census Of The Sioux And Cheyenne Indians Of Pine Ridge Agency, South Dakota.
Taken by W. H. Clapp, Captain 16th Infantry, Acting United States Indian Agent,
June 30, 1896.   (Porcupine District)

Key: Number; Indian Name *(if given)*; English Name; Sex; Relation; Age

1217 Tasunke Ota; Her Many Horses; F; Mother; 41
1218 Osungye Erpeyapi; Destroyed; M; Son; 11
1219 Sunkska Agli; Brings White Horses; M; Son; 9
1220 Lily; F; Niece; 20

1221 Mato C. Inyanka; Jno. Bear Runs IN Woods; M; Father; 49
1222 Mato C. Inyanka; Jennie Bear R.I. Woods; F; Wife; 46
1223 Mato C. Inyanka; Ada Bear Runs In Woods; F; Dau; 2-4
1224 James Provost; M; S.Son; 16

1225 Anpetu; Day; M; Father; 42
1226 Anpetu; Lizzie Day; F; Wife; 31
1227 Anpetu; Millie Day; F; Dau; 10
1228 Anpetu; Lizzie Day; F; Dau; 8
1229 Okawinr Mani; Circle Walker; M; Son; 2-10
1230 Tezi Ska; Willard White Belly; M; Nephew; 16

1231 Tatanka Waste; Pretty Bull; M; Father; 38
1232 Tatanka Waste; Jessie Pretty Bull; F; Wife; 34
1233 Sagye Luta; Red Cane; F; Dau; 3-9
1234 Anpetu; Julia Day; F; S.Dau; 17
1235 Tatanka Waste; Carrie Pretty Bull; F; Dau; 0-8

1236 Catka; Left Hand; M; Father; 33
1237 He Luta; Red Horn; F; Wife; 31
1238 Wasaka; Stout; F; Dau; 0-8

1239 Wahacanka Wakcuwa; Wallace Charging Shield; M; Father; 28
1240 Wahacanka Wakcuwa; Lucy Charging Shield; F; Wife; 27
1241 Wakacanka[sic] Wakcuwa; Lucy Charging Shield; F; Dau; 1-5

1242 Wagmeza; William Corn; M; Father; 34
1243 Wagmeza; Roza Corn; F; Wife; 37
1244 Wagmeza; Emma Corn; F; S.Dau; 10
1245 Sina Gi; Yellow Blanket; F; Dau; 4-4

1246 Otoran; Gives Away; F; Mother; 32
1247 Zintkala Luta; Red Bird; F; Dau; 9

1248 Tucuhu Wicasa; Rib Man; M; Father; 52
1249 Asapi; Shouted At; F; Wife; 53
1250 Tucuhu Wicasa; Thomas Rib Man; M; Son; 23
1251 Tucuhu Wivasa[sic]; Alfred Rib Man; M; Son; 16
1252 Sahunwinla; Cheyenne Woman; F; 74

1253 Maza Sica; Bad Iron; M; Father; 32
1254 Canhaupi; Sugar; F; Wife; 30
1255 Glinapa; Comes Out; F; Dau; 6
1256 Mati Hin Waste; Good Haired Bear; F; Dau; 4

1257 Caje Oglaka[sic]; Tells His Name; M; Father; 31
1258 Warpe Wakan; Medicine Leaf; F; Wife; 28
1259 Wanbli Tokahe; Leading Eagle; F; Dau; 3-6

1260 Mary Romero; F; G.Mo; 62
1261 Maggie Romero[sic]; F; G.Dau; 6

1262 James Bissonette; M; Father; 29
1263 Susy Ramero; F; Wife; 22
1264 Joseph Bissonette; M; Son; 1-7

Census Of The Sioux And Cheyenne Indians Of Pine Ridge Agency, South Dakota. Taken by W. H. Clapp, Captain 16th Infantry, Acting United States Indian Agent, June 30, 1896. (Porcupine District)

Key: Number; Indian Name *(if given)*; English Name; Sex; Relation; Age

1265 Wanbli Cincala; Young Eagle; M; Father; 61
1266 Topa Canupa; Smokes Four Times; F; Wife; 58
1267 Miyogli; Nellie Whetstone; F; Dau; 31
1268 Alice Garcia; F; Mother; 26
1269 Si; Foot; M; Uncle; 39
1270 Nicholas Garcia; M; Son; 3
1271 Wakinyan Ska; White Thunder; M; Father; 63
1272 Wamniomni Koyaka; Wears Whirlwind; F; Wife; #1; 55
1273 Pa Wayatkau; Drinks Bitters; F; Wife #2; 52
1274 Wakinyan Ska; Harry White Thunder; M; Son; 20
1275 Zintkala Luta; Paul Red Bird; M; Son; 20
1276 Wakinyan Ska; Bessie White Thunder; F; Dau; 17
1277 Wamniomni; Whirlwind; M; Son; 14
1278 Tiglisni; Left Her Home; F; G.Dau; 3-2

1279 Itonkala Ska; White Mouse; M; Father; 36
1280 Hakikta; Looks Back; F; Wife; 32
1281 Itonkala Ska; Ella White Mouse; F; Dau; 6
1282 Wanbli Hinapa; Comes Out Eagle; F; Dau 3-1
1283 Ohitika; Brave; M; Son; 1-1

1284 Heraka Sica; John Bad Elk; M; Father; 24
1285 Miyogli; Ida Whetstone; F; Wife; 23
1286 Heraka Sica; Joseph Bad Elk; M; Son; 0-5

1287 Akicita Ciqala; Little Soldier; M; Father; 31
1288 Marpiya Sna; Rattling Cloud; F; Wife; 32
1289 Sina Wakan; Medicine Blanket; F; Dau; 8
1290 Anpetu Luta; Red Day; M; Son; 7

1291 Maka Mani; Walks Under Ground; M; Father; 42
1292 Sna Win; Rattling Woman; F; Wife; 41
1293 Canihanke; John End Of Timber; M; S.Son; 18
1294 Maggie; F; S.Dau; 16
1295 Miuwanca Win; Ocean Woman; F; S.Dau; 10
1296 Taanpetu; Her Good Day; F; Dau; 2-10
1297 Wicincala; Girl; F; Dau; 0-9

1298 Maka Mahel Mani; Amos Walks U. Ground; M; Husb; 19
1299 Alice; F; Wife; 19
1300 Kapojela; Light Woman; F; G.Mo; 69

1301 Tatanka Ska; White Bull #2; M; Husb; 37
1302 Marpuya To; Emma Blue Cloud; F; Wife; 30
1303 Wahacanke Wicarca; Alfred Old Shield; M; Husb; 26
1304 Hotain Win; Hears Voice; F; Wife; 32

1305 Joseph Smith; M; Father; 30
1306 Janette Smith; F; Wife; 26
1307 Effie Smith; F; Dau; 6
1308 Joseph Smith, Jr; M; Son; 1-5

1309 Tatanka Hauska; Long Bull; M; Father; 48

Census Of The Sioux And Cheyenne Indians Of Pine Ridge Agency, South Dakota. Taken by W. H. Clapp, Captain 16th Infantry, Acting United States Indian Agent, June 30, 1896. (Porcupine District)

Key: Number; Indian Name *(if given)*; English Name; Sex; Relation; Age

1310 Ista Wiyakpa; Bright Eyes; F; Wife; 34
1311 Mila Hanska; Long Knife; F; Dau; 17
1312 Kiyela Opi; Shot Close; F; Dau; 8
1313 Wicasa Isnala; Lone Man; M; Son; 6
1314 Canupa Waste; Good Pipe; F; Dau; 3-5
1315 Ciqala Wicakte; Henry Kills Small; M; Father; 21
1316 Ciqala Wicakte; Anna Kills Small; F; Wife; 20
1317 Ciqala Wicakte; Susie Kills Small; F; Dau; 1-5
1318 Mato Wanjila; Oliver Lone Bear; M; Father; 44
1319 Tibloku Ota; Plenty Brothers; F; Wife; 46
1320 Mato Wanjila; Julia Lone Bear; F; Dau; 22
1321 Mato Wanjila; Samuel Lone Bear; M; Son; 17
1322 Mato Wanjila; Abraham Lone Bear; M; Son; 16
1323 Mato Wanjila; Benjamin Lone Bear; M; Son; 14
1324 Mato Wanjila; Henry Lone Bear; M; Son; 9
1325 Mato Wanjila; Susie Lone Bear; F; Dau; 2
1326 Ite Ska; White Face; M; Father; 54
1327 Ti Tani; Old Lodge; F; Wife #1; 43
1328 Keya Cagu; Terropin[sic] Lights; F; Wife; #2; 45
1329 Icospincala; Swallow; M; Son; 16
1330 Rante Zi; Adelin[sic] Yellow Cedar; F; Dau; 13
1331 Tasunke Wakuwa; Willian[sic] Charging Horse; M; Son; 12
1332 Wicincala; Girl; F; Dau; 5
1333 Canku Waste; Good Road; F; Dau; 2-10
1334 Sinte; Tail; M; Father; 22
1335 Sunk Hinto; Fannie Blue Horse; F; Wife; 23
1336 Sunk Hinto; Jack Blue Horse; M; Son; 1-8
1337 Ite Ska; Thomas White Face; M; Husb; 19
1338 Ista Uni; Susie Crooked Eyes; F; Wife; 16
1339 Hoksila Ciqala; Little Boy; M; Father; 27
1340 Hoksila Ciqala; Cicila Little Boy; F; Wife; 23
1341 Ispa; Elbow; M; Son; 6
1342 Charlie; M; Son; 0-1-1
1343 Tasunke Iyanka; Wm. Running Horse; M; Father; 35
1344 Tasunke Maza; Iron Horse; F; Wife; 30
1345 Tasunke Iyanka; Samuel R. Horse; M; Son; 5
1346 Loe[sic]; M; Cousin; 2-10
1347 Mato Wicakte; Bear Killer; M; Father; 44
1348 Nape Sicamna; Hand Dont[sic] Smell; F; Wife; 41
1349 Mato Wicakte; Albert Bear Killer; M; Son; 22
1350 Mato Wicakte; Louise Bear Killer; F; Dau; 14
1351 Mato Wicakte; John Bear Killer; M; Son; 18
1352 Hoksila Waste; Good Boy; M; Son; 2-4

Census Of The Sioux And Cheyenne Indians Of Pine Ridge Agency, South Dakota. Taken by W. H. Clapp, Captain 16th Infantry, Acting United States Indian Agent, June 30, 1896. (Porcupine District)

Key: Number; Indian Name *(if given)*; English Name; Sex; Relation; Age

1353 Ista Gi; Brown Eyes; M; Father; 26
1354 Yamni; Three; F; Wife; 30
1355 Ayustaupi; Let Her Go; M; Son; 7
1356 Iyanka; Runs; M; Son; 5
1357 Witansna On; Single Woman; F; Dau; 2-6
1358 Pehin Ji; Yellow Haired; M; Son; 0-1
1359 Cante Maza; Iron Heart; M; Husb; 59
1360 Wanbli Sun; Eagle Feather; F; Wife; 50
1361 Ohitika; Brave; M; Bro; 44
1362 John; M; G.Son; 15

1363 Haupa Sica; Bad Moccosin[sic]; F; Sister; 65
1364 Maya Ole; Looks For Bank; F; Sister; 81

1365 Marpiya Maza; Iron Cloud; M; Father; 40
1366 Wanapin Luta; Red Necklace; F; Wife #1; 39
1367 Paha Anakitan; Runs For Hill; F; Wife #2; 30
1368 Marpiya Maza; Eddie Iron Cloud; M; Son; 12
1369 Kute; Shoots; M; Son; 8
1370 Pejuta Waste; Good Medicine; F; Dau; 7
1371 Coka Glisni; Never Comes Without; M: Son; 5
1372 Iyuha Wicaku; Gives Them All; F; Dau; 9
1373 Najinhau Ku; Comes Standing; M; Son; 2-2
1374 Wankal Kte; Kills Above; M; Son; 0-7

1375 Wanbli Koyaka; Wears Eagle; M; G.Son; 34

1376 Sina Karwoka; Blowing Blanket; F; G.Mo; 71
1377 Sunkmanu Sa; Steals Horses; M; 36

1378 Mato Wanbli; Bear Eagle; M: Father; 38
1379 Canupa Waci; Pipe Dance; F; Wife; 29
1380 Wanbli He; Eagle Horn; M; Son; 13
1381 Nopa Wakita; Looks Twice; M; Son; 10
1382 Wanbli Ite; Eagle Face; F; Dau; 6
1383 Mato Wanbli; Louis Bear Eagle; M; Son; 1-1

1384 Wahacauka Wanbli; Eagle Shield; M; Father; 40
1385 Heraka Waste; Good Elk; F; Wife #2; 34
1386 Tacanku Waste; Her Good Road; F; Wife #1; 44
1387 Wahacanka Wanbli; Lucy Eagle Shield; F; Dau; 10
1388 Ptesan Gleska; Spotted White Cow; F; Dau; 9
1389 Canwegna Najin; Stands In The Wood; M; Son; 5
1390 Ite Wanbli; Eagle Face; F; Dau; 2-2
1391 Tinga; Grunting; F; Dau; 1-9

1392 Kangi Witko; Fool Crow; M; Husb; 29
1393 Kangi Witko; Lizzie Fool Crow; F; Wife; 24

1394 Heraka Ska; White Elk; M; Father; 34
1395 Heraka Ska; Maggie White Elk; F; Wife; 34
1396 Heraka Ska; Lucy White Elk; F; Dau; 11

Census Of The Sioux And Cheyenne Indians Of Pine Ridge Agency, South Dakota. Taken by W. H. Clapp, Captain 16th Infantry, Acting United States Indian Agent, June 30, 1896. (Porcupine District)

Key: Number; Indian Name *(if given)*; English Name; Sex; Relation; Age

1397 Ehuke Gli; Returned Lost; M; Son; 8
1398 Okinyan; Flies About; M; Son; 5
1399 Tasunke Opi; Wounded Horse; F; Dau; 4
1400 Poge Tanka; Wm. Big Nostrils; M; Son; 2-2
1401 Heraka Ska; Ellis White Elk; M; Son; 0-05

1402 Ituhu Suta; Hard Forehead; M; Father; 63
1403 Winyan Waste; Good Woman; F; Wife; 49
1404 Hoksila Sica; Bad Boy; M; Son; 18

1405 Oye Wakan; Medicine Track; F; Mother; 32
1406 Oye Wakan; Andrew Medicine Track; M; Son; 0-1-6

1407 Zintkala Maza; Iron Bird; M; Father; 40
1408 Pehin Ji; Yellow Hair; F; Wife; 33
1409 Zintkala Maza; Bessie Iron Bird; F; Dau; 16

1410 Cante Ohitika; Brave Heart; M; Father; 54
1411 Tasunke Waste; Her Good Horse; F; Wife; 50
1412 Cante Ohitika; John Brave Heart; M; Son; 23
1413 Cante Ohitika; Pugh Brave Heart; M; Son; 18
1414 Tiyopa Waste; Good Door; F; Dau; 9

1415 Cante Ohitika; James Brave Heart; M; Father; 28
1416 Wanagi Tokeya; First Ghost; F; Wife; 20
1417 Cante Ohitika; Moses Brave Heart; M; Son; 0-5

1418 Maza Cincala; Iron Child; M; Husb; 48
1419 Warpe Mato; Bear Leaf; F; Wife; 34
1420 Hunska To; Blue Leggins; F; Mother; 74
1421 Wicegna Iyanka; Runs Among Them; M; B. in L. 36
1422 Tiglake Waste; Good Mover; F; Sister; 45

1423 Conica Wanica; No Flesh; M; Father; 51
1424 Pankeska Win; Shell Woman; F; Wife; 47
1425 Conica Wanica; Lucy No Flesh; F; Dau; 18
1426 Conica Wanica; Emma No Flesh; F; Niece; 16

1427 Wahacanka Wakuwa; Charging Shield; M; Husb; 64
1428 Wahacanka Wakuwa; Julia Charging Shield; F; Wife; 54
1429 Sungmanitu W; Clayton High Wolf; M; Father; 21
1430 Wahacankuwa; Lizzie Charging Shield; F; Wife; 17
1431 Tasunke Ota; Plenty Horses; F; Dau; 0-7

1432 Tatanka Ote Ska; White Face Bull; M; Father; 51
1433 Iasina Wakan; Her Holy Blanket; F; Wife; 50
1434 Wayank Hipe; Comes To See Her; F; Dau; 5

1435 Ehake Gli; Jennie Comes Last; F; 25
1436 Psito; Beads; F; G.Mo; 74
1437 Canupa Wanbli; Eagle Pipe; M; Father; 40
1438 Cetan; Hawk; F; Wife; 40

Census Of The Sioux And Cheyenne Indians Of Pine Ridge Agency, South Dakota. Taken by W. H. Clapp, Captain 16th Infantry, Acting United States Indian Agent, June 30, 1896. (Porcupine District)

Key: Number; Indian Name *(if given)*; English Name; Sex; Relation; Age

1439 Canupa Wanbli; Maggie Eagle Pipe; F; Dau; 13
1440 Wanbli Waste; Good Eagle; M; Nephew; 3
1441 Wazi Zintkala; Pine Bird; M; Father; 42
1442 Tawicincala; Her Girl; F; Wife; 39
1443 Wazi Zintkala; Samuel Pine Bird; M; Son; 15
1444 Sungmanitu Sica; Bad Wolf; M; Son; 8
1445 Wazi Zintkala; Jack Pine Bird; M; Son; 5
1446 Wazi Zintkala; Willie Pine Bird; M; Son; 2-10

1447 Wiciyela Win; Yankton Woman; F; G.Mo; 51
1448 Wojosa; Farmer; F; G.Mo; 56
1449 Ciqala Kte; Kills Small; M; G.Son; 5

1450 Wapaha; Conrad War Bonnet; M; Father; 25
1451 Ista Gi; Yellow Eyes; F; Wife; 23
1452 Tipi; Lizzie Lodge; F; Dau; 2-4

1453 Mato Wanwicayanka; Sees The Bear; M; Father; 55
1454 Marpiya Waste; Good Cloud; F; Wife; 45
1455 Kangi Kte; Kills Crow Indian; M; Son; 24

1456 Tate Sina; Wind Shawl; F; 75

1457 Peji Rota; Gray Grass; F; 69

1458 Tatanka Wapaha; Bull Bonnet; M; Father; 52
1459 Tasunke Tokeya H.; Horse Goes Ahead; F; Wife; 42

1460 Tatanka Wapaha; Emma Bull Bonnet; F; Dau; 26

1461 Mato Hanska; Long Bear; M; Father; 60
1462 Kiyaksa; Cut Off; F; Wife; 49
1463 Huhu; Walter Bone; M; Son; 24
1464 Tasunke Opi; Her Wounded Horse; F; Dau; 12

1465 Ptesan Wicasa; White Cow Man; M; Father; 46
1466 Wakan Hinapa; Comes Out Holy; F; Wife; 39
1467 Yuhomni; Turns; F; Dau; 17
1468 Warpiya Sna Win; Rattling Cloud; F; Dau; 4-5

1469 Wacapa; Thomas Stabber; M; Husb; 22
1470 Rlola; Nora Growler; F; Wife; 17

1471 Cetan Wakuwa; Chasing Hawk; M; Husb; 35
1472 Ptesan Waste; Good White Cow; F; Wife; 32

1473 Heraka Najin; Standing Elk; M; Father; 40
1474 Tainyan Ti; Lives In Sight; F; Wife; 37
1475 Tasunke Wayankapi; Looks At Her Horses; F; Dau; 11
1476 Cetan Akicita; Hawk Soldier; M; Son; 7
1477 Heraka Najin; George Standing Elk; M; Son; 1-5

1478 Tezi Ska; White Belly; M; Father; 47
1479 Hu Ptecela; Short Leg; F; Wife; 43
1480 Tezi Ska; William White Belly; M; Son; 20

Census Of The Sioux And Cheyenne Indians Of Pine Ridge Agency, South Dakota. Taken by W. H. Clapp, Captain 16th Infantry, Acting United States Indian Agent, June 30, 1896. (Porcupine District)

Key: Number; Indian Name *(if given)*; English Name; Sex; Relation; Age

1481 Tezi Ska; Louise White Belly; F; Dau; 5
1482 Tezi Ska; Jessie White Belly; F; Dau; 1-7

1483 Wosla Najin; Stand Up; M; Father; 25
1484 Sunsunla Agli; Brings Mule; F; S.Dau; 12
1485 Winyan; Woman; F; Wife; 31
1486 Pahin Sinte; Porcupine Tail; M; Son; 5 day

1487 Tatanka Sapa; Thomas Black Bull; M; S.Fath; 33
1488 Tatanka Sapa; Susie Black Bull; Wife; 35
1489 Tatanka Sapa; James Black Bull; M; S.Son; 16

1490 Charles Jones; M; Father; 25
1491 Lizzie Jones; F; Wife; 22
1492 Katie Jones; F; Mother; 69
1493 Alice Jones; F; Dau; 2-10
1494 Laura Jones; F; Dau; 0-2

1495 Akicita Hanska; Long Soldier; M; Father; 49
1496 Wahukeza; Lance; F; Wife; 52
1497 Jennie; F; Dau; 20
1498 Ruth; F; Dau; 18
1499 Oscar; M; Son; 14

1500 Psa Win; Crow Woman; F; 81

1501 Alexander Mousseau; M; Father; 38
1502 Alice Mousseau; F; Wife; 31
1503 Julia Mousseau; F; Dau; 14
1504 Louis Mousseau; M; Son; 12
1505 Sophia Mousseau; F; Dau; 9
1506 James Mousseau; M; Son; 6
1507 Agnes Mousseau; F; Dau; 4-0
1508 Susie Mousseau; F; Dau; 1-4

1509 Ista Rmi; Crooked Eyes; M; Father; 61
1510 Piya Icaga; New Growth; F; Wife; 56
1511 Frank Cross; M; Son; 24

1512 Mila Gi; Yellow Knife; M; S.Father; 53
1513 Tasina Luta Win; Her Red Blanket; F; Wife; 45
1514 Pahin; Edward Porcupine; M; S.Son; 21
1515 Wapaha; War Bonnet; M; S.Son; 10

1516 Heraka Ho Waste; Good Voice Elk; M; Husb; 27
1517 Wazi Eyutan; Touches Pine; F; Wife; 24

1518 Taspan Sapa; Black Apple; F; 60

1519 Wagmu Su; Pumpkin Seed; M; Father; 64
1520 Winyan Hanska; Tall Woman; F; Wife; 44
1521 Wagmu Su; William Pumpkin Seed; M; Son; 10
1522 Wagmu Su; Nicholas Pumpkin Seed; M; Son; 16

1523 Mato Hinapa; Bear Comes Out; M; Father; 38
1524 Kangi; Crow; F; Wife; 34
1525 Mato Hinapa; Jennie Bear Comes Out; F; Dau; 14
1526 Mato Ahan Apapi; Knock O Head; F; Dau; 4-4

1527 Joseph Twiss; M; Son; 30
1528 Frank Twiss; M; Bro; 32
1529 Mary Twiss; F; Mother; 64

1530 Joseph Richard; M; Father; 48
1531 Julia Richard; F; Wife; 39
1532 Alexander Richard; M; Son; 19

Census Of The Sioux And Cheyenne Indians Of Pine Ridge Agency, South Dakota. Taken by W. H. Clapp, Captain 16th Infantry, Acting United States Indian Agent, June 30, 1896. (Porcupine District)

Key: Number; Indian Name *(if given)*; English Name; Sex; Relation; Age

1533 Benjamin Richard; M; Son; 16
1534 Lucy Richard; F; Dau; 13
1535 Julia Richard; F; Dau; 5
1536 Josephine Richard; F; Dau; 3-4

1537 Ota Agli; Brings Plenty; M; Father; 74
1538 Mato Cincala; Young Bear Joe; M; Son; 22
1539 Ota Agli; Philip Brings Plenty; M; Son; 20

1540 Nakiwizipi; Jealous Of Him; M; Husb; 31
1541 Mary Gay; F; Wife; 23
1542 Emma; F; Dau; 4

1543 Cetan Wakinyan; Thunder Hawk; M; Father; 60
1544 Tapankeska; Her Shell; F; Wife; 53
1545 Sunk Sapa; Albert Black Horse; M; Son; 18
1546 Cetan Win; Mary Thunder Hawk; F; Dau; 14
1547 Frank Yego; M; G.Son; 13

1548 Zuya Isnala; Lone War; M; Father; 24
1549 Sunk Hinto Agli; Brings Blue Horses; F; Wife; 20
1550 Wanbli Oyate; Tribe Eagle; F; Dau; 3-2

1551 Heraka Wanbli; Eagle Elk; M; Father; 41
1552 Wakan Hinapa; Comes Out Medicine; F; Wife; 23
1553 Effie; F; Dau; 1-3

1554 Psa Win; Crow Woman; F; Mother; 59
1555 James Lock; M; Son; 15

1556 Nite Waste; Pretty Back; M; Father; 55

1557 Huska Narco; Legging Down; F; Wife; 59
1558 Nite Waste; Maggie Pretty Back; F; Dau; 24
1559 Nite Waste; Thomas Pretty Back; M; Son; 14

1560 Oscar Worden; M; 25

1561 Tasunke Wakuwa; Charging Horse; M; Father; 33
1562 Winyan Waste; Helen Pretty Woman; F; Wife; 19
1563 Nopa; Two; M; Son; 11
1564 Ohitika; Brave; M; Son; 0-7

1565 Wahacauka; Shield; M; Father; 30
1566 Alice Shield; F; Wife; 28
1567 Wahacauka; Julia Shield; F; Dau; 7

1568 Peji; James Grass; M; Father; 31
1569 Peji; Ellen Grass; F; Wife; 26
1570 Peji; William Grass; M; Son; 3-11
1571 Peji; Jennie Grass; F; Dau; 2-6
1572 Peji; Victoria Grass; F; Dau; 0-9

1573 Cetan Wakakesya; Troublesome Hawk; M; Father; 31
1574 Cetan Wakakesya; Bessie T. Hawk; F; Wife; 25
1575 Sunk Hinsa Ota; Mary Red Horses; F; Dau; 5
1576 Heraka Ho Waste; Good Voice Elk; F; Dau; 3-1
1577 Cetan Wakakisya[sic]; Phillip T. Hawk; M; Son; 0-10

1578 Charles Richard; M; Father; 45
1579 Anna Richard; F; Wife; 40
1580 Julia Hornbeck; F; S.Dau; 20
1581 Joseph Hornbeck; M; S.Son; 15
1582 Edward Richard; M; Son; 6

Census Of The Sioux And Cheyenne Indians Of Pine Ridge Agency, South Dakota. Taken by W. H. Clapp, Captain 16th Infantry, Acting United States Indian Agent, June 30, 1896. (Porcupine District)

Key: Number; Indian Name *(if given)*; English Name; Sex; Relation; Age

1583 Mato Sapa; Black Bear; M; Father; 36
1584 Mato Sapa; Emma Black Bear; F; Wife; 31
1585 Mato Sapa; Joseph Bear; M; Son; 10
1586 Sunk Karnir Agli; Brings Picked Horses; M; Son; 4-5
1587 Mato Sapa; Charles Black Bear; M; Son; 1-9

1588 Ista Ogna Opi; Shot In The Eye; M; Husb; 60
1589 Sungmonitu Waukat; Susan High Wolf; F; Wife; 61

1590 Mila Yatpi; Knife Chief; M; Father; 60
1591 Wawokiya; Helps; F; Wife #1; 60
1592 Ona Otape; Follows Prairie Fire; F; Wife #2; 54
1593 Sunk Ole; Looks For Horses; M; Son; 24
1594 Mila; Andrew Knife; M; Son; 23
1595 Tasunke Ska; Her White Horse; F; Dau; 9
1596 Sicaya Ecun Sni; Never Does Wrong; M; Son; 7
1597 Waste Agli; Brings Good; F; G.Dau; 3-8

1598 Mato Wakan; Medicine Bear; M; Father; 24
1599 Hoksi Tokapa; Lucy First Born; F; Wife; 22
1600 Tasunke Gliyunka; Horse Lays Down; M; Son; 1-9

1601 Wapin Orlate; Under The Baggage; M; Father; 34
1602 Winyan Tanka; Big Woman; F; Wife; 28
1603 Cetan Hoksila; Hawk Boy; M; Son; 7

1604 Wakin[sic] Orlate; Alice Under T. Baggage; F; Dau; 2
1605 Ikomi[sic]; Mark Spider; M; Father; 33
1606 Iktomi; Sallie Spider; F; Wife; 23
1607 Iktomi; Nellie Spider; F; Dau; 3-6
1608 Iktomi; Albert Spider; M; Son; 1-5

1609 Wanbli Wakan; Medicine Eagle; M; Father; 32
1610 Wanbli Wakan; Josephin[sic] M Eagle; F; Wife; 30
1611 Maku Wakan; Holy Breast; M; Son; 8
1612 Marpiya Wicasa; Cloud Man; M; Son; 7
1613 Glogli; Brings Back; M; Son; 5
1614 Toka Kte; Kills Enemy; F; Dau; 2-3
1615 Wanbli Wakan; Katie M. Eagle; F; Dau; 10
1616 Wanbli Wakan; Lucy M. Eagle; M; Dau; 0-5

1617 Anpo Wicasa; Daylight Man; M; Father; 68
1618 Wasu Sna Win; Rattling Hail; F; Wife; 56
1619 Putinkin; Simon Beard; M; Son; 19
1620 Putinhin[sic]; Carrie Beard; F; Dau; 16
1621 Pte Wakan; Stella Medicine Cow; F; Dau; 9
1622 Putinhin; John Beard; M; Son; 23
1623 Putinhin; Andrew Beard; M; Son; 25

1624 Mato Gi; Yellow Bear; M; Husb; 41

Census Of The Sioux And Cheyenne Indians Of Pine Ridge Agency, South Dakota. Taken by W. H. Clapp, Captain 16th Infantry, Acting United States Indian Agent, June 30, 1896. (Porcupine District)

Key: Number; Indian Name *(if given)*; English Name; Sex; Relation; Age

1625	Tasunke Ota; Plenty Horses; F; Wife; 50	1649	Roka; Lizzie Badger; F; Dau; 5
		1650	Roka; Sallie Badger; F; Dau; 1-6
1626	Pehan Catka; Left Heron; M; Father; 46	1651	Wantauyeya; Good Shot; M; Father; 24
1627	Pehan Catka; Lottie Left Heron; F; Wife; 41	1652	Wantauyeya; Emily Good Shot; F; Wife; 24
1628	Pehan Catka; Bene[sic] Left Heron; F; Dau; 17	1653	Wantauyeya; Harry Good Shot; M; Son; 2-10
1629	Pehan Catka; Emma Left Heron; F; Dau; 12	1654	Asapi; Shout At; M; Father; 25
1630	Mato Kuwapi; Bear Runs After; M; Son; 5	1655	Asapi; Emma Shout At; F; Wife; 24
1631	Pehan Catka; Amelia Left Heron; F; Dau; 0-7	1656	Asapi; John Shout At; M; Son; 7
		1657	Asapi; Frank Shout At; M; Son; 1-5
1632	Paha Wanjila; Amos Lone Hill; M; Father; 40	1658	Mato Taopi; Wounded Bear; M; Father; 56
1633	Paha Wanjila; Sallie Lone Hill; F; Wife; 31	1659	Yesipi; Sent; F; Wife; 57
1634	Paha Wanjila; Ellen Lone Hill; F; Dau; 8	1660	Mato Taopi; Vina Wounded Bear; F; Dau; 18
1635	Paha Wanjila; Laura Lone Hill; F; Dau; 6	1661	Mato Taopi; Susie Wounded Bear; F; Dau; 15
1636	Paha Wanjila; Sidney Lone Hill; M; Son; 3-1	1662	Canupa Nawizi; Jealous Pipe; F; Mother; 66
1637	Paha Wanjila; Hobart Lone Hill; M; Son; 1-11	1663	Scili; Pawnee; F; Dau; 19
		1664	Ite Wanbli; Eagle Face; F; G.Dau; 16
1638	Tatanka Maza; Iron Bull; M; Husb; 32		
1639	Sunk Agli; Bringing Horses; F; Wife; 28	1665	Eulala Conroy; F; 61
		1666	Sungmanitu Wanka; Victoria High Wolf; F; Sister; 23
1640	Louis Bush; M; Father; 27		
1641	Ella Bush; F; Wife; 22	1667	Sungmanitu Wanka; Kittie High Wolf; F; Sister; 20
1642	Sophia Bush; F; Dau; 4-4		
1643	Frank Bush; M; Son; 2-10	1668	Sungmanitu Wanka; Mattie High Wolf; F; Sister; 18
1644	William Bush; M; Son; 1-3		
1645	Roka; Fred Badger; M; Father; 35	1669	Cetan Wakinyan; Martin Thunder Hawk; M; Father; 38
1646	Roka; Mary Badger; F; Wife; 28	1670	Cetan Wakinyan; Fannie Thunder Hawk; F; Wife; 39
1647	Roka; Jennie Badger; F; Dau; 10		
1648	Zintkala To; Fannie Blue Bird; F; Dau; 5	1671	Rachael Brewer; F; S.Dau; 19
		1672	William Brewer; M; S.Son; 16

Census Of The Sioux And Cheyenne Indians Of Pine Ridge Agency, South Dakota. Taken by W. H. Clapp, Captain 16th Infantry, Acting United States Indian Agent, June 30, 1896. (Porcupine District)

Key: Number; Indian Name *(if given)*; English Name; Sex; Relation; Age

1673	Ellen Brewer; F; S.Dau; 11	1698	Kangi Winyan; Esther Crow Woman; F; Wife; 29
1674	Robert Brewer; M; S.Son; 9	1699	Takuni Olesni; Looks For Nothing; F; Dau; 6
1675	Cetan Wakinyan; Charles Thunder Hawk; M; Son; 2-10	1700	Cin; Wants It; F; Dau; 3-7
1676	Cetan Wakinyan; Joseph Thunder Hawk; M; Son; 1-1	1701	Kangi Winyan; Joseph Crow Woman; M; son; 0-6
1677	Winyan Waste; Pretty Woman; F; Mother; 44	1702	Zintkala Nata; Bird Head; M; Father; 36
1678	Wasu; Hail; F; Dau; 11	1703	Tipi Zi; Yellow Lodge; F; Wife; 28
1679	Tasunke Opi; Shot Her Horses; M; Son; 14	1704	Zintkala Pa; Edith Bird Head; F; Dau; 16
1680	Wagmu Su; Asa Pumpkin Seed; M; Father; 32	1705	Hanhepi; Night; M; Son; 6
1681	Wagmu Su; Julia Pumpkin Seed; F; Wife; 31	1706	Zintkala Pa; Bismarck Bird Head; M; Son; 6-6
1682	Wagmu Su; Eliza Pumpkin Seed; F; Dau; 11	1707	Aiyapi; Talks About; F; Dau; 2-8
1683	Wagmu Su; James Pumpkin Seed; M; Son; 10	1708	Hudson; M; Son; 4
1684	Wagmu Su; Robert Pumpkin Seed; M; Son; 7	1709	Lucy; F; Dau; 06[sic]
1685	Wagmu Su; John Pumpkin Seed; M; Son; 5	1710	Zintkala Pa; Alice Bird Head; F; Dau; 10
1686	Wagmu Su; Joseph Pumpkin Seed; M; Son; 3-10	1711	Frank Lock; M; Father; 31
		1712	Hope Lock; F; Wife; 29
1687	Wagmu Su; Mary Pumpkin Seed; F; Dau; 1-5	1713	Mary Lock; F; Dau; 0-6
		1714	Ite Po; Swollen Face; F; Mother; 38
1688	John Boyer; M; Father; 27	1715	Wayank Najin; Stands Looking; F; Dau; 2-10
1689	Lucy Boyer; F; Wife; 28		
1690	Maggie Boyer; F; Dau; 4-4	1716	Tasunke Wakita; Looking Horse; F; Dau; 2-10
1691	James Boyer; M; Son; 2-1		
1692	Alice Boyer; F; Dau; 0-5	1717	Maggie Palmer; F; Mother; 48
1693	Nite Ciqala; Small Back; M; Father; 30	1718	William Palmer; M; Son; 22
		1719	Taylor Palmer; M; Son; 21
1694	Tasunke Waste Win; Her Good Horse; F; Wife; 29	1720	Olive Palmer; F; Dau; 18
		1721	Charles Palmer; M; Son; 15
1695	Agli; Fetches; M; Son; 5	1722	Julia Palmer; F; Dau; 12
1696	Annie; F; Dau; 0-7	1723	Albert Palmer; M; Son; 11
1697	Kangi Winyan; Crow Woman; F; Father; 31	1724	Ohomni Sni; Dont Go Around; M; Husb; 75

Census Of The Sioux And Cheyenne Indians Of Pine Ridge Agency, South Dakota. Taken by W. H. Clapp, Captain 16th Infantry, Acting United States Indian Agent, June 30, 1896. (Porcupine District)

Key: Number; Indian Name *(if given)*; English Name; Sex; Relation; Age

1725 Glinajin; Comes To Stand; F; Wife; 65

1726 Mastincala; Rabbit #2; M; Husb; 75
1727 Zuzeca Owin; Snake Ear Ring; F; Wife; 65

1728 Kate Gibbons; F; Mother; 35
1729 Lizzie Gibbons; F; Dau; 21
1730 Annie Gibbons; F; Dau; 14
1731 Mary Gibbons; F; Dau; 9
1732 William Gibbons; M; Son; 7
1733 Agnes Gibbons; F; Dau; 5
1734 Winfield Gibbons; M; Son; 3-2
1735 Maggie Gibbons; F; Dau; 1-1

1736 Mato Oyate; Bear Tribe; F; Mother; 35
1737 Psica Wanbli; Hollie Jumping Eagle; F; Dau; 17
1738 Psica Wanbli; Jessie Jumping Eagle; F; Dau; 15
1739 Psica Wanbli; Irene Jumping Eagle; F; Dau; 11
1740 Psica Wanbli; Lizzie Jumping Eagle; F; Dau; 9
1741 Canzeka; Gets Mad; F; Dau; 4-4
1742 Psica Wanbli; Oliver Jumping Eagle; M; Son; 13
1743 Ojutunpi; Bagged; F; Dau; 12

1744 Maya Cunsoka; Timber Bank; M; Son; 34
1745 Nawizi Ehaubla; Dreams Jealous; F; Mother; 49
1746 Winyan Waste; Pretty Woman; F; Sister; 20
1747 Grover; M; Bro; 12

1748 Hogan Tucuhu; Fish Ribs; M; Son; 26
1749 Iwasicu; Talks Too Much; F; Mother; 46
1750 Annie; F; Sister; 16

1751 Ca Ptecela; Short Step; M; Bro; 15

1752 Rlola; Growler; M; Father; 45
1753 Otakeye Nica; Has No Relation; F; Wife; 50
1754 Tipi Wakan; Holy Lodge; F; Dau; 9

1755 Kangi Luta; Red Crow; M; Husb; 38
1756 Wanbli Ska; White Eagle; F; Wife; 35

1757 Wacinhin Waste; Good Plume; M; Son; 34
1758 Wamniomni Hunku; Whirlwind Mother; F; Mother; 62

1759 Inyan Sala; George Red Rock; M; 38

1760 Cante Sapa; Black Heart; M; Father; 71
1761 Rante; James Cedar; M; Son; 29
1762 Wapaha Luta; Red War Bonnet; F; Wife; 54

1763 James Richard; M; Father; 34
1764 Sophia Richard; F; Wife; 36
1765 Louise Richard; F; Dau; 14
1766 Daniel Richard; M; Son; 9
1767 Thomas Richard; M; Son; 5
1768 Anna Richard; F; Dau; 8
1769 Nellie Richard; F; Dau; 2-4
1770 Alfred Richard; M; Son; 0-4

1771 George Harvy; M; Father; 34
1772 Maggie Harvy; F; Wife; 36
1773 Julia Harvy; F; Dau; 11
1774 John Harvy; M; Son; 8
1775 Jacob Harvy; M; Son; 5-6
1776 Susie Harvy; F; Dau; 3
1777 Joseph Harvy; M; Son; 0-3

Census Of The Sioux And Cheyenne Indians Of Pine Ridge Agency, South Dakota. Taken by W. H. Clapp, Captain 16th Infantry, Acting United States Indian Agent, June 30, 1896. (Porcupine District)

Key: Number; Indian Name *(if given)*; English Name; Sex; Relation; Age

1778 Mary Martinis; F; Mother; 45
1779 Philip Martinis; M; Son; 9
1780 Joseph Martinis; M; Son; 6
1781 Netta Eldridge; F; Dau; 18
1782 Emma Martinis; F; Sau; 13
1783 Nora Martinis; F; Dau; 2-9

1784 Mary White; F; Mother; 31
1785 Frank White; M; Husb; 35
1786 Emma White; F; Dau; 12
1787 Frank White, Jr; M; Son; 6
1788 Susie White; F; Dau; 4

1789 Sunk Ska Tanka; Big White Horse; M; Father; 54
1790 Ite Ska; White Face; F; Wife; 44
1791 Wahacanka Sna; Ringing Shield; M; Son; 24
1792 Akan Mani; Susie Walks On; F; Dau; 17
1793 Ptecela; Short; M; Son; 12
1794 Ptesah Nopa; Two White Cows; F; Dau; 5

1795 Wanbli Wankatuya; High Eagle; M; Husb; 27
1796 Mazaska Agli; Brings Money; F; Wife; 22

1797 Taopi Ota; Plenty Wounds; M; Husb; 25
1798 Ituhu Suta; Ada Hard Forehead; F; Wife; 17
1799 Tipi Wanbli; Eagle Lodge; F; Dau; 0-1

1800 Wikan Wanapin; Rope Necklace; M; Father; 54
1801 Canzeka; Gets Angry; F; Wife; 46
1802 Wikan Napin; Lizzie Rope Necklace; F; Dau; 20
1803 Sunk Tokeca; Different Horse; F; Dau; 11

1804 Waste Agli; Brings Good; M; Son; 9
1805 Reyapa Icu; Taken Off; M; Son; 7
1806 Onkcekira; Magpie; M; Son; 4-3

1807 Philip Romero; M; Father; 27
1808 Katie Romero; F; Wife; 25
1809 Emmanuel Romero; M; Son; 3-5

1810 Tasunke Maza; Iron Horse; M; Father; 66
1811 Maza Win; Iron Woman; F; Wife; 57
1812 Niyan Skuya; Myrtle Sweet Bustle; F; Dau; 13
1813 Canhanpa; Shoes; F; M. in L.; 98

1814 Frank Hornbeck; M; Father; 24
1815 Mato Sapa; Jessie Black Bear; F; Wife; 18
1816 Susie Hornbeck; F; Dau; 0-9

1817 Naca Wankatuya; High Chief; M; Husb; 36
1818 Naca Wankatuya; Mary High Chief; F; Wife; 26
1819 Kangi Gleska; William Spotted Cow; M; Nephew; 24
1820 Kangi Gleska; Susie Spotted Cow; F; Niece; 22
1821 Kangi Gleska; Martha Spotted Cow; F; Sister; 40
1822 Kangi Gleska; Tracy Spotted Cow; M; Nephew; 7
1823 Sahumwinla Winorca; Old Cheyenne Woman; F; Mother; 77
1824 Kangi Gleska; Rupert Spotted Cow; M; Nephew; 17

1825 John Mesteth; M; Father; 20
1826 Amanda Marshall; F; Wife; 26
1827 Alice Mesteth; F; Dau; 3-2
1828 George Mesteth; M; Son; 0-2

Census Of The Sioux And Cheyenne Indians Of Pine Ridge Agency, South Dakota. Taken by W. H. Clapp, Captain 16th Infantry, Acting United States Indian Agent, June 30, 1896. (Porcupine District)

Key: Number; Indian Name *(if given)*; English Name; Sex; Relation; Age

1829 Tacanupa Waste; Her Good Pipe; F; Mother; 54
1830 Carrie; F; Dau; 16
1831 Wasu; Hail; F; Dau; 9
1832 Susie Russell; F; G.Dau; 11

1833 Palani Win; Ree Woman; F; 73

1834 Aglagla Inyanka; Runs Along The Edge; M; Father; 27
1835 Aglagla Inyanka; Jennie Runs A. T. Edge; F; Wife; 23
1836 Wopotapi; Shot To Pieces; M; Son; 5
1837 Heraka Nopa; Two Elk; M; Son; 3-2

1838 John Sickler; M; 28

1839 Elizabeth Dixon; F; Mother; 26
1840 William H Dixon; M; Son; 6
1841 James G Dixon; M; Son; 4-6
1842 Alice M Dixon; F; Dau; 2-9
1843 John Y Dixon; M; Son; 1-2

1844 Susan Sears; F; Mother; 42
1845 Vincent Sears; M; Son; 21
1846 Clarence Sears; M; Son; 18
1847 Maud Sears; F; Dau; 12
1848 Lulu Sears; F; Dau; 10
1849 Susie Sears; F; Dau; 8
1850 Leander Sears; M; Son; 6
1851 William Sears; M; Son; 4
1852 Cora Sears; F; Dau; 2-6
1853 Matilda Sears; F; Dau; 0-7

1854 Julia Clifford; F; Mother; 30
1855 Charles Clifford; M; Son; 6
1856 Maggie Clifford; F; Dau; 3
1857 Henry Clifford; M; Son; 0-4

1858 Tanyan Kte; Kills Right; M; Husb; 24

1859 Kangi Winyan; Crow Woman; F; 74

1860 Sungmanitu Gi; Susie Yellow Wolf; F; [blank]; 14
1861 Wanbli Waste; Harrison Good Eagle; M; [blank]; 12
1862 Edward Gerry; M; [blank]; 13
1863 Tasunke Hinzi; Joseph Yellow Horse; M; [blank]; 15
1864 Tasunke Ehakela; Millie Lost Horse; F; [blank]; 16
1865 Si Kahunpi; Mary Cut Foot; F; [blank]; 21
1866 Mato Wanbli; James Eagle Bear; M; [blank]; 15
1867 Sungmanitu Hanska; Amos Long Wolf; M; [blank]; 16

1868 Canupa Wakan; Holy Pipe; F; Mother; 43
1869 Maza Ho Waste; Good Voice Iron; M; Son; 15
1870 Waonsila; Takes Pity; F; Dau; 6
1871 Hinopa; Comes Out; F; Dau; 4
1872 Inyanke Sni; Dont[sic] Run; M; Son; 1

1873 Sunk Ole; Rosa Hunts Horses; F; 22

1874 William Provost; M; 40

Census of the Sioux And Cheyenne Indians
Of Pine Ridge Agency, South Dakota.
June 30, 1896

Wounded Knee District

Census Of The Sioux And Cheyenne Indians Of Pine Ridge Agency, South Dakota. Taken by W. H. Clapp, Captain 16th Infantry, Acting United States Indian Agent, June 30, 1896. (Wounded Knee District)

Key: Number; Indian Name *(if given)*; English Name; Sex; Relation; Age

1875	Mato Wahacanka; Bear Shield; M; Father; 38	1897	Wahukeza Waste; Frank Good Lance; M; Son; 15
1876	Ptesan Hinapa; White Cow Comes Out; F; Wife; 35	1898	Wahukeza Waste; James Good Lance; M; Son; 14
1877	Wopotapi; Charles Shot To Pieces; M; Son; 20	1899	Mni Agli; Brings Water; F; Dau; 13
1878	Mato Wahacanka; William Bear Shield; M; Son; 16	1900	Tokeya Kte; Kills First; M; Nephew; 21
1879	Mato Wahacanka; John Bear Shield; M; Son; 12	1901	Gleska Agli; Brings Spotted; F; 32
1880	Mato Wahacanka; Nellie Bear Shield; F; Dau; 14		
1881	Siyotanka Yuha; Keeps Flute; F; Dau; 2-5	1902	Wahacanka Iyanka; Running Shield; M; Father; 49
1882	Mato Wahacanka; Mary Bear Shield; F; Dau; 0-3	1903	Ptesan Ska; White Cow; F; Wife; 38
		1904	Wahacanka Iyanka; Louis Running Shield; M; Son; 12
1883	Sunkole; Hunts His Horses; M; Father; 52		
1884	Wahinkpe Ska; White Arrow; F; Wife; #1; 64	1905	Wahacanka Iyanka; Leon Running Shield; M; Father; 23
1885	Warpe; Leaf; F; Wife; #2; 49	1906	Sunk Hinrota; Anna Roan Horse; F; Wife; 20
1886	Wakinyan Tasunke; Thunder Horse; M; Son; 22	1907	Anna; F; Dau; 1-8
1887	Sunkole; Lucy Hunts His Horses; F; Dau; 16	1908	Wahukeza Nupa; Two Lance, Jr; M; Father; 42
1888	Waste Wickte; Kills Good; M; Son; 5	1909	Mato Pejuta; Medicine Bear; F; Wife; 34
1889	Kangi Maza; William Iron Crow; M; Father; 47	1910	Wahukeza Nupa; Thomas Two Lance; M; Son; 13
1890	Kangi Maza; Mary Iron Crow; F; Wife; 47	1911	Wahukeza Nupa; Two Lance, Sr; M; Father; 68
1891	Kangi Maza; Nicholas Iron Crow; M; Son; 19	1912	Cega Ska; White Kettle; F; Wife; 54
1892	Kangi Maza; Cecilia Iron Crow; F; Dau; 18	1913	Fannie; F; Dau; 15
1893	Kangi Maza; Emily Iron Crow; D; Dau; 11	1914	George; M; Son; 9
1894	Nape Kahunpi; Cut Hand; F; Cousin; 4-8	1915	Tatanka Wanbli; Eagle Bull; M; Father; 47
		1916	Wigmuke; Rainbow; F; Wife; 39
1895	Wahukeza Waste; Good Lance; M; Father; 50	1917	Tatanka Wanbli; Effa Eagle Bull; F; Dau; 20
1896	Wanbli Nape; Eagle Hand; F; Wife; 48	1918	Tatanka Wanbli; Ella Eagle Bull; F; Dau; 11

Census Of The Sioux And Cheyenne Indians Of Pine Ridge Agency, South Dakota. Taken by W. H. Clapp, Captain 16th Infantry, Acting United States Indian Agent, June 30, 1896. (Wounded Knee District)

Key: Number; Indian Name *(if given)*; English Name; Sex; Relation; Age

1919 Tatanka Wanbli; Henry Eagle Bull; M; Son; 17
1920 Wawokiya; Helps; F; 69
1921 Igmu Hanska; Long Cat; M; Father; 48
1922 Wayartaka; Bites; F; Wife; 42
1923 Sunk Otoran; Bessie Gives Away Horses; F; Dau; 14
1924 Kiyukan; Makes Room; F; Dau; 12
1925 Igmu Hanska; George Long Cat; M; Son; 10
1926 I Tanka; John Big Mouth; M; Husb; 39
1927 Winyan Waranicila; Proud Woman; F; Wife; 34
1928 Caga; Ice; M; Husb; 37
1929 Mazaska Win; Money Woman; F; Wife; 33
1930 Itunkasan; Weasel; F; Dau; 10
1931 Lucy; F; Niece; 15
1932 Wakinyan Peta; Fire Lightning; M; Husb; 61
1933 Canku; Road; F; Wife; 60
1934 Julia; F; G.Dau; 18
1935 Sica Wicakte; Kills Bad; M; G.Son; 3
1936 Cokab Iyaya; Joseph Goes In Center; M; Father; 30
1937 Cokab Iyaya; Maggie Goes In Center; F; Wife; 23
1938 Cokab Iyaya; Wm Goes In Center; M; Son; 6
1939 Cokab Iyaya; Victoria Goes I. Center; Dau; 1-8
1940 He Wotoka; John Blunt Horn; M; Father; 39
1941 He Wotoka; Jessie Blunt Horn; F; Dau; 16
1942 He Wotoka; Louise Blunt Horn; F; Dau; 11
1943 He Wotoka; George Blunt Horn; M; Son; 12
1944 He Wotoka; Susy Blunt Horn; F; Dau; 10
1945 He Wotoka; Joseph Blunt Horn; M; Son; 2-6
1946 Cetan Rabyapi; Paul Scares Hawk; M; Husb; 25
1947 Cetan Rabyapi; Louise Scare[sic] Hawk; F; Wife; 23
1948 Cetan Rabyapi; Stephen Scare Hawk; M; Son; 2-7
1949 Cetan Rabyapi; Joseph Scare Hawk; M; Son; 0-5
1950 Wahacanka Gi; Henry Yellow Shield; M; Father; 28
1951 Wahacanka Gi; Grace Yellow Shield; F; Wife; 26
1952 Wahacanka Gi; Lame Yellow Shield; F; Mother; 59
1953 Canupa Ota; Plenty Pipe; F; Dau; 2-8
1954 Wahacanka Gi; Millie Yellow Shield; F; Dau; 0-4
1955 Wazi Kontke; Bush Top Pine; M Husb; 24
1956 Hakikta; Looks Back; F; Wife; 24
1957 Ite Wanbli; Eagle Face; F; Mother; 36
1958 John; M; Son; 1-3
1959 Sungmanitu Gi; Yellow Wolf; M; Father; 50
1960 Kansu Cepa; Fat Ticket; F; Wife; 52
1961 Sungmanitu Gi; Charles Yellow Wolf; M; Son; 14
1962 Tasunke Wakita; George Looking Horse; M; G.Son; 14

Census Of The Sioux And Cheyenne Indians Of Pine Ridge Agency, South Dakota. Taken by W. H. Clapp, Captain 16th Infantry, Acting United States Indian Agent, June 30, 1896. (Wounded Knee District)

Key: Number; Indian Name *(if given)*; English Name; Sex; Relation; Age

1963 Pehin Ji; Yellow Hair; M; G.Son; 6
1964 Rante Si; Yellow Cedar; F; 66
1965 Cekiyapi; Pray To Her; F; Mother; 54
1966 Henry; M; Son; 14
1967 Anpetu Waste; Good Day; F; Dau; 17
1968 Kokipe Sni; Not Afraid; M; Son; 23
1969 Mato Wakinyan; John Thunder Bear; M; Father; 49
1970 Iyankahan Mani; Running Walker; M; B. in L.; 33
1971 Itonkasan; Weasel; F; Wife; 49
1972 Mato Wakinyan; Alice Thunder Bear; F; Dau; 16
1973 Ellen; F; Niece; 16
1974 Mato Wakinyan; Julia Thunder Bear; F; Dau; 12
1975 Mato Wakinyan; John Alder T. Bear; M; Son; 6
1976 Mato Wakinyan; Victoria Thunder Bear; F; Dau; 0-2
1977 Wiyaka Pegnaka; Feather On Head; M; Father; 51
1978 Lote; Throat; F; Wife; 57
1979 Wiyaka; Cecilia Feather O. Head; F; Dau; 24
1980 Wiyaka Pegnaka; Wm Feather On Head; M; Son; 18
1981 Wiyaka Peynaka[sic]; Emma Feather On Head; F; Dau; 15
1982 Maza Sna; Ringing Iron; F; 84
1983 Wiyaka Sakpe; Six Feather; M; Father; 39
1984 Tacanku; Her Road; F; Wife #1; 44
1985 Tonweya Win; Guide Woman; F; Wife #2; 21
1986 Wiyaka Sakpe; John Six Feathers[sic]; M; Son; 16
1987 Mni Wanca; Ocean; F; Dau; 14
1988 Sunk Ska; White Horse; M; Son; 12
1989 Oye Wakan; Medicine Track; F; Dau; 7
1990 Zintkala Wicasa; Bird Man; M; Son; 2-3
1991 Toka Wayankapi; Seen By Enemy; M; Son; 1-7
1992 Mato Wanagi; John Ghost Bear; M; Father; 41
1993 Maza Wiyokatan; Iron Nail; F; Wife; 40
1994 Mato Wanagi; Charles Ghost Bear; M; Son; 14
1995 Mato Wanagi; Lillie Ghost Bear; F; Dau; 12
1996 Mato Wanagi; Edgar Ghost Bear; M; Son; 7
1997 Mato Wanagi; Thomas Ghost Bear; M; Son; 16
1998 Mato Wanagi; Benjamin Ghost Bear; M; Son; 1-9
1999 Mato Wanagi; William Ghost Bear; M; Husb; [blank]
2000 Inyan Mato; Susie Rocky Bear; F; Wife; 20
2001 Wi Mato; Sun Bear; M; Father; 35
2002 Ista Gi; Brown Eyes; F; Wife; 34
2003 Anpetu Wakan; Sunday; M; Son; 7
2004 Tiowicakte; Kills In Lodge; F; Dau; 5
2005 Susie; F; Dau; 12
2006 Wakan Iyotaka; Sitting Holy; M; Husb; 34
2007 Sina; Blanket; F; Wife; 30
2008 Heyoka; Jennie Clown; F; Sister; 23

Census Of The Sioux And Cheyenne Indians Of Pine Ridge Agency, South Dakota.
Taken by W. H. Clapp, Captain 16th Infantry, Acting United States Indian Agent,
June 30, 1896. (Wounded Knee District)

Key: Number; Indian Name *(if given)*; English Name; Sex; Relation; Age

2009	Peji Kasla; Cut Grass; M; Father; 44	2037	Gleska Icu; Takes Spotted; F; Dau; 4-4
2010	Psito; Bead; F; Wife; 41	2038	Cante Maza; Iron Heart; M; Son; 2-4
2011	Hin Tokesa; Different Color; F; Dau; 9	2039	Mniowicakte; Geo. Kills In The Water; M; S.Son; 18
2012	Hoksila Tanka; Big Boy; M; Son; 5	2040	Caji Nakirun; Hears His Name; M; Son; 9
2013	Sota Win; Smoke Woman; F; Dau; 2-2		
2014	Peji Kasla; Fred Cut Grass; M; Son; 11	2041	Maka Mahel Mani; Wm. Walks Under Ground; M; Father; 54
		2042	Maka Mahel Mani; Jacob Walks U. Ground; M; Son; 26
2015	Mniowicakte; Jas. Kills In The Water; M; Father; 40		
2016	Cetan Oyate; Tribe Hawk; F; Wife; 28	2043	Tasunke Hinrota; His Roan Horse; M; Husb; 40
2017	Kiyan; Flying; M; Son; 10	2044	Toka Kuwa; Charges Enemy; F; Wife; 53
2018	Tuwincu Ota; Plenty Aunts; F; Dau; 5	2045	Sina Luta; Red Blanket; F; Mother; 67
2019	Mniowicakte; Josy[sic] Kills In The Water; F; Dau; 0-2		
		2046	Tokicun; Revenger; M; Husb; 57
2020	Zonie Amiotte; F; Mother; 38	2047	Wanbli Paha; Eagle Hill; F; Wife; 50
2021	Mary Amiotte; F; Dau; 19		
2022	Edward Amiotte; M; Son; 17		
2023	Nettie Amiotte; F; Dau; 15	2048	Wiyukcan; Thinking; F; G.Mo; 65
2024	Walter Amiotte; M; Son; 14		
2025	Oscar Amiotte; M; Son; 11	2049	Wanbli Wankatuya; Joseph High Eagle; M; G.Son; 17
2026	Nora Amiotte; F; Dau; 10		
2027	Bert Amiotte; M; Son; 5		
2028	Maud Amiotte; F; Dau; 7	2050	Yamni Apa; Strikes Three Times; M; 21
2029	Albert Amiotte; M; Son; 2-4		
2030	Mato Ciqala; Little Bear; M; Father; 62	2051	Waniyetu Wicakte; Thomas Kills In Winter; M; Father; 40
2031	Pejuta; Medicine; F; Wife; 50	2052	Rante Maza; Iron Cedar; F; Wife; 33
2032	Mazaska Wicaku; Gives Away Money; F; Dau; 11	2053	Wamniomni; Whirlwind; M; Nephew; 23
2033	Wi Ciqala; Little Moon; M; Father; 39	2054	Waniyetu Wicakte; Jessie Kills In Winter; F; Dau; 13
2034	Rla Win; Rattle Woman; F; Wife; 45	2055	Waniyetu Wicakte; Lizzie Kills In Winter; F; Dau; 8
2035	Wacarpi; Star; F; Dau; 7		
2036	Sina Ska Koyaka; Wears White Robe; F; Dau; 4-4	2056	Tatanka Ciqala; Henry Little Bull; M; Husb; 19

Census Of The Sioux And Cheyenne Indians Of Pine Ridge Agency, South Dakota. Taken by W. H. Clapp, Captain 16th Infantry, Acting United States Indian Agent, June 30, 1896. (Wounded Knee District)

Key: Number; Indian Name *(if given)*; English Name; Sex; Relation; Age

2057	Mato Sapa; Ida Black Bear; F; Wife; 23	2080	Canupa Sapa; Black Pipe; F; Dau; 2-11
2058	Wicayajipa; Hornet; F; GMo; 79		
2059	Mato Pejuta; Medicine Bear; F; Aunt; 49	2081	Sungmanitu Tanka; Big Wolf; M; Father; 38
2060	James; M; Bro; 18	2082	Ceya; Cries; F; Wife; 33
2061	Wagnuni; Looses Things; F; Niece; 13	2083	Sungmanitu Tanka; Samuel Big Wolf; M; Son; 16
		2084	Tokeya Mani; Walks First; F; Dau; 6
2062	Tatanka Wakan; Medicine Bull; M; Husb; 64	2085	Wanbli; Eagle; F; Dau; 4
2063	Huste Win; Lame Woman; F; Wife; 46	2086	Sagye Ska; White Cane; F; Dau; 2-5
2064	Yajuska; Ant; M; B. in L.; 34		
		2087	Onaso; Pacer; M; Husb; 73
2065	Mato Sika; Bear Foot; M; Father; 41	2088	Najinyapa; Surrounded; F; Wife; 68
2066	Hinrota; Roan; F; Wife; 48		
2067	Tasunke Hiychipi; Comes After Her Horses; F; Dau; 10	2089	Itonkasan Ska; White Weasel; F; 59
2068	Wamniomni Sapa; Black Whirlwind; M; Father; 36	2090	Anokasan; Bald Eagle; M; Husb; 34
2069	Wanbli; Eagle; F; Wife; 36	2091	Winyan Waste; Pretty Woman; F; Wife; 27
2070	Tayan Kte; Kills Right; M; Son; 13		
2071	Sunk Agli; Brings Horses; M; Son; 10	2092	Maka Suta; Hard Ground; M; Husb; 57
2072	Ptesan Wicakaga; Makes White Buffalo; F; Dau; 8	2093	Ptesan Nupa; Two White Cows; F; Wife; 51
2073	Canupa Ho; Pipe Voice; F; Dau; 7	2094	Canowicakte; Thomas Kills In Timber; M; Father; 33
2074	Mato Hinapa; Bear Comes Out; M; Son; 4-6	2095	Pejuta Ska; White Medicine; F; Wife; 31
2075	Pejuta Waste; Good Medicine; M; Father; 34	2096	Wacinyapi; Depends On; M; Son; 7
2076	Iciwicayapa; Brings Together; F; Wife; 31	2097	Cetan Oyate; Tribe Hawk; F; Dau; 3-3
2077	Nawicakicizi; Jealous Of Them; M; Bro; 31	2098	Wiyaka Sa; Red Feather; F; Dau; 0-1
2078	Winyan Ska; White Woman; F; Dau; 10	2099	Mato Wanbli; Bear Eagle; M; Father; 41
2079	Rabwicaya; Scares Them Away; M; Son; 6	2100	Wiyaka Luta; Red Feather; F; Wife; 36

Census Of The Sioux And Cheyenne Indians Of Pine Ridge Agency, South Dakota. Taken by W. H. Clapp, Captain 16th Infantry, Acting United States Indian Agent, June 30, 1896. (Wounded Knee District)

Key: Number; Indian Name *(if given)*; English Name; Sex; Relation; Age

2101 Naca; Chief; M; Son; 2-10
2102 Mato Wanbli; Joseph Bear Eagle; M; Son; 0-4
2103 Marpiya Ciqala; Little Cloud; M; Husb; 34
2104 Wakinyan Wikan; Thunder Rope; F; Wife; 32
2105 Cetan Rupahu; Hawk Wing; M; Father; 36
2106 Tokaheya; Leader; F; Wife; 53
2107 Cetan Rupahu; Luke Hawk Wing; M; Son; 10
2108 Cetan Rupahu; James Hawk Wing; M; Son; 9
2109 Samuel Brown; M; 24
2110 Sunka Wanagi; Ghost Dog; M; Father; 33
2111 Siyotauka Yajo; Plays On Flute; F; Wife; 27
2112 Mni Wanca; Ocean; F; Dau; 3-1
2113 Ptesan Win; White Cow Woman; F; Dau; 0-9
2114 Tarca Sa; Red Deer; M; Father; 28
2115 Herlogeca; Hollow Horn; F; Wife; 25
2116 Wanbli; Eagle; F; Dau; 5
2117 Sunk Hinzi; Yellow Horses; F; Dau; 1-4
2118 Rupahu Win; Wing Woman; F; M. in L.; 64
2119 Wiciyela; Yankton; M; Father; 59
2120 Isna Ti; Lives Alone; F; Wife; 51
2121 Wiciyela; Albert Yankton; M; Son; 16
2122 Wiciyela; Creighton Yankton; M; Husb; 24

2123 Wiyaka Wanjila; Jennie One Feather; F; Wife; 17
2124 Kute; Shot; M; Father; 34
2125 Oyate Ota; Plenty Nations; F; Wife; 36
2126 Okawins Kte; Kills Straddle; M; Son; 6
2127 Iyan Ska; White Rock; M; Son; 4
2128 Awagugupi; Roacher; M; Husb; 72
2129 Peji Rota; Sage; F; Wife; 62
2130 Tonweya; Joseph Scout; M; Father; 24
2131 Sungmanitu Gi; Alice Yellow Wolf; M; Wife; 19
2132 Wan On Opi; Arrow Wound; F; Dau; 0-7
2133 Taopi Ota; Plenty Wounds; M; Father; 58
2134 Rla; Rattling; F; Wife; 54
2135 Hanhepi Kte; Kills Enemy At Night; M; Son; 18
2136 Anpetu Sa; Red Day; F; Dau; 15
2137 Winyan Hanska; Tall Woman; F; Dau; 13
2138 Hoksila Zi; Robert Yellow Boy; M; Father; 34
2139 Maka Hunku; Skunks Mother; F; Wife; 23
2140 Onkcekira; Little Magpie; M; Son; 1-8
2141 Kokipe Sni Kte; Kills Without Fear; M; Son; 0-8
2142 Wicarpi; Ruben Star; M; Husb; 26
2143 Wicarpi; Mary Star; F; Wife; 24
2144 Mato Luta; Silver Red Bear; F; S. in L.; 8

Census Of The Sioux And Cheyenne Indians Of Pine Ridge Agency, South Dakota. Taken by W. H. Clapp, Captain 16th Infantry, Acting United States Indian Agent, June 30, 1896. (Wounded Knee District)

Key: Number; Indian Name *(if given)*; English Name; Sex; Relation; Age

2145 Mato Luta; Red Bear; M; Father; 48
2146 Pankeska Win; Shell Woman; F; Wife; 47
2147 Tatanka Huste; Lame Bull; M; Son; 18
2148 Mato Luta; Edgar Red Bear; M; Son; 16
2149 Tacante; Her Heart; F; Dau; 11
2150 Ista Su; Eye Seed; F; Dau; 6
2151 Mata Luta; Maggie Red Bear; F; Dau; 0-3

2152 Mato Luta; Howard Red Bear; M; Father; 23
2153 Winyan Zi; Yellow Woman; F; Wife; 23
2154 Rosa; F; Dau; 0-6

2155 Mato Iyanka; Running Bear; M; Father; 25
2156 Sagye; Come; F; Wife; 22
2157 Winyan Wakan; Holy Woman; F; Dau; 0-6
2158 Kangi Wakan; Holy Crow; M; Son; 4

2159 Waonjinca Huha; Owns Bob Tail; M; Husb; 66
2160 Anpetu Hiyaya; Days Going; F; Wife; 65

2161 Mato Gliyunka; Bear Comes To Lie Down; M; Husb; 45
2162 Ptesan Yuha Mani; Walks With White Cow; F; Wife; 57
2163 William White; M; G.Son; 14
2164 Okicize Tawa; Keeps The Battle; M; Nephew; 5

2165 Mazaska Win; Money Woman; F; Mother; 33
2166 Itunkasan; Weasel; F; Dau; 10

2167 Sina Maza; Iron Robe; F; 59

2168 Winyan Cuwignaka; Womans Dress; M; Father; 50
2169 Winyan Luta; Red Woman; F; Wife #1; 49
2170 Ptesan; White Cow; F; Wife; #2; 34
2171 Akicita Wanjila; Lone Soldier; M; Son; 16
2172 Sungmanitu Peta; Fire Wolf; M; Son; 13
2173 Mato Ciqala; Little Bear; M; Son; 7
2174 Tonweya; Scout; M; Son; 4

2175 Zintkala Napin; George Bird Necklace; M; Father; 48
2176 Wamniomni; Whirlwind; F; Wife; 41
2177 Zintkala Napin; Julia Bird Necklace; F; Dau; 17
2178 Zintkala Napin; Philip Bird Necklace; M; Son; 14
2179 Zintkala Napin; Martha Bird Necklace; F; Dau; 12
2180 Zintkala Napin; Hattie Bird Necklace; F; Dau; 10
2181 Zintkala Napin; Moses Bird Necklace; M; Son; 8
2182 Zintkala Napin; Susen[sic] Bird Necklace; F; Dau; 6
2183 Zintkala Napin; Rosa Bird Necklace; F; Dau; 0-3

2184 Ite; Face; M; Father; 60
2185 Marpiya Topa; Four Cloud; F; Wife #1; 68
2186 Zintkala Luta; Red Bird; F; Wife #2; 58
2187 Zintkala Waste; Pretty Bird; M; Son; 17
2188 Zintkala To; Mary Blue Bird; F; Dau; 17

2189 Jackson Bissonette; M; Husb; 28
2190 Ite; Sally Face; F; Wife; 26

Census Of The Sioux And Cheyenne Indians Of Pine Ridge Agency, South Dakota. Taken by W. H. Clapp, Captain 16th Infantry, Acting United States Indian Agent, June 30, 1896. (Wounded Knee District)

Key: Number; Indian Name *(if given)*; English Name; Sex; Relation; Age

2191 Warpa Tanka; Black Bird; M; Father; 23
2192 Hinapa; Comes Out; F; Wife; 22
2193 Wicarpi Wankatuya; High Star; M; Son; 2-10
2194 Warpa Tanka; Richard Black Bird; M; Son; 0-1

2195 Wasicu Tasunke; American Horse #2; M; Father; 49
2196 Wanbli Wicasa; Eagle Man; M; Son; 12
2197 Wasicu Tasunke; Dawson American Horse; M; Son; 16

2198 Tahu Wanica; No Neck #1; M; Father; 44
2199 KangiMaza[sic]; Ellen Iron Crow; F; Wife; 45
2200 Mato Cincala; Young Cub; M; Son; 11

2201 Aguyapi Soka; Thick Bread; M; Father; 57
2202 Wankal Ti; Lives Above; F; Wife; 44
2203 Mato Gleska; Thomas Spotted Bear; M; Son; 23

2204 Wamniomni Luzahan; Fast Whirlwind; M; Father; 44
2205 Sina Ota; Plenty Blankets; F; Wife; 42
2206 Wamniomni Luzahan; Stella Fast Whirlwind; F; Dau; 9

2207 Tatanka Ciqala; Samuel Little Bull; M; Father; 25
2208 Ninglicu; Comes Out Alive; F; Wife; 39
2209 Ite Wawiyokipi; Pleased Face; F; Dau; 4-5
2210 Emma; F; Dau; 14

2211 Cangleska Waste; Good Ring; F; 67

2212 Zintkala Ota; Plenty Bird; M; Father; 27
2213 Zintkala Ota; Susie Plenty Bird; F; Wife; 27
2214 Zintkala Ota; Nancy Plenty Bird; F; Dau; 7
2215 Zintkala Ota; Julia Plenty Bird; F; Dau; 3-10

2216 Wakinyan Luzahan; Fast Thunder; M; Father; 54
2217 Tasunke Opi; Wounded Horse; F; Wife; #1; 44
2218 Makoce Icu; Locator; F; Wife; #2; 23
2219 Fannie; F; Dau; 25
2220 Stella; F; Dau; 22
2221 Mary; F; Dau; 3-9
2222 Najinyapi; Surrounded; M; Son; 3-7
2223 Otoran; Donating; F; Dau; 1

2224 Wicarpi Luta; Red Star; M; Father; 30
2225 Wicarpi Luta; Sallie Red Star; F; Wife; 30
2226 Sunk Sapa; Black Horse; F; Dau; 10
2227 Wicarpi Luta; David Red Star; M; Son; 5
2228 Wicarpi Luta; Paul Red Star; M; Son; 1-8

2229 Inyan Mato; Rocky Bear; M; Father; 60
2230 Oye; Track; F; Wife #1; 57
2231 Kokab Iyanka; Runs Ahead; F; Wife #2; 52
2232 Lucy; F; Dau; 28
2233 Jessie; F; Dau; 18
2234 Cetan; Silas Hawk; M; Son; 17
2235 Inyan Mato; Lizzie Rocky Bear; F; Dau; 24
2236 Inyan Mato; Thomas Rocky Bear; M; Son; 14

Census Of The Sioux And Cheyenne Indians Of Pine Ridge Agency, South Dakota. Taken by W. H. Clapp, Captain 16th Infantry, Acting United States Indian Agent, June 30, 1896. (Wounded Knee District)

Key: Number; Indian Name *(if given)*; English Name; Sex; Relation; Age

2237	Wabluska Tiyoslola; Mamie Cricket; F; Dau; 12	2258	Anukasan Ciqala; Ada Little Bald Eagle; F; Sister; 15
		2259	Suta; Hard; F; Sister; 12
2238	Mato Wapageyeca; Bluffing Bear; M; Husb; 41	2260	Ohitika Kte; Kills Brave; F; Sister; 10
2239	Mato Wapageyeca; Sophia Bluffing Bear; F; Wife; 29	2261	Anukasan Ciqala; Chas. Little Bald Eagle; M; Bro; 2-10
2240	Tinahel Yanka; Sits In The Lodge; F; G.Mo; 69	2262	Anukasan Ciqala; Moses Little Bald Eagle; M; Father; 22
2241	Si Tanka; Big Foot; M; Husb; 64	2263	Tasunke Oyuspapi; Stop Her Horses; F; Wife; 22
2242	Sunkska Yuha; White Horse Owner; F; Wife; 64	2264	Iyuwer Ekte; Kills Across; F; Dau; 0-9
2243	Heraka Luta; Red Elk; M; Father; 45	2265	Heraka Sapa; Black Elk; M; Father; 32
2244	Mazaska; Money; F; Wife; 36	2266	Wapaha; Kate War Bonnet; F; Wife; 27
2245	Iyan Mato; George Rocky Bear; M; Son; 16	2267	Scu Sni; Never Showed Off; M; Son; 3-3
2246	Heraka Luta; Peter Red Elk; M; Son; 4-5	2268	Wicarpi Ho Waste; Good Voice Star; M; Son; 0-9
2247	Heraka Luta; Emil Red Elk; M; Son; 2-2	2269	Sunka Hanska; John Long Dog; M; Father; 51
2248	Winyan Nuni; Lost Woman; F; G.Mo; 74	2270	Tasunke Hinsa; Her Red Horse; F; Wife; 54
2249	Wamniomni Hinapa; Comes Out Whirlwind; F; G.Dau; 27	2271	Ohitika; Brave; M; Son; 8
		2272	Wicarpi Canku; Star Road; F; Dau; 2-9
2250	Wapaha; War Bonnet; M; Husb; 52	2273	Hanska; Tall; M; Father; 37
2251	Wahacanka Waste; Good Shield; F; Wife; 44	2274	Waste; Good; F; Wife; 42
2252	Sunka Ciqala; Robert Little Dog; M; Nephew; 16	2275	Tokicun; Revenger; F; Dau; 8
		2276	Sunk Mani; Horse Stealer; M; Son; 4-2
2253	Isanyanti; Santee; F; Mother; 56	2277	Naca Win; Chief Woman; F; Dau; 0-3
2254	Lucy; F; Dau; 31		
2255	Naca Kte Rcin; Wished To Be A Chief; M; Bro; 60	2278	Wanbli Iyotaka; Sitting Eagle; M; 47
2256	Anukasan Ciqala; Felix Little Bald Eagle; M: Bro; 20	2279	Ista Ska; White Eyes; M; Father; 48
2257	Tawa Kte; Kills Her Own; F; Mother; 42		

Census Of The Sioux And Cheyenne Indians Of Pine Ridge Agency, South Dakota. Taken by W. H. Clapp, Captain 16th Infantry, Acting United States Indian Agent, June 30, 1896. (Wounded Knee District)

Key: Number; Indian Name *(if given)*; English Name; Sex; Relation; Age

2280 Warpe Zi; Yellow Leaf; F; Wife; 35
2281 Ista Ska; Daniel White Eyes; M; Son; 15
2282 Cangleska Sa; Red Ring; F; Dau; 13
2283 Winyan Ciqala; Small Woman; F; Dau; 13

2284 Winyan Ptecela; Short Woman; F; Mother; 55
2285 Wanbli Hanpa; Eagle Moccosin[sic]; M; Son; 10
2286 Tanyan Kutepi; Shoots Him Right; F; Dau; 7
2287 Hinto Gleska; Gray Spotted Horse; M; Nephew; 13

2288 Witko Winla; Foolish Woman; M; Husb; 63
2289 Tawacin Waste; Free Hearted; F; Wife; 59
2290 Nupa Kte; Kills Twice; F; G.Dau; 13
2291 Sunkgleska; Spotted Horse; F; G.Dau; 12

2292 Tasunke Ota Win; Her Many Horses; F; 68
2293 Wahacanka; Shield; M; Father; 60
2294 Waste Isaga; Grows Good; F; Wife; 60
2295 Tate Sina; Wind Blanket; F; Dau; 23
2296 Tiyopa Luta; Her Red Door; F; Dau; 11

2297 Wahacanka; Shield, Jr; M; Father; 24
2298 Sunkawakan Win; Horse Woman; F; Wife; 23

2299 Hiyete; James Shoulder; M; Father; 21

2300 Wahacanka; Mary Shield; F; Wife; 18
2301 Hiyete; Henry Shoulder; M; Son; 0-9
2302 Iyuwer Ekte; Kills Across; M; Bro; 25
2303 Wanbli Ogle; Eagle Shirt; M; Bro; 24
2304 Tasunke Aglipi; Brings Her Horses; F; Sister; 47
2305 Sinte Conala; Clara Few Tails; F; Niece; 15
2306 Yusiniyeyapi; Scorns Him; M; Nephew; 9
2307 Gli Iyotaka; Comes To Sit; M; Nephew; 8

2308 Ite Rante; Cedar Face; M; Father; 66
2309 Iasunke Hinsa; Her Red Horse; F; Wife; 61
2310 Ite Rante; William Cedar Face; M; Son; 22
2311 Ista Gi; Yellow Eyes; M; Son; 16

2312 Ohitika Kte; Kills Brave; M; Father; 31
2313 Tayan Kte; Comes Right; F; Dau; 2-10
2314 Itunkasan Iyotaka; Sitting Weasel; M; Father 62
2315 Pehin Sakiyapi; Paints Hair; F; Wife; 48
2316 Kiyela Opi; Wounded Close; F; Dau; 15
2317 Itunkasan Iyotaka; Hinman Sitting Weasel; M; Son; 13
2318 Kangi Maza; Iron Crow; F; Dau; 4-3
2319 Itunkasan Sa; Charles Red Weasel; M; G.Son; 10

Census Of The Sioux And Cheyenne Indians Of Pine Ridge Agency, South Dakota. Taken by W. H. Clapp, Captain 16th Infantry, Acting United States Indian Agent, June 30, 1896. (Wounded Knee District)

Key: Number; Indian Name *(if given)*; English Name; Sex; Relation; Age

2320 Herbert Bissonette; M; Bro; 25
2321 Ella Bissonette; F; Mother; 56
2322 Joseph Bissonette; M; Bro; 17
2323 Frank Bissonette; M; Bro; 15
2324 Lucy Bissonette; F; Sister; 12
2325 Fred Bissonette; M; Bro; 10
2326 William Bissonette; M; Nephew; 7
2327 Louise Bissonette; F; Dau; 5

2328 Heyoka; Clown; F; 53

2329 Heraka Wanjila; James Lone Elk; M; Father; 29
2330 Heraka Wanjila; Julia Lone Elk; F; Wife; 27
2331 Conica Wanica; Bert No Flesh; M; B. in L.; 21
2332 Heraka Wanjila; Lucy Lone Elk; F; Dau; 5

2333 Winyan Waste; Good Woman; F; G.Mo; 64
2334 Mato Najin; Anna Standing Bear; F; G.Dau; 12

2335 Hunpeka; Charles Picket Pin; M; Father; 45
2336 Otka; Hanging; F; Wife; 37
2337 Hunpeka; Della Picket Pin; F; Dau; 0-1

2338 Julia Patton; F; Mother; 39
2339 James Patton; M; Son; 21
2340 Susie Patton; F; Dau; 18
2341 Thomas Patton; M; Son; 17
2342 George Patton; M; Son; 15
2343 Laura Patton; F; Dau; 13
2344 Lucy Patton; F; Dau; 9
2345 Emma Patton; F; Dau; 7
2346 Julia Patton; F; Dau; 4-8
2347 William Patton; M; Son; 2-5

2348 Sunka Paha Akan; Dog On Butte; M; Husb; 56
2349 Wanbli; Eagle; F; Wife; 49

2350 Mato Rlola; Growling Bear; M; Father; 34
2351 He Rlogeca; Hollow Horn; F; Mother; 42
2352 Oleku; Comes Hunting; M; Son; 3-8

2353 Mato Najin; Standing Bear; M; Father; 34
2354 Zintkala Sa; Red Bird; F; Dau; 3-6
2355 Wicarpi; Star; F; Dau; 2-1
2356 Imnistan; Saliva; M; G.Fa; 58
2357 Tiglake Waste; Good Mover; F; Wife; 61
2358 Ake Hiyu; Gertie Comes Again; F; G.Dau; 11

2359 Wanbli; Eagle; F; Mother; 43
2360 Ptesan Yatapi; Alice White Cow Chief; F; Dau; 14
2361 Siyo; Prairie Chicken; F; G.Mo; 63

2362 Alexander Adams; M; Father; 44
2364[sic] Tarca Win; Deer Woman; F; Wife; 39
2365 John Adams; M; Son; 19
2366 Nellie Adams; F; Dau; 17
2367 Susy Adams; F; Dau; 14
2368 Joseph Adams; M; Son; 10
2369 Lucy Adams; F; Dau; 14

2370 Sinte Sapela; Black Tail Deer; M; Father; 39
2371 Nisehu; Rum Bone; F; Wife; 38
2372 Ta Rpaya; Lays Dead; M; Son; 10
2373 Zintkala Waste; Pretty Bird; M; Son; 5

2374 Jennie Mesteth; F; Mother; 43
2375 Maggie Mesteth; F; Dau; 8
2376 Willie Mesteth; M; Son; 16
2377 James Mesteth; M; Son; 14

Census Of The Sioux And Cheyenne Indians Of Pine Ridge Agency, South Dakota. Taken by W. H. Clapp, Captain 16th Infantry, Acting United States Indian Agent, June 30, 1896. (Wounded Knee District)

Key: Number; Indian Name *(if given)*; English Name; Sex; Relation; Age

2378	Joseph Mesteth; M; Son; 12	2403	Onpan Hoksila; Huron Elk Boy; M; Father; 47
2379	David Mesteth; M; Son; 10		
2380	Philip Mesteth; M; Son; 7	2404	Itunksan Mato; Weasel Bear; F; Wife; 46
2381	Peter Mesteth; M; Son; 6		
2382	Thomas Mesteth; M; Son; 3-6	2405	Onpan Hoksila; Charles Elk Boy; M; Son; 16
2383	Frank Mesteth; M; Son; 0-3		
		2406	Onpan Hoksila; Joseph Elk Boy; M; Son; 13
2384	Wanbli Sapa; Black Eagle; M; G.Fa; 66	2407	Sagye Wakan; Medicine Cane; F; Dau; 7
2385	Wanbli Sapa; Susy Black Eagle; F; G.Dau; 14	2408	Hoksila Ciqala; Little Boy; M; Son; 3-2
2386	Awicagli; Brings Them; M; Father; 28	2409	Wakinyan Waste; Good Thunder; M; Husb; 64
2387	Onpan Gi; Yellow Elk; F; Wife; 24	2410	Ista San; Grey Eyes; F; Wife #1; 54
2388	Sa; Red; F; Dau; 8	2411	Hunska Narco; Leggins Down; F; Wife #2; 52
2389	Hoksila Wanbli; Eagle Boy; M; Son; 6	2412	Heraka Sapa; Grace Black Elk; F; Dau; 15
2390	Wanbli; Eagle #2; F; Mother; 54		
2391	Sunkhinzi Win; Yellow Horse Woman; F; Dau; 32	2413	Hoksila Tanka; Big Boy; M; Father; 36
2392	Hihan Gleska; Spotted Owl; M; Father; 28	2414	Canku; Road; F; Wife; 55
2393	Cetan Win; Mary Hawk Woman; F; Wife; 21	2415	Hoksila Tanka; Joseph Big Boy; M; Son; 19
2394	Iweosaya; Bloody Mouth; M: Son; 3-3	2416	Hoksila Tanka; Annie Big Boy; F; Dau; 11
2395	Tainyan Yanka; Sits In Sight; F; Dau; 0-4	2417	Tatanka Luta; Red Bull; M; Father; 39
		2418	Tatanka Luta; Sophia Red Bull; F; Wife; 24
2396	Pankeska Hoksila; Shell Boy; M; Husb; 59	2419	Wipata Win; Quilled Woman; F; Dau; 1-3
2397	Tasunke Inajin; Horse Stops; F; Wife; 53		
2398	Toka Kahinrpeya; Runs Over Enemy; M; Nephew; 10	2420	Marpiya Wakita; Looking Cloud; M; Father; 44
		2421	Wazi Sa; Red Pine; F; Wife; 39
2399	Joseph Knight; M; Father; 37	2422	Tawa Agli; Brings Her Own; M; Son; 5
2400	Lizzie Knight; F; Wife; 36		
2401	Ellen Knight; F; Dau; 8		
2402	Oliver Knight; M; Son; 2-1	2423	Nupala; Two Two; M; Father; 37
		2424	Tatanka Wacipi; Buffalo Dance; F; Wife; 34

Census Of The Sioux And Cheyenne Indians Of Pine Ridge Agency, South Dakota. Taken by W. H. Clapp, Captain 16th Infantry, Acting United States Indian Agent, June 30, 1896. (Wounded Knee District)

Key: Number; Indian Name *(if given)*; English Name; Sex; Relation; Age

2425	Nupala; Alexander Two Two; M; Son; 19	2447	Tokala Sapa; Mary Black Fox; F; Wife; 27
2426	Nupala; Joseph Two Two; M; Son; 17	2448	Wakan Najin; Stands Holy; F; Dau; 0-7
2427	Nupala; Eagle Two Two; F; Dau; 15	2449	Itazipa Wakan; Medicine Bow; F; Dau; 7
2428	Ista Gi; Yellow Eyes; F; Dau; 12		
2429	Winyan Ska; White Woman; F; Dau; 9	2450	Inyan Wakan; Kate Holy Rock; F; Mother; 39
2430	Hoksila Tanka; Big Boy; M; Son; 7	2451	Tasunke Opi Wayanka; Looks At Wounded Horse; F; Dau; 4-6
2431	Kute; Shot; M; Son; 7	2452	Itazipa Sica; Bad Bow; M; Son; 0-9
2432	Nupala; Jennie Two Two; F; Dau; 2-6		
2433	Anpetu Wakan; Sunday; F; Dau; 1-7	2453	Ogle Sa; Henry Red Shirt; M; Father; 37
2434	Nupala; Richard Two Two; M; Son; 0-4	2454	Ogle Sa; Emma Red Shirt; F; Wife; 36
		2455	Ogle Sa; John Red Shirt; M; Son; 14
2435	Mato Ota; Plenty Bear; M: Father; 42	2456	Ogle Sa; Mary Red Shirt; F; Dau; 11
2436	Canpa Ista; Cherry Eye; F; Wife; 32	2457	Ogle Sa; Charles Red Shirt; M; Son; 6
2437	Mato Ota; Thomas Plenty Bear; M; Son; 15	2458	Ogle Sa; Alfred Red Shirt; M; Son; 1-6
2438	Maga Isnala; Lone Goose; M; Father; 62	2459	John Pourier; M; Father; 24
2439	Pehin Ji Win; Yellow Hair Woman; F; Wife; 50	2460	Josie Pourier; F; Wife; 21
		2461	Josephin[sic] Pourier; f; Dau; 3-2
2440	Tikanyela Kte; Kills Close To Lodge; M; Son; 27	2462	Ellen Pourier; F; Dau; 0-7
2441	Pasu; Nose; M; Son; 23	2463	Josephin Pourier; f; Mother; 44
2442	Tipi Wakan; Holy Lodge; F; Dau; 22	2464	Joseph Pourier; M; Son; 18
		2465	Louis Pourier; M; Son; 16
2443	Toka Kico; Calls Enemy; M; Son; 7	2466	Emil Pourier; M; Son; 14
		2467	Mary Pourier; F; Dau; 12
2444	Maga Isnala; Susie Lone Goose; F; Dau; 13	2468	Helen Pourier; F; Dau; 10
		2469	Peter Pourier; M; Son; 8
		2470	Rosa Pourier; F; Dau; 6
2445	Maka Sica Win; Bad Land Woman; F; 74	2471	Charlie Pourier; M; Son; 3-2
		2472	Jules Ecoffey; M; Father; 23
2446	Tokala Sapa; Black Fox; M; Father; 36	2473	Alice Ecoffey; F; Wife; 21
		2474	Fred Ecoffey; M; Son; 1-2

Census Of The Sioux And Cheyenne Indians Of Pine Ridge Agency, South Dakota. Taken by W. H. Clapp, Captain 16th Infantry, Acting United States Indian Agent, June 30, 1896. (Wounded Knee District)

Key: Number; Indian Name *(if given)*; English Name; Sex; Relation; Age

2575	Julia Ecoffey; F; Mother; 52		2503	Canpaslatapi Canku; Staked Road; F; Dau; 10
2476	Louise Ecoffey; F; Dau; 19			
2477	Pacifique Ecoffey; F; Dau; 17		2504	Wakita; Looks; F; Dau; 2-10
2478	Albert Ecoffey; M; Son; 13			
2479	Ada Ecoffey; F; Dau; 13		2505	Kangi; Henry Crow; M; Husb; 30
2480	Mary Tway Ecoffey; F; Dau; 29			
2481	Nora Tway; F; G.Dau; 2-3		2506	Tayan Ku; Comes Right; F; Wife; 24
2482	Emma Tway; F; G.Dau; 6			
2483	Thomas Tway; M; G.Son; 0-3		2507	He Rlogeca; Hollow Horn; M; Father; 36
2484	Joseph Ecoffey; M; Father; 19			
2485	Rosa Nelson Ecoffey; F; Wife; 17		2508	Pehin Ji; Yellow Hair; F; Wife; 27
2486	Alvina Ecoffey; F; Dau; 0-2			
			2509	He Rlogeca; Thomas Hollow Horn; M; Son; 9
2487	Ota Agli; Brings Plenty; M; Father; 48			
			2510	Sute Sni; Never Missed; M; Son; 8
2488	Karmi; Bend; F; Wife; 51			
2489	Onyan Glicupi; Robert Left Behind; M; Son; 20		2511	Wan Icarya; Grows Arrows; M; Son; 4-3
2490	Ota Agli; Michael Brings Plenty; M; Son; 16			
			2512	Mato Wakuwa; Chasing Bear; M; Father; 51
2491	Akicizapi; Fights Over Him; M; Son; 10			
			2513	Marpiya; Cloud; F; Wife; 47
			2514	Kokab Hiyaya; Goes In Front; F; Dau; 13
2492	Wakinyan Wanbli; Eagle Thunder; M; Father; 41			
2493	Tasunke Wanbli; Her Horses; F; Wife; 36		2515	Wopotapi; Shot To Pieces; M; Father; 20
2494	Gleska Yuha; Keeps Spotted; F; Dau; 7		2516	Ptan Win; Otter Woman; F; Wife; 18
2495	Napca; Swallow; M; Son; 4		2517	Kiyela Kute; Shoots Close; F; Dau; 1-2
2496	Winyan Punpun; Rotten Woman; F; Dau; 1-4			
			2518	George Ladeau; M; Father; 26
2497	Wanbli Wankatuya; High Eagle; M; Father; 34		2519	Mary Ladeau; F; Wife; 19
			2520	Maggie Ladeau; F; Dau; 1-8
2498	Wakanyan Waste; Good Thunder; F; Wife; 29			
			2521	Wakinyan Witko; Crazy Thunder; M; Father; 40
2499	Asyibone; M; Son; 1-3			
			2522	Wiyaka; Feather; F; Wife; 30
2500	Wawoyuspa; Catches; F; Father; 32		2523	Anukasan; Bald Eagle; M; Son; 9
2501	Wanjila Agli; Brings One; F; Wife; 27		2524	Wasu Luta; Red Hail; F; Dau; 5
			2525	Akayanka Kte; Kills On Horseback; M; Son; 1-7
2502	Magajin Mani; Walking Rain; F; Dau; 5			

Census Of The Sioux And Cheyenne Indians Of Pine Ridge Agency, South Dakota. Taken by W. H. Clapp, Captain 16th Infantry, Acting United States Indian Agent, June 30, 1896. (Wounded Knee District)

Key: Number; Indian Name *(if given)*; English Name; Sex; Relation; Age

2526 Opawinge Kte; John Kills A Hundred; M; Father; 48
2527 Opawinge Kte; Susie Kills A Hundred; F; Wife; 37
2528 Opawinge Kte; Hattie Kills A Hundred; F; Dau; 18
2529 Opawinge Kte; Adelin Kills A Hundred; F; Dau; 15
2530 Opawinge Kte; Elija Kills A Hundred; M; Son; 8
2531 Opawinge Kte; Nancy Kills A Hundred; F; Dau; 7
2532 Opawinge Kte; Annie Kills A Hundred; F; Dau; 1-3
2533 Ite Waste; Jennie Pretty Face; F; 37
2534 Akayanka Kte; Kills On Horseback; M; 27
2535 Tasunke Ota; Plenty Horses; M; Husb; 27
2536 Hinrota Win; Roan Woman; F; Wife; 34
2537 Mato Niyanpi; Living Bear; M; Father; 54
2538 Ptewinyela Sa; Red Cow; F; Wife; 44
2539 Oosica; Hard To Hit; M; Son; 22
2540 Mato Niyanpi; Thomas Living Bear; M; Son; 16
2541 Mato Niyanpi; Sallie Living Bear; F; Dau; 10
2542 Joseph Brown; M; Father; 27
2543 Alice Brown; F; Wife; 26
2544 James Brown; M; Son; 5
2545 Willie Brown; M; Son; 3-9
2546 Joseph Brown, Jr; M; Son; 2-1
2547 Tonie Brown; M; Son; 0-7
2548 Osun Wanica; No Braid; M; Father; 68
2549 Canupa Wiyakpa; Shining Pipe; F; Wife; 60
2550 Osun Wanica; Wilson No Braid; M; Son; 17
2551 Cante Opeyapi; Pleased Heart; F; G.Dau; 4-1
2552 Pamagle; Droops Head; M; 72
2553 Wiyukcan Sni; Dont[sic] Think; M; Father; 60
2554 Otuyacin C[?]ya; Crying Without Cause; F; Wife; 58
2555 Kiyela Ti; Lives By; M; Son; 24
2556 Noge Sa; Red Ear; M; Son; 22
2557 Canpa Su; Cherry Stone; M; Husb; 54
2558 Ptesan; White Cow; F; Wife; 51
2559 Nup Wicakte; Kills Two; M; Father; 22
2560 Zintkala; Bird; F; Wife; 23
2561 Canupa Wicincala; Red Pipe Girl; F; Dau; 0-9
2562 He Rlogeca; Hollow Horn; M; Father; 29
2563 Ptesan Waste; Good White Cow; F; Wife; 26
2564 Itunkasan Wapaha; Weasel Bonnet; M; Son; 2-5
2565 Warca Zi; Sun Flower; F; Dau; 0-3
2566 Wakan Nahomni; Henry Turning Holy; M; Father; 42
2567 Wabliska Zi; Yellow Bug; F; Wife; 33
2568 Heraka Waste; Good Elk; M; B. in L.; 24
2569 Pispiza Luta; Red Prairie Dog; 1 M; Son; 9
2570 Ista Zi; Yellow Eyes; M; Son; 5
2571 Canupa Wakan; Holy Pipe; F; Dau; 2-6

Census Of The Sioux And Cheyenne Indians Of Pine Ridge Agency, South Dakota. Taken by W. H. Clapp, Captain 16th Infantry, Acting United States Indian Agent, June 30, 1896. (Wounded Knee District)

Key: Number; Indian Name *(if given)*; English Name; Sex; Relation; Age

2572 Pehan Wankatuya; High Heron; M; Son; 24
2573 Tankal Woglaka; Talks Outside; F; Mother; 54

2574 Cante Teri; Hard Heart; M; Father; 44
2575 Tasunke Wakan; Medicine Horse; F; Wife; 34
2576 Wan Nupa; Two Arrows; M; B. in L.; 28
2577 Ta Tiyopa; Her Door; F; Dau; 23
2578 Cetan Wanbli; Eagle Hawk; M; Son; 12

2579 Cetan Luta; Red Hawk; M; Husb; 67
2580 Itazipa Cola; No Bow; F; Wife; 63

2581 Wakinyan Ptea; Fire Thunder; M; Father; 48
2582 Timahel Hiyu Okihi; Cant Enter Door; F; Wife; 42
2583 Wiconi Terila; Loves Life; M; Son; 25
2584 Wakinyan Peta; William Fire Thunder; M; Son; 23
2585 Wakinyan Peta; Jennie Fire Thunder; F; Dau; 15
2586 Wakinyan Peta; Earth Fire Thunder; F; Dau; 9
2587 Wakinyan Peta; Charles Fire Thunder; M; Son; 6

2588 Wataga; Foam; M; 69

2589 Sunka Witko; Crazy Dog; M; Husb; 46
2590 Wacinko; Pouting; F; Wife; 54

2591 Cankpe; Knee; M; Father; 64
2592 Wicayajipa; Bumble Bee; F; Wife; 58
2593 Wanbli Wicasa; Eagle Man; M; Son; 32
2594 Cankpe; Wilson Knee; M; Son; 18
2595 Pankeska Maza; Iron Shell; F; G.Dau; 12

2596 He Cinskayapi; Mountain Sheep; M; Father; 31
2597 Hunpeka; Millie Picket Pin; F; Wife; 23
2598 Anpetu Yuha; Keeps Dog Day; F; Dau; 3-6

2599 Taopi; Wounded; M; Husb; 20
2600 Ptesan Nupa; Two White Cows; F; Wife; 18

2601 Hiyete; Shoulder; M; Father; 69
2602 Winyan Yamni; Three Women; F; Wife; 65
2603 Hiyete; Ruben Shoulder; M; Son; 19
2604 Hiyete; Amos Shoulder; M; Son; 17
2605 Hiyete; Paul Shoulder; M; Son; 13
2606 Hiyete; Lucy Shoulder; F; Dau; 12
2607 Witansnaon; Single Woman; F; M. in L.; 84
2608 Tatanka Waste; Good Bull; M; Bro; 39
2609 Orloka Ota; Plenty Hales; M; Father; 22
2610 Hiyete; Mary Shoulder; F; Wife; 22
2611 Tasunke Ska; Her White Horse; F; Dau; 0-4

2612 Maka Luta; Red Earth; F; Mother; 53
2613 Oiyokipiya Najin; Merrily Stands; F; Dau; 22

2614 Wanagi; Ghost; M; Father; 42

Census Of The Sioux And Cheyenne Indians Of Pine Ridge Agency, South Dakota. Taken by W. H. Clapp, Captain 16th Infantry, Acting United States Indian Agent, June 30, 1896. (Wounded Knee District)

Key: Number; Indian Name *(if given)*; English Name; Sex; Relation; Age

2615	Wanagi; Emma Ghost; F; Wife; 34	2638	Wiciyela Win; Yankton Woman; F; M. in L.; 60
2616	Winyan Waste; Good Woman; F; M. in L.; 78	2639	Luzahan; Fast; F; S. in L.; 14
2617	Wanagi; Samuel Ghost; M; Son; 12	2640	Niyan Luta; Road Breath; F; Dau; 0-4
2618	Wanagi; Frank Ghost; M; Son; 8	2641	Heraka Isnala; Lone Elk; M; Father; 44
2619	Wakinyan Watakpe; Charging Thunder; M; Son; 3-11	2642	Sunkhinto Knwa; Runs After Grey Horses; F; Wife; 37
2620	Wanagi; Alexander Ghost; M; Son; 2	2643	Sagye Wanbli; Cane Eagle; F; Dau; 13
2621	Mato Niyanpi; Saves Bear; M; Father; 58	2644	Anpetu Mani; Walking Day; F; Dau; 2-1
2622	Kiza; Fought; F; Wife; 54		
2623	Mato Niyanpi; Ida Saves Bear; F; Dau; 23	2645	Cahrles[sic] Cuny; M; Father; 34
		2646	Louise Cuny; F; Wife; 30
2624	Sunkska Opi; Wounded White Horse; M; Son; 15	2647	Mary Le Rock; F; M. in L.; 71
		2648	Lizzie Cuny; F; Dau; 12
		2649	Eddie Cuny; M; Son; 10
2625	Ozan Mahel; Henry Between Lodges; M; Son; 18	2650	Charles Cuny, Jr; M; Son; 7
		2651	LeRoy Brown Cuny; M; Son; 5
2626	Heraka Ska; White Elk; F; Mother; 43	2652	Wilson Cuny; M; Son; 3
2627	Rabyapi; Scares Away; M; Bro; 6	2653	Mato Gleska; Spotted Bear; M; Father; 29
		2654	Sunkska Yuha; White Horse Owner; F; Wife; 23
2628	Josephin[sic] Cuny; F; Mother; 61		
2629	Jule Cuny; M; Son; 20	2655	Akicisa; Yells For Him; M; Son; 3-5
2630	Lottie Cuny; F; Dau; 20		
		2656	Wicincala Ku; Girls Comes; F; Dau; 0-9
2631	Icanyan Iyanka; Francis Runs Against; M; Father; 43		
2632	Sake Ska; White Finger Nail; F; Wife; 38	2657	Mato Witko; Fool Head; M; Father; 31
2633	Kisun Sni; Jas. Dont[sic] Braid His Hair; M; B. in L.; 26	2658	Onsina Iya; Talks Pitiful; F; Wife; 26
2634	Icayan Iyanka; Jacob Runs Against; M; Son; 23	2659	Maka Patitan; Pushes Ground; F; Dau; 2-6
2635	Kawinga; Turns Back; F; Dau; 2-4	2660	Isnala Wanlatuya; Highest One; M; Son; 0-2
2636	Hiyoya; Goes After; M; Father; 23	2661	Sungmanitu Ska; White Coyote; M; Father; 25
2637	Istina; Sleeper; F; Wife; 38	2662	Sungmanitu Ska; Martha White Coyote; F; Wife; 23

Census Of The Sioux And Cheyenne Indians Of Pine Ridge Agency, South Dakota. Taken by W. H. Clapp, Captain 16th Infantry, Acting United States Indian Agent, June 30, 1896. (Wounded Knee District)

Key: Number; Indian Name *(if given)*; English Name; Sex; Relation; Age

2663 Zintkala Hinapa; Bird Comes Out; F; Dau; 1-8
2664 Tatanka Tamaheca; Poor Buffalo; M; Father; 36
2665 Sa Yuha Mani; Walks With Red; F; Wife; 63
2666 Tatanka Ciqala; Little Bull; M; S.Son; 31
2667 Tasunke Opi; Wounded Horse; M; S.Son; 21
2668 Heraka Luzahan; Fast Elk; M; Father; 59
2669 Tasina Waste Win; Her Good Blanket; F; Wife #1; 58
2670 Wankal Hiyu; Comes Above; F; Wife #2; 54
2671 Tasunke Waste Win; Her Good Horses; F; Dau; 25
2672 Tonweya; Scout; M; Son; 23
2673 Sophia; F; Dau; 21
2674 Sunk Iyanajinca; Runs With Horses; F; Dau; 12
2675 Wapaha Luta; Red War Bonnet; M; Husb; 75
2676 Sagye; Cane; F; Wife; 68
2677 Itonkasan; Weasel; M; G.Son; 11
2678 Emma Webber; F; Mother; 27
2679 Heraka Iyanke; Running Elk; M; Father; 44
2680 Worinyan; Pouting; F; Wife #1; 34
2681 Wawicasi; Asks Them To Do Something; F; Wife #2; 34
2682 Wapaha Wicaku; Gives Away War Bonnet; M; Son; 5
2683 Oyunke Maza; Iron Bed; F; 84
2684 Sam Ladeaux; M; Husb; 24
2685 Hokikta; Looks Behind; F; Wife; 23
2686 Baptiste Ladeaux; M; Husb; 23
2687 Wacinhin; Anna Plume; F; Mother; 52
2688 Julia Ladeaux; F; Sister; 19
2689 Lily Ladeaux; F; Sister; 15
2690 Tipi Luta; Red Lodge; F; Sister; 8
2691 Annie; F; Wife; 23
2692 Mato Lowan; Singing Bear; M; Husb; 70
2693 Tehan Rpaya; Sleeps Late; F; Wife; 53
2694 Palani Kte; John Kills Ree; M; Nephew; 20
2695 Tinpsila Tanka; Big Turnip; M; Father; 48
2696 Winyan Isnala; Lone Woman; F; Wife; 41
2697 Tinpsila Tanka; Luke Big Turnip; M; Son; 20
2698 Wasna; Pemican; M; Bro; 27
2699 Pankeska Win; Shell Woman; F; 79
2700 Pankeska Luta Win; Red Shell Woman; F; 65
2701 Sagye Miwakan; Cane Sword; M; Husb; 60
2702 Iyeska; Interpreter; F; Wife; 49
2703 Mato Wamniomni; Bear Whirlwind; M; Father; 46
2704 Isto Akan Awicapa; Hit Them In The Arm; F; Aunt; 44
2705 Mato Wamniomni; Cora Bear Whirlwind; F; Dau; 21
2706 Oye Tain; Shows The Track; F; Dau; 8
2707 Sunka Luta; Red Dog; M; Father; 47
2708 Pte San; White Cow; F; Wife; 54

Census Of The Sioux And Cheyenne Indians Of Pine Ridge Agency, South Dakota. Taken by W. H. Clapp, Captain 16th Infantry, Acting United States Indian Agent, June 30, 1896. (Wounded Knee District)

Key: Number; Indian Name *(if given)*; English Name; Sex; Relation; Age

2709 Sunkgmuni; Lost Horses; M; Son; 12
2710 Agli; Fetches; M; Son; 7
2711 Hinhan Wanbli; Owl Eagle; M; Father; 64
2712 Sunkgleska Win; Spotted Horse Woman; F; Dau; 54
2713 Tokeya Kte; Kills First; M; G.Son; 11
2714 Isna Wakuwa; Chase Alone; M; G.Son; 1-3

2715 Henry Jones; M; Father; 32
2716 Zintkala Maza; Iron Bird; F; Wife; 40
2717 John Jones; M; Son; 14
2718 Pehin Ji; Yellow Hair; F; Dau; 8
2[sic]
2719 Wicakiza; Fighter; M; Son; 6
2720 Heraka Waste; Good Elk; F; Dau; 1-5

2721 Marpiya Ciqala; Little Cloud #2; M; Father; 47
2722 Marpiya Ciqala; Eli Little Cloud; M; Son; 48

2723 Wacinhin Maza; Iron Plume; M; Father; 52
2724 Pa Oikpemni; Covered Head; F; Wife; 54
2725 Tasunke Tainyan Mani; Horse Walks In Sight; M; Son; 21
2726 Isnala Isarga; Raised Alone; M; Son; 8

2727 Wipi; Full Stomach; M; Father; 35
2728 Cante Waste; Good Heart; F; Wife; 40
2729 Tainyan Ku; Comes In Sight; F; Dau; 5
2730 Mni Kiyela Ti; Lives By Water; F; Dau; 0-4

2731 Huncase; Garter; M; Father; 37
2732 Wazi Ape; Pine Leaf; F; Wife; 39
2733 Icaga; Growth; F; Dau; 8
2734 Oyate Tasunke; Nation Horse; F; Dau; 0-9

2735 Cetan Rcaka; Real Hawk; M; Father; 47
2736 Sinte Tokeca; Different Tail; F; Wife; 45
2737 Tokicun; Revenger; M; Son; 18
2738 Yusineyewicaya; Scares Them; M; Son; 2-3
2739 Tasunke Wopotepi; Her Horses Shot To Pieces; M; Son; 1-3

2740 Toka Wicakte; Kills Enemy; M; Father; 50
2741 Toka Wicakte; Rosa Kills Enemy; F; Wife; 26
2742 Hunska; James Leggins; M; B. in L.; 19
2743 Wapaha Icu; Takes War Bonnet; M; Son; 8
2744 Susuni Kte; Kills Shoshone; M; Son; 1-10
2745 Toka Wicakte; Anna Kills Enemy; F; Dau; 4

2746 Hunska Narco; Leggins Down; F; G.Mo; 69
2747 Toka Ole; Hunts Enemy; M; G.Son; 12
2748 Siyo Winorcala; Old Prairie Hen; F; G.Mo; 59
2749 Karnir Kte; Kills Choice; M; G.Son; 7
2750 Huste; Lame; M; Husb; 39
2751 Ite Witko; Fool Face; F; Wife; 25
2752 Mato Wicakiza; Max Fighting Bear; M; Cousin; 21

Census Of The Sioux And Cheyenne Indians Of Pine Ridge Agency, South Dakota. Taken by W. H. Clapp, Captain 16th Infantry, Acting United States Indian Agent, June 30, 1896. (Wounded Knee District)

Key: Number; Indian Name *(if given)*; English Name; Sex; Relation; Age

2753	Kisun Sni; Abel No Braid; M; Father; 33	2775	Wakinyan Yuha; Owns Thunder; F; Mother; 73
2754	Wanbli Winyan; Eagle Woman; F; Wife; 25	2776	Tasina; Her Blanket; F; Sister; 38
2755	Toka Waste; Good Enemy; F; Dau; 4	2777	Wiyaka Nupa; Two Feathers; M; Son; 4-6
2756	Kangi Winyan; Crow Woman; F; M. in L.; 58	2778	Winyan Hanska; Long Woman; F; G.Mo; 64
2757	Kisun Sni; George No Braid; M; Nephew; 17	2779	Jennie; F; G.Dau; 16
2758	Heraka Wanbli; Eagle Elk; M; Father; 35	2780	Hoksila Maza; Jacob Iron Boy; M; Husb; 22
2759	Winyan Tanka; Grown Woman; F; Wife; 32	2781	Sunka Huste; Mabel Lame Dog; F; Wife; 15
2760	Oyuspapi; Captured; F; Dau; 9		
2761	Wanbli Oyate; Eagle Nation; F; Dau; 2-0	2782	Rloku; Comes Growling; M; Father; 24
2762	Hoksila Sayapi; Red Painted Boy; M; Son; 0-4	2783	Ota Kte; Kills Plenty; F; Wife; 23
		2784	Wasicu Opi; Shot By White Man; M; Son; 6
2763	Aka Hiyu; James Comes Again; M; Father; 26	2785	Ista Gi; Edward Brown Eyes; M; Son; 2-6
2764	Pankeska Luta; Red Shell; F; Wife; 32	2786	Wanjila Agli; Brings One; F; Dau; 1-1
2765	Terilapi; Fond Of Him; F; Dau; 2-4		
		2787	Tasunke Iyanka; Her Running Horse; F; Mother; 58
2766	Anpetu Wakan; Holy Day; F; Mother; 51	2788	Zintkala Sa; Red Bird; M; Son; 18
2767	Mnioyusna; Drops In The Water; F; Mother; 70		
2768	Ptesan Nupa; Two White Cows; F; Dau; 7	2789	Ranhi; Slow; F; 62
		2790	Wapartapi; Packed; F; Mother; 52
2769	Wanagi Witko; Crazy Ghost; M; Father; 44	2791	Jacob; M; Son; 11
2770	Cokab Win; Center Woman; F; Wife; 38	2792	Wanbli Ciqala; Little Eagle; M; Son; 7
2771	Frank; M; Son; 15		
2772	Keya Sa; Red Feather; M; Son; 9	2793	Augustus; M; Father; 19
2773	Tainyan Najin; Stands In Sight; F; Dau; 12	2794	Ota Agli; Brought Plenty; F; Wife; 20
		2795	Rante Maza; Iron Cedar; F; Dau; 0-3
2774	Nawicakicijin; Protector; M; Son; 32		

Census Of The Sioux And Cheyenne Indians Of Pine Ridge Agency, South Dakota. Taken by W. H. Clapp, Captain 16th Infantry, Acting United States Indian Agent, June 30, 1896. (Wounded Knee District)

Key: Number; Indian Name *(if given)*; English Name; Sex; Relation; Age

2796 Tatanka Nupa; Amos Two Bulls; M; Son; 19
2797 Ataya Zintkala; Bird All Over; F; Mother; 49
2798 Tatanka Nupa; Mary Two Bulls; F; Sister; 18
2799 Tatanka Nupa; Anna Two Bulls; F; Sister; 15

2800 Adolph; M; Son; 24
2801 Iya Sica; Bad Talker; F; Mother; 61
2802 Warpe Sna; Falling Leaf; F; Niece; 7

2803 Mastinsala Luta; Red Rabbit; M; Father; 37
2804 Iya Waste; Good Talk; F; Wife; 51
2805 Anna; F; Dau; 18

2806 Kangi Apapi; Struck By Crow; M; Father; 49
2807 Hunkesni; Slow; F; Wife; 46
2808 Gus; M; B. in L.; 23
2809 Kangi Apapi; Harry Struck By Crow; M; Son; 19
2810 Ota Opi; Shot Many Times; M; Son; 7

2811 Heraka Maza; Iron Elk; M; Husb; 20
2812 Pankeska Hoksila; Alice Shell Boy; F; Wife; 17

2813 Ptehe; Cow Horn; F; Mother; 46
2814 Pte Tokahe; Loading Buffalo; F; Dau; 15
2815 Tianatan; Runs For Camp; M; Son; 9
2816 Tokeya Kute; Shoots First; M; Son; 5

2817 Tatanka Nupa; Joseph Two Bulls; M; Father; 30

2818 Tokeya Mani; Walks First; F; Wife; 29
2819 Wapaha Opi; Wounded Bonnet; M; Son; 7
2820 Wanbli Hoksila; Eagle Boy; M; Son; 5
2821 Wanbli Koyaka; Wears Eagle; F; Dau; 2-3

2822 Mato Rabwicaya; Bear Scares; M; Father; 39
2823 Capa Ska; White Beaver; F; Wife; 37
2824 Mato Rabwicaya; Samuel Bear Scares; M; Son; 14

2825 Watakpe; George Charging; M; Father; 35
2826 Watakpe; Louise Charging; F; Wife; 32
2827 Watakpe; Louise Charging; F; Dau; 14
2828 Watakpe; Jackson Charging; M; Son; 12
2829 Watakpe; David Charging; M; Son; 10
2830 Watakpe; Alice Charging; F; Dau; 8
2831 Wanbli Oyate; Eagle Nation; F; Dau; 2-10

2832 Pankeska Maza; Iron Shell; M; Husb; 50
2833 Imaputaka; Kiss Me; F; Wife #1; 48
2834 Pankeska Maza; Lizzie Iron Shell; F; Wife #2; 31

2835 Wanagi Wicakute; Shoots Ghost; M; Father; 74
2836 Scili Kte; Kills Pawnee; F; Wife; 64
2837 Naca; Chief; M; Son; 26
2838 Tainyan Najin; Stand In Sight; F; G.Dau; 10

Census Of The Sioux And Cheyenne Indians Of Pine Ridge Agency, South Dakota. Taken by W. H. Clapp, Captain 16th Infantry, Acting United States Indian Agent, June 30, 1896. (Wounded Knee District)

Key: Number; Indian Name *(if given)*; English Name; Sex; Relation; Age

2839	Najinyapi Kte; Surrounded Killed; M; G.Son; 8	2860	Frank Galligo; M; Father; 34
		2861	Julia Galligo; F; Wife; 28
		2862	Rosa Galligo; F; Dau; 12
2840	Nupa Wakita; Looks Twice; M; Father; 44	2863	Lou Galligo; M; Son; 10
		2864	Alvina Galligo; F; Dau; 7
2841	Wanbli Win; Eagle Woman; F; Wife #1; 41	2865	Minnie Galligo; F; Dau; 5
		2866	Sarah Galligo; F; Dau; 3-1
2842	Winyan Hanska; Long Woman; F; Wife #2; 34	2867	Frank Galligo, Jr; M; Son; 1-7
2843	Icaga; Grows Up; F; Dau; 20	2868	Peter Bissonette; M; Father; 49
2844	Nupa Wakita; Maggie Looks Twice; F; Dau; 16	2869	Susie Bissonette; F; Wife; 45
		2870	Frank Bissonette; M; Son; 22
2845	Oosica; Hard To Hit; M; Son; 14	2871	Jennie Bissonette; F; Dau; 18
		2872	Josephin[sic] Bissonette; F; Dau; 16
2846	Tapi Sagye; Cane Lion; M; Son; 11	2873	Lottie Bissonette; F; Dau; 14
		2874	George Bissonette; M; Son; 10
2847	Sunkska Win; White Horse Woman; F; Dau; 11	2875	Fannie Bissonette; F; Dau; 7
2848	Mato Ota Win; Plenty Bear Woman; F; Dau; 6	2876	Tasunke Maza; Frank Iron Horse; M; Father; 32
2849	Tasina Rlecahan; Her Town Blanket; F; G.Dau; 4-4	2877	Waicu; Takes Things; F; Wife; 31
		2878	Toka Kaga; Makes Enemy; M; Son; 5
2850	Tasunke Gleska; Her Spotted Horse; F; Dau; 3-6	2879	Cante Waste; Feels Good; M; Son; 2-6
2851	Ku Sni; Dont[sic] Come; M; Son; 0-4	2880	Tipi Wakan; Holy Lodge; F; Dau; 0-3
2852	Tasunke Waste; Pretty Horse; F; Dau; 5	2881	Jennie Sires; F; Mother; 29
2853	Tawacin Waste; Good Will; F; Mother; 75	2882	William Provost; M; Son; 11
		2883	Cetan Kiyan; Flying Hawk; M; Father; 40
2854	Sunkgleska Ota; Mary Spotted Horses; F; Dau; 33	2884	Anpetu Ska; White Day; F; Wife #1; 41
2855	Maza; Iron; F; Mother; 66	2885	Wakil Hinapa; Looks Coming Out; F; Wife #2; 34
2856	Ikusan; Mink; F; 81	2886	Canupa Wanbli; Eagle Pipe; M; Nephew; 25
2857	Tarca Luta; Red Deer; F; 69	2887	Tokeya Kte; Kills First; M; Son; 14
2858	Pte Kte; Kills Cow; F; 86		
2859	Pejin Parta; Julia Hay Press; F; 59	2888	Takuni Okola Sni; Respects Nothing; M; Father; 41

Census Of The Sioux And Cheyenne Indians Of Pine Ridge Agency, South Dakota.
Taken by W. H. Clapp, Captain 16th Infantry, Acting United States Indian Agent,
June 30, 1896. (Wounded Knee District)

Key: Number; Indian Name *(if given)*; English Name; Sex; Relation; Age

2889 Ptesan Oyate; White Cow Tribe; F; Wife; 39
2890 Takuni Okola Sni; George Respects Nothing; M; Son; 6
2891 Ilazatan Yanka; Sits Behind; M; Son; 3-2
2892 Wapaha Luta; Red War Bonnet; F; Dau; 0-4
2893 Isna Wakuwa; Chase Alone; M; Father; 33
2894 Okiyakapi; Told To Her; F; Wife; 33
2895 Tasunke Wanbli; Eagle Horse; F; Dau; 6
2896 Tasunke Wanbli; Owns Eagle Horse; F; Dau; 6
2897 Sunk Icu; Takes Horses; F; Dau; 0-1
2898 Zintkala Wicasa; Bird Man; M; Father; 34
2899 Ozan Mahel; Between Lodges; F; Wife; 28
2900 Tasunke Waste; Her Good Horse; F; Dau; 7
2901 Hanhepi Yanka; Night Sitter; M; Son; 4-5
2902 David; M; S.Son; 18
2903 Kangi Luta; Red Crow; M; Husb; 64
2904 Tezi; Belly; F; Wife; 61
2905 Nuwanpi; Swimmer; M; Father; 50
2906 Wakan Mani; Walks Holy; F; Wife; 44
2907 Winyan Waste; Pretty Woman; F; Dau; 35
2908 Nuwanpi; John Swimmer; M; Son; 21
2909 Tasunke Nupa; Two Horses; M; 38
2910 Wacinhin Ska; White Plume; M; Father; 44
2911 Sunkhinsa; Red Horse; F; Wife; 41
2912 Niyanke Kte; Kills Alive; M; Son; 13
2913 Asanpi; Milk; M; Son; 9
2914 Zuya Terila; Loves War; M; Father; 41
2915 Oye Wakan; Holy Track; F; Wife; 35
2916 Nupa Kte; Kills Twice; M; Son; 14
2917 Tasunke Hinapa; Horse Comes Out; F; Dau; 9
2918 Wowasr Yuha; Employer; M; Son; 6
2919 Sunka Mani; Walking Dog; M; Son; 3-6
2920 Canupa Wakita; Looking Pipe; F; Dau; 0-7
2921 Tasunke Witko; Crazy Horse; M; Father; 47
2922 Winyan Waste; Good Woman; F; Wife; 34
2923 Ohitika; Brave; F; Dau; 16
2924 Hinapa; Comes Out; M; Son; 1-11
2925 Ha Wakan; Holy Skin; M; Father; 46
2926 Capa; Beaver; F; Wife; 55
2927 Ha Wakan; Bessie Holy Skin; F; Dau; 16
2928 Winyan Isnala; Lone Woman; F; M. in L.; 79
2929 Tatanka Hanska; Long Bull; M; Husb; 25
2930 Wanbli Luta; Red Eagle; F; Wife; 23
2931 Kangi Maza; Iron Crow #2; M; Father; 36

Census Of The Sioux And Cheyenne Indians Of Pine Ridge Agency, South Dakota. Taken by W. H. Clapp, Captain 16th Infantry, Acting United States Indian Agent, June 30, 1896. (Wounded Knee District)

Key: Number; Indian Name *(if given)*; English Name; Sex; Relation; Age

2932	Tokeya Hiyaya; Goes First; F; Wife; 30	2954	Toka Kuwa; Martha Chasing Enemy; F; Wife; 53
2933	Zintka To; Blue Bird; F; Dau; 8		
2934	Kupi; Gives Him; F; Dau; 5	2955	Wasicu Tasunke; Robert American Horse; M; Husb; 40
2935	Waniyetu Kte; Boy Kills In Winter; M; Nephew; 0-9	2956	Wasicu Tasunke; Nancy American Horse; F; Wife; 27
2936	Canrloyan Win; Needy Girl; F; Dau; 1-4		
		2957	Winyan Hanska; Tail Woman; F; 84
2937	Spayola; Ambrose Mexican; M; Father; 35		
2938	Winyan Waste; Good Woman; F; Wife; 28	2958	Mato Sica; Howard Bad Bear; M; Husb; 19
2939	Kiyela Opi; Shot Close; M; Son; 13	2959	Wasicu Winyan; White Woman; F; Wife; 16
2940	Tasunke Yuhapi; Keeps Her Horses; F; Dau; 11	2960	Glonica; Begs To Keep; F; Mother; 55
2941	Wanjigjila Wicakte; Kills One After Another; M; Son; 1-9	2961	Mato Sica; Henry Bad Bear; M; Bro; 15
2942	Tasunke Wakan; Medicine Horse; M; 45	2962	John Bissonette; M; Father; 24
		2963	Fannie Bissonette; F; Wife; 23
		2964	Jessie Bissonette; F; Dau; 1-2
2943	Wan Taopi; Arrow Wound; M; Father; 40		
2944	Wicincala; Girl; F; Dau; 0-4	2965	Huhu Yuha; Keeps Bone; F; 54
2945	Nape Iyorpeyapi; Boiled Hand; F; Mother; 83	2966	Wikan Yuslohan; Drags Rope; M; Father; 38
		2967	Tasunke Waste; Her Good Horse; F; Wife; 38
2946	Sunkska; John White Horse; M; Father; 57	2968	Cangleska Waste; Good Hoop; M; Son; 1-1
2947	Sunkska; Katie White Horse; F; Dau; 15		
2948	Opanwinge Owicayus; Arrested One Hundred; M; Son; 8	2969	Cante Wicasa; Heart Man; M; Father; 50
2949	Marpiya Wanbli; Eagle Cloud; M; Son; 5	2970	Wacinko; Pouting; F; Wife; 50
		2971	Waonsila; Takes Pity; M; Son; 16
2950	Tate Pejuta; Medicine Wind; F; G.Mother; 87	2972	Sunk Hiyohi; Comes After Horses; F; Dau; 6
2951	Pestola; Painted; F; G.Dau; 18		
		2973	Sahiyela; Cheyenne; M; Father; 49
2952	Opo; Fog; F; 54	2974	Si; Foot; F; Wife; 43
2953	Toka Kuwa; Chasing Enemy; M; Husb; 64	2975	Wapaha; War Bonnet; F; Dau; 8

Census Of The Sioux And Cheyenne Indians Of Pine Ridge Agency, South Dakota. Taken by W. H. Clapp, Captain 16th Infantry, Acting United States Indian Agent, June 30, 1896. (Wounded Knee District)

Key: Number; Indian Name *(if given)*; English Name; Sex; Relation; Age

2976 Tainyan Kte; Kills In Sight; M; Son; 3-5
2977 Zintkala Waste; Pretty Bird; M; Father; 33
2978 Worinyan; Pouting; F; Wife; 41
2979 John; M; Son; 10
2980 Tainyan Mani; Walks In Sight; F; Dau; 7
2981 Tipi Wakan; Her Medicine Lodge; F; Dau; 4
2982 Gleska Wicaku; Gives Spotted; M; Son; 0-4
2983 Canupa Wanbli; Eagle Pipe; M; Father; 47
2984 Tuga; Hump; F; Wife; 35
2985 Kutepi; Shot At; M; Bro; 36
2986 Canupa Wanbli; Mac Eagle Pipe; M; Son; 17
2987 Kasmi Tanka; Big Bend; M; Father; 51
2988 Tonweya Win; Guide Woman; F; Wife; 54
2989 Tainyan Wicakte; Kills In Sight; F; Dau; 9
2990 Isto Wasaka; Lawrence Industrious; M; Father; 26
2991 Isto Wasaka; Alice Industrious; F; Wife; 26
2992 Isto Wasaka; Shell Industrious; F; Dau; 5-6
2993 Zuya Wicakte; Kills Warrior; F; Dau; 0-4
2994 Kuwa Wicakte; Kills Charging; F; Dau; 0-4
2995 Mato Wakatuya[sic]; High Bear; M; Father; 57
2996 Tasina Zi; Yellow Blanket; F; Wife; 59
2997 Mato Wankatuya; Jennie High Bear; F; Dau; 24
2998 Mato Wankatuya; Alice High Bear; F; Dau; 18
2999 Gi; Lucy Yellow; F; Dau; 16
3000 Ota Wicakte; Kills Many; F; Mother; 54
3001 Matoha Sina; Mary Bear Robe; F; Dau; 20
3002 Matoha Sina; Eliza Bear Robe; F; Dau; 11
3003 Nawizi; Jealous; M; G.Son; 8
3004 Wapaha; War Bonnet; M; Father; 29
3005 Nimwicaya; Saves Lives; F; Wife; 23
3006 Kangi Wicakte; Kills Crow; F; Dau; 6
3007 Toka Opi; Wounded By Enemy; F; Dau; 4
3008 Cetan Ho Waste; Good Voice Hawk; M; Son; 2-3
3009 Sota; Wendell Smoke; M; Bro; 21
3010 Sunka Yatapi; Dog Chief; F; Father; 24
3011 Nakiwizipi; Jealous Of Them; F; Wife; 27
3012 Waste; Edgar Good; M; Son; 7
3013 Ninglicu; Comes Alice; F; Dau; 2-7
3014 Hoksila Anatapi; Boy Runs For Him; M; Son; 0-4
3015 Ake Hiyu; Peter Comes Again; M; Father; 51
3016 Ake Hiyu; Lizzie Comes Again; F; Wife; 49
3017 Ake Hiyu; John Come[sic] Again; M; Son; 18
3018 Ake Hiyu; Rachael Comes Again; F; Dau; 14
3019 Mato Ska Sake; White Bear Claws; M; Father; 37

Census Of The Sioux And Cheyenne Indians Of Pine Ridge Agency, South Dakota. Taken by W. H. Clapp, Captain 16th Infantry, Acting United States Indian Agent, June 30, 1896. (Wounded Knee District)

Key: Number; Indian Name *(if given)*; English Name; Sex; Relation; Age

3020	Aiyapi; Talks About Him; F; Wife; 28	3042	Cetan Kokipapi; Albert Afraid Of Hawk; M; Son; 15
3021	Naca Gli; Comes Back Chief; M; Son; 9	3043	Okogna Iyanka; Runs Between; F; Dau; 1-2
3022	Mato Canupa; Bear Pipe; M; Son; 0-5	3044	He Wanjila; Annie Lone Horn; F; Aunt; 36
3023	Wiyaka Raka; Rough Feather; M; Father; 33	3045	Joseph; M; Nephew; 15
		3046	Akicize; Fights Over; F; Niece; 14
3024	Wanbli Cuwignaka; Eagle Dress; F; Wife; 32		
3025	Sunk Iyanajinca; Charles Stampedes Horses; M; Son; 8	3047	Itowe Ro; Straight Forehead; M; Husb; 38
3026	Ptesan Hinapa; White Cow Goes Out; F; Dau; 4	3048	Piya Iglaka; Moves Over; F; Wife; 32
3027	Gi Iciya; Points Yellow; M; Father; 51	3049	Cetan Luta; Austin Red Hawk; M; Father; 37
3028	Gi Iciya; Julia Yellow; F; Wife; 46	3050	Cetan Luta; Alice Red Hawk; F; Wife; 36
3029	Waste Koyaka; Wears Good; F; Dau; 16	3051	Rante Win; Cedar Woman; F; Sister; 44
3030	Ptehincala Ska; White Calf; D; Dau; 5	3052	Akayanka Kte; Kills On Horseback; M; Nephew; 18
		3053	Cetan Luta; Susie Red Hawk; F; Dau; 9
3031	Heraka Lowan; Singing Elk; M; Father; 69	3054	Cetan Luta; James Red Hawk; M; Son; 7
3032	Mato Cankahu; Bear Backbone; M; Cousin; 72	3055	Cetan Luta; Noah Red Hawk; M; Son; 0-5
3033	Ota Koyaka; Wears Plenty; F; Wife; 67		
3034	Wanbli Wakan; Holy Eagle; M; Son; 32	3056	Anukasan Waste; Pretty Bald Eagle; M; Husb; 64
3035	Cetan Wicakte; Kills Hawk; M; Son; 36	3057	Cansi Mna; Smells Gun; F; Wife; 59
		3058	Cante Waste; Good Hearted; F; M. in L.; 81
3036	Cetan Kokipapi; Afraid Of Hawk; M; Father; 48		
3037	Re Ska; White Mountain; F; Wife; 47	3059	Cante Witko; Fool Heart; M; Father; 49
3038	Cetan Kokipapi; Richard Afraid Of Hawk; M; Son; 21	3060	Wayurlata; Scratches; F; Wife #1; 35
3039	Annie; F; Dau; 10	3061	Ble Wakan; Holy Take; F; Wife #2; 43
3040	Wicokuje; Patient; F; Dau; 10		
3041	Wakun; Wished For; F; Dau; 6-6	3062	Iktomni Cankahu; Spider Back Bone; M; Son; 21

Census Of The Sioux And Cheyenne Indians Of Pine Ridge Agency, South Dakota. Taken by W. H. Clapp, Captain 16th Infantry, Acting United States Indian Agent, June 30, 1896. (Wounded Knee District)

Key: Number; Indian Name *(if given)*; English Name; Sex; Relation; Age

3063 Wanbli Ciqala; Little Eagle; M; Father; 53
3064 Tezi; Belly; F; Wife #1; 58
3065 Piya Kaga; Makes Over; F; Wife #2; 53
3066 Sahiyela Waste; Good Cheyenne; M; Son; 24
3067 Ptesan Hinapa; Comes Out White Cow; F; Dau; 17
3068 Cangleska Wanbli; Eagle Ring; M; Husb; 26
3069 Winyan Isnala; Lone Woman; F; Wife; 24
3070 Kangi Waste; Good Crow; M; Father; 42
3071 Wiyaka Ota; Many Feathers; F; Wife; 38
3072 Inyan Hoksila; Rock Boy; M; Son; 11
3073 Inyan Tipi Win; Rock Lodge Woman; F; Dau; 8
3074 Wicincala; Girl; F; Dau; 6
3075 Wasu Cuwignaka; Hail Dress; M; Son; 4
3076 Wicincala Yusna; Drops Down Girl; F; Dau; 0-9
3077 Winyan Gi; Yellow Woman; F; Mother; 43
3078 Hoksila Sica; Bad Boy; M; Son; 22
3079 Iyanka Wicakte; Kills Running; M; Son; 8
3080 Onsiyan Yanka; Sits Poor; M; Father; 47
3081 Oyuspapi; Captured; F; Wife; 38
3082 Onsinyan[sic] Yanka; Franks[sic] Sits Poor; M; Son; 16
3083 Hinzi Agli; Brings Yellow; F; Dau; 6
3084 Tonweya Gli; Returned From Scout; M; Son; 0-8
3085 Istarepi Ska; White Eye Lash; M; Father; 45
3086 Heraka Win; Elk Woman; F; Wife; 37
3087 Toka Tasunke Awica; Brings Enemies Horses; F; Dau; 14
3088 Mazawakan Icu; Takes Gun; M; Son; 7
3089 Sunk Manusa; Horse Thief; M; Son; 2-10
3090 Tatanka Hunke Sni; Slow Bull #1; M; 76
3091 Mniyata Wicasa; William Water Man; M; Father; 23
3092 SkaAgli[sic]; Brings White; F; Wife; 25
3093 Mniyata [sic]; Charles Water Man; M; Son; 1-7
3094 Mniyata Wicasa; Joseph Water Man; M; Son; 0-1
3095 Heraka Ciqala; Little Elk; M; Husb; 24
3096 Hunpeka; Della Picket Pine; F; Wife; 24
3097 Pte San; White Cow; F; Mother; 54
3098 Wanju; Quiver; F; Sister; 42
3099 Ptesan Wanyanka; Sees White Cow; F; Dau; 6
3100 Wanbli Ota; Plenty Eagles; M; Father; 59
3101 Wanbli Tipi; Eagle Lodge; F; Dau; 11
3102 Wakan Lecala; New Holy; M; Father; 34
3103 Wanbli Oye; Eagle Track; F; Wife; 33
3104 Sunkpa Ska Yuha; Owns White Face Horses; F; Sister; 21

Census Of The Sioux And Cheyenne Indians Of Pine Ridge Agency, South Dakota. Taken by W. H. Clapp, Captain 16th Infantry, Acting United States Indian Agent, June 30, 1896. (Wounded Knee District)

Key: Number; Indian Name *(if given)*; English Name; Sex; Relation; Age

3105 Owicale; Hunts Them; F; Dau; 13
3106 Najinyapi; Surrounded; M; Son; 1-4
3107 Wapaha Wicaku; Gives War Bonnet; F; Dau; 3-4
3108 Winyan Zi; Yellow Woman; F; Mother; 25
3109 Canupa Yuha Mani; Walks With Pipe; F; Dau; 0-5
3110 Maku; Breast; M; 43
3111 Wiyaka Wanjila; Moses One Feather; M; Father; 40
3112 Hihan Luta; Red Owl; F; Wife; 39
3113 Wiyaka Wanjila; Ettie One Feather; F; Dau; 13
3114 Re Sapa; Black Hills; F; Dau; 1
3115 Wanbli Gleska; Spotted Eagle; M; Bro; 20
3116 Sota; Smoke; M; Father; 52
3117 Pehin Ji Win; Yellow Haired Woman; F; Wife; 63
3118 Pehin Ji Win; Susie Y. Haired Woman; F; Dau; 18
3119 Ptesan Luta; Red White Cow; F; Dau; 14
3120 Itunkasan Waste; Good Weasel; M; Husb; 24
3121 Ptanka Sina; Otter Blanket; F; Wife; 21
3122 Sunk Iyanajinca; Gets Away With Horses; F; Sister; 8
3123 Sikahunpi; Cut Foot; M; Husb; 72
3124 Wasu; Hail; F; Wife; 68
3125 Wakinyan Tamaheca; Poor Thunder; M; Father; 36
3126 Itunkasan; Weasel; F; Wife; 35
3127 Wakinyan Tamaheca; Lizzie Poor Thunder; F; Dau; 15
3128 Hanpa Spaya; Wet Moccasin; M; Son; 7
3129 Tatanka Catka; Left Hand Bull; M; Son; 4
3130 Tokeya Kte; Kills First; M; Son; 2-5
3131 Kokab Iyaya; Howard Goes In Front; M; Son; 8
3132 Cetan Maza; Iron Hawk; M; Father; 33
3133 Rloku; Comes Growling; F; Wife; 25
3134 Hihan Ska; White Owl; M; G.Father; 6 3
3135 Pejuta; Medicine; F; Dau; 8
3136 Wanbli Sun Pejuta; Medicine Eagle Feather; M; Son; 4
3137 Pejuta Wankatuya; High Medicine; M; Son; 2-7
3138 Sunka Huste; James Lame Dog; M; Father; 42
3139 Marpiya To; Blue Cloud; F; Wife; 39
3140 Sunka Huste; Lizzie Lame Dog; F; Dau; 21
3141 Sunka Huste; William Lame Dog; M; Son; 14
3142 Ho Akatanhan; Voice On Top; M; Son; 14
3143 Icu; Takes; F; Dau; 4
3144 Tokeya Ku; Comes First; F; Dau; 1-11
3145 Wakiya Hanska; John Long Commander; M; Husb; 27
3146 Ake Hiyu; Carrie Comes Again; F; Wife; 19
3147 Heraka Wanbli; Eagle Elk #2; M; Son; 34
3148 Tonweya Ciqala; Little Guide; M; Father; 67

Census Of The Sioux And Cheyenne Indians Of Pine Ridge Agency, South Dakota. Taken by W. H. Clapp, Captain 16th Infantry, Acting United States Indian Agent, June 30, 1896. (Wounded Knee District)

Key: Number; Indian Name *(if given)*; English Name; Sex; Relation; Age

3149	Inyan Topa; Four Rocks; F; Mother; 66	3174	Tasina Nupa; Her Two Blankets; F; Dau; 8
3150	He Hanska; Long Horn; M; Bro; 32	3175	Niyanpi; Saves Him; M; Son; 4
3151	Iglepa; Puke; M; Father; 57	3176	George Brown; M; Father; 25
3152	Oglala; Ogalalla; F; Wife; 53	3177	Susie Brown; F; Wife; 25
3153	Wan Agli; Brings Arrows; M; Son; 27	3178	George Brown, Jr; M; Son; 2-3
		3179	Jennie Brown; F; Dau; 0-9
3154	Ogle Zi; Yellow Shirt; M; Son; 23	3180	Wakinyan Watakpi[sic]; Charging Thunder; M; Father; 27
3155	Tasunke Wankatuya; High Horse; M; Son; 18	3181	Wakinyan Watakpe; Sophia Charging Thunder; F; Wife; 26
3156	Iglepa; Rosa Puke; F; Dau; 12	3182	Wakinyan Watakpe; Columbus C. Thunder; M; Son; 3-3
3157	Inyan Wakan; James Holy Rock; M; Father; 32	3183	Wakinyan Watakpe; Asa Charging Thunder; M; Son; 0-2
3158	Anpetu; Lucy Day; F; Wife; 29		
3159	Nellie Twiss; F; Dau; 13	3184	Helen Garcia; F; Mother; 35
3160	Sally; F; Dau; 1-5	3185	Nupala; Mary Two Two; F; Dau; 2-9
3161	Oye Wakan; Medicine Track; F; 71	3186	Sunk Ska; White Horse; M; Father; 38
3162	Wiyaka Pegnaka; Feather On Head; M; Husb; 64	3187	Tokicun; Revenger; F; Wife; 32
		3188	Iyan Wicasa; Rock Man White Horse; M; Son; 11
3163	Sina To; Blue Blanket; F; Wife; 63		
3164	Mniyata Wicasa; Fannie Waterman; F; G.Dau; 2-9	3189	Hoksila Waste; Pretty Boy; M; Father; 40
		3190	Tasunke; Her Horses; F; Wife; 33
3165	Millie C. Prescott; F; Wife; 26	3191	Keya; Truth; M; Son; 9
3166	Alvina Garcia; F; Sister; 17		
3167	Rosa Garcia; F; Sister; 16	3192	Wakan Hoksila; Medicine Boy; M; Father; 34
3168	Sunday Garcia; F; Sister; 12	3193	Tobloku Ota; Plenty Brothers; F; Wife #1; 36
3169	Thomas Garcia; M; Bro; 9		
3170	Susie Garcia; F; Sister; 6	3194	Ptesan Maza; Iron White Cow; F; Wife #2; 34
3171	Peji Rota; Gray Grass; M; Father; 49	3195	Tasunke Wakan; Medicine Horse; F; Dau; 6
3172	Niyan Kte; Kills Living; F; Wife; 50	3196	Inyan Maza; Iron Rock; F; Dau; 5
3173	Sunk Icu; Takes Horses; F; Dau; 25	3197	Hoksila Wakan; Susie Medicine Boy; F; Dau; 2-10

Census Of The Sioux And Cheyenne Indians Of Pine Ridge Agency, South Dakota. Taken by W. H. Clapp, Captain 16th Infantry, Acting United States Indian Agent, June 30, 1896. (Wounded Knee District)

Key: Number; Indian Name *(if given)*; English Name; Sex; Relation; Age

3198 Cokanyan Iyanka; Runs In Center; F; Wife; 18
3199 Zintkala Sapa; Black Bird; M; Father; 62
3200 Tibloku Ota; Plenty Brothers; F; Wife #1; 59
3201 Tewicarila; Loves Them; F; Wife #2; 62
3202 Takuni Ole Shi; Hunts Nothing; F; Dau; 23
3203 Sunkawakan Wanjila; One Horse; M; Son; 24
3204 Pahi; Picks It Up; M; Son; 14
3205 Sunkawakan Wan; Sees The Horses; F; Dau; 4-6
3206 Tasunke Kinyela; Flying Horse Jr; M; 18
3207 Canhanpa Ohan; Jacob Wears Shoe; M; Husb; 28
3208 Tasina; Her Blanket; F; Wife; 21
3209 Wakan Koyaka; Wears Holy; F; Mother 31
3210 Ista Gonga; Blind Woman; F; Mother; 71
3211 Sunkska Wicao; Shot White Horse; F; Dau; 11
3212 Sunsunla Sa; White Mule; F; Dau; 8
3213 Tokeya Wicakte; Kills First; M; Son; 5
3214 Winyan Wakan; Holy Woman; F; 67
3215 Mato Ciqala; Little Bear; M; Husb; 28
3216 Mato Hu; Bear Legs; F; Wife; 21
3217 Sarah Ingersoll; F; Wife; 31

3218 Cetan Ska; White Hawk; M; Father; 39
3219 Mattie Bissonette; F; Wife; 26
3220 Mato Najin; Clarence Standing Bear; M; Son; 6
3221 Opagila; Silas Fills The Pipe; M; Father; 39
3222 Opagila; Jennie Fills The Pipe; F; Wife; 32
3223 Opagila; Willie Fills The Pipe; M; Son; 16
3224 Opagila; Jessie Fills The Pipe; F; Dau; 3-6
3225 Opagila; Hattie Fills The Pipe; F; Dau; 1-5
3226 Joseph Pablo; M; Father; 42
3227 Rosa Pablo; F; Dau; 23
3228 Fannie Pablo; F; Dau; 20
3229 Alexander Pablo; M; Son; 11
3230 Sungmanitu Ciqala; Little Wolf; M; Father; 48
3231 Sunkska Yuha; Owns White Horses; F; Wife; 44
3232 Asapi; Yells At Him; F; Dau; 11
3233 Kokipeya Kte; Kills With Doubt; M; Son; 8
3234 Tacanku Waste; Her Good Road; F; Dau; 3-2
3235 Maka Luta; Red Earth; F; Dau; 2-8
3236 Tikanyela Kte; Thos. Kills Close To Lodg[sic]; M; Son; 12
3237 John Bissonette; M; Father; 35
3238 Julia Bissonette; F; Wife; 27
3239 Eliza Bissonette; F; Dau; 10
3240 Millie Bissonette; F; Dau; 6
3241 Susie Bissonette; F; Dau; 6
3242 Daniel Bissonette; M; Son; 4
3243 Andrew Bissonette; M; Son; 1-9

Census Of The Sioux And Cheyenne Indians Of Pine Ridge Agency, South Dakota. Taken by W. H. Clapp, Captain 16th Infantry, Acting United States Indian Agent, June 30, 1896. (Wounded Knee District)

Key: Number; Indian Name *(if given)*; English Name; Sex; Relation; Age

3244 James Nelson; M; Father; 20
3245 Okiyakapi Win; Tells Her; F; Wife; 23
3246 Albert Nelson; M; Son; 0-2

3247 Mato Wanartaka; Kicking Bear; M; Father; 44
3248 Wagnuka; Wood Pecker; F; Wife; 43
3249 Sina Wanbli; Eagle Shawl; F; Dau; 12
3250 Wakinyan; Thunder; M; Son; 7
3251 Mazawakan Scu; Takes The Gun; M; Son; 5

3252 Wicakicicute; Shoots For Them; M; Husb; 74
3253 Ska; White; F; Wife #1; 69
3254 Oye Maza; Iron Track; F; Wife #2; 65

3255 Charles Twiss; M; Father; 37
3256 Louise; F; Wife; 25
3257 Jesse; M; Son; 4-3
3258 Florence; F; Dau; 2-6
3259 Clara; F; Dau; 0-3

3260 Nicholas Ruleau; M; Father; 28
3261 Louise; F; Dau; 0-3

3262 Hunkpapa; Unkakapa; F; 67

3263 Tunkanyanke Win; Sitting Rock; F; Mother; 38
3264 Taninyanwin; In Sight; F; Dau; [blank]
3265 Wayakawaste; Good Prisoners; F; G.Mo; 66

Census of the Sioux And Cheyenne Indians
Of Pine Ridge Agency, South Dakota.
June 30, 1896

Medicine Root District

Census Of The Sioux And Cheyenne Indians Of Pine Ridge Agency, South Dakota. Taken by W. H. Clapp, Captain 16th Infantry, Acting United States Indian Agent, June 30, 1896. (Medicine Root District)

Key: Number; Indian Name *(if given)*; English Name; Sex; Relation; Age

3266	Wasicu Tasunke; American Horse; M; Father; 56	3287	Sunkhinsa; Red Horse; F; Wife; 64
3267	Istina; Sleep; F; Wife #1; 51	3288	Teriya Mani; Edward Walks Hard; M; G.Son; 15
3268	Wasicu Tasunke; Josie American Horse; F; Wife #2; 31		
3269	Wasicu Tasunke; Jennie American Horse; F; Dau; 16	3289	Akicita Hanska; Albert Long Soldier; M; Father; 26
3270	Wasicu Tasunke; Benjamin A. Horse; M; Son; 20	3290	Akisita[sic] Hanska; Millie Long Soldier; F; Wife; 32
3271	Wasicu Tasunke; Joseph American Horse; M; Son; 18	3291	Okogna Iyanka; Runs Between; M; Son; 4-3
3272	Wasicu Tasunke; Lucy American Horse; F; Dau; 18	3292	Antoine Herman; M; Father; 35
3273	Wasicu Tasunke; Sophia American Horse; F; Dau; 17	3293	Lizzie Herman; F; Wife; 31
		3294	Winifred Herman; F; Dau; 11
3274	Wasicu Tasunke; Alice American Horse; F; Dau; 15	3295	Nellie Herman; F; Dau; 8
		3296	Cora Herman; F; Dau; 6
3275	Wasicu Tasunke; Charles American Horse; M; Son; 14	3297	Edward Herman; M; Son; 9
		3298	Jacob Herman; M; Son; 4-5
3276	Wasicu Tasunke; Julia American Horse; F; Dau; 9	3299	Taopi Ciqala; Andrew Little Wound; M; 25
3277	Kangi Sapa; Alexander Black Crow; M; Father; 23	3300	Catka Kokipa; Afraid Of Left Hand; M; Son; 34
3278	Kangi Sapa; Millie Black Crow; F; Wife; 21	3301	Winyan Hanska; Tall Woman; F; Mother; 66
3279	Kangi Sapa; Katie Black Crow; F; Dau; 0-8		
		3302	Mato Canali; Bear Climbs; F; 61
3280	Sungmanitu Gi; Alex. Yellow Wolf; M; Father; 34	3303	Siyo Sapa; Black Chicken; M; Husb; 41
3281	Hihan Luta; Amos Red Owl; M; Father; 35	3304	Toka Slipa; Licks Enemy; F; Wife; 41
3282	Hihan Luta; Jessie Red Owl; F; Wife; 31	3305	Sunka Nage Tanka; Big Belly Dog; M; Husb; 56
3283	Hihan Luta; Henry Red Owl; M; Son; 7	3306	Anpetu Waste; Good Day; F; Wife; 44
3284	Ihuni; Levi Gets There; M; Son; 4-6		
3285	Hihan Luta; Hattie Red Owl; F; Dau; 0-11	3307	Mato Sinte; Bear Tail; M; Husb; 34
		3308	Woptura; Chipps; F; Wife; 34
3286	Takuni Kokipesni; Afraid Of Nothing; M; Father; 71	3309	Wahinyan Waste; Good Thunder; M; Son; 8

Census Of The Sioux And Cheyenne Indians Of Pine Ridge Agency, South Dakota. Taken by W. H. Clapp, Captain 16th Infantry, Acting United States Indian Agent, June 30, 1896. (Medicine Root District)

Key: Number; Indian Name *(if given)*; English Name; Sex; Relation; Age

3310	Niyan Luta; Red Breathing; F; Dau; 5	3330	Maza Win; Iron Woman; F; Wife; 49
3311	Nata Tanka; Big Head; M; Husb; 69	3331	Sungmanitu Sapa; Johnson Black Wolf; M; Son; 22
3312	Siyo; Prairie Chicken; F; Wife; 49	3332	Sungmanitu Sapa; Susie Black Wolf; F; Dau; 14
3313	Wanbli Ohitika; Brave Eagle; M; Father; 60	3333	Mato Sapa; Black Bear #2; M; Father; 30
3314	Tokatakiya; Forward; F; Wife; 58	3334	Najinhan Ku; Comes Standing; F; Wife; 24
3315	Wanbli Ohitika; Thomas Brave Eagle; M; G.Son; 12	3335	Marpiya Waste; Good Cloud; F; Dau; 6
		3336	Putinhin; Beard; M; Head; 32
3316	Isto Wegahan; Broken Arm; M; Father; 60	3337	Naca Win; Chief Woman; F; Wife; 42
3317	Hanhepi Gli; Comes Back Night; F; Wife #1; 56	3338	Marpiya He; Joseph Horn Cloud; M; Bro; 22
3318	Siyo; Chicken; F; Wife #2; 57	3339	Putinhin; Earnest Beard; M; Bro; 15
3319	Kangi Sapa; Black Crow; M; Father; 30	3340	Can Yuwega; Breaks Links; M; 67
3320	Wakan Gli; Comes Holy; F; Wife; 26		
3321	Owicale; Hunts Them Up; F; Dau; 5	3341	Tatanka Mato; Bull Bear; M; Husb; 70
3322	Wicegna Glica; Comes Among Them; M; Son; 3-5	3342	Marpiya; Cloud; F; Wife; 59
3323	Sunk Hiwohi; Comes After Horses; F; Dau; 0-4	3343	Tatanka Mato; Lizzie Bull Bear; F; Dau; 19
		3344	Ben Janis; M; Father; 32
3324	Wikan Papsaka; Broken Rope; M; Father; 72	3345	Susie Janis; F; Wife; 36
		3346	James Janis; M; Son; 8
3325	Wikan Papsaka; Sarah Broken Rope; F; Wife; 59	3347	Ben Janis, Jr; M; Son; 1-4
		3348	Bessie Janis; F; Dau; 5
3326	Wikan Papsaka; Joseph Broken Rope; M; Son; 25	3349	Agie Janis; F; Dau; 2-8
3327	Wikan Papsaka; Creighton Creek; M; Son; 12	3350	Ben Roland; M; Father; 30
		3351	Nellie Roland; F; Wife; 27
3328	Kangi Gleska; Edward Spotted Crow; M; Nephew; 14	3352	Mary Roland; F; Dau; 6
		3353	Annie Roland; F; Dau; 1-3
3329	Sungmanitu Sapa; Black Wolf; M; Father; 54	3354	Sicangu Win; Brule Woman; F; G.Mo; 68

Census Of The Sioux And Cheyenne Indians Of Pine Ridge Agency, South Dakota. Taken by W. H. Clapp, Captain 16th Infantry, Acting United States Indian Agent, June 30, 1896. (Medicine Root District)

Key: Number; Indian Name *(if given)*; English Name; Sex; Relation; Age

3355	Hinsma Win; Lucy Haired Woman; F; G.Dau; 10	3377	Tatanka Wakinyan; Shield Thunder Bull; M; Son; 17
3356	Ben Tibbets; M; Head; 22	3378	Tatanka Wakinyan; Joseph Thunder Bull; M: Son; 14
3357	Susie Tibbets; F; Wife; 22	3379	Tatanka Wakinyan; Susie Thunder Bull; F; Dau; 3-7
3358	Marpiya Gi; Brown Cloud; M; 27	3380	Mato Wicakte; Kill The Bear; F; Mo. in L.; 68
3359	Kangi Win; Crow Woman; F; G.Mo; 71	3381	Marpiya Tasunke; Cloud Horse; M; Father; 45
3360	Sunka Nupa; Oscar Two Dogs; M; G.Son; 10	3382	Sagye Waste; Good Cane; F; Wife; 41
3361	Kangi Pegnaka; Crow On Head; M; Father; 80	3383	Marpiya Tasunke; Nancy Cloud Horse; F; Dau; 12
3362	Ikpaptanyan; Turns Over; F; Wife #1; 71	3384	Marpiya Tasunke; Annie Cloud Horse; F; Dau; 8
3363	Inyan Kableca; Breaks Rock; F; Wife #2; 60	3385	Marpiya Tasunke; Minnie Cloud Horse; F; Dau; 2-1
3364	Kangi Pegnaka; Louis Crow On Head; M; Son; 26	3386	Ista Rmi; Crooked Eyes; M; Father; 30
3365	Sungmanitu Nige; Coyote Belly; M; Father; 41	3387	Wacinhin Anatan; Runs For Plume; F; Wife; 28
3366	Rante; Cedar; F; Wife; 34	3388	Maste; Sunshine; M; Son; 6
3367	Okawinr Iyanka; Runs Around; M; Son; 15	3389	Winyan Zi; Yellow Woman; F; Dau; 1-6
3368	Wicaku Sni; Wont[sic] Give Up; M; Son; 11	3390	Wanbli Watakpe; Charging Eagle; M; Father; 62
3369	Tokicun; Revenger; F; Dau; 2-6	3391	Gi Iciya; Paints Herself Yellow; F; Wife; 54
3370	Wanbli Yatapi; Chief Eagle; M; Father; 51	3392	Wanbli Watakpe; Eliza Charging Eagle; F; Dau; 16
3371	Opkiciza; Fights With; F; Wife; 51	3393	Woptura; Chipps; M; Father; 59
3372	Wanbli Yatapi; Otto Chief Eagle; M; Son; 25	3394	Ohomni Yutan; Feels All Around It; F; Wife; 47
3373	Wanbli Yatapi; Peter Chief Eagle; M; Son; 17	3395	Cinpi; Wants Him; F; Dau; 17
		3396	Nup Ewicaya; Takes Away Two; F; Dau; 15
3374	Pehan Win; Crane Woman; F; 68	3397	Kiyukan; Makes Room; M; Son; 15
3375	Tatanka Wakinyan; Charlie Thunder Bull; M; Father; 47	3398	Timahel Wicakte; Kills Within The House; M; Son; 3-4
3376	Mani; Walks; F; Wife; 45		

Census Of The Sioux And Cheyenne Indians Of Pine Ridge Agency, South Dakota. Taken by W. H. Clapp, Captain 16th Infantry, Acting United States Indian Agent, June 30, 1896. (Medicine Root District)

Key: Number; Indian Name *(if given)*; English Name; Sex; Relation; Age

3399	Pejuta Sapa; Coffee; F; G.Mo; 76	3419	Wiciyela; John Yankton; M; Son; 1-4
3400	Sunkgleska Yuha; Owns Spotted Horse; F; G.Dau; 17	3420	Wiciyela; Dollie Yankton; F; Dau; 15
		3421	Wiciyela; Helen Yankton; F; Dau; 9
3401	Sunka Gnaskinyan; Crazy Dog; M; Head; 41		
3402	Sunka Gnaskinyan; Caroline Crazy Dog; F; Wife; 47	3422	Sinte Nupa; Charles Two Tail[sic]; F; Father; 35
		3423	Tarca; Antelope; F; Wife; 42
3403	Sahiyela; Cheyenne; M; Head; 35	3424	Sinte Nupa; Thomas Two Tails; M; Son; 17
3404	Sahiyela; Emma Cheyenne; F; Wife; 30	3425	Cetan Wakuwa; Chasing Hawk; M; 32
3405	Sunk Karniga; Picked Horses; F; Mother; 67		
3406	Cetan Wakuwa; Mattie Chasing Hawk; F; Cousin; 17	3426	Charles Clifford; M; 29
		3427	Cetan Kawinge; Charles T Hawk; M; Father; 38
3407	Sungmanitu Wakuwa; Chasing Wolf; M; Head; 69	3428	Cetan Kawinge; Philomena Turning Hawk; F; Wife; 40
3408	Mato Winyan; Bear Woman; F; Wife; 69	3429	Cetan Kawinge; Hobart Turning Hawk; M; Son; 10
3409	Sikahunpi; Cut Foot; M; Father; 57	3430	Wanbli Heton; Eagle Horn; M; Head; 45
3410	Tasunke Hinto Win; Her Blue Horse; F; Wife; 63	3431	Wanbli Heton; Agnes Eagle Horn; F; Wife; 44
3411	Zintkala Waste; Good Bird; F; Dau; 36	3432	Wanbli Heton; Hattie Eagle Horn; F; Dau; 19
3412	Tarca Ska; Conrad White Deer; M; Head; 39	3433	Wanbli Heton; Fannie Eagle Horn; F; Dau; 18
3413	Tarca Ska; Marget White Deer; F; Wife; 41	3434	Wanbli Heton; Josiah Eagle Horn; M; Son; 16
		3435	Wanbli Heton; Albert Eagle Horn; M; Son; 7
3414	Cuwiosniyanpi; Cold Breast; M; Head; 77	3436	Wanbli Heton; Lizzie Eagle Horn; F; Dau; 10
3415	Wicaku; Gives; F; Wife; 84	3437	Wanbli Heton; Emma Eagle Horn; F; Dau; 1-6
3416	Wiciyela; Charles Yankton; M; Father; 36		
3417	Wiciyela; Julia Yankton; F; Wife; 36	3438	Heraka; Elk; F; Mother; 44
3418	Wiciyela; Fat Yankton; M; Son; 6	3439	Tatanka Wicasa; John Bull Man; M; Son; 18

Census Of The Sioux And Cheyenne Indians Of Pine Ridge Agency, South Dakota. Taken by W. H. Clapp, Captain 16th Infantry, Acting United States Indian Agent, June 30, 1896. (Medicine Root District)

Key: Number; Indian Name *(if given)*; English Name; Sex; Relation; Age

3440 Wanbli Cante; Eagle Heart; M; Father; 29
3441 Wanbli Cante; Jennie Eagle Heart; F; Wife; 28
3442 Marpiya Oranko; Swift Cloud; F; Dau; 0-10

3443 Ellen Mousseau; F; Mother; 64
3444 James Mousseau; M; Son; 24

3445 Edward Janis; M; Father; 28
3446 Sallie Janis; F; Wife; 24
3447 Effie Janis; F; Dau; 6
3448 Elizabeth Janis; F; Dau; 4-3

3449 Emily Tibbets; F; Aunt; 45
3450 Winifred Shangreau; F; Niece; 7

3451 Ellen Farnham; F; Mother; 42
3452 Bessie Farnham; F; Dau; 20
3453 Lizzie Farnham; F; Dau; 18
3454 Ulyses Farnham; M; Nephew; 7

3455 Heraka; Elk #2; M; Head; 25
3456 Tainyan Yanka; Sits In Sight; F; Wife; 30

3457 Wanbli Oranko; Fast Eagle; M; Father; 47
3458 Wangleglega; Spotted Snake; F; Wife; 34
3459 Najinyapi; Surrounded; M; Son; 5
3460 Wkayanka[sic] Kte; Kills On Horseback; M; Son; 4-6

3461 Mato Iyanka; Frank Bear Runner; M; Father; 21
3462 Sina Ska; White Blanket; F; Wife; 20
3463 Mato Iyanka; Howard Bear Runner; M; Son; 3 day

3464 Gnuska; Frog #1; M; Father; 59
3465 Matoha Sina; Bear Robe; F; Wife; 44
3466 Gnuska; Elizabeth Frog; F; Dau; 19
3467 Gnuska; Wounded Frog; M; Son; 15
3468 Gnuska; Warrior Frog; F; Dau; 5

3469 Si; Foot; M; Head; 78
3470 Si; Rosa Foot; F; Wife; 82
3471 Si; Jennis[sic] Foot; F; Dau; 44
3472 Si; Philip Foot; M; Son; 31

3473 Wiyaka; Frank Feather; M; Father; 37
3474 Kiyela Wiyaka; Close Feather; F; Wife; 31
3475 Wiyaka; Mary Feather; F; Dau; 12
3476 Wiyaka; Mabel Feather; F; Dau; 2-6
3477 Wiyaka; Lucy Feather; F; Dau; 12
3478 Wiyaka; John Feather; M; Son; 9
3479 Wiyaka; Daniel Feather; M; Son; 7
3480 Wiyaka; Paul Feather; M; Son; 6
3481 Wiyaka; James Feather; M; Son; 1-6

3482 Wankal Kiyan; Flies Above; M; Father; 41
3483 Wanbli Sun; Eagle Feather; F; Wife; 44
3484 Wiyaka Wicasa; Lewis Featherman; M; Son; 18
3485 Wiyaka Wicasa; Daniel Featherman; M; Son; 16
3486 Wiyaka Wicasa; Blowing Featherman; M; Son; 12

3487 Canupa Yuha; Maggie Owns The Pipe; F; Dau; 12
3488 Ptesan Sina; White Cow Blanket; F; Dau; 3-6

Census Of The Sioux And Cheyenne Indians Of Pine Ridge Agency, South Dakota. Taken by W. H. Clapp, Captain 16th Infantry, Acting United States Indian Agent, June 30, 1896. (Medicine Root District)

Key: Number; Indian Name *(if given)*; English Name; Sex; Relation; Age

3489	Tasunke Iyanke; Fay Running Horse; M; Head; 35	3515	Joseph Morrison; M; Son; 11
3490	Tasunke Iyanka[sic]; Lizzie Running Horse; F; Wife; 34	3516	Cahrles[sic] Morrison; M; Son; 2-9
3491	Tasunke Iyanke; Rock Running Horse; M; Nephew; 11	3517	Jessie Morrison; F; Dau; 2-9
3492	Oowaste; Fine Shot; M; Father; 69	3518	Mato Rlo; Growling Bear; M; Father; 44
3493	Waneca; Rushes; F; Wife; 70	3519	Sahiyela Iya; Talks Cheyenne; F; Wife; 44
3494	Nape Pejuta; Medicine Hand; M; Son; 29	3520	Mato Rlo; Charles Growling Bear; M; Son; 17
3495	Frank Marshall; F; Father; 33	3521	Mato Rlo; Thomas Growling Bear; M; Son; 11
3496	Minnie Marshall; F; Wife; 29	3522	Sungmanitu Hinapa; Comes Out Wolf; M; Son; 7
3497	Louise Marshall; F; Dau; 12	3523	Heraka Ciqala; Little Elk; M; Son; 2-4
3498	Mary Marshall; F; Dau; 9		
3499	Josephin[sic]; Marshall; F; Dau; 2-6	3524	Cetan; Fannie Hawk; F; Dau; 22
3500	Stephen Marshall; M; Son; 4-2	3525	Kangi Ho Waste; Good Voice Crow; M; Father; 37
3501	Walter Garrier; M; Cousin; 37	3526	Kangi Ho Waste; Mollie Good Voice Crow; F; Wife #1; 37
3502	Lizzie Marshall; F; Dau; 0-6		
3503	WabluskWaste[sic]; Good Bug; F; Dau; 38	3527	Sunsunla Yuha; Owns The Mule; F; Wife #2; 51
3504	Rla Win; Rattling Woman; F; Mother; 71	3528	Kangi Ho Waste; Mary Good Voice Crow; F; Dau; 17
3505	Ite Waste; Good Face; F; Niece; 10	3529	Conica Wanica; Della No Flesh; F; Dau; 13
		3530	Wicincala Waste; Good Girl; F; Dau; 7
2506[sic]	Ipiyaka; Guy Belt; M; Father; 40	3531	Cokab Iyaya; Goes In Center; M; Son; 1
3507	Ipiyaka; Maggie Belt; F; Wife; 32	3532	Sunka Ciqala; George Little Dog; M; Head; 33
3508	Ipiyaka; Levi Belt; M; Son; 9		
3509	Ipiyaka; Gertie Belt; F; Dau; 3-6	2533[sic]	Sahinyela Hunku; Cheyenne Mother; F; Wife; 34
3510	Ipiyaka; James Belt; M; Son; 0-11	3534	Tatanka Wakan; Holy Bull; M; Son; 1-1
3511	Tasunke Waste; Good Horse; M; Head; 29	3535	Tasunke Hinzi; Joseph Yellow Horse; M; Nephew; 16
3512	Wasunke[sic] Waste; Josephin[sic] Good Horse; F; Wife; 27		
		3536	Ista Sa; George Red Eyes; M; Head; 27
3513	Ground Morrison; M; Father; 38		
3514	Wing Morrison; F; Wife; 41		

Census Of The Sioux And Cheyenne Indians Of Pine Ridge Agency, South Dakota. Taken by W. H. Clapp, Captain 16th Infantry, Acting United States Indian Agent, June 30, 1896. (Medicine Root District)

Key: Number; Indian Name *(if given)*; English Name; Sex; Relation; Age

3537 Ista Sa; Louise Red Eyes; F; Wife; 26
3538 Winyan Waste; Good Woman; F; Mother; 63
3539 Cuwignaka Ska; Allen White Dress; M; Son; 22
3540 Taopi Ciqala; George Little Wound; M; Head; 28
3541 Taopi Ciqala; Belle Little Wound; F; Wife; 28
3542 Tokeya Ihuni; Gets There First; M; Father; 24
3543 Pehin Zi Win; Yellow Haired Woman; F; Wife; 32
3544 Pehin Zi; Jessie Yellow Hair; F; Dau; 6
3545 Pehin Zi; Emma Yellow Hair; F; Dau; 3-10
3546 Cokab Iyaya; Goes In Center; F; Dau; 1-1
3547 Georgianna O'Rourke; F; Mother; 38
3548 Thomas O'Rourke; M; Son; 19
3549 Charles O'Rourke; M; Son; 13
3550 Samuel O'Rourke; M; Son; 8
3551 John O'Rourke; M; Son; 2-9
3552 Annie O'Rourke; F; Dau; 17
3553 Emma O'Rourke; F; Dau; 11
3554 Nakpogi; Horace Brown Ears; M; Father; 30
3555 Nakpogi; Emma Brown Ears; F; Wife; 23
3556 Nakpogi; Amos Brown Ears; M; Son; 4
3557 Mani Win; Walking Woman; F; Dau; 0-11
3558 Tasunke Wakan; Her Holy Horse; F; Mother; 51
3559 Mato Iyanka; Joseph Bear Runner; M; Son; 18
3560 He Woptura; Horn Chips; M; Head; 24
3561 He Woptura; Rosa Horn Chips; F; Wife; 22
3562 Tipi; House; F; G.Mo; 61
3563 Tasunke Luzahan; Albert Fast Horse; M; G.Son; 14
3564 Tasunke Luzahan; Jessie Fast Horse; F; G.Dau; 18
3565 Nata Rlogeca; Hollow Head; M; Father; 48
3566 Napa Rlogeca; Julia Hollow Head; F; Wife; 44
3567 Nata Rlogeca; George Hollow Head; M; Son; 17
3568 Niniciya; Saves Himself; M; Son; 8
3569 Karniga; Select; M; Son; 7
3570 Naca Win; Chief Woman; F; Dau; 4-2
3571 Sunkole; Henry Looks For Horses; M; Head; 46
3572 Sunkole; Nancy Looks For Horses; F; Wife; 47
3573 Toka Apa; Hits Enemy; M; Father; 24
3574 Toka Apa; Rosa Hits Enemy; F; Wife; 18
3575 Aiyapi; Talks About Him; M; Son; 1-1
3576 Winyan Teri; Hard Woman; F; Mother; 56
3577 Sunk Ole; Maggie Hunts Horses; F; Dau; 27
3578 Ta Kolaku; His Friend; F; G.Son; 3-6
3579 Wanbli Gleska; Harry Spotted Eagle; M; Father; 35
3580 Wanbli Gleska; Millie Spotted Eagle; F; Wife; 28

Census Of The Sioux And Cheyenne Indians Of Pine Ridge Agency, South Dakota. Taken by W. H. Clapp, Captain 16th Infantry, Acting United States Indian Agent, June 30, 1896. (Medicine Root District)

Key: Number; Indian Name *(if given)*; English Name; Sex; Relation; Age

3581	Wanbli Gleska; Sallie Spotted Eagle; F; Dau; 13	3602	Wicakute; Shoots At Them; F; Dau; 10
3582	Wanbli Gleska; Susie Spotted Eagle; F; Dau; 8	3603	Tokicun; Revenger; M; Son; 6
		3604	Wazi Wankatuya; Jessie High Pine; F; Dau; 4
3583	Pehin Maza; Iron Hair; F; Dau; 2-10		
3584	Tokeya Ihuni; Gets There First; M; Son; 4-6	3605	Sahiyela Onca; Imitate Cheyenne; M; Head; 70
		3606	Oturansa; Gives Things; F; Wife; 54
3585	Mato Wankatuya; High Bear; M; Head; 61		
3586	Cunsoka; Timber; F; Wife #2; 45	3607	Joseph Marshall; M; Father; 45
3587	Makata Wakita; Looks At Ground; F; Wife #1; 54	3608	Elizabeth Marshall; F; Wife; 44
		3609	Thomas Marshall; M; Son; 19
3588	Mato Wakatuya; Herbert High Bear; M; Son; 19	3610	Philip Marshall; M; Son; 13
		3611	Harrison Marshall; M; Son; 11
		3612	Charles Marshall; M; Son; 7
3589	Tasina Wakan Win; Her Holy Robe; F; Mother; 68	3613	Alice Marshall; F; Dau; 3-2
		3614	Jennie Marshall; F; Dau; 5
3590	Tasunke Iyanka; George Running Horse; M; Son; 25	3615	John Dillon; M; Nephew; 17
		3616	Peter Dillon; M; Nephew; 17
3591	Wiyaka Wanjila; Lizzie One Feather; F; G.Dau; 13		
		3617	Heraka Wakan; Joshua Medicine Elk #1; M; Father; 43
3592	Henry Morrison; M; Head; 18	3618	Heraka Wakan; Nency[sic] Medicine Elk; F; Wife; 28
3593	Cetan Win; Hawk Woman; F; G.Mo; 64	3619	Heraka Wakan; Cedar Medicine Elk; F; Dau; 7
3594	He Luta; Red Horn; M; G.Son; 3-6	3620	Toka Kokipa; Afraid Of Enemy; M; Son; 4-4
3595	Oksanta; Howard Around It; M; Head; 28	3621	Julia Marshall; F; Head; 68
		3622	Daniel Marshall; M; G.Son; 4
3596	Oksanta; Victoria Around It; F; Wife; 24		
		3623	Marpiya Luta; Jack Red Cloud; M; Father; 38
3597	Tasunke Wakan Win; Her Medicine Horse; F; Dau; 4	3624	Waste; Good; F; Wife; 37
3598	Oksanta; John Around It; M; Son; 0-8	3625	Naca Win; Chief Woman; F; Dau; 11
		3626	Isna Kaga; Makes Alone; F; Son; 7
3599	Wasu Peta; Hail Fire; F; Head; 36		
		3627	Tokeya Hiyaya; Leader; F; Dau; 5
3600	Wazi Wankatuya; High Pine; M; Father; 38	3628	Marpiya Luta; Charles Red Cloud; M; Son; 4
3601	Anpetu; Day; F; Wife; 33		

Census Of The Sioux And Cheyenne Indians Of Pine Ridge Agency, South Dakota. Taken by W. H. Clapp, Captain 16th Infantry, Acting United States Indian Agent, June 30, 1896. (Medicine Root District)

Key: Number; Indian Name *(if given)*; English Name; Sex; Relation; Age

3629 Sunkgleska; John Spotted Horse; M; Head; 28
3630 Waglure; Jennie Loafer; F; Wife; 23

3631 Mato Iyotaka; John Sitting Bear; M; Father; 44
3632 Mato Iyotaka; Lucy Sitting Bear; F; Wife; 39
3633 Mato Iyotaka; Mary Sitting Bear; F; Dau; 22
3634 Mato Iyotaka; Victoria Sitting Bear; F; Dau; 15

3635 Nawizi; Jealous; F; G.Mo; 78
3636 Tasina Wayankapi; Looks At Her Blanket; F; G.Dau; 4

3637 Yamni Hiyuiciya; Jas. Dismounts Thrice; M; Father; 29
3638 Wamni[sic] Hiyuiciya; Susie Dismounts Thrice; F; Wife; 24
3639 Wamni Hiyuiciya; Edward D. Thrice; M; Son; 4-6
3640 Wamni Hiyuiciya; Alfred D. Thrice; M; Son; 9

3641 Mastincala Luta; Jonas Red Rabbit; M; Head; 45

3642 Zintkato[sic]; Jefferson Blue Bird; M; Father; 28
3643 Zintka To; Annie Blue Bird; F; Wife; 25
3644 Zintka To; James Blue Bird; M; Son; 8
3645 Zintka To; Thomas Blue Bird; M; Son; 6
3646 Zintka To; Sarah Blue Bird; F; Dau; 3-4
3647 Zintka To; Mary Blue Bird; F; Dau; 0-6

3648 John Glenn; M; Father; 31
3649 Rosa Glenn; F; Wife; 28
3650 Lena Glenn; F; Dau; 5

3651 Edison Glenn; M; Son; 2-9

3652 John Clifford; M; Father; 25
3653 Hattie Clifford; F; Wife; 17
3654 George Clifford; M; Son; 0-8

3655 Tatanka Hanska; John Long Bull; M; Father; 38
3656 Tatanka Hanska; Julia Long Bull; F; Wife; 37
3657 Tatanka Hanska; Edith Long Bull; F; Dau; 8

3658 James Janis; M; Father; 22
3659 Rosa Janis; F; Wife; 19
3660 Paul Janis; M; Son; 1-1

3661 Osta Ska; Jacob White Eyes; M; Head; 26
3663 Ite Wakan; Holy Face; F; Dau; 6
3664 Mila Hanska; Susy Long Knife; F; Dau; 0-1

3665 Naca Ciqala; Little Chief; M; Father; 37
3666 Pehin Win; Hair Woman; F; Wife; 33
3667 Anpetu Wakan; Sunday; F; Dau; 9
3668 Napca; Swallow; M; Son; 3-5
3669 Sungmanitu Isnala; Oliver Lone Wolf; M; Nephew; 4-4
3670 Wicarpi; Star; F; Dau; 0-3

3671 Tatanka Catka; Left Hand Bull; M; Head; 57

3672 Sungmanitu Gi; Lucy Yellow Wolf; F; Mother; 23
3673 Heraka Luta; Red Elk; F; G.Mo; 79
3674 Sungmanitu Gi; Sally Yellow Wolf; F; Niece; 11
3675 Sungmanitu Gi; Julia Yellow Wolf; F; Dau; 4-6

Census Of The Sioux And Cheyenne Indians Of Pine Ridge Agency, South Dakota. Taken by W. H. Clapp, Captain 16th Infantry, Acting United States Indian Agent, June 30, 1896. (Medicine Root District)

Key: Number; Indian Name *(if given)*; English Name; Sex; Relation; Age

3676	Sungmanitu Gi; Albert Yellow Wolf; M; Son; 4-6	3699	Louis Mousseau; M; Father; 27
		3700	Zonie Mousseau; F; Wife; 27
		3701	Joseph Mousseau; M; Son; 5
3677	Lizzie Sherman; F; Head; 30	3702	Louis Mousseau, Jr; M; Son; 3
3678	William Sherman; M; Son; 11		
3679	Mark Sherman; M; Son; 3-6	3703	Louise L Bianas; F; Head; 36
3680	Rosa Sherman; F; Dau; 8	3704	Paul L Bianas; M; Son; 14
3681	Emily Sherman; F; Dau; 6	3705	Frank L Bianas; M; Son; 11
3682	George Sherman; M; Son; 1	3706	Susie L Bianas; F; Dau; 18
		3707	Frances L Bianas; F; Dau; 16
3683	Zuya Ciqala; Little Warrior; M; Head; 25	3708	Polonia L Bianas; F; Dau; 9
3684	Zuya; Ellen C. H. Warrior; F; Wife; 18	3709	Catka; Left Hand; M; Father; 36
		3710	Mani Wastelaka; Likes To Walk; F; Wife; 54
3685	Mato Wanjila; Lone Bear; M; Father; 42	3711	Ota Kte; Kills Plenty; F; S.Dau; 24
3686	Hanhepi; Lizzie At Night; F; Wife; 42	3712	Winyan Tanka; Big Woman; F; M. in L.; 82
3687	Mato Wanjila; Samuel Lone Bear; M; Son; 19	3713	Taopi Ciqala; Little Wound; M; Father; 67
3688	Mato Wanjila; Alice Lone Bear; F; Dau; 18	3714	Owewakanan; Tells Lies; F; Wife; 64
3689	Mato Tatanka; Lawrence Bull Bear; M; Father; 37	3715	Taopi Ciqala; James Little Wound; M; Son; 22
3690	Mato Tatanka; Julia Bull Bear; F; Wife; 32	3716	Taopi Ciqala; Jennie Little Wound; F; Dau; 20
3691	Mato Tatanka; Dixon Bull Bear; M; Son; 14	3717	Kyaksa Sapa; Black Cut Off; M; Cousin; 51
3692	Mato Tatanka; Jesse Bull Bear; M; Son; 9	3718	Lulu Aschraft; F; Head; 34
3693	Mato Tatanka; Moses Bull Bear; M; Son; 5	3719	Winyan Isnala; Lone Woman; F; Head; 78
3694	Mato Tatanka; Peter Bull Bear; M; Son; 12		
3695	Mato Tatanka; Fannie Bull Bear; F; Dau; 1-6	3720	Louis Shangreau; M; Father; 47
		3721	Louise Shangreau; F; Wife; 42
		3722	Roas[sic] Shangreau; F; Dau; 21
3696	Canku Tanka; Lizzie N. B. Road; F; Head; 31	3723	Nelson Shangreau; M; Son; 19
3697	Canka[sic] Tanka; Bessie N. B. Road; F; Dau; 6	3724	Martin Shangreau; M; Son; 10
		3725	Pearl Shangreau; F; Dau; 2-3
3698	Cetan Winyan; Hawk Woman; F; Mother; 52	3726	Joseph Shangreau; M; Nephew; 18
		3727	Parker Shangreau; M; Son; 0-4

Census Of The Sioux And Cheyenne Indians Of Pine Ridge Agency, South Dakota. Taken by W. H. Clapp, Captain 16th Infantry, Acting United States Indian Agent, June 30, 1896. (Medicine Root District)

Key: Number; Indian Name *(if given)*; English Name; Sex; Relation; Age

3728 Wiyaka Wanjila; Moses One Feather; M; Father; 41
3729 Wiyaka Wanjila; Jennie One Feather; F; Wife; 30
3730 Wiyaka Wanjila; Susie One Feather; f; Dau; 18
3731 Wiyaka Wanjila; Willie One Feather; M; Son; 15
3732 Wabkal Ti; Lives Above; F; Dau; 6
3733 Wiyaka Wanjila; Bessie One Feather; F; Dau; 2-7

3734 Tiglake; Moves Camp; M; Father; 28
3735 Tiglake; Helen Moves Camp; F; Wife; 23
3736 Rlaya Hinapa; Comes Out Rattling; F; Dau; 7
3737 Wanapa Glicu; Comes Out Wounded; M; Son; 2-6

3738 Hu Wegahan; Moses Broken Leg; M; Father; 28
3739 Tainyan Ti; Lives In Sight; F; Wife; 24
3740 Hu Weganhan[sic]; Jack Broken Leg; M; Son; 1-2

3741 Ptesan; Millie White Cow; F; Head; 40

3742 Mato Wakan; Medicine Bear; M; Father; 58
3743 Waci Hiyaya; Goes Dancing; F; Wife; 58
3744 Papta Hinapa; Sticks Out; F; Dau; 25
3745 Wacinyapi; Depends On Them; F; Dau; 16
3746 Teriya Icu; Takes It Hard; F; Dau; 14
3747 Winyan Kte; Kills Woman; F; Dau; 7
3748 Wawokiya; Helps; M; Son; 18

3749 Ninyan Ke Kte; Kills Alive; M; G.Son; 4-3
3750 Tasunke Wakan; Medicine Horse; M; Father; 64
3751 Hu Cancan; Shaking Legs; F; Wife; 64
3752 Taopi Gli; Comes Wounded; F; Dau; 16
3753 Zintka To; Blue Bird; M; G.Son; 8

3754 Wankal Wicasa; Man Above; M; Father; 51
3755 Pehin Sa; Red Hair; F; Wife; 54
3756 Wankal Wicasa; Samuel Man Above; M; Son; 15
3757 Wankal Wicasa; Alexander Man Above; M; Son; 22
3758 Wankal Wicasa; Fannie Man Above; F; Dau; 10

3759 Cega Luta; Moses Red Kettle; M; Father; 36
3760 Cegala[sic] Luta; Mary Red Kettle; F; Wife; 34
3761 Cega Luta; Joseph Red Kettle; M; Son; 7
3762 Cega Luta; Charles A. Red Kettle; M; Son; 4-4

3763 Maggie Clifford; F; Head; 57
3764 Julia Clifford; F; Dau; 18
3765 George Clifford; M; Son; 22

3766 Marthia[sic] Janis; F; Head; 71
3767 Julia Monteleau; F; G.Dau; 20
3768 Emily Monteleau; F; G.Dau; 22

3769 Mary Condelario; F; Head; 52
3770 Sophia Condelario; F; Dau; 22
3771 Clara Candolerio[sic]; F; Dau; 20
3772 Lucy Candelario[sic]; F; Dau; 16
3773 Peter Candelario; M; Son; 18
3774 Joseph Candeloria[sic]; M; Son; 11

Census Of The Sioux And Cheyenne Indians Of Pine Ridge Agency, South Dakota. Taken by W. H. Clapp, Captain 16th Infantry, Acting United States Indian Agent, June 30, 1896.   (Medicine Root District)

Key: Number; Indian Name *(if given)*; English Name; Sex; Relation; Age

3775	Oiyokipiya Ti; Merrily Lives; F; Head; 68
3776	Wasu; Mary Wasu; F; Head; 68
3777	Caga; Mary Ice; F; Dau; 32
3778	Ipiyaka Cola; No Belt; M; Head; 34
3779	Ipiyaka Cola; Ellen No Belt; F; Wife; 34
3780	Nick L Janis; M; Father; 34
3781	Her Head; F; Wife; 28
3782	Thomas Janis; M; Son; 10
3783	Ben Janis; M; Son; 8
3784	Emma Janis; F; Dau; 5
3785	Mary Janis; F; Dau; 1-2
3786	Nancy; F; Head; 88
3787	Sunkgmanitu Wakuwa; Alice Chasing Wolf; F; Niece; 13
3788	Wanbli Ohitika; Oscar Brave Eagle; M; Father; 27
3789	Wicakte Hi; Comes To Kill; F; Wife; 23
3890	Waste Kte; Kills Good; M; Son; 4
3891	Wanbli Ohitka[sic]; Peter Brave Eagle; M; Son; 1-6
3792	Winorcala; Old Bad Wound; F; Head; 72
3793	Aglala Iyanka; Jas. Runs Along T. Edge; M; G.Son; 12
3794	Eyapaha Ota; Plenty Haranguer; M; Father; 46
3795	Psica; Jumper; F; Wife #1; 44
3796	Anptu[sic] Luta; Anna Red Day; F; Wife #2; 52
3797	Eyapaha Ota; Jennie Plenty Haranguer; F; Dau; 14
3798	Pjya Icaga; Second Growth; F; Dau; 6
3799	Wayaka Oyuspa; Captured Prisoner; F; Dau; 3-5
3800	Zintkala Sa; Red Bird; M; Son; 10
3801	Eyapaha Ota; Wm Plenty Haranguer; M; Son; 12
3802	Anpetu Sa; Red Day; F; Mother; 72
3803	Peyozan; Parts His Hair; M; Father; 54
3804	Siha Sapa; Black Feet; F; Wife #1; 53
3805	Peyozan; Susie Parts Her[sic] Hair; F; Wife #2; 42
3806	Peyozan; Isaac Parts His Hair; M; Son; 25
3807	Peyoxan[sic]; Ephriam P. H. Hair; M; Son; 18
3808	Peyozan; Amos Parts His Hair; M; Son; 14
3809	Peyozan; Sarah Parts His Hair; F; Dau; 14
3810	Peyozan; Emma Parts His Hair; F; Dau; 11
3811	Peyozan; Ada Parts His Hair; F; Dau; 8
3812	Peyozan; Winnie Parts His Hair; F; Dau; 8
3813	Wanbli Iyopataka; Albert Sitting Eagle; M; Son; 24
3814	William Gay; M; Nephew; 27
3815	Mato Ota; Plenty Bear; M; Head; 51
3816	Canku; Road; F; Wife; 46
3817	Nite Yazan; Pain On The Rump; M; Head; 36
3818	Tasunke; Her Horse; F; Wife; 34
3819	Nite Yanza[sic]; Chas. Pain O.T. Rump; M; Son; 7
3820	Ti Wegna; In The Crowd; F; Dau; 1-3

Census Of The Sioux And Cheyenne Indians Of Pine Ridge Agency, South Dakota. Taken by W. H. Clapp, Captain 16th Infantry, Acting United States Indian Agent, June 30, 1896. (Medicine Root District)

Key: Number; Indian Name *(if given)*; English Name; Sex; Relation; Age

3821 Sici Tahunska; Pawnee Leggins; M; Father; 48
3822 Ho Naron; Hears The Voice; F; Wife; 49
3823 Scili[sic] Tahunska; Josephine P. Leggins; F; Dau; 15
3824 Scili Tahunska; George P. Leggins; M; Son; 13
3825 Hato Wicakte; Kills The Bear; M; Son; 4-6
3826 Watakpe; Charger; M; G.Son; 0-2

3827 Paddy Star; M; Father; 37
3828 Nellie Star; F; Wife; 28
3829 Phoebe Star; F; Dau; 10
3830 Lydia Star; F; Dau; 3-3
3831 Lucy Star; F; Dau; 1-5

3832 Awicayustanpi; Quits Them; F; Head; 51

3833 Can Sasa; Red Willow; M; Father; 37
3834 Tasunke Hinapa; Her Horse Comes Out; F; Wife; 30
3835 Owicale Hi; Comes To Hunt Them; M; Son; 4-9

3836 Sina Luta; Red Blanket; M; Father; 27
3837 Tasunke; Her Horse; F; Wife; 26
3838 Sina Wakan; Holy Blanket; F; Dau; 0-1

3839 Tasunke Wicarca; Ralph Old Horse; M; Head; 34
3840 Tasunke Nupa; Her Two Horses; F; Wife; 38
3841 Kiyaksa; Cut Off; F; Mother; 84
3842 Taunske[sic] Wacarca[sic]; Mark Old Horse; M; Son; 12
3843 Mato Kokipa; Afraid Of Bear; M; Son; 6

3844 Sungmanitu Isnala; Rosa Lone Wolf; F; Head; 24
3845 Sangmanitu[sic] Isnala; Felix Lone Wolf; M; Son; 2-8
3846 Kici Kiciza; Fights With Him; F; Mother; 61

3847 Anpetu Luta; Red Day; F; Head; 29
3848 Lucy Thomas; F; Dau; 1-4

3849 Akan Iyanka; Runs On; M; Father; 38
3850 Tatanka; Bull; F; Wife; 27
3851 Akan Iyanka; Nellie Runs On; F; Dau; 6
3852 Pekin Hanska; Long Hair; F; Dau; 4
3853 Tasina Wakan; Her Holy Blanket; F; Dau; 1-9

3854 Marpiya Najin; Robert Standing Cloud; M; Father; 30
3855 Tasunke Maza; Iron Horse; M; F. in L.; 71
3856 Wikan; Twine; F; Wife; 51
3857 Susan Johnson; F; Dau; 11
3858 Zuya; Warrior; M; Son; 6
3859 Tasunka Oyate; Dog Tribe; M; Son; 0-8

3860 Oye Luta; Red Track; F; Head; 74
3861 Anpetu; David Day; M; G.Son; 16

3862 Wanbli Luta; Red Eagle #2; F; Head; 44
3863 Wanbli Luta; Julia Red Eagle; F; Dau; 22
3864 Wanbli Luta; Marthia Red Eagle; F; Dau; 3-2
3865 Zuya Terila; Loves War; M; Son; 5

3866 Wanbli Luta; Red Eagle #1; M; Head; 41

Census Of The Sioux And Cheyenne Indians Of Pine Ridge Agency, South Dakota. Taken by W. H. Clapp, Captain 16th Infantry, Acting United States Indian Agent, June 30, 1896. (Medicine Root District)

Key: Number; Indian Name *(if given)*; English Name; Sex; Relation; Age

3867	Sagye; Cane; F; Wife; 24	3890	Marpiya Sna; Rattling Cloud; F; Head; 24
3868	Tikanyela Kte; Kills Close To Lodge; M; Son; 7	3891	Wahacanka; Shield; M; Son; 5
3869	Heraka Luta; Red Elk; M; Head; 62	3892	Wacapa; Stabber #2; M; Father; 26
3870	Heraka Inajin; Stopping Elk; F; Wife; 63	3893	Ite Sna Win; Rattling White Face; F; Wife; 23
3871	Heraka Luta; Millie Red Elk; F; Dau; 32	3894	Zintkala Wanbli; Eagle Bird; M; Son; 3-6
3872	Ayaapi[sic]; Talked About; M; G.Son; 10	3895	Sunk Gliyohi; Comes After Horses; F; Dau; 1-4
3873	Warpe Koyaka; Wears Leaf; M; G.Son; 9	3896	Ota Apela; Strikes Plenty; M; Father; 41
3874	Ista Sa; Red Eyes; M; Father; 49	3897	Winyan Ropa; Pretty Woman; F; Wife; 36
3875	Tasunke Wakan; Medicine Horse; F; Wife; 51	3898	Ota Apeka[sic]; Jefferson Strikes Plenty; M; Son; 17
3876	Ista Sa; Daniel Red Eyes; M; Son; 16	3899	Ota Apela; Lucy Strikes Plenty; F; Dau; 12
3877	Mato; Bear; F; Dau; 8	3900	Toka Ole; Looks For Enemy; F; Dau; 3-6
3878	Ista Sa; Elmore Red Eyes; M; Son; 20	3901	Ota Apela; Paulina Strikes Plenty; F; Dau; 15
3879	Wacinhin Luta; Red Plume; M; Father; 44	3902	Slolyapi; Knew Him; F; Dau; 2-10
3880	Wicincala; Girl; F; Wife; 40	3903	Ota Apela; Rosa Strikes Plenty; F; Dau; 0-6
3881	Ainapi; Talks About Him; M; Son; 8		
3882	Kapojela Win; Light Woman; F; Dau; 2-10	3904	Marpiya Najin; Standing Cloud; M; Father; 58
3883	Rosa Thomas; F; Head; 46	3905	Worinyan; Pouting; F; Wife; 44
3884	Mary Thomas; F; Dau; 5	3906	Marpiya Najin; Cora Stabding[sic] Cloud; F; Dau; 12
3885	Sungmanitu Lute; Red Coyote; M; Father; 49	3907	Wayonk Kte; Julia Kills Looking; F; Dau; 19
3886	Anpetu Ska; White Day; F; Wife; 30		
3887	Tipi Rla Win; Rattling Lodge; F; Dau; 3-3	3908	Wazi Ptecela; Short Pine; M; Head; 73
3888	Tatanka Nata; Bull Head; M; B. in L.; 19	3909	Sa Yuha Mani; Walks With Red; F; Wife; 71
3889	Sunkhinto Nupa; Two Blue Horses; F; S. in L.; 16	3910	Sunka Witko; Julia Crazy Dog; F; G.Dau; 14

Census Of The Sioux And Cheyenne Indians Of Pine Ridge Agency, South Dakota. Taken by W. H. Clapp, Captain 16th Infantry, Acting United States Indian Agent, June 30, 1896. (Medicine Root District)

Key: Number; Indian Name *(if given)*; English Name; Sex; Relation; Age

3911	Kangi Gleska; Spotted Crow; M; Father; 46	3932	Tasunke Ota; Plenty Horses; F; Wife; 34
3912	Marpiya To; Blue Cloud; F; Wife; 62	3933	Kokab Iglonica; Stays In Front; F; Dau; 3-2
3913	Kangi Gleska; Katie Spotted Crow; F; Dau; 14	3934	Can Apaha; Shows The Sticks; F; Mother; 59
3914	Kangi Gleska; Fannie Spotted Crow; F; Dau; 10	3935	Wacapa; Stabber #1; M; Head; 61
3915	Sunka Hunkesni; Slow Dog; M: Head; 82	3936	Wacapa; Julia Stabber; F; Wife #1; 55
3916	Psica; Jumper; F; Wife #1; 64		
3917	Marpiya To; Old Arapahoe; F; Wife #2; 64	3937	Tasunke Ehakela; Samuel Last Horse; M; Father; 44
3918	Ista Ska; Jessie White Eyes; F; G.Dau; 14	3938	Tasunke Ehakela; Samuel Last Horse, Jr; M; Son; 20
3919	Sungmanitu Ska; Herbert White Wolf; M; G.Son; 16	3939	Tasunke Ehakela; Georgiana L. Horse; F; Dau; 13
3920	Sungmanitu Ska; Sarah White Wolf; F; G.Dau; 12	3940	Tasunke Ehakela; Salina Last Horse; F; Dau; 9
		3941	Pehin Hanska; Long Hair; F; Dau; 2-10
3921	Mastiancala Sakow; Seven Rabbits; M; Head; 63		
		3942	Itunkasan Gleska; Spotted Weasel; M; Father; 46
3922	Wanbli Gleska; Spotted Eagle; M; Head; 74	3943	Rante; Cedar; F; Wife #1; 45
3923	Wanbli Gleska; Mollie Spotted Eagle; F; Wife; 65	3944	Wicincala; Girl; F; Wife #2; 35
		3945	Hoksila Wakan; Medicine Boy; M; Son; 11
3924	Wanbli Gleska; Clara Spotted Eagle; F; Dau; 33	3946	Wakinyan Ciqala; Little Thunder; M; Son; 10
3925	Tonweya Gli; Return Scout; M; G.Son; 7		
3926	Kokab Najin; Stands In Front; M; G.Son; 5	3947	Sophia Hermandy; F; Head; 47
		3948	Ambrosis Hermandy; M; Son; 16
3927	Pankeska Napin; Shell Necklace #2; M; Head; 36	3949	Florncis[sic] Hermandy; M; Son; 15
3928	Ninwicaya; Saves Them; F; Wife; 37	3950	Reyes Hermandy; M; Son; 9
		3951	Valentine Hermandy; M; Son; 6
3929	Winyan Tanka; Big Woman; F; Sister; 19	3952	Austacia Hermandy; F; Dau; 6
		3953	Catelina Hermandy; F; Dau; 1-4
3930	Acu; George Frost Over; M; Nephew; 15		
		3954	Panheska Win; Shell Woman; F; Head; 63
3931	Wan On Opi; Shot With Arrows; M; Head; 27	3955	Cetan Rabwicaya; Elizabeth Scares Hawk; F; G.Dau; 16

Census Of The Sioux And Cheyenne Indians Of Pine Ridge Agency, South Dakota. Taken by W. H. Clapp, Captain 16th Infantry, Acting United States Indian Agent, June 30, 1896. (Medicine Root District)

Key: Number; Indian Name *(if given)*; English Name; Sex; Relation; Age

3956 Mary Martinis; F; G.Dau; 10

3957 Sophia Giago; F; Head; 26

3958 Wikan Papsaka; Samuel Broken Rope; M; Head; 35

3959 Casmu; Sand; M; Head; 52
3960 Anpetu; Day; F; Wife; 50

3961 Susie Lamb; F; Head; 26

3962 Oupan Gleska; Spotted Elk; M; Father; 39
3963 Rante Zi; Yellow Cedar; F; Wife; 38
3964 Oupan Gleska; James Spotted Elk; M; Son; 9

3965 Sunkgleska; Spotted Horse; M; Father; 56
3966 Wiciyela Win; Yankton Woman; F; Wife #2; 43
3967 Toka Oyusta; Catches Enemy; F; Wife #1; 53
3968 Sungleska; Robert Spotted Horse; M; Son; 14
3969 Maga Nute; Shoots Ducks; M; Son; 6
3970 Tatanka Mani; Mack Bull Walking; M; Son; 3-5
3971 Nata Kahunpi; Cut Head; F; M. in L.; 73

3972 Sunka Nupa; Two Dogs; M; Head; 49
3973 Tiyopa Luta; Red Door; F; Wife #1; 36
3974 Sunka Nupa; Jenna Two Dogs; F; Wife #2; 34
3975 Wicarpi Wanbli; Star Eagle; M; Son; 17
3976 Nuwan Kte; Jno. Kills Swimming; M; Son; 12
3977 Sunka Nupa; Alice Two Dogs; F; Dau; 6

3978 Sunka Nupa; Lizzie Two Dogs; F; Dau; 13

3979 Thomas Henry; M; Father; 36
3980 Lizzie Henry; F; Wife; 24
3981 Wallace Henry; M; Son; 3-5

3982 Wasicu Tasunke; Thos. American Horse; M; Father; 27
3983 Wasicu Tasunke; Julia American Horse; F; Wife; 27
3984 Wasicu Tasunke; Wm. American Horse; M; Son; 3-6
3985 Heraka Cincala; Young Elk; F; Dau; 1-4

3986 Wankal Mato; Top Bear; M; Head; 64
3987 Lila Yucancan; Shakes Hard; F; Wife #2; 69
3988 Wawokiya; Helps; F; Wife #1; 71

3989 Kangi Nupa; Two Crows; M; Head; 49
3990 Pispiza; Prairie Dog; F; Wife; 42
3991 Ite Ran; Sore Face; F; Dau; 18
3992 Owicalehi; Comes To Hunt Them; F; Dau; 10
3993 Kangi Nupa; John Two Crow[sic]; M; Son; 15
3994 Warpe Sa; Read Leaf; F; Dau; 8
3995 Mato Gi; Brown Bear; F; Dau; 1-2
3996 Wakinyan Tonwanpi; Talks With Lightning; M; Son; 12
3997 Okasake Yukan; Shows White Marks; M; Son; 8
3998 Maka; Dirt; M; Son; 6
3999 Toka Kuwa; Cahrges[sic] The Enemy; M; Son; 5

4000 Wakinyan Gi; Thomas Yellow Thunder; M; Father; 28

Census Of The Sioux And Cheyenne Indians Of Pine Ridge Agency, South Dakota. Taken by W. H. Clapp, Captain 16th Infantry, Acting United States Indian Agent, June 30, 1896. (Medicine Root District)

Key: Number; Indian Name *(if given)*; English Name; Sex; Relation; Age

4001	Wakinyan Gi; Katie Yellow Thunder; F; Wife; 24	4021	Wanbli Gleska Ciqala; Little Spotted Eagle; M; Son; 1-8
4002	Wakinyan Gi; Wm. Yellow Thunder; M; Son; 8	4022	Ite Ska; White Face; M; Father; 45
4003	Wakinyan; Joseph Yellow Thunder; M; Son; 2-3	4023	Tasunke Waste; Her Good Horse; F; Wife; 39
4004	Wakinyan; Wallace Yellow Thunder; M; Son; 0-1	4024	Ite Ska; Mary White Face; F; Dau; 20
4005	Tasunke Luzahan; Thomas Fast Horse; M; Father; 42	4025	Ite Ska; Sallie White Face; F; Dau; 15
4006	Wasicu Winyan; White Woman; F; Wife; 36	4026	Ite Ska; Sophia White Face; F; Dau; 12
4007	Tasunke Luzahan; Mary Fast Horse; F; Dau; 17	4027	Rabwicaya; Scares Them Away; M; Son; 3-3
4008	Hektakiya Ku; Comes Back; F; Dau; 6	4028	Wamniomni Ska; White Whirlwind; M; Head; 28
4009	Mato Ska; White Bear; M; Father; 43	4029	Wanbli Sun; Eagle Feather; F; Wife; 37
4010	Inyan Akan Mani; Walks On Rock; F; Wife; 46	4030	Wankal Mato; Hugh Top Bear; M; Nephew; 20
4011	Mato Ska; Annie White Bear; F; Dau; 15	4031	Honaronpi; Hears Her Voice; F; Niece; 9
4012	Mato Ska; Nellie White Bear; F; Dau; 10	4032	Zintkala Pa; William Bird Head; M; Father; 35
4013	Sungmanitu Halpiya; Wolf Skin Belt; M; Head; 54	4033	Zintkala Pa; Dollie Bird Head; F; Wife; 35
4014	Wakil Hinapa; Goes Out Looking; F; Wife; 59	4034	Zintkala Pa; Burges Bird Head; M; Son; 14
4015	Naca Ciqala; Wing Little Chief; F; G.Dau; 9	4035	Zintkala Pa; Joseph Bird Head; M; Son; 1-9
4016	Cante Sapa; William Black Heart; M; Head; 41	4036	Wahukeza Ska; White Lance; M; Father; 27
4017	Castunpi; Calls Her Name; F; Wife; 50	4037	Wahukeza Ska; Julia White Lance; F; Wife; 23
4018	Tankaya Wakuwa; William Big Charger; M; Father; 25	4038	Wahukeza Ska; Frank White Lance; M; Bro; 17
4019	Sagye Wakan Win; Holy Cain Woman; F; Wife; 33	4039	Tasunke Wayankapi; Looks At Her Horse; F; Dau; 2-6
4020	Zintkaka Naca; Chief Bird; M; Son; 5	4040	Tokeya Mani; Walks Fast; M; Father; 39

Census Of The Sioux And Cheyenne Indians Of Pine Ridge Agency, South Dakota. Taken by W. H. Clapp, Captain 16th Infantry, Acting United States Indian Agent, June 30, 1896. (Medicine Root District)

Key: Number; Indian Name *(if given)*; English Name; Sex; Relation; Age

4041	Kikta Sni; Dont[sic] Get Up; F; Wife; 43	4065	Tatanka Gi; Emma Yellow Bull; F; Wife; 30
4042	Mani Luzahan; Thomas Walks Fast; M; Son; 18	4066	Tatanka Gi; Susie Yellow Bull; F; Dau; 2-7
4043	Nuge Luta; Red Ears Walks Fast; M; Son; 13	4067	Cuwiguaka Ska; White Dress; M; Father; 67
4044	Zintkala Waste; Good Bird Walks Fast; M; Son; 9	4068	Heraka HeWakpa; Elk Horn River; F; Wife; 67
4045	Mani Luzahan; George Walks Fast; M; Son; 7	4069	Ranran Win; Scabby Woman; F; Dau; 41
4046	William Garnett; M; Father; 41	4070	Akan Manipi; Walks On Him; M; G.Son; 11
4047	Filla Garnett; F; Wife; 40		
4048	Charles Garnett; M; Son; 20	4071	Wakinla Ska; White Packet; F; G.Dau; 8
4049	Richard Garnett; M; Son; 11		
4050	William Garnett, Jr; M; Son; 9		
4051	Dollie Garnett; F; Dau; 6	4072	Pahin Ska; White Porcupine; F; Head; 75
4052	Wanbli Ohitika; Warren Brave Eagle; M; Head; 22	4073	John Monroe; M; Father; 27
4053	Wanbli Ohitika; Mary Brave Eagle; F; Wife; 28	4074	Sophia Monroe; F; Wife; 53
		4075	Aloysius Monroe; F; Dau; 1-11
4054	Tainyan Kte; Kills In Sight; F; Dau; 0-3	4076	Lottie Monroe; F; Dau; 0-4
4055	Wiyaka Ska; White Feather; M; Father; 61	4077	Niyan Wakan; Kate Holy Breath; F; Aunt; 30
4056	Rlala; Rattling; F; Wife; 61	4078	Wamniomni Luzahan; Lucy Fast Whirlwind; F; Niece; 13
4057	Wiyaka Ska; Hattie White Feather; F; Dau; 37		
		4079	Peji; John Grass; M; Father; 34
4058	Mato Sapa; William Black Bear; M; Father; 60	4080	Mato Waci; Dancing Bear; F; Wife; 53
4059	Heraka Win; Elk Woman; F; Wife #2; 36	4081	Tasunke Wicopi; Shot Her Horses; F; Dau; 4
4060	Cinpi; Wants Him; F; Wife #1; 47	4082	Sunk Ciqala; Little Dog; M; Father; 45
4061	Zintkala Ciqala; Lone Bird; M; Son; 8	4083	Sa; Red; F; Wife; 54
4062	Mato Sapa; Lucy Black Bear; F; Dau; 14	4084	Heraka Wakan; Joshua Medicine Elk; M; Son; 19
4063	Tasunke Waste; Henry Good Horse; M; Nephew; 16	4085	Heraka Wakan; Lucy Medicine Elk; F; Dau; 18
4064	Tatanka Gi; Wilson Yellow Bull; M; Father; 35	4086	Sicaya Rpaya; Lays Bad; M; Head; 42

Census Of The Sioux And Cheyenne Indians Of Pine Ridge Agency, South Dakota. Taken by W. H. Clapp, Captain 16th Infantry, Acting United States Indian Agent, June 30, 1896.   (Medicine Root District)

Key: Number; Indian Name *(if given)*; English Name; Sex; Relation; Age

4087	Sicaya Rpaya; Frank Lays Bad; M; Son; 27	4108	Wanbli Ota; Plenty Eagle; F; Dau; 7
4088	Sicaya Rpaya; Edward Lays Bad; M; Son; 21	4109	Taista; Her Eyes; F; Dau; 1-9
4089	Sicaya Rpaya; Thomas Lays Bad; M; Son; 12	4110	Nata Opi; William Wounded Head; M; Son; 11
4090	Sicaya Rpaya; Flora Lays Bad; F; Dau; 19	4111	Mato Wamniomni; Whirlwind Bear; M; Father; 36
4091	Sicaya Rpaya; Millie Lays Bad; F; Dau; 18	4112	Enakiya; She Stops; F; Wife; 31
4092	Sicaya Rpaya; Jennie Lays Bad; F; Dau; 11	4113	Canupa Yuha; Keeps The Pipe; F; Dau; 4-9
		4114	Hinhan Sapa; Black Owl; F; Dau; 0-7
4093	Tonweya Ciqala; Little Scout; M; Father; 47	4115	Sungmanitu Ska; White Wolf; M; Father; 42
4094	Haipazaza Tanka; Big Soap; F; Wife; 47	4116	Wicegna Hyaya; Goes Among Them; F; Wife; 39
4095	Marpiya Ska; White Cloud; F; Dau; 8	4117	Sungmanitu Ska; Rosa White Wolf; F; Dau; 10
4096	Louise Girard; F; Head; 24	4118	Oosica; Hard To Hit; F; M. in L.; 84
4097	Tatanka Gnaskinyan; William Crazy Bull; M; Father; 27	4119	Tatanka Gi; Yellow Bull #2; M; Father; 39
4098	Tatanka Gnaskinyan; Lizzie N. Crazy Bull; F; Wife; 28	4120	Tatanka Gi; Julia Yellow Bull; F; Wife; 32
4099	Tatanka Gnaskinyan; May Crazy Bull; Dau; 2-4	4121	Heraka Wakan; Medicine Elk; M; Son; 5
4100	Tatanka Gnaskinyan; Narrows Crazy Bull; M; Son; 0-1	4122	Tatanka Wakan; Medicine Bull; M; Son; 2-10
4101	Ista Ska; White Eyes; M; Head; 71	4123	Wanbli Sun Hoyaka; Wears Eagle Feathers; F; Dau; 0-10
4102	Winorcala; Old Woman; F; Wife; 67	4124	Wakinyan Gi; Yellow Thunder; M; Father; 60
4103	Yusluta; Pulls Out; F; G.Dau; 4-3	4125	Kangi Ska; White Crow; F; Wife; 61
4104	Tatanka Ite Ska; White Face Bull; M; Head; 48	4126	Wakinyan Gi; Andrew Yellow Thunder; M; Son; 18
4105	Tasina; Her Blanket; F; Wife; 50	4127	Wakinyan Gi; Brave Yellow Thunder; M; Son; 9
4106	Nata Opi; Wounded Head; M; Father; 35	4128	Ista Gi; Yellow Eyes; M; Head; 40
4107	Zintakala Zi; Yellow Bird; F; Wife; 29		

Census Of The Sioux And Cheyenne Indians Of Pine Ridge Agency, South Dakota. Taken by W. H. Clapp, Captain 16th Infantry, Acting United States Indian Agent, June 30, 1896. (Medicine Root District)

Key: Number; Indian Name *(if given)*; English Name; Sex; Relation; Age

4129	Petaga; Coal Of Fire; F; Wife; 41		4152	Wankal[sic] Mato; Jessie Top Bear; F; Wife; 21
4130	Ayutapi; Looks At Him; F; Dau; 6		4153	Tasunke Wanica; Has No Horses; M; Head; 20
4131	Zintakala; Bird; F; Dau; 7		4154	Tasunke Wanica; Julia Has No Horses; F; Wife; 24
4132	Gi; Yellow; F; Head; 44			
4133	Hogan Sa; Frank Red Fish; M; Son; 17		4155	Oceti; Fire Place; M: Head; 32
4134	Niyanke Kte; Joseph Kills Alone; M; Son; 14		4156	Oceti; Mary Fire Place; F; Wife; 28
4135	Tatanka Gi; Yellow Bull, Thomas; M; Head; 28		4157	Wacapa; Crandall Stabber; M; Head; 19
4136	Catka; Left Hand; F; Mother; 58		4158	Wacapa; Sallie Stabber; F; Wife; 18
4137	Tinahel Najin; Stands In Side; F; S.Mo; 51		4159	Wacapa; Louise Stabber; F; Mother; 45
4138	Tatanka Gi; Jennie Yellow Bull; F; Sister; 18			
4139	Tatanka Gi; James Yellow Bull; M; Bro; 22		4160	Winyan Ropa; Pretty Woman; F; Head; 38
4140	Tatanka Gi; Lizzie Yellow Bull; F; Sister; 15		4161	Anukasan Mato; Mabel Bald Eagle Bear; F; Dau; 19
			4162	Ptesan; White Cow; F; Dau; 13
4141	Winyan Gi; Yellow Woman; F; Head; 48		4163	Nakipa; Runs Away; F; Dau; 10
			4164	Anukasan Mato; Katie Bald Eagle Bear; F; Dau; 16
4142	Akicita Hanska; Sophia Long Soldier; F; Dau; 14		4165	Ista Tanka; Big Eyes; M; Son; 7
4143	Akicita Hanska; Rose Long Soldier; F; Dau; 9		4166	Keya; Terrapin; M; Son; 3-3
			4167	Winorcala Sica; Bad Old Woman; F; Head; 67
4144	Ska; Robert White; M; Head; 32			
4145	Ska; Jessie White; F; Wife; 24		4168	Zuya Gli; Returned Warrior; F; Dau; 47
4146	Marpiya Najin; Charles Standing Cloud; M; Head; 20		4169	Jessie; F; G.Dau; 18
4147	Marpiya Najin; Bessie Standing Cloud; F; Wife; 23		4170	Mata Rlogeca; Jobson Hollow Head; M; Head; 19
			4171	Mata Rlogeca; Fannie Hollow Head; F; Wife; 20
4148	Huhu Napin; Ella Bone Necklace; M; Head; 77			
4149	Ellen Morrison; F; Dau; 27		4172	George Craven; M; Head; 17
4150	Julia Morrison; F; G.Dau; 5			
			4173	Tasunke Maza; Iron Horse; F; Head; 64
4151	Wanhal Mato; Fred Top Bear; M; Head; 31			

Census Of The Sioux And Cheyenne Indians Of Pine Ridge Agency, South Dakota. Taken by W. H. Clapp, Captain 16th Infantry, Acting United States Indian Agent, June 30, 1896. (Medicine Root District)

Key: Number; Indian Name *(if given)*; English Name; Sex; Relation; Age

4174	Tatanka Ista; Bull Eye; M; Father; 48	4200	Hektakiya Gli; Comes Back; F; Wife; 35
4175	Maza Sa; Red Rod; F; Wife; 42	4201	Louis Twist; M; Son; 15
4176	Cante Wicasa; Heart Man; M; Son; 10	4202	John Twist; M; Son; 7
4177	Wicincala; Girl; F; Dau; 4	4203	Ptesan Wanbli; White Cow Eagle; F; Dau; 5
4178	Woptura; Jefferson Chips; M; Head; 25	4204	Emma Twist; F; Dau; 1-8
4179	Woptura; Katie Chips; F; Wife; 17	4205	Mato Winorcala; Old She Bear; F; Head; 64
4180	William Peno; M; Father; 29	4206	Ota Cinpi Win; Wante[sic] Them Plenty; F; G.Dau; 1-1
4181	Wi Hinapa; Rising Sun; F; Wife; 29	4207	Sungmanitu Peta; John Fire Wolf; M; Head; 21
4182	Naca; Chief; M; Son; 4-6		
4183	Agarota Peno; M; Son; 0-4	4208	He Wanica; No Horn; M; Father; 60
4184	Julia Davidson; F; Head; 42		
4185	John Davidson; M; Son; 18	4209	Winyan Wakin; Holy Woman; F; M. in L.; 76
4186	William Davidson; M; Son; 16		
4187	Emma Davidson; F; Dau; 14	4210	Waksica Kerleca; Breaks Dishes; F; Wife; 54
4188	Edward Davidson; M; Son; 9		
4189	Annie Davidson; F; Dau; 7	4211	Cetan Ska; White Hawk; M; Son; 15
4190	Lali Davidson; F; Dau; 2-2		
4191	David Davidson; M; Son; 0-3		
		4212	Nellie Gallagher; F; Head; 22
4192	Sake Sa; Red Finger Nail; F; Head; 44	4213	Julia Clifford; F; Head; 45
4193	Ptesan Hinapa; White Cow Comes Out; F; Dau; 25	4214	Delila Clifford; F; Dau; 24
		4215	Mary Clifford; F; Dau; 11
4194	Sunkska; White Horse; M; Son; 15	4216	Lily Clifford; F; Dau; 9
		4217	Rosa Clifford; F; Dau; 19
		4218	Hannah Clifford; F; Dau; 18
4195	Wasicu Ciqala; Little White Man; M; Head; 24	4219	John Clifford; M; Son; 15
		4220	James Clifford; M; Son; 13
4196	Hin Rota Win; Roan Woman; F; Wife; 21	4221	Orlando Clifford; M; Son; 23
		4222	Joseph Clifford; M; Son; 6
		4223	Mortimer Clifford; M; Son; 3-7
4197	Anpo Toka Kte; Kills Enemy In The Morning; M; Head; 29	4224	John Pulliam; M; Father; 27
4198	Tonweya Ciqala; Etta Little Scout; F; Wife; 19	4225	Lucinda Pulliam; F; Wife; 23
		4226	James Pulliam; M; Son; 4-8
		4227	Rena Pulliam; F; Dau; 2-8
4199	Hektakiya Gli; Henry Twist; M; Father; 34	4228	Amos Pulliam; m; Son; 0-4

Census Of The Sioux And Cheyenne Indians Of Pine Ridge Agency, South Dakota. Taken by W. H. Clapp, Captain 16th Infantry, Acting United States Indian Agent, June 30, 1896. (Medicine Root District)

Key: Number; Indian Name *(if given)*; English Name; Sex; Relation; Age

4229	Wakinyan Win; Thunder Woman; F; 90
4230	Minnie Thayer; F; Head; 33
4231	Alice Sickler; F; Sister; 20
4232	Lucy Sickler; F; Sister; 17
4233	Robert Morrison; M: Son; 6
4234	Julia Fisher; F; Head; 38
4235	James Wild; M; Son; 20
4236	Anna Fisher; F; Dau; 15
4237	Hattie Fisher; F; Dau; 13
4238	Gracie Fisher; F; Dau; 11
4239	Laura Fisher; F; Dau; 4-5
4240	Amanda Fisher; F; Dau; 2-5
4241	Albert Fisher; M; Son; 9
4242	Stanley H. Fisher; M; Son; 0-1
4243	Mato Tatanka Hoksila; Young Bull Bear; M; Father; 42
4244	Peji Rota; Grey Grass; F; Wife; 35
4245	Mato Tatanka; Henry Bull Bear; M; Son; 12
4246	Wasu Sina; Hail Blanket; F; Dau; 8
4247	Kahinrpeya; Runs Over; F; Dau; 2-4
4248	Kutepi; Shot At Him; M; Son; 5
4249	Wicasa Isnala; Lone Man; M; Head; 40
4250	Winyan Tanka; Big Woman; F; Wife; 51

Census of the Sioux And Cheyenne Indians
Of Pine Ridge Agency, South Dakota.
June 30, 1896

White Clay District

Census Of The Sioux And Cheyenne Indians Of Pine Ridge Agency, South Dakota. Taken by W. H. Clapp, Captain 16th Infantry, Acting United States Indian Agent, June 30, 1896. (White Clay District)

Key: Number; Indian Name *(if given)*; English Name; Sex; Relation; Age

4251 Tasunke Kokipapi; Young Man Afraid; M; Father; 57
4252 Peji Hu; Hay Leg; F; Wife; 42
4253 Tasunke Kokipapi; Minnie Young Man Afraid; F; Dau; 19
4254 Okicize; Battle; M; Son; 14
4255 Akayanka; Rider; M; Son; 11
4256 Ehake Gli; Comes Last; M; Son; 5
4257 Tasunke Kokipapi; Geo. Young Man Afraid; M; Son; 0-11

4258 Tasunka Maza; Iron Horse; F; Head; 71
4259 Tawaste; Her Good Thing; F; G.Dau; 19

4260 Cetan Iyanka; Running Hawk; M; Father; 46
4261 Carli; Powder; F; Wife; 43
4262 Onjinjitka Taspu; Rosebud; M; Son; 14
4263 Nawicakicijin; Defender; M; Son; 17
4264 Mazakan Icu; Takes The Gun; M; Nephew; 14

4265 Taopi; Wounded (Morris); M; Father; 27
4266 Reyap Inajin; Stands Aside; F; Wife; 24
4267 Glihuniki; On Arrival; F; Dau; 7
4268 Mato Cuwignaka; Bear Dress; M; Son; 5
4269 Zintkala Sa; Red Bird; M; Son; 3
4270 Wakpala Ciqala; Little Creek; M; Son; 1-2

4271 Oye Otape; Comes Tracking; M; 23

4272 Tatanka Ciqala; Little Bull #1; M; Father; 44
4273 Winyan Waste; Pretty Woman; F; Wife; 46

4274 Sunkicu; Takes The Horse; F; Dau; 17
4275 Siyo Witko; Fool Grouse; F; M. in L.; 77
4276 Mato Taheya; Bear Louse; M; Father; 40
4277 Wanbli; Eagle; F; Wife; 40
4278 Psa Kte; Kills Crow; F; Dau; 15
4279 Sinte Tanka; Big Tail; F; Dau; 13
4280 Ite Maza; Iron Face; F; Dau; 7
4281 Tatanka Slasla; Hairless Bull; M; Son; 3
4282 Hiyohipi; Comes After Her; F; Dau; 0-3

4283 Ptehincala Ha; Calf Robe; M; Father; 68
4284 Canku Waste; Good Road; F; Wife; 62
4285 Zuyahiyaya Kte; Kills Warrior; M; G.Son; 8
4286 Wayank Kte; Looks And Kills; M; Son; 27

4287 Cega Sapa; Black Kettle; M; Father; 46
4288 Pehin Ji; Yellow Hair; F; Wife; 41
4289 Wiyaka Zi; Yellow Feather; M; Son; 14
4290 Pehin; Hair; F; Dau; 14
4291 Ptan Win; Otter Woman; F; Dau; 4
4292 Sina Wakan; Holy Blanket; M; Son; 1-1
4293 Akicisa; Shoot For; M; Son; 20
4294 Otakuye Ota; Plenty Relation; F; Mother; 61

4295 Pekinji Sica; Bad Yellow Hair; M; Father; 62
4296 Tatiyopa Wakan; Her Holy Door; F; Wife; 50

Census Of The Sioux And Cheyenne Indians Of Pine Ridge Agency, South Dakota. Taken by W. H. Clapp, Captain 16th Infantry, Acting United States Indian Agent, June 30, 1896. (White Clay District)

Key: Number; Indian Name *(if given)*; English Name; Sex; Relation; Age

4297	Wi Ciqala; Little Sun; M; Son; 26	4319	Oko Sna Win; Ringing Crack; F; Wife; 50
4298	Sunka Howaste; Good Voice Dog; M; Son; 24	4320	Hinsma; Hairy; F; Dau; 19
		4321	Pehin Sa; Red Hair; F; Dau; 15
4299	Sunkhin Sa; Red Haired Horse; M; Son; 19	4322	Op Iyayapi; Goes With Them; F; Dau; 4
4300	Jijila; Yellow Yellow; F; Dau; 11	4323	Ptecela; Short; F; Niece; 18
4301	Pehin Ji; Asa Yellow Hair; M; Son; 8	4324	Sunka Glakinyan; Cross Dog; M; Father; 66
		4325	Pejuta; Medicine; F; Wife; 50
4302	Wiyurloka; Bores A Hole; M; Father; 35	4326	Heraka Isnala; Lone Elk; M; Son; 22
4303	Itankasan; Weasel; F; Wife; 27	4327	Canku Terila; Loves His Road; M; Son; 20
4304	Wahosi Hi; Comes And Tells; M; Son; 9	4328	Winyan Ota; Plenty Woman; F; Dau; 10
4305	Ciqala; Little; M; Son; 6		
4306	Winyan Waste; Good Woman; F; Dau; 2-6	4329	Wahacanka Waste; Good Shield; M; Father; 30
4307	Sina Luta; Red Blanket; M; Father; 41	4330	Pte Waste; Good Buffalo; F; Wife; 29
4308	Ptesan Wanbli; White Cow Eagle; F; Wife; 28	4331	Toka Kute; Shoots The Enemy; M; Son; 8
4309	Sina Luta; James Red Blanket; M; Son; 4	4332	Hoksila Waste; Good Boy; M; Son; 5
4310	Witko Winla; Foolish Woman; F; G.Mo; 74	4333	Wakacanka Waste; Jo Good Shield; M; Son; 0-3
4311	Canli; Tobacco; M; Father; 71	4334	Pehin Ska; White Hair; M; Head; 75
4312	Tasunke; Her Horse; F; Wife; 49		
4313	Canli; Adam Tobacco; M; Son; 22	4335	Winyan Rcaka; Pure Woman; F; Wife; 69
4314	Ho Waste; Good Voice; F; Dau; 15	4336	Wakpamnila; Distribution #1; M; Father; 38
4315	Anokasan Wanbli; Good Bald Eagle; M; Head; 31	4337	Piya Icaga; Lives Again; F; Wife; 34
4316	Winyan Hanska; Long Woman; F; Wife; 39	4338	Wakinyan Win; Thunder Woman; F; Dau; 20
4317	Hektakiya Gli; Returned; M; Son; 0-10	4339	Zintka To; Blue Bird; F; Dau; 22
		4340	Najinhan Ku; Comes Standing; F; A. Dau; 2
4318	Kangi Mni Eyeca; Crow Likes Water; M; Father; 45	4341	Tasunke Heton; Horned Horse; M; Head; 74

Census Of The Sioux And Cheyenne Indians Of Pine Ridge Agency, South Dakota. Taken by W. H. Clapp, Captain 16th Infantry, Acting United States Indian Agent, June 30, 1896. (White Clay District)

Key: Number; Indian Name *(if given)*; English Name; Sex; Relation; Age

4342 Tikanyela Wakuwa; Charges Close To Lodge; F; Wife; 84
4343 Waniyetu Wakuwa; Chase In Winter; M; Father; 44
4344 Tasunke Ota; Plenty Horses; F; Wife; 46
4345 He Maza; Iron Horn; M; Son; 12
4346 Hu; Leg; F; Dau; 14
4347 Sunka Yuha; Owns The Dog; F; Dau; 10
4348 Winyan Ciqala; Little Woman; F; Dau; 5
4349 Witko Winla; Foolish Woman; F; Head; 80
4350 Papta Iyaya; Runs Through; F; G.Dau; 18
4351 Wamniomni Wicasa; Whirlwind Man; M; Father; 39
4352 Winyan Tokeca; Different Woman; F; Wife; 43
4353 Warpatanka; Black Bird; M; G.Son; 4
4354 Kokipesni; Kills Without Fear; M; Son; 21
4355 Anokasan; Bald Eagle; M; Head; 24
4356 Winyan Ciqala Waste; Little Good Woman; F; Wife; 19
4357 Sinte Maza; Iron Tail; M; Father; 36
4358 Tipi Luta; Red House; F; Wife; 39
4359 Sinte Maza; Philip Iron Tail; M; Son; 16
4360 Towan Win; Light Woman; F; Dau; 4
4361 Winyan Nawizi; Jealous Woman; F; Dau; 2
4362 Tasunke Wamniomni; Whirlwind Horse; M; Father; 34
4363 Canupa; Pipe; F; Wife; 41
4364 Mniotupi; Born In Water; F; Dau; 14
4365 Tankal Kuwa Eyaya; Chasing Out; F; Dau; 11
4366 Wanbli Sun; Eagle Feather; F; Dau; 5
4367 Tokeya Kihuni; Gets To Lodge First; F; Dau; 2-4
4368 Katonaunka; Running Loper[sic]; F; Head; 68
4369 Winyan Sa; Red Woman; F; G.Dau; 8
4370 Anposka Tunpi; Day Birth; F; Head; 56
4371 Zuya Yesa; Warrior; F; G.Dau; 17
4372 Mato Maza; Iron Bear; M; Father; 34
4373 Ite Wanbli; Face Eagle; F; Wife; 28
4374 Tokeya Kte; Kills First; M; Son; 10
4375 Nup Najinpi; Two Stands; M; Son; 5
4376 Ca Ptecela; Steps Short; M; Son; 1-5
4377 Nuge Wanica; John No Ears; M; Father; 43
4378 Winyan Sapa; Black Woman; F; Wife; 42
4379 Susie; F; Dau; 18
4380 Wanbli Ska; White Eagle; M; Son; 14
4381 Sina Wanbli; Eagle Shawl; F; Dau; 5
4382 Wakan Hinapa; Medicine Out; F; 24
4383 Jolowansa; Whistler; M; Head; 64

Census Of The Sioux And Cheyenne Indians Of Pine Ridge Agency, South Dakota. Taken by W. H. Clapp, Captain 16th Infantry, Acting United States Indian Agent, June 30, 1896. (White Clay District)

Key: Number; Indian Name *(if given)*; English Name; Sex; Relation; Age

4384	Winorcala Ciqala; Little Old Woman; F; Wife; 68	4406	Wakan Gli; Comes Holy; M; Son; 19
4385	Mato Ite Waste; Pretty Face Bear; F; G.Dau; 17	4407	Tatanka Papya Mni; Bull Noise Walker; M; Son; 9
4386	Sunktacanka; Horse Road; M; Head; 72	4408	Hu Wegahan; Mary Broken Leg; F; Dau; 1-2
4387	Nataji Win; Yellow Head Woman; F; Wife; 67	4409	Mato Huhu; Bear Bone; M; Head; 44
4388	Naca; Chief; M; G.Son; 19	4410	Wiciyela Win; Yankton Woman; F; Wife; 30
4389	Wahacanka Maza; Iron Shield; M; Son; 41	4411	Wiyaka Luta; Red Feather; M; Father; 37
4390	Tatanka Hanska; Long Bull; M; Father; 47	4412	Tasina; Her Blanket; F; Wife; 37
4391	Pehin Ji; Yellow Hair; F; Wife; 46	4413	Tasunke Ota; Plenty Horses; F; Dau; 16
4392	James; M; Nephew; 15	4414	Wiyaka Luta; Della B. Red Feather; F; Dau; 9
4393	Mniowicakte; Kills In Water; M; Son; 15	4415	Teriya Kte; Kills Hard; F; Dau; 5
4394	Hukuta Glicu; Gets Down; M; Son; 5	4416	Wasicu Kte; Kills White Man; M; Son; 2
4395	Tikanyela Iyanka; Jos. Runs Close To Edge; M; Father; 31	4417	Charles Smith; M; Head; 29
4396	Wamniomni Sa; Red Whirlwind; F; Wife; 23	4418	Susie Smith; F; Wife; 35
4397	Wasu Sna; Rattling Hail; F; Dau; 4	4419	Ptesan Snia; White Cow Robe; F; Dau; 16
4398	Mato Wamniomni; Whirlwind Bear; M; Son; 0-4	4420	Sina Sapa; Black Shawl; F; 44
4399	Najinyapi; Surrounded; M; Father; 30	4421	Sungmanitu Wakuwa; Charging Wolf; M; Father; 35
4400	Mni Yatkan; Drinks Water; F; Wife; 20	4422	Tahu Rni; Crooked Neck; F; Wife; 23
4401	Rante Win; Cedar Woman; F; Dau; 4	4423	Wanbli Yatapi; Chief Eagle; M; Bro; 38
4402	Mato Hoksila; Bear Boy; M; Son; 2-2	4424	Wanbli Nupa; Two Eagle; F; Father; 53
4403	Hu Wegahan; Broken Leg; M; Father; 42	4425	Sunkakan Win; Horse Woman; F; Wife; 48
4404	Wecoti Yuha; Owns Village; Wife; 38	4426	Isna Kte; Kills Alone; M; Son; 23
4405	Ska Agli; Brings Water; M; Son; 24	4427	Wawayanka; Keeps Guard; M; Son; 7

Census Of The Sioux And Cheyenne Indians Of Pine Ridge Agency, South Dakota. Taken by W. H. Clapp, Captain 16th Infantry, Acting United States Indian Agent, June 30, 1896. (White Clay District)

Key: Number; Indian Name *(if given)*; English Name; Sex; Relation; Age

4428	Mani Ku; Comes Walking; F; Dau; 6	4455	Nata Tanka; Big Head; M; Father; 57
4429	Itazipa Kicun; Uses His Bow; M; Son; 2-3	4456	Tokeya Hinapa; Comes Out First; F; Wife; 50
4430	Catka; Left Hand; M; Head; 31	4457	Hektakiya Ekte; Kills Back; F; Dau; 22
4431	Ota Agli; Brings Plenty; F; Wife; 27	4458	Ohitika; Brave; M; Son; 19
4432	Janjanyela; Clear; M: Father; 36	4459	Marpiya Ciqala; Little Cloud; M; Head; 35
4433	Sina Icu; Takes Robe; F; Wife; 30	4460	Tasunke Najin; Standing Horse; F; Wife; 24
4434	Blotahunka; Leader; F; Dau; 11		
4435	Sunk Wicaku; Gives Horses; F; Dau; 6	4461	Mato Ihanble; Dreaming Bear; M; Father; 29
4436	Wayank Hipi; Comes To See Him; F; Dau; 2	4462	Slecahan; Ella Spirit; F; Wife; 21
		4463	Wakan Hiyaya; Goes Holy; F; Dau; 0-10
4437	William Brown; M; Father; 28		
4438	Lizzie Brown; F; Wife; 25	4464	Tarca Nite; Deer Rump; M; Head; 74
4439	Alice Brown; F; Dau; 7		
4440	Harry Brown; M; Son; 5	4465	Winyan Luta; Red Woman; F; Wife; 54
4441	Nellie Brown; F; Dau; 2-8		
4442	Rosa Brown; F; Dau; 0-9		
4443	Edward Brown; M; Bro; 55	4466	Inyan Pe; Rocky Mountain; M; Father; 44
4444	Gi Iciya; Points Yellow; M; Father; 58	4467	Maka Papta; Shovels Ground; F; Wife; 54
4445	Ite Ska; White Face; F; Wife; 64	4468	Castunpi; Name Him; M; Son; 18
4446	Mato Hinrota; Roan Bear; F; Dau; 30	4469	Zuya Tasunke; War Horse; M; Son; 14
4447	Wincincala Waste; Good Girl; F; G.Dau; 9	4470	Wankal Etonwan; Looks Up; F; Mother; 90
4448	Ptesan; White Cow; F; G.Dau; 5		
4449	Tasunke Opi; Wounded Horse; M; G.Son; 0-8	4471	Termuga Luta; Red Fly; M; Head; 70
4450	Pa Rugahan; Broken Nose; M; Father; 28	4472	Kate Iyeyapi; Shot Him; F; Wife; 58
4451	Tokala; Fox; F; Wife; 36	4473	Inupa; Two Mouths; F; Dau; 13
4452	Cetan Ho Tanka; Loud Voice Hawk; M; B. in L.; 27	4474	Mato Nakpa; Bear Ear; M; F. in L.; 74
4453	Canupa; Pipe; M; Nephew; 7		
4454	Kicaksa; Knocks In Two; M; Son; 3	4475	Heraka Tamaheca; Poor Elk; M; Father; 42

Census Of The Sioux And Cheyenne Indians Of Pine Ridge Agency, South Dakota.
Taken by W. H. Clapp, Captain 16th Infantry, Acting United States Indian Agent,
June 30, 1896. (White Clay District)

Key: Number; Indian Name *(if given)*; English Name; Sex; Relation; Age

4476	Heraka Tamaheca; Martin Poor Elk; M; Son; 16	4498	Zintkala Hinsma; James Hairy Bird; M; Father; 32
4477	Si Wanica; No Foot; M; Son; 13	4499	Winyan Sica; Bad Woman; F; Wife; 27
4478	Tasunke Nupa; Two Horses; F; Dau; 6	4500	Anpo Wicakte; Kills In The Morning; F; Dau; 0-11
4479	Mastincala Gleska; Spotted Rabbit; M; Son; 0-11	4501	Tasunke Najin; Standing Horse; F; Head; 65
4480	Wakpamnila; Distribution #2; M; Father; 25	4502	Sina Gleglega; Spotted Blanket; F; Dau; 20
4481	Mila Tanka; Butcher Knife; F; Wife; 19	4503	Canupa Wakan; Medicine Pipe; F; G.Dau; 7
4482	Inyan Win; Rock Woman; F; Dau; 2	4504	Wakte Gli; Kills And Comes Back; M; Father; 26
4483	Wajaja; Wajaja; F; Head; 84	4505	Tacanku; Her Road; F; Wife; 21
4484	Waste; Good; F; Sister; 74	4506	Mato Hinwaste; Good Hair Bear; M; Son; 3
4485	Spayola Wicarca; Old Mexican; M; B. in L.; 70	4507	Heyoka Tasunke; Clown Horse; M; Father; 53
4486	Napi Wikcemna; Ten Fingers; M; Father; 37	4508	Canku Waste; Good Road; F; Wife; 49
4487	Wapaha; War Bonnet; F Wife; 29	4509	Nup Wicakte; Kills Two; M; Son; 18
4488	Toka Ole; Looks For Enemy; M; Son; 15	4510	Tipi Luta; Red Lodge; F; Dau; 14
4489	Tokeya Kte; Kills First; M; Son; 8	4511	Poge Opi; Wounded Nose; M; Son 3-6
4490	Okiciza Yuha; Keeps The Battle; M; Son; 5	4512	Wicarpi Luta; Red Star; M; Father; 47
4491	Harnir Kte; Picks Out And Kills; F; Dau; 11	4513	Ptehincala Win; Calf Woman; F; Wife; 34
4492	Tinyata Wota; Eats At Home; F; Dau; 2	4514	Wan Kicun; Used Arrow; M; Son; 8
4493	Tokeya Kte; Kills First #2; M; Son; 0-5	4515	Iyuha Wicaku; Gives All; M; Son; 3
4494	Paorpa; Breaks In; M; Head; 74	4516	Anokasan Wanbli; Bald Eagle; M; Son; 0-3
4495	Rante Luta; Red Cedar; F; Wife; 61	4517	Winyan Wakan; Holy Woman; F; Head; 68
4496	Hektakiya Ekte; Kills Back; M; G.Son; 14	4518	Oiciglaka; Tells Herself; F; Dau; 148
4497	Tasunke Opi; Wounded Horse; M; G.Son; 11		

Census Of The Sioux And Cheyenne Indians Of Pine Ridge Agency, South Dakota. Taken by W. H. Clapp, Captain 16th Infantry, Acting United States Indian Agent, June 30, 1896. (White Clay District)

Key: Number; Indian Name *(if given)*; English Name; Sex; Relation; Age

4519	Maka Wiyakpa; Nellie Shining Ground; F; G.Dau; 24	4541	Tiwegna Iyanka; Runs Through Camp; F; Dau; 1-3
4520	Wanbli Waste; Good Eagle; F; Niece; 5	4542	Wapaha Ciqala; Little War Bonnet; M; Father; 60
4521	Maka Cincala; Young Skunk; M; Father; 30	4543	Topa; Four Times; F; Wife; 52
4522	Wamniomni; Whirlwind; F; Wife; 33	4544	Winyan Hunkesne; Slow Woman; F; Wife #2; 50
4523	Anpetu; Day; F; Dau; 11	4545	Wapaha Ciqala; Alice Little War Bonnet; F; Dau; 19
4524	Mniowicakte; Kills In Water; F; Dau; 6	4546	Wapaha Ciqala; Jesse Little War Bonnet; M; Son; 19
4525	Tasunke Kokipapi; Jennie Young Man Afraid; F; Head; 19	4547	Wapaha Ciqala; Dolly Little War Bonnet; F; Dau; 7
4526	Hektakiya Kute; Shoots Back; M; Bro; 14	4548	Wicakarpa; Drive Them; F; Dau; 7
4527	Hunska Waste; Good Leggins; F; Mother; 48	4549	Wanbli Hinapa; Eagle Out; F; Dau; 29
4528	Kokipeya Kte; Kills With Fear; M; Bro; 18	4550	Wapaha Luta; Red Hat; F; Head; 42
4529	Mato Canwegna Iyank[sic]; Bear Runs In The Wood; M; Father; 51	4551	Heraka Bloke; Peter Male Elk; M; Son; 16
4530	Wasu Ska; White Hail; F; Wife; 39	4552	Pehan Zi; Nettie Yellow Crane; F; Dau; 9
4531	Wicincala Hanska; Tall Girl; F; Dau; 15	4553	Wicincala; Girl; F; Dau; 6
4532	Wicakute; Charles Shooter; M; Son; 9	4554	Tipi Wayanka; Sees The Lodge; F; Dau; 0-7
4533	Anowan; Swims For; M: Son; 4	4555	Tankal Ti; Living Outside; M; Father; 40
4534	Tezi Rlecahan; Torn Belly; M; Father; 68	4556	Canupa; Pipe; F; Wife; 41
4535	Wahukeza; Lance; F; Wife; 54	4557	Toka Wicakte; Kills Enemy; M; Son; 11
4536	Wakinyan Marpiya; Cloud Thunder; M; Son; 22	4558	Pankeska Ota; Plenty Shell; F; Dau; 7
4537	Toka Icu; Takes Enemy; F; Dau; 34	4559	Sungmanitu Sica; Bad Wolf; M; Son; 4
4538	Toka Kte; Kills The Enemy; F; G.Dau; 5	4560	Susie; F; Dau; 0-4
		4561	Warapya; Scares; M; Head; 19
4539	Caste; Little Finger; M; Father; 23	4562	To Obtain; Sight Of Lodge; F; Wife; 21
4540	Nawiza; Jealous; F; Wife; 25	4563	Tasunke Hoton; Howling Horse; M; Father; 47

Census Of The Sioux And Cheyenne Indians Of Pine Ridge Agency, South Dakota. Taken by W. H. Clapp, Captain 16th Infantry, Acting United States Indian Agent, June 30, 1896. (White Clay District)

Key: Number; Indian Name *(if given)*; English Name; Sex; Relation; Age

4564 Ptesan; White Cow; F; Wife; 31
4565 Cekiyapi; Prays For Her; F; Dau; 4
4566 Aiyapi; Talks About Her; F; Dau; 1-2
4567 Ptesan Wicakte; Kills White Cow; M; Head; 65
4568 Tainyan Ku; Comes In Light; F; Wife; 55
4569 Ptesan Wicakte; James Kills White Cow; M; Son; 16
4570 Oye Luta; Red Track; M; Mother; 37
4571 Wicegna Iyanka; Runs Among Them; F; Dau; 9
4572 Canowicakte; Kills In Wood; F; Dau; 4-3
4573 Niyan Wakan; Holy Breath; F; Dau; 2-4
4574 Wahukeza Kicun; Uses Her Lance; F; Dau; 0-1
4575 Ota Agli; Brings Plenty; F; Mother; 33
4576 Toka Waste; Good Enemy; F; Dau; 5
4577 Pte Ole; Herder; M; Son; 2-6
4578 Canhu; Tree Leg; M; Father; 38
4579 Wamniomni Sapa; Black Whirlwind; F; Wife; 35
4580 Emma Carson; F; Dau; 16
4581 Lizzie Carson; F; Dau; 13
4582 Wazi; Pine; F; Dau; 5
4583 Pankeska Win; Shell Woman; F; Dau; 0-3
4584 Wicarpi Hinapa; Star Comes Out; M; Husb; 21
4585 Tasina Ota; Her Good Blanket; F; Wife; 19
4586 Aiyapi; Talks About Him; F; Mother; 58
4587 Wazi; Pine; M; Bro; 17
4588 Tainyan Hinapa; Comes Out In Sight; F; Niece; 8
4589 Marpiya Wakan; Holy Cloud; M; Father; 46
4590 Winyan Tanka; Big Woman; F; Wife; 64
4591 Marpiya Wakan; Isaac Holy Cloud; M; Son; 17
4592 Heraka Mani; Walking Elk; M; Father; 34
4593 Toka Kte; Kills Enemy; F; Wife; 64
4594 Tacanupa Ota; Her Plenty Pipe; F; Dau; 12
4595 Mahel Eyayapi; Takes Him In; M; Son; 9
4596 Nupa Kte; Kills Twice; F; Dau; 4
4597 Sina Kute; Shoots Blanket; M; Son; 6
4598 Pizo; Gall; M; Father; 66
4599 Winula; Winola; F; Wife; 44
4600 Mato Glasla; Shaving Bear; M; Son; 19
4601 Mato Luta; Red Bear; F; Dau; 14
4602 Zintkala Waste; Pretty Bird; F; Dau; 21
4603 Pankeska Win; Shell Woman; F; G.Mo; 64
4604 Wagmu Su; Pumpkin Seed; M; G.Son; 7
4605 Istima Ta; Sound Sleeper; M; Father; 53
4606 Wicarpi Win; Star Woman; F; Wife; 47
4607 Najinhan Kte; Kill Standing; M; Son; 10
4608 Ptehincala Ska; White Calf; M; Father; 39

Census Of The Sioux And Cheyenne Indians Of Pine Ridge Agency, South Dakota. Taken by W. H. Clapp, Captain 16th Infantry, Acting United States Indian Agent, June 30, 1896. (White Clay District)

Key: Number; Indian Name *(if given)*; English Name; Sex; Relation; Age

4609	Sunk Sapa; Black Horse; F; Wife; 31	4632	Ti Wicakte; Kills At Lodge; M; Husb; 31
4610	Ista Gi; Brown Eyes; M; Son; 17	4633	Agli; Brings; F; Wife; 29
4611	Canupa Wakan; Holy Pipe; F; Dau; 13	4634	Zintkala; Jay Bird; F; Dau; 0-2
4612	Heraka Isnala; Lone Elk; M; Son; 9	4635	Mato Istima; Sleeping Bear; M; Husb; 39
4613	Otoran; Gives Away; F; Dau; 3-4	4636	Tasina Zi; Her Yellow Blanket; F; Wife; 51
4614	Pijuta Win; Medicine Woman; F; M. in L.; 84	4637	Mato Tokeya; Bear Leader; M; Son; 8
4615	Wanbli Waste; Pretty Eagle; M; 47	4638	Kahinrpeya; Rides Over; M; Son; 11
		4639	Tahu Maza; Iron Neck; F; 71
4616	Oleje Win; Chamber Woman; F; Mother; 53	4640	Mato Ruwimna; Stinking Bear; M; Father; 49
4617	Ptesan Wicakte; Kills White Cow; M; Son; 19	4641	Tarca Hinapa; Deer Goes Out; f; Wife; 49
4618	Cankuhu; Back; M; Father; 57	4642	Najinyapi; Surrounded; M; Son; 26
4619	Waha Parpa; Scrapes The Hide; F; Wife; 56	4643	Gleska Agli; Brings Spotted; F; Dau; 13
4620	Pankeska; Shell; F; Dau; 22	4644	Mato Ska; White Bear; M; Son; 12
4621	Wanbli; Eagle; M; Son; 18		
4622	Marpiya Ciqala; James Little Cloud; M; Father; 36	4645	Mazaska; White Silver; M; Son; 5
4623	Anpetu; Day; F; Wife; 57		
4624	Pehin Waste; Pretty Hair; F; Dau; 18	4646	Sota Win; Smoke Woman; F; Mother; 35
4625	Wazi; Pine; F; Dau; 13	4647	Kiyan Win; Flying Woman; F; G.Mo; 64
4626	Warpe To; Green Leaf; F; Dau; 7	4648	Iktomi Gi; Yellow Spider; M; Son; 19
4627	Pehan Sapa; Black Hair; M; Husb; 38	4649	Rlo Kiyapi; Makes Growl; M; Son; 15
4628	Akicita Ota; Plenty Soldier; F; Wife; 22	4650	Kokipeya Kte; Kills Afraid; M; Son; 13
4629	Tarca Win; Deer Woman; F; G.Mo; 57	4651	Ninglicu; Comes Alive; M; Son; 8
4630	Zi; Yellow; F; G.Dau; 9	4652	Pehan Wankatuya; High Crane; M; Father; 22
4631	Kokipa; Afraid; F; G.Dau; 3	4653	Ptehincala Win; Calf Woman; F; Wife; 21

Census Of The Sioux And Cheyenne Indians Of Pine Ridge Agency, South Dakota. Taken by W. H. Clapp, Captain 16th Infantry, Acting United States Indian Agent, June 30, 1896. (White Clay District)

Key: Number; Indian Name *(if given)*; English Name; Sex; Relation; Age

4654 Sunkska; White Horse; M; Son; 3
4655 Itonkasan Win; Weasel Woman; F; Dau; 0-11

4656 Mato Ska; White Bear; M; Father; 44
4657 Anpetu; Day; F; Wife; 36
4658 Pahi; Picks; M; Son; 14
4659 Hoksila; Boy; M; Son; 5

4660 Kokipapi; Afraid Of Him; M; Husb; 19
4661 Ota Kte; Kills Plenty; F; Wife; 20

4662 Cega Ogle; Joe Kettle Coat; M; Husb; 54
4663 Tacanku Ota; Her Plenty Road; F; Wife; 56

4664 Huhu Napin; Bone Necklace; M; Husb; 64
4665 Tasunke Win; Her Horse; F; Wife; 59

4666 Sungmanitu Sapa; Black Wolf #1; Father; 60
4667 Anpetu; Day; F; Wife; 53
4668 Wahacanka Icu; Takes Shield; M; Son; 24
4669 Iyapi Tawa; Her Talk; F; Dau; 20

4670 Ite Nupa; Two Faces; M; Father; 34
4671 TasunkeAGli[sic]; Horse Comes Out; F; Wife; 33
4672 Ninwicaya; Saves The Life; M; Son; 6
4673 Winyan Kte; Kills Woman; F; Dau; 9
4674 Anatanpi; Run At Him; M; Son; 4

4675 Can Mazawakan; Wooden Gun; M; Husb; 27
4676 Winyan Ptecela; Short Woman; F; Wife; 49

4677 Wasicu Mato; American Bear; M; Father; 67
4678 Capigmuke Maza; Iron Trap; F; Wife; 49
4679 Wasicu Ota; Plenty White Man; F; Dau; 20
4680 Wicasu Yatapi; Philip Chief Man; M; Son; 16
4681 Icanyan Iyanka; Runs Against; M; G.Son; 4
4682 Toka Oyuspa; Catches Enemy; F; G.Dau; 0-4

4683 Canupa Pegnaka; Pipe On Head; M; Father 55
4684 Apepi; Wait For Him; F; Wife; 45
4685 Ota Kte; Kills Plenty; F; Dau; 18
4686 Si Tanka; Big Foot; M; Son; 14

4687 Tipi Wankatuya; High Lodge; M; Father; 70
4688 Jolowan; Whistler; F; Wife; 44
4689 Tawa Iki Hcu; Takes Her Own; F; Dau; 16

4690 Ohitika; Charles Brave #2; M; Husb; 26
4691 Teriya Ku; Comes Hard; F; Wife; 23

4692 Nata Ohomni Ska; White Around Head; M; Father; 72
4693 Mato Kawinge; Turning Bear; M; Father; 58
4694 Marpiya Sapa; Black Cloud; F; Wife; 52
4695 Wiyaka Win; Feather Woman; F; Dau; 29
4696 Okicize Tawa; Owns Fight; M; Son; 17

Census Of The Sioux And Cheyenne Indians Of Pine Ridge Agency, South Dakota. Taken by W. H. Clapp, Captain 16th Infantry, Acting United States Indian Agent, June 30, 1896. (White Clay District)

Key: Number; Indian Name *(if given)*; English Name; Sex; Relation; Age

4697	Marpiya Wicasa; Cloud Man; M; Father; 39	4719	Tainyan Najin; Stands In Sight; F; Dau; 0-9
4698	Wahacanka Waste; Good Shield; F; Wife; 41	4720	Pahin; Porcupine; M; Father; 39
4699	Zintkala Koyaka; Wears The Bird; F; Dau; 6	4721	Hunska Sa; Red Socks; F; Wife; 33
4700	Amapsica; Jumps Over Me; F; M. in L.; 69	4722	Kutepi; Shot At; M; Son; 10
		4723	Wakan Waglaka; Talks Holy; F; Dau; 4
4701	Luzahan; Fast; M; Father; 31		
4702	Sunkhinsa; Red Horse; F; Wife; 32	4724	Mani; Walking; F; Mother; 60
		4725	Kiwoksapi; Shot In Two; M; Son; 16
4703	Tokeya; First; M; Son; 9		
4704	Ti El Kte; Kills At Lodge; F; Dau; 7	4726	Nup Yusna; Drops Two; M; Son; 30
4705	Toka Kte; Kills Enemy; F; Dau; 5	4727	Wanbli Sica; Bad Eagle; F; Niece; 3
4706	Sunkska; White Horse; F; Dau; 0-7	4728	Winyan Waste; Good Woman; F; Mother; 49
4707	Toka Takpe; Charges Enemy; M; Bro; 29	4729	Winorcala; Old Woman; F; G.Mo; 73
4708	Taopi Ota; Plenty Wound; M; Bro; 18	4730	Ninyapi; Makes Alive; F; Sister; 21
4709	Toka Wicaki; Takes Away From Enemy; M; Bro; 17	4731	Wawohiya; Helper; M; Bro; 20
4710	Ite Waste; Good Face; F; Mother; 54	4732	Akicita Waste; Good Soldier; M; Father; 28
		4733	Naca Win; Chief Woman; F; Wife; 24
4711	Tatanka Nata; Bull Head; F; Mother; 44	4734	Ptesan Yatapi; Chief White Cow; F; Dau; 4-6
4712	Pte Wakan; Holy Cow; F; Dau; 18	4735	Hoksila; Boy; M; Son; 3
4713	Heraka Win; Elk Woman; F; Dau; 9	4736	Psa Kte; Kills Crow; M; Husb; 28
4714	Winorcala; Old Woman; F; Mother; 87	4737	Wasicu Winyan; White Woman; F; Wife; 19
4715	Isna Wicakte; Kills Alone; M; Father; 24	4738	Hoksila Luta; Red Boy; M; Father; 38
4716	Wicegna Glicu; Comes From Amongst Them; F; Wife; 23	4739	Tankal Najin; Stands Outside; F; Wife; 38
4717	Mastincala Stola; Sleek Rabbit; M; Son; 4	4740	Hoksila Luta; George Red Boy; M; Son; 1-4
4718	Zintkala Wanbli; Eagle Bird; M; Son; 0-9		

Census Of The Sioux And Cheyenne Indians Of Pine Ridge Agency, South Dakota. Taken by W. H. Clapp, Captain 16th Infantry, Acting United States Indian Agent, June 30, 1896. (White Clay District)

Key: Number; Indian Name *(if given)*; English Name; Sex; Relation; Age

4741	Timahel Yanka; Sits In Lodge; F; Mother; 49	4764	Capa Win; Beaver Woman; F; Wife; 30
4742	Hiyuiciya; Dismounts; M; Son; 15	4765	Sunkska Tawa; His White Horse; M; Son; 3-6
4743	Slohan Ku; Comes Crawling; M; Son; 11	4766	Kici Najin; Stands With Him; F; Dau; 6
4744	Psica; Jumper; M; Father; 49	4767	Tatanka Luta; Red Bull; M; Son; 0-4
4745	Hinhan Ska; White Owl; F; Wife; 60	4768	Hankepi Wicakte; Kills At Night; M; Father; 37
4746	Hinhan Ska; Ida White Owl; F; S.Dau; 21	4769	Wanbli Luta; Red Eagle; F; Dau; 9
4747	Antoine Provost; M; G.Son; 33		
4748	Oliver; M; G.Son; 29		
4749	Beth; F; G.Dau; 28	4770	Itonkasan Waste; Pretty Weasel; M; Father; 49
4750	Charles; M; S.Son; 22		
4751	Jimmie; M; G.Son; 0-5	4771	Awicasa; Shout At; F; Wife; 43
		4772	Ayustanpi; Lets Alone; F; Dau; 17
4752	Tasunke Tokeya Iyan; Horse Runs First; M; Father; 37	4773	Wanupa; Two Arrows; M; Son; 5
4753	Tasunke Tokeya Iyank[sic]; Horse Runs Ahead; M; Son; 16		
		4774	Tatanka; Bull #2; M; Father; 34
4754	Sunkgleska; Spotted Horse #2; M; Father; 23	4775	Ptecela; Short; F; Wife; 25
		4776	Ptesan Tokaheya; Cow Leader; F; Dau; 7
4755	Wakan Najin; Stands Holy; F; Wife; 20	4777	Tasunke Wicasa; His Horse Man; M; Son; 3
4756	Hokipi; Stripped; F; Dau; 1-1		
4757	Kiyan Luta; Flying Red; M; Husb; 65	4778	Winyan Waste; Pretty Woman; F; Head; 59
4758	Sunk Yuha; Owns The Horse; F; Wife; 59	4779	Noge Sa; Red Ear; F; Dau; 30
		4780	Naca Win; Chief Woman; M; G.Son; 5
4759	Cetan Maza; Iron Hawk; M; Father; 61	4781	Heraka Luta Win; Red Elk Woman; F; 66
4760	Tainyan Najin Win; Woman In Sight; F; Wife; 63		
4761	Ohomni Iyanka; Runs Around; M; Son; 32	4782	Rante Luta; Red Cedar; F; Mother; 48
4762	Sunkska Win; White Horse Woman; F; Dau; 19	4783	Kangi Sagye; Crow Cane; F; Dau; 22
		4784	Anpetu; Day; F; Dau; 15
4763	Kici Istima; Sleeps With Him; M; Father; 34	4785	Wicarpi Hinapa; Star Comes Out; F; Dau; 6

Census Of The Sioux And Cheyenne Indians Of Pine Ridge Agency, South Dakota. Taken by W. H. Clapp, Captain 16th Infantry, Acting United States Indian Agent, June 30, 1896.   (White Clay District)

Key: Number; Indian Name *(if given)*; English Name; Sex; Relation; Age

4786 Taku Yuha; Owns Somethings; F; Dau; 3-6
4787 Mato Wawiyokipiya; Pleasing Bear; M; Father; 57
4788 Heraka Mani; Walking Elk; F; Wife; 56
4789 Wawokiye Sni; Not Helps Him; M; Father; 33
4790 Inyan Iyotaka; Sitting Rock; F; Wife; 23
4791 Tanyan Hute; Shoots Good; M; Son; 0-5
4792 Tikanyela Kuwa; Charles Close To Lodge; M; Husb; 42
4793 Sagye Wanbli; Eagle Cane; F; Wife; 38
4794 SihaSrpa[sic]; Black Foot; F; Mother; 67
4795 Wanbli Taheya; Eagle Louse; M; Father; 37
4796 Wasicu Winyan; White Woman; F; Wife; 39
4797 Sunkaiyphi; Comes After Horse; M; Son; 13
4798 Reyap Eyaya; Takes Away; M; Son; 12
4799 Wawiyokipiya; Please; F; Dau; 8
4800 Suwial Kute; Shoots At Side; F; Dau; 6
4801 Pasu Hanska; Long Nose Dawson; F; Dau; 3
4802 Sungleska Ciqala; Little Spotted Horse; M; Father; 33
4803 Eliza; F; Wife; 34
4804 Wapiya Itacan; Chief Medicine Boy; M: Son; 7
4805 Wolota; Borrower; F; Dau; 6
4806 Sunkgleska Ciqala; Louis Little Spotted H.; M; Son; 3-6
4807 Makaicu; Takes The Earth; F; Mother; 63
4808 Hinzi Agli; Brings Yellow; F; Dau; 2
4809 Sunka Bloka; He Dog; F; Father; 59
4810 Inyan; Rock; F; Wife; 52
4811 Sunka Gluha; Keeps Her Horse; F; Dau; 22
4812 Sunka Witko; Crazy Dog; M; B. in L.; 63
4813 Canupa Wakan; Holy Pipe; M; Father; 44
4814 Ska Sapa; Black White; F; Wife; 41
4815 Tokeya Mani; First Walk; M; Son; 17
4816 Naca; Chief; F; Dau; 13
4817 Cosiyo Ciqala; Little Prairie Chicken; F; Mother; 74
4818 Najin; Stands; M; Father; 24
4819 Najin; Smauel[sic] Stands; M; Son; 1-4
4820 Ciqala; Little; M; Father; 46
4821 Onpan Gi; Yellow Elk; F; Wife; 29
4822 Matoha Sina; Bear Robe; F; Dau; 20
4823 Waniyaka; Savior; M; Son; 14
4824 Ogle Wakan; Holy Shirt; M; Son; 4-4
4825 Ptesan; White Cow; F; Dau;2
4826 Ciqala; Amos Comes Little; M; Son; 18
4827 Mato Wicincala; Young Bear; M; Father; 37
4828 Nige Win; Belly Woman; F; Wife; 29
4829 Tokeya Kte; Kills First; M; Son; 18
4830 Wincincala; Girl; F; Dau; 5

Census Of The Sioux And Cheyenne Indians Of Pine Ridge Agency, South Dakota. Taken by W. H. Clapp, Captain 16th Infantry, Acting United States Indian Agent, June 30, 1896. (White Clay District)

Key: Number; Indian Name *(if given)*; English Name; Sex; Relation; Age

4831	Tokeya Hinapa; Comes Out First; F; Mother; 58	4856	Wapostan; Hat; M; Father; 29
4832	Tibloke Ota; Plenty Brothers; F; G.Dau; 14	4857	Heyoka Win; Clown Woman; F; Wife; 24
4833	Sagye Zi; Yellow Cane; F; G.Dau; 12	4858	Waposton; Henry Hat; M; Son; 3
		4859	Itonkasan Mato; Weasel Bear; M; Father; 42
4834	Icimani Hanska; Long Visitor; M; Father; 57	4860	Tasunke Waste Win; Her Good Horse; F; Wife; 41
4835	Tikanyla Wakiwa; Runs Close To Lodge; M; Son; 29	4861	Ista Ska; White Eyes; F; G.Dau; 14
4836	Tipi Luta; Red Lodge; F; Wife; 61	4862	Najinyapi; Surrounded; M; Son; 10
4837	Wipata; Porcupine Work; F; G.Dau; 7	4863	Ciqala Wicakte; Kills Little; M; Son; 17
		4864	Wahacanka Icu; Takes Shield; F; Dau; 5
4838	Igmu Wankatuya; High Cat; M; Father; 54	4865	Hoksila Waste; Good Boy; M; Son; 2
4839	Marpiya Win; Cloud Woman; F; Wife; 54		
4840	Ayutapi; Looks At Him; M; Son; 22	4866	Wakinyan Putinhin; Thunder Beard; M; Father; 43
		4867	Wakinyan Putinhin; Emma Thunder Beard; F; Dau; 12
4841	Grace Jarvis; F; Mother; 43		
4842	May Jarvis; F; Dau; 21	4868	Wakinyan Putinhin; Lizzie Thunder Beard; F; Dau; 8
4843	Frank Jarvis; M; Son; 12		
4844	Joseph Jarvis; M; Son; 18		
4845	Mitchell Jarvis; M; Son; 16	4869	Tatanka Ptecela; Short Bull #1; M; Father; 40
4846	Tatanka Ciqala; Little Bull #3; M; Father; 44	4870	Cetan Heton; Horned Hawk; F; Wife; 41
4847	Wanbli Hinapa; Eagle Comes Out; F; Wife; 41	4871	Nakipa; Runs Away; M; Son; 9
4848	Mato Canwegna; Bear In Wood; M; Son; 9	4872	Makata Wakita; Looks At Ground; F; Dau; 0-11
4849	Wicarpi Zi; Yellow Star; F; Dau; 7	4873	Heraka Sapa; Henry Black Elk; M; Father; 39
4850	Wiconi; Life; M; Son; 4	4874	Heraka Sapa; Louisa C. Black Elk; F; Wife; 36
4851	Zica; Squirrel; F; Dau; 0-10		
		4875	Tayan Kte; Kills Well; M; Son; 3
4852	Ite Ranran; Johnson Scabby Face; M; Son; 24		
4853	Tasina Maza Win; Iron Shawl Woman; F; Mother; 54	4876	Wakinyan Ciqala; Little Thunder; M; Son; 1-1
4854	Bert Janis; M; Nephew; 14	4877	Winyan Ciqala; Little Woman; F; 67
4855	John Buckman; M; Nephew; 9		

Census Of The Sioux And Cheyenne Indians Of Pine Ridge Agency, South Dakota. Taken by W. H. Clapp, Captain 16th Infantry, Acting United States Indian Agent, June 30, 1896. (White Clay District)

Key: Number; Indian Name *(if given)*; English Name; Sex; Relation; Age

4878	Igmu Wakewa; Charging Cat; M; Father; 58	4899	Anokatan Kte; Kills Two Sides; M; Son; 18
4879	Wakinyan Ktepi; Kills By Lightning; F; Wife; 58	4900	Anposkan Tonpi; Born in Day; F; Dau; 11
4880	Waniyetu Wakuwa; Charging Winter; M; Son; 22	4901	Tasunke Wakan; Holy Horse; F; Dau; 6
4881	Najinyapi; Surrounded; M; Son; 17	4902	Susie; F; Dau; 2
		4903	Wincakableca; Scatters Them; M; Father; 34
4882	Cangleska Luta; Red Ring; M; Father; 55	4904	Inyan Maza; Iron Rock; F; Niece; 8
4883	Winyan Gi; Brown Woman; F; Wife; 50	4905	Aiyapi; Talks About; F; Dau; 5
4884	Waonjica Yuha; Owns Bodtail[sic] Horse; M; Son; 23	4906	Hinhan Gi; Brown Owl; M; Son; 1-6
4885	Narcan; Deaf And Dumb; M; Son; 21	4907	Cuwi; Sides; M; Father; 43
4886	Ranran Win; Scabby Woman; F; Dau; 18	4908	Cante Waste; Good Heart; F; Wife; 44
		4909	Sagye; Cane; F; Dau; 11
4887	Mato Niyan Luta; Red Breath Bear; M; Father; 46	4910	Tacanku Ota Win; Her Many Roads; F; Dau; 2-2
4888	Ptesan; White Cow; F; Wife; 36		
4889	Sunk Sapa; Black Horn; F; Dau; 16	4911	Wiyaka Gleska; Spotted Feather; M; Father; 33
4890	Wosica; Makes Trouble; M; Son; 6	4912	Kisun; Braided; F; Wife; 33
		4913	Scili; Pawnee; M; Son; 6
4891	Sina Wakan; Medicine Blanket; F; Dau; 3-6	4914	Tarca Win; Deer Woman; F; `- Dau; 3
4892	Sica Kutepi; Bad Shot Him; M; Son; 0-4	4915	Ihanblesa; Dreamer; M; Father; 28
4893	Tatanka Psica; Thomas Jumping Bull; M; Bro; 23	4916	Ninglicu; Comes Alive; F; Wife; 28
4894	Cokata Mani; Walks In Center; M; Bro; 25	4917	Ogli Wakan; Holy Shirt; M; Son; 5
4895	Tibloku Ota; Plenty Brother; F; Sister; 19	4918	Wahinkpelyanajinca; Carries Off Arrows; M; Son; 1-3
4896	Pehin Ji; Yellow Hair; F; Mother; 57	4919	Mato Niwicaya; Bear Saves Life; M; Father; 27
4897	Tarca Sunkala Sapa; Black Sheep; M; Father; 45	4920	Ptesan Waste; Good White Cow; F; Wife; 38
4898	Onpan Hinska; Elk Tusk; F; Wife; 44	4921	Zintkala Ska; White Bird; M; B. in L.; 27

Census Of The Sioux And Cheyenne Indians Of Pine Ridge Agency, South Dakota. Taken by W. H. Clapp, Captain 16th Infantry, Acting United States Indian Agent, June 30, 1896. (White Clay District)

Key: Number; Indian Name *(if given)*; English Name; Sex; Relation; Age

4922 Mato Cangleska; Bear Ring; M; Son; 5
4923 Psa Wicoti Ole; Hunts Crow Village; M; Son; 3
4924 Sahinyela; Cheyenne; M: Father; 34
4925 Blotahunska Ciqala; Leader; F; Wife; 31
4926 Tokeya Wicakte; Kills First; M; Son; 3
4927 Ite Wanbli; Eagle Face; F; Dau; 0-2
4928 Maza Kawega; Breaks Iron; F; Mo. in L.; 68

4929 Tonweya Gli; Returns From Scout; M; Father; 56
4930 Pankska; Shell; F; Wife; 53
4931 Wawokiya; Helps; M; Son; 19
4932 Blowanjila; Lone Ridge; M; Son; 12
4933 Pte Icarya; Raising Cow; F; Dau; 15

4934 Mato Ohitika; Brave Bear; M; Husb; 64
4935 Heraka Waste; Good Elk; F; Wife; 54

4936 Zuya Yesa; Warrior; M; Father; 28
4937 Kawicapa; Beats Them; F; Wife; 22
4938 Najin Ku; Comes Standing; F; Dau; 14
4939 Tokicun; Retainor[sic]; M; Son; 0-2
4940 Mata Rugahan; Busted Head; F; Mother; 73

4941 Petaga; Fire #1; M; Father; 44
4942 Mato Hinapa; Bear Comes Out; F; Wife; 45
4943 Sunkakan Isnala; Lone Horse; M; Son; 19

4944 Teriya Kte; Kills Hard; F; Dau; 12
4945 Gloku; Brings; F; Dau; 8
4946 Najinyapi; Surrounded; M; Son; 4

4947 Wakinyan Tacanksa; Thunder Club; M: Bro; 27
4948 Canli; Tobacco; M; Bro; 21
4949 Ptesan Sagye; White Cow Cane; F; Mother; 63
4950 Wa Iwoblu; Snow Flies; F; Sister; 29
4951 Wanbli Waste; Pretty Eagle; M; Bro; 34
4952 Wanbli Oye; Eagle Track; F; Niece; 2-4

4953 Tasunke Mato; Bear Horse; M; Father; 39
4954 Tasina Wanbli; Eagle Blanket; F; Wife; 50
4955 Wahacanka Waste; Good Shield; F; Dau; 15
4956 Kawinge; Turns Back; F; Dau; 5

4957 Ista Gonga; Silas Blind; M; Father; 32
4958 Warpe Sna Win; Falling Leaf; F; Wife; 35

4959 Naca; Chief #3; M; Father; 61
4960 Onpan Ite Waste; Good Face Elk; F; Wife; 51
4961 Wakinyan Wanagi; Ghost Thunder; M; Son; 23
4962 Oye Waste; Good Track; F; Dau; 12
4963 Maka Oyate; Earth Nation; F; Dau; 11
4964 Ho Najin; Standing Voice; M; Son; 6

4965 Wicegna Glicu; Comes From Among Them; M; Father; 28

Census Of The Sioux And Cheyenne Indians Of Pine Ridge Agency, South Dakota.
Taken by W. H. Clapp, Captain 16th Infantry, Acting United States Indian Agent,
June 30, 1896. (White Clay District)

Key: Number; Indian Name *(if given)*; English Name; Sex; Relation; Age

4966 Taoyanke Waste Win; Her Red Seat; F; Wife; 25
4967 Wanbli Win; Eagle Woman; F; Dau; 0-9
4968 Wasu Mani; Walking Hail; F; Mother; 52
4969 Icanyan Wica Iyanka; Runs Against Them; M; Son; 12
4970 Sinkakan Isnala; Lone Horse; M; Son; 7
4971 Sunkgleska; Spotted Horse #1; M; Father; 38
4972 Waonjinca; Bobtail; F; Wife; 39
4973 Kangi Wakan; Holy Crow; M; Son; 4-6
4974 Cuwignaka Cola; No Dress; M; Father; 38
4975 Wakan Ota; Plenty Holy; F; Wife; 62
4976 Hinzi Agli; Brings Yellow; F; Dau; 22
4977 Tatanka Cante Sica; Bad Heart Bull; M; Father; 56
4978 Wiciyela Win; Yankton Woman; F; Wife; 48
4979 Wahukeza Wanbli; Eagle Lance; M; Son; 27
4980 Ninwicaya; Makes Alive; F; Dau; 24
4981 Wiyaka Sapa; Black Feather; M; Father; 34
4982 Kokipapi; Afraid Of Him; F; Wife; 23
4983 Ota Wicakte; Kills Plenty; M; Son; 16
4984 Tatanka Cangleska; Ring Buffalo; F; Dau; 12
4985 Canupa Sapa; Black Pipe; M; Son; 10
4986 Pehin Sa; Red Hair; F; Dau; 9

4987 Ptesan Hinapa; White Cow Out; F; Dau; 5
4988 Tasunke Opi; Wounded Horse; M; Son; 1-5
4989 Tasunke Ota Win; Her Plenty Horses; F; 45
4990 Okicize; Battle; M; Father; 31
4991 Ptehincala Ska; White Calf; F; Wife; 24
4992 Timahel Ti; Lives In Lodge; M; Son; 4
4993 Taoyanke Waste Win; Her Good Seat; F; G.Mo; 89
4994 Zintkala; Bird; F; G.Dau; 16
4995 Olepi; Looks For Him; M; Son; 13
4996 Wawoslata; Hair Pipe; M; Father; 47
4997 Cetan Win; Hawk Woman; F; Wife; 49
4998 Wapaha; War Bonnet; F; Dau; 17
4999 Ipiyaka; Belt; M; Father; 37
5000 Tarca Win; Deer Woman; F; Wife; 32
5001 Caje Wanica; No Name; M; Son; 15
5002 Pistola; Sharp Pointed; M; Father; 43
5003 Tipi Win; Woman Lodge; F; Wife; 44
5004 Hoksila; Boy; M; Son; 12
5005 Janjanyela; Clear; F; Dau; 2
5006 Pankeska Luta; Red Shell; M; Father; 55
5007 Pankeska Win; Shell Woman; F; Wife; 51
5008 Tiyopa; Door; F; Dau; 30

Census Of The Sioux And Cheyenne Indians Of Pine Ridge Agency, South Dakota. Taken by W. H. Clapp, Captain 16th Infantry, Acting United States Indian Agent, June 30, 1896. (White Clay District)

Key: Number; Indian Name *(if given)*; English Name; Sex; Relation; Age

5009	Karlok Iyaya; Goes Through; M; Son; 18		5032	Hoksila Ciqa; Loafer Joe; M; Father; 39
5010	Anpetu Hinapa; Day Comes Out; F; Mother; 59		5033	Wanbli Situpi; Eagle Tail; F; Wife; 36
5011	Pehin Sa; Red Hair; F; Dau; 3		5034	Canupa Apa; Hits Pipe; F; Wife; 30
5012	Cetan Akicita; Soldier Hawk; M; Son; 19		5035	Karape Win; Driver; F; Dau; 17
5013	Hanpa Sapa; Black Moccasin; M; Son; 10		5036	Tasina Wakan; Holy Shawl; F; Dau; 13
			5037	Inyan Hinapa; Rock Comes Out; F; Dau; 10
5014	Tatanka Witko; Crazy Bull; M; Father; 58		5038	Ikusan; Mink; M: Son; 7
5015	Tipi Waste; Good Lodge; F; Dau; 18		5039	Maga Tasunke; Duck Horse; M; Son; 4-6
			5040	Okiyakapi; Tells Him; F; Dau; 1-1
5016	Ptehincala Cincala; Young Calf; M; Mother; 53		5041	Agatha Loafer Joe; F; Dau; 15
5017	Hinzi Agli; Brings Yellow; F; Dau; 14		5042	Tatanka Ohitika; Brave Bull; M; Father; 57
			5043	Tipi Rla; Rattler House; F; Wife; 56
5018	Sunk Nakpogi; Red Eagle Horse; M; Father; 60		5044	Teriya Mani; Walks Hard; F; G.Dau; 5
5019	Canku; Road; F; Wife; 59			
5020	Isto; Arm; M; Son; 18		5045	Mato Hanska; Long Bear; M; Son; 27
5021	Tasunke Maza; Iron Horse; M; Son; 15			
5022	Tasunke Opi; Shot His Horse; M; G.Son; 11		5046	Heraka Ska; White Elk; M; Father; 41
5023	Tonweya; Scout; M: G.Son; 4		5047	Ehake Win; Last Woman; F; Wife; 34
5024	Cetan Wanbli; Eagle Hawk #2; M; Father; 63		5048	Tasunke Opi; Wounded Horse; F; Dau; 6
5025	Itonkasan; Weasel; F; Wife; 55		5049	Hanhepi Sni Kte; Kills Before Night; M; Son; 4
5026	Warpe Sa; Red Leaf; F; Dau; 21			
5027	Kangi; Crow; M; Son; 15		5050	Nata Ciqala; Little Head; M; Son; 2
5028	Sa Iciya; Painted Red; M; Son; 11			
5029	Tasunke Sica; Bad Horse; M: Son; 6		5051	Ogle Sa; Red Shirt #2; M; Father; 50
			5052	Winyan Waste; Good Woman; F; Wife; 45
5030	Nakpa Zi; Yellow Ear; F; Mother; 38		5053	Psin Sa; Red Onion; M; Son; 25
5031	Sa Apa; Strikes Red; F; Dau; 4		5054	Sitokapa; Front Fort; M; Son; 12
			5055	Tianatan; Runs For Lodge; M; G.Son; 3

Census Of The Sioux And Cheyenne Indians Of Pine Ridge Agency, South Dakota. Taken by W. H. Clapp, Captain 16th Infantry, Acting United States Indian Agent, June 30, 1896. (White Clay District)

Key: Number; Indian Name *(if given)*; English Name; Sex; Relation; Age

5056	Tasunke Hinzi; Yellow Horse; M; Father; 49	5078	Kiya; Turtle; M; Son; 21
5057	Wikan Iciyakaskapi; Strings Untied; F; Wife; 50	5079	Cinpi; Wants Him; F; Dau; 16
5058	Wosica Kuwa; After Trouble; F; Dau; 28	5080	Tatanka He Luta; Red Horn Bull; M; Father; 44
5059	Ehake; Last; F; Dau; 17	5081	Mazawakan Win; Gun Woman; F; Wife; 44
5060	Naca Ciqala; Elmore Little Chief; M; Father; 24	5082	Tatanka Luta; Red Bull; M; Son; 18
5061	Naca Ciqala; Elva May Little Chief; F; Dau; 0-1	5083	Tasunke Wayankapi; Looks At Her Horses; F; Aunt; 48
5062	Narcan Win; Deaf Woman; F; 47	5084	Wayank Najinpi; Stands Looking At Her; F; Mother; 48
5063	Wicincala; Girl; F; 7	5085	Sunkmanusa; Horse Thief; F; Dau; 21
5064	Ptesan Mani; Walking White Cow; F; Mother; 44	5086	Wataga; Foam; F; Dau; 19
5065	Okihipi Sni; Cant[sic] Get Her; F; Dau; 10	5087	Pejin Zi; Yellow Grass; M; Son; 9
5066	Toka Icu; Takes Enemy; M; Father; 30	5088	Tasunke Opi; Wounded Horse; M; Son; 7
5067	Isna Wicakte; Lone Killer; F; Wife; 29	5089	Ptehincala; Calf; F; Dau; 5
5068	Kokipe Sni Wickte; Kills Without Doubt; F; Dau; 4	5090	Siyotanka Waste; Good Flute; M; Father; 53
5069	Henupin Wanica; No Two Horses #1; M; Father; 52	5091	Winyan Orlate; Woman Under; F; Wife; 42
5070	Naron; Hears It; F; Wife; 49	5092	Zuyaya Wicakte; Hills Warrior; M; Son; 20
5071	Nuge Sa Win; Red Ear Woman; F; Dau; 29	5093	Nata Ska; White Head; M; Son; 11
5072	Marpiya To; Blue Cloud; F; Dau; 17	5094	Wicakaonka; Knock Down; M; Son; 6
5073	Wanbli Cincala; Young Eagle; M; Son; 13	5095	Wanjila Agli; Brings One; F; Dau; 2
5074	Oye Wanbli; Eagle Track; F; Dau; 14	5096	Tasupke Ciqala; Little Horse; M; Son; 22
5075	Sunkhinto Yuha; Blue Horse Owner; M; Father; 53	5097	Cetan Kokipapi; Afraid Of Hawk; M; Bro; 53
5076	Sina On Waapa; Strikes With Blanket; F; Wife; 53	5098	Mato Onjinca; Bob Tail Bear; F; Sister; 73
5077	Winorcala Catka Win; Left Hand Old Woman; M; Son; 28	5099	Sarah Gellispie; F; Mother; 43
		5100	Betty Gellispie; F; Dau; 16
		5101	Jennie Gellispie; F; Dau; 15

Census Of The Sioux And Cheyenne Indians Of Pine Ridge Agency, South Dakota. Taken by W. H. Clapp, Captain 16th Infantry, Acting United States Indian Agent, June 30, 1896. (White Clay District)

Key: Number; Indian Name *(if given)*; English Name; Sex; Relation; Age

5102	George Gellispie; M; Son; 14	5128	Tasunke Gleska Win; Her Spotted Horse; F; Dau; 35
5103	Robert Gellispie; M; Son; 12	5129	Tasunke Waste; Good Horse; F; Dau; 34
5104	Margie Gellispie; F; Dau; 6		
5105	Henry Gellispie; M; Son; 4		
5106	Lizzie Gellispie; F; Dau; 18		
5107	Emma Gellispie; F; Dau; 0-7	5130	Onpan Gleska; Spotted Elk; M; Father; 48
5108	Iku Hanska; Long Chain; F; Mother; 63	5131	Otawicapa; Follower; F; Wife; 38
5109	Cetan; Hawk; M; Son; 34	5132	Gleska Agli; Brings Spotted; F; Dau; 16
5110	Iku Hanska; Long Chain ; M; Son; 24	5133	Toka Oyuspa; Catches Enemy; F; Dau; 12
5111	Onpan Ho Tainyan; Elk Voice Walking; M; Father; 53	5134	Tawapaha; His Bonnet; M; Son; 8
5112	Maka Hukuciyela; Close To Ground; F; Wife; 41	5135	Wapaha Nupa; Two War Bonnet; F; Dau; 0-3
5113	Op Iyanka; Runs With Them; M; Son; 24	5136	Wasicu Wankatuya; High White Man; M; Father; 66
5114	Hoksila; Boy; M; Son; 12		
5115	Ptesan Win; White Cow Woman; F; Dau; 1-6	5137	Ota Kte; Kills plenty[sic]; F; G.Dau; 18
5116	Wanbli Iyanka; Running Eagle; M; Father; 44	5138	Gnuska; Frog #2; M; Father; 56
5117	Roka; Badger; F; Wife; 42	5139	Tasunke Waste Win; Her Good Horse; F; Wife; 57
5118	Wapaha; Bonnet; M; Son; 21		
5119	Ihakap Omani NaKte; Follows And Kills; M; Son; 5	5140	Sunkicu; Takes Horse; M; Son; 28
		5141	Wicakico; Calls; F; Dau; 25
5120	Naca; Chief #2; M; Father; 52	5142	Ta Owicale; Looks For The Dead; M; Son; 21
5121	Pejuta; Medicine; F; Wife; 48		
5122	Itonkasan; Weasel; M; Son; 10	5143	Siyo; Prairie Chicken #1; M; Son; 34
5123	Tasunke Ciqala; Little Horse; M; Son; 8	5144	Karape; Driver; F; Mother; 54
		5145	Nupa Kte; Kills Twice; M; Bro; 19
5124	Wahacanka Ciqala; Little Shield; M; Father; 46		
5125	Waste Mna; Smells Good; F; Wife; 43	5146	Mato Wanbli; Bear Eagle; M; Father; 54
5126	Toka Waste; Good Enemy; F; Dau; 1-6	5147	Capa Luta; Red Beaver; F; Wife; 52
		5148	Wanapa Iyanka; Runs Wounded; M; Son; 22
5127	Wahosi Gli; Brings Word; F; Mother; 64	5149	Niniciya; Saves His Life; M; Son; 14

Census Of The Sioux And Cheyenne Indians Of Pine Ridge Agency, South Dakota. Taken by W. H. Clapp, Captain 16th Infantry, Acting United States Indian Agent, June 30, 1896. (White Clay District)

Key: Number; Indian Name *(if given)*; English Name; Sex; Relation; Age

5150	Heraka Luta; Red Elk; f; Dau; 16	5173	Mato Witko; Crazy Bear; M; Father; 62
5151	Wiyaka Waste; Good Feather; F; Dau; 6	5174	Pehinji Win; Yellow Hair Woman; F; Wife; 57
5152	Wicakte; Kills Them; M; Son; 2	5175	Cangleska Maza; Iron Ring; F; G.Dau; 6
5153	Sungmanitu Sapa; Black Wolf #2; M; Father; 48	5176	Maya; Bank; M; Father; 29
5154	Terilapi; Loves Him; F; Wife; 34	5177	Pehinji; Yellow Hair; F; Wife; 22
5155	Oosica; Hard To Hit; M; Son; 22	5178	Heraka Luzahan; Fast Elk; M; Son; 1-2
5156	Wanbli Yuha; Keeps The Eagle; M; Son; 10	5179	Ptesan Tatanka; White Cow Bull; M; Father; 40
5157	Tanatan; Runs At Lodge; M; Son; 6	5180	Nurcan[sic] Win; Deaf Woman; F; Wife; 49
5158	Tezi Tanka; Big Belly; F; Mother; 74	5181	Ku; Comes; F; Dau; 14
5159	Toka Kokipapi; Afraid Of Enemy; M; Father; 49	5182	Wanbli Nupa; Two Eagle; M; Son; 9
5160	Ista Gi; Brown Eyes; F; Wife; 32	5183	Yokata Hiya; Comes To Front; F; Dau; 3
5161	Sunkgleska Waste; Pretty Spotted Horse; F; Dau; 16	5184	Ohitika; Brave; M; Father; 32
5162	Cetan Wakuwa; Chasing Hawk; M; Son; 12	5185	Sina To; Blue Cloth; F; Wife; 34
5163	Teriya Kte Sni; Kills Without Difficulty; M; Son; 5	5186	Gloglipi; Brings Him Back; M; Nephew; 22
5164	Hanhepi Nakipa; Runs Out At Night; F; Dau; 0-2	5187	Hoksila; Boy; M; Son; 8
5165	Wasicu Mato; White Man Bear; M; Father; 33	5188	Hihan Wanbli; Owl Eagle; M; Son; 6
5166	Ite Ska Win; White Face Woman; F; Wife; 21	5189	Caji Wanica; No Name; F; Mother; 52
5167	Sunkhin Sa; Red Horse; M; Son; 1-3	5190	Siyotanka Sapa; Black Whistler #2; M; Father; 29
5168	Iyuwer Ekte; Kills Across; F; Sister; 19	5191	Ninwicaya; Loves Life; F; Wife; 42
5169	Kangi Wicasa Kte; Kills Crow; M; Nephew; 2	5192	Sunkhinsa Agli; Brings Red Horse; M; Son; 11
5170	Onzihektakiya; Backward; M; Father; 23	5193	Tonweya; Scout; M; Son; 10
5171	Cokab Iyaya; Goes In Center; F; Wife; 18	5194	Toka Ole; Hunts Enemy; M; Father; 40
5172	Tata Wabluska; Dragon Fly; F; Dau; 0-3	5195	Ira; Laugh; F; Wife; 26
		5196	Wicakte; Kills; M; Son; 14

Census Of The Sioux And Cheyenne Indians Of Pine Ridge Agency, South Dakota. Taken by W. H. Clapp, Captain 16th Infantry, Acting United States Indian Agent, June 30, 1896. (White Clay District)

Key: Number; Indian Name *(if given)*; English Name; Sex; Relation; Age

5197	Okiciza Tawa; His Fight; M; Son; 2	5219	Ptewinyela Hinzi; Yellow Cow; F; Dau; 2-8
5198	Sina Topa; Four Blanket; F; Mother; 49	5220	Zintkala Ogle; Bird Shirt; M; Son; 0-4
5199	Nahicipapi; Runs Away From Him; M; Son; 21	5221	Wasu Maza; Iron Hail; F; 66
		5222	Wasin Wanica; No Fat; M; Father; 45
5200	Ptesan Wanbli; White Cow Eagle; M; Father; 53	5223	Siyotanka Sa; Red Flute; F; Wife; 39
5201	Maka Wkan Rpaya; Lays On Ground; F; Wife; 48	5224	Toapi Wicakte; Kills Wounded; M; Son; 17
5202	Kangi Wanjila; One Crow; M; Son; 13	5225	Hektekiya Kte; Kills Enemy Back; M; Son; 13
5203	Tasunke Ota; Plenty Horses; F; Dau; 9	5226	Isnala Ti; Lives Alone; F; Dau; 6
		5227	Rla Win; Rattling; F; Dau; 4
5204	Nurcan; Deaf And Dumb; M; Son; 29	5228	Tasunke Waste; Pretty Horse; F; Dau; 0-10
5205	Oyate Ole; Looks For Nation; F; Mother; 69	5229	Cetan Wanbli; Eagle Hawk #1; M; Father; 54
5206	Psica Iyanka; Running Jumper; M; Bro; 34	5230	Hanska; Leggins Down; F; Wife; 43
5207	Hoksila; Boy; M; Bro; 21	5231	Nasula Witko; Crazy Brain; M; Son; 22
5208	Iglonica; Resist; F; Mother; 47	5232	Nupa Wicaki; Takes Away Twice; F; Dau; 12
5209	Nakpogi Awicagli; Brings Brown Ears; M; Son; 21	5233	Kici Eti; Camp With; M; Son; 4
5210	Pehinji; Yellow Hair; M; Son; 12	5234	Nuwesa; Swimmer; F; Dau; 13
5211	Sunk Mani; Steals Horses; F; Dau; 6	5235	Wicasa Isnala; Lone Man; M; Father; 46
5212	Ogle Maza; Iron Shirt; M: Son; 0-10	5236	Sunk Ska; White Horse; F; Wife; 37
5213	Sungmanitu Mato; Wolf Bear; M G.Son; 0-10	5237	Zuya Wanbli; War Eagle; F; Dau; 22
5214	Sungmanitu Isnala; Lone Wolf; M; Father; 36	5238	Onkcekira Ska; White Magpie; M; Father; 54
5215	Marpiya To; Blue Cloud; F; Wife; 37	5239	Wahuwapa Luta; Red Cob; F; Wife; 47
5216	Sunk Ska; White Horse; F; Dau; 16	5240	Sagye Maza; Iron Cane; F; Dau; 24
5217	Toka Kte; Kills Enemy; F; Dau; 10	5241	Nakipa; Runs Away; M; Son; 15
5218	Sally; F; Dau; 6		

Census Of The Sioux And Cheyenne Indians Of Pine Ridge Agency, South Dakota. Taken by W. H. Clapp, Captain 16th Infantry, Acting United States Indian Agent, June 30, 1896. (White Clay District)

Key: Number; Indian Name *(if given)*; English Name; Sex; Relation; Age

5242	Olepi; Looks For Him; F; Dau; 12		5263	Cetan Iyotaka; Sitting Hawk; M; Father; 43
5243	Wayata; Chewing; M; Son; 10		5264	Wanbli Yuha; Owns Eagle; F; Wife; 33
5244	Winyan Tanka; Big Woman; F; 78		5265	Kiciza; Fight; F; Dau; 11
			5266	Cetan Iyoyaka[sic]; Levi Sitting Hawk; M; Son; 8
5245	Wase Sa; Red Paint; M; Father; 38		5267	Hoksila; Boy; M; Son; 5
5246	Mato Wicoti; Bear Village; F; Wife; 34		5268	Mato Tawa Ku; Her Bear Comes; F; Dau; 0-4
5247	Olepi; Looks For Him; M; Son; 10		5269	Mato Poge; Frank Bear Nose; M; Father; 40
5248	Iogna Opi; Shot In The Mouth; M; Son; 5		5270	Wakan Hiyaga; Goes Holy; F; Wife; 41
5249	Zuya Wicakte; Kills Warrior; F; Dau; 3-6		5271	Matoha Sina; John Bear Robe; M; Bro; 17
			5272	Kutepi; Shoots Him; F; Dau; 7
5250	Kagla Opi; Shot Close; M; Father; 38		5273	Hoksila; Boy; M; Bro; 33
5251	Sunkwakaw Win; Horse Woman; F; Wife; 36		5274	Kuwa; Runs After; M; Father; 34
			5275	Sa Apa; Strikes Red; F; Wife; 33
5252	Lizzie Provost; F; Dau; 22		5276	Hinzi Gleska; Yellow Spotted; F; Dau; 2-5
5253	Suyotanka Sapa; Black Whistler #1; M; Husb; 38		5277	Hurmi; Crooked Leg; F; Mother; 62
5254	Marpiya Sapa; Black Cloud; F; Wife; 33		5278	Okicize Tawa; His Fight; M; Nephew; 12
			5279	Waniyetu Opi; Wounded In Winter; M; Son; 0-10
5255	Heraka Wakita; Looking Elk; M; Husb; 43			
5256	Caku[sic]; Road; F; Wife; 33		5280	Zintkala Ciqala; Little Bird; M; Father; 47
5257	Toka Kte; Kills Enemy; F; Dau; 6		5281	Kuwa; Chase; F; Wife; 38
			5282	Kohab Wosica; Makes Trouble Ahead; M; Son; 13
5258	Okicize Tawa; His Fight; M; Husb; 65		5283	Tasunke; Her Horse; F; Dau; 10
5259	Winyan Hunkesni; Slow Woman; F; Wife; 65		5284	Ite Waste; Good Face; F; Dau; 6
			5285	Tainyan Ku; Comes In Sight; F; Dau; 2
5260	Napsukage Topa; Four Finger; M; Father; 60		5286	Mato Ska Sake; White Bear Claw; M; Father; 42
5261	Wanbli; Eagle; F; Wife; 58			
5262	Hinrota Win; Roan Woman; F; Dau; 23		5287	Tipi Wakan; Holy Lodge; F; Wife; 40

Census Of The Sioux And Cheyenne Indians Of Pine Ridge Agency, South Dakota. Taken by W. H. Clapp, Captain 16th Infantry, Acting United States Indian Agent, June 30, 1896. (White Clay District)

Key: Number; Indian Name *(if given)*; English Name; Sex; Relation; Age

5288 Hutkan; Root; M; Son; 14
5289 Toka Oyuspa; Catches Enemy; M; Son; 12
5290 Mato Wamniomni; Whirlwind Bear; M; Father; 28
5291 Tacangliska Zi Win; Her Yellow Ring; F; Wife; 18
5292 Kicizapi; Fights Each Other; M; Son; 0-4
5293 Hektakiya Ekte; Kills Back; F; Niece; 2

5294 Tahu Wanica; No Neck; M; Father; 60
5295 Kute; Shot At; M; Son; 22

5296 Sunka Ciqala; Little Dog; M; Husb; 44
5297 Mato Winyan; Bear Woman; F; Wife; 64

5298 Mato Wicakiza; Fights Bear; M; Father; 31
5299 Nup Hiyohipi; Two Comes After Her; F; Wife; 28
5300 Waksica Luta; Red Dirt; F; Dau; 9
5301 Tionajinyapi; Surrounded In Lodge; M; Son; 7
5302 Hoksila Wanbli; Eagle Boy; M; Son; 5

5203[sic] Siyo; Prairie Chicken #1; F; Mother; 46
5304 Maggie; F; Dau; 18
5305 Stand; F; Dau; 16
5306 Watage Luta; Red Foam; F; G?Dau[sic]; 5
5307 Wecegna; Among; F; Dau; 23

5308 Ho Tanka; Loud Voice; F; Mother; 34
5309 Sungmanitu Nakpa; Wolf Ears; M; Son; 17

5310 Anpo Wicakte; Kills In Morning; F; Dau; 14
5311 Tehan Gli Sni; Comes In Late; F; Dau; 12
5312 Susuni Kaunka; Knock Down Shoshone; M; Son; 10
5313 Sihasapa Wicakte; Kills Black Feet; M; Son; 8

5314 Paha Nupa; Two Hills; M; Son; 0-11

5315 Pte Waste; Pretty Cow; F; Mother; 43
5316 Tasunke Opi; Shot His Horse; M; Son; 9
5317 Worlokapi Sni; Bullet Proof; M; Son; 5
5318 Sunkgliska Ota; Plenty Spotted Horse; F; Dau; 2

5319 Wasicu Peta; Fire White Man; M; 46

5320 Sunk Nakpo Gli; Brown Eared Horse; M; Uncle 23
5321 Marpiya Waste; Good Cloud; F; Mother; 71
5322 Onpan Hinapa; Elk Comes Out; F; Sister; 26
5323 Hinto Agli; Brings Blue; F; Niece; 15
5324 Pilayapi; Thankful; F; Niece; 9
5325 Ninglicu; Comes Alive; F; Dau; 3-6

5326 Warpe Koyaka; Wears Leaf; F; 78

5327 Hinhan Gi; Brown Owl; M; 61

5328 Lab; Lab; M; 53

5329 Mary Lamont; F; Sister; 14
5330 George Lamont; M; Bro; 12
5331 Frank Lamont; M; Bro; 10

Census Of The Sioux And Cheyenne Indians Of Pine Ridge Agency, South Dakota. Taken by W. H. Clapp, Captain 16th Infantry, Acting United States Indian Agent, June 30, 1896. (White Clay District)

Key: Number; Indian Name *(if given)*; English Name; Sex; Relation; Age

5332	Maggie Lamont; F; Sister; 8	5354	Olepi; Looks For Him; M; Son; 15
5333	Tasunke Wanbli; Eagle Horse; M; Husb; 55	5355	Zintkala; Bird; M; Son; 9
5334	Zintkala Zi; Yellow Bird; F; Wife; 74	5356	Nupa Icaga; Lives Twice; F; Dau; 4
		5357	Heraka Gi; Yellow Elk; F; Dau; 0-11
5335	Mato Hinapa; Bear Comes Out; M; Husb; 54	5358	Sunka Ohitika; Brave Dog; M; Husb; 54
5336	Winyan Ocin Sica; Mean Woman; F; Wife; 42	5359	Maka; Dirt; F; Wife; 57
5337	Sunka Wankatuya; High Dog; M; 41	5360	Winkte Onaso; H. Pacer; M; Husb; 53
		5361	Nisehu; Hip; F; Wife; 60
5338	Putinhin Sapa; Black Beard; M; Father; 79	5362	Winyan Hunkesni; Slow Woman; F; 54
5339	Gnuska Ho Waste; Good Voice Frog; F; Wife; 74		
5340	Oceya Wankala; Easy To Cry; F; Dau; 33	5363	Psica Wakuwa; Chasing Jumper; M; Father; 28
5341	Mato Slasla; Hairless Bear; M; G.Son; 3	5364	Ohitika Win; Brave Woman; F; Wife; 23
5342	Wanbli; Eagle; F; G.Dau; 8	5365	Toka Apapi; Struck By Enemy; M; Son; 6
5343	Winyan Cepa; Fat Woman; F; G.Dau; 7		
5344	Canhan Pi; Sugar; M; G.Son; 2	5366	Sinte Ska; White Tail; M; Husb; 69
5345	Wanju Stola; Slick Quiver; M; Husb; 24	5367	Oterika; Hard Times; F; Wife; 53
5346	Sina Karwoka; Flying Blanket; F; Wife; 27	5368	Inyan Sica; Bad Rock; M; G.Son; 19
5347	Terila; Dearly; M; Father; 26	5369	Wicarpi Ota; Plenty Stars; M; Father; 64
5348	Hotain; Noise; F; Wife; 29		
5349	Nica Ole; Looks For None; F; Dau; 7	5370	Anpetu Hinapa; Day Comes Out; F; Wife; 54
5350	Ite Blagahan; Spread Face; M; Son; 5-10	5371	Tasunke Wakita; Looking Horse; M; Son; 26
5351	Tikanyela Iyanka; Runs Close To Lodge; M; Son; 1-3	5372	Wakinyan Tasina; Thunder Robe; M; Son; 18
		5373	Ptesan Iyotaka; Sitting White Cow; F; G.Dau; 3
5352	Cante Ohitika; Brave Heart; M; Father; 41		
5353	Canupa Waste Icu; Gets Good Pipe; F; Wife; 42	5374	Ranhila; Slowly; M; Father; 26
		5375	Hihan; Owl; F; Wife; 24

Census Of The Sioux And Cheyenne Indians Of Pine Ridge Agency, South Dakota. Taken by W. H. Clapp, Captain 16th Infantry, Acting United States Indian Agent, June 30, 1896. (White Clay District)

Key: Number; Indian Name *(if given)*; English Name; Sex; Relation; Age

5376	Wawiyokipiya; Please; F; Dau; 7	5398	Cehupa Maza; Iron Jaw; F; 81
5377	Ska Agli; Brings White; M; Son; 5	5399	Julia Swallow; F; Mother; 48
5378	Gli Wajin; Comes And Stands; F; Dau; 3	5400	Oliver Swallow; M; Son; 26
		5401	Amelia Swallow; F; Dau; 23
		5402	Ida Swallow; F; Dau; 16
5379	Canku Sapa; Black Road; M; Father; 59	5403	Louise Swallow; F; Dau; 13
		5404	Willie Swallow; M; Son; 10
5380	Sican Gu Win; Brule Woman; F; Wife; 54	5405	Antoine Swallow; M; Son; 8
		5406	May Swallow; F; Dau; 5
5381	Miwakan Wakan; Holy Sword; M; Son; 23	5407	Benjamine[sic] Swallow; M; Son; 2
		5408	Lucy Swallow; F; Dau; 0-3
5382	Sunka Heton; Dog Horn; M; Father; 59	5409	Akicita Ciqala; Little Soldier; M; Father; 29
5383	Rlogeca; Hollow; F; Wife; 61	5410	Canowicakte; Kills In Timber; F; Wife; 26
5384	Cokanyan; Center; F; G.Dau; 24		
		5411	Olepi; Looks For Her; F; Dau; 6
5385	Tanka Mani Iyaya; Walks Out; M; Father; 35	5412	Tasunke Wakita; Looking Horse; F; Dau; 3
5386	Pejuta Win; Medicine Woman; F; Wife; 43	5413	Tonweya Sa; Red Scout; M; Son; 0-4
5387	Rlokiyapi; Fixes And Growls; F; Dau; 10	5414	Tatanka Ciqala; Little Bull #4; M; Husb; 52
5388	Ehake Hiyaya Kute; Shoots At Last; M; Son; 6	5415	Tasina Maza; Walking Shawl; F; Wife; 65
5389	Mato Lowan; Singing Bear; M; Father; 66	5416	Mato Hunkesni; Slow Bear; M; Husb; 50
5390	Naca Win; King Woman; F; Wife; 61	5417	Sunk Ska Ota; Plenty White Horses; F; Wife; 49
5391	Gliyunka; Comes And Lays; M; Son; 24	5418	Kiciza; Frank Fight; M; Nephew; 26
5392	Mato Isto Napin; Bear Own Necklace; M; Father; 48	5419	Aiyapi; Talks About; F; Dau; 23
		5420	Mato Hunkesni; John Slow Bear; M; Son; 17
5393	Ptewinyela Ota; Plenty Cow; F; Wife; 49	5421	Iyarpaya; Grabs Him; M: Son; 16
5394	Wanbli Sun; Eagle Feather; F; Dau; 16	5422	Kokipe Sni; Not Afraid; M; Son; 8
5395	Marpiya Hoksila; Cloud Boy; M; Son; 9	5423	Gliyunka; Comes And Lays; F; Dau; 1-7
5396	Ptesan Wokiyaka; Talks To White Cow; F; Dau; 6		
5397	Wahorpi Luta; Red Nest; F; M. in L.; 87	5424	Wiyaka Ska; White Feather; M; Father; 30

Census Of The Sioux And Cheyenne Indians Of Pine Ridge Agency, South Dakota. Taken by W. H. Clapp, Captain 16th Infantry, Acting United States Indian Agent, June 30, 1896. (White Clay District)

Key: Number; Indian Name *(if given)*; English Name; Sex; Relation; Age

5425	Maka Wase; Dirt Paint; F; Wife; 30	5447	Kangi Winyan; Crow Woman; F; 49
5426	Ninglicu; Comes Alive; M; Son; 4	5448	Heraka Iyotaka; Sitting Elk; M; Husb; 54
5427	Wicakupi; Gives Him Up; M; Son; 1-1	5449	Nurcan Win; Deaf Woman; F; Wife 42
5428	Cuwi Bu; Sounding Tide; M; Father; 32	5450	Mastincala; Rabbit; M; Son; 26
5429	Maka San; White Clay; F; Wife; 26	5451	Apapi; Strikes Him; M; Son; 3
5430	Sunk Icu; Takes The Horses; F; Niece; 18	5452	Takuni; Nothing; F; Mother; 55
		5453	Kutepi; Shot At Him; F; Sister; 24
5431	Marpiya Tokaheya; First Cloud; M; Son; 3	5454	Rlaya Wakuwa; Rattling Chase; M; Father; 46
5432	Cokab Iyaya; Goes In Center; F; Sister; 23	5455	Nisehu; Hip; F; Wife; 42
5433	Tokeya Kte; Kills First; F; Sister; 16	5456	Reyap Icu; Takes Away; M; Son; 17
5434	Wasu Kiyan; Flying Hail; F; G.Mo; 63	5457	Tasunke Sica Win; Her Bad Horse; F; Dau; 2
		5458	Tatanka Ciqala; Little Bull #2; M; Husb; 49
5435	Wakinyan Sinte; Thunder Tail; M; Father; 51	5459	Winyan Ocin Sica; Mean Woman; F; Wife; 63
5436	Tasunke Nupa; Two Horse; F; Wife; 41	5460	Heraka; Elk; F; G.Dau; 9
5437	Tikanyela; Runs Close To Lodge; F; Dau; 19	5461	Wasu Mato; Hail Bear; M; Father; 53
5438	Wicakte; Kills; F; Dau; 8		
5439	Rante Tipi; Cedar Lodge; F; Dau; 4	5462	Pejuta Waste; Good Medicine; F; Wife; 54
5440	Wahukeza Waste; Good Lance; M; Son; 0-2	5463	We Eyalase Ku; Comes Bloody; M; Son; 13
		5464	Sunk Mani; Steals Horses; M; Son; 10
5441	Sapa Wicasa; Black Man; M; Father; 33		
5442	Winyan Luta; Red Woman; F; Wife; 39	5465	Tarca Sapa; Black Deer; M; Father; 46
5443	Ocinsica; Cross; M; Son; 9	5466	Wowapa; Flag; F; Wife; 53
5444	Kahinrpeya; Runs Over; M; Son; 7	5467	Heraka Wakinyan; Thunder Elk; M; Son; 23
		5468	Maste; Sunshine; M; Son; 27
5445	Slohan; Crawls; M; Bro; 54	5469	Wicarpi Wanjila; One Star; M; B. in L.; 24
5446	Inyan Janjanyela; Clear Rock; F; Sister; 64		

Census Of The Sioux And Cheyenne Indians Of Pine Ridge Agency, South Dakota. Taken by W. H. Clapp, Captain 16th Infantry, Acting United States Indian Agent, June 30, 1896. (White Clay District)

Key: Number; Indian Name *(if given)*; English Name; Sex; Relation; Age

5470	Si Maza; Iron Foot; F; Mother; 54	5494	Wicakicagluza; Takes Away From Them; F; Mother; 59
5471	Wamniomni Koyake; Wears Whirlwind; F; 63	5495	Sunk Iyanajinca; Runs Away With Horses; M; Son; 22
5472	Pankeska Ota; Plenty Shell; F; Mother; 42	5496	Ciqala Wicakte; Little Killer; M; Father; 48
5473	Makamani Toka Kte; Kills Enemy Afoot; M; Son; 22	5497	Tarca Sapa; Black Deer; F; Wife; 48
5474	Aku; Brings; M; Son; 11	5498	Nuwan Kte; Kills Swimming; M; Son; 17
5475	Wopotapi; Shot To Pieces; M; Son; 9	5499	Nupa Kte; Kills Twice; M; Son; 4
5476	Tiyopa; Door; M; Son; 6	5500	Gliyunka; Comes And Lays; F; Dau; 20
5477	Tatanka Ptecela; Thomas Short Bull; M; Son; 0-4		
		5501	Tasunke Wankatuya; High Horse #1; M; Husb; 74
5478	Tatanka Ptecela; Short Bull #2; M; Father; 49	5502	Winyan Zi; Yellow Woman; F; Wife; 66
5479	Hinapa; Comes Out; F; Wife; 38		
5480	Wan On Opi; Shoots With Arrow; M; Son; 14	5503	Tasunke Wankatuya; High Horse #2; M; Bro; 34
5481	Mato Sake; Bear Claw; M; Son; 9	5504	Tasina; Her Blanket; F; Mother; 56
5482	Ipahin; Pillow; M; Son; 6		
5483	Oyate Sica; Bad Nation; F; Dau; 2	5505	Anpetu Kiyan; Flying Day; F; Dau; 3
5484	Hanpiska; Moccasin Top; M; Father; 45	5506	Lakota; Lakota; M; Father; 56
5485	Witko; Foolish; F; Wife; 44	5507	Alexander; M; Son; 16
5486	Hanpiska; Emma Moccasin Top; F; Dau; 13	5508	Ciqala Wicakiza; Fights Little; M; Father; 32
5487	Isna Wakuwa; Chase Alone; M; Son; 9	5509	Tinga; Grunts; F; Wife; 31
5488	Can Hu; Wooden Leg; M; Son; 3	5510	Wankal Ho; Voice Above; M; Son; 4
5489	Wahinkpe Wicaku; Gives Arrow; F; Dau; 2-6	5511	Mazawakan; Gun; M; Son; 1-5
5490	Anokasan Hoksila; Bald Eagle Boy; M; Son; 0-4	5512	Thomas Tyon; M: Father; 41
		5513	Elizabeth Tyon; F; Wife; 32
		5514	Adelia Tyon; F; Dau; 15
5491	Tasunke Opi; Wounded Horse; M; Father; 26	5515	Oliver Tyon; M; Son; 13
		5516	Susie Tyon; F; Dau; 7
5492	Wowapi; Flag; F; Wife; 21	5517	Eliza Tyon; F; Dau; 3-6
5493	Oyate Woilagyapi; Works For People; F; Dau; 1-4	5518	Adelia Lowe; F; Sister; 24

Census Of The Sioux And Cheyenne Indians Of Pine Ridge Agency, South Dakota.
Taken by W. H. Clapp, Captain 16th Infantry, Acting United States Indian Agent,
June 30, 1896. (White Clay District)

Key: Number; Indian Name *(if given)*; English Name; Sex; Relation; Age

5519 Sungmanitu Hanska; Dennis Long Wolf; M; 37
5520 Tatanka Maza; Iron Bull; M; Father; 40
5521 Oyate Win; Nation Woman; F; Wife; 39
5522 Icanyan; Against; M; Son; 19
5523 Kaunka; Knocks Down; M; Son; 19
5524 Wasicu Ho; White Man Voice; F; Dau; 7
5525 Tatanka Maza; Cora Iron Bull; F; Dau; 0-10

5526 Mato Gi; Yellow Bear; M; Father; 49
5527 Mato Wicarca; Old Bear; F; Wife; 55

5528 Maka Iktomi; Ground Spider; M; Husb; 28
5529 Nape Wakan; Holy Hand; F; Wife; 20

5530 Tasunke Waste; Good Horse; M; Father; 46
5531 Maka Si; Skunk Foot; M; Son; 9

5532 Mato Iyanka; Running Bear; M; Father; 32
5533 Aku; Brings; F; Wife; 32
5534 Anpo Hute; Shoots In Morning; M; Son; 0-2

5535 Sungmanitu Ciqala; Little Wolf; M; 52

5536 Rupahu Maza; Iron Wing; M; Father; 35
5537 Iyokipiyapi; Pleased; F; Wife; 27
5538 Adelia; F; Dau; 0-11

5539 Hakikta; Looks Back; F; 52

5540 Hokisila[sic] Ciqala; Little Boy; M; Father; 31
5541 Nawizi Win; Jealous Woman; F; Wife; 44

5542 Siunk[sic] Sapa; Black Horse; M; Father; 41
5543 Iyokipiyapi; Pleased; F; Wife; 43
5544 Sunk Sapa; William Black Horse; M; Son; 13
5545 Hubert; M; Son; 9
5546 Tibloku; Plenty Brother; F; Sister; 16

5547 Tasunke Ota; Owns Many Horses; M; Father; 26
5548 Pehan; Crane; F; Wife; 20
5549 Hattie; F; Dau; 0-10

5550 Nellie Hudspeth; F; Mother; 35
5551 Zona Hudspeth; F; Dau; 17
5552 Edna Hudspeth; F; Dau; 16
5553 Oliver Hudspeth; M; Son; 8
5554 William Hudspeth; M; Son; 10
5555 Myrtle Hudspeth; F; Dau; 8

5556 Titan Opi; Shot From House; M; Father; 27
5557 Canupa Waste; Good Pipe; F; Wife; 23
5558 Zintka To; Blue Bird; M; Son; 7

5559 Tasunke Luzahan; William Fast Horse; M; Husb; 22
5560 Tasunke Luzahan; Annie Fast Horse; F; Wife; 21

Census of the Sioux And Cheyenne Indians
Of Pine Ridge Agency, South Dakota.
June 30, 1896

Pass Creek District

Census Of The Sioux And Cheyenne Indians Of Pine Ridge Agency, South Dakota. Taken by W. H. Clapp, Captain 16th Infantry, Acting United States Indian Agent, June 30, 1896. (Pass Creek District)

Key: Number; Indian Name *(if given)*; English Name; Sex; Relation; Age

5561	Jennie Brown; F; 23	5598	Kahunpi; Omega Cut; F; Dau; 4
		5599	Kanhumpi[sic]; Lucinda Cut; F; Dau; 1-2
5562	Pute; Lip; M; Father; 51		
5563	Wicarpi; Star; F; Wife; 46		
5564	Pute; George Lip; M; Son; 20	5600	Mato Gleska; Spotted Bear; M: 37
5565	Pute; Ida Lip; F; Dau; 14		
5566	Pute; Bulah Lip; F; Dau; 12	5601	Wosla Iyotaka; Sitting Up; M; Father; 38
5567	Pute; Kate Lip; F; Dau; 10		
5568	Pute; Oliver Lip; M; Son; 5		
5569	Pute; Hat Lip; M; Son; 2-10	5602	Psica Win; Jumping Woman; F; Wife; 47
5570	Pute; Richard Lip; M; Father; 24	5603	Wosla Iyotaka; Homer Sitting Up; M; Son; 18
5571	Pute; Edith Lip; F; Wife; 25		
5572	Pute; John Lip; M; Son; 1-10	5604	Wosla Iyotaka; Cora Sitting Up; F; Dau; 7
5573	Pute; Susie Lip; F; Dau; 0-2		
		5605	Watape Kte; Kills Charger; M; Son; 1-3
5574	Ceya; Paul Crier; M; Father; 32		
5575	Iktomi; Spider; F; Wife; 35		
5576	Ceya; Louis Crier; M; Son; 11	5606	Winyan Wakan; Holy Woman; F; Dau; 38
5577	Ceya; Peter Crier; M; Son; 8		
5578	Ceya; Cleveland Crier; M; Son; 3-3	5607	Wasicu Winyan; White Woman; F; Mother; 67
5579	Ceya; John Crier; M; Son; 1		
		5608	Tasunke Witko; Crazy Horse; M; Father; 44
5580	Cahu Maza; Iron Road; F; 64		
		5609	Tasunke Witko; Ellen Crazy Horse; F; Wife; 44
5581	Gi; Brown; M; Father; 47		
5582	Onkcekira; Magpie; F; Wife; 47	5610	Tasunke Witko; Ella Crazy Horse; F; Dau; 14
5583	Gi; David Brown; M; Son; 17		
5584	Gi; Lizzie Brown; F; Dau; 19	5611	Tasunke Witko; Richard Crazy Horse; M; Son; 1-10
5585	Gi; Susie Brown; F; Dau; 13		
5586	Gi; Benjamin Brown; M; Son; 11		
		5612	Ptesan Wakpa; White Cow River; M; Father; 56
5587	Kahunpi; Cut; F; Father; 45		
5588	Tarcaha Wikan; Buckskin String; F; Wife #1; 48	5613	Wipi Sni; Never Full; F; Wife; 49
5589	Hu Ranran; Scabby Leg; F; Wife #2; 38	5614	Cetan Wakinyan; Thunder Hawk; M; Son; 26
5590	Kahunpi; Mollie Cut; F; Dau; 16	5615	Ptesan Wakpa; Nellie White Cow River; F; Dau; 6
5591	Kahunpi; Samuel Cut; M; Son; 15		
5592	Kahunpi; Ellis Cut; M: Son; 14		
5593	Kahunpi; Ernest Cut; M; Son; 13	5616	Heraka Nupa; Two Elk; M; Father; 46
5594	Kahunpi; Arthur Cut; M; Son; 10		
5595	Kahunpi; Emily Cut; F; Dau; 9	5617	Toka Kte; Kills Enemy; F; Wife; 44
5596	Kahunpi; Chester Cut; M; Son; 9		
5597	Kahunpi; Raymond Cut; M; Son; 7		

Census Of The Sioux And Cheyenne Indians Of Pine Ridge Agency, South Dakota. Taken by W. H. Clapp, Captain 16th Infantry, Acting United States Indian Agent, June 30, 1896. (Pass Creek District)

Key: Number; Indian Name *(if given)*; English Name; Sex; Relation; Age

5618 Heraka Nupa; Nellie Two Elk; F; Dau; 19
5619 Heraka Nupa; James Two Elk; M; Son; 15
5620 Heraka Nupa; Gerald Two Elk; M; Son; 11
5621 Heraka Nupa; Bessie Two Elk; F; Dau; 6

5622 Heraka Nupa; Robert Two Elk; M; Father; 21
5623 Heraka Nupa; Nettie Two Elk; F; Wife; 21
5624 Heraka Nupa; Thomas Two Elk; M; Son; 1-6

5625 Woptura; Geoffrey Chips; M; Father; 32
5626 Ayutapi; Looks At Her; F; Wife #1; 31
5627 Onziheketa Ku; Comes Back Hard; F; Wife #2; 25
5628 Woptura; Andrew Chips; M; Son; 7
5629 Woptura; Alice Chips; F; Dau; 8
5630 Woptura; Gerome Chips; M; Son; 4
5631 Woptura; Lucy Chips; F; Dau; 1-6
5632 Woptura; Philip Chips; M; Son; 0-6

5633 Cangleska Luta; Red Hoop; M; Father; 51
5634 Poge Nupa; Two Nostrils; F; Wife; 47
5635 Cangleska Luta; Grace Red Hoop; F; Dau; 13
5636 Cangleska Luta; Dora Red Hoop; F; Dau; 11
5637 Cangleska Luta; Ophelia Red Hoop; F; Dau; 6
5638 Ehake Gli; Comes Last; M; Son; 2-1
5639 Cangleska Luta; Fannie Red Hoop; F; Dau; 1-1

5640 Mila Topa; Four Knives; M; Bro; 44

5641 Ciqala Wicakte; Little Killer[sic]; M; Husb; 24
5642 Mato Ota; Plenty Bear; F; Mother; 74
5643 Sunk Watogla; Wild Horse; F; Wife; 21

5644 Sungila; Fox; M; Husb; 31
5645 Anpetu Tokaheya; First Day; F; Wife; 24
5646 Akatanhan Iglonica; Stays On Top; F; Niece; 4-6

5647 Cekpa; Fred Twin; M; Son; 28
5648 Taanpetu To; Her Blue Day; F; Mother; 54
5649 Wanbli Ska; Charles White Eagle; M; Bro; 23
5650 Cekpa; Reuben Twin; M; Bro; 20

5651 Sunka Oye Luta; Red Dog Track; M; Father; 40
5652 Nakpo Gi; Brown Ears; F; Wife; 40
5653 Gleska Agli; Hattie Brings Spotted; F; Dau; 17

5654 Wanju; Quiver; M; Father; 43
5655 Cetan Rla; Rattling Hawk; F; Wife; 40
5656 Hinrota; Roan; F; Dau; 10
5657 Pehin Gi; Yellow Hair; M; Son; 7
5658 Pehin Gi[sic]; James Quiver; M; Son; 1

5659 Tawakin; His Package; M; Father; 36
5660 Tawacin Waste; Good Natured; F; Wife; 30
5661 Tawakin; Philip His Package; M; Nephew; 22

Census Of The Sioux And Cheyenne Indians Of Pine Ridge Agency, South Dakota. Taken by W. H. Clapp, Captain 16th Infantry, Acting United States Indian Agent, June 30, 1896. (Pass Creek District)

Key: Number; Indian Name *(if given)*; English Name; Sex; Relation; Age

5662 Sagye; Cane; M; Nephew; 8
5663 Hoksila Cepa; Fat Boy; M; Son; 2-9
5664 James; M; Son; 0-3

5665 Maku; Lucy Breast; F; Dau; 34
5666 Nakiwizi; Jealous At; F; Mother; 54
5667 Maku; John Breast; M; Bro; 22
5668 Maku; William Breast; M; Bro; 20
5669 Maku; Silas Breast; M; Bro; 14

5670 Taopi; Wounded; F; Mother; 27
5671 Marpiya Koyaka; Wears The Cloud; F; Dau; 7
5672 Mato Sinte; Bear Tail; M; Son; 5
5673 Wamniomni; Lucy Whirlwind; F; Dau; 1-1

5674 Wanju; Harry Quiver; M; Father; 26
5675 Agnes; F; Wife; 21
5676 Winyah Ropa; Pretty Woman; F; Dau; 2-6

5677 Mato Cincala; Young Bear; M; Son; 33
5678 Tasunke Hinsa; Her Red Horse; F; Mother; 70

5679 Kangi Wakuwa; Jacob Charging Crow; M; Father; 50
5680 Oye Maza; Iron Track; F; Wife; 34
5681 Wagleksun Luta; Red Turkey; F; Sister; 52
5682 Kangi Wakuwa; Anna Red Turkey; F; Dau; 15
5683 Tokeya Kte; Wallace Kills First; M; Son; 12
5684 Tasina; Hattie Her Blanket; F; Dau; 10
5685 Waniyetu Wicakte; Kills In Winter; M; Son; 7

5686 Kangi Wakuwa; Cecilia Charging Crow; F; Dau; 4
5687 Jack Lapoint; M; Father; 46
5688 Jennie Lapoint; F; Wife; 39
5689 Annie Lapoint; F; Dau; 18
5690 Joseph Lapoint; M; Son; 17
5691 Eva Lapoint; F; Dau; 12
5692 Oliver Lapoint; M; Son; 9
5693 James Lapoint; M; Son; 4-3
5694 Jacob Lapoint; M; Father; 21
5695 Gertie Lapoint; F; Wife; 22
5696 Anna Lapoint; F; Dau; 1-8

5697 Mahel Lapoint; F; Aunt; 68
5698 Miyogli; Joseph Whetstone; M; Nephew; 14
5699 Miyogli; William Whetstone; M; Nephew; 5

5700 Mato Najin; Henry Standing Bear; M; Father; 27
5701 Mato Najin; Elizabeth Standing Bear; F; Wife; 33
5702 Mato Najin; Thomas Flood; M; Nephew; 11
5703 Mato Najin; Henry Standing Bear, Jr; M; Son; 2-10

5704 Wakinyan Watakpe; Charging Thunder; M; Husb; 53
5705 Wakinyan Watakpe; Louise C. Thunder; F; Wife; 36
5706 Kiyan Win; Sarah Flying Woman; F; Niece; 6

5707 Antoine Boyer; M; Husb; 44
5708 Dollie Boyer; F; Wife; 31
5709 Sungmanitu Luzahan; Thomas Fast Wolf; M; S.Son; 15
5710 Eva Randall; F; S.Dau; 11
5711 James Randall; M; S.Son; 9
5712 Patrick Boyer; M; Son; 0-7

141

Census Of The Sioux And Cheyenne Indians Of Pine Ridge Agency, South Dakota. Taken by W. H. Clapp, Captain 16th Infantry, Acting United States Indian Agent, June 30, 1896. (Pass Creek District)

Key: Number; Indian Name *(if given)*; English Name; Sex; Relation; Age

5713	Antoine Randall; M; Father; 31		5748	Louis Peck; M; Son; 16
5714	Jessie Randall; F; Wife; 32		5749	Jessie Peck; F; Dau; 13
5715	Annie Randall; F; Dau; 4-6		5750	Katie Peck; F; Dau; 11
5716	Antoine Randall; M; Son; 1-9		5751	Dora Peck; F; Dau; 9
			5752	Nellie Peck; F; Dau; 6
5717	Mastinska; White Rabbit; M; Husb; 42		5753	Clara Peck; F; Dau; 3-10
			5754	Mary Peck; F; Dau; 1-6
5718	Mastinska; Nellie White Rabbit; F; Wife; 32		5755	Sallie Randall; F; Mother; 35
5719	Cega Luta; Robert Red Kettle; M; Bro in L.; 19		5756	Maggie Randall; F; Dau; 17
			5757	Joseph Randall; M; Son; 13
5720	Cega Luta; Rosa Red Kettle; F; Sister L[sic]; 17		5758	Dollie Randall; F; Dau; 9
			5759	John Randall; M; Son; 5
5721	Miyogli; Thomas Whetstone; M; Cousin; 11		5760	William Randall; M; Son; 3-7
5722	Cega Luta; Alice Red Kettle; F; S. in L.; 28		5761	Sungmanitu Luzahan; Fast Wolf; M; Father; 40
			5762	Sungmanitu Luzahan; Mollie Fast Wolf; F; Wife; 35
5723	Seth Gerry; M; Father; 44			
5724	John Gerry; M; Bro; 22		5763	Sungmanitu Luzahan; Philip Fast Wolf; M; Son; 18
5725	Cynthia Gerry; F; Dau; 12			
5726	Elbridge Gerry; M; Son; 3		5764	Sungmanitu Luzahan; Millie Fast Wolf; F; Dau; 10
5727	Millicent Dubray; F; Mother; 44		5765	Sungmanitu Luzahan; Josephine F. Wolf; F; Dau; 12
5728	William Gerry; M; Nephew; 30			
5729	Jeff Gerry; M; Nephew; 35		5766	Sungmanitu Luzahan; Annie Fast Wolf; F; Dau; 2-10
5730	Benjamin Gerry; M; Nephew; 24			
5731	David Dubray; M; Son; 18			
5732	Baptiste Dubray; M; Son; 10		5767	Charles Randall; M; Father; 25
5733	Irena Dunbray[sic]; F; Dau; 6		5768	Lucy Randall; F; Wife; 32
5734	Mamie Dunbray; F; Dau; 4-3		5769	Nellie Randall; F; Dau; 2-10
			5770	Ella Randall; F; Dau; 1-4
5735	Mary Ruff; F; Mother; 44			
5736	Emma Ruff; D; Dau; 27		5771	Akicita Najin; Elk Standing Soldier; M; Father; 24
5737	George Ruff; M; Son; 23			
5738	Arthur Ruff; M; Son; 12		5772	Akicita Najin; Julia Standing Soldier; F; Wife; 22
5739	William Ruff; M; Son; 9			
5740	Alice Ruff; F; Dau; 21		5773	Wanbli Waste; Joseph Good Eagle; M; Son; 4-1
5741	Lizzie Ruff; F; Dau; 17			
5742	John Ruff; M; Son; 15		5774	Paul; M; Son; 1-6
5743	Gracie Ruff; F; Dau; 11			
5744	Vina Ruff; F; Dau; 4-5		5775	William Randall; M; Father; 28
5745	Edna Ruff; F; Dau; 6		5776	Susie Randall; F; Wife; 26
			5777	Emma Randall; F; Dau; 1-2
5746	Julia; Julia Peck; F; Mother; 39			
5747	Lottie Peck; F; Dau; 19			

Census Of The Sioux And Cheyenne Indians Of Pine Ridge Agency, South Dakota.
Taken by W. H. Clapp, Captain 16th Infantry, Acting United States Indian Agent,
June 30, 1896. (Pass Creek District)

Key: Number; Indian Name *(if given)*; English Name; Sex; Relation; Age

5778	Emma Randall; F; Mother; 62	5801	Sunkole; Looking For Horse; F; 64
5779	Lucy W. Randall; F; G.Dau; 7		
5780	Frank Randall; M; Father; 26	5802	Pte Hoton; Bawling Bull; M; Husb; 57
5781	Millie Randall; F; Wife; 24		
5782	Amanda Randall; F; Dau; 1-3	5803	Hinapa; Comes Out; f; Wife; 63
5783	Cetan Sapa; Black Hawk; M; Father; 54	5804	Sungmanitu Akicita; Wolf Soldier; M; Father; 59
5784	Huncasa Sola; No Garter; F; Wife; 50	5805	Wanbli Sun; Eagle Feather; F; Wife; 44
5785	Oosica Hoksila; Young Bad Wound; M; Husb; 63	5806	Sungmanitu Akicita; Josephin[sic] Wolf Soldier; F; Dau; 24
5786	Pe Luta; Red Top; F; Wife; 44	5807	Sungmanitu Akicita; Edward Wolf Soldier; M; Son; 20
5787	Anpo Wakuwa; Martha Charge In Morning; F; G.Dau; 10	5808	Mato Watakpe; Charging Bear; M; Father; 52
5788	Niyanke Kte; Daniel Kills Alive; M; Father; 34	5809	Mato Watakpe; Anna Charging Bear; F; Wife; 42
5789	Niyanke Kte; Susie Kills Alive; F; Wife; 34	5810	Mato Watakpe; Addie Charging Bear; F; Dau; 11
5790	Niyanke Kte; Emily Kills Alive; F; Dau; 2	5811	Tatanka Hanska; Levi Long Bull; M; S.Son; 23
5791	Oosica; Robert Bad Wound; M; Father; 26	5812	George W. Means; M; Father; 25
		5813	Alice Means; F; Wife; 24
5792	Winyan Waste; Good Woman; F; Mother; 57	5814	Lavina Means; F; Dau; 2-10
		5815	James Blain Means; M; Son; 1-1
5793	Oosica; Day Bad Wound; F; Wife; 20	5816	Mary Carlow; F; Mother; 34
		5817	Lizzie Carlow; F; Dau; 16
5794	Oosica; Ella Bad Wound; F; Dau; 2-6	5818	Nellie Carlow; F; Dau; 14
		5819	Theadore[sic] Carlow; M; Son; 12
5795	Blotahunka Ciqala; Little Leader; M; Father; 34	5820	Jennie Carlow; F; Dau; 10
		5821	Agatha Carlow; F; Dau; 6
5796	Blotahunka Ciqala; Susie Little Leader; F; Wife; 28	5822	Frank Carlow; M; Son; 5
		5823	Anna Carlow; F; Dau; 2-9
5797	Blotahunka Ciqala; Sophia Little Leader; F; Dau; 2-4	5824	Robert Carlow; M; Son; 0-9
5798	Tanyan Wiyukcan; Julia Thinks Well; F; M. in L.; 61	5825	Mato Tamaheca; Poor Bear; M; Father; 54
5799	Tasunke Ehakela; Allen Last Horse; M; B. in L.; 24	5826	Mato Tinga; Grunting Bear; F; Wife #1; 49
5800	Oowaste; Good Shot; M; B. in L.; 22	5827	Iteska; White Face; F; Wife #2; 31

Census Of The Sioux And Cheyenne Indians Of Pine Ridge Agency, South Dakota. Taken by W. H. Clapp, Captain 16th Infantry, Acting United States Indian Agent, June 30, 1896. (Pass Creek District)

Key: Number; Indian Name *(if given)*; English Name; Sex; Relation; Age

5828	Mato Tamaheca; Harry Poor Bear; M; Son; 17	5855	Huhu Ska; White Bone; M; Father; 52
5829	Mato Tamaheca; Albert Poor Bear; M; Son; 14	5856	Iyotaka; Sits; F; Wife; 49
5830	Mato Tamaheca; Stephen Poor Bear; M; Son; 14	5857	Huhu Ska; Lydia White Bone; F; Dau; 12
5831	Tonweya Gli; Returns Scout; M; Son; 9	5858	Cetan Wicasa; Hawk Man; M; Son; 40
5832	Ptehincala; Calf; F; Dau; 7	5859	Toka; Enemy; F; Mother; 69
5833	Mato Tamaheca; George Poor Bear; M; Son; 5	5860	Cokata Iyaya; Goes In Center; M; Father; 49
5834	Asapi; Shout At; M; Son; 2-10	5861	Wakin; Baggage; F; Wife; 53
5835	Tasunke Hinsa; Her Red Horse; F; Dau; 2-2	5862	Cokata Iyaya; John Goes In Center; M; Son; 20
5836	Sunkhunsa[sic]; Red Horse; M; Father; 58	5863	Cokata Iyaya; Alice Goes In Center; F; Dau; 19
5837	Sagye; Cane; F; Wife #1; 54	5864	Cokata Iyaya; Holy Goes In Center; F; Dau; 8
5838	Wamnionmni[sic] Koyaka; Wears Whirlwind; F; Wife #2; 42	5865	John A. Logan; M; Son; 26
5839	Sunkhinsa; Mary Red Horse; F; Dau; 7	5866	Wanbli Yatapi; Eagle Chief; M; Father; 44
5840	Wanbli Ota; Plenty Eagle; F; Dau; 3-5	5867	Wanbli Yatapi; Fannie Eagle Chief; F; Wife; 37
5841	Onkcekira; Magpie; M; Son; 0-9	5868	Ohola; Respects; F; Dau; 2-10
5842	Wikan Maza; Iron Rope; M; Father; 38	5869	Kangi Isnala; Lone Crow; M; Father; 47
5843	Sunk Sapa; Black Horse; F; Wife; 42	5870	Mni Sa; Red Water; F; Wife; 48
5844	Sunk Hinzi; Yellow Horse; F; Dau; 20	5871	Kangi Isnala; Herbert Lone Crow; M; Son; 14
5845	Makoce; Land; M; Son; 8	5872	Najinyapi; Surrounded; M; Son; 3-3
5846	Mni; Water; M; Son; 8		
5847	Wikan Maza; Winnie Iron Rope; F; Dau; 4-4	5873	Sina Ska; White Blanket; M; Father; 42
5848	Wicarpi Wanbli; Eagle Star; M; Son; 2-4	5874	Pte Hinapa; Cow Goes First; F; Wife; 57
5849	Mary Gresh; F; Mother; 34	5875	Sina Ska; Kittie White Blanket; F; Dau; 19
5850	Millie Gresh; F; Dau; 10		
5851	Lizzie Gresh; F; Dau; 8	5876	Mato Sapa; Herman Black Bear; M; Son; 18
5852	Susie Gresh; F; Dau; 6		
5853	Todd Gresh; M; Son; 3-2	5877	Sina Ska; Harry White Blanket; M; Son; 16
5854	John Gresh; M; Son; 0-2		

Census Of The Sioux And Cheyenne Indians Of Pine Ridge Agency, South Dakota. Taken by W. H. Clapp, Captain 16th Infantry, Acting United States Indian Agent, June 30, 1896. (Pass Creek District)

Key: Number; Indian Name *(if given)*; English Name; Sex; Relation; Age

5878	Wahorpi Luta; Red Nest; M; Father; 33	5904	Mato Najin; Emily Standing Bear; F; Dau; 26
5879	Caje Wakan; Medicine Name; M; Son; 9	5905	Mato Najin; Sarah Standing Bear; F; Dau; 18
5880	Tasunke Opi Win; Shot Her Horses; F; Dau; 4	5906	Mato Najin; Annie Standing Bear; F; Dau; 18
5881	Henry Hunter; M; Father; 28	5907	Mato Najin; Edith Standing Bear; F; G.Dau; 8
5882	Lucy Hunter; F; Wife; 23	5908	Mato Najin; George Standing Bear; M; Son; 8
5883	Nicholas Hunter; M; Son; 4-1		
5884	Victoria Hunter; F; Dau; 1-3	5909	Mato Najin; John Standing Bear; M; Son; 15
5885	Mato Iyotaka; Sitting Bear; M; Father; 45	5910	Wicarpi Yamni; Three Stars; M; Father; 54
5886	Nape Wakan; Holy Hand; F; Wife #1; 42	5911	Hoton; Bawling; F; Wife #1; 45
5887	Inyan Win; Rock Woman; F; Wife #2; 57	5912	Sunkawakan Nupa; Two Horses; F; Wife #2; 48
5888	Pehin Ji; Daniel Yellow Hair; M; Nephew; 14	5913	Wicarpi Yamni; Eva Three Stars; F; Dau; 26
5889	Wahukeza Zi; Yellow Lance; F; Dau; 11	5914	Wicarpi Yamni; Susie Three Stars; F; Dau; 18
5890	Jennie Lance; F; Dau; 10		
5891	Sungmanitu Wakan; Medicine Wolf; M; Son; 7	5915	Wicarpi Yamni; Harry Three Stars; M; Father; 24
5892	Ite Wakan; Holy Face; F; Dau; 6	5916	Wicarpi Yamni; Sally Three Stars; F; Wife; 23
5893	George; M; Son; 1-3	5917	Wicarpi Yamni; Jessie Three Stars; F; Dau; 4-4
5894	Frank Conroy; M; Father; 31		
5895	Victoria Conroy; F; Wife; 30	5918	Wicarpi Yamni; Lucy Three Stars; F; Dau; 1-1
5896	Julia Conroy; F; Dau; 4-5		
5897	Harry Conroy; M; Son; 2-7	5919	Wicarpi Yamni; Clarence Three Stars; M; Father; 32
5898	Mato Najin; Ellis Standing Bear; M; Father; 28	5920	Wicarpi Yamni; Jennie Three Stars; F; Wife; 25
5899	Mato Najin; Annie Standing Bear; F; Wife; 24	5921	Wicarpi Yamni; Sophia Three Stars; F; Dau; 3-1
5900	Mato Najin; Jessie Standing Bear; F; Dau; 1-3	5922	Wicarpi Yamni; Paul Three Stars; M; Son; 1-6
5901	Mato Najin; Standing Bear; M; Father; 61	5923	Wicarpi Yamni; Louise Three Stars; F; Dau; 0-5
5902	Mato Najin; Lena Standing Bear; F; Wife #1; 53		
5903	Mato Najin; Ellen Standing Bear; F; Wife #2; 44	5924	He Topa; Four Horns; M; Father; 45

Census Of The Sioux And Cheyenne Indians Of Pine Ridge Agency, South Dakota. Taken by W. H. Clapp, Captain 16th Infantry, Acting United States Indian Agent, June 30, 1896. (Pass Creek District)

Key: Number; Indian Name *(if given)*; English Name; Sex; Relation; Age

5925	He Topa; Alice Four Horns; F; Dau; 17	5946	Yaslo; Sarah Whistler; F; Dau; 4-7
5926	Wicarpi Wanbli; Eagle Star; M; Son; 9	5947	Yaslo; Fannie Whistler; F; Dau; 3-5
5927	Can Raka; Rough Wood; F; Mother; 71	5948	Wakacanka; Robert Shield; M; Bro; 32
		5949	Canonajinyapi; Surrounded In Wood; M; Bro In L.; 29
5928	Marpiya Luta; Red Cloud; M; Son; 32	5950	Carolus Whistler; M; Son; 0-2
5929	Hakikta; Looks Back; F; Mother; 67	5951	Sunk Icu; Takes Horses; F; Sister; 19
5930	Wanbli Ciqala; Lawrence Little Eagle; M; Nephew; 20	5952	Kangi Ska; White Crow; M; Father; 54
5931	Mato Najin; Luther Standing Bear; M; Father; 34	5953	Kanta Sapa; Prune; F; Wife #1; 50
5932	Mato Najin; Nellie Standing Bear; F; Wife; 25	5954	Canhanpi; Sugar; F; Wife #2; 50
		5955	Edward Crow; M; Son; 30
5933	Mato Najin; Lillie Standing Bear; F; Dau; 10	5956	Sunkgleska; Spotted Horse; M; Bro; 30
5934	Mato Najin; Arthur Standing Bear; M; Son; 8	5957	Tasunke; Her Horses; F; Dau; 24
5935	Mato Najin; Paul F. Standing Bear; M; Son; 6	5958	Wanapa Gli; Comes Back Wounded; M; Son; 11
5936	Mato Najin; Emily Standing Bear; F; Dau; 4	5959	Kokipa; Afraid; M; G.Son; 5
		5960	Peter Ladeaux; M; Father; 46
5937	Mato Najin; Julia Standing Bear; F; Dau; 2-1	5961	Jennie Ladeaux; F; Wife; 38
		5962	Emma Ladeaux; F; Dau; 20
		5963	Alice Ladeaux; F; Dau; 18
5938	Mato Najin; Willard Standing Bear; M; Father; 28	5964	Sarah Ladeaux; F; Dau; 16
		5965	John Ladeaux; M; Son; 12
5939	Mato Najin; Lizzie Standing Bear; F; Wife; 23	5966	Rosa Ladeaux; F; Dau; 8
		5967	Jessie Ladeaux; F; Dau; 2-5
5940	Mato Najin; Esther Standing Bear; F; Dau; 7	5968	Katie Ladeaux; F; 35
5941	Mato Najin; Stephen Standing Bear; M; Son; 4-7	5969	Robert Randall; M; Father; 42
5942	Mato Najin; Oliver Standing Bear; M; Son; 2-2	5970	Mollie Randall; F; Wife; 38
		5971	Mary Randall; F; Dau; 20
		5972	Cetan Gi; Yellow Hawk; M; B. in L.; 24
5943	Yaslo; Julian Whistler; M; Father; 35	5973	Julia; F; S. in L.; 14
5944	Tatiyopa; Her Door; F; Wife; 37		
5945	Yaslo; Newman Whistler; M; Son; 10	5974	Nape Akicita; Moses Hand Soldier; M; Father; 40

Census Of The Sioux And Cheyenne Indians Of Pine Ridge Agency, South Dakota. Taken by W. H. Clapp, Captain 16th Infantry, Acting United States Indian Agent, June 30, 1896. (Pass Creek District)

Key: Number; Indian Name *(if given)*; English Name; Sex; Relation; Age

5975 Nape Akicita; Julia Hand Soldier; F; Wife; 46
5976 Nape Akicita; John Hand Soldier; M; Son; 15
5977 Nape Akicita; Stephen Hand Soldier; M; Son; 13
5978 Nape Akicita; Louise Hand Soldier; F; Dau; 10

5979 Kiyan Hiyaya; Flying By; F; 63

5980 Ista Sapa; Black Eyes; M; Father; 82
5981 Wanbli Luta; Red Eagle; F; Wife; 49
5982 Tayan Kte; Kills Well; M; Nephew; 24
5983 Ista Sapa; Thomas Black Eyes; M; Son; 17

5984 Anpo Wakuwa; Howard Charge In Morning; M; Father; 35
5985 Anpo Wakuwa; Maggie C. In Morning; F; Wife; 35
5986 Anpo Wakuwa; Oliver C. I. Morning; M; Son; 8
5987 Anpo Wakuwa; Agnes C. I. Morning; F; Dau; 5
5988 Anpo Wakuwa; Edward C. I. Morning; M; Son; 1-6

5989 Wakinyan Peta; Edgar Fire Thunder; M; Father; 37
5990 Wakinyan Peta; Susie Fire Thunder; F; Wife; 28
5991 Wakinyan Peta; Julia Fire Thunder; F; Dau; 7
5992 Wakinyan Peta; Lydia Fire Thunder; F; Dau; 3-11
5993 Wakinyan Peta; William Fire Thunder; M; Son; 1-9

5994 Itunkasan Mato; Mary Weasel Bear; F; 61

5995 Anpetu Hinapa; Day Comes Out; F; 59

5996 Sungmanitu Isnala; Charles Lone Wolf; M; Father; 36
5997 Sungmanitu Isnala; Eva Lone Wolf; F; Wife; 42
5998 Sungmanitu Isnala; Stephen Lone Wolf; M; Son; 11
5999 Sungmanitu Isnala; Emma Lone Wolf; F; Dau; 9
6000 Sungmanitu Isnala; Agnes Lone Wolf; F; Dau; 7
6001 Sungmanitu Isnala; Abraham Lone Wolf; M; Son; 3-6

6002 Scili Wicakte; Allen Pawnee Killer; M; Father; 22
6003 Scili Wicakte; Jennie Pawnee Killer; F; Wife; 21
6004 Scili Wicakte; Marthia Pawnee Killer; F; Dau; 1-1

6005 Wicasa Hanska; Long Man; M; Father; 64
6006 Oinkpa; Head Of Creek; F; Wife; 60
6007 Wicasa Hanska; Charles Long Man; M; Son; 19

6008 Ite Sankiya; George White Face; M; Father; 41
6009 Ite Sankiya; Lucy White Face; F; Wife; 44
6010 Ite Sankiya; Winnie White Face; F; Dau; 15
6011 Ite Sankiya; Ethel White Face; F; Dau; 13

6012 Mato Wayuhi; Conquering Bear; M; Father; 67
6013 Canku; Road; F; Wife; 61
6014 Col. Scraper; M; B. in L.; 70
6015 Wamniomni; Whirlwind; M; Son; 25

Census Of The Sioux And Cheyenne Indians Of Pine Ridge Agency, South Dakota. Taken by W. H. Clapp, Captain 16th Infantry, Acting United States Indian Agent, June 30, 1896.   (Pass Creek District)

Key: Number; Indian Name *(if given)*; English Name; Sex; Relation; Age

6016	Mato Wayuhi; Abraham C. Bear; M; Son; 25	6045	George Girroux; M; Father; 29
6017	Sinte Jata; Forked Tail; M; Son; 17	6046	Emma Girroux; F; Wife; 27
		6047	Robert Girroux; M; Son; 7
		6048	William Girroux; M; Son; 5
6018	Watakpe; Charger; M; Son; 16	6049	Rena Girroux; F; Dau; 3-1
6019	Asapi; Yells At Him; M; Son; 15	6050	Arthur Girroux; M; Son; 1-9
6020	Pasu Hanska; Long Nose; M; Son; 15	6051	Louis Cottier; M; Father; 25
6021	Ptesan Hiyaya; Goes White Cow; F; Dau; 45	6052	Nettie Cottier; F; Wife; 25
		6053	Gilbert Cottier; M; Son; 5
6022	Pankeska; Shell; F; G.Dau; 4-6	6054	Walter James Cottier; M; Son; 2-10
6023	Winyan Ota; Plenty Woman; F; Dau; 36	6055	Mabel Cottier; F; Dau; 1-2
6024	Talo; Frank Meat; M; Father; 41	6056	Toka Kte; Kills Enemy; M; Husb; 42
6025	Talo; Nellie Meat; F; Wife; 25		
6026	Sank Hinto; James Gray Horse; M; Son; 12	6057	Waste Kaga; Makes Things Good; F; Wife; 40
6027	Talo; Arthur Meat; M; Son; 0-6	6058	Inyan Hoksila; James Rock Boy; M; Nephew; 11
6028	Waglyre[sic]; Loafer; M; Father; 61		
		6059	Peter Richard; M; Father; 48
6029	Ota Wowasi Ecun; Works Plenty; F; Wife; 53	6060	Louise Richard; F; Wife; 38
		6061	Joseph Richard; M; Son; 15
6030	Pahin Yusla; Plucks Porcupine; M; Son; 30	6062	Susanna Richard; F; Dau; 9
		6063	Josephine Richard; F; Dau; 7
6031	Waglure; Thomas Loafer; M; Son; 20	6064	Alfred Richard; M; Son; 6
		6065	Baptiste Richard; M; Son; 20
6032	Waglure; William Loafer; M; Son; 17	6066	Millie Richard; M; Dau; 0-9
		6067	Joseph Rooks; M; Father; 26
6033	Benj. Claymore; M; Father; 32	6068	Mollie Rooks; F; Wife; 21
6034	Lucy Claymore; F; Wife; 27	6069	Mabel Rooks; F; Dau; 5
6035	David Claymore; M; Son; 9	6070	Jessie Rooks; F; Dau; 0-9
6036	Richard Claymore; M; Son; 7		
6037	Garfield Claymore; M; Son; 5	6071	Joseph Bush; M; Father; 58
6038	Egan Claymore; M; Son; 2-9	6072	Joseph Bush, Jr; M; Son; 18
		6073	Sally Bush; F; Wife; 48
6039	Samuel Claymore; M; Father; 27		
6040	Joseph Claymore; M; Son; 9	6074	Mary Williams; F; Mother; 38
6041	Benjamn[sic] Claymore; M; Son; 7	6075	Charlotte Williams; F; Dau; 10
		6076	Annie Williams; F; Dau; 8
6042	Edward Claymore; M; Son; 5	6077	Lizzie Williams; F; Dau; 6
6043	Roy Claymore; M; Son; 2-10	6078	Winnie Williams; F; Dau; 3-6
6044	Gracie Claymore; F; Dau; 0-5	6079	Maurice Williams; M; Son; 1-6

Census Of The Sioux And Cheyenne Indians Of Pine Ridge Agency, South Dakota. Taken by W. H. Clapp, Captain 16th Infantry, Acting United States Indian Agent, June 30, 1896. (Pass Creek District)

Key: Number; Indian Name *(if given)*; English Name; Sex; Relation; Age

6080 Susie Green; F; Mother; 33
6081 Harry Green; M; Son; 12
6082 Loe[sic] Green; M; Son; 10

6083 Kate Rooks; F; Mother; 38
6084 Charles Rooks; M; Son; 20
6085 William Rooks; M; Son; 8
6086 James Rooks; M; Son; 4-6
6087 Rosanna Rooks; F; Dau; 16
6088 Nellie Rooks; F; Dau; 18
6089 Alice Rooks; F; Dau; 22
6090 Nancy Rooks; F; Dau; 14
6091 Mathia[sic] Rooks; F; Dau; 12
6092 Delia Rooks; F; Dau; 8
6093 Cristina Rooks; F; Dau; 6
6094 Maggie Rooks; F; Dau; 2-6
6095 Clara Rooks; F; Dau; 0-2

6096 Mary Cottier; F; Mother; 44
6097 Henry Cottier; M; Son; 19
6098 George Cottier; M; Son; 16
6099 Ollie Cottier; F; Dau; 14
6100 Emma Cottier; F; Dau; 11
6101 Charles Cottier; M; Son; 8
6102 Samuel Cottier; M; Son; 6
6103 Elizabeth Cottier; F; Dau; 4
6104 Florence Cottier; F; Dau; 2

6105 Scili Kte; Pawnee Killer; M; Husb; 70
6106 Winyan Haska; Tall Woman; F; Wife; 64

6107 Peji; Thomas Grass; M; Father; 29
6108 Tikanyela; Close To House; F; Wife; 28
6109 Peji; Edward Grass; M; Son; 7
6110 Anpetu Wakan; Medicine Day; F; Dau; 4-5
6111 Peji; James Grass; M; Son; 1-6

6112 Millie Gleason; F; Mother; 40
6113 Elizabeth Monto; F; Sister; 43
6114 Pearl Gleason; F; Dau; 12

6115 John Ladeaux; M; Husb; 48
6116 Bessie Ladeaux; F; Wife; 35

6117 Asanpi; Milk; M; Husb; 41
6118 Pejuta Win; Medicine Woman; F; Wife; 37
6119 Mniowicakte; John Kills In Water; M; S.Son; 12

6120 Heraka Wanbli; Eagle Elk; M; Father; 60
6121 Waonsila; Takes Pity On Them; F; Wife; 64
6122 Mahel Wayanka; Looks Inside; M; Son; 24
6123 Wicasa Sakpe; Six Men; M; Son; 6
6124 Tacanku Waste; Her Good Road; F; Dau; 12
6125 Heraka Wanbli; Alice Eagle Elk; F; Dau; 16
6126 Heraka Wanbli; Nancy Eagle Elk; F; Dau; 16

6127 Mato Gi; Yellow Bear; M; Father; 53
6128 Sunk Watogla; Wild Horse; F; Wife #1; 48
6129 Anpetu Wakan; Holy Day; F; Wife #2; 41
6130 Iyokipi Iciya; Pleased Herself; F; Dau; 21
6131 Hayapi Waste Koyaka; Wears Good Cloths; F; Dau; 13

6132 Sunka Onca; Imitates Dog; M; Father; 62
6133 Sunka Onca; Wallace Dog; M; Son; 21
6134 Marpiya Win; Cloud Woman; F; Mother; 91

6135 Kangi Ciqala; Little Crow; M; Father; 33
6136 Tipi Ota; Many Camps; F; Wife; 31

Census Of The Sioux And Cheyenne Indians Of Pine Ridge Agency, South Dakota. Taken by W. H. Clapp, Captain 16th Infantry, Acting United States Indian Agent, June 30, 1896. (Pass Creek District)

Key: Number; Indian Name *(if given)*; English Name; Sex; Relation; Age

6137	Ilazata Yu; Comes Behind; F; M. in L.; 74	6163	Cetan Gi; Emma Yellow Hawk; F; Dau; 12
6138	Kangi Ciqala; Bessie Little Crow; F; Dau; 3-6	6164	Cetan Gi; Julia Yellow Hawk; F; Dau; 11
6139	Mato Ptecela; Grover Short Bear; M; Father; 43	6165	Kiyela Rpaya; Lays Close; M; Son; 9
6140	Waoka; Kills Game; F; Wife; 39	6166	Sunk Tokeca; Different Horse; F; Dau; 9
6141	Mato Ptecela; Silas Short Bear; M; Son; 16	6167	Tokeya Kte; Kills First; M; Son; 2-3
6142	Isna Ti; Lives Alone; F; Dau; 15		
6143	Mato Ptecela; Josephine Short Bear; F; Dau; 14	6168	Cangleska Ciqala; Charles Little Hoop; M; Father; 29
6144	Wanbli Cuwignaka; Eagle Dress; F; Dau; 11	6169	Cangleska Ciqala; Elk Little Hoop; F; Wife; 25
6145	Mato Ptecela; Baby Short Bear; F; Dau; 9	6170	Cangleska Ciqala; Samuel Little Hoop; M; Bro; 18
6146	Mato Ptecela; Nettie Short Bear; F; Dau; 4-4	6171	Wincincala Wakan; Holy Girl; F; Dau; 3-2
6147	Mato Ptecela; Cecilia Short Bear; F; Dau; 0-5	6172	Cangleska Ciqala; Little Hoop; M; Father; 61
6148	Frank Salvis, Jr; M; Father; 36	6173	Cokata Wakan; Holy In Center; F; Wife; 43
6149	Lizzie Salvis; F; Wife; 30		
6150	Levi Salvis; M; Son; 8	6174	Ehake Iyanka; Runs Last; M; Son; 22
6151	Lillie Slavis[sic]; F; Dau; 6		
6152	George Salvis; M; Son; 3-7		
6153	William Salvis; M; Son; 1-7	6175	Winyan Nite; Womans[sic] Back; M; Father; 71
6154	Sophia Salvis; F; Dau; 0-1	6176	Winyan Nite; Lizzie Womans Back; F; Wife; 69
6155	Cetan Gi; Yellow Hawk; M; Father; 44	6177	Jessie Bitters; F; Dau; 26
6156	Ta Waste; Her Good Things; F; Wife #1; 47	6178	Patrick Bitters; M; Son; 24
6157	Tasunke Waste Win; Her Good Horse; F; Wife #2; 42	6179	Peter Cazue; M; Husb; 38
		6180	Mary Cazue; F; Wife; 32
6158	Ilazata Yu; Lucy Comes Behind; F; Dau; 23	6181	Frank Salvis, Sr; M; Father; 64
6159	Cetan Gi; John Yellow Hawk; M; Son; 21	6182	Sophia Salvis; F; Wife; 61
		6183	Julia Salvis; F; Dau; 23
6160	Cetan Gi; Frank Yellow Hawk; M; Son; 18	6184	Nancy Salvis; F; Dau; 17
		6185	James Janis, Jr; M; G.Son; 3-3
6161	Cetan Gi; Susie [sic] Hawk; F; Dau; 17	6186	Thomas Nelson; M; Father; 22
6162	Cetan Gi; James Yellow Hawk; M; Son; 15	6187	Susy Nelson; F; Wife; 24
		6188	Francis Nelson; M; Son; 1-6\

Census Of The Sioux And Cheyenne Indians Of Pine Ridge Agency, South Dakota. Taken by W. H. Clapp, Captain 16th Infantry, Acting United States Indian Agent, June 30, 1896. (Pass Creek District)

Key: Number; Indian Name *(if given)*; English Name; Sex; Relation; Age

6189	William Larrabee; M; Father; 36		6213	Sungmanitu Mato; Bear Wolf; M; Father; 59
6190	Alice Larrabee; F; Wife; 33		6214	Ptesan; White Cow; F; Wife; 36
6191	Nancy Larrabee; F; Dau; 11		6215	Mila Ciqala; Little Knife; M; Son; 12
6192	Samuel Larrabee; M; Son; 9			
6193	Louis Larrabee; M; Son; 7		6216	Pte Talo; Buffalo Meat; M; Son; 6
6194	John Shangreau; M; Father; 40		6217	Wakan Mahel Wayanka; Looks In Holy; F; Dau; 3-2
6195	Jules Shangreau; M; Son; 14			
6196	Leon Shangreau; M; Son; 10			
6197	John Shangreau, Jr; M; Son; 2-6		6218	Heraka Ho Waste; Good Voice Elk; M; Father; 32
6198	Ista Yazan; Sore Eyes; M; Husb; 55		6219	Zuya Win; Warrior Woman; F; Wife; 25
6199	Pankeska Wakpa; Shell Creek; F; Wife; 58		6220	Tarca Iyanka; Running Antelope; M; Son; 9
6200	He Hanska; Aaron Long Horns; M; Father; 38		6221	Sunk Tacanku; Horse Road; M; Son; 4
6201	He Hanska; Tribe Long Horns; F; Wife; 37		6222	Sunk Tacanku; John Horse Road; M; Son; 1-1
6202	He Hanska; Hattie Long Horns; F; Dau; 12		6223	Sahiyela Wapata; Cheyenne Butcher; M; Father; 31
6203	Winyan Wicakte; Kills Woman; F; Dau; 2-10		6224	Tasunke Wakita; Her Looking Horse; F; Wife; 31
6204	Kokab Wosica; Trouble In Front; M; Father; 35		6225	Wanbli Waste; Good Eagle; F; Dau; 6
6205	Hihan Sapa; Black Owl; F; Wife; 24		6226	Wanbli Waste; Susie Good Eagle; F; Dau; 3-8
6206	Takuni Olesni; Hunts Nothing; F; Dau; 3-6		6227	Samuel Good Eagle; M; Son; 1-3
6207	Takuni Olesni; John Hunts Nothing; M; Son; 1-1		6228	Winyan Wakan; Holy Woman; F; Aunt; 67
6208	Maga Ite; Goose Face; M; Son; 38		6229	Catka; Left Hand; M; Nephew; 24
6209	Wicarpi Wankatuya; High Star; F; Mother; 81		6230	Louis Richard; M; Father; 54
			6231	Jennie Richard; F; Wife; 40
			6232	Louise Richard; F; Dau; 25
6210	Tawiyaka Waste; Her Good Feather; F; Mother; 48		6233	Jennie Richard; F; Dau; 19
			6234	Millie Richard; F; Dau; 16
6211	Tasunke Opi; Wounded Horse; M; Son; 12		6235	Alfred Richard; M; Son; 14
			6236	Angelina Richard; F; Dau; 10
6212	Tasunke Opi; Paul Wounded Horse; M; Son; 17		6237	Samuel Richard; M; Son; 3-6
			6238	Louise Reynal; F; 50

Census Of The Sioux And Cheyenne Indians Of Pine Ridge Agency, South Dakota. Taken by W. H. Clapp, Captain 16th Infantry, Acting United States Indian Agent, June 30, 1896. (Pass Creek District)

Key: Number; Indian Name *(if given)*; English Name; Sex; Relation; Age

6239	Lizzie Bullard; F; Mother; 49	6273	William Shangreau; M; Father; 34
6240	Mattie Ward; F; Dau; 28		
6241	Walter Bullard; M; Son; 15	6274	Emma Shangreau; F; Wife; 30
6242	Elmus Bullard; M; Son; 13	6275	Mary Shangreau; F; Dau; 9
6243	Frank Bullard; M; Son; 19	6276	Winnie Shangreau; F; Dau; 7
6244	Elbridge Ward; M; Son; 27	6277	William Wallace Shangra[sic]; M; Son; 2
6245	Louis Richard, Jr; M; Father; 21		
6246	Eva Richard; F; Wife; 19	6278	Alice Bowman; F; Sister; 24
6247	Dora Richard; F; Dau; 1-2	6279	Thomas Bowman; M; Bro; 19
		6280	John Lee Jr; M; Nephew; 4
6248	Jane Bettelyoun; F; Mother; 41		
6249	George W. Bettelyoun; M; Son; 23	6281	Anarlatapi; James Clincher; M; Father; 40
6250	Harry W. Bettelyoun; M; Son; 19	6282	Napsukaga Waste; Goood[sic] Finger; F; Wife; 23
6251	Ida M Bettelyoun; F; Dau; 17	6283	Anarlatapi; George Clincher; M; Son; 18
6252	Fred W Bettelyoun; M; Son; 14		
6253	Lucy M Bettelyoun; F; Dau; 13	6284	Anarlatapi; Calvin Clincher; M; Son; 14
6254	Ellen J Bettelyoun; F; Dau; 11		
6255	Cleveland B Bettelyoun; M; Son; 8	6285	Anarlatapi; Charles Clincher; M; Son; 10
6256	Marthia[sic] L Bettelyoun; F; Dau; 7	6286	Anarlatapi; John Clincher; M; Son; 0-1
6257	Lillie Bettelyoun; F; Dau; 4		
6258	Chester Bettelyoun; M; Son; 1-1	6287	Tarca Gi; Yellow Deer; M; Father; 24
6259	Clara Bettelyoun; F; Dau; 21		
		6288	Wakukeza Win; Lamp Woman; F; Wife; 22
6260	Charlotte Chausse; F; 59		
		6289	Sunk Iyanajinca; Gets Away With Horses; F; Dau; 5
6261	Ohomni Iyanka; Runs Around; F; 63		
		6290	Sunka Hunkesni; Philip Slow Dog; M; Father; 35
6262	Beaver Monto; M; Father; 48		
6263	Agnes Monto; F; Wife; 37	6291	Ska Koyaka; Wears White; F; Wife; 32
6264	Ella Monto; F; Dau; 10		
6265	Enoch Monto; M; Son; 20	6292	Wanbli Waste; Good Eagle; M; Son; 3-6
6266	Emma Vlandry; F; Mother; 30	6293	Tacanupa Wakan; Her Holy Pipe; F; Dau; 2-3
6267	Sadie Vlandry; F; Dau; 12		
6268	Jennie Vlandry; F; Dau; 11		
6269	William Vlandry; M; Son; 9	6294	Wahinkpe Ota; Plenty Arrows; M; Father; 38
6270	Robert C Vlandry; M; Son; 7		
6271	Hattie Vlandry; F Dau; 4-8	6295	Warpe Koyaka; Wears Leaf; F; Wife; 34
6272	Owen H Vlandry; M; Son; 0-8		
		6296	Yusluta; Pulls It Out; M; Son; 3-10

Census Of The Sioux And Cheyenne Indians Of Pine Ridge Agency, South Dakota. Taken by W. H. Clapp, Captain 16th Infantry, Acting United States Indian Agent, June 30, 1896. (Pass Creek District)

Key: Number; Indian Name *(if given)*; English Name; Sex; Relation; Age

6297 Isnala Ti; Lone Life; F; 71
6298 Mato Sapa; Paul Black Bear; M; Father; 32
6299 Otoran; Gives Away; F; Dau; 16
6300 Mato Sapa; Black Bear; M; Father; 43
6301 Tasunke Waste; Owns Good Horses; F; Wife; 36
6302 Mato Sapa; Belle Black Bear; F; Dau; 19
6303 Mato Sapa; William Black Bear; M; Son; 16
6304 Mato Sapa; Susie Black Bear; F; G.Dau; 0-5
6305 Mato Wicagnayan; Fooling Bear; M; Father; 23
6306 Cekiyapi; Pray To Her; F; Wife; 23
6307 Nape Maza; Iron Hand; M; Son; 3-5
6308 Mato Wicagnyan[sic]; Paul Fooling Bear; M; Son; 1-10
6309 Mato Wicagnayan; Lucy Fooling Bear; F; Dau; 0-3
6310 Scili Kokipesni; Mat Afraid Of Pawnee; M; Husb; 41
6311 Hinapa; Comes Out; F; Wife; 33
6312 Sagye; Cane; F; 70
6313 Wanbli Gleska; Felix Spotted Eagle; M; Father; 33
6314 Wanbli Gleska; Amelia Spotted Eagle; F; Wife; 24
6315 Wanbli Gi; Mary Yellow Eagle; F; Dau; 4
6316 Wanbli Gleska; Charles Spotted Eagle; M; Son; 2-6
6317 Sungmanitu Isnala; Lone Wolf; M; Father; 64
6318 Canku Maza; Iron Road; F; Wife; 63
6319 Sungmanitu Isnala; Felix Lone Wolf; M; Son; 25
6320 Sungmanitu Isnala; Nathan Lone Wolf; M; Son; 19
6321 Sungmanitu Isnala; Willard Lone Wolf; M; Son; 18
6322 Mary Selwin; F; G.Dau; 10
6323 Sunk Hinsa Yuka; Red Horse Owner; M; Husb; 65
6324 Ptan Luta; Red Ottar[sic]; F; Wife; 38
6325 Petaga; William P. Fire; M; B. in L.; 63
6326 Jennie; F; Niece; 10
6327 Hanpa Hunaka; Moccason[sic] Mother; F; 83
6328 Pehin Sica; Bad Hair; M; Father; 29
6329 Nupa Opi; Wounded Twice; F; Wife; 24
6330 Pte Luta; Red Cow; F; Dau; 2-10
6331 Tatanka Isnala; Lone Bull; M; 59
6332 Hihan Tatanka; Owl Bull; M; Father; 56
6333 Rante; Cedar; F; Wife; 49
6334 Ayuta; Looked At; F; Dau; 10
6335 Naca; Chief; F; 81
6336 Tiglake; Moves Lodges; F; Mother; 39
6337 Pankeska Waste; Good Shell; F; Dau; 2-8
6338 Waste Kaga; Makes Good; M; Father; 37
6339 Waste Kaga; Eliza Makes Good; F; Wife; 23

Census Of The Sioux And Cheyenne Indians Of Pine Ridge Agency, South Dakota. Taken by W. H. Clapp, Captain 16th Infantry, Acting United States Indian Agent, June 30, 1896. (Pass Creek District)

Key: Number; Indian Name *(if given)*; English Name; Sex; Relation; Age

6340	Heraka Isnala; Lone Elk; M; Son; 7		6367	Henry Young; M; Son; 0-1
6341	Psito Win; Bead Woman; F; Dau; 6		6368	George Young; M; 24
6342	Paul Bead Woman; M; Son; 2-3		6369	Mato Winyan; Bear Woman; F; 60
6343	Waste Kaga; Richard Makes Good; M; Son; 0-1		6370	Susan Robinson; F; 77
6344	Winyan Ska; White Woman; F; Mother; 26		6371	James Hawkins; M; 35
6345	Wanbli Ska; White Eagle; M; Son; 5		6372	Andrew Russell; M; 19
6346	Tainyan Hiyaya; Goes In Light; F; Mother; 68		6376[sic]	Charles Means; M; Father; 29
			6374	Emma Means; F; Wife; 27
6347	Han Glawa; Lucy Counts Her Nights; F; Niece; 13		6375	George Means; M; Son; 8
			6376	Wankal Kte; Kills Above; M; Father; 31
6348	Wazi Ptecela; James Short Pine; M; Husb; 28		6377	Takpe; Charges At; F; Wife; 34
6349	Carli Win; Powder Woman; F; Wife; 32		6378	Aglagla Iyanka; Runs Close To Edge; M; Son; 3-5
6350	Sungmanitu Luzahan; John Fast Wolf; M; Husb; 24		6379	Naca Ciqala; Little Chief; M; Husb; 25
6351	Sungmanitu Luzahan; Jessie Fast Wolf; F; Wife; 19		6380	Naca Ciqala; Louise Little Chief; F; Wife; 18
			6381	Wakinyan Peta; Zoy Fire Thunder; F; Dau; 1-3
6352	Jacob Ladeaux; M; 23			
6353	Charles Dubray; M; Father; 23		6382	Alex Lebuff; M; Father; 36
6354	Elizabeth Dubray; F; Wife; 18		6383	Zonie Lebuff; F; Dau; 8
6355	Eugene Dubray; M; Son; 0-6		6384	Roda Lebuff; F; Dau; 2-6
6356	Wakinyan Kokipapi; Afraid Of Thunder; M; 58		6385	Mila Pe Sni; Dull Knife; m; Husb; 25
			6386	Mila Pe Sni; Mary Dull Knife; F; Wife; 20
6357	Louise Young; F; Mother; 44			
6358	Amelia Young; F; Dau; 26			
6359	Victor Young; M; Son; 19		6387	Nacupa Yuha Mani; Walks With Pipe; F; Mother; 26
6360	Lizzie Young; F; Dau; 18			
6361	Mary Young; F; Dau; 16		6388	Waqupi; Gives Him S. To Eat; M; Son; 7
6362	William Young; M; Son; 14			
6363	Edward Young; M; Son; 12		6389	Warpe Sa; Red Leaf; M; Son; 1-5
6364	Frank Young; M; Son; 11			
6365	Alfred Young; M; Son; 8			
6366	Philip Young; M; Son; 4-2			

Census Of The Sioux And Cheyenne Indians Of Pine Ridge Agency, South Dakota. Taken by W. H. Clapp, Captain 16th Infantry, Acting United States Indian Agent, June 30, 1896. (Pass Creek District)

Key: Number; Indian Name *(if given)*; English Name; Sex; Relation; Age

6390 Mato Sapa; Thomas Black Bear; M; 27
6391 Ole; Ole; M; 69
6392 Canupa Wanbli; Pipe Eagle; M: Father; 43
6393 Panpanla; Tender; F; Wife; 36
6394 Winyan Sapa; Black Woman; F; Dau; 2-10
6395 Oosica; Noah Bad Wound; M; Father; 28
6396 Oosica; Mary Bad Wound; F; Wife; 23
6397 Oosica; Gilbert Bad Wound; M; Son; 3-6
6398 Oosica; Vincent Bad Wound; M; Son; 1-5
6399 Wiyaka Mato Feather Bear; M; Husb; 34
6400 Cetan Win; Hawk Woman; F; Wife; 24

6401 Mato Cante Wanica; Heartless Bear; M; Son; 45
6402 Otakuye Wanica; No Relation; F; Mother; 85

6403 Sunk Manu; Steals Horses; M; Son; 36
6404 Hunkpapa; Hunkpapa; F; Mother; 79

6405 Jennie Stover; F; Mother; 47
6406 Edward Stover; M; Son; 20
6407 William Stover; M; Son; 18
6408 Edith Stover; F; Dau; 7
6409 Laura Stover; F; Dau; 4-6
6410 Grace Stover; F; Dau; 1-4
6411 George Stover; M; Son; 2-5

6412 John Swallow; M; Husb; 25
6413 Hattie Swallow; F; Wife; 22

6414 Samuel Smith; M; Father; 36
6415 Julia Smith; F; Wife; 31
6416 Alice Smith; F; Dau; 11

6417 Wapaha Sapa; Joseph Black N. Bonnet; M; 21

6418 Jessie Craven; F; Mother; 31
6419 Hattie Craven; F; Dau; 14
6420 John Craven; M; Son; 12
6421 Teddie Craven; M; Son; 9
6422 Edith Craven; F; Dau; 5
6423 Isabel Oma Craven; F; Dau; 1-5

6424 Emma Allen; F; Mother; 41
6425 Nellie Allen; F; Dau; 21
6426 Joseph Allen; M; Son; 20
6427 Sophia Allen; F; Dau; 17
6428 Charles Allen; M; Son; 15
6429 Samuel Allen; M; Son; 14
6430 Jessie Allen; F; Dau; 12
6431 Lizzie Allen; F; Dau; 10
6432 Robert Allen; M; Son; 8
6433 Julia Allen; F; Dau; 7

6434 Louis Hawkins; M; Father; 38
6435 Julia Hawkins; F; Wife; 34
6436 Susie Hawkins; F; Dau; 16
6437 James Hawkins; M; Son; 14
6438 Joseph Hawkins; M; Son; 12
6439 Lottie Hawkins; F; Dau; 11
6440 William Hawkins; M; Son; 5
6441 Lottie D Hawkins; F; Dau; 9

6442 Emily Lesserts; F; G.Mo; 54
6443 Belle McWilliams; F; G.Dau; 11
6444 Benny McWilliams; M; G.Son; 9
6445 Mag McWilliams; F; G.Dau; 5
6446 Butterfly; F; Mother; 77

6447 Philip F Wells; M; Father; 45
6448 Thomas H. Wells; M; Son; 10
6449 Alma A. Wells; F; Dau; 7
6450 Philip Wells; M; Son; 5
6451 Mark Wells; M; Son; 2-6

Census Of The Sioux And Cheyenne Indians Of Pine Ridge Agency, South Dakota. Taken by W. H. Clapp, Captain 16th Infantry, Acting United States Indian Agent, June 30, 1896. (Pass Creek District)

Key: Number; Indian Name *(if given)*; English Name; Sex; Relation; Age

6452 George Randall; M; Husb; 20
6453 Lucy Randall; F; Wife; 19

6454 Charles Richard; M; Husb; 23
6455 Louise Richard; F; Wife; 21
6456 Theresa Flesher; F; Niece; 4-8

6457 Maka Hanska; Long Skunk; M: Husb; 25
6458 Nellie Skunk; F; Wife; 26

6459 Tasunke Ciqala; Little Horse; M; Husb; 21
6460 Tasunke Ciqala; Mary Little Horse; F; Wife; 20

6461 Kangi Wakuwa; William Charging Crow; M; Husb; 26
6462 Kangi Wakuwa; Nancy Charging Crow; F; Wife; 21

6463 Louis Provost; M; Husb; 23
6464 Alma Provost; F; Wife; 19

6465 Wasicu Ciqala; Little White Man; M; Father; 24
6466 Hinrota Win; Roan Woman; F; Wife; 21
6467 Lowan Mani; Sings And Walks; M; Son; 1-9

6468 Napa; Hand; M; Father; 57
6469 Ninwicakaga; Makes Life; F; Wife; 48
6470 Nape; Julia Hand; F; Dau; 22
6471 Hakikta; Looks Back; F; Dau; 13

Census Of The Sioux And Cheyenne Indians Of Pine Ridge Agency, South Dakota. Taken by W. H. Clapp, Captain 16th Infantry, Acting United States Indian Agent, August 15, 1896.

- E R R A T A -

Wounded Knee District.

No.	English Name.	Sex.	Relation.	Age.
6473	Frank Webber	M	Son	4-2
6474	Julia Webber	F	Dau	1-5

Being children of No. 2678.

6475	John Sires	M	Son	4
6476	James Sires	M	Son	2-8
6477	Josephine Sires	F	Dau	0-2

Being children of No. 2881.

Medicine Root District.

6480	Jules Lamb	M	Son	1-3
6481	Adolph Lamb	M	Son	1-3

Being children of No. 3957.

6482	Belnore Girard	F	Dau	4-6
6483	Ethel Josephine Girard	F	Dau	2-2

Being children of No. 4096.

The foregoing were omitted from classification in body of census under provision Act of Congress August 9, 1888.

For other children coming under provision of this Act, see numbers 159, 160, 869, 871, 877, 1062, 1063, and 1270.

No. 2363, page 53 omitted.

No. 944, Susie Bullock, Wakpamini District, to be dropped, being enrolled as Susie Tibbetts, No. 3357, Medicine Root District.

No. 6472, Tasunka Luza, Susie Fast Horse, F. Dau, Age 7 years, daughter of No. 992, erroneously reported dead.

The foregoing is believed to be correct.

W. H. Clapp
Captain 16th Infantry,
Acting Indian Agent.

Pine Ridge Agency, August 15, 1896.

Census of the Sioux and Cheyenne Indians Of Pine Ridge Agency, South Dakota.

1897

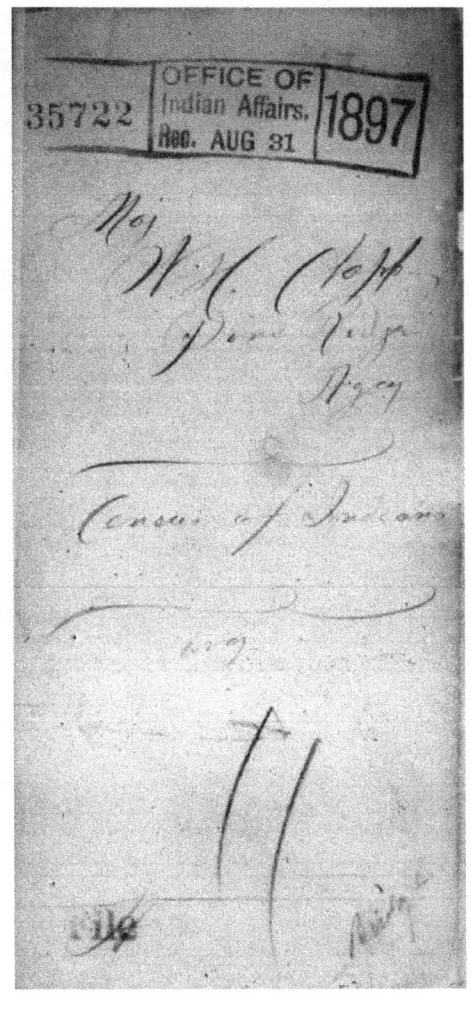

Census Of The Sioux And Cheyenne Indians Of Pine Ridge Agency, South Dakota. Taken by W. H. Clapp, Captain 16th Infantry, Acting United States Indian Agent, 1897

PINE RIDGE RESERVATION. S. D.

-CENSUS-

June 30, 1897.

Total population	6386
Males	3058
Females	3328
Children of school age	1597
Number of day schools	26
Children enrolled in day schools	929
Children at Holy Rosary Mission	152
Children at Non-Reservation Schools	174
Children not attending school	489

Census Of The Sioux And Cheyenne Indians Of Pine Ridge Agency, South Dakota. Taken by W. H. Clapp, Captain 16th Infantry, Acting United States Indian Agent, 1897

PINE RIDGE RESERVATION.

Census, June 30, 1897.

Wakpamini District.

Population	937
Males	447
Females	490
Children of school age	240
Number of day schools	3
Children enrolled in day schools	102
Children at Non-Reservation Schools	49
Children not attending school	89

---•---

Charles Dalkenberger,
Additional Farmer.

Census Of The Sioux And Cheyenne Indians Of Pine Ridge Agency, South Dakota. Taken by W. H. Clapp, Captain 16th Infantry, Acting United States Indian Agent, 1897

PINE RIDGE RESERVATION.

Census, June 30, 1897.

Porcupine District.

Population	794
Males	375
Females	419
Children of school age	191
Number of day schools	3
Children enrolled in day schools	101
Children at non-reservation schools	29
Children not attending school	55

B. J. Gleason,
Additional Farmer.

Census Of The Sioux And Cheyenne Indians Of Pine Ridge Agency, South Dakota. Taken by W. H. Clapp, Captain 16th Infantry, Acting United States Indian Agent, 1897

PINE RIDGE RESERVATION.

Census, June 30, 1897.

Wounded Knee District.

--•--

Population	1326
Males	642
Females	684
Children of school age	335
Number of day schools	6
Children enrolled in day schools	235
Children at non-reservation schools	25
Children not attending school	118

B. J. Gleason,
Additional Farmer.

----•---

Census Of The Sioux And Cheyenne Indians Of Pine Ridge Agency, South Dakota. Taken by W. H. Clapp, Captain 16th Infantry, Acting United States Indian Agent, 1897

PINE RIDGE RESERVATION.

Census, June 30, 1897.

Medicine Root District.

Population	1026
Males	476
Females	550
Children of school age	249
Number of day schools	4
Children enrolled in day schools	146
Children at non-reservation schools	29
Children not attending school	69

James Smalley,
Additional Farmer.

Census Of The Sioux And Cheyenne Indians Of Pine Ridge Agency, South Dakota. Taken by W. H. Clapp, Captain 16th Infantry, Acting United States Indian Agent, 1897

PINE RIDGE RESERVATION.

Census, June 30, 1897.

White Clay District.

Population	1279
Males	623
Females	656
Children of school age	313
Number of day schools	5
Children enrolled in day schools	181
Children at non-reservation schools	6
Children not attending school	94

John H. Bosel,

Additional Farmer.

Census Of The Sioux And Cheyenne Indians Of Pine Ridge Agency, South Dakota. Taken by W. H. Clapp, Captain 16th Infantry, Acting United States Indian Agent, 1897

PINE RIDGE RESERVATION.

Census, June 30, 1897.

Pass Creek District.

Population	1024
Males	495
Females	529
Children of school age	269
Number of day schools	5
Children enrolled in day schools	164
Children at non-reservation schools	36
Children not attending school	67

Joseph Rooks,
Additional Farmer.

Census of the Sioux And Cheyenne Indians
Of Pine Ridge Agency, South Dakota.
June 30, 1897

Wakpamini District

Census Of The Sioux And Cheyenne Indians Of Pine Ridge Agency, South Dakota. Taken by W. H. Clapp, Captain 16th Infantry, Acting United States Indian Agent, June 30, 1897. (Wakpamini District)

Key: Number; Indian Name *(if given)*; English Name; Sex; Relation; Age

1 Jennie Whalen; F; Head; 45
2 Nellie Whalen; F; Dau; 18
3 James Wahlen[sic]; M; Son; 16
4 Jennie Whalen; F; Dau; 13
5 Mary Whalen; F; Dau; 11
6 Richard Whalen; M; Son; 6

7 Winyan Sica; Bad Looking Woman; F; Head; 84

8 E. G. Bettelyoun; M; Head; 27
9 Josephine Bettelyoun; F; Wife; 26
10 Isaac Bettelyoun; M; Son; 4-7
11 Susie Janis; F; Niece; 14
12 Howard Bettelyoun; M; Son; 2
13 Lucinda Bettelyoun; F; Dau; 1mo

14 Mato Hinsma; Hairy Bear; M; Head; 69
15 Winorcala Sica; Bad Old Woman; F; Wife; 62
16 Gliyopsica; Jumps Off; M; Son; 25

17 Waslipa; Licks; M; Head; 68
18 Wiciyela Win; Yankton Woman; F; Wife; 66
19 Zintkala Wanbli; Eagle Bird; M; Son; 21
20 Winyan Tanka; Big Woman; F; Dau; 16

21 Peter Shangreau; M; Head; 37
22 Lucy Shangreau; F; Wife; 27
23 Antonio Shangreau; M; Son; 13
24 Rosa Shangreau; F; Dau; 14
25 Jessy Shangreau; F; Dau; 8
26 Sarah Shangreau; F; Dau; 5
27 Angeline Shangreau; F; Dau; 2-4
28 Myrtle Shangreau; F; Dau; 4mo

29 Akicita Najin; Standing Soldier #1; M; Head; 46
30 Akicita Najin; Katie S. Soldier; F; Wife; 47

31 Akicita Najin; Philip S. Soldier; M; Son; 20
32 Akicita Najin; Henry S. Soldier; M; Son; 15
33 Akicita Najin; Mary S. Soldier; F; Dau; 13
34 Akicita Najin; Dinah S. Soldier; F; Dau; 10
35 Akicita Najin; Victoria S. Soldier; F; Dau; 4-6

36 James D. Janis; M; Head; 40
37 Mollie Janis; F; Wife; 42
38 Minnie Janis; F; Dau; 8
39 Louise Janis; F; Dau; 5-6
40 Julia Janis; F; Dau; 1-6

41 Wankal Iyanka; Runs Above; M; Head; 50
42 Marpiya Hinapa; Cloud Comes Out; F; Wife; 50
43 Caje Wanica; No Name; M; Son; 18
44 Nakipa; Runs Away; M; Son; 14

45 Taka Kute; Shoots Enemy; M; Head; 70

46 Maka Nabu; Noisy Walk; M; Head; 35
47 Peta; Fire; F; Wife; 27
48 Okicize Tawa; Owns The Fight; M; Son; 9
49 Ptesan Hoksila; White Cow Boy; M; Son; 6

50 Tasunke Maza; Iron Horse; M; Head; 47
51 Nata; The Head; F; Wife; 35
52 Wicegna Glicu; Comes From Amongst; F; Dau; 16
53 Ehake Gli; Comes Last; F; Dau; 5-6

54 Sungmanitu Ska; White Wolf; M; Head; 52

Census Of The Sioux And Cheyenne Indians Of Pine Ridge Agency, South Dakota. Taken by W. H. Clapp, Captain 16th Infantry, Acting United States Indian Agent, June 30, 1897. (Wakpamini District)

Key: Number; Indian Name *(if given)*; English Name; Sex; Relation; Age

55 Sunsunla Sapa; Black Mule; F; Wife; 40
56 Sungmanitu Ska; Wm. White Wolf; M; Son; 25
57 Kimimila; Butter Fly; M; S.Son; 15
58 Wamniomni; Whirlwind; F; Dau; 15
59 Pankeska Win; Shell Woman; F; Dau; 9
60 Sungmanitu Ska; Georgiana W. Wolf; F; Dau; 7

61 Oye Luta; Red Track; F; Head; 79

62 Nacaka; Chief #1; M; Head; 34
63 Nacaka; Lucie Chief; F; Wife; 35
64 Marpiya Wanjila; Lone Cloud; M; Son; 15
65 Sunkitacan Agli; Brings Chief Horse; F; Dau; 8
66 Nacaka; Mollie Chief; F; Dau; 1-4

67 Miwakan; George Sword; M; Head; 50
68 Miwakan; Lucy Sword; F; Wife; 31
69 Miwakan; Jessie Sword; F; Dau; 9
70 Miwakan; Archie Sword; M; Neph; 22

71 Manstincala Ska; White Rabbit; M; Head; 60
72 Witko Win; Crazy Woman; F; Wife; 49
73 Hinrota; Roan; M; Son; 25
74 Mastincala Ska; Julia White Rabbit; F; Dau; 19
75 Mastincala Ska; Annie White Rabbit; F; Dau; 16
76 Kutepi; Shoots At Him; M; Son; 14

77 Peji Rota Win; Grey Grass Woman; F; Dau; 4-4

78 Mato Kokipapi; Afraid Of Bear; M; Head; 55
79 Tiglake; Moves Lodge; F; Wife; 40
80 Pankeska Waste; Good Shell; F; Dau; 3-8
81 Mato Kokipapi; Lucy Afraid Of Bear; F; Dau; 14

82 Tucuku; Ribs; M; Head; 39
83 Ipiyaka Cola; No Belt; F; Wife; 40
84 Oksanta Kte; Kills Around; M; Son; 12
85 Cetan; Hawk; M; Son; 8
86 Kiyela; Close; M; S.Son; 22

87 Tasunke Luzahan; Fast Horse; M; Head; 45
88 Wamniomni; Whirlwind; F; Wife; 43
89 Tasunke Luzahan; Julia Fast Horse; F; Dau; 14
90 Wicakico; Calls Them; F; Dau; 12
91 Toka Kute; Shoots Enemy; M; Son; 9
92 Gluka; Keeps; M; Son; 2-1

93 Gertie Janis; F; Head; 39
94 Susie Janis; F; Dau; 5-6
95 Alice; F; Dau; 1-4

96 Charles Janis; M; Head; 50
97 Lives Well; F; Wife; 45
98 Susanna Janis; F; Dau; 19
99 Louis Janis; M; G.Son; 7
100 Henry Janis; M; G.Son; 3-4

101 Cetan Oranko; Quick Hawk; M; Head; 35
102 Mato Hinapa; Bear Comes Out; F; Wife; 23

Census Of The Sioux And Cheyenne Indians Of Pine Ridge Agency, South Dakota. Taken by W. H. Clapp, Captain 16th Infantry, Acting United States Indian Agent, June 30, 1897.   (Wakpamini District)

Key: Number; Indian Name *(if given)*; English Name; Sex; Relation; Age

103   Nagwaka; Kicks; F; M. in L.; 55
104   Sunka Ska; White Dog; M: Head; 63

105   Mary Deon #1; F; Head; 64
106   William Deon; M; Son; 24
107   Cecilia Deon; F; Dau; 21
108   Sophia Deon; F; Dau; 20

109   Sam Deon; M; Head; 25
110   Susie Deon; F; Wife; 23
111   Herold Deon; M; Son; 24 da.

112   Sunymanitu Ska; John White Wolf; M; Head; 26
113   Sunymanitu Ska; Alice White Wolf; F; Wife; 24
114   Sunymanitu Ska; Red White Cow[sic]; F; Dau; 2-10
115   Sunymanitu Ska; Charles White Wolf; M; Son; 11-1/2 mo

116   Wanbli Rota; Roan Eagle; M; Head; 34
117   Rabya Mani; Noisy Walk; F; Wife; 26
118   Wanapa Gli; Comes Wounded; M; Son; 13
119   Anpo Wakuwa; Charges In Morning; M; Son; 3-4
120   Zintkala Hinsma; Mrs. Hairy Bird #2; F; Mother; 60
121   Wanbli Rota; Annie Roan Eagle; F; Dau; 8-2/3 mo

122   Tiglake; Traveler; F; Head; 41
123   Cecelia Armstrong; F; Dau; 14
124   Heraka Nupa; Julia Two Elk; F; Dau; 1-4

125   Louise Allman; F; Head; 42
126   Charles Allman; M; Son; 15
127   Sam Allman; M; Son; 12
128   Nora Allman; F; Dau; 10
129   Lilly Allman; F; Dau; 17

130   Lydia Allman; F; Dau; 6
131   Lorina Allman; F; Dau; 4
132   Myrtle Allman; F; Dau; 1-2

133   Julia Richard; F; Head; 71

134   Maste Kaga; Makes Shine; M; Head; 29
135   Anpetu Hinapa; Day Comes Out; F; Wife; 29
136   Ciyeku; Oldest Brother; M; Son; 5
137   Isna Wakuna; Chase Alone; M; Son; 2-6

138   Zintkala; Charles Bird; M; Head; 31
139   Zintkala; Jennie Bird; F;   Wife; 23
140   Zintkala; Rosa Bird; F; Dau; 4-6
141   Pankeska Win; Shell Woman; F; Mother; 59
142   Eugene; M; Bro; 17
143   Zintkala; Nettie Bird; F; Dau; 6 1/2 mo

144   Sunkgleska Win; Spotted Horse Woman; F; Head; 68

145   Tasunke Wanbli; Eagle Horse; M; Head; 42
146   Onpan Win; Elk Woman; F; Wife; 34
147   Sinte Sapa; Black Tail; M; Son; 17
148   Seven Up; M; Son; 11
149   Wasicu Wayankapa; Looks White; F; Dau; 6
150   Tasunke; Her Horse; F; Dau; 2-6

151   Itunkasan Kte; Kills White Weasel; M; Head; 32
152   David; M; Bro; 10

153   Anpo Wakuwa; Charge In Morning; M; Head; 24

Census Of The Sioux And Cheyenne Indians Of Pine Ridge Agency, South Dakota. Taken by W. H. Clapp, Captain 16th Infantry, Acting United States Indian Agent, June 30, 1897. (Wakpamini District)

Key: Number; Indian Name *(if given)*; English Name; Sex; Relation; Age

154   Sahunwin Tanka; Big Cheyenne Woman; F; Head; 66
155   Wakan Waci; Medicine Dance; M; Son; 22
156   Pankeska Win; Shell Woman; F; Dau; 8
157   Cekpa; Twin; F; Dau; 8

158   Alice Pallardy; F; Head; 50

159   Jennie Pugh; F; Head; 27
160   Stanley R. Pugh; M; Son; 7
161   William G. Pugh; M; Son; 5

162   Victoria Adams; F; Head; 77
163   Sunkowa; Painted Horse; M; Son; 49

164   Mato Lowan; Singing Bear; M; Head; 55
165   Wanbli Sun; Eagle Feather; F; Wife 65
166   Sunkhinsa Yuha; Red Horse Owner; M; Son; 7

167   Taopi Ota; Moses Plenty Wounds; M; Head; 43
168   Hinwaste Win; Good Haired Woman; F; Wife; 30

169   Ska Agli; Brings White; F; Head; 28
170   Naron; Hears; F; Dau; 6

171   Sunkska Win; White Horse Woman; F; Head; 57

172   Joseph Mosseau[sic]; M; Head; 32
173   Nellie Mousseau; F; Wife; 31
174   Ellen Mousseau; F; Dau; 8
175   Maglor'd Mousseau; M; Son; 5-7

176   Sunkmanitu Gi; Yellow Wolf; M; Head; 67

177   Kangi Tanka; Big Crow; M: Head; 60
178   Sina Ksupi Koyaka; Bears Beaded Blanket; F; Wife; 58
179   Kangi Tanka; Ida Big Crow; F; Dau; 26
180   Kangi Tanka; Susie Big Crow; F; Dau; 24
181   Kangi Tanka; Mary Big Crow; F; Dau; 22
182   Kangi Tanka; Lucy Big Crow; F; Dau; 20
183   Takolaku Ota; Many Friends; M; G.Son; 4

184   Sunkhinto; Blue Horse; M; Head; 76
185   Peta Omniciye; Council Fire; F; Wife; 67
186   Sunkhinto; Jennie Blue Horse; F; Dau; 26
187   Sunkhinto; Lizzie Blue Horse; F; G.Dau; 1-3

188   Tokala Win; Sophia Fox; F; Head; 49

189   Mary Janie; F; Head; 58
190   Louis Matthews; M; G.Son; 26

191   Mato Luta; Red Bear; M; Head; 55
192   Wanbli Koyaka; Wears The Eagle; F; Wife; 40
193   Mato Luta; Dick Red Bear; M; Son; 12
194   Zuya Ciqala; Little Warrior; M; Son; 6
195   Wicoti Maza; Iron Village; M; Son; 9 days

196   Tonweya Gli; Comes From Scout; M: Head; 23
197   Julia; F; Wife; 19

Census Of The Sioux And Cheyenne Indians Of Pine Ridge Agency, South Dakota. Taken by W. H. Clapp, Captain 16th Infantry, Acting United States Indian Agent, June 30, 1897. (Wakpamini District)

Key: Number; Indian Name *(if given)*; English Name; Sex; Relation; Age

198 Pesla; Bald Head; M; Head; 20
199 Kangi Maza; Cecilia Iron Crow; F; Wife; 19

200 Cokula; Flesh; M; Head; 56
201 Wakau Win; Holy Woman; F; Wife 46
202 Toka Kute; Shoots The Enemy; M; Son; 4

203 Zintkala Oranko; Swift Bird; M; Head; 64
204 Zintkala Oranko; Marion Swift Bird; F; Dau; 21
205 Zintkala Wakan; Holy Bird; M; G.Son; 2-4

206 Inyan Wicasa; Rock Man; M; Head; 34
207 Oye Sapa; Black Tracks; F; Wife; 37

208 Mato Hinapa; Bear Comes Out; F; Head; 40

209 Wanbli Kokipa; Afraid Of Eagle; M; Head; 55
210 Tipi Tanka; Big Lodge; F; Wife; 61
211 Tanyan Hinapa; Comes Out Good; F; G.Dau; 10

212 Marpiya Luta; Red Cloud; M; Head; 74
213 Marpiya Luta; Mary Red Cloud; F; Wife; 66
214 Mato Hunhesni; Luke Slow Bear; M; G.Son; 14

215 Hektakiya Gli; Comes Back; M; Head; 20
216 Taspau; Dora Apple; F; Wife; 17

217 Sunkhinsa; Susie Red Horse; F; Head; 33

218 Cage Wanica; No Name; F; Sis; 45
219 Gleska Agli; Brings Spotted; F; G.Mo; 85
220 Sunkhinsa; George Red Horse; M; Neph; 13
221 Sunkhinsa; Louise Red Horse; F; Niece; 11

222 Snia Rota; Gray Blanket; M; Head; 36
223 Pankeska; Shell; F; Wife; 41
224 James Galligo; M; Son; 13
225 Winyan Ciqala; Little Woman; F; Dau; 13
226 Wanbli Waste; Good Eagle; F; Dau; 6

227 Wiciyela; Edward Yankton; M; Head; 27
228 Wi Ite; Woman Face; F; Wife; 34
229 Wicarpi Wanjila; One Star; M; Bro; 26

230 Sapa Ska; White Beaver; F; Head; 71

231 Sungmanitu Nakpa; Wolf Ears; M; Head; 63
232 Itunkasan; Weasel; F; Wife; 58
233 Wawokiya; Helper; M; Son; 15

234 Frank McMahon; M; Head; 33
235 Julia McMahon; F; Wife; 34

236 Hoksila Waste; Frank Good Boy; M; Head; 26
237 Wanita; F; Sis; 19

238 Tasunke Hinzi; Yellow Horse; M; Head; 37
239 Aiyapi; Talks About; F; Wife; 33
240 Wayank Hipi; Comes To See Her; F; Dau; 15

Census Of The Sioux And Cheyenne Indians Of Pine Ridge Agency, South Dakota. Taken by W. H. Clapp, Captain 16th Infantry, Acting United States Indian Agent, June 30, 1897. (Wakpamini District)

Key: Number; Indian Name *(if given)*; English Name; Sex; Relation; Age

241 Tonweya Gli; Comes From Scout; M; Son; 8	266 Hektakiya Ekte; Kills Back; M; Head; 31
242 Howaste Win; Good Voice Woman; F; Head; 59	267 Kpazo; Show; F; Wife; 29
243 Ninyan Ke Kte; Kills Alive; F; Dau; 26	268 Mato Hoksila; Bear Boy; M; Son; 5-6
244 Sallie Janis; F; G.Dau; 14	269 Marpiya Wahacanka; Cloud Shield; M; Head; 56
245 Tawa Kte; Kills Her Own; F; G.Dau; 3-5	270 Pehin; Hair; F; Wife; 41
	271 Tipi Zi Win; Yellow House; F; Dau; 18
246 John Nelson; M; Head; 27	272 Hinhan Wakan; Holy Owl; M; Son; 11
247 Lizzie Nelson; F; Wife; 28	
248 William Nelson; M; Son; 9	273 Sunktacanku; Horse Road; M; Son; 8
249 Samuel Nelson; N[sic]; Son; 7	
250 John Nelson, Jr; M; Son; 10 mo	274 Marpiya Wahacanka; Thos. Cloud Shield; M; Son; 5-6
251 Julia Nelson; F; Head; 25	
252 Annie Nelson; F; Dau; 1-4	275 Maza Ciqala; Little Iron; M; Head; 38
253 Maka Cega; Dirt Kettle; M; Head; 49	276 Ptesan; White Cow; F; Wife; 38
254 Wanbli Win; Eagle Woman; F; Wife; 34	277 Nata Witko; Fool Head; M; Head; 29
255 Wahacanka; Shield; M; Son; 8	278 Canku Maza; Iron Road; F; Wife; 21
256 Wapsakapi; Cut From Rope; F; Dau; 5	279 Mni Hinapa; Water Comes Out; F; Dau; 2-10
257 Cetan Wakuwa; Chasing Hawk; M; Father; 66	
	280 Sunk Ska; White Horse; M; Head; 50
258 Naca Agli; Brings The Chief; M; Son; 24	281 Ite Owakita; Looks In Face; F; Wife; 52
259 Hunska Tanka Narco; Big Leggins Down; F; Mother; 65	
	282 Ehake Gli; Comes Last; M; Head; 22
260 Iya Wasaka; Strong Talk; M; Head; 34	283 Anpo Kte; Kills In Morning; F; Wife; 24
261 Tatiyopa; Her Door; F; Wife; 25	
262 Wicarpi Luta; Red Star; F; Dau; 6	284 Hin Tani; Old Hair; M; Head; 34
263 Onpan Luta; Red Elk; F; Dau; 4-6	285 Zintka To; Blue Bird; F; Wife; 31
264 Hinzi Agli; Brings Yellow; M; Nephew; 24	286 Pahin; Porcupine; M; Son; 10
	287 Wapaha Luta; Red War Bonnet; F; Dau; 8
265 Mata; Mata; F; Head; 77	

Census Of The Sioux And Cheyenne Indians Of Pine Ridge Agency, South Dakota.
Taken by W. H. Clapp, Captain 16th Infantry, Acting United States Indian Agent,
June 30, 1897. (Wakpamini District)

Key: Number; Indian Name *(if given)*; English Name; Sex; Relation; Age

288	Tasunke Opi; Wounded Horse; M; Son; 4-8		316	Jessie Mills; F; Wife; 23
289	Agli Ti; Comes And Camps; F; Dau; 2-5		317	Okute; Shoots In; M; Head; 28
			318	Tasina; Her Blanket; F; Wife; 27
			319	Mazaska Ole; After Money; F; Dau; 3-10
290	Toka Kaga; Makes Enemy; M; Head; 39		320	Okute; Wallace Shoots In; M; Son; 8 mo
291	Tacanupa; Her Pipe; F; Wife; 37			
292	Toka Kaga; John Makes Enemy; M; Son; 6 mo		321	Maka Okawinr Mani; Country Traveler; M; Head; 54
293	Petaga; Coal Of Fire; F; G.Mo; 64		322	Sahunwinla; Cheyenne Woman; F; Wife; 59
294	Zintkala Maza; Iron Bird; M; G.Son; 13		323	Maka Okawinr Mani; Beny[sic] Traveler; M; G.Son; 19
295	Capa Maza; Iron Beaver; M; Head; 36		324	Mato Najin; Standing Bear; M; Head; 46
296	Tacanupa Wanbli; Her Eagle Pipe; F; Wife; 29		325	Tasina Wanbli; Hattie Eagle Shawl; F; Dau; 20
			326	Zintkala; Bird; M; Son; 12
297	Nunwanpi; Swimmer; M; Head; 64		327	Mato Najin; Annie Standing Bear; F; Dau; 1 mo
298	Winyan Tanka; Big Woman; F; Wife; 60		328	Pte Sapa Win; Black Cow; F; Head; 39
299	Sunkicu; Takes The Horse; F; Dau; 13			
			329	Kimimila Ska; White Butter Fly; M; Head; 32
300	Alexander Salvis; M; Head; 41			
301	Mollie Salvis; F; Wife; 39		330	Zintkala Waste; Pretty Bird; F; Wife; 28
302	Alice Salvis; F; Dau; 18			
303	Charles Salvis; M; Son; 17		331	Kimimila Ska; Annie W. Butter Fly; F; Dau; 12
304	Willie Salvis; M; Son; 14			
305	Julia Salvis; F; Dau; 12			
306	Alexander Salvis; M; Son; 9		332	Mato Ska; Wm. White Bear; M; Head; 24
307	Stacy Salvis; M; Son; 7			
308	Frank Salvis; M; Son; 5-6		333	Mato Ska; Jennie White Bear; F; Wife; 25
309	Lucy Salvis; F; Dau; 1-2			
			334	Mato Ska; Alice White Bear; F; Dau; 2-2
310	Thomas Mills; M; Head; 34			
311	Nellie Mills; F; Wife; 28		335	Mato Ska; Lucy White Bear; F; Dau; 1-18 da
312	Richard Mills; M; Son; 7			
313	Annie Mills; F; Dau; 2-5			
314	Benj. Mills; M; Son; 7 mo		336	Tatanka Wankatuya; High Bull; M; Head; 39
315	Benjamin Mills; M; Head; 26		337	Sina; Shawl; F; Wife; 40

Census Of The Sioux And Cheyenne Indians Of Pine Ridge Agency, South Dakota.
Taken by W. H. Clapp, Captain 16th Infantry, Acting United States Indian Agent,
June 30, 1897. (Wakpamini District)

Key: Number; Indian Name *(if given)*; English Name; Sex; Relation; Age

338 Cangleska Wanbli; Eagle Hoop; M; Son; 15
339 Pejuta Win; Medicine Woman; F; Dau; 8
340 Tazunke Iyanke; Running Horse; M; Head; 37
341 Hin Waste Win; Good Voiced Woman; F; Wife; 34
342 Itunkasan Luta; Red Weasel; M; Son; 12
343 Naroupi; Hear Him; M; Son; 10
344 Wahacanka To; Blue Shield; M; Head; 56
345 Taanpetu; Her Day; F; Wife; 56
346 Ehake Win; Last Woman; F; Dau; 12
347 Wicapaoskica; Fills The Hole; M; Son; 17
348 Frank Goings; M; Head; 25
349 Can Wanjila; Lone Tree; F; Wife; 19
350 Earl Goings; M; Son; 3-2
351 Garnett Goings; M; Son; 1-8
352 Tainyan Wakuwa; Chase In Light; M; Head; 31
353 Wayank Najin; Stands And Looks; M; Son; 4-6
354 Cetan Waste Win; Good Hawk Woman; F; Mother; 63
355 Ptesan Luta Win; Red White Cow; F; Head; 40
356 Wanbli Sun; Eagle Feather; F; Dau; 15
357 Wayankapi; Looks At Him; F; Dau; 7
358 Martha Dun; F; Head; 79
359 Wasicu Maza; Iron White Man; M; Head; 28
360 Tokaheya Win; Leading Woman; F; Wife; 31
361 Cante Waste; Good Heart; F; Dau; 12
362 Canupa Kupi; Gives Pipe; M; Son; 7
363 Tainyan Najin; Stands In Sight; M; Son; 1-10
364 Wakan Hinapa; Comes Out Holy; M; Head; 31
365 Sunk Sapa; Black Horse; F; Wife; 39
366 Agli; Brings; M; Bro; 25
367 Hanpa Nasica; Bad Moccasin; M; Head; 61
368 Wanbli Luta; Red Eagle; F; Wife; 50
369 Zintkala Mato; Bear Eagle; M; Son; 25
370 Ninglicu; Comes Alive; F; Dau; 23
371 Sunkhinsa; Red Horse; F; Dau; 17
372 Agliti; Comes and Camps; F; Niece; 12
373 Anpo Wakuwa; Chase In Morning; M; Head; 26
374 Tatank[sic] Wicota; Bull Villate[sic]; F; Wife; 29
375 Nakicipapi; Runs Away From Him; M; Son; 15
376 Najinyapi; Surrounded; M; Son; 9
377 Sunkicu; Takes Horses; F; Dau; 6
378 Maskablaska; Flat Iron; M; Head; 68
379 Maza Sna Win; Rattling Iron; F; Wife; 61
380 Tacanku Waste Win; Her Good Road; F; Dau; 18

Census Of The Sioux And Cheyenne Indians Of Pine Ridge Agency, South Dakota.
Taken by W. H. Clapp, Captain 16th Infantry, Acting United States Indian Agent,
June 30, 1897. (Wakpamini District)

Key: Number; Indian Name *(if given)*; English Name; Sex; Relation; Age

381 Tokeya Kte; Kills Leader; M; G.Son; 12

382 Toka Kte; Kills Enemy; M; Head; 34

383 Okogna Iyanka; Runs Between; F; Wife; 32

384 Wanbli Taheya; Eagle Louse; M; Head; 28

385 Kangi Sagye; Crow Cane; F; Wife; 43

386 Tarca Ska; White Deer; M; Head; 38

387 Winyan Luta; Red Woman; F; Wife; 40

388 Cangleska Waste; Good Ring; M; Son; 9

389 Tonwan; Light; M; Son; 5

390 Najin; Lizzie Stands; F; Dau; 28

391 Sungmanitu Tanka; Big Wolf; M; Head; 73

392 Caje Wanica; No Name; F; Wife; 72

393 Mato Istima; John Sleeping Bear; M; G.Son; 21

394 Mato Ehakela; Last Bear; M; Head; 58

395 Cekpa; Twin; F; Wife; 48

396 Wicarpi; Edward Star; M; Head; 28

397 Wicarpi; Anna Star; F; Wife; 25

398 Pejuta Win; Medicine Woman; F; Dau; 1-6

399 Onanya; Burns Prairie; M; Head; 32

400 Ptesan Hinapa; White Cow Out; F; Wife; 32

401 Wanbli Isnala; Lone Eagle; M; Son; 3-9

402 Tokeya Hinapa; Comes Out First; M; Son; 3mo

403 Wamniomni; Whirlwind; M; Head; 71

404 Pte Waste Win; Good Cow; F; Head; 73

405 Cetan Ciqala; Little Hawk; M; Head; 62

406 Tipi Ska Win; White House; F; Wife; 62

407 Cetan Ciqala; Wm. Little Hawk; M; G.Son; 15

408 Mazasu Ota; Many Cartridges; M; Head; 24

409 Kangi Sagye; Crow Cane; F; Wife; 23

410 Mato Sapa; Black Bear; M; Head; 71

411 Wiciyela Win; Yankton Woman; F; Wife; 48

412 Pehinji; Yellow Hair; F; Dau; 11

413 Hokisla[sic] Ska; White Boy; M; Son; 11

414 Kokab Najin; Stands In Front; M; Son; 15

415 Itazipa Kicun; Uses Bow; M; Head; 38

416 Cante Win la; Heart; F; Wife; 28

417 Ota Hinapa Win; Comes Out Plenty; F; Niece; 10

418 Mato; John Bear; M; Head; 59

419 Anpo Wakita; Looks At Daylight; F; Wife; 46

420 Mato; Louise Bear; F; Dau; 17

421 Sila; Philip Foot; M; Head; 32

422 Sallie Hunter; F; Wife; 38

423 John Hunter; M; Neph; 13

Census Of The Sioux And Cheyenne Indians Of Pine Ridge Agency, South Dakota. Taken by W. H. Clapp, Captain 16th Infantry, Acting United States Indian Agent, June 30, 1897. (Wakpamini District)

Key: Number; Indian Name *(if given)*; English Name; Sex; Relation; Age

424 Kokab Ekte; Kills Ahead; M; Head; 49
425 Heraka Sapa; Black Elk; F; Wife; 49
426 John Ladeaux; M; Son; 23
427 John Brooks; M; Son; 20
428 Gluha; Keeps; M; Son; 13
429 Sunkmanu; Steals Horses; M; Son; 10

430 Mato Ciqala; Bob Little Bear; M; Head; 47
431 Mato Ciqala; Zuzella L. Bear; F; Wife; 38
432 Mato Ciqala; Henry L. Bear; M; Son; 22
433 Mato Ciqala; James .[sic] Bear; M; Son; 15

434 Wosla Najin; Stands Up; M; Head; 54
435 Akiyan Win; Flies Over Her; F; Wife; 49
436 Kawicapa; Beats All; F; Dau; 13
437 Hunka Hoksila; Pipe Dance Boy; M; Son; 3-11

438 Wizipan; Frank Baggage; M; Son; 25
439 Peggie; F; Mother; 50
440 James Richard; M; Bro; 22

441 Louis Martin; M; Head; 28
442 Winyan Cuwignake; Mary Womans'[sic] Dress; F; Wife; 35
443 Santa Rosa Martin; M; Bro; 19

444 Sunka Isna; Lone Dog; M; Head; 46
445 Cante Win; Heart Woman; F; Wife; 40
446 Tatanka Ptecela; Short Bull; M; Son; 14
447 Pehin Sa; Red Hair; F; Dau; 1-1

448 Onpan Waste; Good Elk; F; Head; 75
449 Cetan Luta; Chas. Red Hawk; M; Head; 24
450 Sungmanitu Hanska; Hannah Long Wolf; F; Wife; 21
451 Onpan Win; Elk Woman; M; Mother; 59
452 Sante Maza; George Iron Heart; M; Bro; 18
453 Cetan Luta; Thomas Red Hawk; M; Son; 1

454 Rosa Morrisette; F; Head; 54
455 Joseph Matthews; M; Son; 16
456 Oliver Morrisette; M; Head; 22
457 Lucy Morrisette; F; Wife; 28

458 Wahuwapa Sica; Bad Cob; M; Head; 43
459 Mni Sni; Cold Water; F; Wife; 33
460 Wawakpansni; Rustler; M; Son; 7

461 Wujaka Luta; Red Feather; M; Head; 30
462 Hin Waste Win; Pretty Hair; F; Wife; 19

463 Tasunke Kinyela; Flying Horse; M; Head; 25
464 Gleska Agle; Brings Spotted; F; Wife; 22

465 Cetan Tanka; Big Hawk; M; Head; 34
466 Tingleska; Mary Young Deer; F; Wife; 35
467 James Galligo; M; Son; 18
468 Alice Galligo; F; Dau; 16
469 Ella Galligo; f; Dau; 9
470 Zonie Galligo; F; Dau; 7

Census Of The Sioux And Cheyenne Indians Of Pine Ridge Agency, South Dakota. Taken by W. H. Clapp, Captain 16th Infantry, Acting United States Indian Agent, June 30, 1897. (Wakpamini District)

Key: Number; Indian Name *(if given)*; English Name; Sex; Relation; Age

471 Pejuta Win; Medicine Woman; F; Dau; 5
472 Charles Merrival; M; Head; 26
473 Maggie Merrival; F; Wife; 26
474 Laura Merrival; F; Dau; 3-7
475 Enakiya; Quit; F; Head; 53
476 Kangi Bloka; He Crow; M; Head; 60
477 Sunkagli; Brings Horses; F; Wife; 61
478 Canicipawega Waste; Good Cross; M; Son; 20
479 Kutepi; Mark Putepi; M; Son; 36
480 Olege Win; Chamber Woman; F; Mother; 54
481 Ptesan Kte; Kills White Cow; M; Son; 20
482 Maka Luta Win; Red Earth; F; Head; 67
483 Topa Hunka Win; Four Pipe Dance; F; Niece; 45
484 Mato; Bear; M; G.Son; 14
485 Mato Catka; Left Hand Bear; M; Head; 35
486 Oye Wanbli; Eagle Track; F; Wife; 45
487 Wicincala; Girl; F; Dau; 5-6
488 Wisake; Finger Nail Woman; F; Head; 44
489 Toka Oyuspe; Catches Enemy; M; Son; 11
490 Wapiyela; Doctor; F; Dau; 7
491 Akicita Najin; Standing Soldier #2; M; Head; 69
492 Wanbli Win; Eagle Woman; F; Wife; 60
493 Hi Kapsun; Breaks Teeth; M; Son; 24
494 Mato Win; Bear Woman; F; Dau; 16
495 Tocagla Iyanka; Runs Close To Lodge; M; G.Son; 8
496 Mni Okte; Kills In Water; F; Dau; 17
497 Zuyala; Warrior; F; G.Dau; 1-8
498 Nape; Marshall Hand; M; Head; 29
499 Kange[sic] Ciqala; Mary Little Crow; F; Wife; 29
500 Nape; Joseph Hand; M; Son; 1-6
501 Cetan Ska; White Hawk; M; Head; 79
502 Mama; F; Wife; 55
503 Yutimahel Icu; Brings In; M; G.Son; 1-3
504 Zintkala Wanbli; Bird Eagle; M; Head; 40
505 Blewakan; Holy Lake; F; Wife; 34
506 Toka Kte; Kills Enemy; F; Dau; 9
507 Tiapawicakte; Kills The Village; M; Son; 8
508 Taku Kte; Kills Something; M; Son; 5-6
509 Hoksila Zi; Grover Yellow Boy; M; Head; 27
510 Hoksila Zi; Kittie Yellow Boy; F; Wife; 26
511 Hoksila Zi; Jessie Yellow Boy; F; Dau; 7
512 Hoksila Zi; Lucy Yellow Boy; F; Dau; 5-3
513 Hoksila Zi; George Yellow Boy; M; Son; 3-5
514 Hoksila Zi; Thomas Yellow Boy; M; Son; 1-6
515 Janjanyela; Clear; M; Head; 40

Census Of The Sioux And Cheyenne Indians Of Pine Ridge Agency, South Dakota. Taken by W. H. Clapp, Captain 16th Infantry, Acting United States Indian Agent, June 30, 1897. (Wakpamini District)

Key: Number; Indian Name *(if given)*; English Name; Sex; Relation; Age

516 Tate Rmu Win; Ringing Wind; F; Wife; 35
517 Susie; F; Dau; 15
518 Janjanyela; Thomas Clear; M; Son; 13

519 Ohitika Win; Brave Woman #1; F; Head; 45
520 Rose Morrison; F; Dau; 17
521 Brother Morrison; M; Son; 7
522 Charles; M; Son; 5
523 Frank Martimus; M; Son; 9 mo

524 Hoksila Zi; Yellow Boy; M; Head; 31
525 Topa Win; Four Woman; F; Wife; 40
526 Hoksila Zi; Charles Yellow Boy; M; Son; 14
527 Tainyan Yanke Win; Sits In Sight; F; Dau; 12
528 Ska Gli; Comes White; F; Dau; 5-4
529 Hokisla[sic] Zi; Mary Yellow Boy; F; Dau; 1-9

530 Iyaku Win; Comes Talking; F; Head; 22
531 Rante Icaga; Growing Cedar; f; Dau; 2-8

532 Asapi; Shouts At; M; Head; 22
533 Hoksila Zi; Mamie Yellow Boy; F; Wife; 17

534 Winyan Hanska; Tall Woman #1; F; Head; 69

535 Heraka Ciqala; Paul Little Elk; M; Head; 43
536 Taanpetu; Her Day; F; Wife; 27
537 Maka Mahel Kagapi; Made In The Earth; F; Dau; 7
538 Wicincala; Girl; F; Dau; 4-3
539 Heraka Ciqala; Julia Little Elk; F; Dau; 2 mo

540 Winyan Hanska; Tall Woman #2; F; Head; 53

541 Onaso; Pacer; M; Head; 32
542 Ptesan; White Cow; F; Wife; 31
543 Sina Icu; Takes Blanket; F; Dau; 15
544 Wakan Gli; Comes Holy; F; Dau; 9
545 Inyan Cante; Stone Heart; F; Dau; 5
546 Pahin Luta; Red Porcupine; F; Dau; 1-4

547 Mazawakan Icu; Takes The Gun; F; Head; 77
548 Anpatu Waste; Good Day; M: G.Son; 24

549 Mato Wankatuya; High Bear; M; Head; 36
550 Tasina Wakan Win; Her Holy Blanket; F; Wife; 46

551 Taspan; Apple; M; Head; 50
552 Caje Wanica; No Name; F; Wife; 39
553 Taspan; John Apple; M; Son; 24
554 Taspan; George Apple; M; Son; 18
555 Taspan; Jennie Apple; M[sic]; Son; 16
556 Blaska; Flat; M; Son; 8
557 Ite Tanka; Big Face; M; Son; 4-5
558 Inyan Win; Rock Woman; F; Niece; 18
559 Hoksila Tanka; Big Boy; M; G.Son; 17
560 Naca Ota; Plenty Chief; M; Son; 2

561 Pehin Sa; Red Hair; M; Head; 58
562 Caje Oglaka; Tells Her Name; F; Wife; 44
563 Can Iyumni; Twisted Wood; M; Son; 25

Census Of The Sioux And Cheyenne Indians Of Pine Ridge Agency, South Dakota. Taken by W. H. Clapp, Captain 16th Infantry, Acting United States Indian Agent, June 30, 1897. (Wakpamini District)

Key: Number; Indian Name *(if given)*; English Name; Sex; Relation; Age

564	Kangi Wanbli; Crow Eagle; M; Son; 23
565	Ataya Wakan; All Holy; F; Dau; 19
566	Wagmu; Pumpkin; F; Dau; 11
567	Ite Nupa; Two Face; M; Son; 7
568	Tokeya; Leader; M; Son; 8
569	Ista Gi; Brown Eyes; F; Head; 43
570	Cokab Iyaya; Goes In Center; F; Dau; 15
571	Thomas; M; Son; 8
572	Wiyaka Nupa; Two Feather; M; Son; 5
573	Kangi Ciqala; Little Crow; M; Head; 67
574	Ake; Again; F; Wife; 55
575	Ota Kute; Shoots Plenty; M; Son; 17
576	Lizzie Graham; F; Head; 33
577	Howard Graham; M; Son; 9
578	Alfred Graham; M; Son; 7
579	Ollie Graham; F; Dau; 2-10
580	Henry Moore; M; Head; 23
581	Mary Sierro; F; Head; 35
582	Cemona Sierro; F; Dau; 17
583	Seberina Sierro; M; Son; 14
584	Susie Sierro; F; Dau; 12
585	Bennet Sierro; M; Son; 8
586	Antonia Sierro; F; Dau; 5
587	Santo Sierro; M; Son; 3-8
588	Joseph Sierro; M; Son; 1-4
589	Wanbli Luta; Red Eagle; M; Head; 55
590	Pa Rmi; Crooked Nose; F; Wife; 42
591	Hi Maza; Iron Teeth; F; Dau; 22
592	Pejuta; Medicine; M; Son; 21
593	Abe Summers; M: Nephew; 30
594	Tasunke Ota; Plenty Horses; F; Niece; 24
595	Wanbli Luta; Red Eagle; M; Head; 55
596	Tainyan; In Sight; F; Wife; 43
597	Ogle Sa; Anna Red Shirt; F; Dau; 18
598	Hoksila Waste; Good Boy; M; Son; 16
599	Kolayapi; Friendly; M; Son; 13
600	Oliver Salvis; M; Head; 21
601	Ogle Sa; Mary Red Shirt; F; Wife; 20
602	Can Zi; Yellow Wood; M; Head; 35
603	Tahalo; Hide; F; Wife; 40
604	Pejuta Win; Medicine Woman; F; Dau; 8
605	Ista Ska; Ida White Eyes; F; Niece; 22
606	Tiyopa; Door; F; Head; 48
607	Wicincala; Girl; F; Dau; 6
608	Spayola; Mexican; M; Head; 38
609	Winyan Wasaka; Strong Woman; F; Wife; 36
610	Nancy Bissonette; F; Head; 58
611	Millie Bissonette; F; Dau; 24
612	Lulu Bissonette; F; Dau; 23
613	Archie Long Bull; M; G.Son; 2-3
614	Thomas Spotted Bear; M; Son; 1-1/2 mo
615	Mato Waste; Good Bear; F; Head; 35
616	Inyan Sa; Red Rock; F; Dau; 13
617	Tasunke; Her Horses; F; Dau; 8
618	Wicokanyan Hiyaya; Midday; M; Son; 4
619	Kagla Kte; Kills Close; M; Son; 4-2/3 mo

Census Of The Sioux And Cheyenne Indians Of Pine Ridge Agency, South Dakota.
Taken by W. H. Clapp, Captain 16th Infantry, Acting United States Indian Agent,
June 30, 1897. (Wakpamini District)

Key: Number; Indian Name *(if given)*; English Name; Sex; Relation; Age

620 Ista Ska; Addie White Eyes; F; Head; 20
621 Piya Icaga; Lives Again; F; Head; 70
622 Can Ptecela; Short Wood; M; G.Son; 19
623 Can Ptecela; Bell Short Tree; F; G.Dau; 16
624 Mni; Water; M; Head; 31
625 Paha Wakan; Holy Hill; F; Wife; 30
626 Napca; Swallow; F; Dau; 15
627 Toka Ku; Gives Enemy; M; Son; 7
628 Wakuwa Kte; Kills Charging; F; Dau; 4-6
629 Heraka Wakinyan; Thunder Elk; M; Son; 2-5
630 Mni; Maggie Water; F; Dau; 2 mo
631 Wakinyan Peta; George Fire Thunder; M: Head; 35
632 Wakinyan Peta; Mary Fire Thunder; F; Wife; 32
633 Wakinyan Peta; Bessie Fire Thunder; F; Dau; 6
634 Wakinyan Peta; George Fire Thunder; M; Son; 4-1
635 Wakinyan Peta; Prudy Fire Thunder; F; Dau; 9 mo
636 Lucy Bissonette; F; Niece; 15

637 Termuga; Fly; M; Head; 53
638 Tasunke; Her Horse; F; Wife; 44
639 Glinajin; Comes And Stands; F; Dau; 16
640 Termuga; Peter Fly; M; Son; 5-6
641 Termuga; Susie Fly; F; Dau; 1-7

642 Emma Merrivall; F; Head; 31
643 Opo; Rosa Fog; F; Dau; 2 days

644 Ho Yekiya; Throws Her Voice; F; Head; 77
645 Wi Isna; Lone Woman; F; G.Dau; 26
646 Hyosipi; Comes After Him; M; G.Son; 14
646[sic] Cansu; Kittie Card; F; Head; 75
648 Canku Maza; Iron Road; F; Dau; 30
649 Akicita Ciqala; Little Soldier; M; Head; 50
650 Canku Waste; Good Road; F; Wife; 49
651 Wanju; Arrow Quiver; M; Son; 19
652 Ptesau[sic]; White Cow; F; Dau; 12
653 Tasunke Ciqala; Little Horse; M; Head; 40
654 Onpan Hinske; Elk Tooth; F; Head; 75
655 Ehake Gli; Comes Last; M; G.Son; 16
656 Sunkhinto; Baldwin Blue Horse; M; Head; 41
657 Marpiya Wakan; Stephen Medicine Cloud; [blank]; Head; 24
658 Catka; Left Hand; M; Head; 66
659 Winorcala Sica; Bad Old Woman; F; Wife; 60
660 Tarca Luta; Red Deer; F; Head; 48
661 Tacupa; Marrow Bone; M; Head; 43
662 Ranhi Win; Slow Woman; F; Wife; 50

Census Of The Sioux And Cheyenne Indians Of Pine Ridge Agency, South Dakota. Taken by W. H. Clapp, Captain 16th Infantry, Acting United States Indian Agent, June 30, 1897. (Wakpamini District)

Key: Number; Indian Name *(if given)*; English Name; Sex; Relation; Age

663 Tacupa; Joshua Marrow Bone; M; Son; 20
664 Wanbli Heton; Eagle Horn; M; Son; 10
665 Wakinyan Omani; Thunder Traveler; M; Son; 8
666 Wanbli Win; Eagle Woman; F; Dau; 14
667 Zintkala Maza; Iron Bird; M; Son; 6
668 Wasicu Winyan Waste; Good White Woman; F; Dau; 3-1
669 Tacupa; John Marrow Bone; M; Son; 4 days

670 Ohitika; Brave Woman #1; F; Head; 71

671 Mary Armigo; F; Head; 49
672 Lamott Armigo; M; G.Son; 19

673 Muiruha; Calico; M; Head; 54
674 Sunka Waste; Good Dog; F; Wife; 56
675 Mato Gnaskinyan; Crazy Bear; M; Son; 18
676 Hogan Wanbli; Eagle Fish; M; Son; 9

677 Ate Ciqa; Little Feather; M; Head; 53
678 Mani; Walking; F; Wife; 57
679 Kicopi; Calls Him; M; Son; 24

680 Ojuha Sa; Red Sack; M; Head; 58
681 Winorcala Wakan; Holy Old Woman; F; Wife; 54
682 Ojuha Sa; Sallie Red Sack; F; Dau; 22
683 Gunkhinsa[sic]; Red Horse; F; Dau; 14
684 Tacanku; His Road; M; Son; 9

685 Wicasa Ptecela; Short Man; M; Head; 37

686 Tasina Ota; Plenty Shawl; F; Wife; 35

687 Hanes Buckman; M; Head; 39
688 Susie Buckman; F; Wife; 29
689 Gives Up On Him; F; Dau; 12
690 Millie Buckman; F; Dau; 7
691 George Buckman; M; Son; 5-6
692 Benjamin Buckman; M; Son; 1-2

693 Yuselaka; Dripping; M; Head; 65
694 Sasa; Reddy; F; Wife; 35
695 Witke Kte; Kills A Fool; M; Son; 13
696 Sina Wakan; Medicine Sheet; M; Son; 6

697 Tatanka Najin; Standing Bull; M; Nephew; 61
698 Wasicu Kte; Kills White Man; M; Uncle; 65

699 Tasunke Wayanka; Sees Her Horse; F; Head; 45
700 Zintkala Ska; Leon White Bird; M; Head; 24
701 Ptesan Win; White Cow Woman; F; Wife; 25
702 Tasunke Wanbli; Eagle Horse; M; Son; 3-10

703 Tacanku Waste; Her Good Road; F; Head; 22
704 Taopi; Wounded; M; Son; 3-3
705 Can Nupyuha; John Two Sticks; M; Son; 1 mo 10 days

706 Mato Nupa; Two Bears; M; Head; 62
707 Joseph; M: Son; 15

708 Mato Hakikta; Bear Looks Back; M; Head; 52
709 Wanbli; Eagle; F; Wife; 45

Census Of The Sioux And Cheyenne Indians Of Pine Ridge Agency, South Dakota. Taken by W. H. Clapp, Captain 16th Infantry, Acting United States Indian Agent, June 30, 1897. (Wakpamini District)

Key: Number; Indian Name *(if given)*; English Name; Sex; Relation; Age

710 Anpetu Hinapa; Day Comes Out; F; Head; 65
711 Matoha Sina; Paul Bear Robe; M; Head; 28
712 Ptesan Rla Win; Rattling White Cow; F; Wife; 22
713 Tatanka Iyotaka; Sitting Bull; M; Son; 5
714 Winyan Waste; Good Woman; F; Dau; 2-7
715 Matoha Sina; Julia Bear Robe; F; Dau; 9 mo.

716 Antone Janis; M; Head; 38
717 Fannie Janis; F; Wife; 34
718 Lucy Janis; F; Dau; 15
719 Bessy Janis; F; Dau; 13
720 Herbert Janis; M; Son; 7
721 Peter Janis; M; Son; 3-3
722 Fanny Janis; F; Dau; 1-3
723 Julia Godwin; F; S. in Law; 23

724 Mary Colhoff; F; Head; 34
725 John R. Colhoff; M; Son; 17
726 Elizabeth Colhoff; F; Dau; 15
727 George Colhoff; M; Son; 13
728 Anna Colhoff; F; Dau; 11
729 William Colhoff; M; Son; 7
730 Bessy Means; F; Niece; 6-1/2mo

731 Sna Win; Rattler; F; Head; 45

732 Wanbli Nupa; Two Eagle; M; Head; 35
733 Canowicakte; Kills In Timber; F; Wife; 33
734 Pankeska Win; Shell Woman; F; Dau; 11
735 Wanbli; Eagle; F; Dau; 7
736 Oyate Kte; Kills Tribe; M; Son; 3-2
737 Wanbli Nupa; John Two Eagle; M; Son; 6 mo.

738 Berry Martin; M; Head; 22

739 Zintkala Gleska; Spotted Bird; M; Head; 41
740 Winyan Isnala; Lone Woman; F; Wife; 38
741 Zintkala Gleska; Fred Spotted Bird; M; Son; 20
742 Taopi Ota; Plenty Wounds; M; Son; 7
743 Wosla Najin; Stands Up; F; Dau; 9 mo.

744 John Lee; M; Head; 32
745 Sophia Lee; F; Wife; 27
746 Emma Lee; F; Dau; 10
747 James Lee; M; Son; 8
748 Anna Lee; F; Dau; 3-1

749 Mary Merrivall; F; Head; 62
750 Deaf And Dumb; M; Son; 23
751 Jennie Merrivall; F; Dau; 20
752 Rosa Lee White; F; G.Dau; 16

753 Sungmanitu Nakpa Hoksila; Young Wolf Ears; M; Head; 32
754 Pejuta Win; Medicine Woman; F; Wife; 36
755 Tawa Agli; Brings Her Own; F; Dau; 3-5

756 Wamniomni Ska White Whirlwind; M; Head; 46
757 Ataya Waste; All Good; F; Wife; 43
758 Onyan Glicupi; Leaves Him; M; Son; 11
759 Tonweya Kte; Kills Scout; M; Son; 9
760 Wicegna; Among; M; Son; 8
761 Tasunke Ota; Her Plenty Horses; F; Dau; 4-1
762 Tasunke Wayankapi; Looking At Horses; F; Dau; 11 mo.

763 Charles Giroux; M; Head; 35
764 Rosa Giroux; F; Wife; 39
765 Mary Giroux; F; Dau; 12

Census Of The Sioux And Cheyenne Indians Of Pine Ridge Agency, South Dakota. Taken by W. H. Clapp, Captain 16th Infantry, Acting United States Indian Agent, June 30, 1897. (Wakpamini District)

Key: Number; Indian Name *(if given)*; English Name; Sex; Relation; Age

766	Lottie Giroux; F; Dau; 9	792	Maggie Cottier; f; Dau; 1mo8da
767	Lizzie Giroux; F; Dau; 7	793	Nick S. Janis; M; Head; 36
768	Sungmanitu Ota; Plenty Wolf; M; Head; 46	794	Emma Janis; F; Wife; 38
		795	Susie Garnett; F; Dau; 18
769	Icaga; Grows; F; Wife; 35	796	Bertha Janis; F; Dau; 13
770	Tipi Yuha; Own Horse; M; Son; 11	797	John Janis; M; Son; 10
		798	Vinna Janis; F; Dau; 7
771	Oye Wanbli; Eagle Track; F; Dau; 3-10	799	Joseph Janis; M; Son; 6
		800	Lizzie Janis; F; Dau; 2-1
772	Sungmanitu Ota; Sam Plenty Wolf; M; Son; 1-8	801	Julia Manard; F; S. in Law; 21
		802	Emma Stirk; F; Head; 37
773	Sagye Win; Cane Woman; F; Head; 29	803	Tony Stirk; M; Son; 18
		804	James Stirk; M; Son; 16
		805	Prudy Stirk; F; Dau; 14
774	Huhu Napin; Bone Necklace #2; M; Head; 29	806	Ellen Stirk; F; Dau; 11
		807	Richard Stirk; M; Son; 8
775	Ptesan Wayanka; Looks At White Cow; F; Mother; 61	808	Louisa Stirk; F; Dau; 6
		809	George Stirk; M; Son; 4-2
		810	Nellie Stirk; F; Dau; 1-10
776	Romania Jansen; F; Head; 19		
777	Minnie Jansen; F; Dau; 2-2	811	Ellen Irving; F; Head; 31
778	Antoine Jansen; M; Son; 2 mo.	812	Benjamin Irving; M; Son; 17
		813	William Irving; M; Son; 14
779	Sunk Sapa; Charles Black Horse; M; Head; 34	814	Elizabeth Irving; F; Dau; 12
		815	Julia Irving; F; Dau; 1-2
780	Winyan Luta; Red Woman; F; Wife; 31	816	Raymond Smith; M; Head; 27
781	John Lamott; M; Son; 7	817	Josephine Smith; F; Sister; 22
782	Sunk Sapa; Chas. Black Horse, Jr; M; Son; 1		
		818	Nettie Goings; F; Head; 42
		819	Louie Goings; M; Son; 23
783	Heraka Wanbli; Eagle Elk; M: Head; 45	820	Blanch Goings; F; Dau; 21
		821	James Goings; M; Son; 15
784	Sagye Luta; Red Cane; F; Wife; 37	822	Baby Goings; F; Dau; 13
785	Ho Naron; Hears His Voice; M; Son; 4-4	823	Louie Deon; M; Head; 27
		824	Mary Deon; F; Wife; 26
		825	Maria Johns; F; Dau; 7-6
786	John Cottier; M; Head; 32	826	Ward Deon; M; Son; 2-4
787	Susie Cottier; F; Wife; 34	827	Louie Deon, Jr; M; Son; 6 mo.
788	Lucy Cottier; F; Dau; 8		
789	John Cottier, Jr; M; Son; 9	828	Alexander Merrivall; M; Head; 29
790	Esther Cottier; F; Dau; 3-8		
791	Eddie Cottier; M; Son; 2-2	829	Susie Merrivall; F; Wife; 26

Census Of The Sioux And Cheyenne Indians Of Pine Ridge Agency, South Dakota. Taken by W. H. Clapp, Captain 16th Infantry, Acting United States Indian Agent, June 30, 1897. (Wakpamini District)

Key: Number; Indian Name *(if given)*; English Name; Sex; Relation; Age

830 Kira Merrivall; F; Dau; 2-10
831 Herman Merrivall; M; Son; 1-2

832 Mary Rando; F; Head; 50
833 William Bullock; M; Son; 32
834 Julia; F; Dau; 25
835 William Rando; M; Son; 10
836 Silvester Rando; M; Son; 9
837 Josephine Rando; F; Dau; 5
838 Onpan Win; Elk Woman; F; Mother; 89

839 Talo Kaksa; Cut Flesh; M; Head; 44
840 Osun Saka; Thick Braid; F; Wife; 58
841 Tasunka Yukan; Owns Horse; M; Son; 12

842 Zintkala Zi; Herbert J. Zintkaka; M; Head; 9

843 Tasunke Ehakela; Fannie Last Horse; F; Head; 12

844 Tatanka Nupa; Two Bulls; M; Head; 45

845 Lucy Chamberlain; F; Head; 42

846 Louise Henderson; F; Head; 27
847 Stella L. Henderson; F; Dau; 1-9
848 May Louise Henderson; F; Dau; 4 mo.

849 Maggie Young; F; Head; 24
850 Walter Young; M; Son; 5
851 Louise Young; F; Dau; 2-10
852 Frank Young; M; Son; 4 mo.

853 Itagonga; Blind Man; M; Head; 46
854 Wamniomni To; Blue Whirlwind; F; Wife; 50
855 Mahel Cuwignaka; Dress Inside; M; Son; 12

856 Taopi Ciqala; Little Wound; M; Son; 10

857 Huhu Napin; Bone Nechlace[sic] #1; M; Head; 75

858 Wanbli Wicarca; Henry Old Eagle; M; Head; 26
859 Kici Yanka; Sists[sic] With Her; F; Wife; 19
860 Wanbli Wicarca; Rosa Old Eagle; F; Dau; 6 mo 20 day

861 Sunkawakan; Robert Horse; M; Head; 24
862 Wanbli Wicarca; Maggie Old Eagle; F; Wife; 25
863 Sunkawakan; Stella Horse; F; Dau; 1-3

864 Tasunke Luzahan; Joseph Fast Horse; M; Head; 51
865 Tasunke Luzahan; Jennie Fast Horse; F; Wife; 42
866 Tasunke Luzahan; Thomas Fast Horse; M; Son; 15
867 Tasunke Luzahan; Alice Fast Horse; F; Dau; 14
868 Tasunke Luzahan; Amos Fast Horse; M; Son; 14
869 Tasunke Luzahan; Charles Fast Horse; M; Son; 11
870 Tasunke Luzahan; Cecilia Fast Horse; F; Dau; 2-4
871 Tasunke Luzahan; Susie Fast Horse; F; Dau; 8

872 Wanbli Koyaka; Wears Eagle Feather; F; Head; 44

873 Cetan Ciqala; Luke Little Hawk; M; Head; 26
874 Wowapi Yuha; Carry Flag; F; Wife; 23
875 Tasunke Opi; Wounded Horse; M; Son; 2-9

Census Of The Sioux And Cheyenne Indians Of Pine Ridge Agency, South Dakota. Taken by W. H. Clapp, Captain 16th Infantry, Acting United States Indian Agent, June 30, 1897. (Wakpamini District)

Key: Number; Indian Name *(if given)*; English Name; Sex; Relation; Age

876 Hinwaste Win; Good Hair; F; Dau; 11 mo.
877 Kicopi; Calls Her; F; Head; 36
878 Jennie; F; Dau; 3-4
879 Tasunke Wayankapi; Looks At Her Horse; F; Dau; 1-2

880 Baptiste Garnier; M; Head; 50
881 Julia Garnier; F; Wife; 33
882 John Garnier; M; Son; 16
883 Lizzie Garnier; F; Dau; 15
884 Lucy Garnier; F; Dau; 14
885 Ellen Garnier; F; Dau; 13
886 Emma Garnier; F; Dau; 9
887 Sophia Garnier; F; Dau; 8
888 Sallie Garnier; F; Dau; 7

889 Wicegna Glicu; Harry C. A. Them; M; Head; 26
890 Niyan; Breathing; F; Wife; 20

891 Naca; James Chief; M; Head; 21
892 Puca Oyate; Jumping Nation; F; Wife; 17

893 John Galligo; M; Head; 20
894 Toka Kte Win; Kills Enemy; F; Wife; 30
895 John Galligo; M; Son; 1-1

896 Tatanka Wanagi; Ghost Bull; M; Head; 40

897 Heraka Nupa; Richard Two Elk; M; Head; 42
898 Wanbli Conica; Eagle Flesh; F; Wife; 23

899 Ohitika; Charles Brave; M; Head; 25
900 Tasunke Kpazo; Shows Her Horse; F; Wife; 41
901 Zintkala Napin; Frank Bird Necklace; M; G.Son; 21\

902 Hankepi Kte; Kills At Night; F; Head; 85
903 Kanyela Opi; Shot Close; M; G.Son; 11
904 Osun Luta; Red Braid; F; Head; 86

905 Tasunke Luzahan; William Fast Horse; M; Head; 23
906 Tasunke Luzahan; Annie Fast Horse; F; Wife; 22
907 Tasunke Luzahan; Wilber Fast Horse; M; Son; 11 mo.

908 Mato Kokipapi; Robert Afraid Of Bear; M; Head; 20
909 Anpo Kte; Kills In Morning; F; Wife; 16

910 Wapaha Nupa; Two Bonnete[sic]; M; Head; 23
911 Tasunke Hinzi; Yellow Horse; F; Wife; 21
912 Thomas Horse; M; Son; 6 mo.

913 Tarca Win; Deer Woman; F; Head; 39

914 George Ladeau; M; Head; 27
915 Mary Ladeau; F; Wife; 20
916 Maggie Ladeau; F; Dau; 2-8

917 Joseph Knight; M; Head; 38
918 Lizzie Knight; F; Wife; 27
919 Ellen Knight; F; Dau; 9
920 Oliver Knight; M; Son; 3-1
921 Joseph E. Knight; M; Son; 5 mo.

922 Ptesan Kte; Kills White Cow; M; Head; 66
923 Tainyan Ku Win; Comes In Light; F; Wife; 56
924 Ptesan Kte; James Kills White Cow; M; Son; 17

Census Of The Sioux And Cheyenne Indians Of Pine Ridge Agency, South Dakota. Taken by W. H. Clapp, Captain 16th Infantry, Acting United States Indian Agent, June 30, 1897. (Wakpamini District)

Key: Number; Indian Name *(if given)*; English Name; Sex; Relation; Age

925 Eugene Means; M; Head; 23
926 Nellie Means; F; Wife; 22

927 Glinajin; Comes To Stand; F; Head; 66

928 John Sickler; M; Head; 29

929 Julia Ladeaux; F; Head; 20

930 Frank Hornbeck; M; Head; 25
931 Jessie Black Bear; F; Wife; 19
932 Susie Hornbeck; F; Dau; 1-9

933 Jennie Brown; F; Head; 24

934 Lulu Ashcraft; f; Head; 35

935 James Nelson; M: Head; 21
936 Okiyakapi Win; Tells Her; F; Wife; 24
937 Albert Nelson; M; Son; 1-2

Census of the Sioux And Cheyenne Indians
Of Pine Ridge Agency, South Dakota.
June 30, 1897

Porcupine District

Census Of The Sioux And Cheyenne Indians Of Pine Ridge Agency, South Dakota. Taken by W. H. Clapp, Captain 16th Infantry, Acting United States Indian Agent, June 30, 1897. (Porcupine District)

Key: Number; Indian Name *(if given)*; English Name; Sex; Relation; Age

938 Miyogle; Whetstone; M; Head; 60
939 Mato Bloha; He Bear; M; Son; 6
940 James Twiss; M; Head; 39
941 Rosella Twiss; F; Wife; 41
942 Fannie Twiss; F; Dau; 19
943 Thomas Twiss; M; Son; 8
944 Frank Twiss; M; Son; 4-6
945 Hoksila Waste; Good Boy; M; Son; 1-9
946 Maggie Twiss; F; Dau; 12

947 Julia Kocer; F; Head; 52
948 Ruth Kocer; F; Dau; 16
949 Rena Kocer; F; Dau; 11
950 Frank Kocer; M; Son; 14
951 Hobart Kocer; M; Son; 13
952 Joanna Kocer; F; Dau; 3-5

953 Wanbli Wiyake; William Eagle Feather; M; Head; 34
954 Iwasicu; Talks Too Much; F; Wife; 47
955 Hogan Tucuhu; Fish Ribs; M; St.Son; 27
956 Ca Ptecela; Short Step; M; St.Son; 16

957 John Conroy; M; Head; 36
958 Lucy Conroy; F; Wife; 28
959 Maggie Conroy; F; Dau; 15
960 Benjamin Conroy; M: Son; 11
961 Annie Conroy; F; Dau; 9
962 Millie Conroy; F; Dau; 6
963 Taylor Conroy; M; Son; 4-3
964 Lena Conroy; F; Dau; 1-8

965 Ella Russell; F; Head; 35
966 Louise Russell; F; Dau; 16
967 Amelia Russell; F; Dau; 18
968 Ruth Russell; F; Dau; 4-1
969 Nellie Russell; F; Dau; 1-7

970 Mato Gi; James Yellow Bear; M; Head; 23

971 William D. McGaa; M; Head; 38
972 Anna Clifford McGaa; F; Wife; 24
973 Etta McGaa; F; Dau; 12
974 William McGaa; M; Son; 13
975 Charlotte McGaa; F; Dau; 10
976 Albert McGaa; M; Son; 9
977 Agnes McGaa; F; Dau; 7
978 George Leroy McGaa; M; Son; 4-7

979 Wasu Isnala; Lone Hail; F; Head; 75

780[sic] Pasu On Waapa; Strikes With; Nose; M; Head; 50
981 Tacanku Waste; Her Good Road; F; Wife; 58

982 Zintkala Sapa; Cora Black Bird; F; Head; 24
983 Zintkala Sapa; Louis Black Bird; M; Son; 3-6
984 Heraka Maza; David Iron Elk; M; Son; 10 mo.

985 Hihan Tonka; Big Owl; M; Head; 40
986 Hihan Tonka; Lucy Big Owl; F; Wife; 29
987 Hihan Tonka; Edward Big Owl; M; Son; 16
988 Hihan Tonka; Thomas Big Owl; M; Son; 7

989 Pankeska Hoksila; Shell Boy; M; Head; 40
990 Herakawin; Elk Woman; F; Wife; 50
991 Pankeska Hoksila; Ida Shell Boy; F; Dau; 13

992 Heraka Ciqala; Little Elk; M; Head; 64
993 Peji Rota; Sage Bush; F; Wife; 51

Census Of The Sioux And Cheyenne Indians Of Pine Ridge Agency, South Dakota. Taken by W. H. Clapp, Captain 16th Infantry, Acting United States Indian Agent, June 30, 1897. (Porcupine District)

Key: Number; Indian Name *(if given)*; English Name; Sex; Relation; Age

994 Heraka Ciqala; John Little Elk; M; Son; 16
995 Nica; Has None; F; Dau; 10
996 Opan; Paul Moose; M; Head; 24
997 Pehan Catka; Grace Left Heron; F; Wife; 21
998 Opan; Bena Moose; F; Dau; 7mo
999 Hektakuja Ekte; John Kills Back; M; Head; 33
1000 Inyan; Samuel Rock; M; Head; 36
1001 Zintkala Luta; Red Bird; F; Wife; 38
1002 Inyan; Charles Rock; M; Son; 11
1003 Inyan; John Rock; M; Son; 9
1004 Inyan; Bessie Rock; F; Dau; 6
1005 Palani Sica; Bad Ree; M; Head; 72
1006 Tipi; House; F; Wife; 69
1007 Kutepi; Charles Shot At; M; Head; 29
1008 Huhu Yuha; Keeps The Bone; M; Father; 69
1009 Heraka Ska; White Elk; F; Wife; 44
1010 Ozan Mahel; Henry Between Lodges; M; St.Son; 19
1011 Robya; Scares Away; M; St.Son; 7
1012 Mato Bloka; He Bear; M; Head; 51
1013 Winyan Hanska; Tall Woman; F; Wife; 43
1014 Mato Bloka; Mary He Bear; F; Dau; 13
1015 Mato Bloka; George He Bear; M; Son; 10
1016 Tokeya Inyanka; Runs First; F; Dau; 7
1017 Tokala Wanbli; Eagle Fox; M; Head; 25
1018 Pezpiza; Mary Prairie Dog; F; Head; 67
1019 Wohiteka; Has Courage; F; Dau; 1-4
1020 Tatanka Kte; Kille[sic] The Bull; M; Head; 67
1021 Pankeska Luta; Red Shell; F; Wife; 56
1022 Tatanka Kte; Hellen Kills T. Bull; F; Dau; 13
1023 Tatanka Kte; Annie Kills T. Bull; F; G.Dau; 7
1024 Tasunke Taninya Naji; Horse Stands In Sight; M; Head; 36
1025 Tarca Ha; Buckskin; F; Wife; 39
1026 Yawa; Count; M; Son; 7
1027 Taninya Naji; Robert Stands I. Sight; M; Son; 1-5
1028 Itowe Suta; Frank Hard Forehead; M; Head; 27
1029 Itowe Suta; Louisa Hard Forehead; F; Wife; 26
1030 Itowe Suta; Thomas Hard Forehead; M; Son; 3-10
1031 Heraka Waste; Pretty Elk; M; Head; 38
1032 Heraka Waste; Robert Pretty Elk; M; Son; 14
1033 Heraka Waste; Jessie Pretty Elk; F; Dau; 12
1034 Heraka Waste; Lillie Pretty Elk; F; Dau; 10
1035 Heraka Waste; Maggie Pretty Elk; F; Dau; 6
1036 Heraka Waste; Lizzie Pretty Elk; F; Dau; 3-5
1037 Tatanka Site; Bull Tail; M; Head; 28

Census Of The Sioux And Cheyenne Indians Of Pine Ridge Agency, South Dakota. Taken by W. H. Clapp, Captain 16th Infantry, Acting United States Indian Agent, June 30, 1897. (Porcupine District)

Key: Number; Indian Name *(if given)*; English Name; Sex; Relation; Age

1038 Tatanka Site; Sarah Bull Tail; F; Wife; 24
1039 Wakil Naji; Stands And Looks; F; Dau; 7
1040 Mato Can Wegna Imanka; Ada Bear Runs In Woods; F; Dau; 3-4
1041 Tatanka Site; Stella Bull Tail; F; Dau; 8 mo.
1042 Sunk Manu; Steals Horses; M; Head; 39
1043 Tawanibli; Her Eagle; F; Wife; 43
1044 Itunkasan Luta; Red Weasel; F; Dau; 2-1
1045 Tatanka Ciqala; Little Bull; M; Head; 54
1046 Znya Ahake; Late Warrior; F; Wife; 40
1047 Mato Watakpe; Emma Charging Bear; F; Niece; 18
1048 Maka Yublu; Julia Breaks Land; F; Head; 47
1049 Emma; F; Dau; 19
1050 Oscar; M; Son; 16
1051 Mollie; F; Dau; 14
1052 Wahancanka Wicarca; Old Shield; M; Head; 69
1053 Nazuspe Tanka; Big Ax; F; Wife; 64
1054 Topa Oynspa; Lucy Catches Enemy; F; G.Dau; 15
1055 Hotain; Voice In Sight; M; G.Son; 10
1056 Wahacanka Wicarca; George Old Shield; M; G.Son; 5
1057 Julia O.S. Woodruff; F; Head; 31
1058 Tatanka Ska; White Bull; M; Head; 40
1059 Tarca; Deer; F; Wife; 39
1060 Tatanka Ska; Clara White Bull; F; Dau; 14
1061 Wakan Win; Holy Woman; F; Dau; 7
1062 Tasunke Opi; Wounded Horse; M; Son; 5
1063 Mato Hanska; Long Bear; M; Son; 2-2
1064 Tatanka Ska; Richard White Bull; M; Head; 18
1065 Wazi Zintkala; Ella Pine Bird; F; Wife; 20
1066 Aglagla Inyanka; Peter Runs A.T. Edge; M; Head; 31
1067 Tasunke Hinsa; Her Red Horse; F; Wife; 25
1068 Pte Naji; Standing White Cow; F; Dau; 6
1069 Mato Isnala; Lone Bear #2; M; Head; 68
1070 Palani Win; Ree Woman; F; Cousin; 75
1071 Tezi Ska; Frank White Belly; M; G.Son; 21
1072 Kici Kiciza; Jacob Fights With; M; G.Son; 13
1073 Mato Yatapi; Chief Bear; M; Head; 30
1074 Mato Yatapi; Susie Chief Bear; F; Wife; 27
1075 Hoksila Waste; Good Boy; M; Son; 2-5
1076 Honomani; Night Walker; F; Head; 66
1077 Blaska Rpaya; Lays On His Belly; M; Head; 62
1078 Iglake; Moves; F; Wife; 55
1079 Kingi; Thomas Crow; M; Head; 34

Census Of The Sioux And Cheyenne Indians Of Pine Ridge Agency, South Dakota. Taken by W. H. Clapp, Captain 16th Infantry, Acting United States Indian Agent, June 30, 1897. (Porcupine District)

Key: Number; Indian Name *(if given)*; English Name; Sex; Relation; Age

1080 Alice Crow; F; Wife; 34
1081 Lucy Crow; F; Dau; 7
1082 James Crow; M; Son; 4-8
1083 Anna Crow; F; Dau; 1mo1day

1084 Tatanka Mato; Bulls Bear; M; Head; 80

1085 Kte Aou; Comes Killing; M; Head; 20
1086 Canku Wakan; Holy Road; F; Mother; 51

1087 Wanbli Situpi; Eagle Tail Feather; M; Head; 43
1088 Taninya; Standing In Sight; F; Wife; 29
1089 Pejuta Waste; Good Medicine; F; Dau; 2-5
1090 Najinyapi; Surrounded; F; Niece; 16
1091 Ni Glecu; Comes Alice; F; Niece; 13

1092 Marpiyato; David Arapahoe; M; Head; 22
1093 Sinte Nupa; Ada Two Tails; F; Wife; 21
1094 Karolyeyapi; Throws Him; M; Son; 1-7

1095 Marpiya Tucuhu; Cloud Ribs; F; Head; 48
1096 Marpiya To; William Arapahoe; M; Son; 12
1097 Marpiya To; Jennie Arapahoe; F; Dau; 7
1098 Marpiya To; Girl Arapahoe; F; Dau; 4-6
1099 Ctan[sic]; Florence Hawk; F; Niece; 25

1100 Cetan; Lizzie Hawk; F; Head; 20

1101 Tiowicakte; Kills In Lodge; M; Son; 29

1102 Winurcala; Old Woman; F; Mother; 65
1103 Angeline Yates; F; Niece; 25

1104 Wicasa Ktercin; Wants To Be A Man; F; Head; 57
1105 Lucy; F; Dau; 24

1106 Wahacanka Wicarca; Isaac Old Shield; M; Head; 26
1107 Winya Waste; Pretty Woman; F; Wife; 27
1108 Kinya Win; Flying Woman; F; S.Dau; 8
1109 Wahacanka Wicarca; Susie Old Shield; F; Dau; 1-7

1110 Can Wegna; Among Timber; F; Head; 64

1111 Tokeya Naji; Stands First; M; Head; 46
1112 Tokeya Naji; Nancy Stands First; F; Wife; 41
1113 Tokeya Naji; Alexander Stands First; M; Son; 22
1114 Hoksila Waste; Hood Boy; M; Son; 6
1115 Tokeya Naji; Ella Stands First; F; Dau; 2-8

1116 Wan Opi; George Wounded Arrow; M; Head; 23
1117 Wahacanka Win; Shield Woman; F; Wife; 21
1118 Oye Luta; Holy Track; M; Son; 2 mo.

1119 Tasunke Otawin; Her Many Horses; F; Head; 42
1120 Osungya Erpeyapi; Destroyed; M; Son; 16
1121 Sunkska Agli; Brings White Horses; M; Son; 10
1122 Lilly; F; Niece; 21

Census Of The Sioux And Cheyenne Indians Of Pine Ridge Agency, South Dakota. Taken by W. H. Clapp, Captain 16th Infantry, Acting United States Indian Agent, June 30, 1897. (Porcupine District)

Key: Number; Indian Name *(if given)*; English Name; Sex; Relation; Age

1123 MatocanWegnaInyouka; Jno. Bear Runs I. Woods; M; Head; 50
1124 MatocanWegnaInyouka; Jennie Bear Runs I. Woods; F; Wife; 47
1125 Sunka; Dog; M; Head; 43
1126 Sunka; Lizzie Dog; F; Wife; 32
1127 Sunka; Millie Dog; F; Dau; 11
1128 Sunka; Lizzie Dog; F; Dau; 9
1129 Okanwer Mani; Circle Walker; M; Son; 3-10
1130 Tezi Ska; Willard White Belly; M; Head; 19
1131 Cetan Wakinya; Mary Thunder Hawk; F; Wife; 17
1132 Tatanka Waste; Pretty Bull; M; Head; 39
1133 Tatanka Waste; Jessie Pretty Bull; F; Wife; 35
1134 Sagye Luta; Red Cane; F; Dau; 4-9
1135 Tatanka Waste; Carrie Pretty Bull; F; Dau; 1-8
1136 Catka; Left Hand; M; Head; 34
1137 He Luta; Red Horn; F; Wife; 32
1138 Wasaka; Stout; F; Dau; 1-8
1139 Wahasanka Wakuwa; Wallace Charging Shield; M; Head; 29
1140 Wahasanka Wakuwa; Lucy Charging Shield; F; Wife; 28
1141 Wahasanka Wakuwa; Lucy Charging Shield; F; Dau; 2-5
1142 Wagneza[sic]; William Corn; M; Head; 35
1143 Wagneza; Rosa Corn; F; Wife; 38
1144 Wagneza; Emma Corn; F; St.Dau; 11
1145 Sina Zi; Yellow Blanket; F; Dau; 5-4
1146 Wagmeza; William Corn, Jr; M; Son; 7 mo.
1147 Oturan; Gives Away; F; Head; 33
1148 Zintkala Luta; Red Bird; F; Dau; 10
1149 Sahuwinla; Cheyenne Woman; F; Head; 75
1150 Maza Sica; Bad Iron; M; Head; 33
1151 Canhanpi; Sugar; F; Wife; 31
1152 Glenapa; Comes Out; F; Dau; 7
1153 Mato Hin Waste; Good Haired Bear; F; Dau; 5
1154 Maza Sica; Hattie Bad Iron; f; Dau; 5mo
1155 Caji Iglata; Tells His Name; M; Head; 33
1156 Ape Wakan; Medicine Leaf; F; Wife; 29
1157 Wanbli Tokeya; Leading Eagle; F; Dau; 4-6
1158 Mary Romero; F; Head; 63
1159 James Bissonette; M; Head; 30
1160 Susy Romero; F; Wife; 23
1161 Joseph Bissonette; M; Son; 2-7
1162 Wanbli Cincala; Young Eagle; M; Head; 62
1163 Topa Canupa; Smokes Four Times; F; Wife; 59
1164 Wakinya Ska; White Thunder; M; Head; 64
1165 Wamniyomni Koyaka; Wears Whirlwind; F; Wife #1; 56
1166 Pa Wayatkan; Drinks Bitters; F; Wife #2; 53
1167 Zintkala Luta; Paul Red Bird; M; Son; 21

Census Of The Sioux And Cheyenne Indians Of Pine Ridge Agency, South Dakota. Taken by W. H. Clapp, Captain 16th Infantry, Acting United States Indian Agent, June 30, 1897. (Porcupine District)

Key: Number; Indian Name *(if given)*; English Name; Sex; Relation; Age

1168 Wakinya Ska; Bessie White Thunder; F; Dau; 18
1169 Wamniyomni; Whirlwind; M; Son; 15
1170 Tiglisni; Left Her Home; F; G.Dau; 4-2
1171 Heraka Sica; Susie Bad Elk; F; G.Dau; 1-7
1172 Wakinya Ska; Harrison White Thunder; M; Head; 21
1173 Mato Opi; Vina Wounded Bear; F; Wife; 19

1174 Itunkala Ska; White Mouse; M; Head; 37
1175 Hakekta; Looks Back; F; Wife; 33
1176 Itunkala Ska; Ella White Mouse; F; Dau; 7
1177 Wanbli Hinapa; Comes Out Eagle; F; Dau; 4-1
1178 Ohitika; Brave; M; Son; 2-1

1179 Heraka Sica; John Bad Elk; M; Head; 25
1180 Miyogli; Ida Whetstone; F; Wife; 24

1181 Akicita Ciqala; Little Soldier; M; Head; 32
1182 Mrpiya[sic] Rla; Rattling Cloud; F; Wife; 33
1183 Sina Wakan; Medicine Blanket; F; Dau; 9
1184 Anpitu Luta; Red Day; M; Son; 8

1185 Maka Mahel Mani; Walks Under Ground; M; Head; 43
1186 Sna Win; Rattling Woman; F; Wife; 42
1187 Canihanke; John End Of Timber; M; S.Son; 19
1188 Mniwanca Win; Ocean Woman; F; S.Dau; 11

1189 Taanpitu Waste; Her Good Day; F; Dau; 3-10
1190 Wincala; Girl; F; Dau; 1-9
1191 Maka Mahel Mani; Amos Walks U. Ground; M; Head; 20
1192 Maka Mahel Mani; Alice Walks U. Ground; F; Wife; 20
1193 Maka Mahel Mani; Joshaway Walks U. Ground; M; Son; 2 mo.
1194 Kapojela Win; Light Woman; F; Head; 70

1195 Tatanka Ska; White Bull #2; M; Head; 38
1196 Marpiya To; Emma Blue Cloud; F; Wife; 31
1197 Wahacanka Wicarca; Alfred Old Shield; M; head; 27
1198 Honaronpi; Hears Voice; F; Wife; 33
1199 Wahacanka Wicarca; John Old Shield; M; Son; 5 mo.

1200 Joseph Smith; M; Head; 31
1201 Janette Smith; F; Wife; 27
1202 Effie Smith; F; Dau; 7
1203 Joseph Smith, Jr; M; Son; 2-5

1204 Tatanka Hanska; Long Bull; M; Head; 49
1205 Ista Wiyakpa; Bright Eyes; F; Wife; 35
1206 Kanyela Kute; Shot Close; F; Dau; 9
1207 Wicasa Isnala; Lone Man; M; Son; 7
1208 Canupa Waste; Good Pipe; F; Dau; 4-5

1209 Mila Hanska; Long Knife; F; Dau; 18

Census Of The Sioux And Cheyenne Indians Of Pine Ridge Agency, South Dakota. Taken by W. H. Clapp, Captain 16th Infantry, Acting United States Indian Agent, June 30, 1897. (Porcupine District)

Key: Number; Indian Name *(if given)*; English Name; Sex; Relation; Age

1210 Ciqala Kte; Henry Kills Small; M; Head; 22
1211 Ciqala Kte; Anna Kills Small; F; Wife; 21
1212 Ciqala Kte; James Kills Small; M; Son; 10 mo.

1213 Mato Wanjila; Oliver Lone Bear; M; Head; 45
1214 Tiblopu Ota; Plenty Brothers; F; Wife; 47
1215 Mato Wanjila; Samuel Lone Bear; M; Son; 18
1216 Mato Wanjila; Abraham Lone Bear; M; Son; 17
1217 Mato Wanjila; Henry Lone Bear; M; Son; 10
1218 Mato Wanjila; Susie Lone Bear; F; Dau; 3
1219 Si; Foot; M; Bro; 40

1220 Ite Ska; White Face; M; Head; 55
1221 Te Tani; Old Lodge; F; Wife #1; 44
1222 Keya Cagu; Terropin Lights; F; Wife #2; 46
1223 Ieapinpsinsala; Swallow; M; Son; 18
1224 Rante Gi; Adelin Yellow Cedar; F; Dau; 15
1225 Tasunke Watakpe; William Charging Horse; [M]; Son; 13
1226 Wicincala; Girl; F; Dau; 6
1227 Canku Waste; Good Road; F; Dau; 3-10

1228 Sinte; Tail; M; Head; 23
1229 Ruth; F; Wife; 19

1230 Sunk Hinto; Fannie Blue Horse; F; Head; 24
1231 Sinte; John[?] Tail; M; Son; 7mo
1232 Sunk Hinto; Jack Blue Horse; M; Son; 2-8

1233 Ite Ska; Thomas White Face; M; Head; 20
1234 Ista Rmi; Susie Crooked Eyes; F; Wife; 17
1235 Ite Ska; John White Face; M; Son; 10 mo.

1236 Hoksila Ciqala; Little Boy; M; Head; 28
1237 Hoksila Ciqala; Cecilia Little Boy; F; Wife; 24
1238 Ispa Hoksila Ciqala; Elbow; M; Son; 7
1239 Charlie; M; Son; 1-1
1240 Loe[sic]; M; Son; 3-10

1241 Tasunke Maza; Iron Horse #2; F; Head; 31
1242 Tasunke Inyanka; Samuel Running Horse; M; Son; 6
1243 Tasunke Inyanka; Felix Running Horse; M; Son; 7 mo

1244 Mato Kte; Bear Killer; M; Head; 45
1245 Nape Sicamnd; Hand Dont[sic] Smell; F; Wife; 42
1246 Mato Kte; Albert Bear Killer; M; Son; 23
1247 Mato Kte; Louise Bear Killer; F; Dau; 17
1248 Mato Kte; John Bear Killer; M; Son; 19
1249 Hoksila Waste; Good Boy; M; Son; 3-4

1250 Tsta Gi; Brown Eyes; M; Head; 27
1251 Yamni; Three; F; Wife; 31
1252 Wynstanpi; Let Her Go; M; Son; 8
1253 Inyanka; Runs; M; Son; 6
1254 Winyan Isnala; Single Woman; F; Dau; 3-6
1255 Pehin Ji; Yellow Haired; M; Son; 1-1

Census Of The Sioux And Cheyenne Indians Of Pine Ridge Agency, South Dakota. Taken by W. H. Clapp, Captain 16th Infantry, Acting United States Indian Agent, June 30, 1897. (Porcupine District)

Key: Number; Indian Name *(if given)*; English Name; Sex; Relation; Age

1256	Cante Maza; Iron Heart; M; Head; 60	1277	Nupa Wakita; Looks Twice; M; Son; 11
1257	Wanbli Sun; Eagle Feather; F; Wife; 51	1278	Ite Wambli[sic]; Eagle Face; F; Dau; 7
1258	Ohitika; Brave; M; Bro; 45	1279	Mato Wambli; Louis Bear Eagle; M; Son; 2-1
1259	John; M; G.Son; 16		
1260	Hanpa Sica; Bad Moccasin; F; Head; 66	1280	Wambli Wahancanka; Eagle Shield; M; Head; 41
1261	Marpiya Maza; Iron Cloud; M; Head; 41	1281	Tacanku Waste; Her Good Road; F; Wife; 45
1262	Wanapin Luta; Red Necklace; F; Wife #1; 40	1282	Ita Wambli; Lucy Eagle Face; F; Dau; 15
1263	Paha Anatan; Runs For Hill; F; Wife #2; 31	1283	Ptesan Gleska; Spotted White Cow; F; Dau; 10
1264	Marpiya Maza; Eddie Iron Cloud; M; Son; 15	1284	Canroegna Naji; Stands In T. Woods; M; Son; 6
1265	Pijuta Waste; Good Medicine; F; Dau; 8	1285	Ite Wambli; Eagle Face; F; Dau; 3-2
1266	Coka Glisni; Never Comes Without; M; Son; 6	1286	Tinga; Grunting; F; Dau; 2-9
1267	Iyuha Wicaku; Gives Them All; F; Dau; 10	1287	Kangi Witko; Fool Crow; M; Head; 30
1268	Najinhan Ku; Comes Standing; M; Son; 3-2	1288	Kangi Witko; Lizzie Fool Crow; F; Wife; 25
1269	Wankal Kte; Kills Above; M; Son; 1-7	1289	Heraka Ska; White Elk; M; Head; 35
		1290	Heraka Ska; Maggie White Elk; F; Wife; 35
1270	Wanbli Koyaka; Wears Eagle; M; Head; 35	1291	Heraka Ska; Lucy White Elk; f; Dau; 14
1271	Mato Wanjila; Julia Lone Bear; F; Wife; 23	1292	Ahape Gli; Returned Last; M; Son; 9
1272	Sina Karwoka; Blowing Blanket; F; Head; 72	1293	Okinya; Flies About; M; Son; 6
		1294	Tasunke Opi; Wounded Horse; F; Dau; 5
1273	Sunkmano Sa; Steals Horses #2; M; Head; 37	1295	Poge Tanka; Wm. Big Nostrils; M; Son; 3-2
1274	Mato Wanbli; Bear Eagle; M; Head; 39	1296	Ituhu Suta; Hard Forehead; M; Head; 64
1275	Hunkawin; Pipe Dance; F; Wife; 30	1297	Winyan Waste; Good Woman; F; Wife; 50
1276	Wanbli He; Eagle Horn; M; Son; 14	1298	Hoksila Sica; Bad Boy; M; Son; 14

Census Of The Sioux And Cheyenne Indians Of Pine Ridge Agency, South Dakota.
Taken by W. H. Clapp, Captain 16th Infantry, Acting United States Indian Agent,
June 30, 1897. (Porcupine District)

Key: Number; Indian Name *(if given)*; English Name; Sex; Relation; Age

1299 Oye Wakan; Medicine Track; F; Head; 33
1300 Oye Wakan; Andrew Medicine Track; M; Son; 1-1
1301 Zintkala Maza; Iron Bird; M; Head; 41
1302 Pehin Ji; Yellow Hair; F; Wife; 34
1303 Tohicun; Revenger; M; Head; 19
1304 Zintkala Maza; Bessie Iron Bird; F; Wife; 17
1305 Cante Okikeka[sic]; Brave Heart; M; Head; 55
1306 Tasunke Waste; Her Good Horse; F; Wife; 51
1307 Cate Ohitika; Pugh Brave Heart; M; Son; 19
1308 Tiyopa Waste; Good Door; F; Dau; 10
1309 Cante Ohitika; James Brave Heart; M; Head; 29
1310 Wanagi Tokeya; First Ghost; F; Wife; 21
1311 Cante Ohitika; Moses Brave Heart; M; Son; 1-5
1312 Maza Cincala; Iron Child; M; Head; 49
1313 Warpe Mato; Bear Leaf; F; Wife; 35
1314 Hanska To; Blue Leggins; F; Mother; 75
1315 Wecegna Inyan; Runs Among Them; M; B. in L.; 37
1316 Tiglake Waste; Good Mover; F; Sister; 46
1317 Conica Waste; No Flesh; M; Head; 52
1318 Pankeska Win; Shell Woman; F; Wife; 48
1319 Wahancanka Wakuwa; Charging Shield; M; Head; 65
1320 Wahancanka Wakuwa; Julia Charging Shield; F; Wife; 55
1321 Sungmanitu Wankatuya; Clayton High Wolf; M; Head; 22
1322 Wahancanka Wakuwa; Lizzie C. Shield; F; Wife; 18
1323 Tasunke Ota; Plenty Horses; F; Dau; 1-7
1324 Tatanka Ite Ska; White Face Bull; M; Head; 54
1325 Tasina Wakan; Her Holy Blanket; F; Wife; 51
1326 Wayank Hopi; Comes To See Her; F; Dau; 6
1327 Ahake Hi; Jennie Comes Last; F; Head; 26
1328 Wanbli Waste; Good Eagle; M; Son; 4
1329 Ahake Hi; Susie Comes Last; F; Dau; 2 mo.
1330 Wambli[sic] Waste; Eagle Pipe; M; Head; 41
1331 Cetan; Hawk; F; Wife; 41
1332 Wambli Tacanupa; Maggie Eagle Pipe; F; Dau; 16
1333 Psito; Beads; F; G.Mo; 75
1334 Wazi Zintkala; Pine Bird; M; Head; 43
1335 Tawicincala; Her Girl; F; Wife; 40
1336 Wazi Zintkala; Samuel Pine Bird; M; Son; 16
1337 Sangumanitu Sica; Bad Wolf; M; Son; 9
1338 Wazi Zintkala; Jack Pine Bird; M; Son; 6
1339 Wazi Zintkala; Willie Pine Bird; M; Son; 3-10

Census Of The Sioux And Cheyenne Indians Of Pine Ridge Agency, South Dakota. Taken by W. H. Clapp, Captain 16th Infantry, Acting United States Indian Agent, June 30, 1897. (Porcupine District)

Key: Number; Indian Name *(if given)*; English Name; Sex; Relation; Age

1340 Wazi Zintkala; Henry Pine Bird; M; Son; 11 mo
1341 Wiciyela Winyan; Yankton Woman; F; Head; 52
1342 Wojusa; Farmer; F; G.Mother; 57
1343 Ciqala Kte; Kills Small; M; G.Son; 6

1344 Wapaha; Conrad War Bonnet; M; Head; 26
1345 Ista Gi; Yellow Eyes; F; Wife; 24
1346 Tipi; Lizzie Lodge; F; Dau; 3-4
1347 Najinyapin; Surrounded; M; Son; 8 mo.

1348 Mato Wayanka; Sees The Bear; M; Head; 56
1349 Marpiya Waste; Good Cloud; F; Wife; 46

1350 Psa Kte; Kills Crow Indian; M; Head; 25
1351 Sunk Ole; Rosa Hunts Horses; F; Wife; 23
1352 Cetan Wankatuiya; High Hawk; M; Son; 10 mo.

1353 Tate Sina; Wind Shawl; F; Head; 76

1354 Peji Rota; Gray Grass; F; Head; 70

1355 Tatanka Wapaha; Bull Bonnet; M; Head; 53
1356 Tasunke Tokey Hiyaya; Horse Goes Ahead; F; Wife; 43

1357 Mato Hanska; Long Bear; M; Head; 61
1358 Heyaska; Cut Off; F; Wife; 50
1359 Tasunke Opi; Her Wounded Horses; F; Dau; 15

1360 Huhu; Walter Bone; M; Head; 25
1361 Maka Wiyakpa; Nellie Shinning Ground; F; Wife; 25

1362 Ptesan Wicasa; White Cow Man; M; Head; 47
1363 Wakan Hinapa; Comes Out Holy; F; Wife; 50
1364 Marpiya Sna; Rattling Cloud; F; Dau; 5-5
1365 Oyunke Maza; Iron Bed; F; Aunt; 85

1366 Wacapa; Thomas Stabber; M; Head; 23
1367 Sunka; Julia Dog; F; Wife; 18

1368 Cetan Wakuwa; Chasing Hawk; M; Head; 36
1369 Pte San Waste; Good White Cow; F; Wife; 33

1370 Heraka Naji; Standing Elk; M; Head; 41
1371 Taninya Ti; Lives In Sight; F; Wife; 38
1372 Tasunke Wanglaka; Looks At Her Horses; F; Dau; 12
1373 Cetan Akicita; Hawk Soldier; M; Son; 5
1374 Heraka Naji; George Standing Elk; M; Son; 2-5

1375 Tezi Ska; White Belly; M; Head; 48
1376 Hu Ptecela; Short Leg; F; Wife; 44
1377 Tezi Ska; Wm White Belly; M; Son; 21
1378 Tezi Ska; Louise White Belly; F; Dau; 6
1379 Tezi Ska; Jessie White Belly; F; Dau; 2-7

Census Of The Sioux And Cheyenne Indians Of Pine Ridge Agency, South Dakota. Taken by W. H. Clapp, Captain 16th Infantry, Acting United States Indian Agent, June 30, 1897. (Porcupine District)

Key: Number; Indian Name *(if given)*; English Name; Sex; Relation; Age

1380	Tatanka Sapa; Thomas Black Bull; M; Head; 34	1408	Heraka Ho Waste; Good Voice Elk; M; Head; 28
1381	Tatanka Sapa; Susie Black Bull; F; Wife; 36	1409	Wazi Eyutan; Touches Pine; F; Wife; 22
1382	Tatanka Sapa; James Black Bull; M; S.Son; 17	1410	Taspan Sapa; Black Apple; F; Head; 61
1383	Charles Jones; M; Head; 26		
1384	Lizzie Jones; F; Wife; 23	1411	Wagmy[sic] Su; Pumpkin Seed; M; Head; 65
1385	Katie Jones; F; Mother; 70		
1386	Alice Jones; F; Dau; 3-10	1412	Winyan Hanska; Tall Woman; F; Wife; 45
1387	Laura Jones; F; Dau; 1-2		
1388	Louise Jones; F; Dau; 1 mo.	1413	Wagmu Su; Wm. Pumpkin Seed; M: Son; 11
1389	Akicita Hanska; Long Soldier; M; Head; 50	1414	Wagmu Su; Nicholas Pumpkin Seed; M; Son; 18
1390	Wahukeza; Lance; F; Wife; 53		
1391	Oscar; M; Son; 15	1415	Mato Hinapo; Bear Comes Out; M; Head; 39
1392	Psawinyan; Crow Woman #2; F; Head; 82	1416	Kangi; Crow; F; Wife; 33
		1417	Mato Akan Apapi; Knock On Head; F; Dau; 5-4
1393	Alexander Mousseau; M; Head; 39	1418	Joseph Twiss; M; Head; 31
1394	Alice Mousseau; F; Wife; 32	1419	Mary Twiss; F; Mother; 65
1395	Julia Mousseau; F; Dau; 15		
1396	Louis Mousseau; M; Son; 13	1420	Frank Twiss; M; Head; 33
1397	Sophia Mousseau; F; Dau; 10	1421	Adelia Twiss; F; Wife; 25
1398	James Mousseau; M; Son; 7		
1399	Agnes Mousseau; F; Dau; 5	1422	Ota Agli; Brings Plenty; M; Head; 75
1400	Susie Mousseau; F; Dau; 2-6	1423	Mato Cicala; Young Bear Joe; M; Son; 23
1401	Ista Rmi; Crooked Eyes; M; Head; 62		
1402	Piya Icaga; New Growth; F; Wife; 57	1424	Nakiwizi Pi; Jealous Of Him; M; Head; 32
1403	Frank Cross; M; Son; 25	1425	Mary Gay; F; Wife; 24
		1426	Emma; F; S.Dau; 5
1404	Mila Gi; Yellow Knife; M; Head; 54	1427	Cetan Wakinyan; Thunder Hawk; M; Head; 61
1405	Tasina Luta; Her Red Blanket; F; Wife; 46	1428	Pankeska Taway; Her Shell; F; Wife; 54
1406	Pahin; Edward Porcupine; M; St.Son; 22	1429	Sunk Sapa; Albert Black Horse; M; Son; 19
1407	Wapaha; War Bonnet; M; St.Son; 11		

Census Of The Sioux And Cheyenne Indians Of Pine Ridge Agency, South Dakota. Taken by W. H. Clapp, Captain 16th Infantry, Acting United States Indian Agent, June 30, 1897. (Porcupine District)

Key: Number; Indian Name *(if given)*; English Name; Sex; Relation; Age

1430	Frank Gego; M; G.Son; 14
1431	Zuya Isnala; Lone War; M; Head; 25
1432	Sunkhinto Agli; Brings Blue Horse; F; Wife; 21
1433	Wanbli Oyate; Tribe Eagle; F; Dau; 4-2
1434	Zintkala Luta; Red Bird; F; Dau; 8 mo.
1435	Heraka Wanbli; Eagle Elk; M; Head; 42
1436	Wakan Hinapa; Comes Out Medicine; F; Wife; 24
1437	Effie; F; Dau; 2-3
1438	Psa Winyan; Crow Woman #3; F; Head; 60
1439	James Lock; M; Son; 16
1440	Cankahu Waste; Pretty Back; M; Head; 56
1441	Hanska Narco; Legging Down; F; Wife; 60
1442	Cankahu Waste; Thomas Pretty Back; M; Son; 18
1443	Oscar Warden; M; Head; 26
1444	Winyan Waste; Helen Pretty Woman; F; Head; 20
1445	Nupa; Two; M; S.Son; 12
1446	Ohitika; Brave; M; Son; 1-7
1447	Wahacanka; Shield; M; Head; 31
1448	Wahacanka; Alice Shield; F; Wife; 29
1449	Wahacanka; Julia Shield; F; Dau; 8
1450	Wahacanka; Hobert Shield; M; Son; 11 mo.
1451	Peji; James Grass; M; Head; 32
1452	Peji; Ellen Grass; F; Wife; 27
1453	Peji; Wm. Grass; M; Son; 4-11
1454	Peji; Jennie Grass; F; Dau; 3-6
1455	Peji; Victoria Grass; F; Dau; 1-9
1456	Cetan Wosica; Troublesome Hawk; M; Head; 32
1457	Cetan Wosica; Bessie Troublesome Hawk; F; Wife; 26
1458	Tasunke Hinsa; Mary Red Horse; F; Dau; 6
1459	Heraka Ho Waste; Good Voice Elk; F; Dau; 4-1
1460	Cetan Wosica; Phillip T. Hawk; M; Son; 1-10
1461	Chales[sic] Richard; M; Head; 46
1462	Anna Richard; F; Wife; 41
1463	Julia Hornbeck; F; S.Dau; 21
1464	Joseph Hornbeck; M; S.Son; 16
1465	Edward Richard; M; Son; 7
1466	Venny Richard; M; Son; 2 mo.
1467	Mato Sapa; Black Bear; M; Head; 37
1468	Mato Sapa; Emma Black Bear; F; Wife; 32
1469	Mato Sapa; Joseph Black Bear; M; Son; 11
1470	Sunk Karnir Agli; Brings Picked Horses; M; Son; 5-5
1471	Mato Sapa; Charles Black Bear; M; Son; 2-9
1472	Mato Sapa; Jennie Black Bear; F; Dau; 2 mo.
1473	Ista Ogna Opi; Shot In The Eye; M; Head; 61
1474	Sungmanitu Wankatuya; Susan High Wolf; F; Wife; 62
1475	Mila Yatapi; Knife Chief; M; Head; 61
1476	Wawokiya; Helps; F; Wife #1; 61
1477	Ona Otape; Follows Prairie Fire; F; Wife #2; 55

Census Of The Sioux And Cheyenne Indians Of Pine Ridge Agency, South Dakota. Taken by W. H. Clapp, Captain 16th Infantry, Acting United States Indian Agent, June 30, 1897. (Porcupine District)

Key: Number; Indian Name *(if given)*; English Name; Sex; Relation; Age

1478 Sunk Ole; Looks For Horses; M; Son; 25
1479 Mila; Andrew Knife; M; Son; 24
1480 Tasunke Ska; Her White Horse; F; Dau; 13
1481 Waste Agli; Brings Good; F; G.Dau; 4-8
1482 Mato Wakan; Medicine Bear; M; Head; 35
1483 Hoksi Tokapa; Lucy First Born; F; Wife; 23
1484 Tasunke Iyunka; Horse Lays Down; M; Son; 2-9

1485 Wakin Orlate; Under The Baggage; M; Head; 35
1486 Winyan Tanka; Big Woman; F; Wife; 29
1487 Cetan Hoksila; Hawk Boy; M; Son; 8
1488 Wakin Orlate; Alice U.T. Baggage; F; Dau; 3
1489 Wakin Orlate; Susie U.T. Baggage; F; Dau; 10 mo.

1490 Iktomni; Mark Spider; M; Head; 34
1491 Iktomni; Sallie Spider; F; Wife; 24
1492 Iktomni; Nellie Spider; F; Dau; 4-6
1493 Iktomni; Albert Spider; M; Son; 2-5

1494 Wambli[sic] Wakan; Medicine Eagle; M; Head; 33
1495 Wambli Wakan; Josephine M. Eagle; F; Wife; 31
1496 Maku Wakan; Holy Breast; M; Son; 9
1497 Marpuya Wicasa; Cloud Man; M; Son; 8
1498 Toka Kte; Kills Enemy; F; Dau; 3-3

1499 Wanbli Wakan; Katie M. Eagle; F; Dau; 11
1500 Anpo Wicasa; Daylight Man; M; Head; 69
1501 Wasu Sna Win; Rattling Hail; F; Wife; 57
1502 Putihin; Simon Beard; M; Son; 20
1503 Pte Wakin; Stella Medicine Cow; F; Dau; 10
1504 Putihin; John Beard; M: Son; 24
1505 Putihin; Andrew Beard; M: Son; 26

1506 Mato Gi; Yellow Bear; M; Head; 42
1507 Tasunke Ota; Plenty Horses; F; Wife; 51
1508 Pehan Catka; Left Heron; M; Head; 47
1509 Pehan Catka; Lottie Left Heron; F; Wife; 42
1510 Pehan Catka; Bene Left Heron; F; Dau; 18
1511 Pehan Catka; Emma Left Heron; F; Dau; 14
1512 Mato Wakuwa; Bear Runs After; M; Son; 6

1513 Paha Wanjila; Amos Lone Hill; M; Head; 41
1514 Paha Wanjila; Sallie Lone Hill; F; Wife; 32
1515 Paha Wanjila; Hellen Lone Hill; F; Dau; 9
1516 Paha Wanjila; Florence Lone Hill; F; Dau; 7
1516[sic] Paha Wanjila; Sidney Lone Hill; M; Son; 4-1
1518 Paha Wanjila; Hobort[sic] Lone Hill; M; Son; 2-11
1519 Paha Wanjila; Lester Lone Hill; M; Son; 5 mo.

Census Of The Sioux And Cheyenne Indians Of Pine Ridge Agency, South Dakota. Taken by W. H. Clapp, Captain 16th Infantry, Acting United States Indian Agent, June 30, 1897. (Porcupine District)

Key: Number; Indian Name *(if given)*; English Name; Sex; Relation; Age

1520 Tatanka Maza; Iron Bull; M; Head; 33
1521 Sunk Agli; Bringing Horses; F; Wife; 29

1522 Louis Bush; M; Head; 38
1523 Ella Bush; F; Wife; 24
1524 Sophia Bush; F; Dau; 5-4
1525 Frank Bush; M; Son; 3-10
1526 William Bush; M; Son; 2-3
1527 Julia Bush; F; Dau; 1 mo.

1528 Roka; Fred Badger; M; Head; 36
1529 Roka; Mary Badger; F; Wife; 29
1530 Roka; Jennie Badger; F; Dau; 11
1531 Zintkala To; Fannie Blue Bird; F; Dau; 10
1532 Roka; Lizzie Badger; F; Dau; 6
1533 Roka; Sallie Badger; F; Dau; 2-5
1534 Roka; Josephine Badger; F; Dau; 2 mo.

1535 Watanweya; Good Shot; M; Head; 25
1536 Watanweya; Emily Good Shot; F; Wife; 25
1537 Watanweya; Harry Good Shot; M; Son; 3-10
1538 Watanweya; Oscar Good Shot; M; Son; 11 mo.

1539 Asapi; Shout At; M; Head; 26
1540 Asapi; Emma Shout At; F; Wife; 25
1541 Asapi; John Shout At; M; Son; 6
1542 Asapi; Frank Shout At; M; Son; 2-5

1543 Mato Opi; Wounded Bear; M; Head; 57
1544 Yesipi; Sent; F; Wife; 28 (58)[sic]
1545 Mato Opi; Susie Wounded Bear; F; Dau; 16

1546 Canupa Nawizi; Jealous Pipe; F; Head; 67

1547 Ite Wanbli; Eagle Face; F; G.Dau; 17

1548 Eulala Conroy; F; Head; 62

1549 Sungmanitu Wankatuya; Victoria High Wolf; F; Head; 24
1550 Sungmanitu Wankatuya; Mattie High Wolf; F; Sister; 19
1551 Sungmanitu Wankatuya; Kittie High Wolf; F; Sister; 21

1552 Cetan Wakinyan; Martin Thunder Hawk; M; Head; 30
1553 Cetan Wakinyan; Fannie Thunder Hawk; F; Wife; 40
1554 Cetan Wakinyan; Rachel Brewer; F; S.Dau; 20
1555 William Brewer; M; S.Son; 17
1556 Ellen Brewer; F; S.Dau; 12
1557 Robert Brewer; M; S.Son; 10
1558 Cetan Wakinyan; Charles Thunder Hawk; M; Son 3-10
1559 Cetan Wakinyan; Joseph Thunder Hawk; M; Son; 2-1

1560 Winyan Waste; Pretty Woman; F; Head; 45
1561 Wasu; Hail; F; Dau; 14
1562 Tasunke Opi; Shot His Horses; M; Son; 15
1563 He Ptecela; Frank Short Horn; M; Son; 11 mo.

1564 Wagmu Su; Asa Pumpkin Seed; M; Head; 33
1565 Julia Pumpkin Seed; F; Wife; 32
1566 Eliza Pumpkin Seed; F; Dau; 12
1567 James Pumpkin Seed; M; Son; 11
1568 Robert Pumpkin Seed; M; Son; 8
1569 John Pumpkin Seed; M; Son; 6
1570 Joseph Pumpkin Seed; M; Son; 4-10
1571 Mary Pumpkin Seed; F; Dau; 2-5

Census Of The Sioux And Cheyenne Indians Of Pine Ridge Agency, South Dakota. Taken by W. H. Clapp, Captain 16th Infantry, Acting United States Indian Agent, June 30, 1897. (Porcupine District)

Key: Number; Indian Name *(if given)*; English Name; Sex; Relation; Age

1572 Jackson Pumpkin Seed; M; Son; 8 mo.
1573 John Boyer; M; Head; 28
1574 Lucy Boyer; F; Wife; 29
1575 Maggie Boyer; F; Dau; 5-4
1576 James Boyer; M; Son; 3-1
1577 Alice Boyer; F; Dau; 1-5
1578 Cankaku Ciqala; Smalll[sic] Back; M; Head; 31
1579 Tasunke Waste; Her Good Horse; F; Wife; 30
1580 Cankahu[sic] Ciqala; Louis Small Back; M; Son; 1 mo.
1581 Psa Winyan; Crow Woman #1; M; Head; 32
1582 Psa Winyan; Esther Crow Woman; F; Wife; 30
1583 Takuni Ole Sni; Looks For Nothing; F; Dau; 7
1584 Cin; Wants It; F; Dau; 4-7
1585 Zintkala Nata; Bird Head; M; Head; 37
1586 Tizi; Yellow Lodge; F; Wife; 29
1587 Zintkala Nata; Edith Bird Head; F; Dau; 17
1588 Hanhepi; Night; M; Son; 7
1589 Zintkala Nata; Bismarck B. Head; M; Son; 7-6
1590 Aiyapi; Talks About; F; Dau; 3-8
1591 Hudson; M; Son; 5
1592 Lucy; F; Dau; 1-6
1593 Zintkala Nata; Alice Bird Head; F; Dau; 11
1594 Frank Locke; M; Head; 32
1595 Hope Locke; F; Wife; 30
1596 Mary Locke; F; Dau; 3-10
1597 Ite Po; Swollen Face; F; Head; 39
1598 Wakil Naji; Stands Looking; F; Dau; 3-10
1599 Sunk Waketa; Looking Horse; F; Dau; 3-10
1600 Conica Wahica; Emma No Flesh; F; Dau; 17
1601 Mastnicala[sic]; Rabbit #2; M; Head; 77
1602 Zuzeca Owin; Snake Ear Ring; F; Wife; 66
1603 Kate Gibbons; F; Head; 36
1604 Lizzie Gibbons; F; Dau; 22
1605 Annie; Annaie[sic] Gibbons; F; Dau; 15
1606 Mary Gibbons; F; Dau; 10
1607 William Gibbons; M; Son; 8
1608 Agnes Gibbons; F; Dau; 6
1609 Winfield Gibbons; M; Son; 4-2
1610 Maggie Gibbons; F; Dau; 2-1
1611 Rante; James Cedar; M; Head; 30
1612 Mato Oyate; Bear Tribe; F; Wife; 36
1613 Wanbli Psisa[sic]; Nellie Jumping Eagle; F; S.Dau; 18
1614 Wanbli Psisa; Jessie Jumping Eagle; F; S.Dau; 16
1615 Wanbli Psisa; Irene Jumping Eagle; F; S.Dau; 12
1616 Wanbli Psisa; Lizzie Jumping Eagle; F; S.Dau; 10
1617 Canzeka; Gets Mad; F; S.Dau; 5-4
1618 Wanbli Psica; Oliver Jumping Eagle; M; S.Son; 14
1619 Ojutunpi; Bagged; F; S.Dau; 13
1620 Maya Consoke; Timber Bank; M; Son; 35
1621 Nawizi Ihanbla; Dreams Jealous; F; Mother; 50
1622 Winyan Waste; Pretty Woman; F; Sister; 21
1623 Grover; M; Bro; 18
1624 Rlola; Growler; M; Head; 46

Census Of The Sioux And Cheyenne Indians Of Pine Ridge Agency, South Dakota.
Taken by W. H. Clapp, Captain 16th Infantry, Acting United States Indian Agent,
June 30, 1897. (Porcupine District)

Key: Number; Indian Name *(if given)*; English Name; Sex; Relation; Age

1625 Otakuye Nica; Has No Relative; F; Wife; 51
1626 Te Wakan; Holy Lodge; F; Dau; 10
1627 Rlola; Nora Growler; F; Dau; 18
1628 Kangi Luta; Red Crow; M; Head; 39
1629 Wanbli Ska; White Eagle; F; Wife; 36
1630 Kangi Luta; Levi Red Crow; M; Son; 4 mo.
1631 Wacihin Waste; Good Plume; M; Son; 35
1632 Wamniyamni Hunku; Whirlwind Mother; F; Mother; 63
1633 Inyan Sala; George Red Rock; M; Head; 39
1634 Cante Sapa; Black Heart; M; Head; 72
1635 Wapaha Luta; Red War Bonnet; F; Wife; 55
1636 George Harvy; M; Head; 35
1637 Maggie Harvy; F; Wife; 37
1638 Julia Harvy; F; Dau; 12
1639 John Harvy; M; Son; 9
1640 Jacob Harvy; M; Son; 6-6
1641 Susie Harvy; F; Dau; 4
1642 Joseph Harvy; M; Son; 1-3
1643 Mary Martinis; F; Head; 46
1644 Philip Martinis; M; Son; 10
1645 Joseph Martinis; M; Son; 7
1646 Emma Martinis; F; Dau; 14
1647 Nora Martinis; F; Dau; 3-9
1648 Mary White; F; Head; 32
1649 Frank White; M; Husband; 36
1650 Emma White; F; Dau; 13
1651 Frank White Jr; M; Son; 7
1652 Susie White; F; Dau; 6
1653 Sunk Ska Tanka; Big White Horse; M; Head; 55
1654 Ite Ska; White Face; F; Wife; 45
1655 Wahacanka Sna; Ringing Shield; M; Son; 25
1656 Akan Mani; Susie Walks On; F; Dau; 18
1657 Ptecela; Short; M; Son; 13
1658 Ptesan Nupa; Two White Cows; F; Dau; 6
1659 Wanbli Wankatuya; High Eagle; M; Head; 28
1660 Mazaska Agli; Brings Money; F; Wife; 23
1661 Taopi Ota; Plenty Wounds; M; Head; 26
1662 Ituhu Suta; Ada Hard Forehead; F; Wife; 18
1663 Tipi Wanbli; Eagle Lodge; F; Dau; 1-1
1664 Wikan Napin; Rope Necklace; M; Head; 55
1665 Canzeka; Gets Angry; F; Wife; 47
1666 Sunk Tokeca; Different Horse; F; Dau; 12
1667 Waste Agli; Brings Good; M; Son; 10
1668 Reyap Icu; Taken Off; M; Son; 8
1669 Onkcekira; Magpie; M; Son; 5-3
1670 Philip Romero; M; Head; 28
1671 Katie Romero; F; Wife; 26
1672 Emanuel Romero; M; Son; 4-6
1673 Maggie Romero; F; Dau; 7
1674 Philip Romero Jr; M; Son; 11 mo.
1675 Tasunke Maza; Iron Horse; M; Head; 67
1676 Winyan Maza; Iron Woman; F; Wife; 58
1677 Niyan Skuya; Myrtle Sweet Breath; F; Dau; 14

Census Of The Sioux And Cheyenne Indians Of Pine Ridge Agency, South Dakota. Taken by W. H. Clapp, Captain 16th Infantry, Acting United States Indian Agent, June 30, 1897. (Porcupine District)

Key: Number; Indian Name *(if given)*; English Name; Sex; Relation; Age

1678 Naca Wankatuya; High Chief; M: Head; 37
1679 Naca Wankatuya; Mary High Chief; F; Wife; 27
1680 Kangi Gleska; Susie Spotted Crow; F; Niece; 23
1681 Kangi Gleska; Martha Spotted Crow; F; Sister; 41
1682 Kangi Gleska; Tracy Spotted Crow; M; Nephew; 8
1683 Sahunwila Winurca; Old Cheyenne Woman; F; Mother; 78
1684 Kangi Gleska; Robert Spotted Crow; M; Nephew; 18
1685 Kangi Gleska; William Spotted Crow; M; Head; 25
1686 Tacanupa Waste; Her Good Pipe; F; Head; 55
1687 Carrie; F; Dau; 17
1688 Wasu; Hail; F; Dau; 10
1689 Susie Russel; F; Dau; 12
1690 Palaniwin; Ree Woman; F; Head; 74
1691 Elizabeth Dixon; F; Head; 27
1692 William H. Dixon; M; Son; 7
1693 James G Dixon; M; Son; 5-6
1694 Alice M Dixon; F; Dau; 3-9
1695 John Y Dixon; M; Son; 2-2
1696 Susan Sears; F; Head; 43
1697 Vincent Sears; M; Son; 22
1698 Clarence Sears; M; Son; 19
1699 Maud Sears; F; Dau; 13
1700 Lulu Sears; F; Dau; 11
1701 Susie Sears; F; Dau; 9
1702 Leander Sears; M; Son; 7
1703 William Sears; M; Son; 5
1704 Cora Sears; f; Dau; 3-6
1705 Matilda Sears; F; Dau; 1-7
1706 John Sears; M; Son; 2 mo.
1707 Tanyan Kte; Kills Right; M; Head; 25
1708 Wikan Napin; Lizzie Rope Necklace; F; Wife; 21
1709 Anpitu Agli; Brings Day; M; Son; 3 mo.
1710 Psa Winyan; Crow Woman #4; F; Head; 75
1711 William Provost; M; Head; 41
1712 Wahacanka Waste; Good Shield; M; Head; 31
1713 Tatanka Waste; Good Buffalo; F; Wife; 41
1714 Toka Kute; Shot The Enemy; M; S.Son; 9
1715 Hoksila Waste; Good Boy; M; S.Son; 6
1716 Wahacanka Waste; Joseph Good Shield; M; Son; 1-3
1717 Ite Wanbli; Eagle Face; F; Head; 37
1718 Peji; Thomas Grass; M; Head; 30
1719 Ti Kiyela; Close To House; F; Wife; 29
1720 Peji; Edward Grass; M; Son; 8
1721 Anpitu Wakan; Medicine Day; F; Dau; 5-5
1722 Peji; James Grass; M; Son; 2-6
1723 Peji; John Grass; M; Son; 6 mo.
1724 Lallie Janis; F; Head; 25
1725 Effie Janis; F; Dau; 7
1726 Elizabeth Janis; F; Dau; 5-3
1727 Marpiya Ciqala; Little Cloud; M; Head; 35
1728 Wakinyan Wikau; Thunder Rope; F; Wife; 33

Census Of The Sioux And Cheyenne Indians Of Pine Ridge Agency, South Dakota. Taken by W. H. Clapp, Captain 16th Infantry, Acting United States Indian Agent, June 30, 1897.   (Porcupine District)

Key: Number; Indian Name *(if given)*; English Name; Sex; Relation; Age

6383   Lizzie Hill; F; Head; 23
6384   Robert Hill; M; Bro; 20
6385   Susie Hill; F; Sister; 17

Census of the Sioux And Cheyenne Indians
Of Pine Ridge Agency, South Dakota.
June 30, 1897

Wounded Knee District

Census Of The Sioux And Cheyenne Indians Of Pine Ridge Agency, South Dakota.
Taken by W. H. Clapp, Captain 16th Infantry, Acting United States Indian Agent,
June 30, 1897.   (Wounded Knee District)

Key: Number; Indian Name *(if given)*; English Name; Sex; Relation; Age

1729	Mato Wahacanka; Bear Shield; M; Head; 39	1750	Wanbli Napi; Eagle Hand; F; Wife; 49
1730	Ptesan Hinapa; White Cow Comes Out; F; Wife; 36	1751	Wahacanka Waste; James Good Lance; M; Son; 15
1731	Mato Wahacanka; Wm. Bear Shield; M; Son; 17	1752	Wini Aku; Brings Water; F; Dau; 4
1732	Mato Wahacanka; John Bear Shield; M; Son; 13	1753	Wahacanka Waste; Frank Good Lance; M; Head; 18
1733	Mato Wahacanka; Nellie Bear Shield; F; Dau; 15	1754	Igluhomni; Turns; F; Wife; 18
1734	Siyotanka Yuha; Keeps Flute; F; Dau; 3-5	1755	Tasunke Tunua; Looking Horse; M; Head; 27
1735	Mato Wahacanka; Mary Bear Shield; F; Dau; 1-3	1756	Gleska Agli; Brings Spotted; F; Wife; 33
1736	Wopotapi; Charles Shot To Pieces; [M]; Head; 21	1757	Heracka Gi; Yellow Elk; F; Dau; 2 mo
1737	Annie; F; Wife; 17		
1738	Sunkokile; Hunts His Horses; M; Head; 53	1758	Wahacanka Inyaka; Running Shield; M; Head; 50
1739	Wahinkpe Ska; White Arrow; F; Wife #1; 65	1759	Pte San; White Cow; F; Wife; 39
1740	Warpe; Leaf; F; Wife #2; 50	1760	Wahacanka Inyaka; Louis R. Shield; M; Son; 13
1741	Sunkokile; Lucy Hunts [sic] Horses; F; Dau; 17	1761	Isnala Inyaka; Runs Alone; M; Son; 1 mo.
1742	Tanya Kte; Kills Good; M; Son; 6	1762	Wahacanka Inyaka; Leon Running Shield; M; Head; 24
1743	Wakinya Tasunke; Thunder Horse; M; Head; 23	1763	Wahacanka Inyaka; Anna Running Shield; F; Dau; 2-8
1744	Sunk Icu; Takes Horses; F Wife; 26	1764	Wahacanka Inyaka; Nellie Running Shield; F; Dau; 7 mo.
1745	Kangi Maza; William Iron Crow; M; Head; 48	1765	Tasunke Hinrota; Anna Roan Horse; F; Head; 21
1746	Kangi Maza; Mary Iron Crow; F; Wife; 48	1766	Wahukeza Nupa; Two Lance, Jr; M; Head; 43
1747	Kangi Maza; Nicholas Iron Crow; M; Son; 20	1767	Mato Wakan; Medicine Bear; F; Wife; 35
1748	Kangi Maza; Emily Iron Crow; F; Dau; 12	1768	Wahukeza Nupa; Thomas Two Lance; M; Son; 14
1749	Wahacanka Waste; Good Lance; M; Head; 51	1769	Wahukeza Nupa; Two Lance, Sr; M; Head; 69

Census Of The Sioux And Cheyenne Indians Of Pine Ridge Agency, South Dakota. Taken by W. H. Clapp, Captain 16th Infantry, Acting United States Indian Agent, June 30, 1897. (Wounded Knee District)

Key: Number; Indian Name *(if given)*; English Name; Sex; Relation; Age

1770 Cega Ska; White Kettle; F; Wife; 55
1771 George; M; Son; 10
1772 Wegnuke; Rainbow; F; Head; 40
1773 Tatanka Wanbli; Effa Eagle Bull; F; Dau; 21
1774 Tatanka Wanbli; Ella Eagle Bull; F; Dau; 12
1775 Waokiya; Helps; F; Mother; 70
1776 Tatanka Wanbli; Henry Eagle Bull; M; Head; 18
1777 Tatanka Wangli; Lucy; F; Wife; 18
1778 Igmu Hanska; Long Cat; M; Head; 49
1779 Wayartaka; Bites; F; Wife; 43
1780 Sunk Oturan; Bessie Gives Away Hors[sic]; F; Dau; 13
1782[sic] Igmu; George Long Cat; M; Son; 11
1783 Itanka; John Big Mouth; M; Head; 40
1784 Waste Icela; Proud Woman; F; Wife; 35
1785 Cega; Ice; M; Head; 38
1786 Manzaska Win; Money Woman; F; Wife; 34
1787 Itunkasan; Weasel; F; Dau; 11
1788 Wakinya Peta; Fire Lightning; M; Head; 62
1789 Canku; Road; F; Wife; 61
1790 Sicaya Kte; Kills Bad; M; G.Son; 4
1791 Cokab Iyaya; Joseph Goes I. Center; M; Head; 31
1792 Cokab Iyaya; Maggie Goes I. Center; F; Wife; 24
1793 Cokab Iyaya; William Goes I. Center; M; Son; 7
1794 Cokab Iyaya; Victoria G.I. Center; F; Dau; 1 mo.
1795 He Wotoka; John Blunt Horn; M; Head; 40
1796 Miyogli; Nellie Whetstone; F; Wife; 32
1797 He Wotoka; Jessie Blunt Horn; F; Dau; 17
1798 He Wotoka; Louise Blunt Horn; F; Dau; 12
1799 He Wotoka; George Blunt Horn; M; Son; 13
1800 He Wotoka; Susie Blunt Horn; F; Dau; 11
1801 He Wotoka; Joseph Blunt Horn; M; Son; 3-6
1802 Cetan Rabya; Paul Scares Hawk; M; Head; 26
1803 Cetan Rabya; Louise Scares Hawk; F; Wife; 24
1804 Cetan Rabya; Stephen Scares Hawk; M; Son; 3-7
1805 Cetan Rabya; Joseph Scares Hawk; M; Son; 1-5
1806 Wahacanka Gi; Henry Yellow Shield; M; Head; 29
1807 Wahacanka Gi; Grace Yellow Shield; F; Wife; 27
1808 Wahacanka Gi; Lame Yellow Shield; F; Mother; 60
1809 Tacannupa Ota; Plenty Pipe; F; Dau; 3-8
1810 Millie Yellow Shield; F; Dau; 1-4
1811 Wazi Konatke; Bush Top Pine; M; Head; 25
1812 Hakikta; Looks Back; F; Wife; 25
1813 Sungmanitu Gi; Yellow Wolf; M; Head; 51

Census Of The Sioux And Cheyenne Indians Of Pine Ridge Agency, South Dakota.
Taken by W. H. Clapp, Captain 16th Infantry, Acting United States Indian Agent,
June 30, 1897. (Wounded Knee District)

Key: Number; Indian Name *(if given)*; English Name; Sex; Relation; Age

1814 Kansu Sepa; Fat Ticket; F; Wife; 53
1815 Sungmanitu Gi; Chas. Yellow Wolf; M; Son; 15
1816 Wosla Naji; Stand Up; M; Head; 26
1817 Winya; Woman; F; Wife; 32
1818 Sunsula Agli; Brings Mule; M; S.Son; 14
1819 Sungwakita; George Looking Horse; M; S.Son; 15
1820 Pehin Zi; Yellow Hair; M; S.Son; 5 (7)
1821 Pahin Site; Porcupine Tail; M; Son; 1mo 5da
1822 Rante Gi; Yellow Cedar; F; Head; 67
1823 Cekeyapi Win; Pray To Her; F; Head; 55
1824 Henry; M; Son; 15
1825 Anpitu Waste; Good Day; F; Dau; 18
1826 Kokipesni; Not Afraid; M; Son; 24
1827 Mato Wakinya; John Thunder Bear; M; Head; 50
1828 Inyag Mani; Running Walker; M; B. In Law; 34
1829 Itunkasan; Weasel; F; Wife; 50
1830 Mato Wakinya; Alice Thunder Bear; F; Dau; 17
1831 Mato Wakinya; Julia Thunder Bear; F; Dau; 13
1832 Mato Wakinya; Jno. Alder Thunder Bear; M; Son; 7
1833 Mato Wakinya; Victoria Thunder Bear; F; Dau; 1-2
1834 Wiyake Pegnaka; Feather On Head; M; Head; 52
1835 Lote; Throat; F; Wife; 58

1836 Wiyake Pegnaka; Wm. Feather On Head; M; Son; 19
1837 Wiyake Pegnaka; Emma Feather On Head; F; Dau; 16
1838 Mauza Sna; Ringing Iron; F; Head; 85
1839 Mato Wanagi; John Ghost Bear; M; Head; 42
1840 Shake Manza; Iron Nail; F; Wife; 41
1841 Mato Wanagi; Charles Ghost Bear; M; Son; 15
1842 Mato Wanagi; Lillie Ghost Bear; F; Dau; 13
1843 Mato Wanagi; Edgar Ghost Bear; M; Son; 7
1844 Mato Wanagi; Thomas Ghost Bear; M; Son; 17
1845 Mato Wanagi; Benj. Ghost Bear; M; Son; 2-9
1846 Mato Wanagi; Wm. Ghost Bear; M; Head; 20
1847 Iyan Mato; Susie Rocky Bear; F; Wife; 21
1848 Mato Wanagi; Charles Ghost Bear; M; Son; 8 mo.
1849 Wi Mato; Sun Bear; M; Head; 36
1850 Ista Gi; Brown Eyes; F; Wife; 55
1851 Anpitu Wakan; Sunday; M; Son; 8
1852 Tiowicakte; Kills In Lodge; F; Dau; 6
1853 Susie; F; Dau; 13
1854 Zintkala Luta; Red Bird; F; Dau; 1 mo.
1855 Wakanya Yanka; Sitting Holy; M; Head; 35
1856 Sina; Blanket; F; Wife; 31
1857 Iktomni; Jennie Clown; F; Sister; 24

Census Of The Sioux And Cheyenne Indians Of Pine Ridge Agency, South Dakota. Taken by W. H. Clapp, Captain 16th Infantry, Acting United States Indian Agent, June 30, 1897. (Wounded Knee District)

Key: Number; Indian Name *(if given)*; English Name; Sex; Relation; Age

1858 Peji Naksa; Cut Grass; M; Head; 45
1859 Psito; Bead; F; Wife; 42
1860 Hin Tokeca; Different Color; F; Dau; 10
1861 Hoksila Tanka; Big Boy; M; Son; 6
1862 Osota Win; Smoke Woman; F; Dau; 3-2
1863 Peji Naksa; Fred Cut Grass; M; Son; 13

1864 Miniowicakte; Jas. Kills I.T. Water; M; Head; 41
1865 Cetan Oyate; Tribe Hawk; F; Wife; 29
1866 Kinya; Flying; M; Son; 11
1867 Tonwica Ota; Plenty Aunts; F; Dau; 6
1868 Miniowicakte; Josy K. I. T. Water; F; Dau; 1-2

1869 Zoie Ammiotte; F; Head; 39
1870 Mary Ammiotte; F; Dau; 20
1871 Edward Ammiotte; M; Son; 18
1872 Nettie Ammiotte; F; Dau; 16
1873 Walter Ammiotte; M; Son; 15
1874 Oscar Ammiotte; M; Son; 12
1875 Nora Ammiotte; F; Dau; 11
1876 Bert Ammiotte; M; Son; 6
1877 Maud Ammiotte; F; Dau; 8
1878 Albert Ammiotte; M; Son; 3-4
1879 Emery Ammiotte; M; Son; 2 mo.

1880 Mato Ciqala; Little Bear; M; Head; 63
1881 Pejuta; Medicine; F; Wife; 51

1882 Wi Ciqala; Little Moon; M; Head; 40
1883 Rlawin; Rattle Woman; F; Wife; 46
1884 Wicarpi; Star; F; Dau; 8
1885 Sinaska In; Wears White Robe; F; Dau; 5-4

1886 Gleska Icu; Takes Spotted; F; Dau; 5-4
1887 Canta Manza; Iron Heart; M; Son; 3-4
1888 Minowicakte; Geo. Kills I.T. Water; M; S.Son; 19
1889 Caze Nakinrun; Hears His Name; m; Son; 10
1890 Wanbli Ite; Eagle Face; F; Dau; 11 mo.

1891 Maka Makelmani; Wm. Walks Under Ground; M; Head; 55
1892 Tasunke Hinrota; His Roan Horse; M; Head; 41
1893 Toka Kuwa; Charges Enemy; F; Wife; 54
1894 Sina Luta; Red Blanket; F; Mother; 68

1895 Weyukcan; Thinking; F; Head; 66
1896 Wambli Wankatuya; Joseoh[sic] High Wolf; M; G.Son; 18

1897 Tatanka Wakan; Medicine Bull; M; Head; 65
1898 Winya Huste; Lame Woman; F; Wife; 47
1899 Tazuska; Ant; M; B. in Law; 35

1900 Mato Si; Bear Foot; M; Head; 42
1901 Hinrota; Roan; F; Wife; 49
1902 Tasunke Hiyohi; Comes After H. Horses; F; Dau; 15

1903 Wamnyomni Sapa; Black Whirlwind; M; Head; 37
1904 Wanbli; Eagle; F; Wife; 37
1905 Tanya Kte; Kills Right; M: Son; 14
1906 Sungali; Brings Horses; M; Son; 11
1907 Tatanka Ska Kaga; Makes White Buffalo; F; Dau; 9

Census Of The Sioux And Cheyenne Indians Of Pine Ridge Agency, South Dakota. Taken by W. H. Clapp, Captain 16th Infantry, Acting United States Indian Agent, June 30, 1897. (Wounded Knee District)

Key: Number; Indian Name *(if given)*; English Name; Sex; Relation; Age

1908 Siyotanka Ho; Pipe Voice; F; Dau; 8
1909 Wamniyomni[sic] Sapa; Joseph B. Whirlwind; M; Son; 1 mo.
1910 Pejuta Waste; Good Medicine; M; Head; 35
1911 Pteyela Agli; Brings Together; F; Wife; 32
1912 Nanwocakiwizi; Jealous Of Them; M; Bro; 32
1913 Wasicu Winyan; White Woman; F; Dau; 11
1914 Rabwicaya; Scares Them Away; M; Son; 7
1915 Canupa Sapa; Black Pipe; F; Dau; 3-11
1916 Pejuta Waste; Louis G. Medicine; M; Son; 8 mo.
1917 Sungmanitu Tanka; Big Wolf; M; Head; 39
1918 Ceyesa; Cries; F; Wife; 34
1919 Sungmanitu Tanka; Samuel B. Wolf; M; Son; 17
1920 Tokeya Mani; Walks First; F; Dau; 7
1921 Wanbli; Eagle; F; Dau; 5
1922 Saga Ska; White Cane; F; Dau; 3-5
1923 Cetan Hoksila; Hawk Boy; M; Son; 8 mo.
1924 Onanso; Pacer; M: Head; 74
1925 Najinyapi; Surrounded; F; Wife; 69
1926 Itunkasan Ska; White Weasel; F; Head; 60
1927 Anukasan; Bald Eagle; M; Head; 35
1928 Winya Waste; Pretty Woman; F; Wife; 28
1929 Maka Suta; Hard Ground; M; Head; 58
1930 Pte San Nupa; Two White Cows; F; Wife; 52
1931 Can Wehna Wicakte; Thos. Kills I. Timber; M; Head; 34
1932 Pejuta Ska; White Medicine; F; Wife; 32
1933 Wacinwapi; Depneds[sic] On; M; Son; 8
1934 Cetan Oyate; Tribe Hawk; F; Dau; 4-3
1935 Wiyaka Luta; Red Feather; F; Dau; 1-1
1936 Mato Wanbli; Bear Eagle; M; Head; 42
1937 Wiyaka Luta; Red Feather; F; Wife; 37
1938 Nanca; Chief; M; Son; 3-10
1939 Mato Wanbli; Joseph Bear Eagle; M; Son; 1-4
1940 Wamniyomni; Whirlwind; M; B. in Law; 24
1941 Cetan Ropahu; Hawk Wing; M; Head; 47
1942 Tokaheya; Leader; F; Wife; 54
1943 Cetan Ropahu; Luke Hawk Wing; M; Son; 11
1944 Cetan Ropahu; James Hawk Wing; M; Son; 10
1945 Samuel Brown; M; Head; 25
1946 Sunka Wanagi; Ghost Dog; M; Head; 34
1947 Siyotanka Yajo; Plays On Flute; F; Wife; 28
1948 Wniwanca; Ocean; F; Dau; 4-1
1949 Presan[sic] Win; White Cow Woman; F; Dau; 1-9
1950 Tarca Luta; Red Deer; M; Head; 29

Census Of The Sioux And Cheyenne Indians Of Pine Ridge Agency, South Dakota. Taken by W. H. Clapp, Captain 16th Infantry, Acting United States Indian Agent, June 30, 1897. (Wounded Knee District)

Key: Number; Indian Name *(if given)*; English Name; Sex; Relation; Age

1951 He Rlogeca; Hollow Horn; F; Wife; 26
1952 Wambli; Eagle; F; Dau; 6
1953 Sunk Hinzi; Yellow Horses; F; Dau; 2-4
1954 Rupahu Win; Wing Woman; F; M. in Law; 65
1955 Wiciyela; Albert Yankton; M; Head; 17
1956 Isnala Ti; Lives Alone; F; Mother; 52
1957 Wiciyela; Creighton Yankton; M; Head; 25
1958 Wiyaka Luta; Jennie One Feather; F; Wife; 18
1959 Nanjiya Kte; Stands Killing; M; Son; 4 mo.
1960 Wicakute; Shot; M; Head; 35
1961 Oyate Ota; Plenty Nations; F; Wife; 37
1962 Akanwis Kte; Kills Straddle; M; Son; 7
1963 Inya Ska; White Rock; M; Son; 5
1964 Wicakute; Cora Shot; F; Dau; 8 mo.
1965 Awagugupi; Roacher; M; Head; 73
1966 Pejirota; Sage; F; Wife; 63
1967 Tunweya; Joseph Scout; M; Head; 25
1968 Sungmanitu Gi; Alice Yellow Wolf; F; Wife; 20
1969 Wan On Opi; Arrow Wound; F; Dau; 1-7
1970 Hanepi Kte; Kills Enemy At Night; M; Head; 19
1971 Rla; Rattling; F; Mother; 55
1972 Anpitu Luta; Red Day; F; Sister; 16
1973 Winya Hanska; Tall Woman; F; Sister; 14
1974 Kokipesn Kte; Kills Without Fear; M; Nephew; 8
1975 Hoksila Kte; Robert Yellow Boy; M; Head; 35
1976 Manka Hunku; Skunks Mother; F; Wife; 24
1977 Onkcekira Ciqala; Little Magpie; M; Son; 2-8
1978 Wicarpi; Ruben Star; M; Head; 27
1979 Wicarpi; Mary Star; F; Wife; 25
1980 Mato Luta; Silver Red Bear; F; S. in Law; 9
1981 Mato Luta; Red Bear; M; Head; 49
1982 Pankeska Win; Shell Woman; F; Wife; 48
1983 Tatanka Huste; Lame Bull; M; Son; 19
1984 Mato Luta; Edgar Red Bear; M; Son; 17
1985 Ta Cante; Her Heart; F; Dau; 12
1986 Ista Su; Eye Seed; F; Dau; 7
1987 Mato Luta; Maggie Red Bear; F; Dau; 1-3
1988 Mato Inyaka; Running Bear; M; Head; 26
1989 Sagye; Cane; F; Wife; 23
1990 Winya Wakan; Holy Woman; F; Dau; 1-6
1991 Kangi Wakan; Holy Crow; M: Son; 5
1992 Waonjica Yuha; Ownes[sic] Bob Tail; M; Head; 67
1893[sic] Anpitu Hiyaya; Days Going; F; Wife; 66
1994 Mato Hinyuka; Bear Comes To Lay Down; M; Head; 46

Census Of The Sioux And Cheyenne Indians Of Pine Ridge Agency, South Dakota. Taken by W. H. Clapp, Captain 16th Infantry, Acting United States Indian Agent, June 30, 1897. (Wounded Knee District)

Key: Number; Indian Name *(if given)*; English Name; Sex; Relation; Age

1995	Ptesan Kici Mani; Walks With White Cow; F; Wife; 58	2017	Zintkala Waste; Pretty Bird; M; Son; 18
1996	William White; M; G.Son; 15	2018	Zintkala To; Mary Blue Bird; F; Dau; 18
1997	Okicuze Yuha; Keeps The Bottle; M; Nephew; 6		
		2019	Jackson Bissonette; M; Head; 29
1998	Sina Manza; Iron Robe; F; Head; 60	2020	Sally Face; F; Wife; 27
		2021	Joseph Bissonette; M; Son; 4mo.
1999	Winya Cuwegnaka; Womans' Dress; M; Head; 51	2022	Zintkala Sapa; Black Bird; M; Head; 24
2000	Winya Luta; Red Woman; F; Wife #1; 50	2023	Hinapa; Comes Out; F; Wife; 23
2001	Pte San; White Cow; F; Wife #2; 35	2024	Wicarpi Wankatuya; High Star; M; Son; 3-10
2002	Apicita Isnala; Lone Soldier; M; Son; 18	2025	Zintakala[sic] Sapa; Richard Black Bird; M; Son; 1-1
2003	Sugmnaitu Peta; Fire Wolf; M; Son; 15	2026	Wasicu Tasunke; American Horse #2; M; Head; 50
2004	Mato Ciqala; Little Bear; M; Son; 8	2027	Wanbli Wicasa; Eagle Man; M; Son; 13
2005	Tonweya; Scout; M; Son; 5	2028	Wasicu Tasunke; Dawson A. Horse; M; Son; 17
2006	Zintkala Nanpi; George Bird Nechlace[sic]; M; Head; 49	2029	Tahu Wanica; No Neck #1; M; Head; 45
2007	Wamniyomni; Whirlwind; F; Wife; 42	2030	Kangi Manza; Ellen Iron Crow; F; Wife; 46
2008	Zintkala Nanpi; Philip Bird Necklace; M; Son; 15	2031	Mato Cincala; Young Cub; M; Son; 12
2009	Zintkala Nanpi; Mary Bird Necklace; Dau; 13		
2010	Zintkala Nanpi; Hattie Bird Necklace; F; Dau; 11	2032	Aguyapi Soka; Thick Bread; M; Head; 58
2011	Zintkala Nanpi; Moses Bird Necklace; M; Son; 9	2033	Wankal Ti; Lives Above; F; Wife; 45
2012	Zintkala Nanpi; Susan Bird Necklace; F; Dau; 7	2034	Mato Gleska; Thos. Spotted Bear; M; Son; 24
2013	Zintkala Nanpi; Rosa Bird Necklace; F; Dau; 1-3	2035	Wamniyomni Luzahan; Fast Whirlwind; M; Head; 45
2014	Ite; Face; M: Head; 61	2036	Sina Ota; Plenty Blankets; F; Wife; 43
2015	Marpuya Topa; Four Cloud; F; Wife #1; 69	2037	Wamniyomni Luzahan; Stella F. Whirlwind; F; Dau; 10
2016	Zintkala Luta; Red Bird; F; Wife #2; 59		

Census Of The Sioux And Cheyenne Indians Of Pine Ridge Agency, South Dakota. Taken by W. H. Clapp, Captain 16th Infantry, Acting United States Indian Agent, June 30, 1897. (Wounded Knee District)

Key: Number; Indian Name *(if given)*; English Name; Sex; Relation; Age

2038 Tatanka Ciqala; Samuel Little Bull; M; Head; 26
2039 Ni Glenapa; Comes Out Alive; F; Wife; 40
2040 Ita Wawiyokepi; Pleasant Face; F; S.Dau; 5-5
2041 Emma; F; S.Dau; 15

2042 Cangleska Waste; Good Ring; F; Head; 68

2043 Zintkala Ota; Plenty Bird; M; Head; 28
2044 Zintkala Ota; Susie Plenty Bird; F; Wife; 28
2045 Zintkala Ota; Nancy Plenty Bird; F; Dau; 8
2046 Zintkala Ota; Julia Plenty Bird; F; Dau; 4-10

2047 Wakinya Luzahan; Fast Thunder; M; Head; 55
2048 Sung Taopi; Wounded Horse; F; Wife #1; 45
2049 Makoce Icu; Locator; F; Wife #2; 24
2050 Stella; F; Dau; 23
2051 Najinyapi; Surrounded; M; Son; 4-7
2052 Oturan; Donating; F; Dau; 2

2053 Wakinya Luzahan; Fannie Fire Thunder; F; Head; 26
2054 Mary; F; Dau; 4-9

2055 Wicarpi Luta; Red Star; M; Head; 31
2056 Wicarpi Luta; Sallie Red Star; F; Wife; 31
2057 Sung Sapa; Black Horse; F; Dau; 11
2058 Wicarpi Luta; David Red Star; M; Son; 6
2059 Wicarpi Luta; Paul Red Star; M; Son; 2-8

2060 Wicarpi Luta; Stella Red Star; F; Dau; 4 mo.

2061 Inya Mato; Rocky Bear; M; Head; 61
2062 Oye; Track; F; Wife #1; 58
2063 Tokeya Inyaka; Runs Ahead; F; Wife #2; 53
2064 Lucy; F; Dau; 29
2065 Jessie; F; Dau; 19
2066 Cetan; Silas Hawk; M; Son; 18
2067 Inya Mato; Lizzie Rocky Bear; F; Dau; 25
2068 Wabluska Tiyoslola; Mamie Cricket; F; Dau; 13

2069 Mato Wapagiueca; Bluffing Bear; M; Head; 42
2070 Mato Wapagiueca; Sophia R[sic] Bear; F; Wife; 30
2071 Taoyanke Waste; Her Good Place; F; Dau; 11 mo.

2072 Heraka Luta; Red Elk; M; Head; 46
2073 Manzaska; Money; F; Wife; 37
2074 Inya Mato; George Rocky Bear; M; Son; 17
2075 Heraka Luta; Peter Red Elk; M; Son; 5-5
2076 Heraka Luta; Emil Red Elk; M; Son; 3-2

2077 Winuni Win; Lost Woman; F; Head; 75
2078 Wamniyomni Win; Comes Out Whirlwind; F; G.Dau; 28

2079 Wapaha; War Bonnet; M; Head; 33
2080 Wahacanku Waster; Good Shield; F; Wife; 45
2081 Sunka Ciqala; Robert Little Dog; M; Nephew; 17

2082 Isanyante; Santee; F; Head; 57

Census Of The Sioux And Cheyenne Indians Of Pine Ridge Agency, South Dakota. Taken by W. H. Clapp, Captain 16th Infantry, Acting United States Indian Agent, June 30, 1897. (Wounded Knee District)

Key: Number; Indian Name *(if given)*; English Name; Sex; Relation; Age

2083	Lucy; F; Dau; 32	2106	Wanbli Iyotaka; Sitting Eagle; M; Head; 48
2084	Naca Kte Pin; Wished To Be A Chief; M; Bro; 61	2107	Ista Ska; White Eyes; M; Head; 49
2085	Amukasan Ciqala; Felix Little Bald Eagle; [blank]; Head; 21	2108	Warpe Gi; Yellow Leaf; F; Wife; 36
2086	Tawa Kte; Kills Her Own; F; Mother; 43	2109	Ista Ska; Daniel White Eyes; M: Son; 16
2087	Anukasan Ciqala; Ada Little Bald Eagle; F; Sister; 16	2110	Cangleska Luta; Red Ring; F; Dau; 14
2088	Suta; Hard; F; Sister; 13		
2089	Ohitika Kte; Kills Brave; F; Sister; 11	2111	Winya Ptecela; Short Woman; F; Head; 56
2090	Anukasan Ciqala; Chas. Little B. Eagle; M; Bro; 3-10	2112	Wambli Hanpa; Wagle[sic] Moccasin; M; Son; 11
2091	Anukasan Ciqala; Moses Little Bald Eagle; M; Head; 23	2113	Tanyan Kutepi; Shoots Him Right; F; Dau; 8
2092	Tasunke Oyespapi; Stop Her Horses; F; Wife; 23	2114	Hinto Gleska; Gray Spotted Horse; M; Nephew; 14
2093	Cante Waste; Good Heart; M; Son; 8 mo.	2115	Witko Win; Foolish Woman; M; Head; 64
2094	Heraka Sapa; Black Elk; M: Head; 33	2116	Tawacin Waste; Free Hearted; F; Wife; 60
2095	Wapaha; Kate War Bonnet; F; Wife; 28	2117	Nupa Kte; Kills Twice; F; G.Dau; 14
2096	Wicarpi Ho Waste; Good Voice Star; M; Son; 1-9	2118	Sunkgleska; Spotted Horse; F; G.Dau; 13
2097	Sunka Hanska; John Long Dog; M: Head; 52	2119	Tasunke Otawin; Her Many Horses; F; Head; 69
2098	Tasunke Hin Sa; Her Red Horse; F; Wife; 55	2120	Wahacanka; Shield; M: Head; 61
2099	Ohitika; Brave; M; Son; 9	2121	Tanyan Icaga; Grows Good; F; Wife; 61
2100	Wicarpi Canku; Star Road; F; Dau; 3-9	2122	Tyopa Luta; Her Red Door; F; Dau; 12
2101	Hanska; Tall; M; Head; 38		
2102	Waste; Good; F; Wife; 43	2123	Wahacanka; Shield, Jr; M; Head; 25
2103	Tokicun; Revenger; F; Dau; 9		
2104	Sungmanu; Horse Stealer; M; Son; 5-2	2124	Sunkwakan Win; Horse Woman; F; Wife; 24
2105	Naca Win; Cheif[sic] Woman; F; Dau; 1-3	2125	Wastelakapi; Fond Of Him; M; Son; 4 mo.

Census Of The Sioux And Cheyenne Indians Of Pine Ridge Agency, South Dakota. Taken by W. H. Clapp, Captain 16th Infantry, Acting United States Indian Agent, June 30, 1897. (Wounded Knee District)

Key: Number; Indian Name *(if given)*; English Name; Sex; Relation; Age

2126	Hinyete; James Shoulder; M; Head; 22	2146	Herbert Bissonette; M; Head; 18
2127	Wahacanka; Mary Shield; F; Wife; 19	2147	Julia Whalen Bissonette; F; Wife; 23
2128	Hinyete; Henry Shoulder; M; Son; 1-9	2148	William Bissonette; M; Nephew; 8
		2149	Joseph Bissonette; M; Head; 18
2129	Iyuwer Kte; Kills Across; M; Head; 26	2150	Frank Bissonette; M; Bro; 16
		2151	William Bissonette; M; Bro; 11
2130	Tasunke Agli; Brings Her Horses; F; Sister; 48	2152	Pankeska Luta Win; Red Shell Woman; F; Head; 66
2131	Sinte Conala; Clara Few Tails; F; Niece; 16	2153	Louise Bissonette; F; G.Dau; 6
2132	Yusinyeyapi; Scares Him; M; Nephew; 10	2154	Iktomni; Clown; F; Head; 54
2133	Gliyotaka; Comes To Sit; M; Nephew; 9	2155	Heraka Isnala; James Lone Elk; M; Head; 30
2134	Wambli Ogle; Eagle Shirt; M; Head; 25	2156	Heraka Isnala; Julia Lone Elk; F; Wife; 28
2135	Opanwegi Kte; Hattie Kills A Hundred; F; Wife; 19	2157	Heraka Isnala; Lucy Lone Elk; F; Dau; 6
2136	Ite Rante; Cedar Face; M; Head; 67	2158	Win Waste; Good Woman; F; Head; 65
2137	Tasunke Luta Win; Her Red Horse; F; Wife; 62	2159	Mato Naji; Anna Standing Bear; F; G.Dau; 13
2138	Ite Rante; William Cedar Face; M; Son; 23	2160	Honpe; Charles Picket Pin; M; Head; 45
2139	Ista Gi; Yellow Eyes; M; Son; 17	2161	Oktea; Hanging; F; Wife; 38
		2162	Honpe; Della Picket Pin; F; Dau; 1-1
2140	Ohitika Kte; Kills Brave; M; Head; 32	2163	Awicagli; Brings Them; M; B. in Law; 29
2141	Itunkasan Iyotaka; Sitting Weasel; M: Head; 63	2164	Luta; Red; F; Niece; 9
		2165	Wanbli Hoksila; Eagle Boy; M; Nephew; 7
2142	Pehin Sankiya; Paints Hair; F; Wife; 49		
2143	Keyela Taopi; Wounded Close; F; Dau; 16	2166	Julia Patton; F; Head; 40
		2167	James Patton; M; Son; 22
2144	Itunkasan Iyotaka; Herman S. Weasel; M; Son; 14	2168	Susie Patton; F; Dau; 19
		2169	Thomas Patton; M; Son; 18
2145	Itunkasan Luta; Chas. Red Weasel; M; G.Son; 11	2170	George Patton; M; Son; 16
		2171	Louise Patton; F; Dau; 14
		2172	Lucy Patton; F; Dau; 10

Census Of The Sioux And Cheyenne Indians Of Pine Ridge Agency, South Dakota. Taken by W. H. Clapp, Captain 16th Infantry, Acting United States Indian Agent, June 30, 1897. (Wounded Knee District)

Key: Number; Indian Name *(if given)*; English Name; Sex; Relation; Age

2173	Emma Patton; F; Dau; 8		2199	Zintkala Waste; Pretty Bird; M; Son; 6
2174	Julia Patton; F; Dau; 5-8			
2175	William Patton; M; Son; 3-5			
2176	Charles Patton; M; Son; 8 mo.		2200	Jennie Mesteth; F; Head; 44
			2201	Maggie Mesteth; F; Dau; 19
2177	Sunka Paha Akan Naji; Dog On Bute[sic]; M; Head; 57		2202	Willie Mesteth; M; Son; 17
			2203	James Mesteth; M; Son; 15
			2204	Joseph Mesteth; M; Son; 13
2178	Mato Rlola; Growling Bear; M; Head; 35		2205	David Mesteth; M; Son; 11
			2206	Philip Mesteth; M; Son; 8
2179	He Rlogua; Hollow Horn; F; Wife; 43		2207	Peter Mesteth; M; Son; 7
			2208	Thomas Mesteth; M; Son; 4-6
2180	Oleku; Comes Hunting; M; Son; 4-8		2209	Frank Mesteth; M: Son; 1-3
			2210	Wambli Sapa; Black Eagle; M; Head; 67
2181	Mato Naji; Standing Bear; M; Head; 35		2211	Wambli Sapa; Susie Black Eagle; F; G.Dau; 15
2182	Zintkala Luta; Red Bird; F; Dau; 4-6			
2183	Wicarpi; Star; F; Dau; 3-1		2212	Wanbli[sic]; Eagle #2; F; Head; 55
2184	Imnista; Saliva; M; Head; 59		2213	Sunkhinzi Win; Yellow Horse Woman; F; Dau; 33
2185	Teglaka Waste; Good Mover; F; Wife; 62			
2186	Ake Hiyn; Gertie Comes Again; F; G.Dau; 12		2214	Hihan Gleska; Spotted Owl; M; Head; 29
			2215	Cetan Win; Mary Hawk Woman; F; Wife; 22
2187	Wambli; Eagle; F; Head; 44			
2188	Ptesan Yatapi; Alice White Cow Chief; F; Dau; 15		2216	Iwosaya; Bloody Mouth; M; Son; 4-3
2189	Siyo; Prairie Chicken; F; G.Mother; 64		2217	Tainyan Yanka; Sits In Sight; F; Dau; 1-4
2190	Alexander Adams; M; Head; 45		2218	Heraka Hoksila; Huron Elk Boy; M; Head; 48
2191	John Adams; M; Son; 20			
2192	Nellie Adams; F; Dau; 18		2219	Itunhasan Mato; Weasel Bear; F; Wife; 47
2193	Susie Adams; F; Dau; 15			
2194	Joseph Adams; M; Son; 11		2220	Heraka Hoksila; Charles E. Boy; M; Son; 17
2195	Lucy Adams; F; Dau; 15			
			2221	Heraka Hoksila; Joseph E. Boy; M; Son; 14
2196	Sinte Sapela; Black Tail Deer; M; Head; 40		2222	Hoksila Ciqala; Little Boy; M; Son; 4-2
2197	Nisehu; Rum Bone; F; Wife; 39			
2198	Ta Rpaya; Lays Dead; M; Son; 11		2223	Pankeska Hoksila; Shell Boy; M; Head; 60

Census Of The Sioux And Cheyenne Indians Of Pine Ridge Agency, South Dakota. Taken by W. H. Clapp, Captain 16th Infantry, Acting United States Indian Agent, June 30, 1897. (Wounded Knee District)

Key: Number; Indian Name *(if given)*; English Name; Sex; Relation; Age

2224 Tasunke Inajin; Horse Stops; F; Wife; 54
2225 Wainyan Waste; Good Thunder; M; Head; 65
2226 Ista San; Gray Eyes; F; Wife #1; 55
2227 Honska Narco; Leggins Down; F; Wife #2; 53
2228 Heraka Sapa; Grace Black Elk; F; Dau; 16
2229 Hoksila Tanka; Joseph Big Boy; M; Head; 20
2230 Icaga; Grows Up; F; Wife; 21
2231 Tatanka Luta; Red Bull; M; Head; 40
2232 Tatanka Luta; Sophia Red Bull; F; Wife; 25
2233 Wipata Win; Quilled Woman; F; Dau; 2-3
2234 Nupala; Two Two; M; Head; 38
2235 Tatanka Wacipi; Buffalo Dance; F; Wife; 35
2236 Nupala; Alexander Two Two; M; Son; 20
2237 Nupala; Joseph Two Two; M; Son; 18
2238 Nupala; Eagle Two Two; M; Son; 16
2239 Ista Gi; Yellow Eyes; F; Dau; 13
2240 Wasicu Win; White Woman; F; Dau; 10
2241 Hoksila Tanka; Big Boy; M; Son; 8
2242 Kutepi; Shot; M; Son; 8
2243 Nupala; Jennie Two Two; F; Dau; 3-6
2244 Anpitu Wakan; Sundsy[sic]; F; Dau; 2-7
2245 Anpala[sic]; Richard Two Two; M; Son; 1-4
2246 Maga Isnala; Lone Goose; M; Head; 63
2247 Pehinjin Win; Yellow Hair Woman; F; Wife; 51
2248 Poge; Nose; M; Son; 24
2249 Tipi Wakan; Holy Lodge; F; Dau; 23
2250 Toka Kico; Calls Enemy; M; Son; 8
2251 Maga Isnala; Susie Lone Goose; F; Dau; 14
2252 Mako Sica Win; Bad Land Woman; F; Head; 75
2253 Tokala Sapa; Black Fox; M; Head; 37
2254 Tokala Sapa; Mary Black Fox; F; Wife; 28
2255 Wakan Naji; Stands Holy; F; Dau; 1-7
2256 Inyan Wakan; Kate Holy Rock; F; Head; 40
2257 Tasunke Opi Wanyanka; Looks At Wounded Horse; F; Dau; 5-6
2258 Itazipe Sica; Bad Bow; M; Son; 1-9
2259 Ogle Sa; Henry Red Shirt; M; Head; 38
2260 Ogle Sa; Emma Red Shirt; F; Wife; 37
2261 Ogle Sa; John Red Shirt; M; Son; 15
2262 Ogle Sa; Mary Red Shirt; F; Dau; 12
2263 Ogle Sa; Charles [sic] Shirt; M; Son; 7
2264 Ogle Sa; Alfred Red Shirt; M; Son; 2-6
2265 John Purier[sic]; M; Head; 25
2266 Josie Pourier; F; Wife; 22
2267 Josephine Pourier; F; Dau; 4-2
2268 Ellen Pourier; F; Dau; 1-7
2269 Josephine Pourier; F; Head; 45

Census Of The Sioux And Cheyenne Indians Of Pine Ridge Agency, South Dakota. Taken by W. H. Clapp, Captain 16th Infantry, Acting United States Indian Agent, June 30, 1897. (Wounded Knee District)

Key: Number; Indian Name *(if given)*; English Name; Sex; Relation; Age

2270	Joseph Pourier; M; Son; 19		2296	Hihan Gleska; Red Owl; M; Son; 7 mo.
2271	Louis Pourier; M; Son; 17		2297	Kangi; Henry Crow; M; Head; 31
2272	Emil Pourier; M; Son; 15		2298	Tanya Ku; Comes Right; F; Wife; 25
2273	Mary Pourier; F; Dau; 13			
2274	Helen Pourier; F; Dau; 11		2299	Kangi; Sally Crow; F; Dau; 2 mo
2275	Peter Pourier; M; Son; 9		2300	He Rlogeca; Hollow Horn; M; Head; 37
2276	Rosa Pourier; F; Dau; 7			
2277	Charlie Pourier; M; Son; 4-2		2301	Pehin Ji; Yellow Hair; F; Wife; 28
2278	OtaAgli[sic]; Brings Plenty; M; Head; 49		2302	He Rlogeca; Thomas H. Horn; M; Son; 10
2279	Karmi; Bend; F; Wife; 52			
2280	Irpeya Glecupi; Robert Left Behind; M; Son; 21		2303	Kute Sni; Never Missed; M; Son; 9
2281	Ota Agli; Michael Brings Plenty; [M]; Son; 17		2304	Wan Icarya; Grows Arrows; M; Son; 5-3
2282	Okicizapi; Fights Over Him; M; Son; 11		2305	He Rlogeca; Mary H. Horn; F; Dau; 2 mo.
2283	Wakinya Wambli; Eagle Thunder; M; Head; 42		2306	Mato Wakuwa; Chasing Bear; M; Head; 52
2284	TaSunkawakan[sic]; Her Horses; F; Wife; 37		2307	Marpiya; Cloud; F; Wife; 48
2285	Gleska Yuha; Keeps Spotted; F; Dau; 8		2308	Cokab Iyaya; Goes In Front; F; Dau; 14
2286	Napca; Swallow; M; Son; 5		2309	Wapatapi; Shot To Pieces; M; Head; 21
2287	Winya Pupun; Rotten Woman; F; Dau; 2-4			
2288	Wambli Wankatuya; High Eagle; M; Head; 35		2310	Wakinya Witko; Crazy Thunder; M; Head; 41
2289	Wakinya Waste; Good Thunder; F; Wife; 30		2311	Wiyaka; Feather; F; Wife; 31
2290	Astibone; M; Son; 2-3		2312	Anukasan; Bald Eagle; M; Son; 10
2291	Oynspa; Catches; M; Head; 33		2313	Wasu Luta; Red Hail; F; Dau; 6
2292	Wanjila Agli; Brings One; F; Wife; 28		2314	Akanyaka Kte; Kills On Horseback; M; Son; 2-7
2293	Mangaju Mani; Walking Rain; F; Dau; 6		2315	Opanwege Kte; Jno Kills A Hundred; M; Head; 49
2294	Canpaslatapi Canku; Staked Road; F; Dau; 11		2316	Opanwege Kte; Susie Kills A Hundred; F; Wife; 33
2295	Wakita; Looks; F; Dau; 3-10		2317	Opanwege Kte; Adeline Kills A Hundred; F; Dau; 16

Census Of The Sioux And Cheyenne Indians Of Pine Ridge Agency, South Dakota. Taken by W. H. Clapp, Captain 16th Infantry, Acting United States Indian Agent, June 30, 1897. (Wounded Knee District)

Key: Number; Indian Name *(if given)*; English Name; Sex; Relation; Age

2318 Opanwege Kte; Elija Kills A Hundred; M; Son; 9
2319 Opanwege Kte; Nany Kills A Hundred; F; Dau; 8
2320 Ite Waste; Jennie Pretty Face; F; Head; 38
2321 Tasunke Ota; Plenty Horses; M; Head; 28
2322 Hinrota Win; Roan Woman; F; Wife; 35
2323 Mato Minyapi; Living Bear; M; Head; 55
2324 Ptewinyela Sa; Red Cow; F; Wife; 45
2325 Mato Minyapi; Thomas Living Bear; M; Son; 17
2326 Mato Minyapi; Sallie Living Bear; F; Dau; 11
2327 Akanyaka Kte; Kills On Horseback; M; Son; 28
2328 Osica; Hard To Hit; M; Head; 23
2329 Mato Hu; Bear Legs; F; Wife; 22
2330 Joseph Brown; M; Head; 28
2331 Alice Brown; F; Wife; 27
2332 James Brown; M; Son; 6
2333 Willie Brown; M; Son; 4-9
2334 Joseph Brown Jr; M; Son; 3-1
2335 Tonie Brown; M; Son; 1-7
2336 Lilly Brown; F; Dau; 5 mo.
2337 Osun Wanica; No Braid; M; Head; 69
2338 Canupa Wiyakpa; Shining Pipe; F; Wife; 61
2339 Osun Wanica; Wilson No Braid; M; Son; 18
2340 Cante Waste; Pleased Heart; F; G.Dau; 5-1
2341 Pamagle; Drops Head; M; Head; 73
2342 Wiyunkca Sni; Dont[sic] Think; M; Head; 61
2343 OtuyaCinya[sic] Ceya; Crying Without Cause; F; Wife; 59
2344 Isakib Ti; Lives By; M; Son; 25
2345 Nakpa Luta; Red Ear; M; Son; 23
2346 Canpa Su; Cherry Stone; M: Head; 55
2347 Pte San; White Cow; F; Wife; 52
2348 Nupa Kte; Kills Two; M; Head; 23
2349 Zintkala; Bird; F; Wife; 24
2350 Canupa Luta Win; Red Pipe Girl; F; Dau; 1-9
2351 He Rlogeca; Hollow Horn; M; Head; 30
2352 Pte San Waste; Good White Cow; F; Wife; 27
2353 Itunkasan Wapacha; Weasel Bonnet; M; Son; 3-5
2354 Warca Ji; Sun Flower; F; Dau; 1-3
2355 Pehan Wankatuya; High Heron; M; Son; 25
2356 Tankal Woglaka; Talks Outside; F; Mother; 55
2357 Cante Suta; Hard Heart; M; Head; 45
2358 Tasunke Wakan; Medicine Horse; F; Wife; 35
2359 Wahinkpe Nupa; Two Arrows; M; B. in Law; 29
2360 Tiyopa Taway; Her Door; F; Dau; 24
2361 Cetan Wambli; Eagle Hawk; M; Son; 13

Census Of The Sioux And Cheyenne Indians Of Pine Ridge Agency, South Dakota. Taken by W. H. Clapp, Captain 16th Infantry, Acting United States Indian Agent, June 30, 1897. (Wounded Knee District)

Key: Number; Indian Name *(if given)*; English Name; Sex; Relation; Age

2362 Wakinya Peta; Fire Thunder; M; Head; 49
2363 Timahel You Okihisni; Cant[sic] Enter Door; F; Wife; 43
2364 Wiconi Terila; Loves Life; M; Son; 26
2365 Wakinya Peta; Wm. Fire Thunder; M; Son; 24
2326[sic] Jennie F. Thunder; F; Dau; 17
2367 Wakinya Peta; Earth F. Thunder; F; Dau; 10
2368 Wakinya Peta; Charles F. Thunder; M; Son; 7

2369 Watage; Foam; M; Head; 70

2370 Sunka Witko; Crazy Dog; M; Head; 47
2371 Wacinko; Pouting; F; Wife; 55

2372 Cankpe; Knee; M; Head; 65
2373 Wicayajipe; Bumble Bee; F; Wife; 59
2374 Wambli Wicasa; Eagle Man; M; Son; 33
2375 Cankpe; Wilson Knee; M; Son; 19
2376 Pankeska Maza; Iron Shell; F; G.Dau; 16

2377 He Cinsakayapi; Mountain Sheep; M; Head; 32
2378 Hunpi; Millie Picket Pin; F; Wife; 24
2379 Anpetu Yuha; Keeps Day; F; Dau; 4-6

2380 Taopi; Wounded; M; Head; 21
2381 Ptesan Nupa; Two White Cows; F; Wife; 19
2382 Inya Wakinya; Thunder Rock; M; Son; 4 mo.

2383 Hinyete; Shoulder; M; Head; 70

2384 Winyan Yamni; Three Woman; F; Wife; 66
2385 Hinyete; Ruben Shoulder; M; Son; 20
2386 Hinyete; Amos Shoulder; M; Son; 18
2387 Hinyete; Paul Shoulder; M; Son; 14
2388 Hinyete; Lucy Shoulder; F; Dau; 13

2389 Orloka Ota; Plenty Holes; M; Head; 23
2390 Hinyete; Mary Shoulder; F; Wife; 23
2391 Tasunka Ska; Her White Horse; F; Dau; 1-4

2392 Maka Luta; Red Earth; F; Head; 54
2393 Oiyokipiya Naji; Merrily Stands; F; Dau; 23
2394 Keyela Kute; Shoots Close; F; G.Dau; 2-2

2395 Wanagi; Ghost; M; Head; 43
2396 Wanagi; Emma Ghost; F; Wife; 35
2397 Wanagi; Samuel Ghost; M: Son; 13
2398 Wanagi; Frank Ghost; M: Son; 9
2399 Wakinya Wakuwa; Charging Thunder; M; Son; 4-11
2400 Wanagi; Alexander Ghost; M; Son; 3
2401 Wanagi; Henry Ghost; M; Son; 2 mo.

2402 Winya Waste; Wood[sic] Woman; F; Head; 79

2403 Mato Niyanpi; Saves Bear; M; Head; 59
2404 Wacakize; Fought; F; Wife; 55
2405 Mato Niyanpi; Ida Saves Bear; F; Dau; 24

Census Of The Sioux And Cheyenne Indians Of Pine Ridge Agency, South Dakota. Taken by W. H. Clapp, Captain 16th Infantry, Acting United States Indian Agent, June 30, 1897. (Wounded Knee District)

Key: Number; Indian Name *(if given)*; English Name; Sex; Relation; Age

2406 Sunkaka Opi; Wounded White Horse; M; Son; 17

2407 Josephine Cuny; F; Head; 62
2408 Jule Cuny; M; Son; 21
2409 Lottie Cuny; F; Dau; 21

2410 Kepas Inyaka; Francis Runs Against; M; Head; 44
2411 Shake Ska; White Finger Nail; F; Wife; 39
2412 Kesunsni; Jas Dont[sic] Braid H. Hair; [M]; B. in Law; 27
2413 Kanwinga; Turns Back; F; Dau; 3-4

2414 Kepas Inyaka; Jacob Runs Against; M; Head 24
2415 Sophia; F; Wife; 22

2416 Hiyoya; Goes After; M; Head; 24
2417 Itima; Sleeper; F; Wife; 24

2418 Wiciyela Win; Yankton Woman; F; Head; 61
2419 Luzahan; Fast; F; Dau; 25

2420 Heraka Isnala; Lone Elk; M; Head; 45
2421 Sunkhinto Kuwa; Runs A. Gray Horses; F; Wife; 38
2422 Sagye Wambli; Cane Eagle; F; Dau; 16
2423 Anpetu Mani; Walking Day; F; Dau; 3-1

2424 Charles Cuny; M; Head; 35
2425 Louise Cuny; F; Wife; 31
2426 Mary LeRock; F; M. in Law; 72
2427 Lizzie Cuny; F; Dau; 13
2428 Eddie Cuny; M; Son; 11
2429 Charles Cuny Jr; M; Son; 8
2430 Leroy Brown Cuny; M; Son; 6
2431 Wilson Cuny; M; Son; 4
2432 Adolph Cuny; M; Son; 11 mo.

2433 Mato Gleska; Spotted Bear; M; Head; 30
2434 Sunkska Yuha; White Horse Owner; F; Wife; 24
2435 Nata Witko; Fool Head; M; Head; 32
2436 Onsiya Iya; Talks Pitiful; F; Wife; 27
2437 Maka Potitan; Pushes Ground; F; Dau; 3-6
2438 Isnala Wankatuya; Highest One; M; Son; 1-2

2439 Sungmanitu Ska; White Coyote; M; Head; 26
2440 Sungmanitu Ska; Martha W. Coyote; F; Wife; 24
2441 Zintkala Hinapa; Bird Comes Out; F; Dau; 2-8
2442 Sungmanitu Ska; Susie White Coyote; F; Dau; 10 mo.

2443 Tatanka Tamaheca; Poor Buffalo; M; Head; 44
2444 Sa Yuha Wani; Walks With Red; F; Wife; 55

2445 Tatanka Ciqala; Little Bull; M; Head; 32
2446 Tasunke Waste; Her Good Horses; F; Wife; 26
2447 Tasunke Opi; Wounded Horse; M; Brother; 22

2448 Hehaka Luzahan; Fast Elk; M; Head; 60
2449 Tasina Waste; Her Good Blanket; F; Wife #1; 59
2450 Wankal On; Comes Above; F; Wife #2; 55
2451 Sunk Iyanajica; Runs With Horses; F; Dau; 14

2452 Wapaha Luta; Red War Bonnet; M; Head; 76
2453 Sagye; Cane; F; Wife; 69

Census Of The Sioux And Cheyenne Indians Of Pine Ridge Agency, South Dakota.
Taken by W. H. Clapp, Captain 16th Infantry, Acting United States Indian Agent,
June 30, 1897. (Wounded Knee District)

Key: Number; Indian Name *(if given)*; English Name; Sex; Relation; Age

2454	Itunkasan; Weasel; M; G.Son; 16	2479	Tinpsila Tanka; Luke Big Turnip; M; Son; 21
2455	Heraka Inyaka; Running Elk; M; Head; 45	2480	Wasna; Pemican; M; Bro; 28
		2481	Pankeska Win; Shell Woman; F; Head; 80
2456	Wacinko; Pouting; F; Wife #1; 35	2482	Sagye Muvaka; Cane Sword; M; Head; 61
2457	Wawicasi; Asks Them To Do Something; [F]; Wife #2; 35	2483	Iyeska; Interpreter; F; Wife; 50
2458	Wahaha Wicaku; Gives Away War Bonnet; M; Son; 6	2484	Mato Wamniyomni; Bear Whirlwind; M; Head; 47
2459	Wakinya Oyate; Thunder Nation; F; Dau; 1 mo.	2485	Isto Akanl Apa; Hit Them In The Arm; F; Aunt; 45
2460	Sam Ladeaux; M; Head; 23	2486	Mato Womniyomni[sic]; Cora B. Whirlwind; F; Dau; 22
2461	Hakikta; Looks Behind; F; Wife; 24	2487	Oye Tain; Shows The Track; F; Dau; 9
2462	Tokanl Iglake; Change Place; F; Dau; 8 mo.		
		2488	Sunka Luta; Red Dog; M; Head; 48
2463	Baptiste Ladeaux; M; Head; 24	2489	Pta San; White Cow; F; Wife; 55
2464	Annie Ladeaux; F; Wife; 24	2490	Sunk Gnani; Lost Horses; M; Son; 15
2465	Frank Ladeaux; M; Son; 2 mo.	2491	Agli; Fetches; M; Son; 8
2466	Joseph Pablo; M: Head; 43		
2467	Rosa Pulliam; F; Dau; 24	2492	Hinhan Wambli; Owl Eagle; M; Head; 65
2468	Fannie Pulliam; F; Dau; 21		
2469	Alexander Pablo; M; Son; 12	2493	Sunkgleska Win; Spotted Horse Woman; F; Dau; 45
2470	Anna Plume; F; Wife; 53		
2471	Lilly Ladeaux; F; S.Dau; 16	2494	Tokeya Kte; Kills First; M; G.Son; 12
2472	Tipi Sa; Red Lodge; F; S.Dau; 9		
2473	Mato Lowan; Singing Bear; M; Head; 71	2495	Isnala Wakuwa; Chase Alone; M; G.Son; 2-3
2474	Tehan Rpaya; Sleeps Late; F; Wife; 54	2496	Henry Jones; M; Head; 33
		2497	Zintkala Maza; Iron Bird; F; Wife; 41
2475	Palani Kte; John Kills Re e[sic]; M; Head; 21	2498	John Jones; M; Son; 15
2476	Zintkala Waste; Pretty Bird; F; Wife; 22	2499	Pehin Ji; Yellow Hair; F; Dau; 9
		2500	Wicakeza; Fighter; M; Son; 7
		2501	Heraka Waste; Good Elk; F; Dau; 2-5
2477	Tinpsila Tanka; Big Turnip; M; Head; 49		
2478	Winya Isnala; Lone Woman; F; Wife; 42	2502	Marpiya Ciqala; Little Cloud #2; M; Head; 48

Census Of The Sioux And Cheyenne Indians Of Pine Ridge Agency, South Dakota. Taken by W. H. Clapp, Captain 16th Infantry, Acting United States Indian Agent, June 30, 1897. (Wounded Knee District)

Key: Number; Indian Name *(if given)*; English Name; Sex; Relation; Age

2503 Wacinhin Maza; Iron Plume; M; Head; 53
2504 Pa Okemni; Covered Head; F; Wife; 55
2505 Sunk Tainya Mani; Horse Walks In Sight; M; Son; 22
2506 Isnala Icaga; Raised Alone; M; Son; 9
2507 Wipi; Full Stomach; M; Head; 36
2508 Cante Waste; Good Heart; F; Wife; 41
2509 Tainya Ku; Comes in Sight; F; Dau; 6
2510 Huncase; Garter; M; Head; 38
2511 Wazi Ape; Pine Leaf; F; Wife; 40
2512 Isaga; Growth; F; Dau; 9
2513 Oyata Tasunke; Nation Horse; F; Dau; 1-9
2514 Cetan Rca[sic]; Real Hawk; M; Head; 48
2515 Sinte Tokeca; Different Tail; F; Wife; 46
2516 Toka Kte; Kills Enemy; M; Head; 30
2517 Toka Kte; Rosa K. Enemy; F; Wife; 27
2518 Wapaha Icu; Takes War Bonnet; M; Son; 9
2519 Susuni Kte; Kills Shoshone; M; Son; 2-10
2520 Toka Kte; Anna Kills Enemy; F; Dau; 5
2521 Toka Kte; Jennie Kills Enemy; F; Dau; 7 mo.
2522 Hunska Narso[sic]; Leggins Down; F; Head; 70
2523 Toka Ole; Hunts Enemy; M; G.Son; 13
2524 Siyo Winurca; Old Prairie Hen; F; Head; 60
2525 Karnir Kte; Kills Choice; M; G.Son; 8
2526 Mato Wicakiza; Max Fighting Bear; M; Head; 22
2527 Osun Wanrca[sic]; Abel No Braid; M; Head; 34
2528 Wambli Winya; Eagle Woman; F; Wife; 26
2529 Toka Waste; Good Enemy; F; Dau; 5
2530 Psa Win; Crow Woman; F; M. in Law; 59
2531 Osun Wanica; George No Braid; M; Nephew; 18
2532 Heraka Wambli; Eagle Elk; M; Head; 36
2533 Winyan Tanka; Grown Woman; F; Wife; 33
2534 Oyuspapi; Captured; F; Dau; 10
2535; Wanbli Oyate; Eagle Nation; F; Dau; 3-9
2536 Hoksila Sayapi; Red Painted Boy; M; Son; 1-4
2537 Ake Hi; James Comes Again; M; Head; 27
2538 Pankeska Luta; Red Shell; F; Wife; 33
2539 Terilapi; Fond Of Him; F; Dau; 3-4
2540 Anpitu Wakan; Holy Day; F; Head; 52
2541 Mni Oyusna; Drops In The Water; F; Mother; 71
2542 Pte San; Two White Cows; F; Dau; 8
2543 Waagi[sic] Witko; Crazy Ghost; M; Head; 45
2544 Cokab Win; Center Woman; F; Wife; 39

Census Of The Sioux And Cheyenne Indians Of Pine Ridge Agency, South Dakota. Taken by W. H. Clapp, Captain 16th Infantry, Acting United States Indian Agent, June 30, 1897. (Wounded Knee District)

Key: Number; Indian Name *(if given)*; English Name; Sex; Relation; Age

2545	Frank; M; Son; 16		2566	Wapartapi; Packed; F; Head; 53
2546	Wiyaka Luta; Red Feather; M; Son; 10		2567	Jacob; M; Son; 12
2547	Taininya[sic] Naji; Stands In Sight; F; Dau; 13		2568	Wambli Ciqala; Little Eagle; M; Son; 8
2548	Nawicakijin[sic]; Protector; M; Head; 33		2569	Augustus; M; Head; 20
2549	Wakinya Yuha; Owns Thunder; F; Mother; 74		2570	Ota Agli; Brought Plenty; F; Wife; 21
2550	Ta Sina; Her Blanket; F; Sister; 39		2571	Tatanka Nupa; Amos Two Bulls; M; Head; 20
2551	Wiyaka Nupa; Two Feathers; M; Son; 5-6		2572	Conica Wanica; Lucy No Flesh; F; Wife; 19
2552	Winyan Hanska; Long Woman; F; Head; 65		2573	Ataya Zintkala; Bird All Over; F; Head; 50
2553	Jennie; F; G.Dau; 18		2575[sic]	Tatanka Nupa; Mary Two Bull[sic]; F; Dau; 19
2554	Hoksila Maza; Jacob Iron Boy; M; Head; 23		2575	Tatanka Nupa; Anna Two Bull; F; Dau; 16
2555	Sunka Huste; Mable Lame Dog; F; Wife; 18		2576	Adolph; M; Head; 25
2556	Keyela Kute; Shot Close; M; Son; 5 mo.		2577	Iya Sica; Bad Talker; F; Mother; 62
			2578	ApeApe[sic] Hinrpaya; Falling Leaf; F; Niece; 8
2557	Rlo Ku; Comes Growling; M; Head; 25			
2558	Ota Kte; Kills Plenty; F; Wife; 24		2579	Mastincala Luta; Red Rabbit; M; Head; 42
2559	Wasicu Opi; Shot By White Man; M; Son; 7		2580	Iya Waste; Good Talk; F; Wife; 52
2560	Ista Gi; Edward Brown Eyes; M; Son; 3-6		2581	Anna; F; Dau; 19
2561	Wanjila Agli; Brings One; F; Dau; 2-1		2582	Kangi Apapi; Struck By Cow[sic]; M; Head; 50
2562	Rlo Ku; John Comes Growling; M; Son; 2 mo.		2583	Ranhi; Slow; F; Wife; 47
			2584	Gus; M; B. in Law; 24
2563	Zintkala Luta; Red Bird; M; Son; 19		2585	Kangi Apapi; Harry S. B. Crow; M; Son; 20
2564	Tasunke Inyaka; Her Running Horse; F; Mother; 59		2586	Ota Opi; Shot Many Times; M; Son; 8
			2587	Heraka Maza; Iron Elk; M; Head; 21
2565	Ranhi; Slow; F; Head; 63			

Census Of The Sioux And Cheyenne Indians Of Pine Ridge Agency, South Dakota. Taken by W. H. Clapp, Captain 16th Infantry, Acting United States Indian Agent, June 30, 1897. (Wounded Knee District)

Key: Number; Indian Name *(if given)*; English Name; Sex; Relation; Age

2588	Pankeska Hoksila; Alice Shell Boy; F; Wife; 18		2610	Pankeska Maza; Iron Shell; M; Head; 51
2589	Tokeya Mani; Walks Ahead; F; Dau; 2 mo.		2611	Imaputaka; Kiss Me; F; Wife #1; 50
2590	Pte He; Cow Horn; F; Head; 47		2612	Pankeska Maza; Lizzie Iron Shell; F; Wife #2; 42
2591	Pte Tokahe; Loading Buffalo; F; Dau; 16		2613	Wanagi Kute; Shoots Ghost; M; Head; 75
2592	Teana Ketan; Runs For Camp; M; Son; 10		2614	Scili Kte; Kills Pawnee; F; Wife; 65
2593	Tokeya Kute; Shoots First; M; Son; 6		2615	Naca; Chief; M; Son; 27
2594	Tatanka Nupa; Joseph Two Bulls; M; Head; 31		2616	Tainya Naji; Stands In Sight; F; G.Dau; 11
2595	Tokeya Mani; Walks First; F; Wife; 30		2617	Najiyapi[sic] Kte; Surrounded Killed; M; G.Son; 9
2596	Wapaha Opi; Wounded Bonnet; M; Son; 8		2618	Nupa Wakita; Looks Twice; M; Head; 45
2597	Wambli Hoksila; Eagle Boy; M; Son; 6		2619	Wambli Winyan; Eagle Woman; F; Wife #1; 42
2598	Wambli Koyaka; Wears Eagle; F; Dau; 3-3		2620	Winyan Hanska; Long Woman; F; Wife #2; 35
2599	Tatanka Nupa; Charles Two Bulls; M; Son; 7 mo.		2621	Nupa Wakita; Maggie Looks Twice; F; Dau; 17
2600	Mato Rabwicaya; Bear Scares; M; Heads; 40		2622	Oosica; Hard To Hit; M; Son; 15
2601	Capa Ska; White Beaver; F; Wife; 38		2623	Tapi Sagye; Cane Liver; M; Son; 12
2602	Mato Rabwicaya; Samuel Bear Scares; M; Son; 15		2624	Sunkska Win; White Horse Woman; F; Dau; 12
2603	Watakpe; George Charging; M; Head; 36		2625	Mato Ota Win; Plenty Bear Woman; F; Dau; 7
2604	Watakpe; Louise Charging; F; Wife; 33		2626	Tasunke Gleska; Her Spotted Horse; F; Dau; 4-6
2605	Watakpe; Louise Charging; F; Dau; 15		2627	Ku Sni; Dont[sic] Come; M; Son; 1-4
2606	Watakpe; Jackson Charging; M; Son; 13		2628	Tasunke Waste; Pretty Horse; F; Head; 56
2607	Watakpe; David Charging; M; Son; 11		2629	Sunkgleska Ota; Many Spotted Horses; F; Head; 34
2608	Watakpe; Alice Charging; F; Dau; 9		2630	Maza; Iron; F; Mother; 67
2609	Wambli Oyate; Eagle Nation; F; Dau; 3-10		2631	Ikunsan; Mink; F; Head; 82

Census Of The Sioux And Cheyenne Indians Of Pine Ridge Agency, South Dakota. Taken by W. H. Clapp, Captain 16th Infantry, Acting United States Indian Agent, June 30, 1897. (Wounded Knee District)

Key: Number; Indian Name *(if given)*; English Name; Sex; Relation; Age

2632 Tarca Luta; Red Deer; F; Head; 70
2633 Pte Kte; Kills Cow; F; Head; 87
2634 Peji Parta; Julia Hay Press; F; Head; 67
2635 Frank Galligo; M: Head; 35
2636 Julia Galligo; F; Wife; 29
2637 Rosa Galligo; F; Dau; 13
2638 Thomas Galligo; M; Son; 11
2639 Alvina Galligo; F; Dau; 8
2640 Minnie Galligo; F; Dau; 6
2641 Sarah Galligo; F; Dau; 4-1
2642 Francis Galligo; F; Dau; 2 mo.
2643 Peter Bissonette; M; Head; 50
2644 Susie Bissonette; F; Wife; 46
2645 Frank Bissonette; M; Son; 23
2646 Jennie Bissonette; F; Dau; 19
2647 Josephine Bissonette; F; Dau; 17
2648 Lottie Bissonette; F; Dau; 15
2649 George Bissonette; M; Son; 11
2650 Fannie Bissonette; F; Dau; 8
2651 Tasunke Maza; Frank Iron Horse; M; Head; 33
2652 Waicu; Takes Things; F; Wife; 32
2653 Toka Kaga; Makes Enemy; M; Son; 6
2654 Tipi Wakan; Holy Lodge; F; Dau; 1-3
2655 Jennie Sires; F; Head; 30
2656 William Provost; M; Son; 12
2657 John Sires; M; Son; 4
2658 James Sires; M; Son; 3
2659 Josephine Sires; F; Dau; 2
2660 Cetan Kinya; Flying Hawk; M; Head; 41
2661 Anpitu Ska; White Day; F; Wife #1; 42
2662 Wakil Hinapa; Looks Coming Out; F; Wife #2; 35
2663 Wambli Tacanupa; Eagle Pipe; M; Nephew; 26
2664 Tokeya Kte; Kills First; M; Son; 15
2665 Takuni Oholasni; Respects Nothing; M; Head; 42
2666 Pte San Oyate; White Cow Tribe; F; Wife; 40
2667 Tokuni[sic] Oholasni; George R. Nothing; M; Son; 7
2668 Wapaha Luta; Red War Bonnet; F; Dau; 1-4
2669 Isnala Wakuwa; Chase Alone; M; Head; 34
2670 Okiyakapi; Told To Her; F; Wife; 34
2671 Tasunke Wambli; Eagle Horse; F; Dau; 7
2672 Zintkala Wicasa; Bird Man; M; Head; 35
2673 Ozan Mahel; Between Lodges; F; Wife; 29
2674 Tasunke Waste; Her Good Horse; F; Dau; 8
2675 David; M; S.Son; 19
2676 Kangi Luta; Red Crow; M: Head; 65
2677 Belly; F; Wife; 62
2678 Nuwanpi; Swimmer; M; Head; 51
2679 Wakan Mani; Walks Holy; F; Wife; 45
2680 Winyan Waste; Pretty Woman; F; Dau; 29
2681 Nuwanpi; John Swimmer; M; Son; 22

Census Of The Sioux And Cheyenne Indians Of Pine Ridge Agency, South Dakota. Taken by W. H. Clapp, Captain 16th Infantry, Acting United States Indian Agent, June 30, 1897. (Wounded Knee District)

Key: Number; Indian Name *(if given)*; English Name; Sex; Relation; Age

2682 Tasunke Nupa; Two Horses; M; Head; 39
2683 Wacinhin Ska; White Plume; M; Head; 45
2684 Tasunke Hinsa; Red Horse; F; Wife; 42
2685 Niyan Kte; Kills Alive; M; Son; 14
2686 Asanpi; Milk; M: Son; 10
2687 Wambli Heto; Eagle Horn; M; Son; 5 mo.

2688 Zuya Terila; Loves War; M; Head; 42
2689 Oye Wakan; Holy Track; F; Wife; 36
2690 Nupa Kte; Kills Twice; M; Son; 15
2691 Tasunke Hinapa; Horse Comes Out; F; Dau; 10
2692 Wowasi Yuha; Employer; M; Son; 7
2693 Sunka Mani; Walking Dog; M; Son; 4-6
2694 Canupa Wakita; Looking Pipe; F; Dau; 1-7

2695 Tasunke Witko; Crazy Horse; M; Head; 48
2696 Winyan Waste; Good Woman; F; Wife; 35
2697 Ohitika; Brave; F; Dau; 17
2698 He Napa; Comes Out; M; Son; 2-11

2699 Ha Wakan; Holy Skin; M; Head; 47
2700 Capa; Beaver; F; Wife; 56
2701 Ha Wakan; Bessie Holy Skin; F; Dau; 17

2702 Tatanka Hanska; Long Bull; M; Head; 26
2703 Wambli Luta; Red Eagle; F; Wife; 24

2704 Kangi Maza; Iron Crow #2; M; Head; 37
2705 Tokeya Ya; Goes First; F; Wife; 31
2706 Zintkala To; Blue Bird; F; Dau; 9
2707 Kupi; Gives Him; F; Dau; 6
2708 Canrloga Hoksila; Needy Boy; M; Son; 2-4
2709 Itazipe Wakan; Medicine Bow; F; Dau; 8

2710 Spayola; Ambrose Mexican; M; Head; 36
2711 Winyan Waste; Good Woman; F; Wife; 29
2712 Kiyela Kute; Shot Close; M; Son; 14
2713 Sunk Gluha; Keeps Her Horses; F; Dau; 12
2714 Wanjigjila Wicakte; Kills One After Another; M; Son; 2-9

2715 Tasunke Wakan; Medicine Horse; M; Head; 46

2716 Wan Taopi; Arrow Wound; M; Head; 41
2717 Wicincala; Girl; F; Dau; 1-4
2718 Nape Iyorpeyapi; Boiled Hand; F; Mother; 84

2719 Mani Ku; Comes Walking; F; Head; 28
2720 Congleska Zi; Yellow Ring; F; Dau; 7

2721 Sunk Ska; John White Horse; M; Head; 58
2722 Sunk Ska; Katie White Horse; F; Dau; 16
2723 Opanwige Owicayuspa; Arrested One Hundred; M; Son; 9
2724 Marpiya Wambli; Eagle Cloud; M; Son; 6

Census Of The Sioux And Cheyenne Indians Of Pine Ridge Agency, South Dakota.
Taken by W. H. Clapp, Captain 16th Infantry, Acting United States Indian Agent,
June 30, 1897. (Wounded Knee District)

Key: Number; Indian Name *(if given)*; English Name; Sex; Relation; Age

2725 Tate Wakan; Medicine Wind; F; Head; 88
2726 Pestola; Painted; F; G.Dau; 19
2727 Opo; Fog; F; Head; 55
2728 Toka Kuwa; Chasing Enemy; M; Head; 65
2729 Toka Kuwa; Martha Chasing Enemy; F; Wife; 54
2730 Wasicu Tasunke; Robt. Anerican[sic] Horse; M; Head; 41
2731 Wasicu Tasunke; Nancy Anerican Horse; F; Wife; 28
2732 Wasicu Tasunke; Susie Anerican Horse; F; Dau;; 11 mo.
2733 Winyan Hanska; Tall Woman; F; Head; 85
2734 Akisja; Begs To Keep; F; Head; 56
2735 Mato Sica; Henry B. Bear; M; Son; 16
2736 Wasicu Winyan; White Woman; F; Head; 17
2737 John Bissonette; M: Head; 25
2738 Fannie Bissonette; F; Wife; 24
2739 Jessie Bissonette; F; Dau; 2-2
2740 Huhu Yuha; Keeps Bone; F; Head; 55
2741 Wikan Ynslohan; Drags Rope; M; Head; 39
2742 Tasunke Waste; Her Good Horse; F; Wife; 39
2743 Cante Wicasa; Heart Man; M; Head; 51
2744 Worinya; Pouting; F; Wife; 51
2745 Onsilaka; Takes Pity; M: Son; 17
2746 Sunk Hiyo Hi; Comes After Horses; F; Dau; 7
2747 Sahiyela; Cheyenne; M; Head; 50
2748 Si; Foot; F; Wife; 44
2749 Wapaha; War Bonnet; F; Dau; 9
2750 Taniya Kte; Kills In Sight; M; Son; 4-5
2751 Zintkala Waste; Pretty Bird; M; Head; 34
2752 Worinya; Pouting; F; Wife; 42
2753 John; M: Son; 11
2754 Taninya Mani; Walks In Sight; F; Dau; 8
2755 Te Wakan; Her Medicine Lodge; F; Dau; 5
2756 Gleska Wicaku; Gives Spotted; M; Son; 1-4
2757 Wambli Tacanupa; Eagle Pipe; M; Head; 48
2758 Tuga; Hump; F; Wife; 36
2759 Kutepi; Shot At; M; Bro; 37
2760 Wambli Tacanupa; Mac Eagle Pipe; M; Son; 18
2761 Karmi Tanka; Big Bend; M; Head; 52
2762 Toweya Win; Guide Woman; F; Wife; 55
2763 Tainyan Kte; Kills In Sight; F; Dau; 10
2764 Isto Wasake; Lawrence Industrious; M: Head; 27
2765 Isto Wasake; Alice Industrious; F; Wife; 27
2766 Isto Wasake; Shell Industrious; F; Dau; 6-6
2767 Zuya Kte; Kills Warrior; F; Dau; 1-4
2768 Kuwa Wicakte; Kills Charging; F; Dau; 1-4

Census Of The Sioux And Cheyenne Indians Of Pine Ridge Agency, South Dakota. Taken by W. H. Clapp, Captain 16th Infantry, Acting United States Indian Agent, June 30, 1897. (Wounded Knee District)

Key: Number; Indian Name *(if given)*; English Name; Sex; Relation; Age

2769	Mato Wankatuya; High Bear; M; Head; 58	2791	Ake Hiyu; John Comes Again; M; Son; 19
2770	Tasina Zi; Yellow Blanket; F; Wife; 60	2792	Ake Hiyu; Rachael Comes Again; F; Dau; 15
2771	Mato Wankatuya; Jennie High Bear; F; Dau; 25	2793	Mato Ska Sake; White Bear Claws; M; Head; 38
2772	Mato Wankatuya; Alice High Bear; F; Dau; 19	2794	Aiyapa; Talks About Him; F; Wife; 29
2773	Zi; Lucy Yellow; F; Dau; 17	2795	Naca Gli; Comes Back Chief; M; Son; 10
2774	Ota Kte; Kills Many; F; Head; 55	2796	Mato Canupa; Bear Pipe; M; Son; 1-5
2775	Mato Sina; Mary Bear Robe; F; Dau; 21	2797	Wiyaka Rara; Rough Feather; M; Head; 34
2776	Mato Sina; Eliza Bear Robe; F; Dau; 16	2798	Wambli Cuwignaka; Eagle Dress; F; Wife; 33
2777	Wapaha; War Bonnet; M; Head; 30	2799	Sunk Iyanajica; Chas. Stampeeds[sic] Horses; [blank]; Son; 9
2778	Niwicaya; Saves Lives; F; Wife; 24	2800	Ptesan Kinapa; White Cow Goes Out; F; Dau; 5
2779	Psa Kte; Kills Crow; F; Dau; 7	2801	Anpo Wakute; Shoots At Daylight; M; Son; 7 mo.
2780	Toka Opi; Wounded By Enemy; F; Dau; 5	2802	Toka Kahinrpeya; Runs Out Enemy; M; B. in Law; 11
2781	Cetan Ho Waste; Good Voice Hawk; M; Son; 3-3	2803	Gi Iciya; Paints Yellow; M; Head; 52
2782	Oshota; Wendell Smoke; M; Bro; 22	2804	Julia Yellow; F; Wife; 47
2783	Wambli Si; Eagle Foot; M; Son; 10 mo.	2805	Waste Koyaka; Wears Good; F; Dau; 20
2784	Sunka Yatapi; Dog Chief; M; Head; 25	2806	Herakalowan; Singing Elk; M; Head; 70
2785	Nakiwi Zi Pi; Jealous Of Them; F; Wife; 28	2807	Mato Cankalan; Bear Backbone; M; Cousin; 73
2786	Waste; Edgar Good; M; Son; 8	2808	Ota Koyaka; Wears Plenty; F; Wife; 68
2787	Ni Flicu[sic]; Comes Alive; F; Dau; 3-7	2809	Wambli Wakan; Holy Eagle; M; Son; 33
2788	Nawizi; Jealous; M; S.Son; 9	2810	Cetan Kte; Kills Hawk; M; Son; 37
2789	Ake Hiyu; Peter Comes Again; M; Head; 52		
2790	Ake Hiyu; Lizzie Comes Again; F; Wife; 50		

Census Of The Sioux And Cheyenne Indians Of Pine Ridge Agency, South Dakota. Taken by W. H. Clapp, Captain 16th Infantry, Acting United States Indian Agent, June 30, 1897. (Wounded Knee District)

Key: Number; Indian Name *(if given)*; English Name; Sex; Relation; Age

2811	Cetan Kokipa; Afraid Of Hawk; M; Head; 49		2833	Cante Witko; Fool Heart; M; Head; 50
2812	Re Ska; White Mountain; F; Wife; 48		2834	Wayurlata; Scratches; F; Wife #1; 36
2813	Cetan Kokipa; Richard Afraid O. Hawk; [blank]; Son; 22		2835	Ble Wakan; Holy Lake; F; Wife #2; 44
2814	Annie; F; Dau; 13			
2815	Wicokuje; Patient; F; Dau; 11		2836	Iktomni Cankahu; Spider Back Bone; M; Son; 22
2816	Wakun; Wished For; F; Dau; 7-6		2837	Wambli Ciqala; Little Eagle; M; Head; 54
2817	Cetan Kokipa; Albert A. O. Hawk; M; Son; 18		2838	Tezi; Belly; F; Wife #1; 59
2818	Okogna Inyanka; Runs Between; F; Dau; 2-2		2839	Peya Kaga; Makes Over; F; Wife #2; 54
			2840	Sahœyela[sic] Waste; Good Cheyenne; M; Son; 25
2819	He Nupa; Anna Lone Horn; F; Head; 37		2841	Ptesan Hinapa; Comes Out White Cow; F; Dau; 18
2820	Joseph; M; Nephew; 16			
2821	Akicize; Fights Over; F; Wife; 33		2842	Wambli Cangleska; Eagle Ring; M; Head; 27
2822	Itowe Ro; Straight Forehead; M; Head; 39		2843	Winyan Isnala; Lone Woman; F; Wife; 25
2823	Piya Iglake; Mooves[sic] Over; F; Wife; 33		2844	Kangi Waste; Good Crow; M; Head; 43
2824	Cetan Luta; Austin Red Hawk; M; Head; 38		2845	Wiyaka Ota; Many Feathers; F; Wife; 39
2825	Alice Red Hawk; F; Wife; 37		2846	Ire Hoksila; Rock Boy; M; Son; 12
2826	Ranie Win; Cedar Woman; F; Sister; 45		2847	Ire Tipi Win; Rock Lodge Woman; F; Dau; 9
2827	Akanwanka Kte; Kills On Horseback; M; Nephew; 20		2848	Wicincala; Girl; F; Dau; 7
2828	Ceta[sic] Luta; Susie Red Hwk[sic]; F; Dau; 10		2849	Wicincala Yusna; Drops Down Girl; F; Dau; 1-9
2829	Ceta Luta; James Red Hwk; M; Son; 8		2850	Winyan Zi; Yellow Woman; F; Head; 44
2830	Ceta Luta; Noah Red Hwk; M; Son; 1-5		2851	Hoksila Sica; Bad Boy; M; Son; 23
2831	Anukansan Waste; Pretty Bald Eagle; M; Head; 65		2852	Inyang Kte; Kills Running; M; Son; 9
2832	Maza Wakan Omna; Smells Gun; F; Wife; 60		2853	Onsiya Yanka; Sits Poor; M; Head; 48
			2854	Oyuspapi; Captured; F; Wife; 39

Census Of The Sioux And Cheyenne Indians Of Pine Ridge Agency, South Dakota. Taken by W. H. Clapp, Captain 16th Infantry, Acting United States Indian Agent, June 30, 1897. (Wounded Knee District)

Key: Number; Indian Name *(if given)*; English Name; Sex; Relation; Age

2855 Onseya[sic] Yanka; Franks[sic] Sits Poor; M; Son; 17
2856 Zi Agli; Brings Yellow; F; Dau; 7
2857 Tunweya Gli; Returned From Scout; M; Son; 1-8
2858 Ista Re Ska; White Eye Lash; M; Head; 46
2859 Heraka Win; Elk Woman; F; Wife; 38
2860 Toka Tasunke Awicagli; Brings Enemies Horses; F; Dau; 15
2861 Maza Wakan Icu; Takes Gun; M; Son; 8
2862 Sunk Manusa; Horse Thief; M; Son; 3-10
2863 Tatanka Hunkesni; Slow Bull #1; M; Head; 77
2864 Mni Wicasa; William Water Man; M; Head; 24
2865 Ska Agli; Brings White; F; Wife; 26
2866 Mni Wicasa; Joseph W. Man; M; Son; 1-1
2867 Heraka Ciqala; Little Elk; M; Head; 25
2868 Humpe; Della Picket Pin; F; Wife; 25
2869 Pte San; White Cow; F; Head; 55
2870 Wanyu; Quiver; F; Head; 43
2871 Ptesan Wanyaka; Sees White Cow; F; Dau; 7
2872 Wambli Ota; Plenty Eagles; M; Head; 60
2873 Wambli Tipi; Eagle Lodge; F; Dau; 12
2874 Wakan Lecala; New Holy; M; Head; 35
2875 Wambli Oye; Eagle Track; F; Wife; 34
2876 Sunkiteska Yuha; Ownes[sic] White Face Horse; F; Sister; 23
2877 Owicale; Hunts Them; F; Dau; 14
2878 Najinyapi; Surrounded; M; Son; 2-4
2879 Wapaha Wicaku; Gives War Bonnet; F; Dau; 4-4
2880 Caje Wanica; No Name; M; Son; 2 mo.
2881 Winya Zi; Yellow Woman; F; Head; 26
2882 Maku; Breast; M; Head; 44
2883 Wiyaka Wanjila; Moses One Feather; M; Head; 41
2884 Hinhan Luta; Red Owl; F; Wife; 40
2885 Wiyaka Wanjila; Etta One Feather; F; Dau; 16
2886 Re Sape; Black Hills; F; Dau; 2
2887 Tiole; Eats At Her House; F; Dau; 8 mo.
2888 Wambli Gleska; Spotted Eagle; M; Head; 28
2889 Sota; Smoke; M; Head; 53
2890 Pehin Ji Qin; Yellow Haired Woman; F; Wife; 64
2891 Pehin Ji Win; Susie Y. H. Woman; F; Dau; 19
2892 Ptesan Luta; Red White Cow; F; Dau; 15
2893 Anukasan Waste; Good Weasel; M; Head; 25
2894 Ptan Ha; Otter Blanket; F; Wife; 22
2895 Sunk Iyanajica; Gets Away With Horses; F; Sister; 9
2896 Tokaheya; Leader; F; dau; 7 mo.

Census Of The Sioux And Cheyenne Indians Of Pine Ridge Agency, South Dakota. Taken by W. H. Clapp, Captain 16th Infantry, Acting United States Indian Agent, June 30, 1897. (Wounded Knee District)

Key: Number; Indian Name *(if given)*; English Name; Sex; Relation; Age

2897	Seka Hunpi; Cut Foot; M; Head; 73		2920	Wakinya Hanska; Jno. Long Commander; M; Head; 28
2898	Wasu; Hail; F; Wife; 69		2921	Ake Ku; Carrie Come Again; F; Wife; 20
2899	Wakinya Tamaheca; Poor Thunder; M; Head; 37		2922	Heraka Wambli; Eagle Elk #2; M; Head; 35
2900	Itukacan; Weasel; F; Wife; 36			
2901	Wakinya Tamahe; Lizzie P. Thunder; F; Dau; 16		2923	Tonweya Ciqala; Little Guide; M; Father; 68
2902	Hanpa Spaya; Wet Moccasin; M; Son; 8		2924	Inyan Topa; Four Rocks; F; Mother; 67
2903	Tatanka Catka; Left Hand Bull; M; Son; 5		2925	He Hanska; Long Horn; M; Bro; 33
2904	Tokeya Kte; Kills First; M; Son; 3-8		2926	Glepa; Puke; M; Head; 58
2905	Kokab Iyaya; Howard Goes In Front; M; Son; 9		2927	Oglala; Ogalalla; F; Wife; 54
			2928	Wan Agli; Brings Arrows; M; Son; 28
2906	Hoksila Ciqala; Little Boy; M; Son; 11 mo.		2929	Ogle Zi; Yellow Shirt; M; Son; 24
2907	Cetan Maza; Iron Hawk; M; Head; 34		2930	Tasunke Wankatuya; High Horse; M; Son; 19
2908	Rlo Ku; Comes Growling; F; Wife; 26		2931	Glepa; Rosa Puke; F; Dau; 13
2909	Hihan Ska; White Owl; M: G.Fa; 64		2932	Ire Wakan; James Holy Rock; M; Head; 33
2910	Pejuta; Medicine; F; Dau; 9		2933	Anpitu; Lucy Day; F; Wife; 30
2911	Wambli Sun Pejuta; Medicine Eagle Feather; [M]; Son; 5		2934	Nellie Twiss; F; S.Dau;; 14
			2935	Sally; F; Dau; 2-5
2912	Pejuta Wankatuya; High Medicine; M; Son; 3-7		2936	Ire Wakan; Moses Holy Rock; M; Son; 5 mo.
2913	Sunka Huste; James Lame Dog; M; Head; 43		2937	Wye Wakan; Medicine Track; F; Head; 72
2914	Marpiya To; Blue Cloud; F; Wife; 40		2938	Wiyake Pegnaka; Feather On Head; M; Head; 65
2915	Sunka Huste; Lizzie Lame Dog; F; Dau; 22		2939	Sina To; Blue Blanket; F; Wife; 64
2916	Sunka Huste; William Lame Dog; M; Son; 15		2940	Mniyata Wicasa; Fannie Waterman; F; G.Dau; 3-9
2917	Ho Akatanhan; Voice On Top; M; Son; 15			
2918	Icu; Takes; F; Dau; 5		2941	Millie C. Prescott; F; Wife; 27
2919	Tokeya Ku; Comes First; F; Dau; 2-11		2942	Alvina Gracia[sic]; F; Head; 18
			2943	Rosa Garcia; F; Sister; 17

Census Of The Sioux And Cheyenne Indians Of Pine Ridge Agency, South Dakota. Taken by W. H. Clapp, Captain 16th Infantry, Acting United States Indian Agent, June 30, 1897. (Wounded Knee District)

Key: Number; Indian Name *(if given)*; English Name; Sex; Relation; Age

2944	Sunday Garcia; F; Sister; 13	2968	Tasunke Wakan; Medicine Horse; F; Dau; 7
2945	Thomas Garcia; M; Bro; 10		
2946	Susie Garcia; F; Sister; 7	2969	Ire Maza; Iron Rock; F; Dau; 6
		2970	Hoksila Wakan; Susie Medicine Boy; F; Dau; 3-10\
2947	Peji Rota; Gray Grass; M; Head; 50		
		2971	Cokanya Inyanka; Runs In Center; F; Dau; 19
2948	Niya Kte; Kills Living; F; Wife; 51		
		2972	Pejuta Waste; Good Medicine; F; Dau; 4 mo.
2949	Tasina Nupa; Her Two Blankets; F; Dau; 19		
2950	Niyapi; Saves Him; M; Son; 5	2973	Zintkala Sapa; Black Bird; M; Head; 63
2951	Wakinyan Watakpe; Charging Thunder; M; Head; 28	2974	Tibloku Ota; Plenty Brothers; F; Wife #1; 60
2952	Wakinyan Watakpe; Sophia C. Thunder; F; Wife; 27	2975	Tiwicarila; Loves Them; F; Wife #2; 63
2953	Wakinyan Watakpe; Columbus C. Thunder; M; Son; 4-3	2976	Tahuni Ole Sni; Hunts Nothing; F; Dau; 24
2954	Wakinyan Watakpe; Asa C. Thunder; M; Son; 1-2	2977	Tasunke Wanjila; One Horse; M; Son; 25
		2978	Pahi; Picks It Up; M; Son; 15
2955	Helen Garcia; F; Head; 36	2979	Sunkawakan Wanwicayanka; Sees The Horses; F; Dau; 5-6
2956	Mary Two Two; F; Dau; 3-0		
2957	Louise; F; Dau; 10 mo.		
		2980	Tasunke Kinyela; Flying Horse, Jr; M; Head; 19
2958	Sunka Ska; White Horse; M; Head; 39		
2959	Tokicun; Revenger; F; Wife; 33	2981	Wakan Koyaka; Wears Holy; F; Head; 32
2960	Inyan Wicasa; Rock Man White Horse; M; Son; 12	2982	Winyan Istagonga; Blind Woman; F; Mother; 72
2961	Hoksila Waste; Pretty Boy; M; Head; 41	2983	Sunkska Wicao; Shot White Horses; F; Dau; 12
2962	Tasunke; Her Horses; F; Wife; 34	2984	Sunsula Ska; White Mule; F; Dau; 9
2963	Keya; Truth; M; Son; 10	2985	Tokeya Kte; Kills First; M; Son; 6
2964	Wakan Mani; Walking Holy; M; Son; 4 mo.		
		2986	Winyan Wakan; Holy Woman; F; Head; 68
2965	Hoksila Wakan; Medicine Boy; M; Head; 35		
2966	Tibloku Ota; Plenty Brothers; F; Wife #1; 37	2987	Sarah Ingersoll; F; Head; 32
2967	Pte San Maza; Iron White Cow; F; Wife #2; 35	2988	Cetan Ska; White Hawk; M; Head; 40
		2989	Mattie Bissonette; F; Wife; 27

Census Of The Sioux And Cheyenne Indians Of Pine Ridge Agency, South Dakota. Taken by W. H. Clapp, Captain 16th Infantry, Acting United States Indian Agent, June 30, 1897. (Wounded Knee District)

Key: Number; Indian Name *(if given)*; English Name; Sex; Relation; Age

2990 Mato Naji; Clarence Standing Bear; M; Son; 7
2991 Opagela; Silas Fills The Pipe; M; Head; 40
2992 Opagela; Jennie Fills The Pipe; F; Wife; 33
2993 Opagela; Willie Fills The Pipe; M; Son; 17
2994 Opagela; Mattie Fills The Pipe; F; Dau; 2-5
2995 Opagela; Oliver Fills The Pipe; M; Son; 1 mo.
2996 Sungmanitu Ciqala; Little Wolf; M; Head; 49
2997 Sukska Yuha; Ownes White Horses; F; Wife; 45
2998 Asapi; Yells At Him; F; Dau; 12
2999 Kokepeya Kte; Kills With Doubt; M; Son; 9
3000 Tatanka Waste; Her Good Road; F; Dau; 4-2
3001 Maka Luta; Red Earth; F; Dau; 3-8
3002 Tikanyela Kte; Thos. Kills Close T. Lodge; [M]; Son; 17
3003 John Bissonette; M; Head; 36
3004 Julia Bissonette; F; Wife; 28;
3005 Eliza Bissonette; F; Dau; 11
3006 Mille Bissonette; F; Dau; 7
3007 Susie Bissonette; F; Dau; 7
3008 Daniel Bissonette; M; Son; 5
3009 Andrew Bissonette; M; Son; 2-9
3010 Mato Wanrtaka; Kicking Bear; M; Head; 45
3011 Wagnuka; Woodpecker; F; Wife; 44
3012 Wambli Tasma; Eagle Shawl; F; Dau; 14
3013 Wakinya; Thunder; M; Son; 8
3014 Mazawakan Icu; Takes The Gun; M; Sun; 6

3015 Wicakicikuta; Shoots For Them; M; Head; 75
3016 Ska; White; F; Wife #1; 70
3017 Oye Maza; Iron Track; F; Wife #2; 66
3017[sic] Charles Twiss; M; Head; 38
3019 Louise Twiss; F; Wife; 26
3020 Jesse Twiss; M; Son; 5-3
3021 Flowrence[sic] Twiss; F; Dau; 3-6
3022 Clara Twiss; F; Dau; 1-3
3023 Hunkpapa; Unkakapa; F; Head; 68
3024 Mato Sapa; Thomas Black Bear; M; Head; 28
3025 Tatanka Wapaha; Emma Bull Bonnet; F; Wife; 27
3026 Wambli Naca; Otto Chief Eagle; M; Head; 25
3027 Zezela; Yellow Bird; M; Head; 39
3028 Anna Y. Bird; F; Wife; 38
3029 Zizila[sic]; David Y. Bird; M; Son; 19
3030 Lizzie Y. Bird; F; Dau; 15
3031 Josephine Y. Bird; F; Dau; 13
3032 Harry Y. Bird; M; Son; 10
3033 Eddie Y. Bird; M; Son; 7
3034 Alex Y. Bird; M; Son; 2-8
3035 Frank Y. Bird; M; Son; 9 mo.
3036 Tima Wakita; Looks Inside; M; Head; 26
3037 Wiyaka Pegnake; Cecilie Feather O. H.; F; Wife; 25
3038 Tucuhu Wicasa; Rib Man; M; Head; 53
3039 Asapi; Shouted At; F; Wife; 54
3040 Tucuhu Wicasa; Alfred R. Man; M; Son; 17

Census Of The Sioux And Cheyenne Indians Of Pine Ridge Agency, South Dakota. Taken by W. H. Clapp, Captain 16th Infantry, Acting United States Indian Agent, June 30, 1897. (Wounded Knee District)

Key: Number; Indian Name *(if given)*; English Name; Sex; Relation; Age

3041 Tucuhu Wacasa[sic]; Thomas Rib Man; M; Head; 24
3042 Jennie Rib Man; F; Wife; 21

3043 William Twiss; M; Head; 35
3044 Lizzie Cuny; F; Wife; 32
3045 Stella Dora Twiss; F; Dau; 2 mo.

3046 Aglagla Inyanka; Runs Along T. Edge; M; Head; 28
3047 Aglagla Inyanka; Jennie R.A.T. Edge; F; Wife; 24
3048 Wopotapi; Shot To Pieces; M; Son; 6
3049 Heraka Nupa; Two Elk; M; Dau; 4-2

3050 Winya Tanka; Big Woman; F; Head; 79

3051 Wapaha; War Bonnet; F; Head; 18

3052 Mato Sina; John Bear Robe; M; Head; 18

3053 Spayola Wicarca; Old Mexican; M; Head; 70

Census of the Sioux And Cheyenne Indians
Of Pine Ridge Agency, South Dakota.
June 30, 1897

Medicine Root District

Census Of The Sioux And Cheyenne Indians Of Pine Ridge Agency, South Dakota. Taken by W. H. Clapp, Captain 16th Infantry, Acting United States Indian Agent, June 30, 1897. (Medicine Root District)

Key: Number; Indian Name *(if given)*; English Name; Sex; Relation; Age

3054 Wasicu Tasunke; American Horse; M; Head; 57
3055 Tisina; Sleep; F; Wife #1; 52
3056 Wasicu Tasunke; Josie A. Horse; F; Wife #2; 32
3057 Wasicu Tasunke; Jennie A. Horse; F; Dau; 17
3058 Wasicu Tasunke; Beny American Horse; M; Son; 21
3059 Wasicu Tasunke; Jos. American Horse; M; Son; 19
3060 Wasicu Tasunke; Lucy American Horse; F; dau; 19
3061 Wasicu Tasunke; Sopjia[sic] American Horse; F; Dau; 18
3062 Wasicu Tasunke; Alice American Horse; F; Dau; 16
3063 Wasicu Tasunke; Charles American Horse; M; Son; 15
3064 Wasicu Tasunke; Julia; F; Dau; 10

3065 Kangi Sapa; Alexander Black Crow; M; Head; 24
3066 Kangi Sapa; Millie Black Crow; F; Wife; 22
3067 Kangi Sapa; Katie Black Crow; F; Dau; 1-8
3068 Kangi Sapa; Lucy Black Crow; F; Dau; 11 mo.

3069 Sungmanitu Gi; Alex Yellow Wolf; M; Head; 34

3070 Hinhan Luta; Amos Red Owl; M; Head; 36
3071 Hinhan Luta; Jessie Red Owl; F; Wife; 32
3072 Hinhan Luta; Henry Red Owl; M; Son; 8
3073 Ihuni; Levi Gets There; M; Son; 5-6
3074 Hinhan Luta; Hattie Red Owl; F; Dau; 1-11

3075 Tahuni Kokipesni; Afraid Of Nothing; M; Head; 72
3076 Sunkhinsa; Red Horse; F; Wife; 65
3077 Suntaya Mani; Edward Walk Hard; M; G.Son; 16

3078 Akicita Hanska; Albert Long Soldier; M; Head; 27
3079 Akicita Hanska; Millie Long Soldier; F; Wife; 33
3080 Okogna Inyanka; Runs Between; M; Son; 5-3
3081 Akicita Hanska; Bessie Long Soldier; F; Dau; 2 days

3082 Antoine Herman; M; Head; 36
3083 Lizzie Herman; F; Wife; 32
3084 Winfred Herman; F; Dau; 12
3085 Nellie Herman; F; Dau; 8
3086 Cora Herman; F; Dau; 7
3087 Edward Herman; M; Son; 10
3088 Jacob Herman; M; Son; 5-5

3089 Catka Kokepa; Afraid Of Left Hand; M; Head; 35
3090 Winyan Hanska; Tall Woman; F; Mother; 67

3091 Alice Garcia; F; Head; 28
3092 Nicholas Garcia; M; Son; 4
3093 Virginia Garcia; F; Dau; 6 mo.

3094 Mato Canali; Bear Climbs; F; Head; 62

3095 Siye Sapa; Black Chicken; M; Head; 42
3096 Toka Slipa; Licks Enemies; F; Wife; 42

3097 Sunka Nige Tanka; Big Belly Dog; M; Head; 57
3098 Anpitu Waste; Good Day; F; Wife; 45

Census Of The Sioux And Cheyenne Indians Of Pine Ridge Agency, South Dakota. Taken by W. H. Clapp, Captain 16th Infantry, Acting United States Indian Agent, June 30, 1897. (Medicine Root District)

Key: Number; Indian Name *(if given)*; English Name; Sex; Relation; Age

3099	Mato Sinte; Bear Tail; M; Head; 35	3120	Kangi Gleska; Edward Spotted Crow; M; Nephew; 15
3100	Woptura; Chipps; F; Wife; 35	3121	Wikan Papsaka; Sam'l Broken Rope; M; Son; 34
3101	Wakinyan Waste; Good Thunder; M; Son; 9		
3102	Niyan Luta; Red Breathing; F; Dau; 5	3122	Sungmanitu Sapa; Black Wolf; M; Head; 55
		3123	Maza Winyan; Iron Woman; F; Wife; 50
3103	Siyo; Prairie Chicken; F; Head; 50	3124	Sungmanitu Sapa; Johnson B. Wolf; M; Son; 23
3104	Wambli Ohititka; Brave Eagle; M; Head; 61	3125	Sungmanitu Sapa; Susie B. Wolf; F; Dau; 15
3105	Tokatakiya; Forward; F; Wife; 59	3126	Mato Sapa; Black Bear #2; M; Head; 31
3106	Wambli Okitika[sic]; Thos. Brave Eagle; M; G.Son; 13	3127	Najinhan Ku; Comes Standing; F; Wife; 25
3107	Wambli Okitika; Peter Brave Eagle; M; G.Son; 2-6	3128	Marpiya Waste; Good Cloud; F; Dau; 7
3108	Isto Weyahan; Broken Arm; M; Head; 61	3129	Hanpa Sapa; Black Moccasin; M; Son; 11 mo.
3109	Hankepi Gli; Comes Back Night; F; Wife #1; 57	3130	Putinhin; Beard; M; Head; 33
3110	Siyo; Chicken; F; Wife #2; 58	3131	Naca Win; Chief Woman; F; Wife; 43
3111	Kangi Sapa; Black Crow; M; Head; 31	3132	Marpiya He; Joseph Horn Cloud; M; Bro; 23
3112	Wakan Gli; Comes Holy; F; Wife; 27	3133	Putinhin; Ernest Beard; M; Bro; 16
2113[sic]	Owicale; Hunts Them Up; F; Dau; 6	3134	Can Yuwega; Breaks Limbs; M; Head; 68
2114	Wecegna Ku; Comes Among Them; M; Son; 4-5		
3115	Sunk Heyohe; Comes After Horses; F; Dau; 1-5	3135	Tatanka Mato; Bull Bear; M; Head; 71
		3136	Marpiya; Cloud; F; Wife; 60
3116	Wikan Papsaka; Broken Rope; M; Head; 73	3137	Tatanka Mato; Lizzie Bull Bear; F; Dau; 20
3117	Wikan Papsaka; Sarah B. Rope; F; Wife; 60	3138	Benjamin Janis; M; Head; 33
3118	Wikan Papsaka; Jos. B. Rope; M; Son; 26	3139	Susue[sic] Janis; F; Wife; 37
		3140	James Janis; M; Son; 9
3119	Nakpala; Creighton Creek; M; Son; 13	3141	Benj. Janis; M; Son; 2-4
		3142	Bessie Janis; F; Dau; 6
		3143	Aggie Janis; F; Dau; 3-8

Census Of The Sioux And Cheyenne Indians Of Pine Ridge Agency, South Dakota. Taken by W. H. Clapp, Captain 16th Infantry, Acting United States Indian Agent, June 30, 1897. (Medicine Root District)

Key: Number; Indian Name *(if given)*; English Name; Sex; Relation; Age

3144	Ben Roland; M; Head; 31	3169	Tokicun; Revenger; F; Dau; 3-6
3145	Nellie Roland; F; Wife; 28	3170	Tokala Nige; Noah Coyote Belly; M; Son; 7 mo.
3146	Mary Roland; F; Dau; 7		
3147	Annie Roland; F; Dau; 2-3	3171	Wambli Naca; Chief Eagle; M; Head; 52
3148	Sicangu Win; Brule Woman; F; Head; 69	3172	Kici Kiciza; Fight With; F; Wife; 52
3149	Tokahiya; Leader; F; G.Dau; 6	3173	Wambli Naca; Peter Chief Eagle; M; Son; 18
3150	Benj. Tibbitts; M; Head; 23		
3151	Susie Tibbitts; F; Wife; 23		
3152	Thomas Tibbitts; M; Son; 7 mo.	3174	Pehan Win; Crane Woman; F; Head; 69
3153	Marpiya Gi; Brown Cloud; M: Head; 28	3175	Tatankan[sic] Wakinyan; Chas. Thunder Bull; M; Head; 48
3154	Taopi; Wounded; F; Wife; 28		
3155	Tunweya Gli; Return Scout; M; Son; 8	3176	Tatankan Wakinyan; Walks; F; Wife; 46
3156	Wicitokab Naji; Stands In Front; M; Son; 6	3177	Shield; M; Son; 18
		3178	Jos.; M; Son; 15
		3179	Susie; F; Dau; 4-7
3157	Wayartha; Bite; M; Head; 75	3180	Mato Kte; Kills The Bear; F; M. in Law; 69
3158	Hoksila Tanka; Big Boy; M; Head; 37	3181	Marpiya Tasunke; Cloud Horse; M; Head; 46
3159	Canku; Road; F; Wife; 56		
3160	Hoksila; Anna Big Boy; F; Dau; 12	3182	Sagye Waste; Good Cane; F; Wife; 42
		3183	Marpiya Tasunke; Nancy Cloud Horse; F; Dau; 13
3161	Psa Winyan; Cow Woman; F; Head; 72	3184	Marpiya Tasunke; Annie Cloud Horse; F; Dau; 9
3162	Sunka Nupa; Oscar Two Dogs; M; G.Son; 11	3185	Marpiya Tasunke; Minnie Cloud Horse; F; Dau; 3-1
3163	Ikapaptanyan; Turns Over; F; Head; 72	3186	Ista Rmi; Crooked Eyes; M; Head; 31
3164	Inyan Kableca; Breaks Rock; F; Sister; 61	3187	Wacihin Anatan; Runs For Plume; F; Wife; 29
3165	Tokala Nige; Coyote Belly; M; Head; 42	3188	Maste; Sunshine; M; Son; 7
		3189	Winyan Zi; Yellow Woman; F; Dau; 2-6
3166	Rante; Cedar; F; Wife; 35		
3167	Achomni; Runs Around; M; Son; 16		
3168	Wicaku Sni; Wont[sic] Give Up; M; Son; 13	3190	Wambli Watapki; Charging Eagle; M; Head; 63

Census Of The Sioux And Cheyenne Indians Of Pine Ridge Agency, South Dakota. Taken by W. H. Clapp, Captain 16th Infantry, Acting United States Indian Agent, June 30, 1897. (Medicine Root District)

Key: Number; Indian Name *(if given)*; English Name; Sex; Relation; Age

3191 Ge Iciyawin; Paints Herself Yellow; F; Wife; 55
3192 Woptura; Chips; M; Head; 60
3193 Ohomni Yutantan; Feels All Around It; F; Wife; 48
3194 Nup Ewicaya; Takes Away Two; F; Dau; 16
3195 Kiynkan; Makes Room; M; Son; 16
3196 Pejuta Sapa; Coffee; F; Head; 77
3197 Sunk Gleska Yuha; Owns Spotted Horse; F; G.Dau; 18
3198 Sunka Witko; Crazy Dog; M; Head; 42
3199 Sunka Witko; Caroline Crazy Dog; F; Wife; 48
3200 Sahiyela; Cheyenne; M; Head; 36
3201 Sahiyela; Emma Cheyenne; F; Wife; 31
3202 Sunk Karnige; Picked Horses; F; Mother; 68
3203 Mato Winyan; Bear Woman; F; Head; 60
3204 Wambli Heton; Eagle Horn; M; Head; 46
3205 Wambli Heton; Agnes E. Horn; F; Wife; 45
3206 Wambli Heton; Hattie Eagle Horn; F; Dau; 20
3207 Wambli Heton; Fannie Eagle Horn; F; Dau; 19
3208 Wambli Heton; Josiah Eagle Horn; M: Son; 17
3209 Wambli Heton; Albert Eagle Horn; M; Son; 8
3210 Wambli Heton; Lizzie Eagle Horn; F; Dau; 11
3211 Wambli Heton; Emma Eagle Horn; F; Dau; 2-6

3212 Heraka; Elk; F; Head; 45
3213 Wambli Cante; Eagle Heart; M; Head; 30
3214 Wambli Cante; Jennie Eagle Heart; F; Wife; 29
3215 Marpiya Oronko; Swift Cloud; F; Dau; 1-10
3216 Ellen Mousseau; F; Head; 65
3217 James Mousseau; M; Son; 25
3218 Edward Janis; M; Head; 29
3219 Emily Tibbitts; F; Head; 46
3220 Winifred Shangrau; F; Niece; 8
3221 Ellen Farnham; F; Head; 43
3222 Bessie Farnham; F; Dau; 21
3223 Lizzie Farnham; F; Dau; 19
3224 Ulyses Farnham; M; Nephew; 8
3225 Wambli Oranko; Fast Eagle; M; Head; 48
3226 Zuzeca Gleska; Spotted Snake; F; Wife; 35
3227 Najinyapin; Surrounded; M; Son; 6
3228 Akomyaka Kte; Kills On Horseback; M; Son; 5-6
3229 Wambli Oranko; Sally Fast Eagle; F; Dau; 6 mo.
3230 Se Kaksa; Cut Foot; M; Head; 58
3231 Tarca Ska; Conrad White Deer; M; Head; 40
3232 Tarca Ska; Margret White Deer; F; Wife; 42
3233 Tarca Ska; Dan'l Marshall; M; Nephew; 5
3234 Cuwisnyanpi; Cold Breast; M; Head; 78
3235 Wicaku; Gives; F; Wife; 85

Census Of The Sioux And Cheyenne Indians Of Pine Ridge Agency, South Dakota. Taken by W. H. Clapp, Captain 16th Infantry, Acting United States Indian Agent, June 30, 1897. (Medicine Root District)

Key: Number; Indian Name *(if given)*; English Name; Sex; Relation; Age

3236 Tasunke Waste; Henry Good Horse; M; G.Son; 17
3237 Wiciyela; Charles Yankton; M; Head; 37
3238 Wiciyela; Julia Yankton; F; Wife; 37
3239 Wiciyela; Fat Yankton; M; Son; 6
3240 Wiciyela; John Yankton; M; Son; 2-4
3241 Wiciyela; Dollie Yankton; F; Dau; 16
3242 Wiciyela; Helen Yankton; F; Dau; 10

3243 Sinte Nupa; Charles Two Tails; M; Head; 36
3244 Tarca; Antelope; F; Wife; 43
3245 Sinte Nupa; Thomas Two Tails; M; Son; 18

3246 Cetan Wakuwa; Chasing Hawk; M; Head; 33

3247 Charles Clifford; M; Head; 30
3248 Julia Clifford; F; Wife; 30
3249 Charles Clifford Jr; M; Son; 6
3250 Maggie Clifford; F; Dau; 3
3251 William Clifford; M; Son; 3 mo.

3252 Cetan Kanwega; Charles Turning Hawk; M; Head; 39
3253 Cetan Kanwega; Philamena Turning Hawk; F; Wife; 41
3254 Cetan Kanwega; Hobart Turning Hawk; M; Son; 11

3255 Mato Inyanka; Frank Bear Runner; M; Head; 22
3256 Sina Ska; White Blanket; F; Wife; 21
3257 Mato Inyanka; Howard B. Runner; M; Son; 1

3258 Gnaska; Frog #1; M; Head; 60

3259 Mato Sina; Bear Robe; F; Wife; 45
3260 Gnaska; Elizabeth Frog; F; Dau; 20
3261 Taopi; Wounded; M; Son; 16
3262 Zuya; Warrior; F[sic]; Son; 6

3263 Si; Foot; M; Head; 79
3264 Si; Rosa Foot; F; Wife; 83
3265 Si; Jennie Foot; F; Dau; 45

3266 Wiyaka; Frank Feather; M; Head; 38
3267 Wiyaka; Close Feather; F; Wife; 32
3268 Wiyaka; Mary Feather; F; Dau; 13
3269 Wiyaka; Mable Feather; F; Dau; 3-6
3270 Wiyaka; Lucy Feather; F; Dau; 13
3271 Wiyaka; John Feather; M; Son; 10
3272 Wiyaka; Daniel Feather; M; Son; 8
3273 Wiyaka; Paul Feather; M; Son; 7
3274 Wiyaka; James Feather; M; Son; 2-6
3275 Wiyaka; Antoine Feather; M; Son; 6 mo.

3276 Wankal Kinyan; Flies Above; M; Head; 42
3277 Wanbli Sun; Eagle Feather; F; Wife; 35
3278 Wiyaka Wicasa; Louis Featherman; M; Son; 19
3279 Wiyaka Wicasa; Daniel Featherman; M; Son; 17
3280 Wiyaka Wicasa; Blowing Featherman; M; Son; 13
3281 Canupa Yuka; Maggie Owns The Pipe; F; Dau; 13
3282 Pte San Sina; White Cow Blanket; F; Dau; 4-6

Census Of The Sioux And Cheyenne Indians Of Pine Ridge Agency, South Dakota. Taken by W. H. Clapp, Captain 16th Infantry, Acting United States Indian Agent, June 30, 1897. (Medicine Root District)

Key: Number; Indian Name *(if given)*; English Name; Sex; Relation; Age

3283	Tasunke Inyanke; Fay Running Horse; M; Head; 36
3284	Tasunke Inyanke; Lizzie Running Horse; F; Wife; 35
3285	Tasunke Inyanke; Rock Running Horse; M; Nephew; 12
3286	Oowaste; Fine Shot; M; Head; 70
3287	Wanyeca; Rushes; F; Wife; 71
3288	Nape Wakan; Medicine Hand; M; Son; 30
3289	Wasicu; Kate White Man; F; G.Dau; 8 mo.
3290	Frank Marshall; M; Head; 34
3291	Minnie Marshall; F; Wife; 30
3292	Louisa Marshall; F; Dau; 13
3293	Mary Marshall; F; Dau; 10
3294	Josephine Marshall; F; Dau; 3-6
3295	Stephen Marshall; M; Son; 5-2
3296	Lizzie Marshall; F; Dau; 1-6
3297	Wabluska Waste; Good Bug; F; Head; 39
3298	Rla Win; Rattling Woman; F; Mother; 72
3299	Ite Waste; Good Face; F; Niece; 11
3300	Ipiyaka; Guy Belt; M: Head; 41
3301	Ipiyaka; Maggie Belt; F; Wife; 33
3302	Ipiyaka; Levi Belt; M; Son; 10
3303	Ipiyaka; Gertie Belt; F; Dau; 4-6
3304	Ipiyaka; James Belt; M; Son; 1-11
3305	Tasunke Waste; Good Horse; M; Head; 29
3306	Tasunke Waste; Josephine G. Horse; F; Wife; 28
3307	Ground Morrison; M; Head; 39
3308	Wing Morrison; F; Wife; 42
3309	Joseph Morrison; M; Son; 12
3310	Charles Morrison; M; Son; 3-9
3311	Josie Morrison; F; Dau; 3-9
3312	Mato Rlo; Growling Bear; M; Head; 45
3313	Sahiyela Iya; Talks Cheyenne; F; Wife; 45
3314	Mato Rlo; Charles G. Bear; M; Son; 18
3315	Mato Rlo; Thomas G. Bear; M; Son; 12
3316	Sungmanitu Hinapa; Comes Out Wolf; M; Son; 8
3317	Heraka Ciqala; Little Elk; M; Son; 3-4
3318	Cetan; Fannie Hawk; F; Dau; 23
3319	Kangi Ho Waste; Good Voice Crow; M; Head; 38
3320	Kangi Ho Waste; Mollie G.V. Crow; F; Wife #1; 38
3321	Sunsula Yuha; Owns The Mule; F; Wife #2; 52
3322	Kangi Ho Waste; Mary G.V. Crow; F; Dau; 18
3323	Conica Wanica; Della No Flesh; F; Dau; 16
3324	Wicincala Waste; Good Girl; F; Dau; 8
3325	Cokab Iyaya; Goes In Center; M; Son; 2
3326	Sunka Ciqala; George Little Dog; M; Head; 34
3327	Sahiyela Hunku; Cheyenne Mother; F; Wife; 35
3328	Tatanka Waka; Holy Bull; M; Son; 2-1
3329	Tasunke Hinzi; Joseph Yellow Horse; M; Nephew; 17
3330	Ista Sa; George Red Eyes; M; Head; 28
3331	Ista Sa; Louisa Red Eyes; F; Wife; 27

Census Of The Sioux And Cheyenne Indians Of Pine Ridge Agency, South Dakota. Taken by W. H. Clapp, Captain 16th Infantry, Acting United States Indian Agent, June 30, 1897. (Medicine Root District)

Key: Number; Indian Name *(if given)*; English Name; Sex; Relation; Age

3332	Winyan Waste; Good Woman; F; Head; 64	3355	Nakpa Ogi; Amos Brown Ears; M; Son; 5
3333	Cuwegna Ka Ska; Allen White Dress; M; Son; 23	3356	Winyan Mani; Walking Woman; F; Dau; 1-11
3334	Pehin Hanska; Long Hair; F; G.Dau; 3-10	3357	Tasunke Wakan; Her Holy Horse; F; Head; 52
3335	Taopi Ciqala; George Little Woman; M; Head; 29	3358	Mato Inyanka; Joseph Beae[sic] Runner; M; Son; 19
3336	Tasunke Kokipa[sic]; Belle Little Woman; F; Wife; 29	3359	Akan Manipa; Walks On Him; M; Son; 12
3337	Tasunke Kokipa; Jennie Young Man Afraid; [F]; Niece; 20	3360	He Woptura; Horn Chip; M; Head; 25
3338	Tokeya Ihuni; Gets There First; M; Head; 25	3361	He Woptura; Rosa Horn Chip; F; Wife; 23
3339	Pehin Ji Win; Yellow Haired Woman; F; Wife; 33	3362	He Woptura; Nellie H. Chip; F; Dau; 7 mo.
3340	Pehin Ji Win; Jessie Y. Hair; F; Dau; 7	3363	Tipi; House; F; Head; 62
3341	Pehin Ji [sic]; Emma Y. Hair; F; Dau; 4-10	3364	Tasunke Luzahan; Albert Fast Horse; M; Son; 15
3342	Cokab Iyaya; Goes In Center; F; Dau; 2-1	3365	Nato Rlogeca; Hollow Head; M; Head; 49
3343	Hinsma Win; Lucy Hair Woman; F; Dau; 11	3366	Nato Rlogeca; Julia Hollow Head; F; Wife; 45
3344	Tokeya Ihuni; Maggie Gets There First; F; Dau; 5 da.	3367	Nato Rlogeca; George Hollow Head; M; Son; 18
3345	Georgiana O'Rourke; F; Head; 39	3368	Niniciya; Saves Himself; M; Son; 9
3346	Thomas O'Rourke; M; Son; 20	3369	Karniga; Select; M; Son; 8
3347	Charkes[sic] O'Rourke; M; Son; 14	3370	Naca Win; Cheif[sic] Woman; F; Dau; 5-2
3348	Samuel O'Rourke; M; Son; 9		
3349	John O'Rourke; M; Son; 3-9	3371	Sunkole; Henry Looks F. Horses; M; Head; 47
3350	Annie Lang O'Rourke; F; Dau; 18	3372	Sunkole; Nancy Looks F. Horses; F; Wife; 48
3351	Emma O'Rourke; F; Dau; 12		
3352	Walter O'Rourke; M; Son; 23 da.	3373	Toka Apa; Hits Enemy; M; Head; 25
3353	Nakpa Ogi; Horace Brown Ears; M; Head; 31	3374	Toka Apa; Rosa Hits Enemy; F; Wife; 19
3354	Nakpa Ogi; Emma Brown Ears; F; Wife; 24	3375	Aiyapi; Talks About Him; M; Son; 2-1

Census Of The Sioux And Cheyenne Indians Of Pine Ridge Agency, South Dakota. Taken by W. H. Clapp, Captain 16th Infantry, Acting United States Indian Agent, June 30, 1897. (Medicine Root District)

Key: Number; Indian Name *(if given)*; English Name; Sex; Relation; Age

3376	Winyan Suta; Hard Woman; F; Head; 57	3397	Wazi Wankatuya; High Pine; M; Head; 39
3377	Sunkole; Maggie Hunts Horses; F; Dau; 28	3398	Anpetu; Day; F; Wife; 34
3378	Takolakai; His Friend; M; G.Son; 4-6	3399	Wicakute; Shoots At The; F; Dau; 11
		3400	Tokicun; Revenger; M; Son; 7
3379	Wambli Gleska; Harry Spotted Eagle; M; Head; 36	3401	Wazi Wankatuya; Jessie High Pine; F; Dau; 5
3380	Wambli Gleska; Nellie Spotted Eagle; F; Wife; 29	3402	Wazi Wankatuya; James High Pine; M; Son; 6 mo.
3381	Wambli Gleska; Sally Spotted Eagle; F; Dau; 14	3403	Sahiyela Obca[sic]; Imatates[sic] Cheyenne; M; Head; 71
3382	Pehin Maza; Iron Hair; F; Dau; 3-10	3404	Oturansa; Gives Things; F; Wife; 55
3383	Tokeya Shuni; Gets There First; M; Son; 5-6	3405	Joseph Marshall; M; Head; 46
		3406	Elizabeth Marshall; F; Wife; 45
3384	Mato Wankatuya; High Bear; M; Head; 62	3407	Thomas Marshall; M; Son; 20
		3408	Philip Marshall; M; Son; 14
3385	Cunsoka; Timber; F; Wife #2; 46	3409	Harrison Marshall; M; Son; 12
3386	Makata Wakita; Looks At Ground; F; Wife #1; 55	3410	Charles Marshall; M; Son; 8
		3411	Alie Marshall; F; Dau; 4-2
3387	Mato Wankatuya; Herbert H. Bear; M; Son; 20	3412	Jennie Marshall; F; Dau; 6
		3413	John Dillon; M; Nephew; 18
		3414	Peter Dillon; M; Nephew; 18
3388	Tasina Wakan; Her Holy Robe; F; Head; 69	3415	McGee Morris Marshall; M; Son; 7 mo.
3389	Wiyaka Wanjila; Lizzie One Feather; F; G.Dau; 14	3416	Heraka Wakan; Nancy Medicine Elk; F; Head; 29
3390	Henry Morrison; M; Head; 19	3417	Heraka Wakan; Cedar Medicine Elk; F; Dau; 8
3391	Cetan Win; Hawk Woman; F; Head; 65	3418	Toka Kokipa; Afraid Of Enemy; M; Son; 5-4
3392	He Luta; Red Horn; M; G.Son; 4-6	3419	Marpiya Luta; Jack Red Cloud; M; Head; 39
3393	Oksanta; Howard Around It; M; Head; 29	3420	Waste; Good; F; Wife; 38
3394	Oksanta; Victoria Around It; F; Wife; 25	3421	Naca Wni[sic]; Chief Woman; F; Dau; 16
3395	Tasunek Wakan; Medicine Horse; F; Dau; 5	3422	Isnala Kaga; Makes Alone; M; Son; 5
3396	Oksanta; John Around It; M; Son; 1-8	3423	Marpiya Luta; Charles Red Cloud; M; Son; 8

Census Of The Sioux And Cheyenne Indians Of Pine Ridge Agency, South Dakota. Taken by W. H. Clapp, Captain 16th Infantry, Acting United States Indian Agent, June 30, 1897. (Medicine Root District)

Key: Number; Indian Name *(if given)*; English Name; Sex; Relation; Age

3424 Marpiya Luta; Alfred Red Cloud; M; Son; 9 mo.
3425 Sunk Gleska; John Spotted Horse; M; Head; 29
3426 Waglure; Jennie Loafer; F; Wife; 24
3427 Mato Iyoyaka; John Sitting Bear; M; Head; 45
3428 Mato Iyoyaka; Lucy Sitting Bear; F; Wife; 40
3429 Mato Iyoyaka; Mary Sitting Bear; F; Dau; 23
3430 Mato Iyoyaka; Victoria[sic] Sitting Bear; F; Dau; 16
3431 Nawizi; Jealous; F; Head; 79
3432 Tasina Wanyankapi; Looks At Her Blanket; F; G.Dau; 5
3433 Yamni Hiyuciya; James Dismounts Thrice; M; Head; 30
3434 Yamni Hiyuciya; Susie Dismounts Thrice; F; Wife; 25
3435 Yamni Hiyuciya; Edward Dismounts Thrice; M; Son; 5-6
3436 Yamni Hiyuciya; Alfred Dismounts Thrice; M; Son; 1-9
3437 Mastincala Luta; Jonas Red Rabbit; m: Head; 46
3438 Zintakala Waste; Good Bird; F; Wife; 37
3439 Tasunke Hin To; Her Blue Horse; F; M. in Law; 64
3440 Zintkala To; Jefferson Blue Bird; M; Head; 29
3441 Zintkala To; Annie Blue Bird; F; Wife; 26
3442 Zintkala To; James Blue Bird; M; Son; 9
3443 Zintkala To; Thomas Blue Bird; M; Son; 7
3444 Zintkala To; Sarah Blue Bird; F; Dau; 4-4
3445 Zintkala To; Mary Blue Bird; F; Dau; 1-6
3446 John Glenn; M; Head; 32
3447 Rosa Glenn; F; Wife; 29
3448 Lena Glenn; F; Dau; 6
3449 Edison Glenn; M; Son; 3-9
3450 Annie Glenn; F; Dau; 9 mo.
3451 John Clifford; M; Head; 26
3452 Hattie Clifford; F; Wife; 18
3453 George Clifford; M; Son; 1-8
3454 Tatanka Hanska; John Long Bull; M; Head; 39
3455 Tatanka Hanska; Julia Long Bull; F; Wife; 38
3456 Tatanka Hanska; Edith Long Bull; F; Dau; 9
3457 James Janis; M; Head; 23
3458 Rosa Janis; F; Wife; 20
3459 Paul Janis; M; Son; 2-1
3460 Edward Janis; M; Son; 6 mo.
3461 Ista Ska; Jacob White Eyes; M; Head; 27
3462 Tatanka Gi; Jennie Yellow Bull; F; Wife; 19
3463 Ista Ska; Edith White Eyes; F; Dau; 2 mo.
3464 Mila Hanska; Long Knife; F; Head; 33
3465 Ite Wakan; Holy Face; F; Dau; 7
3466 Mila Hanska; Susie Long Knife; F; Dau; 1-1
3467 Naca Ciqala; Little Chief; M; Head; 38
3468 Pehin Win; Hair Woman; F; Wife; 34
3469 Anpetuwakan; Sunday; F; Dau; 10

Census Of The Sioux And Cheyenne Indians Of Pine Ridge Agency, South Dakota. Taken by W. H. Clapp, Captain 16th Infantry, Acting United States Indian Agent, June 30, 1897. (Medicine Root District)

Key: Number; Indian Name *(if given)*; English Name; Sex; Relation; Age

3470 Napca; Swallow; M; Son; 4-5
3471 Sungmanitu Wanjila; Oliver Lone Wolf; M; Nephew; 5-4
3472 Wicarpi; Star; F; Dau; 1-3
3473 Naca Ciqala; Wing Little Chief; F; Dau; 10

3474 Tatanka Catka; Left Hand Bull; M; Head; 58

3475 Sungmanitu Gi; Lucy Yellow Wolf; F; Head; 24
3476 Herakaluta; Red Elk; F; G.Mo; 80
3477 Singmanitu[sic] Gi; Sally Yellow Wolf; F; Niece; 12
3478 Singmanitu Gi; Julia Yellow Wolf; F; Dau; 5-5

3479 Zuya Ciqala; Little Warrior; M; Head; 26
3480 Zuya; Ellen Warrior; F; Wife; 19

3481 Mato Wanjila; Lone Bear; M; Head; 43
3482 Hankepi; Lizzie At Night; F; Wife; 43
3483 Mato Wanjila; Samuel Lone Bear; M; Son; 20
3484 Mato Wanjila; Alice Lone Bear; F; Dau; 19

3485 Tatanka Mato; Lawrence Bull Bear; M; Head; 38
3486 Tatanka Mato; Julia Bull Bear; F; Wife; 33
3487 Tatanka Mato; Dixon Bull Bear; M; Son; 15
3488 Tatanka Mato; Jesse Bull Bear; M; Son; 10
3489 Tatanka Mato; Moses Bull Bear; M; Son; 6
3490 Tatanka Mato; Peter Bull Bear; M; Son; 13
3491 Tatanka Mato; Fannie Bull Bear; F; Dau; 2-6

3492 Tatanka Mato; Henry Bull Bear; M; Son; 10 mo.
3493 Canku Tanka; Lizzie M.B.Road; F; Head; 32
3494 Canku Tanka; Bessie M.B.Road; F; Dau; 7
3495 Cetan Win; Hawk Woman; F; Mother; 53

3496 Louis Mousseau; M; Head; 28
3497 Zoey Mousseau; F; Wife; 28
3498 Joseph Mousseau; M; Son; 6
3499 Louis Mousseau Jr; M; Son; 4
3500 John Mousseau; M; Son; 11mo 17da

3501 Louisa L. Baines; F; Head; 37
3502 Paul Baines; M; Son; 15
2503[sic] Frank L. Baines; M; Son; 12
2504[sic] Susie L. Baines; F; Dau; 19
2505[sic] Francis L. Baines; F; Dau; 17
3506 Polonia L. Baines; F; Dau; 10

2507[sic] Catka; Left Hand; M; Head; 37
2508[sic] Mani Wastelaka; Likes To Walk; F; Wife; 55
3509 Ota Kte; Kills Plenty; F; S.Dau; 25
3510 Winyan Tanka; Big Woman; M[sic]; M. in Law; 83
3511 Taopi Ciqala; Little Wound; M; Head; 68
3512 Owewakankan; Tells Lies; F; Wife; 55
3513 Taopi Ciqala; James Little Wound; M; Son; 23
3514 Hektakeya Kute; Shoots Back; M; G.Son; 15

3515 Louis Shangreau; M; Head; 48
3516 Louisa Shangreau; F; Wife; 42
3517 Rosa Shangreau; F; Dau; 22
3518 Nelson Shangreau; M; Son; 20

Census Of The Sioux And Cheyenne Indians Of Pine Ridge Agency, South Dakota. Taken by W. H. Clapp, Captain 16th Infantry, Acting United States Indian Agent, June 30, 1897. (Medicine Root District)

Key: Number; Indian Name *(if given)*; English Name; Sex; Relation; Age

3519 Martin Shangreau; M; Son; 11
3520 Pearl Shangreau; F; Dau; 3-3
3521 Joseph Montileau; M; Nephew; 19
3522 Parker Shangreau; M; Son; 1-4
3523 Wiyaka Wanjila; Moses One Feather; M; Head; 42
2524[sic] Wiyaka Wanjila; Jessie One Feather; F; Wife; 31
3525 Wiyaka Wanjila; Susie One Feather; F; Dau; 19
3526 Wiyaka Wanjila; Willie One Feather; M; Son; 16
3527 Wiyaka Wanjila; Bessie One Feather; F; Dau; 3-7
3528 Tiglake; Moves Camp; M; Head; 29
3529 Tiglake; Helen Moves Camp; F; Wife; 24
3530 Rla O; Comes Rattling; F; Dau; 8
3531 Taopi Glinapa; Comes Out Wounded; M; Son; 3-6
3532 Hu Wegahan; Moses Broken Leg; M; Head; 29
3533 Taninyan Ti; Lives In Sight; F; Wife; 25
3534 Hu Wegahan; Jack Broken Leg; M; Son; 2-2
3535 Ptesan; Millie White Cow; F; Head; 41
3536 Mato Wakan; Medicine Bear; M; Head; 59
3537 Waci Ya; Goes Dancing; F; Wife; 59
3538 Papta Hinapa; Sticks Out; F; Dau; 26
3539 Wacinyapi; Depends On Them; F; Dau; 17
3540 Teriya Icu; Takes It Hard; F; Dau; 15
3541 Winyan Kte; Kills Woman; F; Dau; 8
3542 Niyan Kte; Kills Alive; M; G.Son; 5-3
3543 Wicakicu; Gives Back; F; G.Dau; 11 mo.
3544 Tasunke Wakan; Medicine Horse; M: Head; 65
3545 Hu Can Can; Shaking Legs; F; Wife; 65
3546 Taopi Gli; Come Wounded; F; Dau; 17
3547 Zintkala To; Blue Bird; M; G.Son; 9
3548 Wicasa Wakanl; Man Above; M; Head; 52
3549 Pehin Sa; Red Hair; F; Wife; 55
3550 Wankal Wicasa; Samuel Man Above; M; Son; 16
3551 Wankal Wicasa; Alexander M. Above; M; Son; 23
3552 Wankal Wicasa; Fanny M. Above; F; Dau; 11
3553 Cega Luta; Moses Red Kettle; M; Head; 37
3554 Cega Luta; Mary Red Kettle; F; Wife; 35
3555 Cega Luta; Joseph Red Kettle; M; Son; 8
2556[sic] Cega Luta; Charles A. R. Kettle; M; Son; 5-4
2557[sic] Cega Luta; Nattie R. Kettle; F; Dau; 5mo 28da
3558 Maggie Clifford; F; Head; 58
3559 Julian Clifford; F; Dau; 19
3560 George Clifford; M; Son; 23
3561 Martha Janis; F; Head; 72
3562 Julia Montileau; F; Head; 21
3563 Emily Montileau; F; Sister; 23

Census Of The Sioux And Cheyenne Indians Of Pine Ridge Agency, South Dakota.
Taken by W. H. Clapp, Captain 16th Infantry, Acting United States Indian Agent,
June 30, 1897. (Medicine Root District)

Key: Number; Indian Name *(if given)*; English Name; Sex; Relation; Age

3564 Mary Condelario; F; Head; 53
3565 Sophia Condelario; F; Dau; 23
3566 Clara Condelario; F; Dau; 21
3567 Lucy Condelario; F; Dau; 17
3568 Peter Condelario; M; Son; 19
3569 Joseph Condelario; M; Son; 12

3570 Oiyokipiya Ti; Merrily Lives; F; Head; 69

3571 Wasu; Mary Wasu; F; Head; 69
3572 Caga; Mary Ice; F; Dau; 33

3573 Ipiyaka Nica; No Belt; M; Head; 35
3574 Ipiyaka Nica; Ellen No Belt; F; Wife; 35

3575 Nick L. Janis; M; Head; 35
3576 Her Head; F; Wife; 29
3577 Thomas Janis; M; Son; 11
3578 Ben Janis; M; Son; 9
3579 Emma Janis; F; Dau; 6
3580 Mary Janis; F; Dau; 2-2
3581 Lucy Janis; F; Dau; 9 mo.

3582 Nancy; F; Head; 89
3583 Sungmanitu Wakuwa; Alice Chasing Wolf; F; Niece; 14

3584 Wambli Ohitika; Oscar Brave Eagle; M; Head; 28
3585 Wicakte Hi; Comes To Kill; F; Wife; 24
3586 Tayan Kte; Kills Good; M; Son; 5
3587 Wambli Ohitika; Silas Brave Eagle; M: Son; 9 mo.

3588 Winarca Taopi; Old Bad Wound; F; Head; 73
3589 Aglagla Inyanka; Jas. Runs A.T. Edge; M; G.Son; 13

3590 Peyozan; Parts His Hair; M; Head; 55

3591 Siha Sapa; Black Feet; F; Wife #1; 54
3592 Peyozan; Susie Parts Her Hair; F; Wife #2; 43
3593 Peyozan; Ephraim R[sic].H.Hair; M; Son; 19
3594 Peyozan; Amos P.H.Hair; M; Son; 15
3595 Peyozan; Sarah P.H.Hair; F; Dau; 15
3596 Peyozan; Emma P.H.Hair; F; Dau; 12
3597 Peyozan; Winnie P.H.Hair; F; Dau; 9
3598 Wambli Iyotaka; Albert Sitting Eagle; M; Son; 25
3599 William Gay; M; Nephew; 28

3600 Mato Ota; Plenty Bear; M; Head; 52
3601 Canku; Road; F; Wife; 47
3602 Nite Yazan; Pain On The Rump; M; Head; 37
3603 Tasunke; Her Horse; F; Wife; 35
3604 Nite Yazan; Chas. Pain O.T. Rump; M; Son; 8
3605 Te Wegna; In The Crowd; F; Dau; 2-3

3606 Scili Hunska; Pawnee Leggins; M; Head; 49
3607 Honronpi; Hears The Voice; F; Wife; 50
3608 Scili Hunska; Josephin[sic] P. Leggins; F; Dau; 16
3609 Scili Hunska; George P. Leggins; M; Son; 14
3610 Mato Yuha; Kills The Bear; M; Son; 5-6
3611 Watakpe; Charger; M; G.Son; 1-2

3612 Paddy Star; M; Head; 38
3613 Nellie Star; F; Wife; 29
3614 Phoebe Star; F; Dau; 11

Census Of The Sioux And Cheyenne Indians Of Pine Ridge Agency, South Dakota. Taken by W. H. Clapp, Captain 16th Infantry, Acting United States Indian Agent, June 30, 1897. (Medicine Root District)

Key: Number; Indian Name *(if given)*; English Name; Sex; Relation; Age

3615 Lydia Star; F; Dau; 4-3
3616 Lucy Star; F; Dau; 2-5
3617 Paddy Star Jr; M; Son; 3mo16da
3618 Awicayustan; Quits Them; F; Head; 52
3619 Cansasa; Red Willow; M; Head; 38
3620 Tasunke Hinapa; Her Horse Comes Out; F; Wife; 31
3621 Owicalehi; Comes To Hunt Them; M; Son; 5-9
3622 Sina Luta; Red Blanket; M; Head; 28
3623 Tasunke; Her Horse; F; Wife; 27
3624 Sina Wakan; Holy Blanket; F; Dau; 1-1
3625 Tasunke Wicarca; Ralph Old Horse; M; Head; 35
3626 Tasunke Nupa; Her Two Horses; F; Wife; 39
3627 Kiyansa; Cut Off; F; Mother; 85
3628 Tasunke Wesarca; Spark Old Horse; M; Son; 13
3629 Mato Kokepa; Afraid Of Bear; M; Son; 7
3630 Tasunke Wicarca; Katie Old Horse; F; Dau; 5 mo.
3631 Sungmanitu Isnala; Rosa Lone Wolf; F; Head; 25
3632 Sungmanitu Isnala; Felix Lone Wolf; M; Son; 3-8
3633 Kici Kiciza; Fight With Him; F; Mother; 62
3634 Sungmanitu Isnala; Agnes Lone Wolf; F; Dau; 9 mo.
3635 Akan Inyanka; Runs On; M; Head; 39
3636 Tatanka; Bull; F; Wife; 28
3637 Akan Inyanka; Nellie Runs On; F; Dau; 7
3638 Pihin Hanska; Long Hair; F; Dau; 5
3639 Tasina Wakan; Her Holy Blanket; F; Dau; 2-9
3640 Winyan Kte; Kills Woman; F; Dau; 10 mo.
3641 Marpiya Naji; Robert Standing Cloud; M; Head; 31
3642 Tasunke Maza; Iron Horse; M; F. in Law; 72
3643 Wikan; Twine; F; Wife; 52
3644 Susan Johnson; F; Dau; 12
3645 Znya; Warrior; M; Son; 7
3646 Sunka Oyate; Dog Tribe; M; Son; 1-8
3647 Oye Luta; Red Track; F; Head; 75
3648 Anpetu; David Day; M; G.Son; 17
3649 Wambli Luta; Red Eagle #1; M; Head; 42
3650 Sagye; Cane; F; Wife; 25
3651 Tikanyela Kte; Kills Close To Lodge; M; Son; 8
3652 Heraka Luta; Red Elk; M; Head; 63
3653 Heraka Inajin; Stopping Elk; F; Wife; 64
3654 Heraka Luta; Millie Red Elk; F; Dau; 33
3655 Aiyapi; Talked About; M; G.Son; 11
3650[sic] Warpe Koyaka; Wears Leaf; M; G.Son; 10
3657 Ista Sa; Red Eyes; M; Head; 50
3658 Tasunke Wakan; Medicine Horse; F; Wife; 52
3659 Ista Sa; Daniel Red Eyes; M; Son; 17

Census Of The Sioux And Cheyenne Indians Of Pine Ridge Agency, South Dakota. Taken by W. H. Clapp, Captain 16th Infantry, Acting United States Indian Agent, June 30, 1897. (Medicine Root District)

Key: Number; Indian Name *(if given)*; English Name; Sex; Relation; Age

3660 Mato; Bear; F; Dau; 9
3661 Wacihin Luta; Red Plume; M; Head; 45
3662 Wicincala; Girl; F; Wife; 41
3663 Rosa Thomas; F; Head; 47
3664 Mary Thomas; F; Dau; 6
3665 Sungmanitu Luta; Red Coyote; M; Head; 50
3666 Anpetu Ska; White Day; F; Wife; 31
3667 Tirla; Rattling Lodge; F; Dau; 4-3
3668 Marpiya Sna; Rattling Cloud; F; Head; 25
3669 Wahacanka; Shield; M; Son; 6
3670 Wacapa; Stabber #2; M; Head; 27
3671 Ite Ska Rla; Rattling White Face; F; Wife; 24
3672 Zintkala Wambli; Eagle Bird; M; Son; 4-6
3673 Sunkhiyohi; Comes After Horses; F; Dau; 2-4
3674 Ota Apela; Strikes Plenty; M; Head; 42
3675 Winyan Waste; Pretty Woman; F; Wife; 37
3676 Oto Apela; Jefferson S. Plenty; M; Son; 18
3677 Oto Apela; Lucy S. Plenty; F; Dau; 13
3678 Toka Ole; Looks For Enemy; F; Dau; 4-6
3679 Ota Apela; Paulina S. Plenty; F; Dau; 16
3680 Slolyapi; Knows Him; F; Dau; 3-10
3681 Marpiya Naji; Standing Cloud; M; Head; 59

3682 Worinya; Pouting; F; Wife; 45
3683 Naji; Cora Standing; F; Dau; 13
3684 Wayank Kte; Julia Kills Looking; F; Dau; 20
3685 Sa Yuha Mani; Walks With Red; F; Head; 72
3686 Sunk Witko; Julia Crazy Dog; F; G.Dau; 15
3687 Kangi Gleska; Spotted Crow; M; Head; 47
3688 Marpiya To; Blue Cloud; F; Wife; 63
3689 Kangi Gleska; Katie S. Crow; F; Dau; 15
3690 Kangi Gleska; Fannie S. Crow; F; Dau; 10
3691 Sunka Hunkesni; Slow Dog; M; Head; 83
3692 Pseca; Jumper; F; Wife #1; 65
3693 Marpiya To; Old Arapahoe; F; Wife #2; 65
3694 Ista Ska; Jessie White Eyes; F; G.Dau; 15
3695 Sungmanitu Ska; Herbert White Wolf; M; G.Son; 17
3696 Sungmanitu Ska; Sarah White Wolf; F; G.Dau; 13
3697 Mastincala Sakewin; Seven Rabbits; M; Head; 64
3698 Wambli Gleska; Clara Spotted Eagle; F; Head; 34
3699 Pankeska Napin; Shell Necklace #2; M; Head; 37
3700 Niwevaya[sic]; Saves Them; F; Wife; 38
3701 Winyan Tanka; Big Woman; F; Sister; 20
3702 Areyunka; George Frost Over; M; Nephew; 16

Census Of The Sioux And Cheyenne Indians Of Pine Ridge Agency, South Dakota. Taken by W. H. Clapp, Captain 16th Infantry, Acting United States Indian Agent, June 30, 1897.   (Medicine Root District)

Key: Number; Indian Name *(if given)*; English Name; Sex; Relation; Age

3703	Marpiya; Fast Cloud; M; Son; 8 mo.	3723	Florence Hermandez; M; Son; 16
3704	Wan onopi; Shot With Arrows; M; Head; 28	3724	Reyes Hermandez; M; Son; 10
		3725	Valentine Hermandez; M; Son; 7
		3726	Austacia Hermandez; F; Dau; 7
3705	Tasunke Ota; Plenty Horses; F; Wife; 35	3727	Catelina Hermandez; F; Dau; 2-4
3706	Kokab Iglonica; Stays In Front; F; Dau; 4-2	3728	Pankeskawin; Shell Woman; F; Head; 64
3707	Can Apaha; Shows The Sticks; F; Mother; 60	3729	Cetan Rabya; Elizabeth Scares Hawk; F; G.Dau; 17
		3730	Mary Martinez; F; G.Dau; 11
3708	Wacapa; Stabber #1; M; Head; 62	3731	Sophia Giago; F; Head; 27
3709	Wacapa; Julia Stabber; F; Wife #1; 56	3732	Grace Giago; F; Dau; 5
		3733	Timothy Giago; M; Son; 2
3710	Tasunkeajake; Samuel Last Horse; M; Head; 45	3734	Casmu; Sand; M; Head; 53
3711	Tasunkeajake; Georgiana Last Horse; F; Dau; 14	3735	Anpetu; Day; F; Wife; 51
		3736	Heraka Gleska; Spotted Elk; M; Head; 40
3712	Tasunkeajake; Salina Last Horse; F; Dau; 10	3737	Rante Zi; Yellow Cedar; F; Wife; 39
3713	Tasunke Ehakela; Sam'l Last Horse Jr; M; Head; 21	3738	Heraka Gleska; James S. Elk; M; Son; 10
3714	Tasunke Ehakela; Mattie Last Horse; F; Wife; 18	3739	Sunk Gleska; Spotted Horse; M; Head; 57
3715	Itunkasan Gleska; Spotted Weasel; M; Head; 47	3740	Wiciyela Winyan; Yankton Woman; F; Wife #2; 44
3716	Rante; Cedar; F; Wife #1; 45	3741	Toka Oyuspa; Catches Enemy; F; Wife #1; 54
3717	Wicincala; Girl; F; Wife #2; 36	3742	Sunk Gleska; Robert S. Horse; M; Son; 19
3718	Hoksila Wakan; Medicine Boy; M; Son; 12	3743	Maga Kute; Shoots Ducks; M; Son; 7
3719	Wakinya Ciqala; Little Thunder; M; Nephew; 11	3744	Tatanka Mani; Mack Bull Walking; M; Son; 4-5
3720	Tarca; Deer; F; Dau; 8 da.	3745	Nata Kahumpi; Cut Head; F; M. In Law; 74
3721	Sophia Hermandez[sic]; F; Head; 48	3746	Sunk Gleska; James Spotted Horse; M; Son; 5 mo.
3722	Ambrosus Hermandez; M; Son; 17	3747	Sunka Nupa; Two Dogs; M; Head; 50

Census Of The Sioux And Cheyenne Indians Of Pine Ridge Agency, South Dakota. Taken by W. H. Clapp, Captain 16th Infantry, Acting United States Indian Agent, June 30, 1897. (Medicine Root District)

Key: Number; Indian Name *(if given)*; English Name; Sex; Relation; Age

3748 Tiyopa Luta; Red Door; F; Wife #1; 37
3749 Sunka Nupa; Jennie T. Dogs; F; Wife #2; 35
3750 Wambli Wicarpi; Star Eagle; M; Son; 18
3751 Nuwan Kte; Jno. Kills Swimming; M; Son; 13
3752 Sunka Nupa; Alice Two Dogs; F; Dau; 7
3753 Sunka Nupa; Lizzie Two Dogs; F; Dau; 16
3754 Sunka Nupa; Jacob Two Dogs; M; Son; 3 mo.

3755 Thomas Henry; M; Head; 37
3756 Lizzie Henry; F; Wife; 25
3757 Wallace Henry; M; Son; 4-5

3758 Wasicu Tasunke; Thos. American Horse; M; Head; 28
3759 Wasicu Tasunke; Julia American Horse; F; Wife; 28
3760 Wasicu Tasunke; William American Horse; M; Son; 4-6
3761 Heraka Cincala; Young Elk; F; Dau; 2-4

3762 Wankal Mato; Top Bear; M; Head; 65
3763 Lila Yucancan; Shakes Hard; F; Wife #2; 70
3764 Wawokiya; Helps; F; Wife #1; 72

3765 Kangi Nupa; Two Crows; M; Head; 50
3766 Prspiza; Prairie Dog; F; Wife; 43
3767 Owecale Hi; Comes To Hunt Them; F; Dau; 11
3768 Kange[sic] Nupa; John Two Crow[sic]; M; Son; 16
3769 Warpe Luta; Red Leaf; F; Dau; 9

3770 Mato Gi; Brown Bear; F; Dau; 2-2
3771 Wakinyan OpWoglaka; Talks With Lightning; M; Son; 13
3772 Okasaka Yukan; Shows Whip Marks; M; Son; 9

3773 Maka; Dirt; M; Head; 7
3774 Toka Kuwa; Charges The Enemy; M; Son; 6

3775 Wakinyan Gi; Thos. Yellow Thunder; M; Head; 29
3776 Wakinyan Gi; Katie Yellow Thunder; F; Wife; 25
3777 Wakinyan Gi; Wm. Yellow Thunder; M; Son; 9
3778 Wakinyan Gi; Joseph Yellow Thunder; M; Son; 3-3
3779 Wakinyan Gi; Wallace Yellow Thunder; M; Son; 1-1

3780 Tasunke Luzahan; Thos. Fast Horse; M; Head; 43
3781 Wasicu Winyan; White Woman; F; Wife; 37
3782 Tasunke Luzahan; Mary Fast Horse; F; Dau; 18
3783 Hektakeya[sic] Ku; Comes Back; F; Dau; 7
3784 Tasunke Luzahan; Jessie F. Horse; F; Dau; 19

3788[sic] Mato Ska; White Bear; M; Head; 44
3789 Inyan Skan Mani; Walks On Rock; F; Wife; 47
3787[sic] Mato Ska; Annie White Bear; F; Dau; 16

3788 Sunkmanitu Ipiyaka; Wolf Skin Belt; M; Head; 55
3789 Wakil Hinapa; Goes Out Looking; F; Wife; 60

Census Of The Sioux And Cheyenne Indians Of Pine Ridge Agency, South Dakota. Taken by W. H. Clapp, Captain 16th Infantry, Acting United States Indian Agent, June 30, 1897. (Medicine Root District)

Key: Number; Indian Name *(if given)*; English Name; Sex; Relation; Age

3790 Cante Sapa; William Black Heart; M; Head; 42
3791 Castunpi; Calls Her Name; F; Wife; 51
3792 Tankaya Wakawa; Wm. Big Charger; M; Head; 26
3793 Sagye Wakan Win; Holy Cane Woman; F; Head; 23
3794 Zintkala Naca; Chief Bird; M; Son; 6
3795 Wambli Gleska Ciqala; Little Spotted Eagle; [blank]; Son; 2-8
3796 Ite Ska; White Face; M; Head; 46
3797 Tasunke Waste; Her Good Horse; F; Wife; 40
3798 Ite Ska; Mary White Face; F; Dau; 21
3799 Ite Ska; Sophia White Face; F; Dau; 13
3800 Rabwicaya; Scares Them Away; M; Son; 4-3
3801 Tatanka Wicasa; Daniel Bull Man; M; Head; 19
3802 Tatanka Wicasa; Sally Bull Man; F; Wife; 16
3803 Wamniyomni Ska; White Whirlwind; M; Head; 29
3804 Wambli Sun; Eagle Feather; F; Wife; 37
3805 Wankal Mato; Hugh Top Bear; M; Nephew; 21
3806 Honaronpi; Hears Her Voice; F; Niece; 10
3807 Zintkala Pa; William Bird Head; M; Head; 36
3808 Zintkala Pa; Dolly Bird Head; F; Wife; 36
3809 Zintkala Pa; Burgess Bird Head; M; Son; 15
3810 Zintkala Pa; Joseph Bird Head; M; Son; 2-9
3811 Wahukeza Ska; White Lance; M; Head; 28
3812 Wahukeza Ska; Julia White Lance; F; Wife; 24
3813 Wahukeza Ska; Frank White Lance; M; Bro; 18
3814 Tasunke Wanyankapi; Looks At Her Horse; F; Dau; 3-6
3815 Mani Luzahan; Walks Fast; M: Head; 40
3816 Kikta Sni; Dont[sic] Get Up; F; Wife; 44
3817 Mani Luzahan; Red Ears Walks Fast; M: Son; 14
3818 Mani Luzahan; Good Bird Walks Fast; M; Son; 9
3819 Mani Luzahan; George Walks Fast; M; Son; 8
3820 William Garnett; M; Head; 42
3821 Filla Garnett; F; Wife; 41
3822 Charles Garnett; M; Son; 21
3823 Richard Garnett; M; Son; 12
3824 William Garnett Jr.; M; Son; 10
3825 Dolly Garnett; F; Dau; 7
3826 Wambli Ohitika; Warren Brave Eagle; M; Son; 23
3827 Wambli Ohitika; Mary Brave Eagle; F; Wife; 29
3828 Taninya Kte; Kills In Sight; F; Dau; 1-3
3829 Wiyaka Ska; White Feather; M; Head; 62
3830 Rlala; Rattling; F; Wife; 62
3831 Wiyaka Ska; Hattie White Feather; F; Dau; 38
3832 Mato Sapa; William Black Bear; M; Head; 61

Census Of The Sioux And Cheyenne Indians Of Pine Ridge Agency, South Dakota. Taken by W. H. Clapp, Captain 16th Infantry, Acting United States Indian Agent, June 30, 1897. (Medicine Root District)

Key: Number; Indian Name *(if given)*; English Name; Sex; Relation; Age

3833	Heraka Win; Elk Woman; F; Wife #2; 37	3853	Cicaya Rpaya; Frank Lays Bad; M; Head; 28
3834	Cinpi; Wants Him; F; Wife #1; 48	3854	Anpetu Luta; Red Day; F; Wife; 30
3835	Zintkala Isnala; Lone Bird; M; Son; 9	3855	Lucy Thomas; F; Dau; 2-4
3836	Mato Sapa; Lucy Black Bear; F; Dau; 15	3856	Cicaya Rpaya; Edward Lays Bad; M; Head; 22
3837	Tatanka Gi; Wilson Yellow Bull; M; Head; 36	3857	Canupi Agli; Brings Pipe; F; Wife; 23
3838	Tatanka Gi; Etta Yellow Bull; F; Wife; 31	3858	Cante Witko; Fool Heart; F; Dau; 1-7
3839	Ciwignaka Ska; White Dress; M; Head; 68	3859	Tunweya Ciqqla[sic]; Little Scout; M; Head; 48
3840	Heraka He Wakpa; Elk Horn River; F; Wife; 68	3860	Haipagja Tanka; Big Soap; F; Wife; 48
3841	Winyan Ranran; Scabby Woman; F; Dau; 42	3861	Marpiya Tanka; White Cloud; F; Dau; 9
3842	Wakinla Ska; White Pocket; F; G.Dau; 9	3862	Tatanka Witko; William Crazy Bull; M; Head; 28
3843	Pahin Ska; White Porcupine; F; Head; 76	3863	Tatanka Witko; Nellie Crazy Bull; F; Wife; 29
		3864	Tatanka Witko; May Crazy Bull; F; Dau; 3-4
3844	Winyan Wakan; Kate Holy Breath; F; Head; 31	3865	Tatanka Witko; Narrows Crazy Bull; M; Son; 1-1
3845	Wamniyomni Luzahan; Lucy Fast Whirlwind; F; Niece; 14	3866	Ista Ska; White Eyes; M; Head; 72
3846	Sunka Ciqala; Little Dog; M; Head; 46	3867	Winyan Winurcala; Old Woman; F; Wife; 68
3847	Luta; Red; F; Wife; 55	3868	Yuslutapi; Pulls Out; F; G.Dau; 5-3
3848	Heraka Wakan; Lucy Medicine Elk; F; Dau; 19		
		3869	Tatanka Ite Ska; White Face Bull; M; Head; 49
3849	Cicaya Rpaya; Lays Bad; M; Head; 43	3870	Tasina; Her Blanket; F; Wife; 51
3850	Cicaya Rpaya; Thos. Lays Bad; M; Son; 13	3871	Nata Opi; Wounded Head; M; Head; 36
3851	Cicaya Rpaya; Flora L. Bad; F; Dau; 20	3872	Zintkala Zi; Yellow Bird; F; Wife; 30
3852	Cicaya Rpaya; Jennie L. Bad; F; Dau; 12	3873	Wambli Ota; Plenty Eagle; F; Dau; 8

Census Of The Sioux And Cheyenne Indians Of Pine Ridge Agency, South Dakota. Taken by W. H. Clapp, Captain 16th Infantry, Acting United States Indian Agent, June 30, 1897. (Medicine Root District)

Key: Number; Indian Name *(if given)*; English Name; Sex; Relation; Age

3874	Taista; His Eyes; M; Son; 2-9	3896	Gi; Yellow; F; Head; 45
3875	Bata Opi; William W. Head; M; Son; 12	3897	Hogan Luta; Frank Red Fish; M; Son; 18
		3898	Isnala Kte; Joseph Kills Alone; M; Son; 15
3876	Mato Wamniyomni; Whirlwind Bear; F; Head; 37	3899	Tatanka Gi; Thomas Yellow Bull; M; Head; 29;
3877	Enakiye; She Stops; F; Wife; 32		
3878	Canupa Yuha; Keeps The Pipe; F; Dau; 5-9	3900	Tima Naji; Stands Inside; F; S.Mo; 52
3879	Hinhan Sapa; Black Owl; F; Dau; 1-7	3901	Tatanka Gi; James Yellow Bull; M: Bro; 23
		3902	Tatanka Gi; Lizzie Yellow Bull; F; Sister; 16
3880	Sungmanitu Ska; White Wolf; M; Head; 43		
3881	Wicegna Iyaga; Goes Among Them; F; Wife; 40	3903	Catka; Left Hand; F; Head; 59
3882	Sungmanitu Ska; Rosa White Wolf; F; Dau; 11	3904	Winyan Zi; Yellow Woman; F; Head; 49
3883	Oosica; Hard To Hit; F; M in Law; 85	3905	Akicita Hanska; Sophia Long Soldier; F; Dau; 15
		3906	Akicita Hanska; Rosa Long Soldier; F; Dau; 10
3884	Tatanka Gi; Yellow Bull #2; M; Head; 40		
3885	Tatanka Gi; Julia Y. Bull; F; Wife; 33	3907	Ska; Robert White; M; Head; 25
		3908	Ska; Jessie White; F; Wife; 25
3886	Heraka Wakan; Medicine Elk; M; Son; 6	3909	Marpiya Naji; Charles Standing Cloud; [M]; Head; 21
3887	Tatanka Wakan; Medicine Bull; M; Son; 3-10	3910	Marpiya Naji; Bessie S. Cloud; F; Wife; 24
3888	Wakinyan Gi; Yellow Thunder; M; Head; 61	3911	Huhu Napin; Ellen Bone Necklace; F; Head; 78
3889	Pte San; White Cow; F; Wife; 62		
3890	Wahinyan Gi; Andrew Y. Thunder; M; Son; 19	3912	Ellen Morrison; F; Dau; 28
		3913	Julia Morrison; F; G.Dau; 6
3891	Wahinyan Gi; Brave Y. Thunder; M; Son; 10	3914	Wankal Mato; Red Top Bear; M; Head; 32
3892	Ista Gi; Yellow Eyes; M; Head; 41	3915	Wankal Mato; Jessie Top Bear; F; Wife; 22
3893	Petaga; Coal Of Fire; F; Wife; 42	3916	Wankal Mato; Victoria T. Bear; F; Dau; 2 mo.
3894	Ayutapi; Looks At Him; F; Dau; 7		
3895	Zintkala; Bird; F; Dau; 8	3917	Tasunke Wanica; Has No Horse; M; Head; 21

Census Of The Sioux And Cheyenne Indians Of Pine Ridge Agency, South Dakota. Taken by W. H. Clapp, Captain 16th Infantry, Acting United States Indian Agent, June 30, 1897. (Medicine Root District)

Key: Number; Indian Name *(if given)*; English Name; Sex; Relation; Age

3918 Tasunke Wanica; Julia H. N. Horse; F; Wife; 25
3919 Wacapa; Crandall Stabber; M; Head; 20
3920 Wacapa; Sally Stabber; F; Wife; 19
3921 Wacapa; Louisa Stabber; F; Mother; 46
3922 Wacapa; Paul Stabber; M; Son; 9 mo.

3923 Winyan Ropa; Pretty Woman; F; Head; 39
3924 Anukasan Wanbli; Mable Bald Eagle Bear; F; Dau; 20
3925 Pte San; White Cow; F; Dau; 14
3926 Nakipa; Runs Away; F; Dau; 11
3927 Anukasan Wambli; Katy Baldeagle[sic] Bear; F; Dau; 17
3928 Ista Tanka; Big Eyes; M; Son; 8
3929 Keya; Terrapin; M; Son; 4-3

3930 Winurcala Sica; Bad Old Woman; F; Head; 68
3931 Zuya Gli; Return Warrior; F; Dau; 48
3932 Jessie; F; G.Dau; 19

3933 Nata Rlokeca; Jobson Hollow Head; M; Head; 20
3934 Nata Rlokeca; Fannie Hollow Head; F; Wife; 21
3935 Nata Rlokeca; Stephen Hollow Head; M; Son; 3 mo.

3936 Tasunke Maza; Iron Horse; F; Head; 65

3937 Tatanka Ista; Bull Eye; M; Head; 49
3938 Sagye Luta; Red Rod; F; Wife; 43
3939 Cante Wicasa; Heart Man; M; Son; 11
3940 Wicincala; Girl; F; Dau; 5

3941 Woptura; Jefferson Chips; M; Head; 26
3942 Woptura; Katie Chips; F; Wife; 18

3943 William Pine; M; Head; 30
3944 Wi Hinapa; Rising Sun; F; Wife; 30
3945 Naca; Chief; M; Son; 5-6
3946 Agarota Peno; M; Son; 1-4

3947 Julia Davidson; F; Head; 43
3948 John Davidson; M; Son; 19
3949 William Davidson; M; Son; 17
3950 Emma Davidson; F; Dau; 15
3951 Edward Davidson; M; Son; 10
3952 Annie Davidson; F; Dau; 8
3953 Lalie E. Davidson; F; Dau; 3-2
3954 David Davidson; M; Son; 1-3

3955 Sake Luta; Red Finger Nail; F; Head; 45
3956 Pte San Gli; White Cow Comes Out; F; Dau; 26
3957 Sunk Ska; White Horse; M; Son; 16

3958 Wacicu Ciqala; Little White Man; M; Head; 25
3959 Hinrota Win; Roan Woman; F; Wife; 22

3960 Anpo Toka Kte; Kills Enemy I. T. Morn; M; Head; 30
3961 Tunweya Ciqala; Etta Little Scout; F; Wife; 20

3962 Henry Twist; M; Head; 35
3963 Hektakiya Gli; Comes Back; F; Wife; 36
3964 Louis Twist; M; Son; 16
3965 John Twist; M; Son; 7
3966 Ptesan Wambli; White Cow Eagle; F; Dau; 6
3967 Emma Twist; F; Dau; 2-8

Census Of The Sioux And Cheyenne Indians Of Pine Ridge Agency, South Dakota. Taken by W. H. Clapp, Captain 16th Infantry, Acting United States Indian Agent, June 30, 1897. (Medicine Root District)

Key: Number; Indian Name *(if given)*; English Name; Sex; Relation; Age

3968 Mato Winurcala; Old She Bear; F; Head; 65
3969 Ota Cinpi Win; Wants Them Plenty; F; G.Dau; 2-1
3970 Sungmanitu Peta; John Fire Wolf; M; Head; 22
3971 He Wanica; No Horn; M; Head; 61
3972 Waksica Karleca; Breakes[sic] Dishes; F; Wife; 55
3973 Cetan Ska; White Hawk; M; Son; 16

3974 Nellie Gallagher; F; Head; 23

3975 Julia Clifford; F; Head; 46
3976 Kary Clifford; F; Dau; 12
3977 Lillie Clifford; F; Dau; 10
3978 Rosa Clifford; F; Dau; 20
3979 Hannah Clifford; F; Dau; 19
3980 John Clifford; M; Son; 16
3981 James Clifford; M; Son; 14
3982 Orlando [sic]; M; Son; 24
3983 Joseph Clifford; M; Son; 7
3984 Mortimer Clifford; M; Son; 4-7

3985 Delila Midkiff; F; Head; 26

3986 John Pulliam; M; Head; 28
3987 Lucinda Pulliam; F; Wife; 24
3988 James Pulliam; M; Son; 5-8
3989 Rena Pulliam; F; Dau; 3-8
3990 Amos Pulliam; M; Son; 1-4

3991 Wakinyan Win; Thunder Woman; F; Head; 91

3992 Julia Fisher; F; Head; 39
3993 James Wilde; M; Son; 21
3994 Anna Fisher; F; Dau; 16
3995 Hattie Fisher; F; Dau; 14
3996 Gracie Fisher; F; Dau; 12
3997 Laura Fisher; F; Dau; 5-5

3998 Amanda Fisher; F; Dau; 3-5
3999 Albert Fisher; M; Son; 10
4000 Stanley H. Fisher; M; Son; 1-1
4001 Mato Tatanka Hoksila; Young Bull Bear; M; Head; 43
4002 Peji Rota; Gray Grass; F; Wife; 36
4003 Mato Tatanka; Henry Bull Bear; M; Son; 13
4004 Kahunrpeyapa; Runs Over; F; Dau; 3-4
4005 Kutepi; Shoots At Him; M; Son; 6
4006 Hunska Hinsma; Wooly Leggins; M; Son; 3 mo.

4007 Wicasa Isnala; Lone Man; M; Head; 41
4008 Wambli Luta; Red Eagle; F; Wife; 45
4009 Wambli Luta; Julia Red Eagle; F; Dau; 23
4010 Wambli Luta; Martha Red Eagle; F; Dau; 4-2
4011 Zuya Wastelaka; Loves War; M; Son; 6

4012 Tokicem; Revenger; M; Head; 58
4013 Wambli Paha; Eagle Hill; F; Wife; 52
4014 Mato Tanka; Bull Head; M; Son; 20
4015 Sunkhinto Nupa; Two Blue Horses; F; Dau; 16

4016 Maggie Palmer; F; Head; 49
4017 William Palmer; M; Son; 23
4018 Olive Palmer; F; Dau; 19
4019 Charles Palmer; M; Son; 17
4020 Julia Palmer; F; Dau; 14
4021 Albert Palmer; M; Son; 13

4022 Taylor Palmer; M: Head; 23
4023 Louisa Palmer; F; Wife; 20

Census Of The Sioux And Cheyenne Indians Of Pine Ridge Agency, South Dakota. Taken by W. H. Clapp, Captain 16th Infantry, Acting United States Indian Agent, June 30, 1897. (Medicine Root District)

Key: Number; Indian Name *(if given)*; English Name; Sex; Relation; Age

4024	William Janis; M; Head; 26	
4025	Mable Janis; F; Wife; 27	
4026	Wilson Janis; M; Son; 2-8	
4027	Thomas Janis; M; Son; 4 mo.	
4028	Tainyan Yanka; Sits In Sight; F; Head; 31	
4029	Taku Oli; Hunts For Something; M; Son; 3 mo.	
4030	John Mesteth; M; Head; 21	
4031	Amanda Marshall; F; Wife; 28	
4032	Alice Mesteth; F; Dau; 4-2	
4033	George Mesteth; M; Son; 1-2	
4034	Wambli Iyotaka; Sitting Eagle; M; Head; 48	
4035	Wasu Peta; Nail Fire; F; Wife; 37	
4036	Marpiya Wakita; Looking Cloud; M; Head; 45	
4037	Wazi Luta; Red Pine; F; Wife; 40	
4038	Glogli; Brings Her Own; M; Son; 6	
4039	Peyozan; Isaac Parts His Hair; M; Head; 45	
4040	Nite Waste; Maggie Pretty Back; F; Wife; 25	
4041	Peyozan; Ada Parts His Hair; F; Sister; 9	
4042	Ista Sa; Elmore Red Eyes; M; Head; 21	
4043	Mato Ite Waste; Mollie Pretty F. Bear; F; Wife; 17	
4044	Waokiya; Helps (Joseph); M; Head; 19	
4045	Wambli Wakuwa; Eliza Charging Eagle; F; Wife; 17	
4046	Maka Mahel Mani; Jacob Walks U. Ground; M; Head; 27	
4047	Tokeya Kte; Kills First; M; Head; 22
4048	Conica Wamica; Bert No Flesh; M; Head; 22
4049	Waniyetu Wicakte; Thos. Kills In Winter; M; Head; 41
4050	Rante Maza; Iron Cedar; F; Wife; 34
4051	Waniyetu Wicakte; Jessie K. In Winter; F; Dau; 14
4052	Waniyetu Wicakte; Lizzie K. In Winter; F; Dau; 9
4053	Nape Kicaksapi; Cut Hand; M; Son; 5-8
4054	Tatanka Ciqala; Henry Little Bull; M; Head; 20
4055	Mato Sapa; Ida Black Bear; F; Wife 24
4056	Mato Wakan; Medicine Bear #2; F; Head; 50
4057	Wicayajipa; Hornet; F; Mother; 80
4058	James; M; Nephew; 19
4059	Wakita; Looks Things; F; Nephew; 14
4060	Heraka Sica; Julia Bad Elk; G; Head; 23
4061	Walter Garrier; M: Head; 38
4062	Heraka Wakan; Joshua Medicine Elk; M; Head; 20
4063	Ite Ranran; Sore Face; F; Wife; 19
4064	Tasunke Inyanka; George Running Horse; M; Head; 26
4065	Sophia Somorrow[sic]; F; Wife; 20
4066	Sophia R. Horse; F; Dau; 11 mo.

Census Of The Sioux And Cheyenne Indians Of Pine Ridge Agency, South Dakota. Taken by W. H. Clapp, Captain 16th Infantry, Acting United States Indian Agent, June 30, 1897. (Medicine Root District)

Key: Number; Indian Name *(if given)*; English Name; Sex; Relation; Age

4067 Orankoya Mani; Thos. Walks Fast; M; Head; 19
4068 Heraka Wambli; Alice Eagle Elk; F; Wife; 17

4069 John Monroe; M; Head; 28
4070 Sophia Monroe; F; Wife; 33
4071 Aloyasus Monroe; M; Son; 2-1
4072 Lottie Monroe; F; Dau; 1-2

4073 Peji; John Grass; M; Head; 35
4074 Mato Waci; Dancing Bear; F; Wife; 34
4075 Tasunke Opi; Shot Her Horses; F; Dau; 5

4076 Louisa Girard; F; Head
4077 Belmore Girard; F; Dau; 5-6
4078 Ethel J. Girard; F; Dau; 3-2
4079 Amburu R. Girard; M; Son; 6mo.

Census of the Sioux And Cheyenne Indians
Of Pine Ridge Agency, South Dakota.
June 30, 1897

White Clay District

Census Of The Sioux And Cheyenne Indians Of Pine Ridge Agency, South Dakota. Taken by W. H. Clapp, Captain 16th Infantry, Acting United States Indian Agent, June 30, 1897. (White Clay District)

Key: Number; Indian Name *(if given)*; English Name; Sex; Relation; Age

4080 Tasunke Kokipapi; Young Man Afraid; M; Head; 58
4081 Hu Peji; Hay Leg; F; Wife; 43
4082 Minnie; F; Dau; 20
4083 Okicize; Battle; M; Son; 15
4084 Akanyaka; Rider; M; Son; 12
4085 Ehake gli[sic]; Comes Last; M; Son; 6
4086 Tasunke Kokipapi; Geo. Young Man Afraid; M; Son; 1-11
4087 Tasunke Maza; Iron Horse; F; Head; 72
4088 Tawaste; Her Good Thing; F; G.Dau; 20
4089 Cetan Iyanka; Running Hawk; M; Head; 47
4090 Carli; Powder; F; Wife; 44
4091 Onjinjinkta; Rosebud; M; Son; 15
4092 Nawicakinjin; Defender; M; Son; 18
4093 Mazakan Icu; Takes The Gun; M; Nephew; 181
4094 Kokipeya Kte; Kills With Fear; M; Cousin; 20
4095 Witko Win; Foolish Woman; F; M. in Law; 81
4096 Taopi; Wounded Morris; M; Head; 38
4097 Iyape Najin; Stands Aside; F; Wife; 30
4098 Kihuni; On Arrival; F; Dau; 8
4099 Zintkala Luta; Red Bird; M; Son; 4
4100 Wakpala Ciqala; Little Creek; M; Son; 2-2
4101 Taopi; Bessie Wounded; F; Dau; 1 mo.
4102 Tatanke[sic] Ciqala; Little Bull #1; M; Head; 45
4103 Winyan Waste; Pretty Woman; F; Wife; 47
4104 Sunkicu; Takes The Horse; F; Dau; 18
4105 Siyo Witko; Fool Grouse; F; M. in Law; 78
4106 Wanbli; Eagle; F; Head; 41
4107 Psakte; Kills Crow; F; Dau; 17
4108 Sinye Tonka; Big Tail; F; Dau; 14
4109 Ite Maza; Iron Face; F; Dau; 8
4110 Tatanka Slasla; Hairless Bull; M; Son; 4
4111 Ptehinsa; Calf Robe; M; Head; 69
4112 Canku Waste; Good Road; F; Wife; 63
4113 Zuya Wicakte; Kills Warrior; M; G.Son; 9
4114 Wayanknajin; Looks And Kills; M; Son; 28
4115 Cega Sapa; Black Kettle; M; Head; 47
4116 Pehinji; Yellow Hair; F; Wife; 42
4117 Wiyaka Zi; Yellow Feather; M; Son; 15
4118 Wasu; Hail; F; Dau; 15
4119 Sina Wakan; Holy Blanket; M; Son; 2-1
4120 Awicakicisa; Shout For; M; Son; 21
4121 Otakuye Ota; Plenty Relation; F; G.Mo; 62
4122 Ptan Win; Otter Woman; F; G.Dau; 3 mo.
4123 Pehinji Sica; Bad Yellow Hair; M: Head; 63
4124 Tatiyopa Wakan; Her Holy Door; F; Wife; 51
4125 Kangi Ciqala; Little Crow; M; Son; 27
4126 Sunkhin Sa; Red Haired Horse; M; Son; 20

Census Of The Sioux And Cheyenne Indians Of Pine Ridge Agency, South Dakota. Taken by W. H. Clapp, Captain 16th Infantry, Acting United States Indian Agent, June 30, 1897. (White Clay District)

Key: Number; Indian Name *(if given)*; English Name; Sex; Relation; Age

4127 Jijila; Yellow Yellow; F; Dau; 12
4128 Pehinji; Asa Yellow Hair; M; Son; 9
4129 Wiyurloka; Bores A Hole; F; Head; 36
4130 Itonkasan; Weasel; F; Wife; 38
4131 Wahosigli; Comes And Tells; M; Son; 10
4132 Ciqala; Little; M; Son; 7
4133 Sina Luta; Red Blanket; M; Head; 42
4134 Ptesan Wambli; White Cow Eagle; F; Wife; 29
4135 Pehinji Sica; Bad Yellow Hair; M; Son; 11 mo.
4136 Tasunke; Her Horse; F; Head; 50
4137 Canli; Adam Tobacco; M; Son; 23
4138 Awokasan Waste; Good Bald Eagle; M; Head; 40
4139 Winyan Hanska; Long Woman; F; Wife; 40
4140 Hektakiya gli; Returned; M; Son; 1-4
4141 Kangi Mni Eyeca; Crow Lacks Water; M; Head; 46
4142 Oko Sba Win; Ringing Crack; F; Wife; 45
4143 Hinsma; Hair; F; Dau; 20
4144 Pehin Sa; Red Hair; F; Dau; 16
4145 Op Iyayaya; Goes With Them; F; Dau; 5
4146 Charlie; M; Son; 8 mo.
4147 Sunka Glakinyan; Cross Dog; M; Head; 67
4148 Pejuta; Medicine; F; Wife; 51
4149 Canku Terila; Loves His Road; M; Son; 23
4150 Winyan Ota; Plenty Woman; F; Dau; 11
4151 Wakan Hiyaya; Goes Holy; F; Dau; 42
4152 Kutepi; Shoots Him; F; G.Dau; 8
4153 Wakpamnila; Distribution #1; M; Head; 40
4154 Piya Icaga; Lives Again; F; Wife; 38
4155 Wakinyan Win; Thunder Woman; F; Dau; 21
4156 Zintkala To; Blue Bird; F; Dau; 23
4157 Najinhan Ku; Comes Standing; F; Dau; 3
4158 Tikanyela Wakuwa; Charges Close To Lodge; F; Wife; 85
4159 Waniyetu Wakuwa; Chase In Winter; M; Head; 45
4160 Tasunke Ota; Plenty Horse; F; Wife; 42
4161 Tasunke Maza; Iron Horse; M; Son; 13
4162 Hu; Leg; F; Dau; 16
4163 Sunka Yuha; Ownes[sic] The Dog; F; Dau; 11
4164 Winyan Ciqala; Little Woman; F; Dau; 6
4165 Wamniomni Wicasa; Whirlwind Man; M; Head; 40
4166 Winyan Tokca; Different Woman; F; Wife; 44
4167 Warpa Tanka; Black Bird; M; G.Son; 5
4168 Kokipesni Kte; Kills Without Fear; M; Son; 22
4169 Anukasan; Bald Eagle; M; Head; 25
4170 Winyan Ciqala Waste; Little Good Woman; F; Wife; 20

Census Of The Sioux And Cheyenne Indians Of Pine Ridge Agency, South Dakota.
Taken by W. H. Clapp, Captain 16th Infantry, Acting United States Indian Agent,
June 30, 1897. (White Clay District)

Key: Number; Indian Name *(if given)*; English Name; Sex; Relation; Age

4171 Glohi; Brings With; F; Dau; 3 mo.
4172 Sinte Maza; Iron Tail; M; Head; 37
4173 Sunkhinsa; Red Horse; F; Wife; 40
4174 Sinte Maza; Philip Iron Tail; M; Son; 17
4175 Ojanyan Win; Light Woman; F; Dau; 5
4176 Nawizisa Win; Jealous Woman; F; Dau; 3
4177 Wamniomni Tasunke; Whirlwind Horse; M; Head; 35
4178 Tipi Maza; Iron Lodge; F; Wife; 31
4179 Mniotumpi; Borne In Water; F; Dau; 15
4180 Wambli Sun; Eagle Feather; F; Dau; 6
4181 Joe W. Horse; M; Son; 3 mo.
2182[sic] Ktonaunka; Running Loper; F; Head; 64
4183 Winyan Luta; Red Woman; F; G.Dau; 9

4184 Anposkan Tunpi; Day Birth; F; Head; 57
4185 Zuyala; Warrior; F; G.Dau; 18
4186 Mato Maza; Iron Bear; M; Head; 35
4187 Ite Wambli; Eagle Face; F; Wife; 27
4188 Tokeya Kte; Kills First; M; Son; 11
4189 Nupa Kinajin; Two Stands; M; Son; 61
4190 Captecela; Steps Short; M; Son; 2-5
4191 Ptanwin; Otter; F; Dau; 9 mo.

4192 Nuge Wanica; Jno. No Ears; M; Head; 44
4193 Winyan Sapa; Black Woman; F; Wife; 43
4194 Susie; F; Dau; 19
4195 Wambli Ska; White Eagle; M; Son; 15
4196 Tasina Wambli; Eagle Shawl; F; Dau; 6
4197 Pejuta Hinapa; Medicine Out; F; Head; 25
4198 Jola; Whistler; M; Head; 65
4199 Winurcala Sica; Little Old Woman; F; G.Dau; 18
4200 Pehinji Win; Yellow Head Woman; F; Head; 68
4201 Naca; Chief; M; G.Son; 12
4202 Tatanka Hanska; Long Bull; M; Head; 48
4203 Pehinji; Yellow Hair; F; Wife; 47
4204 Mniowicakte; Kills In Water; M; Son; 16
4205 James; M; Nephew; 16
4206 Ticagla Inyanka; Jos. Runs Close To Lodge; M; Head; 32
4207 Wasusna Win; Rattling Hail; F; Dau; 5
4208 Mato Wamniomni; Whirlwind Bear; M; Son; 1-4
4209 Najinyapa; Surrounded; M; Head; 31
4210 Mniyatkan; Drinks Water; F; Wife; 21
4211 Rante Win; Cedar Woman; F; Dau; 5
4212 Mato Hoksila; Bear Boy; M; Son; 3-2
4213 Tonka Win; Good Rock; F; Dau; 9 mo.

Census Of The Sioux And Cheyenne Indians Of Pine Ridge Agency, South Dakota.
Taken by W. H. Clapp, Captain 16th Infantry, Acting United States Indian Agent,
June 30, 1897. (White Clay District)

Key: Number; Indian Name *(if given)*; English Name; Sex; Relation; Age

4214	Maha Luta Win; Red Clay Woman; F; Dau; 9 mo.	4236	Wambli Nupa; Two Eagle; M; Head; 54
4215	Huwegahan; Broken Leg; M; Head; 43	4237	Sunkakan Win; Horse Woman; F; Wife; 49
4216	Wicoti Yuha; Ownes[sic] Village; F; Wife; 39	4238	Isna Kte; Kills Alone; M; Son; 24
4217	Wakan Gli; Comes Holy; M; Son; 20	4239	Wawanganka; Keeps Guard; M; Son; 10
4218	Tatanka Hotanin Mani; Bull Noise Walking; M; Son; 10	4240	Mani Ku; Comes Walking; F; Dau; 7
4219	Hu Wegahan; Mary Broken Leg; F; Dau; 2-2	4241	Itazipa Kicun; Uses His Bow; M; Son; 3-3
		4242	Janjanyela; Clear; M; Head; 37
4220	Mato Huhu; Bear Bone; M; Head; 45	4243	Sina Icu; Takes Robe; F; Wife; 31
4221	Wiciyela Win; Yankton Woman; F; Wife; 31	4244	Blotahunka Win; Leader; F; Dau; 12
		4245	Sunk Wicaqu; Gives Horses; F; Dau; 7
4222	Wiyaka Luta; Red Feather; M; Head; 38	4246	Wayank Hipi; Comes To See Him; F; Dau; 3
4223	Tasina; Her Blanket; F; Wife; 38	4247	Wicarpi Wakan; Holy Star; M; Son; 4 mo.
4224	Tasunke Ota; Plenty Horses; F; Dau; 17		
4225	Wiyaka Luta; Della B. Red Feather; F; Dau; 11	4248	Edward Brown; M: Head; 23
4226	Teriya Kte; Kills Hard; F; Dau; 6		
4227	Wasicu Kte; Kills White Man; M; Son; 4	4249	Guciya; Paints Yellow; M; Head; 59
4228	Anpo Wicakute; Shoots In the Morning; [M]; Son; 9 da.	4250	Ite Ska; White Face; F; Wife; 55[?]
		4251	Mato Hinrota; Roan Bear; F; Dau; 31
4229	Cahlie[sic] Smith; M; Head; 31		
4230	Susie Smith; F; Wife; 36	4252	Wicincala Waste; Good Girl; F; G.Dau; 10
4231	Ptesanha Sina; White Cow Robe; F; S.Dau; 17	4253	Ptesan; White Cow; F; G.Dau; 6
		4254	Tasunke Opi; Wounded Horse; M; G.Son; 1-8
4232	Tasina Sapa; Black Shawl; F; Head; 45		
		4255	Parugahan; Broken Nose; M; Head; 27
4233	Sungmanitu Wakuwa; Charging Wolf; M; Head; 36	4256	Tokala; Fox; F; Wife; 26
4234	Tahu Rmi; Crooked Neck; F; Wife; 24	4257	Cetan Hotanka; Loud Voice Hawk; M; B. in Law; 28
4235	Wambli Yatapika; Chief Eagle; M; Bro.; 29	4258	Canupa; Pipe; M; Nephew; 9

Census Of The Sioux And Cheyenne Indians Of Pine Ridge Agency, South Dakota. Taken by W. H. Clapp, Captain 16th Infantry, Acting United States Indian Agent, June 30, 1897. (White Clay District)

Key: Number; Indian Name *(if given)*; English Name; Sex; Relation; Age

4259 Kicaksa; Knocks In Two; M; Son; 4
4260 Dick; M; Son; 10 mo.
4261 Nata Tanka; Big Head; M: Head; 58
4262 Tokeya Hinapa; Comes Out First; F; Wife; 51
4263 Hektakiya Ekta; Kills Back; F; Dau; 23
4264 Ohitika; Brave; M; Son; 20
4265 Marpiya Ciqala; Little Cloud; M; Head; 36
4266 Tasunke Najin; Standing Horse; F; Wife; 35
4267 Marpiya Ciqala; Loomis L. Cloud; M; Son; 4 mo.
4268 Mato Shambla; Dreaming Bear; M; Head; 30
4269 Slecahan; Ella Spits; F; Wife; 22
4270 Wakan Hiyaya; Goes Holy; F; Dau; 1-10
4271 Tarca Nite; Deer Rump; M: Head; 75
4272 Winyan Luta; Red Woman; F; Wife; 55
4273 Re Ska; Rocky Mountain; M; Head; 45
4274 Maka Papta; Shovels Ground; F; Wife; 55
4275 Zuya Tasunke; War Horse; M; Son; 14
4276 Wankal Etonwa; Looks Up; F; M. in L.; 91
4277 Termuga Luta; Red Fly; M; Head; 79
4278 Katiyeyapi; Shot Him; F; Wife; 59
4279 Inupa; Two Months; F; Dau; 14
4280 Mato Nakpa; Bear Ear; M; F. in L.; 75

4281 Heraka Tamakeca; Poor Elk; M; Head 44
4282 Tahunska Waste; Good Leggins; F; Wife; 49
4283 Heraka Tamaheca[sic]; Marting[sic] Poor Elk; M: Son; 20
4284 Si Wanica; No Foot; M; Son; 14
4285 Tasunke Nupa; Two Horses; F; Dau; 7
4286 Wakpaminala; Distribution #2; M; Head; 26
4287 Mila Tanka; Butcher Knife; F; Wife; 20
4288 Tonkanwin; Rock Woman; F; Dau; 3
4289 Wajaja; Wajaja; F; Head; 85
4290 Waste; Good; F; Sister; 75
4291 Nape Wikacemna; Ten Fingers; M; Head; 38
4292 Wapaha; War Bonnet; F; Wife; 30
4293 Toka Ole; Looks For Enemy; M; Son; 16
4294 Tokeya Kte; Kills First; M; Son; 9
4295 Okicize Yuha; Keeps The Battle; M; Son; 6
4296 Harnir Kte; Takes Out And Kills; F; Dau; 12
4297 Tiyata Wota; Eats At Home; F; Dau; 3
4298 Tokeya Kte; Kills First #2; M; Son; 1-5
4299 Paorpa; Breaks In; M; Head; 75
4300 Rante Luta; Red Cedar; F; Wife; 62
4301 Hektakiya Ekte; Kills Back; M; G.Son; 16
4302 Tasunke Opi; Wounded Horse; M; G.Son; 14

Census Of The Sioux And Cheyenne Indians Of Pine Ridge Agency, South Dakota. Taken by W. H. Clapp, Captain 16th Infantry, Acting United States Indian Agent, June 30, 1897. (White Clay District)

Key: Number; Indian Name *(if given)*; English Name; Sex; Relation; Age

4303 Zintkala Hinsna; James Hairy Bird; M; Head; 33
4304 Winyan Sica; Bad Woman; F; Wife; 28
4305 Anpo Wicakte; Kills In T. Morning; F; Dau; 1-11

4306 Tasunke Najin; Standing Horse; F; Head; 66
4307 Sina Glegkega; Spotted Blanket; F; Dau; 21
4308 Canupa Wakan; Medicine Pipe; F; G.Dau; 8

4309 Wakte Gli; Kills And Comes Back; M; Head; 27
4310 Tacanku; Her Road; F; Wife; 22
4311 Tasunke Mani; Walking Horse; F; Dau; 8 mo.

4312 Heyaka Tasunke; Clown Horse; M; Head; 54
4313 Canku Waste; Good Road; F; Wife; 50
4314 Nupkte; Kills Two; M; Son; 19
4315 Tipi Luta; Red Lodge; F; Dau; 15
4316 Pa Opi; Wounded Nose; M; Son; 4-6

4317 Wicarpi Luta; Red Star; M; Head; 48
4318 Ptehincala Win; Calf Woman; F; Wife; 35
4319 Wan Kicun; Used Arrow; M; Son; 9
4320 Iyuha Wicaku; Gives All; M; Son; 4
4321 Anukasan; Bald Eagle; M; Son; 1-3

4322 Winyan Wakan; Holy Woman; F; Head; 69
4323 Oeciglaka; Tells Herself; F; Dau; 49

4324 Wambli Waste; Good Eagle; F; Niece; 6

4325 Maka Cincala; Young Skunk; M; Head; 30
4326 Wamniomni; Whirlwind; F; Wife; 34
4327 Anpetu; Day; F; Dau; 12
4328 Mnikokte; Kills In Water; F; Dau; 7
4329 Nica Ole; Looks For None; F; Dau; 4 mo.

4330 Mato Canwegna; Bear Runs In T. Wood; M; Head; 52
4331 Wasu Ska; White Hail; F; Wife; 40
4332 Wicincala Hanska; Tall Girl; F; Dau; 16
4333 Wicakute; Sharles[sic] Shooter; M; Son; 10
4334 Anunwan; Swim For; M; Son; 5

4335 Tezi Yurlecapi; Torn Belly; M; Head; 69
4336 Wahukeza; Lance; F; Wife; 55
4337 Wakinyan Marpiya; Cloud Thunder; M; Son; 23
4338 Toka Icu; Takes Enemy; F; Dau; 35
4339 Toka Wicakte; Kills The Enemy; F; G.Dau; 6

4340 Saste; Little Finger; M; Head; 24
4341 Nawizi; Jealous; F; Wife; 26
4342 Tiwegna Iyanka; Runs Through Camp; F; Dau; 2-3

4343 Wapaha Ciqala; Little War Bonnet; M; Head; 61
4344 Topla; Four Times; F; Wife #1; 53
4345 Ranhi Win; Slow Woman; F; Wife #2; 51
4346 Wapaha Ciqala; Alice Little War B.; Dau; 20

Census Of The Sioux And Cheyenne Indians Of Pine Ridge Agency, South Dakota. Taken by W. H. Clapp, Captain 16th Infantry, Acting United States Indian Agent, June 30, 1897. (White Clay District)

Key: Number; Indian Name *(if given)*; English Name; Sex; Relation; Age

4347 Wapaha Ciqala; Jesse L.W. Bonnet; M; Son; 20
4348 Wapaha Ciqala; Dolly L.W. Bonnet; F; Dau; 8
4349 Wambli Hinapa; Eagle Out; F; Dau; 30
4350 Onpan Howaste; Good Voice Elk; M; Son; 3 mo.
4351 Wapostan Luta; Red Hat; F; Head; 45
4352 Heraka Bloka; Peter Male Elk; M; Son; 17
4353 Pehan Zi; Nettie Yellow Crane; F; Dau; 10
4354 Tankal Ti; Living Outside; M; Head; 41
4355 Canupa; Pipe; F; Wife; 42
4356 Toka Wicakte; Kills Enemy; M; Son; 12
4357 Pankeska Ota; Plenty Shell; F; Dau; 8
4358 Sungmanitu Sica; Bad Wolf; M; Son; 5
4359 Susie; F; Dau; 1-4
4360 Rabya; Scares; M; Head; 20
4361 Tiotawin; Sight Of Lodge; F; Wife; 22
4362 Tasunke Hotan; Howling Horse; M; Head; 48
4363 Ptesan; White Cow; F; Wife; 32
4364 Cekiyapi; Prays For Her; F; Dau; 5
4365 Oye Luta; Red Track; F; Head; 38
4366 Wicegna Iyanka; Runs Among Them; F; Dau; 10
4367 Canowicakte; Kills In Wood; F; Dau; 5-3
4368 Wahukeza Kicun; Uses Her Lance; F; Dau; 1-11
4369 OtaAGli[sic]; Brings Plenty; F; Head; 34
4370 Toka Waste; Good Enemy; F; Dau; 6
4371 Pteyuha Najin; Herder; M; Son; 3-6
4372 Huocan; Tree Leg; M; Head; 39
4373 Wamniomni Sapa; Black Whirlwind; F; Wife; 36
4374 Emma Carson; F; Dau; 17
4375 Lizzie Carson; F; Dau; 14
4376 Wazi; Pine; F; Dau; 6
4377 Wicarpi Hinapa; Star Comes Out; M; Head; 22
4378 Tasina Waste; Her Good Blanket; F; Wife; 20
4379 Aiyapi; Talks About Him; F; Mother; 59
4380 Wazi; Pine; M; Bro; 18
4381 Tainyan Hinapa; Comes Out In Sight; F; Niece; 9
4382 Wicarpi Hinapa; Willie S. C. Out; M; Son; 3 weeks
4383 Marpiya Wakan; Holy Cloud; M; Head; 47
4384 Winyan Tanka; Big Woman; F; Wife; 64
4385 Marpiya Wakan; Isaac Holy Cloud; M; Son; 18
4386 Heraka Mani; Walking Elk; M; Head; 35
4387 Toka Kte; Kills Enemy; F; Wife; 33
4388 Tacanupa Ota; Her Plenty Pipe; F; Dau; 13
4389 Majel Icupi; Takes Him In; M; Son; 10
4390 Nupa Kte; Kills Twice; F; Dau; 5
4391 Sina Kute; Shoots Blanket; M; Son; 7

Census Of The Sioux And Cheyenne Indians Of Pine Ridge Agency, South Dakota. Taken by W. H. Clapp, Captain 16th Infantry, Acting United States Indian Agent, June 30, 1897. (White Clay District)

Key: Number; Indian Name *(if given)*; English Name; Sex; Relation; Age

4392 Pizo; Gall; M; Head; 67
4393 Winula; Winona; F; Wife; 45
4394 Mato glasla[sic]; Shaving Bear; M; Son; 20
4395 Mato Luta; Red Bear; F; Dau; 15
4396 Pankeska Win; Shell Woman; F; Head; 65
4397 Wagmu Su; Pumpkin Seed; M; G.Son; 8
4398 Istimata; Sound Sleeper; M; Head; 54
4399 Wicarpi Win; Star Woman; F; Wife; 48
4400 Najinhan Kte; Kills Standing; M; Son; 11
4401 Ptehincala Ska; White Calf; M; Head; 40
4402 Sunk Sapa; Black Horse; F; Wife; 32
4403 Ista Gi; Brown Eyes; M; Son; 18
4404 Canupa Wakan; Holy Pipe; F; Dau; 15
4405 Heraka Isnala; Lone Elk; M; Son; 10
4406 Pejuta Win; Medicine Woman; F; M. in Law; 85
4407 Oturan; Gives Away; F; Dau; 4-4
4408 Frank; M; Son; 2 mo.
4409 Wanbli Waste; Pretty Eagle; M; Head; 48
4410 Nite; Back; M; Head; 58
4411 Wahaparpa; Scrapes The Hide; F; Wife; 57
4412 Pankeska; Shell; F; Dau; 23
4413 Wanbli; W[sic] Eagle; M; Son; 19
4414 Marpiya Ciqala; James Little Cloud; M; Head; 57
4415 Anpetu; Day; F; Wife; 58

4416 Wazi; Pine; F; Dau; 14
4417 Warpe To; Green Leaf; F; Dau; 8
4418 Pehin Sapa; Black Hair; M; Head; 39
4419 Akicita Ota; Plenty Soldier; F; Wife; 23
4420 Mastincala Ska; White Rabbit; M; Son; 6 mo.
4421 Tarca Win; Deer Woman; F; Head; 58
4422 Kokipa; Afraid; F; G.Dau; 4
4423 Ticagla Kte; Kills At Lodge; M; Head; 32
4424 Agli; Brings; F; Wife; 30
4425 Zintkala; Jay Bird; F; Dau; 1-2
4426 Mato Istima; Sleeping Bear; M; Head; 40
4427 Tasina Zi; Her Yellow Blanket; F; Wife; 52
4428 Mato Tokahe; Bear Leader; M; Son; 9
4429 Kahinrpeya; Rides Over; M; Son; 12
4430 Tahu Maza; Iron Neck; F; Head; 72
4431 Mato Ruwinmna; Stinking Bear; M; Head; 50
4432 Tarca Hinapa; Deer Goes Out; F; Wife; 50
4433 Najinyapi; Surrounded; M; Son; 27
4434 Gleska Agli; Brings Spotted; F; Dau; 17
4435 Mato Ska; White Bear; M; Son; 13
4436 Sota Win; Smoke Woman; F; Head; 36

Census Of The Sioux And Cheyenne Indians Of Pine Ridge Agency, South Dakota.
Taken by W. H. Clapp, Captain 16th Infantry, Acting United States Indian Agent,
June 30, 1897. (White Clay District)

Key: Number; Indian Name *(if given)*; English Name; Sex; Relation; Age

4437 Kiyan Win; Flying Woman; F; G.Mo; 65
4438 Rlo Kiyapi; Makes Growl; M; Son; 16
4439 Kokipeya Kte; Kills Afraid; M; Son; 14
4440 Ninglicu; Come Alice; M; Son; 9
4441 Pehin Wankatuya; High Crane; M; Head; 23
4442 Ptehincala Win; Calf Woman; F; Wife; 22
4443 Itunkasan Win; Weasel Woman; F; Dau; 1-11
4444 Timahel Mani; Walks In Lodge; F; Dau; 1 mo.
4445 Mato Ska; White Bear; M; Head; 45
4446 Napetu; Day; F; Wife; 37
4447 Pahi; Picks; M; Son; 15
4448 Hoksila; Boy; M; Son; 6
4449 Kokipapi; Afraid Of Him; M; Head; 20
4450 Ota Kte; Kills Plenty; F; Wife; 21
4451 Cega Ogle; Joe Kettle Coat; M; Head; 55
4452 Tacanku Ota; Her Plenty Road; F; Wife; 57
4453 Tasunke; Her Horse; F; Wife; 60
4454 Sungmanitu Sapa; Black Wolf #1; M; Head; 61
4455 Anpetu; Day; F; Wife; 64
4456 Wahacanka Icu; Takes Shield; M; Son; 25
4457 Iyapi Tawa; Her Talk; F; Dau; 21
4458 Can Mazakan; Wooden Gun; M; Head; 48
4459 Winyan Ptecela; Short Woman; F; Wife; 50
4460 Ite Nupa; Two Faces; M; Head; 35
4461 Tasunke Hinapa; Horse Comes Out; F; Wife; 34
4462 Ninwicaya; Saves The Life; M; Son; 7
4463 Winyan Kte; Kills Woman; F; Dau; 10
4464 Anatan; Runs At Him; M; Son; 5
4465 Kiyela Iyanka; Runs Close; M; Son; 10 mo.
4466 Wasicu Mato; American Bear; M; Head; 68
4467 Capignuke Maza; Iron Trap; F; Wife; 50
4468 Wasicu Ota; Plenty White Man; F; Dau; 21
4469 Wicasa Yatapi; Philip Chief Man; M; Son; 17
4470 Icanyan Iyanka; Runs Against; M; G.Son; 5
4471 Toka Oyuspa; Catches Enemy; F; G.Dau; 1-4
4472 Canupa Pegnaka; Pipe On Head; M; Head; 56
4473 Apepi; Wait For Him; F; Wife; 46
4474 Si Tanka; Big Foot; M; Son; 15
4475 Witko Win; Foolish Woman; F; Mo.; 75
4476 Tipi Wankatuya; High Lodge; M; Head; 71
4477 Jola; Whistler; F; Dau; 45
4478 Ohitika; Charles Brave #2; M; Head; 27
4479 Teriya Ku; Comes Hard; F; Wife; 24

Census Of The Sioux And Cheyenne Indians Of Pine Ridge Agency, South Dakota. Taken by W. H. Clapp, Captain 16th Infantry, Acting United States Indian Agent, June 30, 1897. (White Clay District)

Key: Number; Indian Name *(if given)*; English Name; Sex; Relation; Age

4480	Mato Kawinga; Turning Bear; M; Head; 59
4481	Marpiya Sapa; Black Cloud; F; Wife; 53
4482	Wiyaka Win; Feather Woman; F; Dau; 30
4483	Okicize Yuha; Ownes[sic] Flight; M; Son; 18
4484	Marpiya Wicasa; Cloud Man; M; Head; 40
4485	Wahacanka Waste; Good Shield; F; Wife; 42
4486	Zintkala Koyaka; Wears The Bird; F; Dau; 7
4487	Amapsica; Jumps Over Me; F; M. in Law; 70
4488	Luzahan; Fast; M; Head; 32
4489	He Luta; Red Horse; F; Wife; 33
4490	Tokeya; First; M; Son; 10
4491	Ticagla Kte; Kills At Lodge; F; Dau; 8;
4492	Toka Kte; Kills Enemy; F; Dau; 6
4493	Toka Kinwa; Charges Enemy; M; Head; 30
4494	Taopi Ota; Plenty Wound; M; Bro.; 19
4495	Toka Wicaki; Takes Away From Enemy; M; Bro.; 17
4496	Ite Waste; Good Face; F; Mo.; 55
4497	Tatanka Nata; Bull Head; F; Head; 45
4498	Pte Wakan; Holy Cow; F; Dau; 19
4499	Onpan Win; Elk Woman; F; Dau; 10
4500	Winorcala; Old Woman; F; Mo.; 88
4501	Isnala Kte; Kills Alone; M; Head; 25
4502	Wicegna Glicu; Comes From Among Them; [F]; Wife; 24
4503	Zintkala Wanbli; Eagle Bird; M; Son; 1-9
4504	Taninyan Najin; Stands In Sight; F; Dau; 1-9
4505	Pahin; Porcupine; M; Head; 40
4506	Hunska Sasa; Red Socks; F; Wife; 34
4507	Kutepi; Shot At; M; Son; 11
4508	Iya Wakan; Talks Holy; F; Dau; 5
4509	Zintkala Wambli; Eagle Bird; M; Son; 3 mo.
4510	Mani; Walking; F; Head; 61
4511	Kiwoksapi; Shot In Two; M; Son; 17
4512	Nup Karpa; Drops Two; M; Head; 31
4513	Wanbli Sica; Bad Eagle; F; Niece; 4
4514	Winyan Waste; Good Woman; F; Mo.; 50
4515	Winorcala; Old Woman; F; G.Mo.; 74
4516	Niyapi; Makes Alive; F; Sister; 22
4517	Akicita Waste; Good Soldier; M; Head; 29
4518	Naca Win; Chief Woman; F; Wife; 25
4519	Ptesan Yatapi; Chief White Cow; F; Dau; 5-6
4520	Hoksila; Boy; M; Son; 4
4521	Psa Kte; Kills Crow; M; Head; 26
4522	Winyan Ska; White Woman; F; Wife; 20
4523	Itunkasan; Weasel; F; Dau; 9mo.

Census Of The Sioux And Cheyenne Indians Of Pine Ridge Agency, South Dakota. Taken by W. H. Clapp, Captain 16th Infantry, Acting United States Indian Agent, June 30, 1897. (White Clay District)

Key: Number; Indian Name *(if given)*; English Name; Sex; Relation; Age

4524	Hoksila Luta; Red Boy; M; Head; 39	4547	Tainyan Najin Win; Woman In Light; F; Wife; 64
4525	Tankal Najin; Stands Outside; F; Wife; 39	4548	Okawinr Iyanka; Runs Around; M; Son; 33
4526	Hoksila Luta; George Red Boy; M; Son; 2-4	4549	Sunk Ska Win; White Horse Woman; F; Dau; 20
4527	Timahel Yanka; Sists[sic] In Lodge; F; Head; 50	4550	Kici Rpaya; Sleeps With Him; M; Head; 35
4528	Hiyuiciya; Dismount; M; Son; 16	4551	Capa Win; Beaver Woman; F; Wife; 31
4529	Slohan Ku; Comes Crawling; M; Son; 12	4552	Tasunke Ska; His White Horse; M; Son; 4-6
4530	Psica; Jumper; M; Head; 50	4553	Kici Najin; Stands With Him; F; Dau; 7
4531	Hihan Ska; White Owl; F; Wife; 61	4554	Tatanke[sic] Luta; Red Bull; M; Son; 1-4
4532	Hihan Ska; Ida White Owl; F; S.Dau; 22	4555	Hanhepi Kte; Kills At Night; M; Head; 38
4533	Hihan Ska[sic]; Antoine Provost; M; Son; 34	4556	Wambli Luta; Red Eagle; F; Dau; 10
4534	Oliver Provost; M; Son; 30		
4535	Beth; F; Dau; 29		
4536	Charles; M; Son; 23	4557	Itunkasan Waste; Pretty Weasel; M; Head; 40
4537	Jimmie; M; G.Son; 1-5	4558	Asapi; Shout At; F; Wife; 46
4538	Tasunke Tokaheya; Horse Runs Ahead; M; Head; 37	4559	Ayustampi; Lets Alone; F; Dau; 18
4539	Tasunke Tokaheya; Horse Runs First; M; Son; 17	4560	Wan Nup; Two Arrows; M; Son; 5-4
4540	Sunkgleska; Spotted Horse #2; M; Head; 24	4561	Winyan Ropa; Pretty Woman; F; Head; 60
4541	Hakipi; Stepped; F; Dau; 2-2	4562	Nuge Sa; Red Ear; F; Dau; 31
4542	Wakan Najin; Stands Holy; F; Wife; 21	4563	Zuya Itacan; Chief Warrior; M; G.Son; 6
4543	Alice; F; Dau; 2 mo.		
4544	Kiyan Luta; Flying Red; M; Head; 66	4564	Onpan Luta Win; Red Elk Woman; F; Head; 67
4545	Sunk Yuha; Ownes[sic] The Horse; F; Wife; 60	4565	Ttanka[sic]; Bull #2; M; Head; 35
4546	Cetan Maza; Iron Hawk; M; Head; 62	4566	Rante Luta; Red Cedar; F; Head; 49
		4567	Napetu; Day; F; Dau; 16

Census Of The Sioux And Cheyenne Indians Of Pine Ridge Agency, South Dakota. Taken by W. H. Clapp, Captain 16th Infantry, Acting United States Indian Agent, June 30, 1897. (White Clay District)

Key: Number; Indian Name *(if given)*; English Name; Sex; Relation; Age

4568	Wicarpi Hinapa; Star Comes Out; F; Dau; 7	4590	Hinzi Agli; Bring Yellow; F; Dau; 3
4569	Mato Waunsila; Pleasing Bear; M; Head; 58	4591	Sunka Bloka; He Dog; M; Head; 60
4570	Heraka Mani; Walking Elk; F; Wife; 57	4592	Inyan; Rock; F; Wife; 53
		4593	Sunkterila; Keeps Her Horse; F; Dau; 23
4571	Waokiye Sni; Not Help Him; M; Head; 34	4594	Sunka Witko; Crazy Dog; M; B. in Law; 64
4572	Tonkan Yanke Win; Sitting Rock; F; Wife; 34	4595	Canupa Wakan; Holy Pipe; M; Head; 45
4573	Tikanyela Wakuwa; Chase Close To Lodge; M; Head; 43	4596	Ska Sapa; Black White; F; Wife; 42
4574	Sagye Wanbli; Eagle Cane; F; Wife; 39	4597	Tokeya Mani; First Walk; M; Son; 18
4575	Siha Sapa; Black Foot; F; Mo.; 68	4598	Naca; Chief; F; Dau; 15
		4599	Siyo Ciqala; Little Prairie Chicken; [F]; Mother; 75
4576	Wanbli Taheya; Eagle Louse; M; Head; 38	4600	Kinajin; Peter Stands; M; Head; 25
4577	Wasicu Winyan; White Woman; F; Wife; 40	4601	Kinajin; Samuel Stands; M; Son; 2-4
4578	Sunkgliyohi; Comes After Horse; M; Son; 14	4602	Iyuwer Ekte; Kills Across; F; Wife; 19
4579	Ikikcu; Takes Away; M; Son; 13	4603	Psa Kte; Kills Crow; M; Son; 3
4580	Wawiyokipiya; Please; F; Dau; 9		
4581	Cuwi Kute; Shoots At Side; F; Dau; 11	4604	Ciqala; Little; M; Head; 47
4582	Pasu Hanska; Long Nose Dawson; F; Dau; 4	4605	Heraka Gi; Yellow Elk; F; Wife; 30
4583	Hoksila Wambli; Eagle Boy; M; Son; 9 mo.	4606	Matoha Sina; Bear Robe; F; Dau; 21
		4607	Wanikiya; Savior; M; Son; 15
4584	Sunkgleska Ciqala; Little Spotted Horse; M; Head; 34	4608	Ogle Wakan; Holy Shirt; M; Son; 5-4
4585	Eliza; F; Wife; 35	4609	Ciqala Ku; Comes Little; M; Son; 19
4586	Wapiya Itacan; Chief Medicine Boy; M; Son; 8		
4587	Wolotesa; Borrower; F; Dau; 7	4610	Mato Cincala; Young Bear; M; Head; 38
4588	Sunkgleska Ciqala; Louise L.S. Horse; F; Dau; 4-6	4611	Tezi Win; Belly Woman; F; Wife; 30
4589	Maka Icu; Takes The Earth; F; Mo; 64	4612	Tokeya Kte; Kills First; M; Son; 19

Census Of The Sioux And Cheyenne Indians Of Pine Ridge Agency, South Dakota. Taken by W. H. Clapp, Captain 16th Infantry, Acting United States Indian Agent, June 30, 1897. (White Clay District)

Key: Number; Indian Name *(if given)*; English Name; Sex; Relation; Age

4613 Wicincala; Girl; F; Dau; 6
4614 Sina Gnunipi; Lost Blanket; M; Son; 6 mo.
4615 Tokeya Hinapa; Comes Out First; F; Head; 59
4616 Sagye Gi; Yellow Cane; F; G.Dau; 13
4617 Icimani Hanska; Long Visitor; M; Head; 58
4618 Tikauyela Iyanka; Runs Close TO Lodge; M; Son; 30
4619 Wipatapi; Porcupine Work; F; G.Dau; 8
4620 Igmu Wankatuya; High Cat; M; Head; 55
4621 Marpiya Win; Cloud Woman; F; Wife; 55
4622 Ayutepi; Looks At Him; M; Son; 23
4623 Grace Jarvis; F; Head; 44
4624 Mary Jarvis; F; Dau; 22
4625 Frank Jarvis; M; Son; 13
4626 Joseph Jarvis; M; Son; 19
4627 Mitchell Jarvis; M; Son; 17
4628 Tatanka Ciqala; Little Bull #3; M; Head; 45
4629 Wambli Hinapa; Eagle Comes Out; F; Wife; 42
4630 Mato Canwegna; Bear in Wood; M; Son; 10
4631 Wicarpi Gi; Yellow Star; F; Dau; 8
4632 Zica; Squirrel; F; Dau; 1-10
4633 Ite Ranran; Johnson Scabby Face; M; Son; 25
4634 Tasina Maza Win; Iron Shawl Woman; F; Mo.; 55
4635 Bert Janis; M; Nephew; 15
4636 John Buckman; M; Nephew; 10
4637 Wapostan; Hat; M; Head; 30
4638 Heyoka Win; Clow[sic] Woman; F; Wife; 23
4639 Wapostan; James Hat; M; Son; 5 mo.
4640 Itunksan Mato; Weasel Bear; M; Head; 43
4641 Tasunke Waste Win; Her Good Horse; F; Wife; 42
4642 Ista Ska; White Eyes; F; G.Dau; 16
4643 Najinyapi; Surrounded; M; Son; 11
4644 Ciqala Wicakte; Kills Littel[sic]; M; Son; 18
4645 Wahacanka Icu; Takes Shield; F; Dau; 6
4646 Wakinyan Putinhin; Thunder Beard; M; Head; 44
4647 Wakinyan Putinhin; Emma T. Beard; F; Dau; 13
4648 Wakinyan Putinhin; Lizzie T. Beard; F; Dau; 9
4649 Tonkan Yanke Win; Sitting Rock; F; Wife; 44
4650 Otain Win; In Sight; F; Dau; 3
4651 Wayaka Waste Win; Good Prisoner; F; M. in Law; 66
4652 Tatanka Ptecela; Short Bull; M; Head; 41
4653 Cetan Heton; Horned Hawk; F; Wife; 42
4654 Nakipa; Runs Away; M; Son; 12
4655 Maka Wayanka; Looks At Ground; F; Dau; 1-11
4656 Heraka Sapa; Henry Black Elk; M; Head; 40
4657 Heraka Sapa; Louisa C. Black Elk; F; Wife; 37
4658 Tanyan Kte; Kills Well; M; Son; 4
4659 Wakinyan Ciqala; Little Thunder; M; Son; 2-1

Census Of The Sioux And Cheyenne Indians Of Pine Ridge Agency, South Dakota. Taken by W. H. Clapp, Captain 16th Infantry, Acting United States Indian Agent, June 30, 1897. (White Clay District)

Key: Number; Indian Name *(if given)*; English Name; Sex; Relation; Age

4660 Winyan Ciqala; Little Woman; F; Head; 68
4661 Waniyetu Wakewa; Charging Winter; M; Head; 23
4662 Tawa Ikikcu; Takes Her Own; F; Wife; 17
4663 Wakinyan Wicakte; Kills By Lightning; F; Mo.; 59
4664 Cangleska Luta; Red Ring; M; Head; 56
4665 Winyan Gi; Brown Woman; F; Wife; 51
4666 Waonjica Yuha; Owns Bob Tail Horse; M; Son; 24
4667 Norcan; Deaf And Dumb; M; Son; 22
4668 Ranran Win; Scabby Woman; F; Dau; 19
4669 Mato Niyan Luta; Red Breath Bear; M; Head; 47
4670 Ptesan; White Cow; F; Wife; 37
4671 Sunk Sapa; Black Horse; F; Dau; 18
4672 Wosica; Makes Trouble; M; Son; 7
4673 Tasina Wakan; Medicine Blanket; F; Dau; 4-6
4674 Sica Kutepi; Bad Shot Him; M; Son; 1-4
4675 Tatanka Psica; Thos. Jumping Bull; M; Head; 24
4676 Cokanyan Mani; Walks In Center; M; Bro; 26
4677 Tibloku Ota; Plenty Brothers; F; Sister; 20
4678 Tarca Sapa; Black Sheep; M; Head; 46
4679 Onpan Hinska; Elk Tusk; F; Wife; 45
4680 Anukatan Kte; Kills Two Sides; M; Son; 19
4681 Anposkan Tunpi; Born In Bay; F; Dau; 12
4682 Tasunke Wakan; Holy Horse; F; Dau; 7
4683 Susie; F; Dau; 3
4684 Wicakableca; Scatters Them; M; Head; 45
4685 Inyan Maza; Iron Rock; F; Dau; 9
4686 Canku Win; Road Woman; F; Wife; 24
4687 Cuwi; Sides; M; Head; 44
4688 Cante Waste; Good Heart; F; Wife; 45
4689 Sagye; Cane; F; Dau; 13
4690 Tacanku Ota; Her Many Road; F; Dau; 3-2
4691 Kisun; Braided; F; Head; 34
4692 Scili; Pawnee; M; Son; 7
4693 Tarca Win; Deer Woman; F; Dau; 4
4694 Cetan Iyanka; Running Hawk; M; Son; 9 mo.
4695 Ihanbla; Dreamer; M; Head; 29
4696 Ninglicu; Comes Alive; F; Wife; 29
4697 Ogle Wakin; Holy Shirt; M; Son; 6
4698 Wan Iyanajinca; Carries Off Arrows; M; Son; 2-3
4699 Mato Ohitika; Brave Bear; M; Father; 65
4700 Mato Ninyepi; Bear Saves Life; M; Head; 28
4701 Ptesan Waste; Good White Cow; F; Wife; 28
4702 Zintkala Ska; White Bird; M; B. in Law; 30

Census Of The Sioux And Cheyenne Indians Of Pine Ridge Agency, South Dakota. Taken by W. H. Clapp, Captain 16th Infantry, Acting United States Indian Agent, June 30, 1897. (White Clay District)

Key: Number; Indian Name *(if given)*; English Name; Sex; Relation; Age

4703 Mato Cangleska; Bear Ring; M; Son; 6
4704 Psa Wicoti Ole; Hunts Crow Village; M; Son; 4
4705 Sahiyela; Cheyenne; M; Head; 35
4706 Tokaheya; Leader; F; Wife; 32
4707 Tokeya Kte; Kills First; M; Son; 4
4708 Ite Wanbli; Eagle Face; F; Dau; 1-2
4709 Maza Yuwega; Breaks Iron; F; M. in Law; 69
4710 Tonweya Gli; Returns From Scout; M; Head; 56
4711 Pankeska; Shell; F; Wife; 54
4712 Wawokiya; Helps; M; Son; 20
4713 Blowanjila; Lone Ridge; M; Son; 13
4714 Pte Icarya; Raising Cow; F; Dau; 16
4715 Onpan Waste; Good Elk; F; Head; 55
4716 Zuyala; Warrior; M; Head; 29
4717 Kawicapa; Beats Them; F; Wife; 23
4718 Nata Rugahan; Busted Head; F; Head; 74
4719 Najinhan Ku; Comes Standing; F; G.Dau; 15
4720 Petaga; Fire #2; M; Head; 45
4721 Mato Hinapa; Bear Comes Out; F; Wife; 46
4722 He Wanjila; Lone Horn; M; Son; 20
4723 Teriya Kte; Kills Hard; M; Son; 13
4724 Glogli; Brings; F; Dau; 9
4725 Najinyapi; Surrounded; M; Son; 5

4726 Papta Iyaya; Runs Through; F; D. in Law; 19
4727 Wakinyan Tacanksa; Thunder Club; M; Head; 28
4728 Canli; Tobacco; M; Bro.; 22
4729 Ptesan Sagye; White Cow Cane; F; Mo.; 64
4730 Iwoblu; Snow Flies; F; Sister; 30
4731 Wanbli Waste; Pretty Eagle; M; Bro; 35
4732 Wanbli Oye; Eagle Track; F; Niece; 3-4
4733 Mato Tasunke; Bear Horse; M; Head; 40
4734 Tasina Wanbli; Eagle Blanket; F; Wife; 50
4735 Wahacanka Waste; Good Shield; F; Dau; 16
4736 Kawinga; Tunrs[sic] Back; F; Dau; 6
4737 Ista Gonga; Silas Blind; M; Head; 33
4738 Warpe Kasna; Falling Leaf; F; Wife; 26
4739 Naca; Chief #3; M; Head; 62
4740 Onpan Ite Waste; Good Face Elk; F; Wife; 52
4741 Wakinyan Wangi; Ghost Thunder; M; Son; 24
4742 Oye Waste; Good Track; F; Dau; 14
4743 Maka Oyate; Earth Nation; F; Dau; 12
4744 Wicegna Glicu; Comes F. A. Them; M; Head; 29
4745 Toyanke Luta; Her Red Seat; F; Wife; 26
4746 Wasu Mani; Walking Hail; F; Head; 53

Census Of The Sioux And Cheyenne Indians Of Pine Ridge Agency, South Dakota. Taken by W. H. Clapp, Captain 16th Infantry, Acting United States Indian Agent, June 30, 1897. (White Clay District)

Key: Number; Indian Name *(if given)*; English Name; Sex; Relation; Age

4747	Icanyan Wicainyanka; Runs Against Them; M; Son; 13	4768	Okiciza; Battle; M; Head; 31
4748	Tasunke Wanjila; Lone Horse; M; Son; 8	4769	Ptehincala Ska; White Calf; F; Wife; 25
4749	Sunk Gleska; Spotted Horse #1; M; Head; 39	4770	Timahel Ti; Lives In Lodge; M; Son; 5
4750	Onjinca; Bob Tail; F; Wife; 40	4771	Toyanke; Waste Her Good Seat; F; Head; 70
4751	Kangi Wakan; Holy Crow; M; Son; 5-6	4772	Zintkala; Bird; F; G.Dau; 17
4752	Cuwignaka Cola; No Dress; M; Head; 63	4773	Olepi; Looks For Him; M; G.Son; 14
4753	Ota Wakan; Plenty Holy; F; Wife; 63	4774	Wawoslata; Hair Pipe; M; Head; 48
4754	Hinzi Agli; Brings Yellow; F; Dau; 23	4775	Cetan Win; Hawk Woman; F; Wife; 50
4755	Tatanka Cante Sica; Bad Heart Bull; M; Head; 57	4776	Ipiyaka; Belt; M; Head; 38
		4777	Tarca Win; Deer Woman; F; Wife; 33
4756	Wiciyela Win; Yankton Woman; F; Wife; 49	4778	Caje Wanica; No Name; M; Son; 16
4757	Wahukeza Wanbli; Eagle Lance; M; Son; 28	4779	Petsola; Sharp Pointed; M; Head; 44
4758	Ninyapi; Makes Alive; F; Dau; 25	4780	Winyan Tipi; Woman Lodge; F; Wife; 44
4759	Wiyaka Sapa; Black Feather; M; Head; 35	4781	Hoksila; Boy; M; Son; 13
4760	Kokipapi; Afraid Of Him; F; Wife; 34	4782	Janjanyela; Clear; F; Dau; 3
		4783	Zintkala Waste; Good Bird; M; Son; 3 wks.
4761	Ota Kte; Kills Plenty; M; Son; 17	4784	Pankeska Luta; Red Shell; M; Head; 57
4762	Tatanka Cangleska; Ring Buffalo; F; Dau; 13	4785	Pankeska Win; Shell Woman; F; Wife; 52
4763	Canupa Sapa; Black Pipe; M; Son; 11	4786	Pepta Iyaya; Goes Through; M; Son; 19
4764	Pehin Sa; Red Hair; F; Dau; 10		
4765	Ptesan Hinapa; White Cow Out; F; Dau; 6	4787	Cetan Akicita; Soldier Hawk; M; Head; 20
4766	Tasunke Opi; Wounded Horse; M; Son; 2-5	4788	Ptecela; Short; F; Wife; 19
4767	Tasunke Ota; Her Plenty Horses; F; Head; 46	4789	Anpetu Hinapa; Day Comes Out; F; Mo.; 60
		4790	Pehin Sa; Red Hair; F; Sis; 23

Census Of The Sioux And Cheyenne Indians Of Pine Ridge Agency, South Dakota. Taken by W. H. Clapp, Captain 16th Infantry, Acting United States Indian Agent, June 30, 1897. (White Clay District)

Key: Number; Indian Name *(if given)*; English Name; Sex; Relation; Age

4791	Hanpa; Black Moccasin; M; Son; 11	4813	Sina Wakan; Holy Shawl; F; Dau; 14
4792	Tatanka Witko; Crazy Bull; M; Head; 59	4814	Inyan Hinapa; Rock Comes Out; F; Dau; 14
4793	Ptehincala; Young Calf; F; Head; 54	4815	Ikusan; Mink; M; Son; 8
4794	Hinzi Agli; Brings Yellow; F; Dau; 15	4816	Maga Tasunke; Duck Horse; M; Son; 5-6
		4817	Okiyakapi; Tells Him; F; Dau; 2-1
		4818	Agatha Loafer Joe; F; Dau; 16
4795	Sunknakpo Gi; Red Eared Horse; M; Head; 61	4819	Tatanka Ohitika; Brave Bull; M; Head; 48
4796	Canku; Road; F; Wife; 60	4820	Tipi Rla Win; Rattling House; F; Wife; 57
4797	Isto; Arm; M; Son; 19	4821	Teriya Mani; Walks Hard; F; Dau; 6
4798	Tasunke Maza; Iron Horse; M; Son; 16		
4799	Tasunke Opi; Shot His Horse; M; G.Son; 12	4822	Heraka Ska; White Elk; M; Head; 42
4800	Tonweya; Scout; M; G.Son; 5	4823	Ehake Win; Last Woman; F; Wife; 35
4801	Cetan Wanbli; Eagle Hawk; M; Head; 64	4824	Tasunke Opi; Wounded Horse; F; Dau; 7
4802	Itunksan; Weasel; F; Wife; 56	4825	Hanhepi Sni Kte; Kills Before Night; M; Son; 5
4803	Kangi; Crow; M; Son; 16		
4804	Siciya; Painted Red; M; Son; 12	4826	Nata Ciqala; Little Head; M; Son; 3
4805	Sungmanitu Ohitika; Brave Wolf; M; Son; 6 mo.	4827	Ogle Sa; Red Shirt #2; M; Head; 51
4806	Mato Sica; Howard Bad Bear; M; Head; 21	4828	Winyan Waste; Good Woman; F; Wife; 46
4807	Warpe Luta; Red Leaf; F; Wife; 22	4829	Psin Sa; Red Onion; M; Son; 26
4808	Nakpogi; Yellow Ear; F; M. In Law; 58	4830	Si Tokapatan; Front Foot; M; Son; 13
4809	Saapa; Strikes Red; F; S. in Law; 5	4831	Tianatan; Runs For Lodge; M; G.Son; 4
4810	Waglure; Loafer Joe; M; Head; 40	4832	Tasunke Hinzi; Yellow Horse; Head; 50
4811	Wanbli Sinte; Eagle Tail; F; Wife #1; 37	4833	Wikan Iciyakaskapi; Strings Untied; F; Wife; 51
4812	Canupa Apa; Hits Pipe; F; Wife #2; 31	4834	Wosica Kuwa; After Trouble; F; Dau; 29
		4835	Ehake; Last; F; Dau; 18
		4836	Deaf Woman; F; Wife #2; 52

Census Of The Sioux And Cheyenne Indians Of Pine Ridge Agency, South Dakota. Taken by W. H. Clapp, Captain 16th Infantry, Acting United States Indian Agent, June 30, 1897. (White Clay District)

Key: Number; Indian Name *(if given)*; English Name; Sex; Relation; Age

4837 Naca Ciqala; Elmore Little Chief; M; Head; 25
4838 Naca Ciqala; Elva May Little Chief; F; Dau; 1-1

4839 Ptesan Mani; Walking White Cow; F; Head; 45
4840 Okihipi Sni; Cant[sic] Get Her; F; Dau; 13

4841 Toka Icu; Takes Enemy; M; Head; 31
4842 Isnala Kte; Lone Killer; F; Wife; 30
4843 Kokipesni Kte; Kills Without Doubt; F; Dau; 5

4844 He Nupin Wanica; No Two Horns #1; M; Head; 53
4845 Naron; Hears It; F; Wife; 50
4846 Nakpogi Win; Red Eared Woman; F; Dau; 30
4847 Narpiya[sic] To; Blue Cloud; F; Dau; 18
4848 Wanbli Cincala; Young Eagle; M; Son; 14
4849 Oye Wanbli; Eagle Track; F; Dau; 15

4850 Sunkhinto Yuha; Blue Horse Owner; M; Head; 54
4851 Sina On Apa; Strikes With Blanket; F; Wife; 54
4852 Winorcala Catka Win; Left Hand Old Woman; M; Son; 29
4853 Keya; Turtle; M; Son; 22
4854 Cinpi; Wants Him; F; Dau; 17

4855 Tatanka Heluta; Red Horned Bull; M; Head; 45
4856 Mazawakan Win; Gun Woman; F; Wife; 45

4857 Tatanka Luta; Red Bull; M; Son; 22

4858 Tasunke Wayankapi; Looks At Her Horses; F; Aunt; 49
4859 Cokata Iyaya; Goes In Center; F; D. in Law; 24

4860 Wayank Najinpi; Stands Looking At Her; F; Head; 49
4861 Sunkmanu; Horse Thief; F; Dau; 22
4862 Tingleska; Fawn; F; Dau; 20
4863 Peji Zi; Yellow Grass; M; Son; 10
4864 Tasunke Opi; Wounded Horse; M; Son; 8
4865 Ptehincala; Calf; F; Dau; 5-6

4866 Siyotanka Waste; Good Flute; M; Head; 54
4867 Winyan Orlate; Woman Under; F; Wife; 43
4868 Zuya Wicakte; Kills Warrior; M; Son; 21
4869 Nata Ska; White Head; M; Son; 12
4870 Kaunkapi; Knocked Down; M; Son; 7
4871 Wanjila Agli; Brings One; F; Dau; 3
4872 Tipi Waste; Good Lodge; F; D. in Law; 19

4873 Cetan Kokipapi; Afraid of Hawk; M; Head; 54

4874 Mato Onjinca; Bob Tail Bear; F; Head; 74

4875 Sarah Gillespie; F; Head; 44
4876 Bettie Gillespie; F; Dau; 17
4877 Jennie Gillespie; F; Dau; 17
4878 George Gillespie; M; Son; 15
4879 Robert Gillespie; M: Son; 13
4880 Margie Gillespie; F; Dau; 7
4881 Henry Gillespie; M; Son; 5
4882 Lizzie Gillespie; F; Dau; 19
4883 Emma Gillespie; F; Dau; 1-7

Census Of The Sioux And Cheyenne Indians Of Pine Ridge Agency, South Dakota.
Taken by W. H. Clapp, Captain 16th Infantry, Acting United States Indian Agent,
June 30, 1897. (White Clay District)

Key: Number; Indian Name *(if given)*; English Name; Sex; Relation; Age

4884	Iku Hanska; Long Chin; F; Head; 64	4907	Gleska Agli; Brings Spotted; F; Dau; 18
4885	Cetan; Hawk; M; Son; 35	4908	Toka Oyuspa; Catches Enemy; F; Dau; 13
4886	Iku Hanska; Long Chin; M; Son; 24	4909	Tawapaha; His Bonnet; M; Son; 9
4887	Onpan Hotan Mani; Elk Voice Walking; M; Head; 54	4910	Wapaha Nupa; Two War Bonnets; F; Dau; 1-3
4888	Maka Kanyela; Close To Ground; F; Wife; 42	4911	Wasicu Wankatuya; High White Man; M; Head; 67
4889	Op Iyanka; Runs With Them; M; Son; 25	4912	Ota Kte; Kills Plenty; F; G.Dau; 19
4890	Hoksila; Boy; M; Son; 13	4913	Gnaska; Frog #2; M; Head; 57
4891	Ptesan Win; White Cown[sic] Woman; F; Dau; 2-6	4914	Tasunke Waste; Her Good Horse; F; Wife; 58
4892	Wanbli Iyanke; Running Eagle; M; Head; 45	4915	Kico; Calls; F; Dau; 26
4893	Hoka; Badger; F; Wife; 43	4916	Ta Ole; Looks For The Dead; M; Son; 22
4894	Wapaha; Bonnet; M; Son; 22		
4895	Najinwicaya Kte; Follows And Kills; M; Son; 6	4917	Siyo; Prairie Chicken #1; M; Head; 35
4896	Pejuta; Medicine; F; Head; 49	4918	Karape Win; Driver; F; Mother; 55
4897	Itunkasan; Weasel; M; Son; 11		
4898	Tasunke Ciqala; Little Horse; M; Son; 9	4919	Nupa Kte; Kills Twice; M; Bro; 20
4899	Wahacanka Ciqala; Little Shield; M; Head; 47	4920	Mato Wanbli; Bear Eagle; M; Head; 55
4900	Waste Mna; Smells Good; F; Wife; 44	4921	Capa Luta; Red Beaver; F; Wife; 53
4901	Toka Waste; Good Enemy; F; Dau; 2-6	4922	Wanapa Iyanka; Runs Wounded; M; Son; 23
		4923	Niwicaya; Saves His Life; M; Son; 15
4902	Wahosi Gli; Brings Wood; F; Head; 65	4924	Onpan Luta; Red Elk; F; Dau; 17
4903	Tasunke Gleska; Her Spotted Horse; F; Dau; 36	4925	Wiyaka Waste; Good Feather; F; Dau; 7
4904	Tasunke Waste; Good Horse; F; Dau; 34	4926	Wicakte; Kills Them; M; Son; 3
		4927	Sungmanitu Sapa; Black Wolf #2; M; Head; 49
4905	Onpan Gleska; Spotted Elk; M; Head; 49	4928	Terilapi; Loves Him; F; Wife; 35
4906	Otawicapa; Follower; F; Wife; 39		

Census Of The Sioux And Cheyenne Indians Of Pine Ridge Agency, South Dakota. Taken by W. H. Clapp, Captain 16th Infantry, Acting United States Indian Agent, June 30, 1897. (White Clay District)

Key: Number; Indian Name *(if given)*; English Name; Sex; Relation; Age

4929 Oosica; Hard To Hit; M; Son; 23
4930 Wanbli Yuha; Keeps The Eagle; M; Son; 11
4931 Tianatan; Runs At Lodge; M; Son; 7
4932 Tezi Tanka; Big Belly; F; Mo.; 75

4933 Toka Kokipa; Afraid Of Enemy; M; Head; 41
4934 Ista Gi; Brown Eyes; F; Wife; 42
4935 Sunkgleska Waste; Pretty Spotted Horse; F; Dau; 18
4936 Cetan Wakuwa; Chasing Hawk; M; Son; 13
4937 Teriya Kte Sni; Kills Without Difficulty; [M]; Son; 6
4938 Hanomani; Runs Out At Night; F; Dau; 1-2

4939 Wasicu Mato; White Man Bear; M; Head; 34
4940 Iteska Win; White Face Woman; F; Wife; 22
4941 Sunkhinsa; Red Horse; M; Son; 2-3

4942 Hektakiya; Backward; M; Head; 24
4943 Cokata Iyaya; Goes In Center; F; Wife; 19
4944 Tota Wabluska; Dragon Fly; F; Dau; 1-3

4945 Mato Gnaskinyan; Crazy Bear; M; Head; 63
4946 Pehinji Win; Yellow Hair Woman; F; Woman[sic]; 58

4947 Maya; Bank; M; Head; 30
4948 Pehinji Win; Yellow Hair; F; Wife; 23

4949 Heraka Luzahan; Fast Elk; M; Son; 2-2

4950 Tipi Wakita; Looking Lodge; F; Dau; 3 mo.

4951 Ptesan Tatanka; White Cow Bull; M; Head; 41
4952 Norcan Win; Deaf Woman; F; Wife; 40
4953 Ku; Comes; F; Dau; 15
4954 Wanbli Nupa; Two Eagles; M; Son; 10
4955 Tokata Hiyu; Comes To Front; F; Dau; 4

4956 Ohitika; Brave; M; Head; 33
4957 Sina To; Blue Cloth; F; Wife; 35
4958 Aglipi; Brings Him Back; M; Nephew; 23
4959 Hoksila; Boy; M; Son; 10
4960 Hihan Wanbli; Owl Eagle; M; Son; 7
4961 Caje Wanica; No Name; F; Mo.; 63

4962 Siyotanka Sapa; Black Whistler #2; M; Head; 36
4963 Ninwicaya; Saves Life; F; Wife; 43
4964 Sunkhinsa; Brings Red Horse; M; Son; 12
4965 Tonweya; Scout; M; Son; 11
4966 Can; Wood; F; Dau; 4 mo.

4967 Toka Ole; Hunts Enemy; M; Head; 41
4968 Ira; Laugh; F; Wife; 36
4969 Wicakte; Kills; M; Son; 15
4970 Okiciza Tawa; His Fight; M; Son; 3

4971 Sina Topa; Four Blanket; F; Head; 50
4972 Nakicipa; Runs Away From Him; M; Son; 22

4973 Ptesan Wanbli; White Cow Eagle; M; Head; 54

Census Of The Sioux And Cheyenne Indians Of Pine Ridge Agency, South Dakota. Taken by W. H. Clapp, Captain 16th Infantry, Acting United States Indian Agent, June 30, 1897. (White Clay District)

Key: Number; Indian Name *(if given)*; English Name; Sex; Relation; Age

4974	Maka Akan Epaya; Lays On Ground; F; Wife; 49	4996	Tasunke Waste; Pretty Horse; F; Dau; 1-10
4975	Kangi Wanjila; One Crow; M; Son; 14	4997	Cetan Wanbli; Eagle Hawk #1; M; Head; 55
4976	Tasunke Ota; Plenty Horses; F; Dau; 12	4998	Hunska Narco; Leggins Down; F; Wife; 49
4977	Norcan; Deaf And Dumb; M; Son; 30	4999	Nasula Witko; Crazy Brain; M; Son; 23
4978	Oyate Ole; Looks For Nation; F; Mo.; 60	5000	Nupa Iyanajinca; Takes Away Twice; F; Dau; 13
		5001	Kici Eti; Camp With; M; Son; 5
4979	Psica Iyanka; Running Jumper; M; Head; 35	5002	Wuwanpi; Swimmer; F; Dau; 14
		5003	Wicasa Isnala; Lone Man; M; Head; 47
4980	Oglonica; Resist; F; Head; 48		
4981	Pehinji; Yellow Hair; M; Son; 14	5004	Sunkska; White Horse; F; Wife; 38
4982	Sunkmanu; Steels Horse; F; Dau; 7	5005	Zuya Wanbli; War Eagle; F; Dau; 23
4983	Sugmanitu Isnala; Lone Wolf; M; Head; 36	5006	Onkcekira; White Magpie; M; Head; 55
4984	Marpiya To; Blue Cloud; F; Wife; 38	5007	Wahuwapa Luta; Red Cob; F; Wife; 48
4985	Sunkska; White Horse; F; Dau; 17	5008	Sagye Maza; Iron Cane; F; Dau; 25
4986	Toka Kte; Kills Enemy; F; Dau; 11	5009	Nakipa; Runs Away; M; Son; 18
4987	Pte Hinzi; Yellow Cow; F; Dau; 3-8	5010	Olepi; Looks For Him; F; Dau; 14
4988	Zintkala Ogle; Bird Shirt; M; Son; 1-4	5011	Yata; Chewing; M; Son; 11
		5012	Psa Kte; Kills Crow; F; Dau; 1 mo.
4989	Wasu Maza; Iron Hail; F; Head; 80	5013	Maka Wasa; Red Paint; M; Head; 30
4990	Wasin Wanica; No Fat; M; Head; 46	5014	Mato Wicoti; Bear Village; F; Wife; 35
4991	Siyotanka Luta; Red Flute; F; Wife; 40	5015	Olepi; Looks For Him; M; Son; 11
4992	Toapi Kte; Kills Wounded; M; Son; 18	5016	Iogna Opi; Shot In The Mouth; M; Son; 6
4993	Hehtakiya Toka Kte; Kills Enemy Back; M; Son; 14	5017	Yuya Kte; Kills Warrior; F; Dau; 4-5
4994	Isanti; Lives Alone; F; Dau; 7	5018	Winyan Rcaka; Pure Woman; F; M. in Law; 70
4995	Rlawin; Rattling; F; Dau; 5		

Census Of The Sioux And Cheyenne Indians Of Pine Ridge Agency, South Dakota. Taken by W. H. Clapp, Captain 16th Infantry, Acting United States Indian Agent, June 30, 1897. (White Clay District)

Key: Number; Indian Name *(if given)*; English Name; Sex; Relation; Age

5019	Kiyela Opi; Shot Close; M; Head; 39		5042	Kuwa; Runs After; M; Head; 35
5020	Sunkahan Win; Horse Woman; F; Wife; 39		5043	Sa Apa; Strikes Red; F; Wife; 34
			5044	Hinzi Gleska; Yellow Spotted; F; Dau; 3-5
5021	Siyotanka Sapa; Black Whistler #1; M; Head; 39		5045	Waniyetu Taopi; Wounded In Winter; M; Son; 1-10
5022	Marpiya Sapa; Black Cloud; F; Wife; 45		5046	Hu Rni; Crooked Leg; F; Head; 63
5023	Heraka Wakita; Looking Elk; M; Head; 44		5047	Okicize Tawa; His Fight; M; G.Son; 13
5024	Canku; Road; F; Wife; 38		5048	Zintkala Ciqala; Little Bird; M; Head; 48
5025	Toka Kte Win; Kills Enemy; F; Dau; 7		5049	Kuwa; Chase; F; Wife; 39
5026	Najinhan Ku; Cokes[sic] Standing; M; Bro[sic]; 11 mo.		5050	Kokab Wosica; Makes Trouble Ahead; M; Son; 16
			5051	Tasunke; Her Horse; F; Dau; 11
5027	Okicize Tawa; His Fight; M; Head; 65		5052	Ite Waste; Good Face; F; Dau; 8
5028	Ranhi Win; Slow Woman; F; Wife; 67		5053	Tainyan Ku Win; Comes In Sight; F; Dau; 3
			5054	Mato Ska Sake; White Bear Claws; M; Head; 43
5029	Napsukaga Topa; Four Finger; M; Head; 61		5055	To Wakan; Holy Lodge; F; Wife; 40
5030	Wanbli; Eagle; F; Wife; 59			
5031	Ptecela; Short; F; Dau; 26		5056	Hutkan; Root; M; Son; 16
5032	Pte Tokahe; Cow Leader; F; G.Dau; 8		5057	Toka Oyuspe; Catches Enemy; M; Son; 12
5033	Cetan Iyotaka; Sitting Hawk; M; Head; 44		5058	Mato Wamniomni; Whirlwind Bear; M; Head; 29
5034	Wanbli Yuha; Own Eagle; F; Wife; 34		5059	Tacangleska Gi; Her Yellow Ring; F; Wife; 23
5035	Kiciza; Fight; F; Dau; 12		5060	Kicizapi; Fight Each Other; M; Son; 1-3
5036	Cetan Iyoyaka; Levi Sitting Hawk; M; Son; 9		5061	Hektakiya Ekte; Kills Back; F; Niece; 3
5037	Hoksila; Boy; M; Son; 6			
5038	Mato Tawa Ku; Her Bear Comes; F; Dau; 1-4		5062	Tahu Wanica; No Neck; M; Father; 61
5039	Mato Poge; Frank Bear Nose; M; Head; 41		5063	Sunka Ciqala; Little Dog; M; Head; 45
5040	Sunkicu; Takes Horses; F; Wife; 30		5064	Mato Winyan; Bear Woman; F; Wife; 65
5041	Hoksila; Boy; M; Bro; 34			

Census Of The Sioux And Cheyenne Indians Of Pine Ridge Agency, South Dakota. Taken by W. H. Clapp, Captain 16th Infantry, Acting United States Indian Agent, June 30, 1897. (White Clay District)

Key: Number; Indian Name *(if given)*; English Name; Sex; Relation; Age

5065	Mato Wicakiza; Fights Bear; M; Head; 32	5087	Heraka Hinapa; Elk Comes Out; F; Sister; 27
5066	Nup Hiyokipi; Two Comes After Her; F; Wife; 29	5088	Hinto Agli; Brings Blue; F; Niece; 16
5067	Maka Luta; Red Dirt; F; Dau; 10	5089	Pilayapi; Thankful; F; Niece; 10
5068	Tionajinyapi; Surrounded In Lodge; M: Son; 8	5090	Ninglicu; Comes Alive; F; Niece; 4-6
5069	Wanbli Hoksila; Eagle Boy; M; Son; 6	5091	Warpe Koyaka; Wears Leaf; F; Head; 79
5070	Siyo; Prairie Chicken #2; F; Head; 47	5092	Hihan Gi; Brown Owl; M; Head; 62
5071	Maggie; F; Dau; 19		
5072	Najin; Stands; F; Dau; 17		
5073	Watage Luta; Red Foam; F; Dau; 6	5093	Lab; Lob; M; Head; 54
5074	Tasunke Najin; Standing Horse; F; G.Dau; 11 mo.	5094	Mary Lamont; F; Head; 15
		5095	George Lamont; M; Bro; 13
5075	Akicize; Fights Over; M; S. in Law; 21	5096	Frank Lamont; M; Bro; 11
		5097	Maggie Lamont; F; Sis; 9
5076	Hotanka; Loud Voice; F; Head; 43	5098	Wanbli Heton; Eagle Horn; M; Head; 56
5077	Sungmanitu Nakpa; Wolf Ears; M; Son; 18	5099	Zintkala Zi; Yellow Bird; F; Wife; 75
5078	Tehan Gli Sni; Comes In Late; F; Dau; 14	5L100[sic]	Mato Hinapa; Bear Comes Out; M; Head; 55
5079	Susuni Haunka; Knocks Down Shoshone; M; Son; 11	5101	Ocinsica Win; Mean Woman; F; Wife; 43
5080	Sihasapa Kte; Kills Blackfeet; M; Son; 9		
5081	Paha Nupa; Two Hills; M; Son; 1-11	5102	Sunka Wankatuya; High Dog; M; Head; 42
5082	Ptewaste Win; Pretty Cow; F; Head; 44	5103	Putinhin Sapa; Black Beard; M; Head; 80
5083	Tasunke Opi; Shot His Horse; M; Son; 10	5104	Gnaska Ho Waste; Good Voice Frog; F; Wife; 75
5084	Worlokapi Sni; Bullet Proof; M; Son; 6	5105	Oceya Wankala; Easy To Cry; F; Dau; 34
5085	Sunknakpogi; Brown Eared Horse; M; Son; 24	5106	Mato Slasla; Hairless Bear; M; G.Son; 4
		5107	Wanbli; Eagle; F; G.Dau; 9
5086	Marpiya Waste; Good Cloud; F; Mo; 72	5108	Sepa Win; Fat Woman; F; G.Dau; 8
		5109	Canhanpi; Sugar; M; G.Son; 3

Census Of The Sioux And Cheyenne Indians Of Pine Ridge Agency, South Dakota. Taken by W. H. Clapp, Captain 16th Infantry, Acting United States Indian Agent, June 30, 1897. (White Clay District)

Key: Number; Indian Name *(if given)*; English Name; Sex; Relation; Age

5110 Tatanka Ciqala; Little Bull; M; G.Son; 4 mo.
5111 Wanju Stola; Slick Quiver; M; Head; 25
5112 Sina Harwoka; Flying Blanket; F; Wife; 28
5113 Wanju; Joseph Quiver; M; Son; 8 mo.
5114 Terilapi; Dearly; M; Head; 27
5115 Hotain; Noise; F; Wife; 30
5116 Nica Ole; Looks For None; F; Dau; 8
5117 Ite Blagahan; Spread Face; M; Son; 6-10
5118 Tikanyela Iyanka; Runs Close TO Lodge; M; Son; 2-3

5119 Cante Ohitika; Brave Heart; M; Head; 42
5120 Canupa Waste Icu; Gets Good Pipe; F; Wife; 32
5121 Olepi; Looks For Him; M; Son; 16
5122 Zintkala; Bird; M; Son; 10
5123 Nupa Icaga; Lives Twice; F; Dau; 5
5124 Onpan Gi; Yellow Elk; F; Dau; 1-11

5125 Sunka Ohitika; Brave Dog; M; Head; 55
5126 Maka; Dirt; F; Wife; 58
5127 Winkte Onaso; H. Pacer; M; Head; 54
5128 Nite; Hip; F; Head[sic]; 61

5129 Ranhi Win; Slow Woman; F; Head; 55

5130 Psica Wakuwa; Chasing Jumper; M; Head; 29
5131 Ohitika Win; Brave Woman; F; Wife; 26

5132 Toka Apapi; Struck By Enemy; M; Son; 7

5133 Sinte Ska; White Tail; M; Head; 70
5134 Oterika; Hard Times; F; Wife; 60

5135 Wicarpi Ota; Plenty Stars; M; Head; 65
5136 Anpetu Hinapa; Day Come Out; F; Wife; 55
5137 Wakinyan Tasina; Thunder Robe; M; Son; 19
5138 Ptesan Iyotaka; Sitting White Cow; F; G.Dau; 4

5139 Ranhiya; Slowly; M; Head; 27
5140 Hinhan; Owl; F; Wife; 25
5141 Wawiyokipiya; Please; F; Dau; 8
5142 Ska Agli; Brings White; M; Son; 6
5143 Gli Najin; Comes And Stands; F; Dau; 4
5144 Roka; Badger; F; Dau; 10 mo.

5145 Canku Sapa; Black Road; M; Head; 60
5146 Sicangu Win; Brule Woman; F; Wife; 55
5147 Miwakan Wakan; Holy Sword; M; Son; 25

5148 Sunka Heton; Dog Horn; M; Head; 60
5149 Orlogeca; Hollow; F; Wife; 61
5150 Cokanyan; Center; F; G.Dau; 25

5151 Tankal Mani; Walk Out; M; Head; 36
5152 Pejuta Win; Medicine Woman; F; Wife; 33
5153 Rlokiyapi; Fixes And Growls; F; Dau; 11
5154 Ehake Kute; Shoots At Last; M; Son; 7

Census Of The Sioux And Cheyenne Indians Of Pine Ridge Agency, South Dakota. Taken by W. H. Clapp, Captain 16th Infantry, Acting United States Indian Agent, June 30, 1897. (White Clay District)

Key: Number; Indian Name *(if given)*; English Name; Sex; Relation; Age

5155	Hoksila Luta; Red Boy; M; Son; 9 mo.	5180	Inyan Sica; Red Rock; M; Cousin; 20
5156	Mato Lowan; Singing Bear; M; Head; 67	5181	Tatanka Ciqala; Little Bull #4; M; Head; 54
5157	Naca Win; King Woman; F; Wife; 67	5182	Tasina Mani; Walking Shawl; F; Wife; 56
5158	Gliyunka; Comes And Lays; M: Son; 25	5183	Mato Hunkesni; Slow Bear; M; Head; 51
5159	Mato Isto Napin; Bear Arm Necklace; M; Head; 49	5184	Sunkska Ota Win; Plenty White Horse; F; Wife; 50
5160	Pte Ota Win; Plenty Cow; F; Wife; 50	5185	Kiciza; Frank Fight; M; Nephew; 27
5161	Wanbli Sun; Eagle Feather; F; Dau; 17	5186	Aiyapi; Talks About; F; Dau; 24
5162	Marpiya Hoksila; Cloud Boy; M; Son; 10	5187	Mato Hunkesni; John Slow Bear; M; Son; 18
5163	Ptesan Wokiyaka; Talks To White Cow; F; Dau; 7	5188	Iyar payapi[sic]; Grabs Him; M; Son; 17
5164	Wahorpi Luta; Red Nest; F; M. in Law; 88	5189	Kokipesni; Not Afraid; M; Son; 10
5165	Cehupa Maza; Iron Jaw; F; Head; 82	5190	Gliyunka; Comes And Lays; F; Dau; 2-7
5166	Julia Swallow; F; Head; 49	5191	Wiyaka Ska; White Feather; M; Head; 31
5167	Oliver Swallow; M; Son; 27	5192	Maka Wase; Dirt Paint; F; Wife; 31
5168	Amelia Swallow; F; Dau; 24	5193	Ninglicu; Comes Alive; M; Son; 5
5169	Ida Swallow; F; Dau; 17		
5170	Susie Swallow; F Dau; 14	5194	Ayustanpi; Gives Him Up; M; Son; 2-1
5171	Willie Swallow; M; Son; 11		
5172	Antoine Swallow; M; Son; 9		
5173	May Swallow; F; Dau; 6	5195	Maka San; White Clay; F; Head; 27
5174	Benjamin Swallow; M; Son; 3	5196	Marpiya Tokalu; First Cloud; M; Son; 4
5175	Akicita Ciqala; Little Soldier; M; Head; 30		
5176	Canowicakte; Kills In Timber; F; Wife; 27	5197	Wasu Kiyan; Flying Hail; F; Head; 64
5177	Olepi; Looks For Her; F; Dau; 7	5198	Tokeya Kte; Kills First; F; G.Dau; 18
5178	Tasunke Wakita; Looking Horse; F; Dau; 4	5199	Wakinyan Sinte; Thunder Tail; M; Head; 42
5179	Tonweya Luta; Red Scout; M; Son; 1-4	5200	Tasunke Nupa; Two Horse; F; Wife; 42

Census Of The Sioux And Cheyenne Indians Of Pine Ridge Agency, South Dakota. Taken by W. H. Clapp, Captain 16th Infantry, Acting United States Indian Agent, June 30, 1897. (White Clay District)

Key: Number; Indian Name *(if given)*; English Name; Sex; Relation; Age

5201	Ticagla Iyanka; Runs Close TO Lodge; F; Dau; 20	5225	Tatanka Ciqala; Little Bull #2; M; Head; 50
5202	Wicakte; Kills; F; Dau; 9	5226	Ocinsica Win; Mean Woman; F; Wife; 54
5203	Rante Tipi; Cedar Lodge; F; Dau; 5	5227	Heraka; Elk; F; G.Dau; 10
5204	Wahukeya Waste; Good Lance; M; Son; 3	5228	Wasu Mato; Hail Bear; M; Head; 54
5205	Wicasa Sapa; Black Man; M; Head; 34	5229	Pejuta Waste; Good Medicine; F; Wife; 55
5206	Winyan Luta; Red Woman; F; Wife; 40	5230	We Eyalase Gli; Comes Bloody; M; Son; 14
5207	Ocinsica; Cross; M; Son; 10	5231	Sunkmanu; Steals Horse; M; Son; 11
5208	Kahinrpeya; Runs Over; M; Son; 8		
5209	Tiole; Looks For Lodge; F; Dau; 5 mo.	5232	Tarca Sapa; Black Deer; M; Head; 47
		5233	Wowapi; Flag; F; Wife; 54
5210	Slohan; Crawls; M; Head; 55	5234	Heraka Wakinyan; Thunder Elk; M; Son; 24
5211	Kakikte; Looks Back; F; Wife; 53	5235	Maste; Sunshine; M; Son; 28
5212	Psa Win; Crow Woman; F; Head; 43	5236	Wicarpi Wanjila; One Star; M; B. in Law; 25
		5237	Si Maza; Iron Foot; F; Head; 70
5213	Heraka Iyotaka; Sitting Elk; M; Head; 50	5238	Wamniomni Koyaka; Wears Whirlwind; F; Head; 64
5214	Nurcan Win; Deaf Woman; F; Wife; 43	5239	Pankeska Ota; Plenty Shell; F; Head; 43
5215	Mastincala; Rabbit; M; Head; 27		
5216	Wicegna; Among; F; Wife; 24	5240	Makamani Toka Kte; Kills Enemy Afoot; M; Son; 23
5217	Waste Karniga; Picks Out Best; M; Son; 2 mo.	5241	Aku; Brings; M: Son; 13
		5242	Wopotapi; Shot To Pieces; M Son; 10
5218	Takuni; Nothing; F; Head; 54	5243	Tiyopa; Door; M: Son; 6
5219	Kutepi; Shot At Him; F; Dau; 25	5244	Tatanka Ptecela; Thos. Short Bull; M: Son; 1-4
5220	Apapi; Strikes Him; M; G.son; 4		
5221	Rlaya Wakuwa; Rattling Chase; M; Head; 47	5245	Tatanka Ptecela; Short Bull #2; M; Head; 45
5222	Nisehu; Hip; F; Wife; 43	5246	Hinapa; Comes Out; F; Wife; 39
5223	Kicigluca; Takes Away; M; Son; 18	5247	Wahinkpe On Kute; Shoots With Arrow; M; Son; 15
5224	Tasunke Sica; Her Bad Horse; F; Dau; 3		

Census Of The Sioux And Cheyenne Indians Of Pine Ridge Agency, South Dakota. Taken by W. H. Clapp, Captain 16th Infantry, Acting United States Indian Agent, June 30, 1897. (White Clay District)

Key: Number; Indian Name *(if given)*; English Name; Sex; Relation; Age

5248 Mato Sake; Bear Claw; M; Son; 10
5249 Ipahin; Pillow; M; Son; 6-6
5250 Oyate Sica; Bad Nation; F; Dau; 3
5251 Hanpiska; Moccasin Top; M; Head; 46
5252 Witko; Foolish; F; Wife; 45
5253 Hanpiska; Emma Moccasin Top; F; Dau; 12
5254 Isna Wakuwa; Chase Alone; M; Son; 10
5255 Can Hu; Wood Let; M; Son; 4
5256 Wan Wicaqu; Gives Arrow; F; Dau; 6
5257 Anukasan Hoksila; Bald Eagle Boy; M; Son; 1-6

5258 Tasunke Opi; Wounded Horse; M; Head; 27
5259 Wowapi; Flag; F; Wife; 22
5260 Tasunke Opi; Mabel Ogalalla W. H.; F; Dau; 1 mo.

5261 Wicakicigluza; Takes Away From Them; F; Head; 60
5262 Sunk Iyanajinca; Runs Away With Horses; M: Son; 23

5263 Ciqala Wicakte; Little Killer; M; Head; 49
5264 Tarca Sapa; Black Deer; F; Wife; 49
5265 Nuwan Kte; Kills Swimming; M: Son; 18
5266 Nupa Kte; Kills Twice; M; Son; 5

5267 Tasunke Wankatuya; High Horse #1; M; Head; 75
5268 Winyan Gi; Yellow Woman; F; Wife; 67

5269 Tasunke Wankatuya; High Horse #2; M; Head; 35

5270 Tasina; Her Blanket; F; Mother; 57
5271 Anpetu Kiyan; Flying Day; F; Dau; 4

5272 Lakota; Lakota; M: Head; 57
5273 Alexander; M: Son; 17

5274 Ciqala Kiza; Fights Little; M; Head; 33
5275 Cayanka; Grunts; F; Wife; 32
5276 Wankal Ho; Voice Above; M; Son; 5
5277 Mazakan; Gun; M; Son; 2-5

5278 Thomas Tyon; M; Head; 42
5279 Elizabeth Tyon; F; Wife; 33
5280 Adelia Tyon; F; Dau; 16
5281 Oliver Tyon; M: Son; 14
5282 Susie Tyon; F; Dau; 8
5283 Eliza Tyon; F; Dau; 4-6

5284 Sungmanitu Hanska; Dennis Long Wolf; M; Head; 38

5285 Tatanka Maza; Iron Bull; M; Head; 41
5286 Icanyan; Against; M; Son; 20
5287 Kaunka; Knocks Down; M; Son; 19
5288 Wasicu Ho; White Man Voice; F; Dau; 8
5289 Tatanka Maza; Cora Iron Bull; F; Dau; 1-10

5290 Mato Gi; Yellow Bear; M; Head; 50
5291 Maro[sic] Winorcala; Old Bear; F; Wife; 56

5292 Maka Iktomi; Ground Spider; M; Head; 26
5293 Nape Wakan; Holy Hand; F; Wife; 21
5294 Wicakte; Kills; M; Son; 8 mo.

Census Of The Sioux And Cheyenne Indians Of Pine Ridge Agency, South Dakota. Taken by W. H. Clapp, Captain 16th Infantry, Acting United States Indian Agent, June 30, 1897. (White Clay District)

Key: Number; Indian Name *(if given)*; English Name; Sex; Relation; Age

5295 Tasunke Waste; Good Horse; M; Head; 47
5296 Maka Siha; Skunk Foot; M; Son; 10
5297 Mato Iyanka; Running Bear; M; Head; 33
5298 Glogli; Brings; F; Wife; 33
5299 Anpo Wicakute; Shoots In Morning; M; Son; 1-2
5300 Rupahu Maza; Iron Wing; M; Head; 42
5301 Pilayapi; Pleased; F; Wife; 28
5302 Adelia; F; Dau; 1-11
5303 Hoksila Ciqala; Little Boy; M; Head; 32
5304 Nawizi Win; Jealous Woman; F; Wife; 38
5305 Sunk Sapa; Black Horse; M: Head; 42
5306 Pilayapi; Pleased; F; Wife; 44
5307 Sunk Sapa; William Black Horse; M; Son; 14
5308 Hobert; M; Son; 10
5309 Tibloku Ota; Plenty Brother; F; Dau; 17
5310 Tasunke Ota; Ownes[sic] Many Horses; M; Head; 27
5311 Pehan; Crane; F; Wife; 21
5312 Hattie; F; Dau; 1-10
5313 Hannah; F; Dau; 1 mo.
5314 Lizzie; F; Dau; 1 mo.
5315 Nellie Hudspeth; F; Head; 36
5316 Oliver Hudspeth; M; Son; 13
5317 William Hudspeth; M; Son; 11
5318 Myrtle Hudspeth; F; Dau; 9
5319 Thetna Hudspeth; F; Dau; 2 mo.
5320 Zona Wilson; F; Wife; 18
5321 Edna Wilson; F; Head; 17
5322 James John Wilson; M: Son; 9 mo.
5223[sic] Titan Opi; Shot From House; M; Head; 28
5324 Canupa Waste; Good Pipe; F; Wife; 24
5325 Zintkala To; Blue Bird; M; Son; 8
5326 Wahacanka Maza; Iron Shield; M: Head; 42
5327 Ite Ska Win; White Faced Woman; F; Wife; 35
5328 Ota Agli; Brings Plenty; F; Head; 28
5329 Oktomi Gi; Yellow Spider; M; Head; 20
5330 Tibloku Ota; Plenty Brothers; F; Wife; 15
5331 Castunpi; Name Him; M; Head; 20
5332 Harape Win; Driver; F; Wife; 18
5333 Sunka Ho Waste; Good Voice Dog; M: Head; 25
5334 Putinhin; Carrie Beard; F; Wife; 18
5335 Wawokiya; Helper; M: Head; 21
5336 Sunkicu; Takes The Horses; F; Wife; 19
5337 Ticagla Kte; Kills Close To Lodge; M; Head; 29
5338 Gliyunka; Comes And Lays; F; Wife; 21
5339 Heraka Isnala; Lone Elk; M; Head; 23
5340 Tate Sina Win; Wind Blanket; F; Wife; 25
5341 Taanpetu Waste; Her Good Day; F; Dau; 6 mo.

Census Of The Sioux And Cheyenne Indians Of Pine Ridge Agency, South Dakota. Taken by W. H. Clapp, Captain 16th Infantry, Acting United States Indian Agent, June 30, 1897. (White Clay District)

Key: Number; Indian Name *(if given)*; English Name; Sex; Relation; Age

5342 Huste; Lame; M: Head; 40
5343 Ite Witko; Fool Face; F; Wife; 26

5344 Cetan Luta; Red Hawk; M: Head; 68
5345 Itazipa Cola; No Bow; F; Wife; 64

5346 Mato Hanska; Long Bear; M; Head; 28
5347 Tiyopa; Door; F; Wife; 31

5348 Ohitiku; Clayton Brave; M; Head; 32
5349 Ituhu Suta; Holy Forehead; F; Wife; 38

5350 Tipi Luta; Red Lodge; F; Head; 26
5351 Sunkhiyohi; Comes After Horse; F; Dau; 6
5352 Zintkala Wakan; Julia Holy Bird; F; Dau; 3

5353 Wickte; Kills; F; Head; 32

5354 Canupa Wakan; Holy Pipe; F; Head; 44
5355 Maza Ho Waste; Good Voice Iron; M; Son; 16
5356 Waonsila; Takes Pity; F; Dau; 7
5357 Hinapa; Comes Out; F; Dau; 5
5358 Iyanke Sni; Dont[sic] Run; M; Son; 2

Census of the Sioux And Cheyenne Indians
Of Pine Ridge Agency, South Dakota.
June 30, 1897

Pass Creek District

Census Of The Sioux And Cheyenne Indians Of Pine Ridge Agency, South Dakota.
Taken by W. H. Clapp, Captain 16th Infantry, Acting United States Indian Agent,
June 30, 1897. (Pass Creek District)

Key; Number; Indian Name *(if given)*; English Name; Sex; Relation; Age

5359	Wi Isna; Lone Woman; F; Head; 23	5392	Kahunpi; Samuel Cut; M; Son; 16
		5393	Kahunpi; Ellis Cut; M; Son; 15
5360	Pute; Lip; M; Head; 52	5394	Kahunpi; Arthur Cut; M; Son; 11
5361	Wicarpi; Star; F; Wife; 47		
5362	Pute; George Lip; M; Son; 21	5395	Kahunpi; Emily Cut; F; Dau; 10
5363	Pute; Ida Lip; F; Dau; 15	5396	Kahunpi; Chester Cut; M; Son; 10
5364	Pute; Bulah Lip; F; Dau; 13		
5365	Pute; Kate Lip; F; Dau; 11	5397	Kahunpi; Raymond Cut; M; Son; 8
5366	Pute; Oliver Lip; M; Son; 6		
5367	Pute; Hat Lip; M; Son; 3-10	5398	Kahunpi; Lucinda Cut; F; Dau; 2-2
5368	Pute; Richard Lip; M; Head; 25	5399	Kahunpi; Rosa Cut; F; Dau; 1
5369	Pute; Edith Lip; F; Wife; 26		
5370	Pute; John Lip; M; Son; 2-10	5400	Mato Gleska; Spotted Bear; M; Head; 38
5371	Pute; Susie Lip; F; Dau; 1-2		
5372	Ceya; Paul Crier; M; Head; 33	5401	Wosla Yanka; Sitting Up; M; Head; 39
5373	Iktomi; Spider; F; Wife; 36		
5374	Ceya; Louis Crier; M; Son; 12	5402	Psica Win; Jumping Woman; F; Wife; 48
5375	Ceya; Peter Crier; M; Son; 9		
5376	Ceya; Cleveland Crier; M; Son; 4-3	5403	Wosla Yanka; Homer Sitting Up; M; Son; 19
5377	Ceya; John Crier; M; Son; 2	5405	Wosla Yanka; Cora Sitting Up; F; Dau; 8
5378	Ceya; Guy Crier; M; Son; 6	5406	Ellen; F; Dau; 17
5379	Canku Maza; Iron Road; F; Head; 65	5407	Winyan Wakan; Half Woman; F; Head; 39
5380	Gi; Brown; M; Head; 48	5408	Ska Win; White Woman; F; Mo.; 68
5381	Onkcekira; Magpie; F; Wife; 48		
5382	Gi; David Brown; M; Son; 18		
5383	Gi; Susie Brown; F; Dau; 14	5409	Tasunke Witko; Crazy Horse; M; Head; 45
5384	Gi; Benjamin Brown; M; Son; 12	5410	Tasunke Witko; Ellen Crazy Horse; F; Wife; 45
5385	John A Logan; M; Head; 27	5411	Tasunke Witko; Ella Crazy Horse; F; Dau; 15
5386	Lizzie Logan; F; Wife; 20		
5387	Angelina Logan; F; Dau; 6 mo.	5412	Tasunke Witko; Richard Crazy Horse; Son; 2-10
5388	Kahunpi; Cut; M; Head; 46		
5389	Tarcaha Wikan; Buckskin String; F; Wife #1; 49	5413	Ptesan Wakpa;; White Cow River; M; Head; 57
5390	Hu Ranran; Scabby Leg; F; Wife #2; 39	5414	Wipisni; Never Full; F; Wife; 50
5391	Kahunpi; Mollie Cut; F; Dau; 17	5415	Cetan Wakinyan; Thunder Hawk; M; Son; 27

Census Of The Sioux And Cheyenne Indians Of Pine Ridge Agency, South Dakota.
Taken by W. H. Clapp, Captain 16th Infantry, Acting United States Indian Agent,
June 30, 1897. (Pass Creek District)

Key; Number; Indian Name *(if given)*; English Name; Sex; Relation; Age

5416 Ptesan Wakpa; Nellie W.C. River; F; Dau; 7
5417 Cetan Wakinyan; Eva Thunder Hawk; F; G.Dau; 4-6

5418 Heraka Nupa; Two Elk; M; Head; 47
5419 Toka Kte; Kills Enemy; F; Wife; 45
5420 Heraka Nupa; James Two Elk; M; Son; 16
5421 Heraka Nupa; Bessie Two Elk; F; Dau; 7

5422 Heraka Nupa; Robert Two Elk; M; Head; 22
5423 Heraka Nupa; Nettie Two Elk; F; Wife; 22
5424 Heraka Nupa; Thomas Two Elk; M; Son; 2-6

5425 Woptura; Geoffrey Chips; M; Head; 33
5426 Wayankapi; Looks At Her; F; Wife #1; 32
5427 Teriya Ku; Comes Back Hard; F; Wife #2; 26
5428 Woptura; Andrew Chips; M; Son; 8
5429 Woptura; Alice Chips; F; Dau; 9
5430 Woptura; Lucy Chips; F; Dau; 2-6
5431 Woptura; Philip Chips; M; Son; 1-6

5432 Cangleska Luta; Red Hoop; M; Head; 52
5433 Pogerloka Nup; Two Nostrils; F; Wife; 48
5434 Cangleska Luta; Grace Red Hoop; F; Dau; 14
5435 Cangleska Luta; Dora Red Hoop; F; Dau; 12
5436 Cangleska Luta; Ophelia R. Hoop; F; Dau; 7

5437 Cangleska Luta; Fanny R. Hoop; F; Dau; 2-1
5438 Mila Nupa; Four Knives; M; Bro; 45

5439 Ciqala Wicakte; Little Killer; M; Head; 25
5440 Mato Ota; Plenty Bear; F; Mo.; 75
5441 Sunkmun; Wild Horse; F; Wife; 22
5442 Carry; F; Dau; 6 mo.

5443 Tokala; Fox; M; Head; 32
5444 Anpetu Tokeya; First Day; F; Wife; 25
5445 Akatankan On; Stays On Top; F; Niece; 5-6

5446 Cekpa; Fred Twin; M; Head; 29
5447 Taanpetu To; Her Blue Day; F; Mo.; 55
5448 Wanbli Ska; Chas. White Eagle; M; Bro; 24
5449 Cekpa; Reuben Twin; M; Bro; 21

5450 Sunka Oye Luta; Red Dog Track; M; Head; 41
5451 Nakpogi; Brown Ears; F; Wife; 41
5452 Gleska Agli; Hattie Brings Spotted; F; Dau; 18

5453 Wanju; Quiver; M; Head; 44
5454 Cetan Rla Win; Rattling Hawk; F; Wife; 41
5455 Hinrota; Roan; F; Dau; 11
5456 Pehinji; Yellow Hair; M; Son; 8
5457 Wanju; James Quiver; M; Son; 2

5458 Tawakin; His Package; M; Head; 37
5459 Tawacin Waste; Good Natured; F; Wife; 31

Census Of The Sioux And Cheyenne Indians Of Pine Ridge Agency, South Dakota. Taken by W. H. Clapp, Captain 16th Infantry, Acting United States Indian Agent, June 30, 1897. (Pass Creek District)

Key; Number; Indian Name *(if given)*; English Name; Sex; Relation; Age

5460	Tawakin; Philip His Package; M; Nephew; 23	5484	Kangi Wakuwa; Cecilia Charging Crow; F; Dau; 5
5461	Sagye; Cane; M; Nephew; 9	5485	Samuel; M; Son; 7 mo.
5462	Hoksila Cepa; Fat Boy; M; Son; 3-9	5486	Jack Lapoint; M; Head; 47
5463	James; M; Son; 1-3	5487	Jennie Lapoint; F; Wife; 40
		5488	Joseph Lapoint; M; Son; 18
5464	Maku; Lucy Breast; F; Head; 35	5489	Eva Lapoint; F; Dau; 13
5465	Anawizi; Jealous At; F; Mo; 55	5490	Oliver Lapoint; M; Son; 10
5466	Maku; John Breast; M; Bro; 23	5491	James Lapoint; M; Son; 5-3
5467	Maku; William Breast; M; Bro; 21	5492	Verax Lapoint; F; Dau; 1
5468	Maku; Silas Breast; M; Bro; 15	5493	Charles Rooks; M; Head; 21
		5494	Annie Rooks; F; Wife; 19
5469	Marpiya Koyaka; Wears The Cloud; F; Head; 8	5495	Jacob Lapoint; M; Head; 22
5470	Mato Sinte; Bear Tail; M; Bro; 6	5496	Gertie Lapoint; F; Wife; 23
		5497	Annie Lapoint; F; Dau; 2-8
5471	Wanju; Harry Quiver; M; Head; 27	5498	Mabel Lapoint; F; Head; 69
5472	Wanju; Agnes Quiver; F; Wife; 22	5499	Miyogli; Joseph Whetstone; M; Nephew; 15
5473	Winyan Waste; Pretty Woman; F; Dau; 3-6	5500	Miyogli; William Whetstone; M; Nephew; 6
5474	Wanju; Dennis Quiver; M; Son; 1-3	5501	Mato Najin; Henry Standing Bear; M; Head; 28
5475	Mato Cincala; Young Bear; M; Head; 34	5502	Mato Najin; Mary Standing Bear; F; Wife; 21
5476	Tasunke Hinsa; Her Red Horse; F; Mo; 71	5503	Elizabeth Flood; F; Head; 34
		5504	Thomas Flood; M; Son; 12
5477	Kangi Wakuwa; Jacob Charging Crow; M; Head; 51	5505	Mato Najin; Henry Standing Bear, Jr; M; Son; 3-10
5478	Oye Maza; Iron Track; F; Wife; 35	5506	Wakinyan Watakpe; Charging Thunder; M; Head; 54
5479	Wagleksun Luta; Red Turkey; F; Sis; 53	5507	Wakinyan Watakpe; Louise C. Thunder; F; Wife; 37
5480	Wagleksun Luta; Annie Red Turkey; F; Dau; 16		
5481	Tokeya Kte; Wallace Kills First; M; Son; 13	5508	Antoine Boyer; M; Head; 45
		5509	Dolly Boyer; F; Wife; 32
5482	Tasina; Hattie Her Blanket; F; Dau; 11	5510	Eva Randall; F; S.Dau; 12
		5511	James Randall; M; S.Son; 10
5483	Waniyetu Kte; Kills In Winter; M; Son; 8	5512	Antoine Randall; M; Head; 32

Census Of The Sioux And Cheyenne Indians Of Pine Ridge Agency, South Dakota. Taken by W. H. Clapp, Captain 16th Infantry, Acting United States Indian Agent, June 30, 1897. (Pass Creek District)

Key; Number; Indian Name *(if given)*; English Name; Sex; Relation; Age

5513	Jessie Randall; F; Wife; 33	5548	Jessie Peck; F; Dau; 14
5514	Annie Randall; F; Dau; 5-6	5549	Katie Peck; F; Dau; 12
5515	Antoine Randall, Jr; M; Son; 2-9	5550	Dora Peck; F; Dau; 10
		5551	Nellie Peck; F; Dau; 7
5516	Mastin Ska; White Rabbit; M; Head; 43	5552	Clara Peck; F; Dau; 4-10
		5553	Mary Peck; F; Dau; 2-6
5517	Mastin Ska; Nellie W. Rabbit; F; Wife; 33	5554	Owen Walter Peck; M; Son; 4 mo.
5518	Cega Luta; Robert Red Kettle; M; B. in Law; 20	5555	Sallie Randall; F; Head; 36
5519	Cega Luta; Rosa Red Kettle; F; S. in Law; 18	5556	Maggie Randall; F; Dau; 18
		5557	Joseph Randall; M; Son; 14
5520	Miyogli; Thos. Whetstone; M; Cousin; 12	5558	Dolly Randall; F; Dau; 10
		5559	John Randall; M; Son; 6
5521	Cega Luta; Alice Red Kettle; F; S. in Law; 29	5560	William Randall; M; Son; 4-7
		5561	Sungmanitu Luzahan; Fast Wolf; M; Head; 41
5522	Seth Gerry; M; Head; 45		
5523	John Gerry; M; Bro; 23	5562	Sungmanitu Luzahan; Mollie Fast Wolf; F; Wife; 36
5524	Cynthia Gerry; F; Dau; 13		
5525	Elbridge Gerry; M; Son; 4	5563	Sungmanitu Luzahan; Philip Fast Wolf; M; Son; 19
5526	Millicent Dubray; F; Head; 45	5564	Sungmanitu Luzahan; Mollie Fast Wolf; F; Dau; 11
5527	William Gerry; M; Nephew; 31		
5528	Jef[sic] Gerry; M; Nephew; 36	5565	Sungmanitu Luzahan; Josephine Fast Wolf; F; Dau; 13
5529	Benjamin Gerry; M; Nephew; 25		
5530	David Dubray; M; Son; 19	5566	Sungmanitu Luzahan; Annie Fast Wolf; F; Dau; 3-10
5531	Baptiste Dubray; M; Son; 11		
5532	Irene Dubray; F; Dau; 7		
5533	Mamie Dubray; F; Dau; 5-3	5567	Charles Randall; M; Head; 26
		5568	Lucy Randall; F; Wife; 33
5534	Mary Ruff; F; Head; 45	5569	Nellie Randall; F; Dau; 3-10
5535	Emma Ruff; F; Dau; 28	5570	Ella Randall; F; Dau; 2-4
5536	George Ruff; M; Son; 24	5571	Catherine Randall; F; Wife[sic]; 3 mo.
5537	Arthur Ruff; M; Son; 13		
5538	William Ruff; M; Son; 10		
5539	Alice Ruff; F; Dau; 22	5572	Heraka Akicita Najin; Elk Standing Soldier; M; Head; 25
5540	Lizzie Ruff; F; Dau; 18		
5541	John Ruff; M; Son; 16	5573	Heraka Akicita Najin; Julia E.S. Soldier; F; Wife; 23
5542	Gracie Ruff; F; Dau; 12		
5543	Vina Ruff; F; Dau; 5-5	5574	Wanbli Waste; Joseph Good Eagle; M; Son; 5-1
5544	Edna Ruff; F; Dau; 7		
		5575	Paul; M; Son; 2-6
5545	Julia Peck; F; Head; 40		
5546	Lottie Peck; F; Dau; 20	5576	William Randall; M; Head; 29
5547	Louis Peck; M; Son; 17	5577	Susie Randall; F; Wife; 27

Census Of The Sioux And Cheyenne Indians Of Pine Ridge Agency, South Dakota.
Taken by W. H. Clapp, Captain 16th Infantry, Acting United States Indian Agent,
June 30, 1897. (Pass Creek District)

Key; Number; Indian Name *(if given)*; English Name; Sex; Relation; Age

5578	Emma Randall; F; Dau; 2-2	5601	Tanyan Wiyukcan; Julia Thinks Well; F; M. in Law; 62
5579	Sungmanitu Luzahan; Thomas Fast Wolf; M; Nephew; 16	5602	Tasunke Ehake; Allen Last Horse; M; B. in Law; 25
5580	Emma Randall; F; Head; 63	5603	Oowaste; Good Shot; M; B. in Law; 23
5581	Lucy W. Randall; F; G.Dau; 8		
5582	Frank Randall; M; Head; 27	5604	Sunkole; Looking For Horses; F; Head; 65
5583	Millie Randall; F; Wife; 25		
5584	Amanda Randall; F; Dau; 2-3		
5585	Richard Randall; M; Son; 1 mo.	5605	Pte Hoton; Bawling Bull; M; Head; 58
5586	Cetan Sapa; Black Hawk; M; Head; 55	5606	Hinapa; Comes Out; F; Wife; 64
5587	Huncasa Cola; No Garter; F; Wife; 51	5607	Sungmanitu Akicita; Wolf Soldier; M; Head; 60
		5608	Wanbli Sun; Eagle Feather; F; Wife; 45
5588	Oosica Hoksila; Young Bad Wound; M; Head; 64		
5589	Pesa; Red Top; F; Wife; 45	5609	Sungmanitu Akicita; Josephine Wolf Soldier; [F]; Dau; 25
5590	Anpo Wakuwa; Martha C.I. Morning; F; G.Dau; 11	5610	Mato Wakuwa; Charging Bear; M; Head; 53
5591	Niyanke Kte; Daniel Kills Alive; M; Head; 35	5611	Mato Wakuwa; Annie C. Bear; F; Wife; 43
5592	Niyanke Kte; Susie Kills Alive; F; Wife; 35	5612	Mato Wakuwa; Addie C. Bear; F; Dau; 12
5593	Niyanke Kte; Emily Kills Alive; F; Dau; 3	5613	Tatanka Hanska; Levi Long Bull; M; S.Son; 24
5594	Osica; Robert Bad Wound; M; Head; 27	5614	George W. Means; M; Head; 26
		5615	Alice Means; F; Wife; 25
5595	Winyan Waste; Good Woman; F; Mo; 58	5616	Lavina Means; F; Dau; 3-10
		5617	James Blaine Means; M; Son; 2-1
5596	Oosica[sic]; Day B. Wound; F; Wife; 21	5618	Mary Carlow; F; Head; 35
5597	Oosica; Ella B. Wound; F; Dau; 3-6	5619	Lizzie Carlow; F; Dau; 17
		5620	Nellie Carlow; F; Dau; 15
		5621	Theodore Carlow; M; Son; 13
5598	Blotahunka Ciqala; Little Leader; M; Head; 35	5622	Jennie Carlow; F; Dau; 11
		5623	Agatha Carlow; F; Dau; 7
5599	Blotahunka Ciqala; Susie Little Leader; F; Wife; 29	5624	Frank Carlow; M; Son; 6
		5625	Annie Carlow; F; Dau; 3-9
5600	Blotahunka Ciqala; Sophia Little Leader; F; Dau; 3-4	5626	Robert Carlow; M; Son; 1-9
		5627	Abraham Carlow; M; Son; 1 mo.

Census Of The Sioux And Cheyenne Indians Of Pine Ridge Agency, South Dakota. Taken by W. H. Clapp, Captain 16th Infantry, Acting United States Indian Agent, June 30, 1897. (Pass Creek District)

Key; Number; Indian Name *(if given)*; English Name; Sex; Relation; Age

5628	Mato Tamaheca; Poor Bear; M; Head; 55	5654	Lizzie Gresh; F; Dau; 9
5629	Mato Cayanka; Grunting Bear; F; Wife #1; 50	5655	Susie Gresh; F; Dau; 7
		5656	Todd Gresh; M; Son; 4-2
5630	Ite Ska; White Face; F; Wife #2; 32	5657	John Gresh; M; Son; 1-1
		5658	Huhu Ska; White Bone; M; Head; 53
5631	Mato Tamaheca; Harry Poor Bear; M; Son; 18	5659	Iyotaka; Sits; F; Wife; 50
5632	Mato Tamaheca; Albert Poor Bear; M; Son; 15	5660	Cetan Wicasa; Hawk Man; M; Head; 41
5633	Mato Tamaheca; Stephen Poor Bear; M; Son; 15	5661	Toka; Enemy; F; Mo; 70
5634	Tonweya Gli; Return Scout; M; Son; 10	5662	Cokab Iyaya; Goes In Center; M; Head; 50
5635	Ptehincala; Calf; D; Dau; 8		
5636	Mato Tamaheca; George Poor Bear; M; Son; 6	5663	Wakin; Baggage; F; Wife; 54
		5664	Cokab Iyaya; Jno. Goes In Center; M; Son; 21
5637	Asapi; Shout At; M; Son; 3-10		
5638	Tasunke Hinsa; Her Red Horse; F; Dau; 3-2	5665	Cokab Iyaya; Alice G. In Center; F; Dau; 20
5639	Mato Tamaheca; Philip Poor Bear; M; Son; 3 mO/[sic]	5666	Cokab Iyaya; Holy G.I. Center; F; Dau; 9
5640	Sunkhinsa Yuha; Red Horse; M; Head; 59	5667	Wanbli Yatapi; Eagle Chief; M; Head; 45
5641	Sagye; Cane; F; Wife #1; 55	5668	Wanbli Yatapi; Fanny E. Chief; F; Wife; 38
5642	Wamniomni Koyaka; Wears Whirlwind; F; Wife #2; 43	5669	Ohola; Respects; F; Dau; 3-10
5643	Sunkhinsa Yuha; Mary Red Horse; F; Dau; 8	5670	Wanbli Yatapi; Thos. Eagle Chief; M; Son; 1
5645[sic]	Onkcekira; Magpie; M; Son; 1-9	5671	Kangi Isnala; Lone Crow; M; Head; 48
5646	Wikan Maza; Iron Rope; M; Head; 39	5672	Mni Sa; Red Water; F; Wife; 49
		5673	Kange Isnala; Herbert Lone Crow; M; Son; 15
5647	Sunk Sapa; Black Horse; F; Wife; 43	5674	Najinyapi; Surrounded; M; Son; 4-3
5648	Maka; Land; M; Son; 9		
5649	Mni; Water; M; Son; 9		
5650	Wikan Maza; Winnie Iron Rope; F; Dau; 5-4	5675	Sina Ska; White Blanket; M; Head; 43
5651	Wicarpi Wanbli; Eagle Star; M; Son; 3-4	5676	Pte Tokaheya; Cow Goes First; F; Wife; 58
		5677	Mato Sapa; Herman Black Bear; M; Son; 19
5652	Mary Gresh; F; Head; 35		
5653	Millie Gresh; F; Dau; 11		

Census Of The Sioux And Cheyenne Indians Of Pine Ridge Agency, South Dakota. Taken by W. H. Clapp, Captain 16th Infantry, Acting United States Indian Agent, June 30, 1897. (Pass Creek District)

Key; Number; Indian Name *(if given)*; English Name; Sex; Relation; Age

5678	Sina Ska; Harry White Blanket; M; Son; 17	5704	Ista Sapa; Jessie Black Eye; F; Dau; 2-3
5679	Wamniomni; Whirlwind; M; Head; 26	5705	Mato Najin; Ellis Standing Bear; M; Head; 29
5680	Hattie; F; Wife; 20	5706	Mato Najin; Standing Bear; M; Head; 62
5681	Wahorpi Luta; Red Nest; M; Head; 34	5707	Mato Najin; Lena S. Bear; F; Wife #1; 54
5682	Cage Wakan; Medicine Name; M; Son; 10	5708	Mato Najin; Ellen S. Bear; F; Wife #2; 45
5683	Tasunke Opi; Shot Her Horses; F; Dau; 5	5709	Mato Najin; Emily S. Bear; F; Dau; 27
5684	Henry Hunter; M; Head; 29	5710	Mato Najin; Sarah S. Bear; F; Dau; 19
5685	Lucy Hunter; F; Wife; 24		
5686	Nicholas Hunter; M; Son; 5-1	5711	Mato Najin; Annie S. Bear; F; Dau; 19
5687	Victoria Hunter; F; Dau; 2-3		
5688	Mary Hunter; F; Dau; 1 mo.	5712	Mato Najin; Edith S. Bear; F; G.Dau; 9
5689	Mato Iyotaka; Sitting Bear; M; Head; 46	5713	Mato Najin; George S. Bear; M; Son; 9
5690	Nape Wakan; Holy Hand; F; Wife #1; 43	5714	Mato Najin; John S. Bear; M; Son; 16
5691	Tonkau Win; Rock Woman; F; Wife #2; 58	5715	Wicarpi Yamni; Three Stars; M; Head; 55
5692	Pehinji; Daniel Yellow Hair; M; Nephew; 15	5716	Hotun; Bawling; F; Wife #1; 46
5693	Wahukeza Zi; Yellow Lance; F; Dau; 12	5717	Tasunke Nupa; Two Horses; F; Wife #2; 49
5694	Wahukeza Zi; Jennie Lance; F; Dau; 11	5718	Wicarpi Yamni; Eva Three Stars; F; Dau; 27
5695	Sungmanitu Wakan; Medicine Wolf; M; Son; 8	5719	Wicarpi Yamni; Susie Three Stars; F; Dau; 19
5696	Ite Wakan; Holy Face; F; Dau; 7		
5697	George; M; Son; 2-3	5720	Wicarpi Yamni; Harry Three Stars; M; Head; 25
5698	Frank Conroy; M; Head; 32	5721	Wicarpi Yamni; Sallie Three Stars; F; Wife; 24
5699	Victoria Conroy; F; Wife; 31		
5700	Julia Conroy; F; Dau; 5-5	5722	Wicarpi Yamni; Jessie Three Stars; F; Dau; 5-4
5701	Harry Conroy; M; Son; 3-7		
5702	Walter Conroy; M; Son; 7 Mo.	5723	Wicarpi Yamni; Lucy Three Stars; F; Dau; 2-1
5703	Ista Sapa; Annie Black Eye; F; Head; 25	5724	Wicarpi Yamni; Martha Three Stars; F; Dau; 3 mo.

Census Of The Sioux And Cheyenne Indians Of Pine Ridge Agency, South Dakota.
Taken by W. H. Clapp, Captain 16th Infantry, Acting United States Indian Agent,
June 30, 1897. (Pass Creek District)

Key; Number; Indian Name *(if given)*; English Name; Sex; Relation; Age

5725 Wicarpi Yamni; Clarence Three Stars; M; Head; 33
5726 Wicarpi Yamni; Jennie Three Stars; F; Wife; 26
5727 Wicarpi Yamni; Sophia Three Stars; F; Dau; 4-1
5728 Wicarpi Yamni; Paul Three Stars; M; Son; 2-6
5729 Wicarpi Yamni; Louise Three Stars; F; Dau; 1-5

5730 He Topa; Four Horns; M; Head; 46
5731 He Topa; Alice Four Horns; F; Dau; 18
5732 Wicarpi Wanbli; Eagle Star; M; Son; 10
5733 Can yuri[sic]; Rough Wood; F; Mother; 72

5734 Marpiya Luta; Red Cloud; M; Son; 33
5735 Hokikta; Looks Back; F; Mother; 68
5736 Wanbli Ciqala; Lawrence Little Eagle; M; Nephew; 21

5737 Mato Najin; Luther Standing Bear; M; Head; 35
5738 Mato Najin; Nellie Standing Bear; F; Wife; 26
5739 Mato Najin; Lillie Standing Bear; F; Dau; 11
5740 Mato Najin; Arthur Standing Bear; M; Son; 9
5741 Mato Najin; Paul F. Standing Bear; M; Son; 7
5742 Mato Najin; Emily Standing Bear; F; Dau; 5
5743 Mato Najin; Julia Standing Bear; F; Dau; 3-1

5744 Mato Najin; Willard Standing Bear; M; Head; 29
5745 Mato Najin; Lizzie Standing Bear; F; Wife; 24

5746 Mato Najin; Esther Standing Bear; F; Dau; 8
5747 Mato Najin; Stephen Standing Bear; M; Son; 5-7
5748 Mato Najin; Oliver Standing Bear; M; Son; 3-2

5749 Yeslo[sic]; Julia[sic] Whistler; M; Head; 36
5750 Tatiyopa; Her Door; F; Wife; 38
5751 Yaslo; Newman Whistler; M; Son; 11
5752 Yaslo; Sarah Whistler; F; Dau; 5-7
5753 Wahacanka; Robert Shield; M; Bro; 33
5754 Can Onajinyapi; Surrounded In Woods; M; B. in Law; 30
5755 Yaslo; Charles Whistler; M; Son; 1-2

5756 Kangi Ska; White Crow; M; Head; 55
5757 Kanta; Prune; F; Wife #1; 51
5758 Canhanpi; Sugar; F; Wife #2; 51
5759 Sunkgleska; Spotted Horse; M; Bro; 31
5760 Tasunke; Her Horses; F; Dau; 25
5761 Wanapa Gli; Comes Back Wounded; M; Son; 12
5762 Kokipa; Afraid; M; G.Son; 6

5763 Peter Ladeaux; M; Head; 47
5764 Jennie Ladeaux; F; Wife; 39
5765 Emma Ladeaux; F; Dau; 21
5766 Alice Ladeaux; F; Dau; 19
5767 Sarah Ladeaux; F; Dau; 17
5768 John Ladeaux; M; Son; 13
5769 Rosa Ladeaux; F; Dau; 9
5770 Jessie Ladeaux; F; Dau; 3-5
5771 Peter Ladeaux Jr; M; Son; 2 mO/[sic]

5772 Katie Ladeaux; F; Head; 36

5773 Robert Randall; M; Head; 43
5774 Mollie Randall; F; Wife; 39

Census Of The Sioux And Cheyenne Indians Of Pine Ridge Agency, South Dakota. Taken by W. H. Clapp, Captain 16th Infantry, Acting United States Indian Agent, June 30, 1897. (Pass Creek District)

Key; Number; Indian Name *(if given)*; English Name; Sex; Relation; Age

5775	Cetan Gi; Yellow Hawk; M; B. in Law; 25		5795	Wakinyan Peta; Lydia Fire Thunder; F; Dau; 4-11
5776	Cetan Gi; Jullia[sic] Yellow Hawk; F; S. in Law; 15		5796	Wakinyan Peta; William Fire Thunder; M; Son; 2-9
5777	Nape Akicita; Moses Hand Soldier; M; Head; 41		5797	Itunkasan Mato; Mary Weasel Bear; F; Head; 62
5778	Nape Akicita; Julia Hand Soldier; F; Wife; 47		5798	Anpetu Hinapa; Day Comes Out; F; Head; 60
5779	Nape Akicita; John Hand Soldier; M; Son; 16			
5780	Nape Akicita; Stephen H. Soldier; M; Son; 14		5799	Sungmanitu Isnala; Charles Lone Wolf; M; Head; 37
5781	Nape Akicita; Lauise[sic] H. Soldier; F; Dau; 11		5800	Eva Lone Wolf; F; Wife; 43
			5801	Stephen Lone Wolf; M; Son; 12
			5802	Emma Lone Wolf; F; Dau; 10
5782	Kiyan Hiyaya; Flying By; F; Head; 64		5803	Agnes Lone Wolf; F; Dau; 8
			5804	Abraham Lone Wolf; M; Son; 4-6
5783	Ista Sapa; Black Eyes; M; Head; 83		5805	John Lone Wolf; M; Son; 6 mo.
5784	Wanbli Luta; Red Eagle; F; Wife; 50		5806	Scili Kte; Allen Pawneee[sic] Killer; M; Head; 23
5785	Tanyan Kte; Kills Well; M; Nephew; 25		5807	Jennie; F; Wife; 22
			5808	Martha; F; Dau; 2-1
5786	Ista Sapa; Thomas Black Eyes; M; Son; 18		5809	Eliza; F; Dau; 6 mo.
			5810	Wicasa Hanska; Long Man; M; Head; 65
5787	Anpo Wakuwa; Howard C. I. Morning; M; Head; 36		5811	Wakpa Oinkpa; Head Of Creek; F; Wife; 61
5788	Anpo Wakuwa; Maggie C. I. Morning; F; Wife; 36		5812	Wicasa Hanska; Charles Long Man; M; Son; 20
5789	Anpo Wakuwa; Oliver C. I. Morning; M; Son; 9			
5790	Anpo Wakuwa; Agnes C. I. Morning; F; Dau; 6		5813	Ite Sankeya; George White Face; M; Head; 42
5791	Anpo Wakuwa; Edward C. I. Morning; M; Son; 2-6		5814	Ite Sankeya; Lucy White Face; F; Wife; 45
			5815	Ite Sankeya; Winnie White Face; F; Dau; 16
5792	Wakinyan Peta; Edgard[sic] Fire Thunder; M; Head; 38		5816	Ite Sankeya; Ethel White Face; F; Dau; 14
5793	Wakinyan Peta; Susie Fire Thunder; F; Wife; 29			
5794	Wakinyan Peta; Julia Fire Thunder; F; Dau; 8		5817	Mato Wayuhi; Conquering Bear; M; Head; 68
			5818	Canku; Road; F; Wife; 62

Census Of The Sioux And Cheyenne Indians Of Pine Ridge Agency, South Dakota. Taken by W. H. Clapp, Captain 16th Infantry, Acting United States Indian Agent, June 30, 1897. (Pass Creek District)

Key; Number; Indian Name *(if given)*; English Name; Sex; Relation; Age

5819	Wahaparpa; Colonel Scraper; M; B. in Law; 71	5850	George Girroux; M; Head; 30
5820	Mato Wayuhi; Abraham C. Bear; M; Son; 25	5851	Emma Girroux; F; Wife; 28
		5852	Robert Girroux; M; Son; 8
5821	Upijata; Forked Tail; M; Son; 25	5853	William Girroux; M; Son; 6
5822	Wakuwa; Charger; M; Son; 17	5854	Rena Girroux; F; Dau; 4-1
5823	Asapi; Yels[sic] At Him; M; Son; 16	5855	Arthur Girroux; M; Son; 2-9
		5856	Annie Girroux; F; Dau; 11 mo.
5824	Pasu Hanska; Long Nose; M; Son; 16	5857	Louis Cottier; M; Head; 26
		5858	Lettie Cottier; F; Wife; 26
5825	Ptesan Hiyaya; Goes White Cow; F; Dau; 46	5859	Gilbert Cottier; M; Son; 6
		5860	Walter J. Cottier; M; Son; 3-10
5826	Pankeska; Shell; F; G.Dau; 5-6	5861	Mabel Cottier; F; Dau; 2-2
5827	Winyan Ota; Plenty Woman; F; Dau; 37	5862	Pearl Cottier; F; Dau; 2 mo.
		5863	Toka Kte; Kills Enemy; M; Head; 43
5828	Talo; Frank Meat; M; Head; 42		
5829	Talo; Nellie Meat; F; Wife; 26	5864	Wakicage Win; Makes Things Good; F; Wife; 41
5830	Sunk Hinto; James Gray Horse; M; Son; 13	5865	Inyan Hoksila; James Rock Boy; M; Nephew; 12
5831	Talo; Arthur Meat; M; Son; 1-6		
5832	Waglure; Loafer; M; Head; 62	5866	Peter Richard; M; Head; 49
5833	Ota Wowasi Ecun; Works Plenty; F; Wife; 54	5867	Louise Richard; F; Wife; 39
		5868	Joseph Richard; M; Son; 16
5834	Pahin Yusla; Plucks Porcupine; M; Son; 31	5869	Susanna Richard; F; Dau; 10
		5870	Josephine Richard; F; Dau; 8
5835	Waglure; Thomas Loafer; M; Son; 21	5871	Alfred Richard; M; Son; 7
		5872	Baptiste Richard; M; Son; 21
5836	Waglure; William Loafer; M; Son; 18	5873	Millie Richard; F; Dau; 1-9
		5874	Joseph Rooks; M; Head; 27
5837	Benj. Claymore; M; Head; 33	5875	Mollie Rooks; F; Wife; 22
5838	Lucy Claymore; F; Wife; 28	5876	Mabel Rooks; F; Dau; 6
5839	David Claymore; M; Son; 10	5877	Jessie Rooks; F; Dau; 1-9
5840	Richard Claymore; M; Son; 8		
5841	Garfield Claymore; M; Son; 6	5878	Joseph Bush; M; Head; 59
5842	Egan Claymore; M; Son; 3-9	5879	James Bush; M; Son; 19
5843	Hobart Claymore; M; Son; 7 mo.	5880	Sallie Bush; F; Wife; 49
		5881	Rosa Bush; F; D. in Law; 26
5844	Samuel Claymore; M; Head; 28		
5845	Joseph Claymore; M; Son; 10	5882	Mary Williams; F; Head; 39
5846	Benj. Claymore; M; Son; 8	5883	Cahrlotte[sic] Williams; F; Dau; 11
5847	Edward Claymore; M; Son; 6		
5848	Roy Claymore; M; Son; 3-10	5884	Annie Williams; F; Dau; 9
5849	Gracie Claymore; F; Dau; 1-3	5885	Lizzie Williams; F; Dau; 7

Census Of The Sioux And Cheyenne Indians Of Pine Ridge Agency, South Dakota. Taken by W. H. Clapp, Captain 16th Infantry, Acting United States Indian Agent, June 30, 1897. (Pass Creek District)

Key; Number; Indian Name *(if given)*; English Name; Sex; Relation; Age

5886	Winnie Williams; F; Dau; 4-6	5922	Mni Owicakte; Jno. Kills IN Water; M; S.Son; 13
5887	Maurice Williams; M; Son; 2-6		
5888	Jennie Williams; F; Dau; 3 mo.	5923	Heraka Wanbli; Eagle Elk; M; Head; 61
5889	Susie Green; F; Head; 34		
5890	Harry Green; M; Son; 13	5924	Waonsila; Takes Pity On Them; F; Wife; 65
5891	Loe Green; M; Son; 11		
5892	Lloyd Green; M; Son; 2 mo.	5925	Wicasa Sakpe; Six Men; M; Son; 7
5893	Kate Rooks; F; Head; 39	5926	Tacanku Waste; Her Good Road; F; Dau; 13
5894	William Rooks; M; Son; 9		
5895	James Rooks; M; Son; 5-6	5927	Heraka Wanbli; Nancy Eagle Elk; F; Dau; 17
5896	Rosana Rooks; F; Dau; 17		
5897	Nellie Rooks; F; Dau; 19		
5898	Alice Rooks; F; Dau; 23	5928	Henry Cottier; M; Head; 20
5899	Nancy Rooks; F; Dau; 15		
5900	Martha Rooks; F; Dau; 13	5929	Mato Gi; Yellow Bear; M; Head; 54
5901	Delia Rooks; F; Dau; 9		
5902	Christina Rooks; F; Dau; 7	5930	Sunknuni; Wild Horse; F; Wife #1; 49
5903	Maggie Rooks; F; Dau; 3-5		
5904	Clara Rooks; F; Dau; 1-2	5931	Anpetu Wakan; Holy Day; F; Wife #2; 42
5905	Mary Cottier; F; Head; 45	5932	Hayapi Waste Koyaka; Wears Good Clothes; F; Dau; 14
5906	George Cottier; M; Son; 17		
5907	Ollie Cottier; F; Dau; 15	5933	Edgar; M; Son; 11 mo.
5908	Emma Cottier; F; Dau; 12		
5909	Charles Cottier; M; Son; 9	5934	Sunka Onca; Imitates Dog; M; Head; 63
5910	Samuel Cottier; M; Son; 7		
5911	Elizabeth Cottier; F; Dau; 5	5935	Sunka Onca; Wallace I. Dog; M; Son; 22
5912	Florence Cottier; F; Dau; 3		
		5936	Marpiya Win; Cloud Woman; F; Mother; 92
5913	Scili Kte; Pawnee Killer; M; Head; 71		
5914	Winyan Hanska; Tall Woman; F; Wife; 65	5937	Kangi Ciqala; Little Crow; M; Head; 34
		5938	Eti; Many Camps; F; Wife; 32
5915	Millie Gleason; F; Head; 41	5939	Ilazata You; Comes Behind; F; M. in Law; 75
5916	Elizabeth Monto; F; Sister; 44		
5917	Pearl Gleason; F; Dau; 13	5940	Kangi Ciqala; Bessie Little Crow; F; Dau; 4-6
5918	John Ladeaux; M; Head; 49		
5919	Bessie Ladeaux; F; Wife; 36	5941	John; M; Son; 11 mo.
		5942	Mato Ptecela; Grover Short Bear; M; Head; 44
5920	Asanpi; Milk; M; Head; 42		
5921	Pejuta Win; Medicine Woman; F; Wife; 38	5943	Wakteka; Kills Game; F; Wife; 40

Census Of The Sioux And Cheyenne Indians Of Pine Ridge Agency, South Dakota. Taken by W. H. Clapp, Captain 16th Infantry, Acting United States Indian Agent, June 30, 1897.   (Pass Creek District)

Key; Number; Indian Name *(if given)*; English Name; Sex; Relation; Age

5944	Mato Ptecela; Silas Short Bear; M; Son; 17	5969	Mato Luta; Julia Red Bear; F; G.Dau; 11 mo.
5945	Isna qu[sic]; Lives Alone; F; Dau; 16	5970	Cangleska Ciqala; Charles Little Hoop; M; Head; 30
5946	Mato Ptecela; Josephine S. Bear; F; Dau; 15	5971	Heraka; Elk; F; Wife; 26
5947	Wanbli Cuwignaka; Eagle Dress; F; Dau; 12	5972	Cangleska Ciqala; Samuel Little Hoop; M; Bro; 19
5948	Mato Ptecela; Baby Short Bear; F; Dau; 10	5973	Wicincala Wakan; Holy Girl; F; Dau; 4-2
5949	Mato Ptecela; Nettie Short Bear; F; Dau; 5-4	5974	Lizzie; F; Dau; 6 mo.
5950	Mato Ptecela; Cecilia Short Bear; F; Dau; 1-5	5975	Cangleska Ciqala; Little Hoop; M; Head; 62
		5976	Cokata Wakan; Holy In Center; F; Wife; 55
5951	Frank Salvis; M; Head; 37		
5952	Lizzie Salvis; F; Wife; 31	5977	Ehake Iyanka; Runs Last; M; Son; 23
5953	Levi Salvis; M; Son; 9		
5954	Lillie Salvis; F; Dau; 7		
5955	George Salvis; M; Son; 4-7	5978	Winyan Nite; Womans[sic] Back; M; Head; 72
5956	William Salvis; M; Son; 2-7		
5957	Sophia Salvis; F; Dau; 1-1	5979	Winyan Nite; Lizzie Womans Back; F; Wife; 70
5958	Cetan Gi; Yellow Hawk; M; Head; 45	5980	Jessie Bittters[sic]; F; Dau; 27
5959	Tawaste; Her Good Things; F; Wife #1; 48	5981	Patrick Bitters; M; Head; 25
		5982	Red Cedar; F; Wife; 19
5960	Tasunke Waste; Her Good Horse; F; Wife #2; 43	5983	Peter Cazue; M; Head; 39
5961	Cetan Gi; Frank Yellow Hawk; M; Son; 19	5984	Mary; F; Wife; 33
5962	Cetan Gi; Susie Yellow Hawk; F; Dau; 18	5985	Frank Salvis, Sr; M; Head; 65
		5986	Sophia Salvis; F; Wife; 62
5963	Cetan Gi; James Yellow Hawk; M; Son; 16	5987	Nancy Salvis; F; Dau; 18
		5988	James Janis/Jr.[sic]; M; G.Son; 4-3
5964	Cetan Gi; Emma Yellow Hawk; F; Dau; 13		
5965	Cetan Gi; Julia Yellow Hawk; F; Dau; 12	5989	Thomas Nelson; M; Head; 23
		5990	Susie Nelson; F; Wife; 25
5966	Kanyela Rpaya; Lays Close; M; Son; 10	5991	Francis Nelson; M; Son; 2-6
		5992	Jennie Nelson; F; Dau; 7 mo.
5967	Sunk Tokca; Different Horse; F; Dau; 10		
		5993	William Larrabee; M; Head; 37
5968	Tokeya Kte; Kills First; M; Son; 3-3	5994	Alice Larrabee; F; Wife; 34
		5995	Nancy Larrabee; F; Dau; 12
		5996	Samuel Larrabee; M; Son; 10

Census Of The Sioux And Cheyenne Indians Of Pine Ridge Agency, South Dakota.
Taken by W. H. Clapp, Captain 16th Infantry, Acting United States Indian Agent,
June 30, 1897. (Pass Creek District)

Key; Number; Indian Name *(if given)*; English Name; Sex; Relation; Age

5997 Louis Larrabee; M; Son; 8
5998 John Shangreau; M; Head; 41
5999 Jules Shangreau; M; Son; 15
6000 Leon Shangreau; M; Son; 11
6001 John Shangreau Jr.; M; Son; 3-6
6002 William Shangreau; M; Son; 1 mo.

6003 Ista Yazan; Sore Eyes; M; Head; 56
6004 Pankeska Wakpa; Shell Creek; F; Wife; 56

6005 He Hanskaska; Aaron Long Horns; M; Head; 39
6006 Oyate; Tribe; F; Wife; 38
6007 Hattie; F; Dau; 13
6008 Winyan Kte; Kills Woman; F; Dau; 3-10
6009 Joseph; M; Son; 11 mo.

6010 Kokab Wosica; Trouble In Front; M; Head; 36
6011 Hihan Sapa; Black Owl; F; Wife; 25
6012 Takuni Ole Sni; Hunts Nothing; F; Dau; 4-6
6013 Takuni Ole Sni; John Hunts Nothing; M; Son; 2-1
6014 Annie; F; Dau; 1 mo.

6015 Maga Ite; Goose Face; M; Head; 39
6016 Wicarpi Wankatuya; High Star; F; Mother; 82

6017 Tawiyaka Waste; Her Good Feather; F; Head; 49
6018 Tasunke Opi; Wounded Horse; M; Son; 13
6019 Tasunke Opi; Paul Wounded Horse; M; Son; 18

6020 Sungmanitu Mato; Bear Wolf; M; Head; 60

6021 Ptesan; White Cow; F; Wife; 37
6022 Mila Ciqala; Little Knife; M; Son; 13
6023 Pte Talo; Buffalo Meat; M; Son; 7
6024 Wakan Mahel Wayanka; Looks In Holy; F; Dau; 4-2

6025 Onpan Ho Waste; Good Voice Elk; M; Head; 33
6026 Zuya Win; Warrior Woman; F; Wife; 26
6027 Tarca Iyanka; Running Antelope; M; Son; 10
6028 Sunktacanku; Horse Road; M; Son; 5
6029 Sunktacanku; John Horse Road; M; Son; 2-1

6030 Sahiyela Wapata; Cheyenne Butcher; M; Head; 32
6031 Tasunke Wakita; Her Looking Horse; F; Wife; 32
6032 Wanbli Waste; Good Eagle; F; Dau; 7
6033 Wanbli Waste; Susie Good Eagle; F; Dau; 4-8
6034 Wanbli Waste; Samuel Good Eagle; M; Son; 2-3

6035 Catka; Left Hand; M; Head; 25
6036 Winyan Wakan; Holy Woman; F; Aunt; 68
6037 Ho Waste; Good Voice; F; Wife; 18

6038 Louis Richard; M; Head; 55
6039 Jennie Richard; F; Wife; 41
6040 Louise Richard; F; Dau; 26
6041 James Richard; M; Son; 20
6042 Mille Richard; F; Dau; 17
6043 Alfred Richard; M; Son; 15
6044 Angelina Richard; F; Dau; 11
6045 Samuel Richard; M; Son; 4-6

6046 Louise Reynal; F; Head; 51

Census Of The Sioux And Cheyenne Indians Of Pine Ridge Agency, South Dakota. Taken by W. H. Clapp, Captain 16th Infantry, Acting United States Indian Agent, June 30, 1897. (Pass Creek District)

Key; Number; Indian Name *(if given)*; English Name; Sex; Relation; Age

6047 Lizzie Bullard; F; Head; 58
6048 Mattier[sic] Ward; F; Dau; 29
6049 Walter Bullard; M; Son; 16
6050 Elmus Bullard; M; Son; 14
6051 Frank Bullard; M; Son; 20
6052 Elbridge Ward; M; Son; 28

6053 Louis Richard, Jr.; M; Head; 22
6054 Eva Richard; F; Wife; 29
6055 Dora Richard; F; Dau; 2-2
6056 Jennie Richard; F; Dau; 2 mo.

6057 Jane Bettelyoun; F; Head; 42
6058 George W. Bettelyoun; M; Son; 24
6059 Harry W. Bettelyoun; M; Son; 20
6060 Fred W. Bettelyoun; M; Son; 15
6061 Lucy M. Bettelyoun; F; Dau; 14
6062 Ellen J. Bettelyoun; F; Dau; 12
6063 Cleveland B. Bettelyoun; M; Son; 9
6064 Martha L. Bettelyoun; F; Dau; 8
6065 Lillie Bettelyoun; F; Dau; 5
6066 Chester Bettelyoun; M; Son; 2-1
6067 Clara Bettelyoun; F; Dau; 22
6068 Lorenzo L. Bettelyoun; M; Son; [?]

6069 Charlotte Chausse; F; Head; 60

6070 Ohomni Iyanka; Runs Around; F; Head; 64

6071 Beaver Monto; M; Head; 49
6072 Agnes Monto; F; Wife; 38
6073 Ella Monto; F; Dau; 11
6074 Enoch Monto; M; Nephew; 21
6075 Belle Monto; F; Dau; 6 mo.

6076 Emma Vlandry; F; Head; 31
6077 Sadie Vlandry; F; Dau; 13
6078 Jennie Vlandry; F; Dau; 12
6079 William Vlandry; M; Son; 10
6080 Robert C. Vlandry; M; Son; 8
6081 Hattie Vlandry; F; Dau; 5-8
6082 Owen H. Vlandry; M; Son; 1-8

6083 William Shangreau; M; Head; 35
6084 Emma Shangreau; F; Wife; 31
6085 Mary Shangreau; F Dau; 10
6086 Winnie Shangreau; F; Dau; 8
6087 William W. Shangreau; M; Son; 3

6088 Alice Bowman; F; Head; 25
6089 Thomas Bowman; M; Bro; 20
6090 John Lee, Jr., M; Nephew; 5

6091 Anarlatapi; James Clincher; M; Head; 41
6092 Napsukaga; Good Finger; F; Wife; 24
6093 Anarlatapi; George Clincher; M; Son; 19
6094 Anarlatapi; Calvin Clincher; M; Son; 15
6095 Anarlatapi; Charles Clincher; M; Son; 11

6096 Tarca Gi; Yellow Deer; M; Head; 25
6097 Wahukeza Win; Lance Woman; F; Wife; 23

6098 Sunka Hunkesni; Philip Slow Dog; M; Head; 36
6099 Ska Koyaka; Wears White; F; Wife; 33
6100 Wanbli Waste; Good Eagle; M; Son; 4-6
6101 Tacanupa Wakan; Her Holy Pipe; F; Dau; 3-3
6102 Sunka Hinkesni[sic]; Susie Slow Dog; F; Dau; 2 mo.

6103 Wan Ota; Plenty Arrows; M; Head; 39
6104 Warpe Koyaka; Wears Leaf; F; Wife; 35
6105 Yusluta; Pulls It Out; M; Son; 4-10

Census Of The Sioux And Cheyenne Indians Of Pine Ridge Agency, South Dakota. Taken by W. H. Clapp, Captain 16th Infantry, Acting United States Indian Agent, June 30, 1897. (Pass Creek District)

Key; Number; Indian Name *(if given)*; English Name; Sex; Relation; Age

6106 Wan Ota; William Plenty Arrows; M; Son; 6 mo.
6107 Isnala Ti; Lone Life; F; Head; 72
6108 Mato Sapa; Paul Black Bear; M; Head; 33
6109 Oyuran; Gives Away; F; Dau; 17
6110 Mato Sapa; Black Bear; M; Head; 44
6111 Tasunke Waste; Ownes[sic] Good Horses; F; Wife; 37
6112 Mato Sapa; Belle Black Bear; F; Dau; 20
6113 Mato Sapa; William Black Bear; M; Son; 17
6114 Mato Sapa; Susie Black Bear; F; G.Dau; 1-5
6115 Mato Wicagnaya; Fooling Bear; M; Head; 24
6116 Cekiyapi; Prays To Her; F; Wife; 24
6117 Nape Maza; Iron Hand; M; Son; 4-5
6118 Mato Wicagnaya; Paul Fooling Bear; M; on; 2-10
6119 Mato Wicagnaya; Lucy Fooling Bear; F; Dau; 1-3
6120 Scili Kokipesni; Not Afraid Of Pawnee; M; Head; 42
6121 Hinapa; Comes Out; F; Wife; 34
6122 Cagye; Cane; F; Head; 71
6123 Wanbli Gleska; Felix Spotted Eagle; M; Head; 34
6124 Wanbli Gleska; Amelia Spotted Eagle; F; Wife; 25
6125 Wanbli Gi; Mary Yellow Eagle; F; Dau; 5
6126 Wanbli Gleska; Charles Spotted Eagle; M; Son; 3-6
6127 Sungmanitu Isnala; Lone Wolf; M; Head; 65
6128 Canku Maza; Iron Road; F; Wife; 64
6129 Sungmanitu Isnala; Felix Lone Wolf; M; Son; 26
6130 Sungmanitu Isnala; Nathan L;. Wolf; M; Son; 20
6131 Sungmanitu Isnala; Willard L. Wolf; M; Son; 19
6132 Mary Selwin; F; G.Dau; 11
6133 Sunkhinsa Yuha; Red Horse Owner; M; Head; 66
6134 Ptan Luta; Red Otter; F; Wife; 39
6135 Petaga; William P. Fire; M; B. in Law; 64
6136 Jennie; F; Niece; 11
6137 Hanpa Hunku; Moccasin Mother; F; Head; 84
6138 Pehin Sica; Bad Hair; M; Head; 30
6139 Pte Luta; Red Cow; F; Dau; 3-10
6140 Ehake Win; Last Woman; F; Wife; 24
6141 Tatanka Isnala; Lone Bull; M; Head; 60
6142 Hihan Tatanka; Owl Bull; M; Head; 57
6143 Rante; Cedar; F; Wife; 50
6144 Wayankapi; Looked At; F; Dau; 11
6145 Naca; Chief; F; Head; 82
6146 Waste Kaga; Makes Good; M; Head; 38
6147 Waste Kaga; Eliza Makes Good; F; Wife; 24
6148 Heraka Isnala; Lone Elk; M; Son; 8

Census Of The Sioux And Cheyenne Indians Of Pine Ridge Agency, South Dakota. Taken by W. H. Clapp, Captain 16th Infantry, Acting United States Indian Agent, June 30, 1897. (Pass Creek District)

Key; Number; Indian Name *(if given)*; English Name; Sex; Relation; Age

6149	Psito Win; Bead Woman; F; Dau; 7	6176	Mato Win; Bear Woman; F; Head; 61
6150	Waste Kaga; Richard Makes Good; M; Son; 1-1	6177	Susan Robinson; F; Head; 78
6151	Ska Win; White Woman; F; Head; 27	6178	James Hawkins; M; Head; 36
6152	Wanbli Ska; White Eagle; M; Son; 6	6179	Andrew Russell; M; Head; 20
6153	Tainyan Hiyaya; Goes In Sight; F; Mother; 69	6180	Charles Means; M; Head; 30
		6181	George Means; M; Son; 9
6154	Hanglawa; Lucy Counts H. Nights; F; Niece; 14	6182	Wankal Ti; Kills Above; M; Head; 32
6155	Carli Win; Powder Woman; F; Head; 33	6183	Wakuwa; Charges At; F; Wife; 35
6156	Wazi Ptecela; James Short Pine, Jr.; M; Son; 11 mo.	6184	Aglagla Iyanka; Runs Close TO Edge; M; Son; 4-5
		6185	Wankal Kte; Maggie Kills Above; F; Dau; 3 mo.
6157	Sungmanitu Luzahan; John Fast Wolf; M; Head; 25		
6158	Sungmanitu Luzahan; Jessie Fast Wolf; F; Wife; 20	6186	Naca Ciqala; Little Chief; M; Head; 26
		6187	Naca Ciqala; Louise L. Chief; F; Wife; 19
6159	Charles Dubray; M; Head; 24		
6160	Elizabeth Dybray[sic]; F; Wife; 19	6188	Wakinyan Peta; Zoy Fire Thunder; F; Dau; 2-3
6161	Eugene Dybray; M; Son; 1-6	6189	Margrette; F; Dau; 2 mo.
6162	Cetan Kokipapi; Afraid Of Thunder; M; Head; 59	6190	Alex Lebuff; M; Head; 37
		6191	Zonie Lebuff; F; Dau; 9
6163	Louise Young; F; Head; 45	6192	Rhoda Lebuff; F; Dau; 3-6
6164	Amelia Young; F; Dau; 27		
6165	Victor Young; M; Son; 20	6193	Mila Pe Sni; Dull Knife; M; Head; 26
6166	Lizzie Young; F; Dau; 19		
6167	Mary Young; F; Dau; 17	6194	Mary; F; Wife; 21
6168	William Young; M; Son; 15	6195	Eliza; F; Dau; 3 mo.
6169	Edward Young; M; Son; 13		
6170	Frank Young; M; Son; 12	6196	Canupa Yuha Mani; Walks With Pipe; F; Head; 27
6171	Alfred Young; M; Son; 9		
6172	Philip Young; M; Son; 5-2	6197	Woqupi; Gives Him S.T. Eat; M; Son; 8
6173	Henry Young; M; Son; 1-1		
		6198	Warpe Sa; Red Leaf; M; Son; 2-5
6174	George Young; M; Head; 25		
6175	Ida Young; F; Wife; 18	6199	Ole; Ole; M; Head; 70

Census Of The Sioux And Cheyenne Indians Of Pine Ridge Agency, South Dakota. Taken by W. H. Clapp, Captain 16th Infantry, Acting United States Indian Agent, June 30, 1897. (Pass Creek District)

Key; Number; Indian Name *(if given)*; English Name; Sex; Relation; Age

6200 Canupa Wanbli; Pipe Eagle; M; Head; 44
6201 Panpanla; Tender; F; Wife; 37
6202 Winyan Sapa; Black Woman; F; Dau; 3-10
6203 Oosica; Noah Bad Wound; M; Head; 29
6204 Oosica; Mary Bad Wound; F; Wife; 24
6205 Oosica; Gilbert Bad Wound; M; Son; 4-6
6206 Oosica; Vincent Bad Wound; M; Son; 2-5
6207 Mato Wiyaka; Feather Bear; M; Head; 35
6208 Cetan Win; Hawk Woman; F; Wife; 25
6209 Mato Cante Wanica; Heartless Bear; M; Son; 46
6210 Otakuye Wanica; No Relation; F; Mother; 86
6211 Sunkmanu; Steals Horses; M; Head; 37
6212 Hunkpapa; Hunkpapa; F; Mother; 80
6213 Jennie Stover; F; Head; 48
6214 Edward Stover; M; Son; 21
6215 William Stover; M; Son; 19
6216 Edith Stover; F; Dau; 8
6217 Laura Stover; F; Dau; 5-6
6218 Grace Stover; F; Dau; 2-4
6219 George Stover; M; Son; 3-5
6220 John Swallow; M; Head; 26
6221 Hattie Swallow; F; Wife; 23
6222 Samuel Smith; M; Head; 37
6223 Julia Smith; F; Wife; 32
6224 Alice Smith; F; Dau; 12
6225 Wapaha Sapa; Joseph B. W. Bonnet; M; Head; 22
6226 Cetan Gi; John Yellow Hawk; M; Head; 22
6227 Sicaya Rpaya; Millie Lays Bad; F; Wife; 19
6228 Jessie Craven; F; Head; 32
6229 Hattie Craven; F; Dau; 15
6230 John Craven; M; Son; 13
6231 Teddy Craven; M; Son; 10
6232 Edith Craven; F; Dau; 6
6233 Isabelle Oma Craven; F; Dau; 2-5
6234 Emma Allen; F; Head; 42
6235 Joseph Allen; M; Son; 21
6236 Sophia Allen; F; Dau; 18
6237 Charles Allen; M; Son; 17
6238 Samuel Allen; M; Son; 15
6239 Jessie Allen; F; Dau; 13
6240 Lizzie Allen; F; Dau; 11
6241 Robert Allen; M; Son; 9
6242 Julia Allen; F; Dau; 8
6243 Louis Hawkins; M; Head; 39
6244 Julia Hawkins; F; Wife; 35
6245 Susie Hawkins; F; Dau; 17
6246 James Hawkins; M; Son; 15
6247 Joseph Hawkins; M; Son; 13
6248 William Hawkins; M; Son; 6
6249 Lottie D. Hawkins; F; Dau; 10
6250 Louis Hawkins; M; Son; 1 mo.
6251 Emily Lesserts; F; Head; 55
6252 Bell McWilliams; F; G.Dau; 12
6253 Benny McWilliams; M; G.Son; 10
6254 Mag McWilliams; F; G.Dau; 6
6255 Butterfly; F; Mother; 78
6256 Philip F. Wells; M; Head; 46
6257 Thomas H. Wells; M; Son; 11
6258 Alma A. Wells; F; Dau; 8
6259 Philip Wells Jr.; M; Son; 6

Census Of The Sioux And Cheyenne Indians Of Pine Ridge Agency, South Dakota. Taken by W. H. Clapp, Captain 16th Infantry, Acting United States Indian Agent, June 30, 1897. (Pass Creek District)

Key; Number; Indian Name *(if given)*; English Name; Sex; Relation; Age

6260 Mark Wells; M; Son; 3-6
6261 Patrick F. Wells; M; Son; 3 mo.
6262 George Randall; M; Head; 21
6263 Lucy Randall; F; Wife; 20
6264 Rosa Randall; F; Dau; 6 mo.

6265 Charles Richard; M; Head; 24
6266 Louise Richard; F; Wife; 22
6267 Theresha[sic] Flesher; F; Niece; 5-8
6268 Louis Richard; M; Son; 5 mo.

6269 Maka Hanska; Long Skunk; M; Head; 26
6270 Nellie; F; Wife; 27
6271 Mary; F; Dau; 11 mo.

6272 Tasunka Ciqala; Little Horse; M; Head; 22
6273 Tasunke Ciqala; Mary L. Horse; F; Wife; 21

6274 Kangi Wakuwa; Wm. Charging Crow; M; Head; 27
6275 Kangi Wakuwa; Nancy Charging Crow; F; Wife; 22

6276 Louis Provost; M; Head; 24
6277 Alma Provost; F; Wife; 20
6278 Emma Provost; F; Dau; 7 mo.

6279 Nape; Hand; M; Head; 58
6280 Nin Kaga; Makes Life; F; Wife; 49
6281 Nape; Julia Hand; F; Dau; 23
6282 Hakikta; Looks Back; F; Dau; 14

6283 William Brown; M; Head; 28
6284 Lizzie Brown; F; Wife; 26
6285 Alice Brown; F; Dau; 8
6286 Harry Brown; M; Son; 6
6287 Rosa Brown; F; Dau; 1-9
6288 Nellie Brown; F; Dau; 3-8

6289 Nicholas Ruleau; M; Head; 30

6290 Louis Ruleau; F; Dau; 2-3

6291 Oceti; Fire Place; M; Head; 33
6292 Oceti; Mary Fire Place; F; Wife; 29
6293 Oceti; Charles Fire Place; M; Son; 8 mo.

6294 Eyapa Ota; Plenty Haranguer; M; Head; 47
6295 Psica; Jumper; F; Wife; #1; 45
6296 Anpetu Luta; Anna Red Day; F; Wife #2; 53
6297 Eyapa Ota; Jennie P. Haranguer; F; Dau; 15
6298 Piya Isaga; Second Growth; F; Dau; 7
6299 Wayaka Oycespapi; Captured Prisoner; F; Dau; 4-5
6300 Zintkala Luta; Red Bird; M; Son; 11
6301 Byapaha Ota; William P. Haranger; M; Son; 13

6302 Susie Lamb; F; Head; 27
6303 Adolph Lamb; M; Don; 2
6304 Jule Lamb; M; Son; 2
6305 Mary Lamb; F; Dau; 10 mo.

6306 Joseph Richard; M; Head; 49
6307 Julia Richard; F; Wife; 40
6308 Alexander Richard; M; Son; 20
6309 Benjamin Richard; M; Son; 17
6310 Lucy Richard; F; Dau; 14
6311 Julia Richard; F; Dau; 6
6312 Josephine Richard; F; Dau; 4-4
6313 Nettie Eldridge; F; D. in Law; 19

6314 Huncase; Garter;; F; Head; 65

6315 James Richard; M; Head; 35
6316 Sophia Richard; F; Wife; 37
6317 Louise Richard; F; Dau; 15
6318 Daniel Richard; F; Son; 10
6319 Thomas Richard; M; Son; 6
6320 Annie Richard; F; Dau; 9

Census Of The Sioux And Cheyenne Indians Of Pine Ridge Agency, South Dakota.
Taken by W. H. Clapp, Captain 16th Infantry, Acting United States Indian Agent,
June 30, 1897. (Pass Creek District)

Key; Number; Indian Name *(if given)*; English Name; Sex; Relation; Age

6321	Nellie Richard; F; Dau; 3-4	6343	Zintkala Wicasa; Bird Man; M; Son; 3-3
6322	Alfred Richard; M; Son; 1-4	6344	Tasunke Ku; Horses Comes[sic]; M; Son; 10 mo.
6323	Yamni Apa; Strikes Three Times; M; Head; 22		
6324	Pilaiciya; Pleased Herself; F; Wife; 22	6345	Si Tanka; Big Foot; M; Head; 65
		6346	Sunkska Yuha; White Horse Owner; F; Wife; 65
6325	Mato Luta; Howard Red Bear; M; Head; 24	6347	Mato Ota; Plenty Bear; M; Head; 43
6326	Winyan Gi; Yellow Woman; F; Wife; 24	6348	Capa Esta; Cherry Eye; F; Wife; 33
6327	Rosa Red Bear; F; Dau; 1-6		
		6349	Mato Ota; Thomas Plenty Bear; M; Son; 16
6328	Tasunke Kinyela; Flying Horse; M; Head; 19		
		6350	Emma Webber; F; Head; 28
6329	Cinpi Win; Wants Him; F; Head; 18	6351	Frank Webber; M; Son; 5
		6352	Julia Webber; F; Dau; 2
6330	Wakan Nahomni; Henry Tunring[sic]; Holy; M; Head; 43	6353	Julia Ecoffey; F; Head; 53
		6354	Pacific Ecoffey; F; Dau; 18
6331	Wabluska Gi; Yellow Bug; F; Wife; 34	6355	Albert Ecoffey; M; Son; 14
		6356	Adie Ecoffey; F; Dau; 14
6332	Heraka Waste; Good Elk; M; B. in Law; 25	6357	Mary Tway; F; Head; 30
6333	Pispiza Luta; Red Prairie Dog; M; Son; 10	6358	Norah Tway; F; Dau; 3-3
		6359	Emma Tway; F; Dau; 7
6334	Ista Gi; Yellow Eyes; M; Son; 6	6360	Thomas Tway; M; Son; 1-3
6335	Canupa Wakan; Holy Pipe; F; Dau; 3-6		
		6361	Joseph Ecoffey; M; Head; 20
		6362	Rosa Ecoffey; F; Wife; 18
6336	Wiyaka Sakpe; Six Feathers; M; Head; 40	6363	Jules Ecoffey; M; Head; 24
6337	Tacanku; Her Road; F; Wife #1; 45	6364	Alice Ecoffey; F; Wife; 22
		6365	Fred Ecoffey; M; Son; 2-2
6338	Tonweya Win; Guide Woman; F; Wife; #2; 22	6366	George Brown; M; Head; 26
6339	Wiyaka Sakpe; John Six Feathers; M; Son; 17	6367	Susie Brown; F; Wife; 26
		6368	George Brown Jr.; M; Son; 3-3
6340	Mniwanca; Ocean; F; Dau; 15	6369	Joseph Brown; M: Son; 2 mO/[sic]
6341	Sunkska; White Horse; M; Son; 13	6370	Jennie Brown; F; Dau; 1-9
6342	Oye Wakan; Medicine Track; F; Dau; 8	6371	Lizzie Means; F; Head; 32
		6372	Robert B. Means; M; S.Son; 19
		6373	William Burgen; M; S.Son; 17

Census Of The Sioux And Cheyenne Indians Of Pine Ridge Agency, South Dakota. Taken by W. H. Clapp, Captain 16th Infantry, Acting United States Indian Agent, June 30, 1897. (Pass Creek District)

Key; Number; Indian Name *(if given)*; English Name; Sex; Relation; Age

6374 Minnie Vlandry; F; Dau; 12
6375 Bert Means; F; Son; 4-10
6376 Frank Means; M; Son; 10
6377 John Means; M; Son; 2

6378 Minnie Thayer; F; Head; 34
6379 Alice Sickler; F; Sister; 21
6380 Lucy Sickler; F; Sister; 18
6381 Robert Morrison; M; S.Son; 7

6382 Inyan Sna Win; Rattling Rock; F; Head; 76

Note.
    For Numbers 6383 - 4-5, see page 54 of census, Porcupine District.

[The page and numbers mentioned above could not be found.]

Index

[CLIFFORD], Orlando 265
ABOVE
   Alexander M 255
   Fanny M 255
ACHOMNI 247
ACU 97
ADAMS
   Alexander 59,223
   John 59,223
   Joseph 59,223
   Lucy 59,223
   Nellie 59,223
   Susie 223
   Susy 59
   Victoria 8,174
ADELIA 135,298
ADOLPH 69,231
AFRAID 115,146,278,310
AFRAID O HAWK, Richard 237
AFRAID OF BEAR 6,95,172,257
   Lucy 6,172
   Robert 6,189
AFRAID OF EAGLE 9,175
AFRAID OF ENEMY 14,90,127,
   252,290
AFRAID OF HAWK . 74,125,237,288
   Albert 74
   Annie 74
   Richard 74
AFRAID OF HIM 116,123,279,286
AFRAID OF LEFT HAND 83,245
AFRAID OF NOTHING 83,245
AFRAID OF PAWNEE, Mat 153
AFRAID OF THUNDER 154,318
AFTER MONEY 12,177
AFTER TROUBLE 125,287
AGAIN 18,183
AGAINST 135,297
AGAROTA PENO 264
AGLAGLA INYANKA 46,195,
   242,256
AGLAGLA IYANKA 31,154,318
AGLALA IYANKA 94
AGLI 16,43,67,115,178,229,278
AGLI TI 11,177
AGLIPI 290
AGLITI 13,178
AGNES 141

AGUYAPI SOKA 56,219
AHAKE HI 201
AHAPE GLI 200
AHPO WAKUWA 13
AHU 13
AINAPI 96
AIYAPA 236
AIYAPI 10,43,74,89,114,121,132,
   175,207,251,257,277,295
AKA HIYU 68
AKAN INYANKA 257
AKAN IYANKA 95
AKAN MANI 45,208
AKAN MANIPA 251
AKAN MANIPI 100
AKANWANKA KTE 237
AKANWIS KTE 218
AKANYAKA 271
AKANYAKA KTE 225,226
AKATANHAN IGLONICA 140
AKATANKAN ON 304
AKAYANKA 107
AKAYANKA KTE 62,63,74
AKE 18,183
AKE HI 230
AKE HIYN 223
AKE HIYU 59,73,76,236
AKE KU 239
AKICIPA CIQALA 20
AKICISA 65,107
AKICITA CIQALA 34,132,184,
   198,295
AKICITA HANSKA 39,83,102,
   203,245,263
AKICITA NAJIN 5,16,142,181
AKICITA OTA 9,115,278
AKICITA WANJILA 55
AKICITA WASTE 117,280
AKICITSA NAJIN 171
AKICIZAPI 62
AKICIZE 11,74,237,293
AKISITA HANSKA 83
AKISJA 235
AKIYAN WIN 180
AKIYANPI 15
AKOMYAKA KTE 248
AKU 134,135,296
ALEXANDER 134,297

Index

ALICE 6,34,92,172,281
ALL GOOD 22,186
ALL HOLY 18,183
ALLEN
    Charles 155
    Emma 155,319
    Jessie 155,319
    Joseph 155,319
    Julia 155,319
    Lizzie 155,319
    Nellie 155
    Robert 155,319
    Samuel 155,319
    Sophia 155,319
ALLMAN
    Alice 7
    Charles 7,173
    Lilly 173
    Lily 7
    Lorina 7,173
    Louise 7,173
    Lydia 7,173
    Myrtle 173
    Nora 7,173
    Sam 7,173
AMAPSICA 117,280
AMBROSE MEXICAN 72
AMERICAN BEAR 116,279
AMERICAN HORSE 83,219,245
    Alice 83,245
    Benny 245
    Charles 83,245
    Dawson 56
    Jennie 83
    Joa 245
    Joseph 83
    Josie 83
    Julia 83,98,260
    Lucy 83,245
    Nancy 72
    Robert 72
    Sophia 83
    Sopjia 245
    Thos 98,260
    William 260
    Wm 98
AMERICAN HORSE #2 56
AMIOTTE

Albert 52
Bert 52
Edward 52
Mary 52
Maud 52
Nettie 52
Nora 52
Oscar 52
Walter 52
Zonie 52
AMMIOTTE
    Albert 216
    Bert 216
    Edward 216
    Emery 216
    Mary 216
    Maud 216
    Nettie 216
    Nora 216
    Oscar 216
    Walter 216
    Zoie 216
AMONG 22,130,186,296
AMONG TIMBER 32,196
AMUKASAN CIQALA 221
ANARLATAPI 152,316
ANATAN 279
ANATANPI 116
ANAWIZI 305
ANERICAN HORSE
    Nancy 235
    Robt 235
    Susie 235
ANILKANSAN WASTE 237
ANNA 49,69,231
ANNAIE 30
ANNIE 43,44,66,207,213,237,315
ANOKASAN 53,109
ANOKASAN HOKSILA 134
ANOKASAN WANBLI 108,112
ANOKATAN KTE 121
ANOWAN 113
ANPATU WASTE 182
ANPETU 33,77,90,95,98,113,115,
...116,118,252,257,259,276,278,279
ANPETU HINAPA 7,21,124,131,147,
.... 173,186,286,294,311
ANPETU HIYAYA 55

Index

ANPETU KIYAN 134,297
ANPETU LUTA 10,34,95,262,320
ANPETU MANI 65,228
ANPETU SA 54,94
ANPETU SKA 70,96,258
ANPETU TOKAHEYA 140
ANPETU TOKEYA 304
ANPETU WAKAN .... 51,61,68,91, ... 149,313
ANPETU WASTE 17,51,83
ANPETU YUHA 64,227
ANPETUWAKAN 253
ANPITU 239
ANPITU AGLI 209
ANPITU HIYAYA 218
ANPITU LUTA 198,218
ANPITU SKA 233
ANPITU WAKAN ... 209,215,224,230
ANPITU WASTE 215,245
ANPO 30
ANPO HUTE 135
ANPO KTE 176,189
ANPO TOKA KTE 103,264
ANPO WAKITA 14,179
ANPO WAKUTE 236
ANPO WAKUWA .... 7,143,147,173, ... 178,307,311
ANPO WATAKPE 7
ANPO WICAKTE 6,112,130,276
ANPO WICAKUTE 274,298
ANPO WICASA 41,205
ANPOSKA TUNPI 109
ANPOSKAN TONPI 121
ANPOSKAN TUNPI 273,284
ANPTU LUTA 94
ANT 53,216
ANTELOPE 86,249
ANTELOPE WOMAN 12,24
ANUKASAN 62,217,225,272,276
ANUKASAN CIQALA 57,221
ANUKASAN HOKSILA 297
ANUKASAN MATO 102
ANUKASAN WAMBLI 264
ANUKASAN WANBLI 264
ANUKASAN WASTE 74,238
ANUKATAN KTE 284
ANUNWAN 276
APAPI 133,296

APE WAKAN 197
APEAPE HINRPAYA 231
APEPI 116,279
APICITA ISNALA 219
APPLE 18,182
   Dora 18,175
   George 18,182
   Jennie 18,182
   John 18,182
ARAPAHOE
   David 32,196
   Girl 32,196
   Jennie 32,196
   William 32,196
AREYUNKA 258
ARM 124,287
ARMIJO
   Lamott 20
   Mary 20
ARMINGO
   Lamott 185
   Mary 185
ARMSTRONG
   Cecelia 173
   Cecilia 7
AROUND IT
   Howard 90,252
   John 90,252
   Victoria 90,252
ARRESTED ONE HUNDRED 72,234
ARROW QUIVER 20,184
ARROW WOUND 54,72,218,234
ASANPI 71,149,234,313
ASAPI .... 22,33,42,78,144,148,182, ... 241,281,308,312
ASCHRAFT, Lulu 92
ASHCRAFT, Lulu 190
ASKS THEM TO DO SOMETHING 66,229
AST 125
ASTIBONE 225
ASYIBONE 62
AT NIGHT, Lizzie 92,254
ATAYA WAKAN 18,183
ATAYA WASTE 186
ATAYA ZINTKALA 69,231
ATAYE WASTE 22
ATE CIQA 185

Index

ATE CIQALA 20
AUGUSTUS 68,231
AWAGUGUPI 54,218
AWEAN 20
    John 20
AWICAGLI 60,222
AWICAKICISA 271
AWICASA 118
AWICAYUSTAN 257
AWICAYUSTANPI 95
AWOKASAN WASTE 272
AYAAPI 96
AYUATAMPI 281
AYUSTANPI 118,295
AYUSTAUPI 36
AYUTA 153
AYUTAPI 13,102,120,140,263
AYUTEPI 283
B HEAD, Bismarck 207
B W BONNET, Joseph 319
BACK 115,278
BACKWARD 127,290
BAD
    Flora L 262
    Jennie L 262
BAD BEAR
    Henry 72
    Howard 72,287
BAD BOW 61,224
BAD BOY 37,75,200,237
BAD COB 15,180
BAD EAGLE 117,280
BAD ELK
    John 34,198
    Joseph 34
    Julia 32,266
    Susie 32,198
BAD HAIR 153,317
BAD HEART BULL 123,286
BAD HORSE 124
BAD IRON 33,197
    Hattie 197
BAD LAND WOMAN 61,224
BAD LOOKING WOMAN 5,171
BAD MOCCASIN 178,200
BAD MOCCOSIN 13,36
BAD NATION 134,297
BAD OLD WOMAN 5,20,102,
.... 171,184,264
BAD REE 30,194
BAD ROCK 131
BAD SHOT HIM 121,284
BAD TALKER 69,231
BAD WOLF 38,113,201,277
BAD WOMAN 112,276
BAD WOUND
    Day 143
    Ella 143
    Gilbert 155,319
    Mary 155,319
    Noad 319
    Noah 155
    Robert 143,307
    Vincent 155,319
BAD YELLOW HAIR ... 107,271,272
BADGER 126,289,294
    Fred 42,206
    Jennie 42,206
    Josephine 206
    Lizzie 42,206
    Mary 42,206
    Sallie 42,206
BAGGAGE 144,308
    Frank 15,180
BAGGED 44,207
BAINES
    Francis L 254
    Frank L 254
    Louisa L 254
    Paul 254
    Polonia L 254
    Susie L 254
BALD EAGLE 53,62,109,112,
.... 217,225,272,276
BALD EAGLE BEAR
    Katie 102
    Mabel 102
    Mable 264
BALD EAGLE BOY 134,297
BALD HEAD 8,175
BALDEAGLE BEAR, Katy 264
BANK 127,290
BATA OPI 263
BATTLE 107,123,271,286
BAWLING 145,309
BAWLING BULL 143,307

Index

BEAD 52,216
BEAD WOMAN 154,318
   Paul 154
BEADS 37,201
BEAE RUNNER, Joseph 251
BEAR 16,96,181,258
   Abraham C 148,312
   Addie 307
   Annie C 307
   Charles G 250
   Henry B 235
   Henry L 180
   Herbert H 252
   James 180
   John 14,179
   Joseph 41
   Josephine S 314
   Louise 14,179
   Sophia R 220
   Thomas G 250
   Victoria T 263
   Zuzella L 180
BEAR ARM NECKLACE 295
BEAR BACKBONE 74,236
BEAR BIRD 13
BEAR BONE 110,274
BEAR BOY 10,110,176,273
BEAR CLAW 134,297
BEAR CLIMBS 83,245
BEAR COMES OUT ... 7,9,39,53,122,
.... 131,172,175,203,285,293
   Jennie 39
BEAR COMES TO LAY DOWN.218
BEAR COMES TO LIE DOWN ... 55
BEAR DRESS 107
BEAR EAGLE 36,53,126,
.... 178,200,217,289
   Joseph 54,217
   Louis 36,200
BEAR EAR 111,275
BEAR FOOT 53,216
BEAR HORSE 122,285
BEAR IN WOOD 120,283
BEAR KILLER 35,199
   Albert 35,199
   John 35,199
   Louise 35,199
BEAR LEADER 115,278

BEAR LEAF 37,201
BEAR LEGS 78,226
BEAR LOOKS BACK 21,185
BEAR LOUSE 107
BEAR NOSE, Frank 129,292
BEAR OWN NECKLACE 132
BEAR PIPE 74,236
BEAR RING 122,285
BEAR ROB, John 242
BEAR ROBE 87,119,249,282
   Eliza 73,236
   John 129
   Julia 186
   Mary 73,236
   Paul 21,186
BEAR RUNNER
   Frank 87,249
   Howard 87
   Joseph 89
BEAR RUNS AFTER 42,205
BEAR RUNS I WOODS
   Jennie 197
   Jno 197
BEAR RUNS IN T WOOD 276
BEAR RUNS IN THE WOOD 113
BEAR RUNS IN WOODS
   Ada 33,195
   Jennie 33
   Jno 33
BEAR SAVES LIFE 121,284
BEAR SCARES 69,232
   Samuel 69,232
BEAR SHIELD 49,213
   John 49,213
   Mary 49,213
   Nellie 49,213
   William 49
   Wm 213
BEAR TAIL 83,141,246,305
BEAR TRIBE 44,207
BEAR VILLAGE 129,291
BEAR WHIRLWIND 66,229
   Cora 66
BEAR WOLF 151,315
BEAR WOMAN 16,86,130,154,
.... 181,248,292,318
BEARD 84,246
   Andrew 41,205

Index

Carrie 41,298
Earnest 84
Emma T 283
Ernest 246
John 41,205
Lizzie T 283
Simon 41,205
BEARS BEADED BLANKET ..8,174
BEATS ALL 15,180
BEATS THEM 122,285
BEAVER 71,234
BEAVER WOMAN 118,281
BEGS TO KEEP 72,235
BELLY 22,71,75,233,237
BELLY WOMAN 119,282
BELT 123,286
   Gertie 88,250
   Guy 88,250
   James 88,250
   Levi 88,250
   Maggie 88,250
BEND 62,225
BENJAMIN 23
BESSIE LITTLE CROW 150
BETH 118,281
BETTELYOUN
   Chester 152,316
   Clara 152,316
   Cleveland B 152,316
   E G 5,171
   Ellen J 152,316
   Fred W 152,316
   George W 152,316
   Harry W 152,316
   Harwood 5
   Howard 171
   Ida M 152
   Isaac 5,171
   Jane 152,316
   Josephine 5,171
   Lillie 152,316
   Lorenzo L 316
   Lucinda 171
   Lucy M 152,316
   Martha L 152,316
BETWEEN LODGES 71,233
   Henry 65,194
BIANAS

Frances L 92
Frank L 92
Louise L 92
Paul L 92
Polonia L 92
Susie L 92
BIG AX 31,195
BIG BELLY 127,290
BIG BELLY DOG 83,245
BIG BEND 73,235
BIG BOY 18,52,60,61,182,
.... 216,224,247
   Anna 247
   Annie 60
   Joseph 60,224
BIG CHARGER
   William 99
   Wm 261
BIG CHEYENNE WOMAN 7,174
BIG CROW 8,174
   Ida 8,174
   Lucy 8,174
   Mary 8,174
   Susie 8,174
BIG EYES 102,264
BIG FACE 18,182
BIG FOOT 57,116,279,321
BIG HAWK 15,180
BIG HEAD 111,275
BIG LEGGINS DOWN 10,176
BIG LODGE 9,175
BIG MOUTH, John 50,214
BIG NOSTRILS, Wm 37,200
BIG OWL 29,193
   Edward 29,193
   George W 29
   John 29
   Lucy 29,193
   Thomas 29,193
BIG SOAP 101,262
BIG TAIL 107,271
BIG TURNIP 66,229
   Luke 66,229
BIG WHITE HORSE 45,208
BIG WOLF 13,53,179,217
   Samuel 53
BIG WOMAN . 5,11,17,41,92,97,104,
114,129,171,177,205,242,254,258,277

Index

BIRD 12,63,102,131,177,
.... 226,263,286,294
   Alex Y 241
   Anna Y 241
   Charles 173
   Chas 7
   David Y 241
   Eddie Y 241
   Frank Y 241
   Harry Y 241
   Jay 278
   Jennie 173
   Josephine Y 241
   Lizzie Y 241
   Nettie 173
   Rosa 173
BIRD ALL OVER 69,231
BIRD COMES OUT 66,228
BIRD EAGLE 16,17,181
BIRD HEAD 43,207
   Alice 43,207
   Bismarck 43
   Burges 99
   Burgess 261
   Dollie 99
   Dolly 261
   Edith 43,207
   Joseph 99,261
   William 99,261
BIRD MAN 51,71,233,321
BIRD NECKLACE
   Frank 26,189
   George 55
   Hattie 55,219
   Julia 55
   Martha 55
   Mary 219
   Moses 55,219
   Philip 55,219
   Rosa 55,219
   Susan 219
   Susen 55
BIRD NICHLACE, George 219
BIRD SHIRT 128,291
BISSONETTE
   Andrew 78,241
   Daniel 78,241
   Eliza 78,241
   Ella 59
   Fannie 70,72,233,235
   Frank 59,70,222,233
   Fred 59
   George 70,233
   Herbert 59,222
   Jackson 55,219
   James 33,197
   Jennie 70,233
   Jessie 72,235
   John 72,78,235,241
   Joseph 33,59,197,219,222
   Josephin 70
   Josephine 233
   Julia 78,241
   Julia Whalen 222
   Lottie 70,233
   Louise 59,222
   Lucy 59,184
   Lulu 19,183
   Mattie 78,240
   Mille 241
   Millie 19,78,183
   Nancy 19,183
   Peter 70,233
   Susie 70,78,233,241
   William 59,222
BITE 247
BITES 50,214
BITTERS
   Jessie 150
   Patrick 150,314
BITTTERS, Jessie 314
BKASKA RPAYA 32
BLACK APPLE 39,203
BLACK BEAR 14,41,153,179,204
   Belle 153,317
   Charles 41,204
   Emma 41,204
   Herman 144,308
   Ida 53,266
   Jennie 204
   Jessie 45,190
   Joseph 204
   Lucy 100,262
   Mary 10
   Paul 153,317
   Susie 153,317

Index

Thomas 155,241
William 100,153,261,317
BLACK BEAR #2 84,246
BLACK BEARD 131,293
BLACK BIRD 24,56,78,109,
.... 219,240,272
   Cora 29,193
   Louis 29,193
   Richard 56,219
BLACK BULL
   James 39,203
   Susie 39,203
   Thomas 39,203
BLACK CHICKEN 83,245
BLACK CLOUD 116,129,280,292
BLACK COW 12,177
BLACK CROW 84,246
   Alexander 83,245
   Katie 83,245
   Lucy 245
   Millie 83,245
BLACK CUT OFF 92
BLACK DEER 133,134,296,297
BLACK EAGLE 60,223
   Susie 223
   Susy 60
BLACK ELK 14,57,180,221
   Grace 60,224
   Henry 120,283
   Louisa C 120,283
BLACK EYE
   Annie 309
   Jessie 309
BLACK EYES 147,311
   Thomas 147,311
BLACK FEATHER 123,286
BLACK FEET 94,256
BLACK FOOT 119,282
BLACK FOX 61,224
   Mary 61,224
BLACK HAIR 115,278
BLACK HAWK 143,307
BLACK HEART 44,208
   William 99,261
BLACK HILLS 76,238
BLACK HORN 121
BLACK HORSE .. 13,56,115,135,144,
.... 178,220,278,284,298,308

Albert 40,203
Charles 23,187
Chas, Jr 187
William 135,298
BLACK KETTLE 107,271
BLACK MAN 133,296
BLACK MOCCASIN 124,246,287
BLACK MULE 20,172
BLACK N. BONNET, Joseph 155
BLACK OWL 101,151,263,315
BLACK PIPE 53,123,217,286
BLACK ROAD 132,294
BLACK SHAWL 110,274
BLACK SHEEP 121,284
BLACK TAIL 7,173
BLACK TAIL DEER 59,223
BLACK TRACKS 9,175
BLACK WHIRLWIND 53,114,
.... 216,277
BLACK WHISTLER 292
BLACK WHISTLER #1 129
BLACK WHISTLER #2 127,290
BLACK WHITE 282
BLACK WOLF 84,116,246,279
   Johnson 84
   Susie 84
BLACK WOLF #2 127,289
BLACK WOMAN ... 109,155,273,319
BLANKET 51,215
BLASKA 18,182
BLASKA RPAYA 195
BLE WAKAN 74,237
BLEWAKAN 16,181
BLICK WHITE 119
BLIND, Silas 122,285
BLIND MAN 25,188
BLIND WOMAN 78,240
BLO WANICLA 19
BLOODY MOUTH 60,223
BLOTAHUNKA 111
BLOTAHUNKA CIQALA ... 143,307
BLOTAHUNKA WIN 274
BLOTAHUNSKA CIQALA 122
BLOWANJILA 122,285
BLOWING BLANKET 36,200
BLUE BIRD ... 11,72,93,108,135,176,
.... 234,255,272,298
   Annie 91,253

Index

Fannie 42,206	BORN IN DAY 121
James 91,253	BORN IN WATER 109
Jefferson 91,253	BORNE IN WATER 273
Mary 55,91,219,253	BORROWER 119,282
Sarah 91,253	BOSEL, John H 166
Thomas 91,253	BOWMAN
BLUE BLANKET 77,239	Alice 152,316
BLUE CLOTH 127,290	Thoma 316
BLUE CLOUD 76,97,125,	Thomas 152
.... 128,239,288,291	BOY 116,117,123,126,127,128,
Emma 34,198	 129,279,280,286,289,290,292
BLUE CLOUS 258	Charles E 223
BLUE HORSE 8,174	Joseph E 223
Baldwin 20,184	BOY KILLS IN WINTER 72
Fannie 35,199	BOY RUNS FOR HIM 73
Jack 35,199	BOYER
Jennie 8,19,174	Alice 43,207
Lizzie 8,174	Antoine 141,305
BLUE HORSE OWNER 125,288	Dollie 141
BLUE LEGGINS 37,201	Dolly 305
BLUE SHIELD 12,178	James 43,207
BLUE WHIRLWIND 25,188	John 43,207
BLUFFING BEAR 57,220	Lucy 43,207
Sophia 57	Maggie 43,207
BLUNT HORN	Patrick 141
George 50,214	BRAIDED 121,284
Jessie 50,214	BRAVE 34,36,40,57,71,111,
John 50,214	... 127,198,200,204,221,234,275,290
Joseph 50,214	Charles 26,116,189
Louise 50,214	Clayton 26,299
Susie 214	BRAVE #2, Charles 279
Susy 50	BRAVE BEAR 122,284
BOB TAIL 286	BRAVE BULL 124,287
BOB TAIL BEAR 125,288	BRAVE DOG 131,294
BOBTAIL 123	BRAVE EAGLE 84,246
BOILED HAND 72,234	Mary 100
BONE, Walter 38,202	Oscar 94,256
BONE NECHLACE 188	Peter 246
BONE NECKLACE 116	Silas 256
Ella 102	Thomas 84
Ellen 263	Thos 246
BONE NECKLACE #1 25	Warren 100,261
BONE NECKLACE #2 23,187	BRAVE HEART 37,131,201,294
BONNET 126,289	James 37,201
Dolly L W 277	John 37
Jesse L W 277	Moses 37,201
BORES A HOLE 108,272	Pugh 37,201
BORN IN BAY 284	BRAVE WOLF 287

Index

BRAVE WOMAN ... 131,182,185,294
BRAVE WOMAN #1 17,20
BREAKES DISHES 265
BREAKS DISHES 103
BREAKS IN 112,275
BREAKS IRON 122,285
BREAKS LAND, Julia 31,195
BREAKS LIMBS 246
BREAKS LINKS 84
BREAKS ROCK 85,247
BREAKS TEETH 16,181
BREAST 76,238
   John 141,305
   Lucy 141,305
   Silas 141,305
   William 141,305
BREATHING 25,189
BREWER
   Ellen 43,206
   Rachael 42
   Rachel 206
   Robert 43,206
   William 42,206
BRIGHT EYES 35,198
BRING HER OWN 22
BRING YELLOW 282
BRINGING HORSES 42,206
BRINGS 13,115,122,134,135,
.... 178,278,285,296,298
BRINGS ARROWS 77,239
BRINGS BACK 41
BRINGS BLUE 130,293
BRINGS BLUE HORSE 204
BRINGS BLUE HORSES 40
BRINGS BROWN EARS 128
BRINGS CHIEF HORSE 6,172
BRINGS DAY 209
BRINGS ENEMIES HORSES.75,238
BRINGS GOOD 41,45,205,208
BRINGS HER HORSES 58,222
BRINGS HER OWN 60,186,266
BRINGS HIM BACK 127,290
BRINGS HORSES 16,53,181,216
BRINGS IN 16,181
BRINGS MONEY 45,208
BRINGS MULE 39,215
BRINGS ONE 62,68,125,225,
.... 231,288

BRINGS PICKED HORSES ... 41,204
BRINGS PIPE 32,262
BRINGS PLENTY 40,62,111,
.... 114,203,225,277,298
   Michael 62,225
   Philip 40
BRINGS RED HORSE 127,290
BRINGS SPOTTED 9,15,49,115,
.... 126,175,180,213,278,289
   Hattie 140,304
BRINGS THE CHIEF 10,176
BRINGS THEM 60,222
BRINGS TOGETHER 53,217
BRINGS WATER 49,110,213
BRINGS WHITE.. 8,132,174,238,294
BRINGS WHITE HORSES 33,196
BRINGS WITH 273
BRINGS WOOD 289
BRINGS WORD 126
BRINGS YELLOW 10,75,119,
.... 123,124,176,238,286,287
BROKEN ARM 84,246
BROKEN LEG 110,274
   Jack 93,255
   Mary 110,274
   Moses 93,255
BROKEN NOSE 111,274
BROKEN ROPE 84,246
   Joseph 84
   Sam'l 246
   Samuel 98
   Sarah 84
BROOKS, John 14,180
BROUGHT PLENTY 68,231
BROWN 139,303
   Alice 63,111,226,320
   Benjamin 139,303
   David 139,303
   Edward 111,274
   George 77,321
   George, Jr 77,321
   Harry 111,320
   James 63,226
   Jennie 77,139,190,321
   Joseph 63,226,321
   Joseph, Jr 63,226
   Lilly 226
   Lizzie 111,139,320

Index

Nellie ... 111,320
Rosa ... 111,320
Samuel ... 54,217
Susie ... 77,139,303,321
Tonie ... 63,226
William ... 111,320
Willie ... 63,226
BROWN BEAR ... 98,260
BROWN CLOUD ... 85,247
BROWN EARED HORSE 130,293
BROWN EARS ... 6,140,304
   Amos ... 89,251
   Emma ... 89,251
   Horace ... 89,251
BROWN ELK ... 23
BROWN EYES ... 18,36,51,115,127,
.... 183,199,215,278,290
   Edward ... 68,231
BROWN OWL ... 121,130,293
BROWN WOMAN ... 121,284
BRULE WOMAN ... 84,132,247,294
BUCKMAN
   Benjamin ... 21,185
   George ... 21,185
   Hanes ... 185
   James ... 21
   John ... 120,283
   Millie ... 21,185
   Susie ... 21,185
BUCKSKIN ... 30,194
BUCKSKIN STRING ... 139,303
BUFFALO DANCE ... 60,224
BUFFALO MEAT ... 151,315
BUFFALO ROAD ... 24
BULL ... 18,95,257
   Julia Y ... 263
BULL #2 ... 118,281
BULL BEAR ... 32,84,246
   Dixon ... 92,254
   Fannie ... 92,254
   Henry ... 104,254,265
   Jesse ... 92,254
   Julia ... 92,254
   Lawrence ... 92,254
   Lizzie ... 84,246
   Moses ... 92,254
   Peter ... 92,254
BULL BONNET ... 38,202
   Emma ... 38,241
BULL EYE ... 103,264
BULL HEAD ... 96,117,265,280
BULL MAN
   Daniel ... 261
   John ... 86
   Sally ... 261
BULL NOISE WALKER ... 110
BULL NOISE WALKING ... 274
BULL TAIL ... 31,194
   Sarah ... 31,195
   Stella ... 195
BULL VILLAGE ... 13
BULL VILLATE ... 178
BULL WALKING
   Bull ... 98
   Mack ... 259
BULLARD
   Elmus ... 152,316
   Frank ... 152,316
   Lizzie ... 152,316
   Walter ... 152,316
BULLET PROOF ... 130,293
BULLOCK
   Susie ... 157
   William ... 24,188
BULLS BEAR ... 196
BUMBLE BEE ... 64,227
BURGEN, William ... 23,321
BURNS PRAIRIE ... 179
BUSH
   Ella ... 42,206
   Frank ... 42,206
   James ... 312
   Joseph ... 148,312
   Joseph, Jr ... 148
   Julia ... 206
   Louis ... 42,206
   Rosa ... 312
   Sallie ... 312
   Sally ... 148
   Sophia ... 42,206
   William ... 42,206
BUSH TOP PINE ... 50,214
BUSTED HEAD ... 122,285
BUTCHER KNIF ... 275
BUTCHER KNIFE ... 112
BUTE ... 30

Index

BUTTER FLY 172
   Annie W 177
BUTTERFLY 20,155,319
BYAPAHA OTA 320
C A THEM, Harry 189
C I MORNING
   Agnes 147,311
   Edward 147,311
   Howard 311
   Maggie 311
   Oliver 147,311
C IN MORNING, Maggie 147
C. THUNDER, Columbus 77
C.A. THEM, Harry 25
CA PTECELA 44,109
CA TPECELA 193
CAGA 50,94,256
CAGE WAKAN 309
CAGE WANICA 175
CAGYE 317
CAHRGES THE ENEMY 98
CAHU MAZA 139
CAJE OGLAKA 18,33,182
CAJE WAKAN 145
CAJE WANICA..... 5,9,13,18,123,171,
.... 179,182,238,286,290
CAJI IGLATA 197
CAJI NAKIRUN, Hears His Name 52
CAJI WANICA 127
CAKU 129
CALF 125,144,288,308
CALF ROBE 107,271
CALF WOMAN 112,115,276,279
CALICO 20,185
CALLS 126,289
CALLS ENEMY 61,224
CALLS HER 25,189
CALLS HER NAME 99,261
CALLS HIM 20,185
CALLS THEM 6,172
CAMP WITH 128,291
CAN 290
CAN APAHA 97,259
CAN HU 134,297
CAN IYUMNI 182
CAN MAZAKAN 279
CAN MAZAWAKAN 116
CAN NUP YUHA 21

CAN NUPYUHA 185
CAN ONAJINYAPI 310
CAN PTECELA 19,184
CAN RAKA 146
CAN SASA 95
CAN WANJILA 12,178
CAN WEGNA 196
CAN WEHNA WICAKTE 217
CAN WIYUMNI 18
CAN YURI 310
CAN YUWEGA 84,246
CAN ZI 19,183
CANDELARIO
   Lucy 93
   Peter 93
CANDELORIA, Joseph 93
CANDOLERIO, Clara 93
CANE 66,96,121,141,144,153,
.... 218,228,257,284,305,308,317
CANE EAGLE 65,228
CANE LION 70
CANE LIVER 232
CANE SWORD 66,229
CANE WOMAN 187
CANGLESKA CIQALA 150,314
CANGLESKA LUTA 121,140,
.... 221,284,304
CANGLESKA MAZA 127
CANGLESKA SA 58
CANGLESKA WANBLI ... 12,75,178
CANGLESKA WASTE 13,56,72,
.... 179,220
CANHAN PI 131
CANHANPA 45
CANHANPA OHAN 78
CANHANPI 146,197,293,310
CANHAUPI 33
CANHU 114
CANICIPAWEGA WASTE 16,181
CANIHANKE 34,198
CANKAHU WASTE 204
CANKAKU CIQALA 207
CANKPE 64,227
CANKU 50,60,94,124,147,214,
.... 247,256,287,292,311
CANKU MAZA 11,20,153,176,
.... 184,303,317
CANKU SAPA 132,294

334

Index

CANKU TANKA 92,254
CANKU TERILA 108,272
CANKU WAKAN 32,196
CANKU WASTE 20,35,107,112,
.... 184,199,271,276
CANKU WIN 284
CANKUHU 115
CANLI 108,122,272,285
CANONAJINYAPI 146
CANOWICAKTE 22,53,114,132,
.... 186,277,295
CANPA ISTA 61
CANPA SU 63,226
CANPASLATAPI CANKU 62,225
CANRLOGA HOKSILA 234
CANRLOYAN WIN 72
CANROEGNA NAJI 200
CANSASA 257
CANSI MNA 74
CANSU 184
CANT ENTER DOOR 64,227
CANT GET HER 125,288
CANTA MANZA 216
CANTA SAPA 99
CANTE MAZA 36,52,200
CANTE OHITIKA 37,131,201,294
CANTE OKIKEKA 201
CANTE OPEYAPI 63
CANTE SAPA 44,208,261
CANTE SICASA 235
CANTE SUTA 15,226
CANTE TERI 64
CANTE WASTE 12,13,67,70,74,121,
.... 178,221,226,230,284
CANTE WICASA 72,103,264
CANTE WIN 14,180
CANTE WIN LA 179
CANTE WITKO 32,74,262
CANTO WITKO 237
CANUPA 109,111,113,274,277
CANUPA AGLI 32
CANUPA APA 124,287
CANUPA HO 53
CANUPA KUPI 178
CANUPA LUTA WIN 226
CANUPA NAWIZI 42,206
CANUPA OTA 50
CANUPA PEGNAKA 116,279

CANUPA QUPI 13
CANUPA SAPA 53,123,217,286
CANUPA WACI 36
CANUPA WACI HOKSILA 15
CANUPA WAKAN ... 46,63,112,115,
.... 119,276,278,282,299,321
CANUPA WAKITA 71,234
CANUPA WANBLI 37,38,70,
.... 73,155,319
CANUPA WASTE 35,135,198,298
CANUPA WASTE ICU 131,294
CANUPA WICINCALA 63
CANUPA WIYAKPA 63,226
CANUPA YUHA 87,101,263
CANUPA YUHA MANI 76,318
CANUPA YUKA 249
CANUPI AGLI 262
CANWEGNA 32
CANWEGNA NAJIN 36
CANZEKA 44,45,207,208
CAPA 71,234
CAPA AKA 9
CAPA ESTA 321
CAPA LUTA 126,289
CAPA MAZA 11,177
CAPA SKA 69,232
CAPA WIN 118,281
CAPIGMUKE MAZA 116
CAPIGNUKE MAZA 279
CAPTECELA 273
CAPTURED 68,75,237
CAPTURED PRISONER 94,320
CAPTURNED 230
CARD, Kittie 8,184
CARLI 107,271
CARLI WIN 154,318
CARLOW
    Abraham 307
    Agatha 143,307
    Anna 143
    Annie 307
    Frank 143,307
    Jennie 143,307
    Lizzie 143,307
    Mary 143,307
    Nellie 143,307
    Robert 143,307
    Theodore 143

Index

Theodore 307
CARRIE 46,209
CARRIES OFF ARROWS 121,284
CARRY 304
CARRY FLAG 25,188
CARSON
   Emma 114,277
   Lizzie 114,277
CASMU 98,259
CASTE 113
CASTUNPI 99,111,261,298
CATCHES 62,225
CATCHES ENEMY ... 16,98,116,126,
.... 130,181,259,279,289,292
   Lucy 31,195
CATER OHITIKA 201
CATHERINE 13
CATKA 20,33,92,102,111,
.... 151,184,197,254,263,315
CATKA KOKEPA 245
CATKA KOKIPA 83
CAYANKA 297
CAZE NAKINRUN 216
CAZUE
   Mary 150
   Peter 150,314
CEDAR 85,97,153,247,259,317
   James 44,207
CEDAR BOY 18
CEDAR FACE 58,222
   William 58,222
CEDAR LODGE 133,296
CEDAR WOMAN 23,74,110,
.... 237,273
   Susie 23
CEGA 214
CEGA LUTA 93,142,255,306
CEGA OGLE 116,279
CEGA SAPA 107,271
CEGA SKA 49,214
CEGALA LUTA 93
CEHUPA MAZA 132,295
CEKEYAPI WIN 215
CEKIYAPI 51,114,153,277,317
CEKPA 8,14,140,174,179,304
CENTER 132,294
CENTER WOMAN 68,230
CERTAN RUPAHU 54

CETA LUTA 237
CETAN 6,32,37,56,88,126,172,
.... 196,201,220,250,289
CETAN AKICITA 38,124,202,286
CETAN CIQALA 14,25,179,188
CETAN GI 146,150,311,314,319
CETAN HETON 120,283
CETAN HO 22
CETAN HO TANKA 111
CETAN HO WASTE 73,236
CETAN HOKSILA 41,205,217
CETAN HOTANKA 274
CETAN IYANKA 107,271,284
CETAN IYOTAKA 129,292
CETAN IYOYAKA 129,292
CETAN KANWEGA 249
CETAN KAWINGE 86
CETAN KINYA 233
CETAN KIYAN 70
CETAN KOKIPA 237
CETAN KOKIPAPI .. 74,125,288,318
CETAN KTE 236
CETAN LUTA 15,64,74,180,237,299
CETAN MAZA 76,118,239,281
CETAN ORANKO 172
CETAN OYATE 52,53,216,217
CETAN RABWICAYA 97
CETAN RABYA 214,259
CETAN RABYAPI 50
CETAN RCA 230
CETAN RCAKA 67
CETAN RLA 140
CETAN RLA WIN 304
CETAN ROPAHU 217
CETAN RUPAHU 54
CETAN SAPA 143,307
CETAN SKA. 16,78,103,181,240,265
CETAN TANKA 15,180
CETAN WAKAKESYA 40
CETAN WAKAKISYA 40
CETAN WAKINYA 197
CETAN WAKINYAN 40,42,43,
.... 139,203,206,303,304
CETAN WAKUWA 10,38,86,127,
.... 176,202,249,290
CETAN WAMBLI 226
CETAN WANBLI64,124,128,287,291
CETAN WANKATUIYA 202

Index

CETAN WASTE WIN............12,178
CETAN WICAKTE...................... 74
CETAN WICASA..................144,308
CETAN WIN...........17,40,60,90,123,
............155,223,252,254,286,319
CETAN WINYAN........................ 92
CETAN WOSICA.........................204
CEYA..............................53,139,303
CEYESA..217
CHAMBER WOMAN...........115,181
CHAMBERLAIN, Lucy..........24,188
CHANGE PLACE........................229
CHARGE IN MORNING...........7,173
   Howard.....................................147
   Martha......................................143
CHARGER................95,148,256,312
CHARGES AT......................154,318
CHARGES CLOSE TO LODGE
....109,272
CHARGES ENEMY..52,117,216,280
CHARGES IN MORNING.........7,173
CHARGES THE ENEMY............260
CHARGING
   Alice.....................................69,232
   David....................................69,232
   George..................................69,232
   Jackson.................................69,232
   Louise...................................69,232
CHARGING BEAR...............143,307
   Addie...143
   Anna...143
   Emma....................................31,195
CHARGING CAT........................121
CHARGING CROW
   Cecilia.................................141,305
   Jacob..................................141,305
   Nancy.................................156,320
   William.....................................156
   Wm..320
CHARGING EAGLE...............85,247
   Eliza......................................85,266
CHARGING ENEMY.................... 14
CHARGING HORSE..................... 40
   William.....................................199
   Willian.. 35
CHARGING SHIELD..............37,201
   Julia......................................37,201
   Lizzie... 37

Lucy......................................33,197
Wallace..................................33,197
CHARGING THUNDER.........65,77,
.....................................141,227,240,305
   Asa... 77
CHARGING WINTER.........121,284
CHARGING WOLF..............110,274
CHARLES.........................118,182,281
CHARLIE........................35,199,272
CHASE..................................129,292
CHASE ALONE............7,67,71,134,
................................173,229,233,297
CHASE CLOSE TO LODGE.......282
CHASE IN LIGHT........................178
CHASE IN MORNING............13,178
CHASE IN SIGHT......................... 12
CHASE IN WINTER............109,272
CHASING BEAR...................62,225
CHASING ENEMY................72,235
   Martha..................................72,235
CHASING HAWJ...........................38
CHASING HAWK............10,86,127,
............................176,202,249,290
   Mattie.. 86
CHASING JUMPER..............131,294
CHASING OUT...........................109
CHASING WOLF........................ 86
   Alice.....................................94,256
CHAUSSE, Charlotte.............152,316
CHEIF WOMAN...................221,251
CHERRY EYE.......................61,321
CHERRY STONE..................63,226
CHEWING.............................129,291
CHEYENNE . 72,86,122,235,248,285
   Emma..................................86,248
CHEYENNE BUTCHER.......151,315
CHEYENNE MOTHER..........88,250
CHEYENNE WOMAN.............12,33,
....177,197
CHICKEN.............................84,246
CHIEF..........54,69,103,110,119,153,
................217,232,264,273,282,317
   James....................................25,189
   Lucie..172
   Mollie...................................6,172
   Susie..6
CHIEF #1..................................6,172
CHIEF #2....................................126

CHIEF #3	122,285
CHIEF BEAR	31,195
Susie	31,195
CHIEF BIRD	99,261
CHIEF EAGLE	85,110,247,274
Otto	85,241
Peter	85,247
CHIEF MAN, Philip	116,279
CHIEF MEDICINE BOY	119,282
CHIEF WARRIOR	281
CHIEF WHITE COW	23,117,280
CHIEF WOMAN	57,84,89,90,117, 118,246,252,280
CHIP, Nellie H	251
CHIPPS	83,85,246
CHIPS	248
Alice	140,304
Andres	304
Andrew	140
Geoffrey	140,304
Gerome	140
Jefferson	103,264
Katie	103,264
Lucy	140,304
Philip	140,304
CICAYA RPAYA	262
CIN	43,207
CINPI	85,100,125,262,288
CINPI WIN	321
CIQALA	108,119,272,282
CIQALA KIZA	297
CIQALA KTE	38,199,202
CIQALA KU	282
CIQALA WICAKIZA	134
CIQALA WICAKTE	35,134,140, 283,297,304
CIQALAQ WICAKTE	120
CIRCLE WALKER	33,197
CIWIGNAKA SKA	262
CIYEKU	7,173
CIYELA	6
CLAPP, W H	157
CLARA	79
CLAYMORE	
Benj	148,312
Benjamn	148
David	148,312
Edward	148,312
Egan	148,312
Garfield	148,312
Gracie	148,312
Hobart	312
Joseph	148
Josph	312
Lucy	148,312
Richard	148,312
Roy	148,312
Samuel	148,312
CLEAR	17,111,123,181,274,286
Thomas	17,182
CLEAR ROCK	133
CLIFFORD	
Charles	46,86,249
Charles, Jr	249
Delila	103
George	91,93,253,255
Hannah	103,265
Hattie	91,253
Henry	46
James	103,265
John	91,103,253,265
Joseph	103,265
Julia	46,93,103,249,265
Julian	255
Kary	265
Lillie	265
Lily	103
Maggie	46,93,249,255
Mary	103
Mortimer	103,265
Orlando	103
Rosa	103,265
William	249
CLINCHER	
Calvin	152,316
Charles	152,316
George	152,316
James	152,316
John	152
CLOSE	6,172
CLOSE FEATHER	87
CLOSE TO GROUND	126,289
CLOSE TO HOUSE	149,209
CLOSE TO LODGE, Charles	119
CLOUD	62,84,225,246
Bessie S	263

Index

Loomis L 275
CLOUD BOY 132,295
CLOUD COME OUT 5
CLOUD COMES OUT 171
CLOUD HORSE 85,247
   Annie 85,247
   Minnie 85,247
   Nancy 85,247
CLOUD MAN 41,117,205,280
CLOUD RIBS 32,196
CLOUD SHIELD 10,176
   Thomas 11
   Thos 176
CLOUD THUNDER 113,276
CLOUD WOMAN ... 120,149,283,313
CLOW WOMAN 283
CLOWN 59,222
   Jennie 51,215
CLOWN HORSE 112,276
CLOWN WOMAN 120
COAL OF FIRD 177
COAL OF FIRE 11,102,263
COFFEE 86,248
COKA GLISNI 36,200
COKAB IYAYA 18,50,88,89,127,
   133,183,214,225,250,251,308
COKAB WIN 68,230
COKANYA INYANKA 240
COKANYAN 132,294
COKANYAN IYANKA 78
COKANYAN MANI 284
COKATA IYAYA 144,288,290
COKATA MANI 121
COKATA WAKAN 150,314
COKES STANDING 292
COKULA 9,175
COLD BREAST 86,248
COLD WATER 15,180
COLHOFF
   Anna 21,186
   Elizabeth 21,186
   George 21,186
   John R 21,186
   Mary 21,186
   William 21,186
COLONEL SCRAPER 312
COME 55
COME AGAIN

Carrie 239
   John 73
COME ALICE 279
COME WOUNDED 255
COMES 127,290
COMES ABOVE 66,228
COMES AFTER H HORSES 216
COMES AFTER HER 107
COMES AFTER HER HORSES 53
COMES AFTER HIM 7,19,184
COMES AFTER HORSE119,282,299
COMES AFTER HORSES 6,10,72,
   84,96,235,246,258
COMES AGAIN
   Carrie 76
   Gertie 59,223
   James 68,230
   John 236
   Lizzie 73,236
   Peter 73,236
   Rachael 73,236
COMES ALICE 73,196
COMES ALIVE .. 13,30,115,121,130,
   133,178,236,284,293,295
COMES AMONG THEM 84,246
COMES AND CAMPS 11,13,177,
   178
COMES AND LAYS 132,134,295,
   298
COMES AND STANDS . 19,132,184,
   294
COMES AND TELLS 108,272
COMES BACK 9,12,99,103,
   175,260,264
COMES BACK CHIEF 74,236
COMES BACK HARD 140,304
COMES BACK NIGHT 84,246
COMES BACK WOUNDED 146,310
COMES BEHIND 150,313
   Lucy 150
COMES BLOODY 133,296
COMES CRAWLING 118,281
COMES F A THEM 285
COMES FIRST 76,239
COMES FROM AMONG THEM
   122,280
COMES FROM AMONGST 5,171
COMES FROM AMONGST THEM .

339

Index

COMES 117
COMES FROM SCOUT 8,10,174,
.... 176
COMES GROWLING . 68,76,231,239
   John 231
COMES HARD 116,279
COMES HOLY 17,84,110,182,
.... 246,274
COMES HUNTING 59,223
COMES IN LATE 130,293
COMES IN LIGHT 114,189
COMES IN SIGHT 67,129,230
COMES KILLING 32,196
COMES LAST 6,11,20,107,140,
.... 171,176,184,271
   Jennie 37,201
   Susie 201
COMES LITTLE 282
   Amos 119
COMES MEDICINE 17
COMES OUT 33,46,56,71,134,143,
... 153,197,219,234,296,299,307,317
COMES OUT ALIVE 56,220
COMES OUT EAGLE 34,198
COMES OUT FIRST 111,120,179,
.... 275,283
COMES OUT GOOD 9,175
COMES OUT HOLY 13,24,38,
.... 178,202
COMES OUT IN SIGHT 114,277
COMES OUT MEDICINE 40,204
COMES OUT PLENTY 14,179
COMES OUT RATTLING 93
COMES OUT RIGHT 14
COMES OUT WHIRLWIND .. 57,220
COMES OUT WHITE COW ... 75,237
COMES OUT WOLF 88,250
COMES OUT WOUNDED 93,255
COMES RATTLING 255
COMES RIGHT 58,62,225
COMES STANDING 36,84,108,
.... 122,200,246,272,285
COMES TALKING 17,182
COMES TO FRONT 127,290
COMES TO HUNT THEM 95,98,
.... 257,260
COMES TO KILL 94,256
COMES TO SEE HER 10,37,175,201
COMES TO SEE HIM 274
COMES TO SIT 58,222
COMES TO STAND 44,190
COMES TRACKING 107
COMES WALKING . 19,111,234,274
COMES WHITE 17,182
COMES WOUNDED 7,93,173
CONDELARIO
   Clara 256
   Joseph 256
   Lucy 256
   Mary 93,256
   Peter 256
   Sophia 93,256
CONGLESKA ZI 234
CONICA WAHICA 207
CONICA WAMICA 266
CONICA WANICA 37,59,88,231,
.... 250
CONICA WASTE 201
CONQUERING BEAR 147,311
CONROY
   Annie 29,193
   Benjamin 29,193
   Eulala 42,206
   Frank 145,309
   Harry 145,309
   John 29,193
   Julia 145,309
   Lena 29,193
   Lucy 29,193
   Maggie 29,193
   Millie 29,193
   Taylor 29,193
   Victoria 145,309
   Walter 309
CORA SHOT 218
CORN
   Emma 33,197
   Rosa 197
   Roza 33
   William 33,197
   William, Jr 197
CORN LEAF 24
COSIYO CIQALA 119
COTTIER
   Charles 149,313
   Eddie 23,187

Index

Elizabeth 149,313	CRAZY BEAR 20,127,185,290
Emma 149,313	CRAZY BRAIN 128,291
Esther 23,187	CRAZY BULL 124,287
Florence 149,313	Lizzie N 101
George 149,313	May 101,262
Gilbert 148,312	Narrows 101,262
Henry 149,313	Nellie 262
John 23,187	William 101,262
John, Jr 23	CRAZY DOG 64,86,119,227,
Lettie 312	 248,282
Louis 148,312	Caroline 86,248
Lucy 23,187	Julia 96,258
Mabel 148,312	CRAZY GHOST 68,230
Maggie 187	CRAZY HORSE 71,139,234,303
Mary 149,313	Ella 139,303
Nettie 148	Ellen 139,303
Ollie 149,313	Richard 139,303
Pearl 312	CRAZY THUNDER 62,225
Samuel 149,313	CRAZY WOMAN 6,172
Susie 23,187	CREEK, Creighton 84,246
Walter J 312	CRICKET, Mamie 57,220
Walter James 148	CRIER
COUNCIL FIRE 8,174	Cleveland 139,303
COUNT 30,194	Guy 303
COUNTRY TRAVELER 12,177	John 139,303
COUNTS H NIGHTS, Lucy 318	Louis 139,303
COUNTS HER NIGHTS, Lucy 154	Paul 139,303
COVERED HEAD 67,230	Peter 139,303
COW GOES FIRST 144,308	CRIES 53,217
COW HORN 69,232	CROOKED EYES 39,85,203,247
COW LEADER 118,292	Susie 35,199
COW WOMAN 247	CROOKED LEG 129,292
COYOTE, Martha W 228	CROOKED NECK 110,274
COYOTE BELLY 85,247	CROOKED NOSE 18,183
Noah 247	CROSS 296
CRANE 135,298	Frank 39,203
CRANE WOMAN 85,247	CROSS DOG 108,272
CRAVEN	CROW 39,124,203,287
Edith 155,319	Alice 32,196
George 102	Anna 32,196
Hattie 155,319	Edward 146
Isabel Oma 155	Fannie S 258
Isabelle Oma 319	Harry S B 231
Jessie 155,319	Henry 62,225
John 155,319	James 32,196
Teddie 155	Katie S 258
Teddy 319	Lucy 32,196
CRAWLS 133,296	Mary G V 250

Index

Mollie G V 250
Sally 225
Thomas 32,195
CROW CANE...................13,118,179
CROW EAGLE 18,183
CROW LACKS WATER 272
CROW LIKES WATER 108
CROW ON HEAD........................ 85
   Louis....................................... 85
CROW WOMAN........39,40,43,46,68,
................................85,133,230,296
   Esther...................................... 43
   Joseph 43
CROW WOMAN #2.....................203
CROW WOMAN #3.....................204
CROW WOMAN #4.....................209
CROWWE 133
CRYING WITHOUT CAUSE.63,226
CTAN 196
CUNSOKA 90,252
CUNY
   Adolph 228
   Cahrles 65
   Charles 228
   Charles, Jr 65,228
   Eddie 65,228
   Josephin 65
   Josephine.............................228
   Jule..................................65,228
   LeRoy Brown........................ 65
   Leroy Brown 228
   Lizzie 29,65,228,242
   Lottie...............................65,228
   Louise 65,228
   Wilson.............................65,228
CUT 139,303
   Arthur..............................139,303
   Chester............................139,303
   Ellis..................................139,303
   Emily...............................139,303
   Ernest 139
   Lucinda 139,303
   Mollie...............................139,303
   Omega...................................139
   Raymond.........................139,303
   Rosa 303
   Samuel 139,303
CUT FLESH 24,188

CUT FOOT................. 76,86,239,248
   Mary 46
CUT FROM ROPE................. 10,176
CUT GRASS 52,216
   Fred 52,216
CUT HAND 49,266
CUT HEAD............................. 98,259
CUT OFF................... 38,95,202,257
CUWEGNA KA SKA................. 251
CUWI 121,284
CUWI BU..................................... 133
CUWI KUTE................................ 282
CUWIGNAKA COLA 123,286
CUWIGNAKA SKA 89
CUWIGUAKA SKA 100
CUWIOSNIYANPI....................... 86
CUWISNYANPI......................... 248
DALKENBERGER, Charles........ 162
DANCING BEAR................ 100,267
DAVID 7,71,173,233
DAVIDSON
   Annie 103,264
   David 103,264
   Edward 103,264
   Emma 103,264
   John 103,264
   Julia 103,264
   Lali 103
   Lalie E 264
   William 103,264
DAWSON 119
DAY 33,90,98,113,115,116,
...........118,252,259,276,278,279,281
   David 95,257
   Julia 33
   Lizzie....................................... 33
   Lucy.................................. 77,239
   Millie 33
DAY BIRTH 109,273
DAY COME OUT....................... 294
DAY COMES OUT....... 7,21,124,131,
.... 147,173,186,286,311
DAYLIGHT MAN 41,205
DAYS GOING 55,218
DEAF AND DUMB 22,121,128,
.... 186,291
DEAF WOMAN............. 125,127,290
DEAR AND DUMB.................... 284

342

Index

DEAR WOMAN 133,287,296
DEARLY 131,294
DEER 31,195,259
DEER GOES OUT 115,278
DEER RUMP 111,275
DEER WOMAN 59,115,121,123,
.... 189,278,284,286
DEFENDER 107,271
DEON
   Cecilia 7,173
   Herold 173
   Louie 187
   Louie, Jr 187
   Louis 24
   Mary 24,173,187
   Mary #1 7
   Sam 7,173
   Sophia 7,173
   Susie 173
   Ward 24,187
   William 7,173
DEPENDS ON 53
DEPENDS ON THEM 93,255
DEPNEDS ON 217
DESTROYED 33,196
DICK 275
DIFFERENT COLOR 52,216
DIFFERENT HORSE 45,150,208,
.... 314
DIFFERENT TAIL 67,230
DIFFERENT WOMAN 109,272
DILLON
   John 90,252
   Peter 90,252
DIRT 98,131,260,294
DIRT KETTLE 9,176
DIRT PAINT 133,295
DISMOUNT 281
DISMOUNTS 118
DISMOUNTS THRICE
   Alfred 253
   Edward 253
   James 253
   Jas. 91
   Susie 91,253
DISTRIBUTION #1 108,272
DISTRIBUTION #2 112,275
DIXON
   Alice M 46,209
   Elizabeth 46,209
   James G 46,209
   John Y 46,209
   William H 46,209
DOCTOR 16,181
DOG 197
   Julia 202
   Lizzie 197
   Millie 197
   Wallace 149
DOG CHIEF 73,236
DOG HORN 132,294
DOG ON BUTE 223
DOG TRIBE 95,257
DOGS, Jennie T 260
DONATING 56,220
DONG ON BUTTE 59
DONT BRAID H HAIR, Jas 228
DONT BRAID HIS HAIR, Jas 65
DONT COME 70,232
DONT GET UP 100,261
DONT RUN 46,299
DONT THINK 63,226
DOOR 19,123,134,183,296,299
DRAGON FLY 127,290
DRAGS ROPE 72,235
DREAMER 121,284
DREAMING BEAR 111,275
DREAMS JEALOUS 44,207
DRESS INDISE 25
DRESS INSIDE 188
DRINKS BITTERS 34,197
DRINKS WATER 110,273
DRIPPING 21,185
DRIPS IN THE WATER 68
DRIVE THEM 113
DRIVER 124,126,289,298
DROOPS HEAD 63
DROPS DOWN GIRL 75,237
DROPS HEAD 226
DROPS IN THE WATER 230
DROPS TWO 117,280
DUBRAY
   Baptiste 142,306
   Charles 154,318
   David 142,306
   Elizabeth 154

Index

Eugene 154
Irene 306
Mamie 306
Millicent 142,306
DUCK HORSE 124,287
DULL KNIFE 154,318
Mary 154
DUN
   Martha 178
   Mary 13
DUNBRAY
   Irena 142
   Mamie 142
DYBRAY
   Elizabeth 318
   Eugene 318
E CHIEF, Fanny 308
EAGLE 21,22,53,54,59,107,115,
.. 129,185,186,216,217,218,223,271,
.... 292,293
   Josephin M 41
   Katie M 41
   Lucy M 41
EAGLE #2 60,223
EAGLE BEAR, James 46
EAGLE BIRD .. 5,96,117,171,258,280
EAGLE BLANKET 122,285
EAGLE BOY 60,69,130,222,
.... 232,282,293
EAGLE BULL 49
   Effa 49,214
   Ella 49,214
   Henry 50,214
EAGLE CANE 119,282
EAGLE CHIEF 144,308
   Fannie 144
   Thos 308
EAGLE CLOUD 72,234
EAGLE COMES OUT 120,283
EAGLE DRESS 74,150,236,314
EAGLE ELK 23,40,68,149,187,
.... 204,230,313
   Alice 149,267
   Joe 23
   Nancy 149,313
EAGLE ELK #2 76,239
EAGLE FACE 36,42,50,122,200,206,
.... 209,216,273,285

Lucy 200
EAGLE FEATHER 8,13,36,87,99,109,
132,143,174,178,200,249,261,273,295
.... ,307
   Jane 13
   William 29,193
EAGLE FISH 20,185
EAGLE FLESH 26,189
EAGLE FOOT 236
EAGLE FOX 30,194
EAGLE HAND 49,213
EAGLE HAWK .. 64,124,226,287,291
EAGLE HAWK #1 128
EAGLE HEART 87,248
   Jennie 87,248
EAGLE HILL 52,265
EAGLE HOOP 12,178
EAGLE HORN 20,36,86,185,
.... 200,234,248,293
   Agnes 86
   Albert 86,248
   Emma 86,248
   Fannie 86,248
   Hattie 86,248
   Josiah 86,248
   Lizzie 86,248
EAGLE HORSE 7,21,71,131,
.... 173,185,233
EAGLE LANCE 123,286
EAGLE LODGE 45,75,208,238
EAGLE LOUSE 13,119,179,282
EAGLE MAN 22,56,64,219,227
EAGLE MOCCOSIN 58
EAGLE NATION 68,69,230,232
EAGLE OUT 113,277
EAGLE PIPE ... 37,70,73,201,233,235
   Mac 73,235
   Maggie 38,201
EAGLE RING 75,237
EAGLE SHAWL 79,109,241,273
   Hattie 12,177
EAGLE SHIELD 36,200
   Lucy 36
EAGLE SHIRT 58,222
EAGLE STAR 14,144,146,308,310
EAGLE TAIL 124,287
EAGLE TAIL FEATHER 32,196
EAGLE THUNDER 225

Index

EAGLE TRACK .... 16,22,75,122,125, ... 181,187,238,285,288
EAGLE WOMAN ...... 10,16,20,68,70, ... 123,176,181,185,230,232
EARTH NATION 122,285
EARTH WOMAN 9
EASY TO CRY 131,293
EATS AT HER HOUSE 238
EATS AT HOME 112,275
ECOFFEY
   Ada 62
   Adie 321
   Albert 62,321
   Alice 61,321
   Alvina 62
   Fred 61,321
   Joseph 62,321
   Jules 61,321
   Julia 62,321
   Louise 62
   Mary Tway 62
   Pacific 321
   Pacifique 62
   Rosa 321
   Rosa Nelson 62
EDGAR 313
EDGE, Jennie R A T 242
EFFIE 40,204
EHAKA WIN 12,178
EHAKE 125,287
EHAKE GLI .... 6,11,20,37,107,140, ... 171,176,184,271
EHAKE HIYAYA KUTE 132
EHAKE IYANKA 314
EHAKE KUTE 294
EHAKE WIN 124,287,317
EHUKE GLI 37
ELBOW 35,199
ELDRIDGE
   Netta 45
   Nettie 320
ELIZA 18,119,282,311,318
ELK 86,133,248,296,314
   George 23
   James S 259
ELK #2 87
ELK BOY
   Charles 60

Huron 60,223
   Joseph 60
ELK COMES OUT 130,293
ELK HORN RIVER 100,262
ELK SOMAN 75
ELK STANDING SOLDIER 306
ELK TOOTH 20,184
ELK TUSK 121,284
ELK VOICE WALKING 126,289
ELK WOMAN .... 7,15,24,29,100, ...117,173,180,188,193,238,262,280
ELLEN 51,303
EMMA 31,40,56,195,203,220
EMPLOYER 71,234
ENAKIYA 16,101,181
ENAKIYE 263
END OF TIMBER, John 34,198
ENEMY 144,308
   Rosa K 230
ETHON DAYLIGHT 30
ETI 313
EUGENE 7,173
EYAPA OTA 320
EYAPAHA OTA 94
EYE SEED 55,218
FACE 55,219
   Sally 55,219
FACE EAGLE 109
FALLING LEAF 69,122,231,285
FANNIE 49,56
FARMER 38,202
FARNHAM
   Bessie 87,248
   Ellen 87,248
   Lizzie 87,248
   Ulyses 87,248
FAST 65,117,228,280
FAST CLOUD 259
FAST EAGLE 87,248
   Sally 248
FAST ELK 66,127,228,290
FAST HORSE 6,172
   Albert 251
   Alic 25
   Alice 188
   Amos 25,188
   Annie 135,189
   Cecilia 25,188

Index

Charles 25,188
Jennie 25,188
Joseph 25,188
Julia 6,172
Mary 99,260
Susie 157,188
Thomas 25,99,188
Thos 260
Wilber 189
William 135,189
FAST HORST
   Albert 89
   Jessie 89
FAST THUNDER 56,220
FAST WHIRLWIND 56,219
   Lucy 100,262
   Stella 56
FAST WOLF 142,306
   Annie 142,306
   Jessie 154,318
   John 154,318
   Josephine 306
   Millie 142
   Mollie 142,306
   Philip 142,306
   Thomas 141,307
FAT BOY 141,305
FAT TICKET 50,215
FAT WOMAN 131,293
FAWN 288
FEATHER 62,225
   Antoine 249
   Close 249
   Daniel 87,249
   Frank 87,249
   James 87,249
   John 87,249
   Lucy 87,249
   Mabel 87
   Mable 249
   Mary 87,249
   Paul 87,249
FEATHER BEAR 319
FEATHER O H, Cecilie 241
FEATHER O. HEAD, Cecilia 51
FEATHER ON HEAD . 51,77,215,239
   Emma 51,215
   Wm 51,215

FEATHER WOMAN 116,280
FEATHERMAN
   Blowing 87,249
   Daniel 87,249
   Lewis 87
   Louis 249
FEELS ALL AROUND IT 85,248
FEELS GOOD 70
FETCHES 43,67,229
FEW TAILS, Clara 58,222
FHUNTS HORSES, Rosa 202
FIGHT 129,292
   Frank 132,295
FIGHT EACH OTHER 292
FIGHT LITTLE 134
FIGHT OVER 11
FIGHT WITH 247
FIGHTER 67,229
FIGHTING BEAR, Max 67,230
FIGHTS BEAR 130,293
FIGHTS EACH OTHER 130
FIGHTS LITTLE 297
FIGHTS OVER 74,237,293
FIGHTS OVER HIM 62,225
FIGHTS WITH 85
   Jacob 195
FIGHTS WITH HIM 95
FILLS THE HOLE 12,178
FILLS THE PIPE
   Hattie 78
   Jennie 78,241
   Jessie 78
   Mattie 241
   Oliver 241
   Silas 78,241
   Willie 78,241
FINE SHOT 88,250
FINGER NAIL WOMAN 16,181
FIRE 5,171
   William P 153,317
FIRE #1 122
FIRE #2 285
FIRE LIGHTNING 50,214
FIRE PLACE 102,320
   Charles 320
   Mary 102,320
FIRE THUNDER 64,227
   Annie 19

Index

Bessie 19,184
Charles 64
Earth 64
Edgar 147
Edgard 311
Fannie 220
George 19,184
George, Jr 19
Jennie 64
Julia 147,311
Lydia 147,311
Mary 19,184
Prudy 184
Susie 147,311
William 64,147,311
Wm 227
Zoy 154,318
FIRE WHITE MAN 130
FIRE WOLF 55,219
 John 103,265
FIRST 117,280
FIRST BORN, Lucy 41,205
FIRST CLOUD 133,295
FIRST DAY 140,304
FIRST GHOST 37,201
FIRST WALK 119,282
FISH RIBS 44,193
FISHER
 Albert 104,265
 Amanda 104,265
 Anna 104,265
 Gracie 104,265
 Hattie 104,265
 Julia 104,265
 Laura 104,265
 Stanley H 104,265
FISHT WITH HIM 257
FIXES AND GROWLS 132,294
FLAG 133,134,296,297
FLAT 18,182
FLAT IRON 13,178
FLESH 9,175
FLESHER, Theresha 320
FLIES ABOUT 37,200
FLIES ABOVE 87,249
FLIES OVER HER 15,180
FLOOD
 Elizabeth 305

 Thomas 141,305
FLORENCE 79
FLY 19,184
 Peter 19,184
 Susie 19,184
FLYING 52,216
FLYING BLANKET 131,294
FLYING BY 147,311
FLYING DAY 134,297
FLYING HAIL 133,295
FLYING HAWK 70,233
FLYING HORSE 15,180,240,321
FLYING HORSE, JR 78
FLYING RED 118,281
FLYING WOMAN ... 32,115,196,279
 Sarah 141
FOAM 64,125,227
FOG 19,72,235
 Rosa 184
FOLLOWER 126,289
FOLLOWS AND KILLS 126,289
FOLLOWS PRAIRIE FIED 41
FOLLOWS PRAIRIE FIRE 204
FOND OF HIM 68,221,230
FOOL CROW 36,200
 Lizzie 36,200
FOOL FACE 67,299
FOOL GROUSE 107,271
FOOL HEAD 11,65,176,228
 Annie 11
FOOL HEART 32,74,237,262
FOOLING BEAR 153,317
 Lucy 153,317
 Paul 153,317
FOOLISH 134,297
FOOLISH WOMAN 58,108,109,
 221,271,279
FOOT 34,72,87,199,235,249
 Jennie 249
 Jennis 87
 Philip 87,179
 Rosa 87,249
FORKED TAIL 148,312
FORWARD 84,246
FOUGHT 65,227
FOUR BLANKET 128,290
FOUR CLOUD 55,219
FOUR FINGER 129,292

347

Index

FOUR HORNS 145,310
   Alice 146,310
FOUR KNIVES 140,304
FOUR PIPE DANCE 16,181
FOUR ROCKS 77,239
FOUR TIMES 113,276
FOUR WOMAN 17,182
FOX 111,140,274,304
   Sophia 8,174
FRANK 68,231,278
FREE HEARTED 58,221
FRIENDLY 18,183
FROG
   Elizabeth 87,249
   Warrior 87
   Wounded 87
FROG #1 87,249
FROG #2 126,289
FRONT FOOT 287
FRONT FORT 124
FROST OVER, George 97,258
FULL STOMACH 67,230
G I CENTER
   Holy 308
   Victoria 214
G IN CENTER, Alice 308
GALL 114,278
GALLAGHER, Nellie 103,265
GALLIGO
   Alice 15,180
   Alvina 70,233
   Ella 15,180
   Francis 233
   Frank 70,233
   James 9,15,175,180
   John 25,189
   John, Jr 25
   Julia 70,233
   Lou 70
   Minie 233
   Minnie 70
   Rosa 70,233
   Sarah 70,233
   Thomas 233
   Zonie 15,180
GARCIA
   Alice 34,245
   Alvina 77

Helen 77,240
Nicholas 34,245
Rosa 77,239
Sunday 77,240
Susie 77,240
Thomas 77,240
Virginia 245
GARNETT
   Charles 100,261
   Dollie 100
   Dolly 261
   Filla 100,261
   Richard 100,261
   Susie 23,187
   William 100,261
   William, Jr 100,261
GARNIER
   Baptiste 25,189
   Baptiste, Jr 25
   Ellen 25,189
   Emma 25,189
   John 25,189
   Julia 25,189
   Lizzie 25,189
   Lucy 25,189
   Sallie 25,189
   Sophia 25,189
GARRIER, Walter 88,266
GARTER 31,67,230,320
GAY
   Mary 203
   William 94,256
GE ICIYAWIN 248
GEGO, Frank 204
GELLISPIE
   Betty 125
   Emma 126
   George 126
   Henry 126
   Jennie 125
   Lizzie 126
   Margie 126
   Robert 126
   Sarah 125
GEORGE 49,214,309
GERRY
   Benjamin 142,306
   Cvynthia 142

Index

Cynthia ... 306
Edward ... 46
Elbridge ... 142,306
Jef ... 306
Jeff ... 142
John ... 142,306
Seth ... 142,306
William ... 142,306
GETAN ORANKO ... 7
GETS ANGRY ... 45,208
GETS AWAY WITH HORSES ... 76,152,238
GETS DOWN ... 110
GETS GOOD PIPE ... 131,294
GETS MAD ... 44,207
GETS THERE, Levi ... 83,245
GETS THERE FIRST .. 89,90,251,252
   Maggie ... 251
GETS TO LODGE FIRST ... 109
GHOST ... 64,227
   Alexander ... 65,227
   Emma ... 65,227
   Frank ... 65,227
   Samuel ... 65,227
GHOST BEAR
   Benj ... 215
   Benjamin ... 51
   Charles ... 51,215
   Edgar ... 51,215
   John ... 51,215
   Lillie ... 51,215
   Thomas ... 51,215
   William ... 51
   Wm ... 215
GHOST BULL ... 25,189
GHOST DOG ... 54,217
GHOST THUNDER ... 122,285
GI ... 73,102,139,263,303
GI ICIYA ... 74,85,111,236
GIAGO
   Grace ... 259
   Sophia ... 98,259
   Timothy ... 259
GIBBONS
   Agnes ... 44,207
   Annaie ... 207
   Annie ... 44
   Kate ... 44,207
   Lizzie ... 44,207
   Maggie ... 44,207
   Mary ... 44,207
   William ... 44,207
   Winfield ... 44,207
GILLESPIE
   Bettie ... 288
   Emma ... 288
   George ... 288
   Henry ... 288
   Jennie ... 288
   Lizzie ... 288
   Margie ... 288
   Robert ... 288
   Sarah ... 288
GIRARD
   Amburu R ... 267
   Belmore ... 267
   Belnore ... 157
   Ethel J ... 267
   Ethel Josephine ... 157
   Louisa ... 267
   Louise ... 101
GIRL ... 16,17,19,34,35,72,75,96, 97,103,113,119,125,181,182,183,198, ... 199,234,258,259,264,283
GIRLS COMES ... 65
GIROUX
   Charles ... 22,186
   Charles, Jr ... 22
   Lizzie ... 22,187
   Lottie ... 22,187
   Mary ... 22,186
   Rosa ... 22,186
GIRROUX
   Annie ... 312
   Arthur ... 148,312
   Emma ... 148,312
   George ... 148,312
   Rena ... 148,312
   Robert ... 148,312
   William ... 148,312
GIVES ... 86,248
GIVES ALL ... 112,276
GIVES ARROW ... 134,297
GIVES AWAY ... 33,115,153,197, ... 278,317
GIVES AWAY HORS, Bessie ... 214

Index

GIVES AWAY HORSES, Bessie .. 50
GIVES AWAY MONEY 52
GIVES AWAY WAR BONNET ...66, ...229
GIVES BACK 255
GIVES ENEMY 19,184
GIVES HIM 72,234
GIVES HIM S T EAT 318
GIVES HIM S. TO EAT 154
GIVES HIM UP 133,295
GIVES HORSES 111,274
GIVES PIPE 13,178
GIVES SPOTTED 73,235
GIVES THEM ALL 36,200
GIVES THINGS 90,252
GIVES UP ON HIM 21,185
GIVES WAR BONNET 76,238
GLEASON
   B J 163,164
   Millie 149,313
   Pearl 149,313
GLENAPA 197
GLENN
   Annie 253
   Edison 91,253
   John 91,253
   Lena 91,253
   Rosa 91,253
GLEPA 239
GLESKA AGLE 180
GLESKA AGLI ....9,15,49,115,126, ... 140,175,213,278,289,304
GLESKA ICU 52,216
GLESKA WICAKU 73,235
GLESKA YUHA 225
GLI IYOTAKA 58
GLI NAJIN 19,294
GLI WAJIN 132
GLIHUNIKI 107
GLINAJIN 44,184,190
GLINAPA 33
GLIYOPSICA 5,171
GLIYOTAKA 222
GLIYUNKA 132,134,295,298
GLOGLI 41,266,285,298
GLOGLIPI 127
GLOHI 273
GLOKU 122

GLONICA 72
GLUHA 180
GLUKA 172
GNASKA 249,289
GNASKA HO WASTE 293
GNUSKA 87,126
GNUSKA HO WASTE 131
GODWIN, Julis 186
GOES AFTER 65,228
GOES AMONG THEM 101,263
GOES DANCING 93,255
GOES FIRST 72,234
GOES HOLY 111,129,272,275
GOES I CENTER
   Joseph 214
   Maggie 214
   William 214
GOES I. CENTER, Victoria 50
GOES IN CENTER ...... 18,88,89,127, ...133,144,183,250,288,290,308
   Alice 144
   Holy 144
   Jno 308
   John 144
   Joseph 50
   Maggie 50
   Wm 50
GOES IN FRONT 62,225
   Howard 76,239
GOES IN LIGHT 154
GOES IN SIGHT 318
GOES ON CENTER 251
GOES OUT BAD 31
GOES OUT LOOKING 99,260
GOES THROUGH 124,286
GOES WHITE COW 148,312
GOES WITH THEM 108,272
GOINGS
   Baby 24,187
   Blanch 187
   Blanche 24
   Earl 12,178
   Frank 12,178
   Garnett 12,178
   James 24,187
   Louie 187
   Louis 24
   Nettie 24,187

Index

GOOD 57,90,112,221,252,275
   Edgar 73,236
GOOD ACTION 30
GOOD BALD EAGLE 108,272
GOOD BEAR 19,183
GOOD BIRD 86,253,286
GOOD BIRD WALKS FAST 100
GOOD BOY 18,29,31,32,35,108,
.... 120,183,193,195,199,209
   Frank 9,175
GOOD BUFFALO 108,209
GOOD BUG 88,250
GOOD BULL 64
GOOD CANE 85,247
GOOD CHEYENNE 75,237
GOOD CLOUD 38,84,130,202,
.... 246,293
GOOD COW 14,179
GOOD CROSS 16,181
GOOD CROW 75,237
GOOD DAY 17,51,83,182,215,245
GOOD DOG 20,185
GOOD DOOR 37,201
GOOD EAGLE 9,38,113,151,152,
.... 175,201,276,315,316
   Harrison 46
   Joseph 142,306
   Samuel 151,315
   Susie 151,315
GOOD ELK 15,36,63,67,122,
.... 180,229,285,321
GOOD ENEMY 68,114,126,
.... 230,277,289
GOOD FACE 88,117,129,250,
.... 280,292
GOOD FACE ELK 122,285
GOOD FEATHER 15,127,289
GOOD FINGER 316
GOOD FLUTE 125,288
GOOD GIRL 88,111,250,274
GOOD HAIR 189
GOOD HAIR BEAR 112
GOOD HAIRED BEAR 33,197
GOOD HAIRED WOMAN 8,174
GOOD HAWK WOMAN 12,178
GOOD HEART 13,67,121,178,
.... 221,230,284
GOOD HEARTED 12,74

GOOD HOOP 72
GOOD HORSE 30,88,126,
.... 135,250,289,298
   Henry 100,249
   Josephin 88
GOOD LANCE 49,133,213,296
   Frank 49,213
   James 49,213
GOOD LEGGINS 113,275
GOOD LODGE 124,288
GOOD MEDICINE 32,36,53,133,
.... 196,200,217,240,296
GOOD MOVER 37,59,201,223
GOOD NATURED 140,304
GOOD PIPE 35,135,198,298
GOOD PLUME 44,208
GOOD PRISONER 283
GOOD PRISONERS 79
GOOD RING 13,56,179,220
GOOD ROAD 20,35,107,112,
.... 184,199,271,276
GOOD ROCK 273
GOOD SHELL 153,172
GOOD SHIELD 57,108,117,
.... 122,209,220,280,285
   Jo 108
   Joseph 209
GOOD SHOT 10,42,143,206,307
   Emily 42,206
   Harry 42,206
   Oscar 206
GOOD SOLDIER 117,280
GOOD TALK 69,231
GOOD THUNDER 60,62,83,
.... 224,225,246
GOOD TRACK 122,285
GOOD VOICE 22,108,315
GOOD VOICE CROW 88,250
   Mary 88
   Mollie 88
GOOD VOICE DOG 108,298
GOOD VOICE ELK 39,151,
.... 203,204,277,315
GOOD VOICE FROG 131,293
GOOD VOICE HAWK 73,236
GOOD VOICE IRON 46,299
GOOD VOICE STAR 57,221
GOOD VOICE WOMAN 10,176

Index

GOOD VOICED WOMAN 12,178
GOOD WEASEL 76,238
GOOD WHITE COW 38,63,121,
 202,226,284
GOOD WHITE WOMAN 20,185
GOOD WILL 70
GOOD WIN, Julia 21
GOOD WOMAN 12,15,21,37,59,65,71,
 72,89,108,117,124,143,186,200,222,
 234,251,280,287,307
GOOOD FINGER 152
GOOSE FACE 151,315
GRABS HIM 132,295
GRACIA, Alvina 239
GRAHAM
   Alfred 18,183
   Howard 18,183
   Lizzie 18,183
   Ollie 18,183
GRASS
   Edward 149,209
   Ellen 40,204
   James 40,149,204,209
   Jennie 40,204
   John 100,209,267
   Thomas 149,209
   Victoria 40,204
   William 40
   Wm 204
GRAY BLANKET 9,175
GRAY EYES 224
GRAY GRASS 38,77,202,240,265
GRAY HORSE, James 148,312
GRAY SPOTTED HORSE 58,221
GREEN
   Harry 149,313
   Lloyd 313
   Loe 149,313
   Susie 149,313
GREEN LEAF 115,278
GRESH
   John 144,308
   Lizzie 144,308
   Mary 144,308
   Millie 144,308
   Susie 144,308
   Todd 144,308
GREY BLANKET, Lucy 9

GREY EYES 60
GREY GRASS 104
GREY GRASS WOMAN 6,172
GROUND SPIDER 135,297
GROVER 44,207
GROWING CEDAR 17,182
GROWLER 44,207
   Nora 38,208
GROWLING BEAR 59,88,223,250
   Charles 88
   Thomas 88
GROWN WOMAN 68,230
GROWS 22,187
GROWS ARROWS 62,225
GROWS GOOD 58,221
GROWS UP 70,224
GROWTH 67,230
GRUNTING 36,200
GRUNTING BEAR 143,308
GRUNTS 134,297
GUCIYA 274
GUIDE WOMAN 51,73,235,321
GUN 134,297
GUN WOMAN 125,288
GUNKHINSA 185
GUS 231
H SOLDIER
   Lauise 311
   Stephen 311
HA WAKAN 71,234
HAIL 43,46,76,206,209,239,271
HAIL BEAR 133,296
HAIL BLANKET 104
HAIL DRESS 75
HAIL FIRE 90
HAIPAGJA TANKA 262
HAIPAZAZA TANKA 101
HAIR 10,107,176,272
   Amoh P H 256
   Emma P H 256
   Emma Y 251
   Ephraim R H 256
   Ephriam P. H. 94
   Jessie Y 251
   Sarah P H 256
   Winnie P H 256
HAIR PIPE 123,286
HAIR WOMAN 91,253

Index

Lucy 251
HAIRED WOMAN, Lucy 85
HAIRLESS BEAR 131,293
HAIRLESS BULL 107,271
HAIRY 108
HAIRY BEAR 5,171
HAIRY BIRD
   James 112,276
   Mrs 173
HAIRY BIRD #2, Mrs 7
HAKEKTA 198
HAKIKTA 25,34,50,135,146,
   156,214,229,320
HAKIPI 281
HALF WOMAN 303
HAN GLAWA 154
HAND 156,320
   Joseph 181
   Josph 16
   Julia 156,320
   Marshall 16,181
HAND DONT SMELL 35
HAND SOLDIER
   John 147,311
   Julia 147,311
   Louise 147
   Moses 146,311
   Stephen 147
HANEPI KTE 218
HANGING 59,222
HANGLAWA 318
HANHEPI 43,92,207
HANHEPI GLI 84
HANHEPI KTE 54,281
HANHEPI NAKIPA 127
HANHEPI SNI KTE 124,287
HANHEPI WICAKTE 26
HANHEPI YANKA 71
HANKEPI 254
HANKEPI GLI 246
HANKEPI KTE 189
HANKEPI WICAKTE 8,118
HANNAH 298
HANOMANI 31,290
HANPA 287
HANPA HUNAKA 153
HANPA HUNKU 317
HANPA NASICA 13,178

HANPA SAPA 124,246
HANPA SICA 200
HANPA SPAYA 76,239
HANPISKA 134,297
HANSKA 57,128,221
   Long Skunk 156
   Maka 156
HANSKA NARCO 204
HANSKA TO 201
HARAPE WIN 298
HARD 57,221
HARD FOREHEAD 37,200
   Ada 45,208
   Frank 30,194
   Louisa 30,194
   Thomas 30,194
HARD GROUND 53,217
HARD HEART 64,226
   George 15
HARD ROBE 24
HARD TIMES 131,294
HARD TO HIT 63,70,101,127,
   226,232,263,290
HARD WOMAN 15,89,252
HARNIR KTE 275
HARVY
   George 44,208
   Jacob 44,208
   John 44,208
   Joseph 44,208
   Julia 44,208
   Maggie 44,208
   Susie 44,208
HAS COURAGE 30,194
HAS NO HORSE 264
HAS NO HORSES 102
   Julia 102
HAS NO RELATION 44
HAS NO RELATIVE 208
HAS NONE 30,194
HAS SPOTTED HORSES 14
HAT 120,283
   Henry 120
   James 283
HATO WICAKTE 95
HATTIE 135,298,309,315
HAUPA SICA 36
HAWK 6,37,126,172,201,289

Index

Albert A O 237
Bessie T 40
Charles T 86
Fannie 88,250
Florence 32,196
Lizzie 32,196
Phillip T 40,204
Silas 56,220
Susie 150
HAWK BOY 41,205,217
HAWK MAN 144,308
HAWK SOLDIER 38,202
HAWK VOICE 22
HAWK WING 54,217
   James 54,217
   Luke 54,217
HAWK WOMAN 17,90,92,123,
.... 155,252,254,286,319
   Mary 60,223
HAWKINS
   James 154,155,318,319
   Joseph 155,319
   Julia 155,319
   Lottie 155
   Lottie D 155,319
   Louis 155,319
   Susie 155,319
   William 155,319
HAY LEG 107,271
HAY PRESS, Julia 70,233
HAYAPI WASTE KOYAKA 149,313
HE BEAR 29,30,193,194
   George 30,194
   Mary 30,194
HE CINSAKAYAPI 227
HE CINSKAYAPI 64
HE CROW 16,181
HE DOG 119,282
HE HANSKA 77,151,239
HE HANSKASKA 315
HE LUTA 33,90,197,252,280
HE MAZA 109
HE NAPA 234
HE NUPA 237
HE NUPIN WANICA 288
HE PTECELA 206
HE RLOGECA 59,62,63,218,225,226
HE RLOGUA 223

HE TOPA 145,146,310
HE WANICA 103,265
HE WANJILA 74,285
HE WOPTURA 89,251
HE WOTOKA 50,214
HEAD, William W 263
HEAD OF CREEK 147,311
HEAR HIM 178
HEARS 8,174
HEARS A VOICE 12
HEARS HER VOICE 99,261
HEARS HIM 12
HEARS HIS NAME 216
HEARS HIS VOICE 23,187
HEARS IT 125,288
HEARS THE VOICE 95,256
HEARS VOICE 34,198
HEART 14,179
HEART MAN 72,103,235,264
HEART WOMAN 180
HEARTLESS BEAR 155,319
HEHAKA LUZAHAN 228
HEHTAKIYA TOKA KTE 291
HEKTAKEYA KU 260
HEKTAKEYE KUTE 254
HEKTAKIYA 290
HEKTAKIYA EKTA 275
HEKTAKIYA EKTE 10,24,30,
.... 111,112,130,176,275
HEKTAKIYA GLI 9,12,103,108,
.... 175,264,272
HEKTAKIYA KU 99
HEKTAKIYA KUTE 113
HEKTAKUJA EKTE 194
HEKTEKIYA KTE 128
HEKTKIYA EKTE 292
HELPER 9,117,175,298
HELPS 19,41,50,93,98,122,
.... 204,214,260,285
   (Joseph) 266
   Jennie 19
   Lucy 19
HENDERSON
   Louise 25,188
   May Louise 188
   Stella L 25,188
HENRY 51,215
   Lizzie 98,260

Index

Thomas 98,260
Wallace 98
Wallack 260
HENUPIN WANICA 125
HER BAD HORSE 133,296
HER BEAR COMES 129,292
HER BLANKET .. 12,68,101,110,134, ... 177,231,262,274,297
Hattie 141,305
HER BLUE DAY 140,304
HER BLUE HORSE 86,253
HER DAY 12,17,178,182
HER DOOR ... 10,64,146,176,226,310
HER EAGLE 11,31,195
HER EAGLE PIPE 177
HER EYES 101
HER GIRL 38,201
HER GOOD BLANKET .. 66,114,228, ... 277
HER GOOD DAY 34,198,298
HER GOOD FEATHER 151,315
HER GOOD HORSE ...... 37,43,71,72, 99,120,126,150,201,207,233,235,261, ... 283,289,314
HER GOOD HORSES 66,228
HER GOOD PIPE 46,209
HER GOOD PLACE 220
HER GOOD ROAD ... 13,21,29,36,78, ... 149,178,185,193,200,241,313
HER GOOD SEAT 123
HER GOOD THING 107,271
HER GOOD THINGS 150,314
HER HEAD 94,256
HER HEART 55,218
HER HOLY BLANKET ...... 17,37,95, ... 182,201,257
HER HOLY DOOR 107,271
HER HOLY HORSE 89,251
HER HOLY PIPE 152,316
HER HOLY ROBE 90,252
HER HORSE ...... 7,19,94,95,108,116, ... 129,173,184,256,257,272,279,292
HER HORSE COMES OUT 95,257
HER HORSES .... 19,77,146, ... 183,225,240,310
HER HORSES SHOT TO PIECES 67
HER LOOKING HORSE 151,315
HER MANY HORSES 33,58,196,221

HER MANY ROAD 284
HER MANY ROADS 121
HER MEDICINE HORSE 90
HER MEDICINE LODGE 73,235
HER PIPE 11,177
HER PLENTY HORSES 22,123,186,286
HER PLENTY PIPE 114,277
HER PLENTY ROAD 116,279
HER RED BLANKET 39,203
HER RED DOOR 58,221
HER RED HORSE .... 31,57,58,141, ... 144,195,221,222,305,308
HER RED SEAT 123,285
HER ROAD 51,112,276,321
HER RUNNING HORSE 68,231
HER SHELL 17,40,203
HER SPOTTED HORSE .... 70,126, ... 232,289
HER TALK 116,279
HER TOWN BLANKET 70
HER TWO BLANKETS 77,240
HER TWO HORSES 95,257
HER WHITE HORSE . 41,64,205,227
HER WOUNDED HORSE 38
HER WOUNDED HORSES 202
HER YELLOW BLANKET .. 115,278
HER YELLOW RING 130,292
HERACKA GI 213
HERAKA 86,87,133,248,296,314
HERAKA AKICITA NAJIN 306
HERAKA BLOKA 277
HERAKA BLOKE 113
HERAKA CINCALA 98,260
HERAKA CIQALA .. 17,29,30,75,88, ... 182,193,194,238,250
HERAKA GI 23,131,282
HERAKA GLESKA 259
HERAKA HE WAKPA 262
HERAKA HEWAKPA 100
HERAKA HINAPA 293
HERAKA HO WASTE ... 39,151,203, ... 204
Good Voice Elk 40
HERAKA HOKSILA 223
HERAKA INAJIN 96,257
HERAKA INYAKA 229
HERAKA ISNALA .. 65,108,115,154,

Index

..........................222,228,278,298,317
HERAKA IYANKE....................... 66
HERAKA IYOTAKA........20,133,296
HERAKA LOWAN 74
HERAKA LUTA 10,57,91,96,
...................................127,220,257
HERAKA LUTA WIN 118
HERAKA LUZAHAN......66,127,290
HERAKA MANI 114,119,277,282
HERAKA MAZA 69,193,231
HERAKA NAJI 202
HERAKA NAJIN 38
HERAKA NOPA 46
HERAKA NUPA 26,139,140,
..................................173,189,242,304
HERAKA SAPA...........14,57,60,120,
..................................180,221,224,283
HERAKA SICA...........32,34,198,266
HERAKA SKA.............36,37,65,124,
..................................194,200,287
HERAKA TAMAHECA 112,275
HERAKA TAMAKECA 275
HERAKA WAKAN......19,22,90,100,
..................101,252,262,263,266
HERAKA WAKINYAN.133,184,296
HERAKA WAKITA..............129,292
HERAKA WAMBLI 230,239,267
HERAKA WANBLI
.... 23,40,68,76,149,187,204,313
HERAKA WANJILA 59
HERAKA WASTE 15,30,31,36,63,
..........................67,122,194,229,321
HERAKA WIN 15,24,29,75,
.................................100,117,238,262
HERAKALOWAN 236
HERAKALUTA 254
HERAKAWIN..............................193
HERDER 114,277
HERLOGECA 54
HERMAN
    Antoine 83,245
    Cora 83,245
    Edward............................83,245
    Jacob 83,245
    Lizzie 83,245
    Nellie...............................83,245
    Winfred 245
    Winifred........................... 83
HERMANDEZ
    Ambrosus 259
    Austacia...................................259
    Catelina...................................259
    Florence...................................259
    Retes...259
    Sophia......................................259
    Valentine 259
HERMANDY
    Ambrosis 97
    Austacia...................................97
    Catelina...................................97
    Florncis....................................97
    Reyes.......................................97
    Sophia......................................97
    Valentine 97
HEYAKA TASUNKE.................276
HEYASKA 202
HEYOKA 51,59
HEYOKA WIN 120,283
HI KAPSUN.......................... 16,181
HI MAZA 18,183
HIDE 19,183
HIGH BEAR ... 17,73,90,182,236,252
    Alice 73,236
    Herbert.................................90
    Jennie................................ 73,236
HIGH BULL............................ 12,177
HIGH CAT 120,283
HIGH CHIEF 45,209
    Mary 45,209
HIGH CRANE....................... 115,279
HIGH DOG 131,293
HIGH EAGLE............. 45,62,208,225
    Joseph.................................. 52
HIGH HERON 64,226
HIGH HORSE..................... 77,239
HIGH HORSE #1 297
HIGH HORSE #2 134,297
HIGH LODGE................... 116,279
HIGH MEDICINE.................. 76,239
HIGH PINE 90,252
    James 252
    Jessie 90,252
HIGH STAR............ 56,151,219,315
HIGH WAWK.............................202
HIGH WHITE MAN 126,289
HIGH WOLF

Index

Clayton..............................37,201
Joseoh 216
Kittie 42,206
Mattie............................42,206
Susan.............................41,204
Victoria..........................42,206
HIGHEST ONE 65,228
HIGHT HORSE #1 134
HIHAN...............................131
HIHAN GI 293
HIHAN GLESKA 60,223,225
HIHAN LUTA 76,83
HIHAN SAPA 151,315
HIHAN SKA...............76,239,281
HIHAN TATANKA 153,317
HIHAN TONKA.........................193
HIHAN WANBLI.................127,290
HILL
   Lizzie 24,210
   Robert 24,210
   Susie...............................24,210
HILLS WARRIOR 125
HIN ROTA WIN........................103
HIN TANI............................176
HIN TOKECA 216
HIN TOKESA............................. 52
HIN WASTE WIN................178,180
HINAPA 56,71,134,143,153,
.....................219,296,299,307,317
HINAPAPI SICA...................... 31
HINHAN.............................294
HINHAN GI......................121,130
HINHAN LUTA 17,238,245
HINHAN SAPA....................101,263
HINHAN SKA..........................118
HINHAN TANKA...................... 29
HINHAN WAKAN...............10,176
HINHAN WAMBLI 229
HINHAN WANBLI...................... 67
HINMAN SITTING WEASEL....... 58
HINOPA 46
HINROTA 6,53,140,172,216,304
HINROTA WIN.. 63,129,156,226,264
HINSMA..........................108,272
HINSMA WIN.....................85,251
HINTANI............................ 11
HINTO AGLI....................130,293
HINTO GLESKA 58,221

HINWASTE WIN 8,174,189
HINYETE..........................222,227
HINZI AGLI........ 10,75,119,123,124,
.... 176,282,286,287
HINZI GLESKA 129,292
HIP 131,133,294,296
HIRD.................................. 123
HIRNIR KTE 112
HIS BONNET 126,289
HIS EYES............................263
HIS FIGHT............. 128,129,290,292
HIS FRIEND 252
HIS HORSE MAN 118
HIS PACKAGE................... 140,304
   Philip 140,305
HIS ROAD 21,185
HIS ROAD HORSE 52
HIS ROAN HORSE 216
HIS WHITE HORSE............ 118,281
HIT THEM IN THE ARM 66,229
HITS ENEMY 89,251
   Rosa............................... 89,251
HITS PIPE............................. 124,287
HIYANKE KTE 10
HIYETE.............................58,64
HIYOHIPI 7,107
HIYOKIPI 19
HIYOYA 65,228
HIYUICIYA......................... 118,281
HO AKATANHAN................. 76,239
HO NAJIN............................. 122
HO NARON 12,95
HO NARPN............................. 187
HO TANKA 130
HO WASTE 22,108,315
HO YEKIYA.............................. 184
HOBERT..............................298
HOGAN LUTA 263
HOGAN SA........................... 102
HOGAN TUCUHU 44,193
HOGAN WANBLI.................20,185
HOKA 289
HOKIKTA.............................66,310
HOKIPI 118
HOKISLA SKA....................... 179
HOKISLA ZI........................ 182
HOKSI TOKAPA.................. 41,205
HOKSILA 116,117,123,126,

Index

.. 127,128,129,247,279,280,286,289, ...290,292
HOKSILA ANATAPI................... 73
HOKSILA CEPA...................141,305
HOKSILA CIQA 124
HOKSILA CIQALA ...35,60,135,199, ...223,239,298
HOKSILA KTE 218
HOKSILA LUTA 117,281,295
HOKSILA MAZA 68,231
HOKSILA SAYAPI................68,230
HOKSILA SICA..........37,75,200,237
HOKSILA SKA 16
HOKSILA TANKA ....18,52,60,61, ...182,216,224,247
HOKSILA WAKAN....77,97,240,259
HOKSILA WAMBLI 282
HOKSILA WANBLI................60,130
HOKSILA WASTE .....9,18,29,31,32, 35,77,108,120,175,183,193,195,196, ...199,209,240
HOKSILA ZI 16,17,54,181,182
HOKSILOA ZI 17
HOL PIPE..................................119
HOLLOW 132,294
HOLLOW HEAD 89,251
   Fannie 102,264
   George.....................................89,251
   Jobson 102,264
   Julia.......................................89,251
   Stephen 264
HOLLOW HORN...........54,59,62,63, ...218,223,225,226
   Thomas 62
HOLY BIRD........................9,10,175
   Julia.....................................10,299
HOLY BLANKET.....95,107,257,271
HOLY BREAST 41,205
HOLY BREATH 114
   Kate 100,262
HOLY BULL 88,250
HOLY CAIN WOMAN................. 99
HOLY CANE WOMAN..............261
HOLY CLOUD....................114,277
   Isaac....................................114,277
HOLY COW 117,280
HOLY CROW 55,123,218,286
HOLY DAY...............68,149,230,313
HOLY EAGLE........................ 74,236
HOLY ELK 22
HOLY FACE............. 91,145,253,309
HOLY FOREHEAD................26,299
HOLY GIRL......................... 150,314
HOLY HAND 135,145,297,309
HOLY HILL........................... 19,184
HOLY HORSE..................... 121,284
HOLY IN CENTER 150,314
HOLY LAKE 16,181,237
HOLY LODGE .... 44,61,70,129, ... 208,224,233,292
HOLY OLD WOMAN 20,185
HOLY OWL........................... 10,176
HOLY PIPE......... 46,63,115,278,282, ... 299,321
HOLY ROAD......................... 32,196
HOLY ROCK
   James............................... 77,239
   Kate 61,224
   Moses.....................................239
HOLY SHAWL.................... 124,287
HOLY SHIRT 119,121,282,284
HOLY SKIN.......................... 71,234
   Bessie 71,234
HOLY STAR................................274
HOLY SWORD.................... 132,294
HOLY TAKE 74
HOLY TRACK 71,196,234
HOLY WOMAN........ 9,31,55,78,103, ..112,139,151,175,195,218,240,276, ... 315
HONARONPI.............. 23,99,198,261
HONOMANI................................ 195
HONPE..222
HONRONPI 256
HONSKA NARCO.......................224
HOOD BOY 196
HOOP
   Fanny R 304
   Ophelia R.................................304
HORN
   Agnes E 248
   Mary H 225
   Thomas H 225
HORN CHIP.................................251
   Rosa...251
HORN CHIPS 89

Index

Rosa 89
HORN CLOUD, Joseph 84,246
HORNBECK
    Edward 204
    Frank 45,190
    Joseph 40,204
    Julia 40,204
    Susie 45,190
HORNED HAWK 120,283
HORNED HORSE 108
HORNET 53,266
HORSE
    Annie 25
    Benjamin A. 83
    Dawson A 219
    Georgiana L 97
    Jennie A 245
    Jessie F 260
    Joe W 273
    Josephine G 250
    Josie A 245
    Julia H N 264
    Louise L S 282
    Robert 25,188
    Robert S 259
    Samuel R 35
    Sophia R 266
    Stella 188
    Thomas 189
HORSE COMES OUT ..... 71,116,234, ... 279
HORSE GOES AHEAD 38,202
HORSE LAYS DOWN 41,205
HORSE ROAD ... 11,110,151,176,315
    John 151,315
HORSE RUNS AHEAD 118,281
HORSE RUNS FIRST 118,281
HORSE STANDS IN SIGHT .. 30,194
HORSE STEALER 57,221
HORSE STOPS 60,224
HORSE THIEF 75,125,238,288
HORSE WALKS IN SIGHT 67,230
HORSE WOMAN .... 58,110,129, ... 221,274,292
HORSES COMES 321
HOTAIN 31,131,195,294
HOTAIN WIN 34
HOTANKA 293
HOTON 145
HOTUN 309
HOUSE 30,89,194,251
HOWASTE WIN 10,12,176
HOWLING HORSE 113,277
HOYEKIYA 19
HU 109,272
HU CAN CAN 255
HU CANCAN 93
HU PEJI 271
HU PTECELA 38,202
HU RANRAN 139,303
HU RNI 292
HU WEGAHAN 93,110,255,274
HUBERT 135
HUDSON 43
HUDSPETH
    Edna 135
    Myrtle 135,298
    Nellie 135,298
    Oliver 135,298
    Thetna 298
    William 135,298
    Zona 135
HUHU 38,202
HUHU NAPIN .... 23,25,102,116, ... 187,188,263
HUHU SKA 144,308
HUHU YUHA 30,72,194,235
HUKUTA GLICU 110
HUMP 73,235
HUMPE 238
HUNCASA COLA 307
HUNCASA SOLA 143
HUNCASE 31,67,230,320
HUNKA HOKSILA 180
HUNKAWIN 200
HUNKESNI 69
HUNKPAPA 79,155,241,319
HUNPEKA 59,64,75
HUNPI 227
HUNSKA 67
HUNSKA HINSMA 265
HUNSKA NARCO 60,67,291
HUNSKA NARSO 230
HUNSKA SA 117
HUNSKA SASA 280
HUNSKA TANKA NARCO ... 10,176

Index

HUNSKA TO 37
HUNSKA WASTE 113
HUNTER
    Henry 145,309
    John 14,179
    Lucy 145,309
    Mary 309
    Nicholas 145,309
    Sallie 14,179
    Victoria 145,309
HUNTS CROW VILLAGE ... 122,285
HUNTS ENEMY 67,127,230,290
HUNTS FOR SOMETHING 266
HUNTS HIS HORSES 49,213
    Lucy 49
HUNTS HORSES 16
    His Friend 89
    Lucy 213
    Maggie 89,252
    Rosa 46
    Ta Kolaku 89
HUNTS NOTHING ... 78,151,240,315
    John 151,315
HUNTS THEM 76,238
HUNTS THEM UP 84,246
HUOCAN 277
HURMI 129
HUSA LUTA 20
HUSKA NARCO 40
HUSTE 67,299
HUSTE WIN 15,53
HUTKAN 130,292
HUWEGAHAN 274
HYOSIPI 184
I DOG, Wallace 313
I TANKA 50
IASINA WAKAN 37
IASUNKE HINSA 58
ICAGA 22,67,70,187,224
ICANYAN 135,297
ICANYAN IYANKA 65,116,279
ICANYAN WICA IYANKA 123
ICANYAN WICAINYANKA 286
ICAPSIPSICALA 19
ICAYAN IYANKA 65
ICE 50,214
    Mary 94,256
ICIMANI HANSKA 120,283

ICIWICAYAPA 53
ICOSPINCALA 35
ICU 76,239
IEAPINPSINSALA 199
IGLAKE 195
IGLAKESA 30
IGLEPA 77
IGLONICA 24,128
IGLUHOMNI 213
IGMU HANSKA 50,214
IGMU WAKEWA 121
IGMU WANKATUYA 120,283
IHAKAP OMANI NAKTE 126
IHAKE IYANKA 150
IHANBLA 284
IHANBLESA 121
IHUNI 83,245
IKAPAPTANYAN 247
IKIKCU 282
IKOMI 41
IKOTMNI 222
IKPAPTANYAN 85
IKTOMI 139,303
IKTOMI GI 115
IKTOMNI 205,215
IKTOMNI CANKAHU 74,237
IKU HANSKA 126,289
IKUNSAN 232
IKUSAN 70,124,287
ILAZATA YOU 313
ILAZATA YU 150
ILAZATAN YANKA 71
IMAPUTAKA 69,232
IMATATES CHEYENNE 252
IMITATE CHEYENNE 90
IMITATES DOG 149,313
IMNISTA 223
IMNISTAN 59
IN SIGHT 18,79,183,283
IN THE CROWN 94,256
INDUSTRIOUS
    Alice 73,235
    Lawrence 73,235
    Shell 73,235
INGERSOLL, Sarah 78,240
INTERPRETER 66,229
INUPA 111,275
INYA MATO 220

Index

INYA SKA 218
INYA WAKINYA 227
INYAG MANI 215
INYAN 30,119,194,282
INYAN AKAN MANI 99
INYAN CANTE 17,182
INYAN HINAPA 124,287
INYAN HOKSILA 75,148,312
INYAN IYOTAKA 119
INYAN JANJANYELA 133
INYAN KABLECA 85,247
INYAN MATO 51,56
INYAN MAZA 77,121,284
INYAN PE 111
INYAN SA 19,183
INYAN SALA 44,208
INYAN SICA 131,295
INYAN SKAN MANI 260
INYAN SNA WIN 322
INYAN TIPI WIN 75
INYAN TOPA 77,239
INYAN WAKAN 61,77,224
INYAN WICASA 9,175,240
INYAN WIN 112,145,182
INYAN WINYAN 18
INYANG KTE 237
INYANKA 199
INYANKE SNI 46
IOGNA OPI 129,291
IPAHIN 134,297
IPIYAKA 88,123,250,286
IPIYAKA COLA 6,94,172
IPIYAKA NICA 256
IRA 127,290
IRE HOKSILA 237
IRE MAZA 240
IRE TIPI WIN 237
IRE WAKAN 239
IRON 70,232
IRON BEAR 109,273
IRON BEAVER 11,177
IRON BED 66,202
IRON BIRD 11,20,37,67,
.... 177,185,201,229
    Bessie 37,201
IRON BOY, Jacob 68,231
IRON BULL 42,135,206,297
    Cora 135,297

IRON CANE 128,291
IRON CEDAR 52,68,266
IRON CHILD 37,201
IRON CLOUD 36,200
    Eddie 36,200
IRON CROW 58
    Cecilia 49,175
    Ellen 56,219
    Emily 49,213
    Mary 49,213
    Nicholas 49,213
    William 49,213
IRON CROW #2 71,234
IRON ELK 69,231
    David 193
IRON FACE 107,271
IRON FOOT 134,296
IRON HAIL 128,291
IRON HAIR 90,252
IRON HAND 153,317
IRON HAWK 76,118,239,281
IRON HEART 36,52,200,216
    George 180
IRON HORN 109
IRON HORSE 35,45,95,102,107,
... 124,171,208,257,264,271,272,287
    Frank 70,233
IRON HORSE #2 199
IRON JAW 295
IRON LODGE 273
IRON NAIL 51,215
IRON NECK 115,278
IRON PLUME 67,230
IRON RING 127
IRON ROAD 11,20,139,153,
.... 176,184,303,317
IRON ROBE 55,219
IRON ROCK 77,121,240,284
IRON ROPE 144,308
    Winnie 144,308
IRON SHAWL WOMAN 120,283
IRON SHELL 64,69,227,232
    Lizzie 69,232
IRON SHIELD 110,298
IRON SHIRT 128
IRON TAIL 109,273
    Philip 109,273
IRON TEETH 18,183

Index

IRON TRACK 79,141,241,305
IRON TRAP 116,279
IRON VILLAGE 174
IRON WHITE COW 77,240
IRON WHITE MAN 13,178
IRON WING 135,298
IRON WOMAN 45,84,208,246
IRPEYA GLECUPI 225
IRVING
    Benjamin 23,187
    Elizabeth 23,187
    Ella 23
    Ellen 187
    Julia 23,187
    William 23,187
ISAGA 230
ISAKIB TI 226
ISANTI 291
ISANYANTE 220
ISANYANTI 57
ISNA KAGA 90
ISNA KTE 110,274
ISNA QU 314
ISNA TI 54,150
ISNA WAKUNA 173
ISNA WAKUWA 7,67,71,134,297
ISNA WICAKTE 117,125
ISNALA ICAGA 230
ISNALA INYAKA 213
ISNALA ISARGA 67
ISNALA KAGA 252
ISNALA KTE 263,280,288
ISNALA TI 128,153,218,317
ISNALA WAKUWA 229,233
ISNALA WANLATUYA 65
ISNLA WANKATUYA 228
ISPA 35
ISPA HOKSILA CIQALA 199
ISTA GI 14,18,36,38,51,58,61,
68,101,115,127,183,202,215,222,224,
.... 231,263,278,290,321
ISTA GONGA 25,78,122,285
ISTA OGNA OPI 41,204
ISTA RE SKA 238
ISTA RMI 39,85,199,203,247
ISTA SA 88,89,96,250,257,266
ISTA SAN 60,224
ISTA SAPA 147,309,311

ISTA SKA 19,57,58,97,101,120,
.... 183,184,221,253,258,262,283
ISTA SU 55,218
ISTA TANKA 102,264
ISTA UNI 35
ISTA WIYAKPA 35,198
ISTA YAZAN 151,315
ISTA ZI 63
ISTAREPI SKA 75
ISTIMA TA 114
ISTIMATA 278
ISTINA 65,83
ISTO 124,287
ISTO AKAN AWICAPA 66
ISTO AKANL APA 229
ISTO WASAKA 73
ISTO WASAKE 235
ISTO WEGAHAN 84
ISTO WEYAHAN 246
ITA WAMBLI 200
ITA WAWIYOKEPI 220
ITAGONGA 188
ITANKA 214
ITANKASAN 108
ITAZIPA COLA 64,299
ITAZIPA KICUN 14,111,179,274
ITAZIPA SICA 61
ITAZIPA WAKAN 61
ITAZIPE SICA 224
ITAZIPE WAKAN 234
ITE 55,219
ITE BLAGAHAN 131,294
ITE MAZA 107,271
ITE NOPA 18
ITE NUPA 116,183,279
ITE OGNA OPI 19
ITE OWAKITA 11,176
ITE PO 43,207
ITE RAN 98
ITE RANRAN 120,266,283
ITE RANTE 58,222
ITE SANKEYA 311
ITE SANKIYA 147
ITE SKA 35,45,99,111,
.... 199,208,261,274,308
ITE SKA RLA 258
ITE SKA WIN 127,298
ITE SKA YUHA 21

Index

ITE SNA WIN 96
ITE TANKA 18,182
ITE WAKAN 91,145,253,309
ITE WAMBLI 200,273
ITE WANBLI 36,42,50,109,
.... 122,206,209,285
ITE WASTE 63,88,117,129,
.... 226,250,280,292
ITE WAWIYOKIPI 56
ITE WITKO 67,299
ITESKA 143
ITESKA WIN 290
ITIMA 228
ITOHU SUTA 30
ITONKALA SKA 34
ITONKASAN 9,51,66,124,126,272
ITONKASAN KTE 7
ITONKASAN LUTA 12,31
ITONKASAN MATO 120
ITONKASAN SKA 53
ITONKASAN WASTE 118
ITONKASAN WIN 116
ITOWE RO 74,237
ITOWE SUTA 194
ITUHU SUTA .. 26,37,45,200,208,299
ITUKACAN 239
ITUNHASAN MATO 223
ITUNKALA SKA 198
ITUNKASAN 50,55,76,175,
.... 214,215,229,280,289
ITUNKASAN GLESKA 259
ITUNKASAN IYOTAKA 58,222
ITUNKASAN KTE 173
ITUNKASAN LUTA 178,195,222
ITUNKASAN MATO 147,311
ITUNKASAN SA 58
ITUNKASAN SKA 217
ITUNKASAN WAPACHA 226
ITUNKASAN WAPAHA 63
ITUNKASAN WASTE 76,281
ITUNKASAN WIN 279
ITUNKSAN 287
ITUNKSAN MATO 60,283
ITUUNKASAN GLESKA 97
IWASICU 44,193
IWEOSAYA 60
IWOBLU 285
IWOSAYA 223

IYA SICA 69,231
IYA WAKAN 280
IYA WASAKA 176
IYA WASTE 69,231
IYAKU WIN 182
IYAKUWIN 17
IYAN MATO 57,215
IYAN SKA 54
IYAN WICASA 77
IYANKA 36
IYANKA WICAKTE 75
IYANKAHAN MANI 51
IYANKE SNI 299
IYAPE NAJIN 271
IYAPI TAWA 116,279
IYAR PAYAPI 295
IYARPAYA 132
IYAWASAKA 10
IYESKA 66,229
IYOKIPI ICIYA 149
IYOKIPIYAPI 135
IYOTAKA 144,308
IYUHA KAWICAPA 15
IYUHA WICAKU 36,112,200,276
IYUWER EKTE 57,58,127,282
IYUWER KTE 222
JACOB 68,231
JAMES ... 17,53,110,141,266,273,305
JAMES RED BLANKET 108
JANIE, Mary 174
JANIS
   Aggie 246
   Agie 84
   Antone 186
   Antonia 21
   Ben 84,94,256
   Ben, Jr. 84
   Benj 246
   Benjamin 246
   Bert 120,283
   Bertha 187
   Berthia 23
   Bessie 84,246
   Bessy 21,186
   Charles 6,172
   Edward 87,248,253
   Effie 87,209
   Elizabeth 87,209

363

Index

Emma 23,94,187,256
Fannie 21,186
Fanny 21,186
Gertie 6,172
Henry 6,172
Herbert 21,186
James 84,91,246,253
James D 5,171
James, Jr 314
John 23,187
Joseph 23,187
Julia 5,171
Lallie 209
Lizzie 23,187
Louis 6,172
Louise 5,171
Lucy 5,21,186,256
Mabel 10
Mable 266
Maggie 8
Martha 255
Marthia 93
Mary 8,94,256
Minnie 5,171
Mollie 5,171
Nick L 94,256
Nick S 23,187
Paul 91,253
Peter 21,186
Rosa 91,253
Sallie 87,176
Susanna 6,172
Susie 6,84,171,172
Susue 246
Thomas 10,94,256,266
Vinna 23,187
William 10,266
Wilson 10,266
JANJANYELA 17,111,123,
.... 181,182,274,286
JANSEN
   Antoine 187
   Minnie 23,187
   Ramania 23
   Romania 187
JARVIS
   Frank 120,283
   Grace 120,283

Joseph 120,283
Mary 283
May 120
Mitchell 120,283
JAY BIRD 115
JEALOUS 73,91,113,236,253,276
JEALOUS AT 141,305
JEALOUS OF HIM 40,203
JEALOUS OF THEM . 53,73,217,236
JEALOUS PIPE 42,206
JEALOUS WOMAN 109,135,273,
.... 298
JENNIE 7,25,39,68,153,
.... 189,231,311,317
JESSE 79
JESSIE 56,102,220,264
JEYOKA TASUNKE 112
JIJILA 108,272
JIMMIE 118,281
JOHN 36,50,200,235,313
JOHN NO EARS 109
JOHNS, Maria 24,187
JOHNSON, Susan 95,257
JOLA 273,279
JOLOWAN 116
JOLOWANSA 109
JONES
   Alice 39,203
   Charles 39,203
   Henry 67,229
   John 67,229
   Katie 39,203
   Laura 39,203
   Lizzie 39,203
   Louise 203
JOS 247
JOSEPH 21,74,185,237,315
JULIA 24,50,142,146,174,188,245
JUMPER 94,97,118,258,281,320
JUMPING BULL
   Thomas 121
   Thos 284
JUMPING EAGLE
   Hollie 44
   Irene 44,207
   Jessie 44,207
   Lizzie 44,207
   Nellie 207

Index

Oliver ... 44,207
JUMPING NATION ... 16,189
JUMPING WOMAN ... 139,303
JUMPS OFF ... 5,171
JUMPS OVER ME ... 117,280
K I T WATER, Josy ... 216
K IN WINTER
   Jessie ... 266
   Lizzie ... 266
KAGLA KTE ... 183
KAHINRPEYA. 104,115,133,278,296
KAHUNPI ... 139,303
KAHUNRPEYAPA ... 265
KAKAB EKTE ... 14
KAKAB WOSICA ... 315
KAKIJA ... 16
KAKIKTE ... 296
KANGE CIQALA ... 181
KANGE NUPA ... 260
KANGI ... 32,39,62,124,203,225,287
KANGI APAPI ... 69,231
KANGI BLOKA ... 16,181
KANGI CIQALA ... 16,18,149,
   ... 150,183,271,313
KANGI GLESKA ... 45,84,97,
   ... 209,246,258
KANGI HO WASTE ... 88,250
KANGI ISNALA ... 144,308
KANGI KTE ... 38
KANGI LUTA ... 44,71,208
KANGI LUTE ... 233
KANGI MANZA ... 219
KANGI MAZA ... 49,58,71,175,
   ... 213,234
KANGI MNI EYECA ... 108,272
KANGI NUPA ... 98,260
KANGI PEGNAKA ... 85
KANGI SAGYE ... 118,179
KANGI SAPA ... 83,84,245,246
KANGI SKA ... 101,146,310
KANGI TANKA ... 8,174
KANGI TASAGYE ... 13
KANGI WAKAN ... 55,123,218,286
KANGI WAKUWA. 141,156,305,320
KANGI WANBLI ... 18,183
KANGI WANJILA ... 128,291
KANGI WASTE ... 75,237
KANGI WICAKTE ... 73
KANGI WICASA KTE ... 127
KANGI WIN ... 85
KANGI WINYAN ... 43,46,68,133
KANGI WITKO ... 36,200
KANGIMAZA ... 56
KANHUMPI ... 139
KANSU ... 8
KANSU CEPA ... 50
KANSU SEPA ... 215
KANTA ... 310
KANTA SAPA ... 146
KANWINGA ... 228
KANYELA KUTE ... 198
KANYELA OPI ... 189
KANYELA RPAYA ... 314
KAPOJELA ... 34
KAPOJELA WIN ... 96,198
KARAPE ... 126
KARAPE WIN ... 124,289
KARLOK IYAYA ... 124
KARMI ... 62,225
KARMI TANKA ... 235
KARNIGA ... 89,251
KARNIR KTE ... 67,230
KAROLIYEYAPI ... 32
KAROLYEYAPI ... 196
KASMI TANKA ... 73
KATE IYEYAPI ... 111
KATONAUNKA ... 109
KAUNK ... 135
KAUNKA ... 297
KAUNKAPI ... 288
KAWICAPA ... 122,180,285
KAWINGA ... 65,285
KAWINGE ... 122
KEEOS ... 180
KEEPS ... 6,14,172
KEEPS BONE ... 72,235
KEEPS DAY ... 64,227
KEEPS FLUTE ... 49,213
KEEPS GUARD ... 110,274
KEEPS HER HORSE ... 119,282
KEEPS HER HORSES ... 72,234
KEEPS SPOTTED ... 225
KEEPS THE BATTLE ... 55,112,275
KEEPS THE BONE ... 30,194
KEEPS THE BOTTLE ... 219
KEEPS THE EAGLE ... 127,290

Index

KEEPS THE PIPE 101,263
KEPAS INYAKA 228
KESUNSNI 228
KETTLE
    Charles A R 255
    Nattie R 255
KETTLE COAT, Joe 116,279
KEYA 77,102,264,288
KEYA CAGU 35,199
KEYA SA 68
KEYA TRUTH 240
KEYELA KUTE 227,231
KEYELA TAOPI 222
KICAKSA 111,275
KICI ETI 128,291
KICI ISTIMA 118
KICI IYANKA 24
KICI KICIZA 95,195,247,257
KICI NAJIN 118
KICI RPAYA 281
KICI YANKA 25,188
KICIGLUCA 296
KICIZA 129,132,292,295
KICIZAPI 130,292
KICK NAJIN 281
KICKING BEAR 79,241
KICKS 7,173
KICO 289
KICOPI 6,25,185,189
KIHUNI 271
KIKTA SNI 100,261
KILL STANDING 114
KILL THE BEAR 85
KILLE THE BULL 194
KILLS ... 25,127,133,290,296,297,299
KILLS A FOOL 21,185
KILLS A HUNDRED
    Adelin 63
    Adeline 225
    Annie 63
    Elija 63,226
    Hattie 63,222
    Jno 225
    John 63
    Nancy 63
    Nany 226
    Susie 63,225
KILLS A MAN 22

KILLS ABOVE 36,154,200,318
    Maggie 318
KILLS ACROSS 57,58,127,282
KILLS ACROWW 222
KILLS AFRAID 115,279
KILLS AHEAD 14,180
KILLS ALIVE 10,71,93,176,234,
.... 255
    Daniel 143,307
    Emily 143,307
    Susie 143,307
KILLS ALONE 110,117,274,280
    Joseph 102,263
KILLS AND COMES BACK 112,276
KILLS AROUND 6,172
KILLS AT LODGE . 115,117,278,280
KILLS AT NIGHT . 8,26,118,189,281
KILLS BACK 10,24,111,112,
.... 130,176,275,292
    John 30,194
KILLS BAD 50,214
KILLS BEE 22
KILLS BEFORE NIGHT 124,287
KILLS BLACK FEET 130
KILLS BLACKFEET 293
KILLS BRAVE 57,58,221,222
KILLS BY LIGHTNING 121,284
KILLS CHARGER 139
KILLS CHARGING 19,73,184,235
KILLS CHOICE 67,230
KILLS CLOSE 183
KILLS CLOSE T LODGE, Thos . 241
KILLS CLOSE TO LODG, Thos ... 78
KILLS CLOSE TO LODGE
.... 61,96,257,298
KILLS COW 70,233
KILLS CROW 73,107,117,127,
.... 236,271,280,291
KILLS CROW INDIAN 38,202
KILLS CROWN 282
KILLS ENEMY 13,16,17,25,41,67,
113,114,117,128,129,139,148,179,181,
189,205,230,277,280,291,292,304,312
    Anna 67,230
    Jennie 230
    Rosa 67
KILLS ENEMY AFOOT 134,296
KILLS ENEMY AT NIGHT ... 54,218

Index

KILLS ENEMY BACK 291
KILLS ENEMY I T MORN 264
KILLS ENEMY IN THE MORNING
....103
KILLS FIRST 49,67,70,76,78,109,
112,119,122,133,150,229,233,239,240,
266,273,275,282,285,295,314
    Wallace 141,305
KILLS FIRST #2 112,275
KILLS GAME 150,313
KILLS GOOD.............. 49,94,213,256
KILLS HARD........... 110,122,274,285
KILLS HAWK........................74,236
KILLS HER OWN........10,57,176,221
KILLS I T WATER
    Geo....................................216
    Jas 216
KILLS I TIMBER, Thos...............217
KILLS IN LODGE........32,51,196,215
KILLS IN MORNING .6,130,176,189
KILLS IN SIGHT 73,100,235,261
KILLS IN T MORNING...............276
KILLS IN THE MORING 112
KILLS IN THE WATER 52
    Geo.................................... 52
    Josy................................... 52
KILLS IN TIBMER......................132
KILLS IN TIMBER..........22,186,295
    Thomas 53
KILLS IN WATER
.... 110,113,181,273,276
    Jno.....................................313
    John...........................……...149
KILLS IN WINTER................141,305
    Jessie 52
    Lizzie 52
    Thomas 52
    Thos 266
KILLS IN WOOD...................114,277
KILLS LEADER 13,179
KILLS LITTEL...............................283
KILLS LITTLE...............................120
KILLS LIVING 77,240
KILLS LOOKING, Julia...........96,258
KILLS MANY 73,236
KILLS ON HORSEBACK ..62,63,74,
..............................87,225,226,237,248
KILLS ONE AFTER ANOTHER72,234

KILLS PAWNEE 69,232
KILLS PLENTY 68,92,116,123,
.... 126,231,254,279,286,289
KILLS RE E, John....................... 229
KILLS REE, John.......................... 66
KILLS RIGHT............. 46,53,209,216
KILLS RUNNING 75,237
KILLS SCOUT....................... 22,186
KILLS SHOSHONE..................... 67
KILLS SMALL 38,202
    Anna................................ 35,199
    Henry............................... 35,199
    James................................... 199
    Susie..................................... 35
KILLS SOMETHING 16,181
KILLS STANDING 278
KILLS STRADDLE................ 54,218
KILLS SWIMMING 134,297
    Jno................................... 98,260
KILLS T BULL
    Annie................................... 194
    Hellen 194
KILLS THE BEAR 95,247,256
KILLS THE BULL....................... 30
    Ellen 30
KILLS THE ENEMY 113,276
KILLS THE VILLAGE........... 16,181
KILLS THEM 127,289
KILLS TRIBE 22,186
KILLS TWICE 58,71,114,126,
.... 134,221,234,277,289,297
KILLS TWO.............. 63,112,226,276
KILLS TWO SIDES.............. 121,284
KILLS WARRIOR................. 73,107,
.... 235,271,288,291
KILLS WELL..... 15,120,147,283,311
KILLS WHITE COW.... 114,115,181,
.... 189
    James............................... 114,189
KILLS WHITE MAN...... 21,110,185,
.... 274
KILLS WHITE WEASEL 7,173
KILLS WITH DOUBT............ 78,241
KILLS WITH FEAR 113,271
KILLS WITHIN THE HOUSE 85
KILLS WITHOUT DIFFICULTY127
KILLS WITHOUT DIFFICUTLY290
KILLS WITHOUT DOUBT.. 125,288

Index

KILLS WITHOUT FEAR 54,109,218,272
KILLS WOMAN .... 93,116,151, ... 255,257,279,315
KILLS WOUNDED 128,291
KIMIMILA 172
KIMIMILA SKA 12,177
KIMNILA 20
KINAJIN 282
KING WOMAN 132,295
KINGI 195
KINGI APAPI 231
KINYA 216
KINYA WIN 196
KIPANPI 20
KISS ME 69,232
KISUN 121,284
KISUN SNI 24,65,68
KIWOKSAPI 117,280
KIYA 125
KIYAKSA 38,95
KIYAN 52
KIYAN HIYAYA 147,311
KIYAN LUTA 118,281
KIYAN WIN 32,115,141,279
KIYANSA 257
KIYELA 172
KIYELA IYANKA 279
KIYELA KUTE 62,234
KIYELA OPI 8,26,35,58,72,292
KIYELA RPAYA 150
KIYELA TI 63
KIYELA WIYAKA 87
KIYNKAN 248
KIYUKAN 50,85
KIZA 65
KLLS SHOSHONE 230
KNEE 64,227
  Wilson 64,227
KNEW HIM 96
KNIFE, Andrew 41,205
KNIFE CHIEF 41,204
KNIGHT
  Ellen 60,189
  Joseph 60,189
  Joseph E 189
  Lizzie 60,189
  Oliver 60,189

KNOCK DOWN 125
KNOCK DOWN SHOSHONE 130
KNOCK O HEAD 39
KNOCK ON HEAD 203
KNOCKED DOWN 288
KNOCKS DOWN 135,297
KNOCKS DOWN SHOSHONE .. 293
KNOCKS IN TWO 111,275
KNOWS HIM 258
KOCER
  Frank 29,193
  Hobart 29,193
  Joanna 29,193
  Julia 29,193
  Rena 29,193
  Ruth 29,193
KOHAB WOSICA 129
KOKAB EKTE 180
KOKAB HIYAYA 62
KOKAB IGLONICA 97,259
KOKAB IYANKA 56
KOKAB IYAYA 76,239
KOKAB NAJIN 97,179
KOKAB WOSICA 151,292
KOKEPEYA KTE 241
KOKIPA 115,146,278,310
KOKIPAPI 116,123,279,286
KOKIPE SNI 51,132
KOKIPE SNI KTE 54
KOKIPE SNI WICKTE 125
KOKIPESN KTE 218
KOKIPESNI 109,215,295
KOKIPESNI KTE 272,288
KOKIPEYA KTE .... 78,113,115, ... 271,279
KOKOB IYANKA 24
KOKOB NAJIN 16
KOLAYAPI 18,183
KPAZO 10,176
KTE AOU 196
KTONAUNKA 273
KU 127,290
KU SNI 70,232
KUPI 72,234
KUTE 36,54,61,130
KUTE SNI 225
KUTEPI 6,16,30,73,104,117, 129,133,172,181,194,224,235,265,272

....,280,296	Mable.. 231
Mack 16	William................................... 76,239
KUWA 129,292	LAME WOMAN................ 15,53,216
KUWA WICAKTE............19,73,235	LAMONT
KYAKSA SAPA............................ 92	Frank 130,293
L CHIEF, Louise...........................318	George............................. 130,293
L HORSE, Mary 320	Maggie............................. 131,293
L WOLF	Mary 130,293
Nathan......................................317	LAMOTT, John..................... 23,187
Willard......................................317	LAMP WOMAN...................... 152
LAB 130,293	LANCE................... 39,113,203,276
LADEAU	Jennie................................ 145,309
George.............................62,189	LANCE WOMAN.................. 20,316
Maggie 62,189	LAND............................... 144,308
Mary.................................62,189	LAPOINT
LADEAUX	Anna...................................... 141
Alice...............................146,310	Annie............................. 141,305
Annie......................................229	Eva................................. 141,305
Baptiste 66,229	Gertie............................. 141,305
Bessie..............................149,313	Jack................................ 141,305
Emma..............................146,310	Jacob.............................. 141,305
Fank.......................................229	James............................. 141,305
Jacob.....................................154	Jennie............................. 141,305
Jennie..............................146,310	Joseph............................ 141,305
Jessie..............................146,310	Mabel.................................. 305
John 14,146,149,180,310,313	Mahel.................................. 141
Julia..................................66,190	Oliver............................. 141,305
Katie...............................146,310	Verax................................... 305
Lilly 229	LARRABEE
Lily.. 66	Alice............................... 151,314
Peter................................146,310	Louis.............................. 151,315
Peter, Jr 310	Nancy 151,314
Rosa................................146,310	Samuel............................ 151,314
Sam...................................66,229	William........................... 151,314
Sarah 146,310	LAST.....................................287
LAKOTA 134,297	LAST BEAR 179
LAMB	LAST HORSE 259
Adolph 157,320	Allen............................... 143,307
Jule..320	Fannie............................... 24,188
Jules 157	Georgiana 259
Mary.......................................320	Mattie 259
Susie................................98,320	Salina............................. 97,259
LAME 67,299	Sam'l, Jr............................. 259
LAME BULL.................................55,218	Samuel................................. 97
LAME DOG	Samuel, Jr............................ 97
James..............................76,239	LAST WOMAN . 12,124,178,287,317
Lizzie 76,239	LATE WARRIOR.................. 31,195
Mabel....................................... 68	LAUGH................................ 127,290

Index

LAYS BAD............................100,262
    Edward...........................101,262
    Flora......................................101
    Frank.............................101,262
    Jennie...................................101
    Millie..............................101,319
    Thomas.................................101
    Thos......................................262
LAYS CLOSE........................150,314
LAYS DEAD...........................59,223
LAYS ON GROUND.............128,291
LAYS ON HIS BELLY.................195
LE ROCK, Mary............................ 65
LEADER.................18,54,90,111,122,
   183,217,238,247,274,285
LEADING EAGLE..................33,197
LEADING WOMAN..........13,16,178
LEAF.................................49,213
LEAVES HIM........................22,186
LEBUFF
    Alex................................154,318
    Rhoda....................................318
    Roda......................................154
    Zonie................................154,318
LEE
    Anna..................................22,186
    Emma.................................22,186
    James.................................22,186
    John...................................22,186
    John, Jr.............................152,316
    Sophia...............................22,186
LEFT BEHIND, Robert............62,225
LEFT HAND..........20,33,92,102,111,
   151,184,197,254,263,315
LEFT HAND BEAR.................16,181
LEFT HAND BULL....76,91,239,254
LEFT HAND OLD WOMAN 125,288
LEFT HER HOME..................34,198
LEFT HERON..........................42,205
    Amelia..................................... 42
    Bene..................................42,205
    Emma................................42,205
    Grace..................................30,194
    Lottie.................................42,205
LEG...109,272
LEGGING DOWN....................40,204
LEGGINS
    George P...........................95,256

James..67
Josephin P.................................256
Josephine P..................................95
LEGGINS DOWN.............60,67,128,
   224,230,291
LEROCK, Mary...........................228
LESSERTS, Emily.......................319
LET HER GO...........................36,199
LETS ALONE......................118,281
LICKS..5,171
LICKS ENEMIES........................245
LICKS ENEMY..............................83
LIFE...120
LIGHT...179
LIGHT WOMAN.34,96,109,198,273
LIKES TO WALK...................92,254
LILA YUCANCAN........................98
LILLY..196
LILS YUCANCAN......................260
LILY..33
LIP...303
    Bulah...............................139,303
    Edith................................139,303
    George.............................139,303
    Hat...................................139,303
    Ida....................................139,303
    John.................................139,303
    Kate.................................139,303
    Oliver...............................139,303
    Richard............................139,303
    Susie................................139,303
LITTE THUNDER........................120
LITTLE....................108,119,272,282
LITTLE BALD EAGLE
    Ada.....................................57,221
    Chas....................................57,221
    Felix....................................57,221
    Moses.................................57,221
LITTLE BEAR.........52,55,78,216,219
    Alice...15
    Bob.................................... 14,180
    Henry..15
    James..15
    Zuzella......................................14
LITTLE BIRD........................129,292
LITTLE BOY..............35,60,135,199,
   223,239,298
    Cecilia.....................................199

Index

Cicila 35
LITTLE BULL 31,66,195,228,294
   Edward 15
   Henry 52,266
   Samuel 56,220
LITTLE BULL #1 107,271
LITTLE BULL #2 133,296
LITTLE BULL #3 120,283
LITTLE BULL #4 132,295
LITTLE CHIEF 91,154,253,318
   Elmore 125,288
   Elva ,Au 125
   Elva May 288
   Louise 154
   Wing 254
LITTLE CLOUD 54,111,209,275
   Eli 67
   James 115,278
LITTLE CLOUD #2 67,229
LITTLE CREEK 107,271
LITTLE CROW .. 18,149,183,271,313
   Bessie 313
   Mary 16,181
LITTLE DOG 100,130,262,292
   George 88,250
   Robert 57,220
LITTLE EAGLE 68,75,231,237
   Lawrence 146,310
LITTLE ELK ... 29,75,88,193,238,250
   John 30,194
   Julia 182
   Paul 17,182
LITTLE FEATHER 20,185
LITTLE FINGER 113,276
LITTLE GOOD WOMAN 109,272
LITTLE GREY WOLF 21
LITTLE GUIDE 76,239
LITTLE HAWK 14,179
   Luke 25,188
   Wm 14,179
LITTLE HEAD 124,287
LITTLE HOOP 150,314
   Charles 150,314
   Elk 150
   Samuel 150,314
LITTLE HORSE 20,125,126,
   156,184,320
   Mary 156

LITTLE IRON 11,176
LITTLE KILER 140
LITTLE KILLER 134,297,304
LITTLE KNIFE 315
LITTLE KNIFE 151
LITTLE LEADER 143,307
   Sophia 143,307
   Susie 143,307
LITTLE MAGPIE 54,218
LITTLE MOON 52,216
LITTLE OLD WOMAN 110,273
LITTLE PRAIRIE CHICKEN 282
LITTLE PRAIRIE CHIDKEN 119
LITTLE SCOUT 101,262
   Etta 103,264
LITTLE SHIELD 126,289
LITTLE SOLDIER 20,34,132,
   184,198,295
LITTLE SPOTTED EAGLE ... 99,261
LITTLE SPOTTED H., Louis 119
LITTLE SPOTTED HORSE . 119,282
LITTLE SUN 108
LITTLE THUNDER 97,259,283
LITTLE WAR B, Alice 276
LITTLE WAR BONNET 113,276
   Alice 113
   Dolly 113
   Jesse 113
LITTLE WARRIOR 9,92,174,254
LITTLE WHITE MAN .. 103,156,264
LITTLE WOLF 78,135,241
LITTLE WOMAN 9,109,120,
   175,272,284
   Belle 251
   George 251
LITTLE WOUND 25,92,188,254
   Andrew 83
   Belle 89
   George 89
   James 92,254
   Jennie 92
LIVE IN SIGHT 93
LIVES ABOVE 56,93,219
LIVES AGAIN 13,19,108,184,272
LIVES ALONE 54,128,150,218,
   291,314
LIVES BY 63,226
LIVES BY WATER 67

Index

LIVES IN LODGE 123,286
LIVES IN SIGHT 38,202,255
LIVES TWICE 131,294
LIVES WELL 6,172
LIVING BEAR 63,226
   Sallie 63,226
   Thomas 63,226
LIVING OUTSIDE 113,277
LIZZIE 298,314
LOADING BUFFALO 69,232
LOAFER 148,312
   Jennie 91,253
   Thomas 148,312
   William 148,312
LOAFER JOE 124,287
   Agatha 124,287
LOB 293
LOCATOR 56,220
LOCK
   Frank 43
   Hope 43
   James 40,204
   Mary 43
LOCKE
   Frank 207
   Hope 207
   Mary 207
LODGE 10
   Lizzie 38,202
LOE 35,199
LOESSERTS, Emily 155
LOGAN
   Angelina 303
   John A 144,303
   Lizzie 303
LONE BEAR 92,254
   Abraham 199
   Alice 254
   Benjamin 35
   Henry 35,199
   Julia 35,200
   Oliver 35,199
   Samuel 35,199,254
   Susie 35,199
LONE BEAR #2 195
LONE BIRD 100,262
LONE BULL 153,317
LONE CLOUD 6,172

LONE CROW 144,308
   Herbert 144,308
LONE DOG 15,180
LONE EAGLE 14,179
LONE ELK 65,108,115,154,
   228,278,298,317
   James 59,222
   Julia 59,222
   Lucy 59,222
LONE GOOSE 61,224
   Susie 61,224
LONE HAIL 29,193
LONE HILL
   Amos 42,205
   Ellen 42
   Florence 205
   Hellen 205
   Hobart 42
   Hobort 205
   Laura 42
   Lester 205
   Sallie 42,205
   Sidney 42,205
LONE HORN 285
   Anna 237
   Annie 74
LONE HORSE 122,123,286
LONE KILLER 125,288
LONE LIFE 153,317
LONE MAN 35,104,128,198,265,
   291
LONE RIDGE 19,122,285
LONE SOLDIER 55,219
LONE TREE 12,178
LONE WAR 40,204
LONE WOLF 128,153,291,317
   Abraham 147,311
   Agnes 147,257,311
   Charles 147,311
   Emma 147,311
   Eva 147,311
   Felix 95,153,257,317
   John 311
   Nathan 153
   Oliver 91,254
   Rosa 95,257
   Stephen 147,311
   Willard 153

Index

LONE WOMAN .... 19,22,66,71,75, ... 92,184,186,229,237,303
LONG BEAR. 31,38,124,195,202,299
LONG BULL. 34,71,110,198,234,273
    Archie 183
    Edith..............................91,253
    John...............................91,253
    Julia................................91,253
    Levi...............................143,307
    Nellie.................................. 19
LONG CAT 50,214
    George...........................50,214
LONG CHAIN 126
LONG CHIN 289
LONG COMMANDER
    Jno 239
    John 76
LONG DOG, John 57,221
LONG HAIR................95,97,251,257
LONG HORN 77,239
LONG HORNS
    Aaron 151,315
    Hattie..................................151
    Tribe 151
LONG KNIFE...................35,198,253
    Susie 253
    Susy 91
LONG MAN 147,311
    Charles 147,311
LONG NOSE 148,312
LONG NOSE DAWSON........119,282
LONG SKUNK 320
LONG SOLDIER....................39,203
    Albert 83,245
    Bessie 245
    Millie..............................83,245
    Rosa 263
    Rose 102
    Sophia 102,263
LONG VISITOR....................120,283
LONG WOLF
    Amos 46
    Dennis............................135,297
    Hannah 15,180
LONG WOMAN ....68,70,108,231, ...232,272
LOOKED AT.........................153,317
LOOKING AT HORSES 186

LOOKING CLOUD 60,266
LOOKING ELK 129,292
LOOKING FOR HORSE 143
LOOKING FOR HORSES........... 307
LOOKING HORSE......... 43,131,132, ... 207,213,295
    George 50,215
LOOKING LODGE 290
LOOKING PIPE..................... 71,234
LOOKS................................... 62,225
LOOKS AND KILLS............ 107,271
LOOKS AT DAYLIGHT........ 14,179
LOOKS AT GROUND ... 90,120,252, ...283
LOOKS AT HER 140,304
LOOKS AT HER BLANKET. 91,253
LOOKS AT HER HORSE 99,189,261
LOOKS AT HER HORSES ..... 25,38, ... 125,202,288
LOOKS AT HIM............. 13,102,120, ... 178,263,283
LOOKS AT WHITE COW 23,187
LOOKS AT WOUNDED HORSE 61,224
LOOKS BACK25,34,50,135,146,156, ... 198,214,296,310,320
LOOKS BEHIND................... 66,229
LOOKS COMING OUT.......... 70,233
LOOKS F HORSES
    Henry 251
    Nancy 251
LOOKS FO ENEMY..................... 275
LOOKS FOR BANK..................... 36
LOOKS FOR ENEMY 96,112,258
LOOKS FOR HER 132,295
LOOKS FOR HIM .... 123,129,131, ... 286,291,294
LOOKS FOR HORSES........... 41,205
    Henry 89
    Nancy 89
LOOKS FOR LODGE................. 296
LOOKS FOR NATION......... 128,291
LOOKS FOR NONE 131,276,294
LOOKS FOR NOTHING 43,207
LOOKS FOR THE DEAD 126,289
LOOKS IN FACE 11,176
LOOKS IN HOLY 151,315
LOOKS INSIDE................... 149,241

Index

LOOKS THINGS..........................266
LOOKS TWICE..........36,70,200,232
   Maggie...............................70,232
LOOKS UP.......................111,275
LOOKS WHITE 7,173
LOOSES THINGS........................ 53
LOST BLANKET..........................283
LOST HORSE, Millie.................... 46
LOST HORSES 67,229
LOST WOMAN.......................57,220
LOTE..51,215
LOUD VOICE 130,293
LOUD VOICE HAWK..........111,274
LOUISE 79,240
LOVES HIM..........................127,289
LOVES HIS ROAD...............108,272
LOVES LIFE 64,127,227
LOVES THEM.........................78,240
LOVES WAR 71,95,234,265
LOWAN MANI............................156
LOWE, Adelia............................134
LUCY 17,32,43,56,57,
  196,207,214,220,221
LUTA.....................................222,262
LUZAHAN................65,117,228,280
M EAGLE
   Josephine...................................205
   Katie..205
MADE IN THE EARTH...........17,182
MAETO HINOPA 7
MAGA ISNALA.......................61,224
MAGA IT 315
MAGA ITE....................................151
MAGA KUTE................................259
MAGA NUTE................................ 98
MAGA TASUNKE.................124,287
MAGAJIN MANI......................... 62
MAGGIE 34,130,293
MAGPIE 45,139,144,208,303,308
MAHA LUTA WIN......................274
MAHEL CUWIGNAKA 25,188
MAHEL EYAYAPI......................114
MAHEL WAYANKA 149
MAJEL ICUPA............................277
MAKA 98,131,260,294,308
MAKA AKAN EPAYA................291
MAKA CEGA 9,176
MAKA CINCALA.................113,276

MAKA HANSKA 320
MAKA HUKUCIYELA............... 126
MAKA HUNKU 54
MAKA ICU..................................282
MAKA IKTOMI 135,297
MAKA KANYELA......................289
MAKA LUTA . 16,64,78,227,241,293
MAKA LUTA WIN 181
MAKA MAHEL KAGAPI........... 182
MAKA MAHEL MANI 17,34,52,
   198,266
MAKA MAKELMANI 216
MAKA MANI 34
MAKA NABU............................. 171
MAKA OKAWINR MANI 12,177
MAKA OYATE 122,285
MAKA PAPTA 111,275
MAKA PATITAN........................ 65
MAKA POTITAN........................228
MAKA SAN 133,295
MAKA SI 135
MAKA SICA WIN........................ 61
MAKA SIHA 298
MAKA SUTA 53
MAKA WASA 291
MAKA WASE..................... 133,295
MAKA WAYANKA....................283
MAKA WIN.................................. 9
MAKA WIYAKPA 113
MAKA WKAN RPAYA............. 128
MAKA YUBLU 195
MAKAICU.................................. 119
MAKAMANI TOKA KTE.... 134,296
MAKATA WAKITA 90,120,252
MAKE SUTA 217
MAKES ALIVE 117,123,280,286
MAKES ALONE..................... 90,252
MAKES ENEMY 11,70,177,233
   John 177
MAKES GOOD..................... 153,317
   Eliza.................................. 153,317
   Richard 154,318
MAKES GROWL 115,279
MAKES LIFE...................... 156,320
MAKES OVER 75,237
MAKES ROOM 50,85,248
MAKES SHINE 7,173
MAKES THINGS GOOD 148,312

Index

MAKES TROUBLE 121,284
MAKES TROUBLE AHEAD 129,292
MAKES WHITE BUFFALO ... 53,216
MAKO SICA WIN 224
MAKOCE 144
MAKOCE ICU 56,220
MAKU 76,141,238,305
MAKU WAKAN 41,205
MAKU YUBLU 31
MALE ELK, Peter 113,277
MAMA 16,181
MAN
   Alfred R 241
   Joseph W 238
MAN ABOVE 93,255
   Alexander 93
   Fannie 93
   Samuel 93,255
MANARD, Julia 187
MANGAJU MANI 225
MANI 20,85,117,185,280
MANI KU 111,234,274
MANI LUZAHAN 100,261
MANI WASTELAKA 92,254
MANI WIN 89
MANIKU 19
MANIRUPA 20
MANKA HUNKU 218
MANSTINCALA SKA 172
MANY CAMPS 149,313
MANY CARTRIDGES 14,179
MANY FEATHERS 75,237
MANY FRIENDS 174
MANY HORSES 17
MANY SPOTTED HORSES 232
MANY WOUNDS 21
MANZASKA 220
MANZASKA WIN 214
MARGRETTE 318
MARO WINORCALA 297
MARPATANKA 24
MARPIYA 62,84,225,246,259
MARPIYA CIQALA .. 54,67,111,115,
.... 209,229,275,278
MARPIYA GI 85,247
MARPIYA HE 84,246
MARPIYA HINAPA 5,171
MARPIYA HOKSILA 132,295

MARPIYA ISNALA 6
MARPIYA KOYAKA 141,305
MARPIYA LUTA 9,90,146,175,
.... 252,253,310
MARPIYA MAZA 36,200
MARPIYA NAJI 257,258,263
MARPIYA NAJIN 95,96,102
MARPIYA ORANKO 87
MARPIYA ORONKO 248
MARPIYA SAPA ... 116,129,280,292
MARPIYA SKA 101
MARPIYA SNA 34,96,202,258
MARPIYA TANKA 262
MARPIYA TASUNKE 85,247
MARPIYA TO 32,76,97,125,128,196,
.... 198,239,258,291
MARPIYA TOKAHEYA 133
MARPIYA TOKALU 295
MARPIYA TOPA 55
MARPIYA TUCUHU 32,196
MARPIYA WAHACANKA 176
MARPIYA WAKAN 20,114,184,277
MARPIYA WAKITA 60,266
MARPIYA WAMBLI 234
MARPIYA WANBLI 72
MARPIYA WANJILA 172
MARPIYA WASTE 38,84,130,
.... 202,246,293
MARPIYA WICASA 41,117,280
MARPIYA WIN 120,149,283,313
MARPIYATO 196
MARPUYA TO 34
MARPUYA TOPA 219
MARPUYA WICASA 205
MARRISETTE
   Joseph 15
   Oliver 15
   Rosa 15
MARROW BONE 20,184
   Joshua 20,185
MARSHALL
   Alice 90
   Alie 252
   Amanda 45,266
   Charles 90,252
   Daniel 90
   Dan'l 248
   Elizabeth 90,252

Index

Frank 88,250
Harrison 90,252
Jennie 90,252
Joseph 90,252
Josephin 88
Josephine 250
Julia 90
Lizzie 88,250
Louisa 250
Louise 88
Mary 88,250
McGee Morris 252
Minnie 88,250
Philip 90,252
Stephen 88,250
Thomas 90,252
MARTHA 311
MARTIMUS, Frank 182
MARTIN
    Berry 22,186
    Louis 22,180
    Santa Rosa 22,180
MARTINEZ, Mary 259
MARTINIS
    Emma 45,208
    Joseph 45,208
    Mary 45,98,208
    Nora 45,208
    Philip 45,208
MARY 56,220,314,318,320
MARY GAY 40
MASKABLASKA 13,178
MASTE 85,133,247,296
MASTE KAGA 173
MASTIANCALA SAKOW 97
MASTIN SKA 306
MASTINCALA 24,44,133,296
MASTINCALA GLESKA 112
MASTINCALA LUTA 91,231,253
MASTINCALA SAKEWIN 258
MASTINCALA SKA 6,278
MASTINCALA STOLA 117
MASTINSALA LUTA 69
MASTINSKA 142
MASTNICALA 207
MATA 10,176
MATA RUGAHAN 122
MATAS RLOGECA 102

MATI HIN WASTE 33
MATI HOKSILA 273
MATO 14,16,96,179,181,258
MATO AHAN APAPI 39
MATO AKAN APAPI 203
MATO BLOHA 193
MATO BLOKA 29,30,194
MATO C INYANKA 33
MATO CAN WEGNA IMANKA 195
MATO CANALI 83,245
MATO CANGLESKA 122,285
MATO CANKAHU 74
MATO CANKALAN 236
MATO CANTE WANICA 155,319
MATO CANUPA 74,236
MATO CANWEGNA 120,276,283
MATO CANWEGNA IYANK 113
MATO CATKA 16,181
MATO CAYANKA 308
MATO CICALA 203
MATO CINCALA 40,56,141,
    219,282,305
MATO CIQALA 14,15,52,55,78,
    180,216,219
MATO CUWIGNAKA 107
MATO EHAKELA 179
MATO GI 29,41,98,135,149,193,
    205,260,297,313
MATO GLASLA 114,278
MATO GLESKA 56,65,139,
    219,228,303
MATO GLIYUNKA 55
MATO GNASKINYAN 185,290
MATO HA SINA 21
MATO HAKIKTA 185
MATO HAKIKTO 21
MATO HANSKA 38,124,195,202,
    299
MATO HAUSKA 31
MATO HIN WASTE 197
MATO HINAPA 9,39,53,122,131,
    172,175,285,293
MATO HINAPO 203
MATO HINROTA 111,274
MATO HINSMA 5,171
MATO HINWASTE 112
MATO HINYUKA 218
MATO HOKSILA 10,110,176

376

Index

MATO HU 78,226
MATO HUHU 110,274
MATO HUNHESNI 175
MATO HUNKESNI 9,132,295
MATO IHANBLE 111
MATO INYAKA 218
MATO INYANKA 249,251
MATO ISNALA 195
MATO ISTIMA 13,115,179,278
MATO ISTO NAPIN 132,295
MATO ITE WASTE 110,266
MATO IYANKA 55,87,89,135,298
MATO IYOTAKA 91,145,309
MATO IYOYAKA 253
MATO KAWINGA 280
MATO KAWINGE 116
MATO KOKEPA 257
MATO KOKIPA 95
MATO KOKIPAPI 6,172,189
MATO KTE 199,247
MATO KUWAPI 42
MATO LOWAN 8,66,132,174,
.... 229,295
MATO LUTA 8,9,54,55,114,
.... 174,218,278,314,321
MATO MAZA 109,273
MATO MINYAPI 226
MATO NAJI 222,223,241
MATO NAJIN 12,59,78,141,145,
.... 146,177,305,309,310
MATO NAKPA 111,275
MATO NINYEPI 284
MATO NIWICAYA 121
MATO NIYAN LUTA 121,284
MATO NIYANPI 63,65,227
MATO NUPA 21,185
MATO OHITIKA 122,284
MATO ONJINCA 125,288
MATO OPI 198,206
MATO OTA... 61,94,140,256,304,321
MATO OTA WIN 232
MATO OTE WIN 70
MATO OYATE 44,207
MATO PEJUTA 49,53
MATO POGE 129,292
MATO PTECELA 150,313,314
MATO RABWICAYA 69,232
MATO RLO 88,250
MATO RLOLA 223
MATO RUWIMNA 115
MATO RUWINMNA 278
MATO SAKE 134,297
MATO SAPA 10,14,41,45,53,84,
100,144,153,155,179,204,241,246,261
.... ,262,266,308,317
MATO SHAMBLA 275
MATO SI 216
MATO SICA 72,235,287
MATO SIKA 53
MATO SINA 236,242,249
MATO SINA KSUPI 8
MATO SINTE 83,141,246,305
MATO SKA 12,99,115,116,
.... 177,260,278,279
MATO SKA SAKE ... 73,129,236,292
MATO SLASLA 131,293
MATO TAHEYA 107
MATO TAMAHECA 143,144,308
MATO TANKA 265
MATO TAOPI 42
MATO TASUNKE 285
MATO TATANKA 32,92
MATO TATANKA HOKSILA104,265
MATO TAWA KU 129,292
MATO TINGA 143
MATO TLOLA 59
MATO TOKAHE 278
MATO TOKEYA 115
MATO WACI 100,267
MATO WAHACANKA 49,213
MATO WAKAN 41,93,205,213,
.... 255,266
MATO WAKATUYA 73
MATO WAKINYA 215
MATO WAKINYAN 51
MATO WAKUWA 31,62,205,
.... 225,307
MATO WAMBLI 200
MATO WAMNIOMNI ... 66,101,110,
.... 130,273,292
MATO WAMNIYOMNI 229,263
MATO WANAGI 51,215
MATO WANARTAKA 79
MATO WANBLI 36,46,53,54,
.... 126,200,217,289
MATO WANJILA 35,92,199,200,254

Index

MATO WANKATUYA..... 17,90,182, ...236,252
MATO WANRTAKA...................241
MATO WANWICAYANKA 38
MATO WAPAGEYECA............... 57
MATO WAPAGIUECA...............220
MATO WASTE........................19,183
MATO WATAKPE 143,195
MATO WAUNSILA.....................282
MATO WAWIYOKIPIYA...........119
MATO WAYANKA.....................202
MATO WAYUHI 147,148,311,312
MATO WICAGNAYA.................317
MATO WICAGNAYAN...............153
MATO WICAGNYAN..................153
MATO WICAKIZA... 67,130,230,293
MATO WICAKTE 35,85
MATO WICARCA.......................135
MATO WICINCALA...................119
MATO WICOTI....................129,291
MATO WIN......................16,181,318
MATO WINORCALA.................103
MATO WINURCALA..................265
MATO WINYAN............86,130,154, ...248,292
MATO WITKO 20,65,127
MATO WIYAKA........................319
MATO WOMNIYOMNI..............229
MATO YAMNI 23
MATO YATAPI.....................31,195
MATO YUHA 256
MATOCANWEGNAINYOUKA .197
MATOHA SINA... 73,87,129,186,282
MATOHAN SINA.......................119
MATTHEWS
    Joseph 180
    Louis 8,174
    Lucy 24
MAUZA SNA..............................215
MAYA....................................127,290
MAYA CONSOKE.....................207
MAYA CUNSOKA 44
MAYA OLE................................... 36
MAZA................................70,232
MAZA CINCALA.................37,201
MAZA CIQALA....................11,176
MAZA HO WASTE 46,299
MAZA KAWEGA........................122

MAZA SA 103
MAZA SICA 33,197
MAZA SNA................................. 51
MAZA SNA WIN 13,178
MAZA WAKAN ICU 238
MAZA WAKAN OMNA.............237
MAZA WIN................................45,84
MAZA WINYAN........................246
MAZA WIYOKATAN................... 51
MAZA YUWEGA.......................285
MAZAKAN..................................297
MAZAKAN ICU.............. 17,107,271
MAZASKA 57,115
MAZASKA AGLI...................45,208
MAZASKA OLE.....................12,177
MAZASKA WICAKU................. 52
MAZASKA WIN 50,55
MAZASU OTA 14,179
MAZAWAKAN 134
MAZAWAKAN ICU 75,182,241
MAZAWAKAN SCU 79
MAZAWAKAN WIN 125,288
MCGAA
    Agnes..................................... 29,193
    Albert......................................29,193
    Anna Clifford 29,193
    Charlotte..............................29,193
    Etta 29,193
    George Leroy.......................29,193
    William..................................29,193
    William D..............................29,193
MCMAHON
    Frank 9,175
    Julia 9,175
MCWILLIAMS
    Bell..319
    Belle...155
    Benny 155,319
    Mag 155,319
MEAN WOMAN 131,133,293,296
MEANS
    Alice 143,307
    Bert......................................23,322
    Bessy 186
    Charles...............................154,318
    Emma 154
    Eugene..............................23,190
    Frank 23,322

Index

George 154,318
George W 143,307
James Blain 143
James Blaine 307
John 23,322
Lavina 143,307
Lizzie 23,321
Nellie 190
Robert B 23,321
MEAT
   Arthur 148,312
   Frank 148,312
   Nellie 148,312
MEDICINE 18,52,76,108,126,
.... 183,216,239,272,289,313
   Louis G 217
MEDICINE BEAR 41,49,53,
.... 93,205,213,255
MEDICINE BEAR #2 266
MEDICINE BLANKET 34,121,
.... 198,284
MEDICINE BOW 61,234
MEDICINE BOY 77,97,240,259
   Susie 77,240
MEDICINE BULL 53,101,216,263
MEDICINE CANE 60
MEDICINE CLOUD, Stephen 20,
.... 184
MEDICINE COW, Stella 41,205
MEDICINE DANCE 8,174
MEDICINE DAY 149,209
MEDICINE EAGLE 41,205
MEDICINE EAGLE FEATHER ... 76,
.... 239
MEDICINE ELK 101,263
   Cedar 90,252
   Joshua 90,100,266
   Lucy 100,262
   Nancy 252
   Nency 90
MEDICINE HAND 88,250
MEDICINE HORSE .. 64,72,77,93,96,
.... 226,234,240,252,255,257
MEDICINE LEAF 33,197
MEDICINE NAME 145,309
MEDICINE OUT 109,273
MEDICINE PIPE 112,276
MEDICINE SHEET 21,185

MEDICINE TRACK
.... 37,51,77,201,239,321
   Andres 37
   Andrew 201
MEDICINE WIND 72,235
MEDICINE WOLF 145,309
MEDICINE WOMAN 12,14,15,19,
22,24,115,132,149,178,179,181,183,
.... 186,278,294
MENARD, Julia 23
MERRILY LIVES 94,256
MERRILY STANDS 64,227
MERRIVAL
   Charles 181
   Laura 181
   Maggie 181
MERRIVALL
   Alexander 24,187
   Charles 15
   Emma 22,184
   Herman 24,188
   Jennie 22,186
   Kira 24,188
   Laura 15
   Maggie 15
   Mary 22,186
   Susie 24,187
MESTETH
   Alice 45,266
   David 60,223
   Frank 60,223
   George 45,266
   James 59,223
   Jennie 59,223
   John 45,266
   Joseph 60,223
   Maggie 59,223
   Peter 223
   Philip 60,223
   Thomas 60,223
   Willie 59,223
MEXICAN 19,183
   Ambrose 234
MIDDAY 19,183
MIDKIFF, Delila 265
MILA 41,205
MILA CIQALA 151,315
MILA GI 39,203

Index

MILA HANSKA 35,91,198,253
MILA NUPA 304
MILA PE SNI 154,318
MILA TANKA 112,275
MILA TOPA 140
MILA YATAPI 204
MILA YATPI 41
MILK 71,149,234,313
MILLS
   Annie 11,177
   Benj 177
   Benjamin 11,177
   Jessie 11,177
   Nellie 11,177
   Richard 11,177
   Thomas 11,177
MINIOWICAKTE 216
MINIWANCA 321
MINK 70,124,232,287
MINNIE 271
MINOWICAKTE 216
MIUWANCA WIN 34
MIWAKAN 172
MIWAKAN WAKAN 132,294
MIWAKAN YULA 6
MIYOGLE 193
MIYOGLI 29,34,142,198,214,
.... 305,306
MIYOGLOI 141
MNI 19,144,184,308
MNI AGLI 49
MNI HINAPA 11,176
MNI KIYELA TI 67
MNI OKTE 181
MNI OWICAKTE 313
MNI OYUSNA 230
MNI SA 144,308
MNI SNI 15,180
MNI WANCA 51,54
MNI WICASA 238
MNI YATKAN 110
MNIKOKTE 276
MNIOTUMPI 273
MNIOTUPI 109
MNIOWICAKTE 52,110,113,
.... 149,273
MNIOYUSNA 68
MNIWANCA WIN 198

MNIYATA WICASA 75,77,239
MNIYATKAN 273
MOCCASIN MOTHER 317
MOCCASIN TOP 134,297
   Emma 134,297
MOCCASON 153
MOLLIE 31,195
MONEY 57,220
MONEY WOMAN 50,55,214
MONROE
   Aloyasus 267
   Aloysius 100
   John 100,267
   Lottie 100,267
   Sophia 100,267
MONTELEAU
   Emily 93
   Julia 93
MONTILEAU
   Emily 255
   Joseph 255
   Julia 255
MONTO
   Agnes 152,316
   Beaver 152,316
   Belle 316
   Elizabeth 149,313
   Ella 152,316
   Enoch 152,316
MOORE, Henry 18,183
MOOSE
   Bena 194
   Paul 194
MOOVES OVER 237
MORNING, Martha C I 307
MORRISETTE
   Lucy 180
   Oliver 180
   Rosa 180
MORRISON
   Brother 17,182
   Cahrles 88
   Charles 17,250
   Ellen 102,263
   Ground 88,250
   Henry 90,252
   Jessie 88
   Joseph 88,250

Index

Josie 250
Julia 102,263
Robert 104,322
Rosa 17
Rose 182
Wing 88,250
MORROW BONE, John 185
MOSSEAU, Joseph 174
MOUNTAIN SHEEP 64
MOUNTAIN SHIIP 227
MOUSEAU
   Ellen 8
   Joseph 8
   Joseph, Jr. 8
   Maglor'd 8
   Nellie 8
MOUSSEAU
   Agnes 39,203
   Alexander 39,203
   Alice 39,203
   Ellen 87,174,248
   James 39,87,203,248
   John 254
   Joseph 92,254
   Julia 39,203
   Louis 39,92,203,254
   Louis, Jr 92,254
   Maglor'd 174
   Nellie 174
   Sophia 39,203
   Susie 39,203
   Zoey 254
   Zonie 92
MOVES 32,195
   Paul 30
MOVES CAMP 93,255
   Helen 93,255
MOVES LODGE 172
MOVES LODGES 153
MOVES OVER 74
MRPIYA RLA 198
MUIRUHA 185
NACA 25,54,69,103,110,119,
  122,126,153,189,232,264,273,282,285
.... ,317
NACA AGLI 10,176
NACA CIQALA 91,99,125,154,
.... 253,254,288,318
NACA GLI 74,236
NACA KTE PIN 221
NACA KTE RCIN 57
NACA OTA 18,182
NACA WANKATUYA 209
NACA WIN 57,84,89,90,117,
.... 118,132,221,246,251,280,295
NACA WNI 252
NACAKA 6,172
NACUPA YUHA MANI 154
NAGWAKA 7,173
NAHICIPAPI 128
NAIL FIRE 266
NAJI 258
NAJIN 13,119,179,293
NAJIN KU 122
NAJINHAN KTE 114,278
NAJINHAN KU 84,108,200,246,
.... 272,285,292
NAJINHAU KU 36
NAJINWICAYA KTE 289
NAJINYAPA 53,273
NAJINYAPI 13,16,30,56,76,87,
110,115,120,122,144,178,196,217,220
.... ,238,278,283,285,308
NAJINYAPI KTE 70
NAJINYAPIN 202,248
NAJIYAPI 121
NAJIYAPI KTE 232
NAKICIPA 290
NAKICIPAPI 178
NAKIPA 5,13,102,120,128,
.... 171,264,283,291
NAKIWI ZI PI 236
NAKIWIZI 141
NAKIWIZI PI 203
NAKIWIZIPI 40,73
NAKPA LUTA 226
NAKPA OGI 251
NAKPA ZI 124
NAKPALA 246
NAKPO GI 140
NAKPOGI 6,89,287,304
NAKPOGI AWICAGLI 128
NAKPOGI WIN 288
NAME HIM 111,298
NANCA 217
NANCY 94,256

Index

NANJIYA KTE 218
NANWOCAKIWIZI 217
NAPA 156
NAPCA 91,184,225,254
NAPE 16,181,320
NAPE AKICITA 146,147,311
NAPE IYORPEYAPI 72,234
NAPE KAHUNPI 49
NAPE KICAKSAPI 266
NAPE MAZA 153,317
NAPE PEJUTA 88
NAPE RUWIMNA 24
NAPE SICAMNA 35
NAPE WAKAN 135,145,250,
.... 297,309
NAPE WIKACEMNA 275
NAPETU 279,281
NAPI WIKCEMNA 112
NAPSUKAGA 316
NAPSUKAGA TOPA 292
NAPSUKAGA WASTE 152
NAPSUKAGE TOPA 129
NARCAN 121
NARCAN WIN 125
NARON 125,174,288
NARONPI 12
NAROUPI 178
NARPIYA TO 288
NASULA WITKO 128,291
NATA 5,171
NATA CIQALA 124,287
NATA KAHUMPI 259
NATA KAHUNPI 98
NATA OHOMNI SKA 116
NATA OPI 101,262
NATA RLOGECA 89
NATA RLOKECA 264
NATA RUGAHAN 285
NATA SKA 125,288
NATA TANKA 84,111,275
NATA WITKO 8,11,176,228
NATAJI WIN 110
NATION HORSE 67,230
NATION WOMAN 135
NATO RLOGECA 251
NAWICAKICIJIN 68,107
NAWICAKICIZI 53
NAWICAKIJIN 231
NAWICAKINJIN 271
NAWIZA 113
NAWIZI 73,91,236,253,276
NAWIZI EHAUBLA 44
NAWIZI IHANBLA 207
NAWIZI WIN 135,298
NAWIZISA WIN 273
NAZUNSPE TANKA 31
NAZUSPE TANKA 195
NEEDY BOY 234
NEEDY GIRL 72
NELLIE 320
NELSON
   Albert 79,190
   Annie 10,176
   Francis 150,314
   James 79,190
   Jennie 314
   John 10,176
   John, Jr 176
   Julia 10,176
   Lizzie 10,176
   Reuben 10
   Samuel 10,176
   Susie 314
   Susy 150
   Thomas 150,314
   William 10,176
NEVER COMES WITHOUT .. 36,200
NEVER DOES WRONG 41
NEVER FULL 139,303
NEVER MISSED 62,225
NEVER SHOWED OFF 57
NEW GROWTH 39,203
NEW HOLY 75,238
NI FLICU 236
NI GLECU 196
NI GLENAPA 220
NICA 30,194
NICA OLE 131,276,294
NIGE WIN 119
NIGHT 43,207
NIGHT SITTER 71
NIGHT WALKER 31,195
NIGLICU 133
NIMWICAYA 73
NIN KAGA 320
NINGLICA 30

Index

NINGLICU 13,56,73,115,121,
.... 130,178,279,284,293,295
NINICIYA 89,126,251
NINWICAKAGA 156
NINWICAYA 97,116,123,127,
.... 279,290
NINYAN KE KTE 93,176
NINYAPI 117,286
NISEHU 59,131,133,223,296
NITE 278,294
NITE CIQALA 43
NITE WASTE 40,266
NITE YANZA 94
NITE YAZAN 94,256
NIWEVAYA 258
NIWICAYA 236,289
NIYA KTE 240
NIYAN 25,189
NIYAN KTE 77,234,255
NIYAN LUTA 65,84,246
NIYAN SKUYA 45,208
NIYAN WAKAN 100,114
NIYANKE KTE 71,102,143,307
NIYANPI 77
NIYAPI 240,280
NO BELT 6,94,172,256
Ellen 94,256
NO BOW 64,299
NO BRAID 63,226
Abel 68,230
George 68,230
Wilson 63,226
NO DRESS 123,286
NO EARS, Jno 273
NO FAT 128,291
NO FLESH 37,201
Bert 59,266
Della 88,250
Emma 37,207
Lucy 37,231
NO FOOT 112,275
NO GARTER 143,307
NO HORN 103,265
NO NAME 5,9,13,18,123,127,
.... 171,175,179,182,238,286,290
NO NECK 56,130,292
NO NECK #1 219
NO RELATION 19,155,319

NO TWO HORNS #1 288
NO TWO HORSES #1 125
NOGE SA 63,118
NOISE 131,294
NOISY WALK 7,171,173
Lena 5
NOISY WALKS 5
NOPA 40
NOPA WAKITA 36
NORCAN 284,291
NORCAN WIN 290
NOSE 61,224
NOT AFRAID 51,132,215,295
NOT AFRAID OF PAWNEE 317
NOT HELP HIM 282
NOT HELPS HIM 119
NOTHING 133,296
George R 233
NUGE LUTA 100
NUGE SA 281
NUGE SA WIN 125
NUGE WANICA 109,273
NUNWANPI 177
NUP EWICAYA 85,248
NUP HIYOHIPI 130
NUP HIYOKIPI 293
NUP KARPA 280
NUP NAJINPI 109
NUP WICAKTE 63,112
NUP YUSNA 117
NUPA 204
NUPA ICAGA 131,294
NUPA IYANAJINCA 291
NUPA KINAJIN 273
NUPA KTE 58,71,114,126,134,
.... 221,226,234,277,289,297
NUPA OPI 153
NUPA WAKITA 70,200,232
NUPA WICAKI 128
NUPALA 60,61,77,224
NUPKTE 276
NURCAN 128
NURCAN WIN 127,133,296
NUWAN KET 260
NUWAN KTE 98,134,297
NUWANPI 71,233
NUWESA 128
NUWMPI 11

Index

OCEAN 51,54,217,321
OCEAN WOMAN 34,198
OCETI 102,320
OCEYA WANKALA 131,293
OCINSICA 133,296
OCINSICA WIN 293,296
OECIGLAKA 276
OGALALLA 77,239
OGALALLA W H, Mabel 297
OGLALA 77,239
OGLE MAZA 128
OGLE SA 18,61,124,183,224,287
OGLE WAKAN 119,282
OGLE WAKIN 284
OGLE ZI 77,239
OGLI WAKAN 121
OGLONICA 291
OHITIKA 26,34,36,40,57,71,111,
.. 116,127,185,189,198,200,204,221,
.... 234,275,279,290
OHITIKA KTE 57,58,221,222
OHITIKA WIN 17,20,131,182,294
OHITIKU 299
OHOLA 144,308
OHOMNI IYANKA 118,152,316
OHOMNI SNI 43
OHOMNI YUTAN 85
OHOMNI YUTANTAN 248
OICIGLAKA 112
OINKPA 147
OIYOKIPIYA NAJI 227
OIYOKIPIYA NAJIN 64
OIYOKIPIYA TI 94,256
OJANYAN WIN 273
OJUHA SA 20,185
OJUTUNPI 44,207
OKANWER MANI 197
OKASAKA YUKAN 260
OKASAKE YUKAN 98
OKAWINR IYANKA 85,281
OKAWINR MANI 33
OKAWINS KTE 54
OKICIZA 286
OKICIZA TAWA 128,290
OKICIZA YUHA 112
OKICIZAPI 225
OKICIZE 107,123,271
OKICIZE TAWA 5,55,116,129,
.... 171,292
OKICIZE YUHA 275,280
OKICUZE YUHA 219
OKIHIPI SNI 125,288
OKINYA 200
OKINYAN 37
OKIYAKAPI 71,124,233,287
OKIYAKAPI WIN 79,190
OKO SBA WIN 272
OKO SNA WIN 108
OKOGNA INYANKA 237,245
OKOGNA IYANKA 13,74,83,179
OKSANTA 90,252
OKSANTA KTE 172
OKSANTAN KTE 6
OKTEA 222
OKTOMI GI 298
OKUTE 12,177
OLD ARAPAHOE 97,258
OLD BAD WOUND 94,256
OLD BEAR 135,297
OLD CHEYENNE WOMAN .. 45,209
OLD EAGLE 14
  Henry 25,188
  Maggie 25,188
  Rosa 188
OLD HAIR 11,176
OLD HORSE
  Katie 257
  Mark 95
  Ralph 95,257
OLD LODGE 35,199
OLD MEXICAN 112,242
OLD PRAIRIE HEN 67,230
OLD SHE BEAR 103,265
OLD SHIELD 31,195
  Alfred 34,198
  George 31,195
  Isaac 32,196
  John 198
  Susie 32,196
OLD WOMAN 32,101,117,196,262,280
OLDEST BROTHER 7,173
OLE 155,318
OLEGE WIN 181
OLEJE WIN 115
OLEKU 59,223
OLEPI 123,129,131,

Index

.... 132,286,291,294,295
OLIVER 118
ON ARRIVAL 107,271
ONA OTAPE 41,204
ONANSO 217
ONANYA 179
ONASO 53,182
ONASOLA 17
ONAYAN 14
ONE CROW 128,291
ONE FEATHER
   Bessie 93,255
   Etta 238
   Ettie 76
   Jennie 54,93,218
   Jessie 255
   Lizzie 90,252
   Moses 76,93,238,255
   Sueie 255
   Susie 93
   Willie 93,255
ONE HORSE 78,240
ONE STAR 9,133,175,296
ONJINCA 286
ONJINJINKTA 271
ONJINJITKA TASPU 107
ONKCEKIRA 45,54,139,144,
.... 208,291,303,308
ONKCEKIRA CIQALA 218
ONKCEKIRA SKA 128
ONPAN GI 60,119,294
ONPAN GLESKA 126,289
ONPAN HINAPA 130
ONPAN HINSKA 121,284
ONPAN HINSKE 20,184
ONPAN HO TAINYAN 126
ONPAN HO WASTE 315
ONPAN HOKSILA 60
ONPAN HOTAN MANI 289
ONPAN HOWASTE 277
ONPAN ITE WASTE 122,285
ONPAN LUTA 176,289
ONPAN LUTA WIN 281
ONPAN WASTE 180,285
ONPAN WIN 173,180,188,280
ONPAU WIN 7
ONSEYA YANKA 238
ONSILAKA 235
ONSINA IYA 65
ONSINYAN YANKA 75
ONSIYA IYA 228
ONSIYA YANKA 237
ONSIYAN YANKA 75
ONYAN GLICUPI 62,186
ONYAN IYAYAPI 22
ONZIHEKETA KU 140
ONZIHEKTAKIYA 127
OOSICA 63,70,101,127,143,
.... 155,232,263,290,319
OOSICA HOKSILA 143,307
OOWASTE 88,143,250,307
OP IYANKA 126,289
OP IYAYAPI 108
OP IYAYAYA 272
OPAGELA 241
OPAGILA 78
OPAN 194
OPAN WEGE KTE 225
OPANWEGE KTE 226
OPANWEGI KTE 222
OPANWIGE OWICAYUSPA 234
OPANWINGE OWICAYUS 72
OPAWINGE KTE 63
OPKICIZA 85
OPO 19,72,184,235
ORANKOYA MANI 267
ORAU WASTE 30
ORLAKA KAOTINZAPI 12
ORLOGECA 294
ORLOKA OTA 64,227
O'ROURKE
   Annie Lang 251
   Charkes 251
   Emma 251
   Georgiana 251
   John 251
   Samuel 251
   Thomas 251
   Walter 251
O'ROURKE
   Annie 89
   Charles 89
   Emma 89
   Georgianna 89
   John 89
   Samuel 89

Index

Thomas 89	OUT, Willie S C 277
OSCAR 31,39,195	OWECALE HI 260
OSHOTA 236	OWEWAKANAN 92
OSICA 226,307	OWEWAKANKAN 254
OSOTA WIN 216	OWICALE 76,84,238,246
OSTA SKA 91	OWICALE HI 95
OSUN LUTA 189	OWICALEHI 98,257
OSUN SAKA 188	OWL 131,294
OSUN SOKA 24	OWL BULL 153,317
OSUN WANICA 63,226,230	OWL EAGLE 67,127,229,290
OSUN WANRCA 230	OWN EAGLE 292
OSUNGYA ERPEYAPI 196	OWN HORSE 187
OSUNGYE ERPEYAPI 33	OWN HOUSE 22
OTA AGLI 40,62,68,111,114,	OWNES BOB TAIL 218
.... 203,225,231,298	OWNES FLIGHT 280
OTA APEKA 96	OWNES GOOD HORSES 317
OTA APELA 96,258	OWNES MANY HORSES........... 298
OTA CINPI WIN 103,265	OWNES THE DOG..................... 272
OTA HINAPA 14	OWNES THE HORSE 281
OTA HINAPA WIN 179	OWNES VILLAGE 274
OTA KOYAKA 74,236	OWNES WHITE FACE HORSE . 238
OTA KTE 68,92,116,126,231,	OWNES WHITE HORSES 241
.... 236,254,279,286,289	OWNS BOB TAIL 55
OTA KUTE 18,183	OWNS BOB TAIL HORSE 284
OTA OPI 69,231	OWNS BODTAIL HORSE 121
OTA WAKAN 286	OWNS EAGLE 129
OTA WICAKTE 73,123	OWNS EAGLE HORSE 71
OTA WOWASI ECUN 148,312	OWNS FIGHT 116
OTAAGLI 225,277	OWNS GOOD HORSES 153
OTACAN 18	OWNS HORSE 24,188
OTAIN WIN 283	OWNS MANY HORSES 135
OTAKEYE NICA 44	OWNS SOMETHINGS 119
OTAKUYE 19	OWNS SPOTTED HORSE 86,248
OTAKUYE NICA 208	OWNS THE DOG 109
OTAKUYE OTA 107,271	OWNS THE FIGHT 5,171
OTAKUYE WANICA 155,319	OWNS THE HORSE 118
OTAWICAPA 126,289	OWNS THE MULE 88,250
OTERIKA 131,294	OWNS THE PIPE, Maggie 87,249
OTKA 59	OWNS THUNDER 68,231
OTORAN 33,56,115,153	OWNS VILLAGE 110
OTTER 273	OWNS WHITE COW 20
OTTER BLANKET 76,238	OWNS WHITE FACE HORSES ... 75
OTTER WOMAN 62,107,271	OWNS WHITE HORSE 20
OTURAN 197,220,278	OWNS WHITE HORSES 78
OTURANSA 90,252	OYATA TASUNKE 230
OTUYACIN C[?]YA 63	OYATE 315
OTUYACINYA CEYA 226	OYATE KTE 186
OUPAN GLESKA 98	OYATE OLE 128,291

Index

OYATE OTA.............................54,218
OYATE SICA........................134,297
OYATE TASUNKE 67
OYATE WICAKTE..................... 22
OYATE WIN.............................135
OYATE WOILAGYAPI..............134
OYE..56,220
OYE LUTA....................6,14,95,114,
................................172,196,257,277
OYE MAZA...............79,141,241,305
OYE OTAPE 107
OYE SAPA...............................9,175
OYE TAIN...................................66,229
OYE WAKAN................37,51,71,77,
...............................201,234,321
OYE WANBLI............16,22,125,181,
.....................................187,288
OYE WASTE..........................122,285
OYNSPA 225
OYUNKE MAZA...................66,202
OYURAN 317
OYUSPAPA 237
OYUSPAPI...................68,75,230
OZAN MAHEL 65,71,194,233
P HARANGER, William 320
P HARANGUER, Jennie 320
PA OIKPEMNI............................. 67
PA OKEMNI 230
PA ON WAAPA........................... 29
PA OPI..276
PA RMI...183
PA RUGAHAN 111
PA WAYATKAN........................197
PA WAYATKAU.......................... 34
PABLO
    Alexander......................78,229
    Fannie 78
    Joseph 78,229
    Rosa 78
PACER........................17,53,182,217
    H 131,294
PACKED 68,231
PAHA ANAKITAN...................... 36
PAHA ANATAN.........................200
PAHA NUPA..........................130,293
PAHA WAKAN 19,184
PAHA WANJILA....................42,205
PAHI........................78,116,240,279

PAHIN........... 11,39,117,176,203,280
PAHIN LUTA 17,182
PAHIN SINTE...............................39
PAHIN SITE 215
PAHIN SKA...................... 100,262
PAHIN YUSLA.................... 148,312
PAIN O T RUMP, Chas 256
PAIN O.T. RUMP-, Chas............... 94
PAIN ON THE RUMP............ 94,256
PAINTED............................... 72,235
PAINTED HORSE................... 8,174
PAINTED RED 124,287
PAINTS HAIR 58,222
PAINTS HERSELF YELLOW 85,248
PAINTS YELLOW 236,274
PALANI KTE.................... 22,66,229
PALANI SICA 30,194
PALANI WIN 46,195
PALANIWIN 209
PALLARDY, Alice.................. 8,174
PALMER
    Albert............................. 43,265
    Charles........................... 43,265
    Julia 43,265
    Louisa................................. 265
    Maggie 43,265
    Olive 43,265
    Taylor 43,265
    William........................... 43,265
PAMAGLE............................. 63,226
PANESKA WIN............................. 7
PANHESKA WIN......................... 97
PANKESK HOKSILA 193
PANKESKA................. 9,22,115,148,
.... 175,278,285,312
PANKESKA HOKSILA 29,60,69,
....223,232
PANKESKA LUTA 30,68,123,
....194,230,286
PANKESKA LUTA WIN 66,222
PANKESKA MAZA ... 64,69,227,232
PANKESKA NAPIN............... 97,258
PANKESKA OTA... 113,134,277,296
PANKESKA TAWAY 203
PANKESKA WAKPA 151,315
PANKESKA WASTE 153,172
PANKESKA WIN......... 6,8,32,37,55,
66,114,123,172,173,174,186,201,218,

Index

..................................229,278,286
PANKESKAWIN 259
PANKSKA...............................122
PANPANLA 155,319
PAORPA.............................112,275
PAPTA HINAPA....................93,255
PAPTA IYAYA....................109,285
PARMI.................................... 18
PARTS HER HAIR, Susie.......94,256
PARTS HIS HAIR..................94,256
   Ada...................................94,266
   Amos...................................... 94
   Emma..................................... 94
   Isaac.................................94,266
   Sarah 94
   Winnie.................................... 94
PARUGAHAN 274
PASU 61
PASU HANSKA......119,148,282,312
PASU ON WAAPA.....................193
PATIENT...............................74,237
PATTON
   Charles.................................223
   Emm....................................223
   Emma.................................... 59
   George................................59,222
   James.................................59,222
   Julia.............................59,222,223
   Laura 59
   Louise 222
   Lucy 59,222
   Susie.................................59,222
   Thomas 59,222
   William 59,223
PAUL 142,306
PAWIYAKPA............................. 7
PAWNEE........................42,121,284
PAWNEE KILLER................149,313
   Allen 147
   Jennie..................................147
   Marthia................................147
PAWNEE LEGGINS...............95,256
PAWNEEE KILLER, Allen..........311
PE LUTA 143
PECK
   Clara................................142,306
   Dora 142,306
   Jessie...............................142,306

   Julia 142,306
   Katie 142,306
   Lottie 142,306
   Louis................................ 142,306
   Mary 142,306
   Nellie 142,306
   Owen Walter........................... 306
PEGGIE................................... 15,180
PEHAN................................. 135,298
PEHAN CATKA 30,42,194,205
PEHAN SAPA............................ 115
PEHAN WANKATUYA.. 64,115,226
PEHAN WIN..........................85,247
PEHAN ZI............................. 113,277
PEHIN 10,107,176
PEHIN GI................................ 140
PEHIN HANSKA....................97,251
PEHIN JI 36,37,51,62,67,107,
...108,110,121,145,199,201,225,229
PEHIN JI QIN 238
PEHIN JI WIN 61,76,251
PEHIN LUTA............................... 18
PEHIN MAZA....................... 90,252
PEHIN SA 93,108,123,124,
.... 180,182,255,272,286
PEHIN SAKIYAPI....................... 58
PEHIN SANKIYA 222
PEHIN SAPA............................. 278
PEHIN SICA 153,317
PEHIN SKA 108
PEHIN WANKATUYA 279
PEHIN WASTE.......................... 115
PEHIN WIN 91,253
PEHIN ZI 89,215
PEHIN ZI WIN............................ 89
PEHINJI 127,128,179,271,
.... 272,273,291,304,309
PEHINJI SICA 271,272
PEHINJI WIN 127,273,290
PEHINJIN WIN........................... 224
PEHINSA 15
PEJI 40,100,149,204,209,267
PEJI HU.................................... 107
PEJI KASLA 52
PEJI NAKSA............................. 216
PEJI PARTA 233
PEJI ROTA................... 29,38,54,77,
.... 104,193,202,240,265

388

Index

PEJI ROTA WIN 6,172
PEJI ZI 288
PEJIN PARTA 70
PEJIN ZI 125
PEJIROTA 218
PEJUTA 18,52,76,108,126,
.... 183,216,239,272,289
PEJUTA HINAPA 273
PEJUTA SAPA 86,248
PEJUTA SKA 53,217
PEJUTA WANKATUYA 76,239
PEJUTA WASTE 32,36,53,133,
.... 196,217,240,296
PEJUTA WIN 12,14,15,22,24,132,
149,178,179,181,183,186,278,294,313
PEKIN HANSKA 95
PEKIN JI 14
PEKINJI SICA 107
PEMICAN 66,229
PENO
  Agarota 103
  William 103
PEPTA IYAYA 286
PESA 307
PESLA 175
PESTOLA 72,235
PETA 171
PETA OMNICIYE 8,174
PETAGA 5,11,102,122,
.... 153,177,263,285,317
PETSOLA 286
PEYA KAGA 237
PEYOZAN 94,256,266
PEZPIZA 194
PICKED HORSES 86,248
PICKET PIN
  Charles 59,222
  Della 59,222,238
  Millie 64,227
PICKET PINE, Della 75
PICKS 116,279
PICKS ARROWS 23
PICKS IT UP 78,240
PICKS OUT AND KILLS 112
PICKS OUT BEST 296
PIHIN HANSKA 257
PIJUTA WASTE 200
PIJUTA WIN 115

PILAICIYA 321
PILAYAPI 130,293,298
PILLOW 134,297
PINE 114,115,277,278
  William 264
PINE BIRD 38,201
  Ella 31,195
  Henry 202
  Jack 38,201
  Samuel 38,201
  Willie 38,201
PINE LEAF 67,230
PIPE 109,111,113,274,277
PIPE DANCE 36,200
PIPE DANCE BOY 15,180
PIPE EAGLE 155,319
PIPE ON HEAD 116,279
PIPE VOICE 53,217
PISPIZA 30,98
PISPIZA LUTA 63,321
PISTOLA 123
PIYA ICAGA 13,19,39,108,
.... 184,203,272
PIYA IGLAKA 74
PIYA IGLAKE 237
PIYA ISAGA 320
PIYA KAGA 75
PIZO 114,278
PJYA ICAGA 94
PLAYS ON FLUTE 54,217
PLEASANT FACE 220
PLEASE 119,132,282,294
PLEASED 135,298
PLEASED FACE 56
PLEASED HEART 63,226
PLEASED HERSELF 149,321
PLEASES 298
PLEASING BEAR 119,282
PLENTY
  Jefferson S 258
  Lucy 258
  Paulina S 258
PLENTY ARROWS 152,316
  William 317
PLENTY AUNTS 52,216
PLENTY BEAR 61,94,140,256,
.... 304,321
  Thomas 61,321

Index

PLENTY BEAR WOMAN 70,232
PLENTY BIRD 56,220
   Julia 56,220
   Nancy 56,220
   Susie 56,220
PLENTY BLANKETS 56,219
PLENTY BROTHER 121,135,298
PLENTY BROTHERS.. 35,77,78,120,
   199,240,284,298
PLENTY CHIEF 18,182
PLENTY COW 132,295
PLENTY EAGLE 101,144,262
PLENTY EAGLES 75,238
PLENTY HALES 64
PLENTY HARANGUER 94,320
   Jennie 94
   Wm 94
PLENTY HOLES 227
PLENTY HOLY 123,286
PLENTY HORSE 272
PLENTY HORSES 18,37,42,63,97,
   .. 109,110,128,183,201,205,226,259,
   274,291
PLENTY NATIONS 54,218
PLENTY PIPE 50
PLENTY RELATION 107,271
PLENTY SHAWL 21,185
PLENTY SHELL 113,134,277,296
PLENTY SOLDIER 9,115,278
PLENTY SPOTTED HORSE 130
PLENTY STARS 131,294
PLENTY WHITE HORSE 295
PLENTY WHITE HORSES 132
PLENTY WHITE MAN 116,279
PLENTY WOLF 22,187
   Sam 22,187
PLENTY WOMAN . 108,148,272,312
PLENTY WOUND 117,280
PLENTY WOUNDS 22,45,54,186,
   208
   Moses 8,174
PLUCKS PORCUPINE 148,312
PLUME, Anna 66,229
POGE 224
POGE NUPA 140
POGE OPI 112
POGE TANKA 37,200
POGERLOKA NUP 304

POINTS YELLOW 74,111
POOR BEAR 143,308
   Albert 144,308
   George 144,308
   Harry 144,308
   Philip 308
   Stephen 144,308
POOR BUFFALO 66,228
POOR ELK 112,275
   Martin 112
   Marting 275
POOR THUNDER 76,239
   Lizzie 76
PORCUPINE 11,117,176,280
   Edward 39,203
PORCUPINE TAIL 39,215
PORCUPINE WORK 120,283
POURIER
   Charlie 61,225
   Ellen 61,224
   Emil 61,225
   Helen 61,225
   John 61
   Joseph 61,225
   Josephin 61
   Josephine 224
   Josie 61,224
   Louis 61,225
   Mary 61,225
   Peter 61,225
   Rosa 61,225
POUTINF 227
POUTING 64,66,72,73,96,
   229,235,258
POWDER 107,271
POWDER WOMAN 154,318
PRAIRIE CHICKEN ... 59,84,223,246
PRAIRIE CHICKEN #1 . 126,130,289
PRAIRIE CHICKEN #2 293
PRAIRIE DOG 98,260
   Mary 30,194
PRAY TO HER 51,153,215
PRAYS FOR HER 114,277
PRAYS TO HER 317
PRESAN WIN 217
PRESCOTT, Millie C 77,239
PRETTY BACK 40,204
   Maggie 40,266

Index

Thomas 40,204
PRETTY BALD EAGLE 74,237
PRETTY BIRD 12,55,59,73,114,
.... 177,219,223,229,235
PRETTY BOY 77,240
PRETTY BULL 33,197
 Carrie 33,197
 Jessie 33,197
PRETTY COW 130,293
PRETTY EAGLE 115,122,278,285
PRETTY ELK 30,194
 Jessie 30,194
 Lillie 30,194
 Lizzie 31,194
 Maggie 31,194
 Robert 30,194
PRETTY F BEAR, Mollie 266
PRETTY FACE, Jennie 63,226
PRETTY FACE BEAR 110
PRETTY HAIR 115,180
PRETTY HORSE 70,128,232,291
PRETTY SPOTTED HORSE 127,290
PRETTY WEASEL 118,281
PRETTY WOMAN32,43,44,53,71,96,
.. 102,107,118,141,196,206,207,217,
.... 233,258,264,271,281,305
 Helen 40,204
PROTECTOR 68,231
PROUD WOMAN 50,214
PROVOST
 Alma 156,320
 Antoine 118,281
 Emma 320
 James 33
 Lizzie 129
 Louis 156,320
 Oliver 281
 William 46,70,209,233
PRSPIZA 260
PRUNE 146,310
PSA KTE 107,117,202,236,280,
.... 282,291
PSA WICOTI OLE 122,285
PSA WIN 39,40,230,296
PSA WINYAN 204,209,247
PSAKTE 271
PSAWINYAN 203
PSECA 258

PSICA 94,97,118,281,320
PSICA IYANKA 128,291
PSICA OYATE 16
PSICA WAKUWA 131,294
PSICA WANBLI 44
PSICA WIN 139,303
PSIN SA 124,287
PSITO 37,52,201,216
PSITO WIN 154,318
PTA SAN 229
PTAN HA 238
PTAN LUTA 153,317
PTAN WIN 62,107,271
PTANKA SINA 76
PTANWIN 273
PTE HE 232
PTE HINAPA 144
PTE HINZI 291
PTE HOTON 143,307
PTE ICARYA 122,285
PTE KTE 70,233
PTE LUTA 153,317
PTE NAJI 195
PTE OLE 114
PTE OTA WIN 295
PTE SAN 66,75,213,219,
.... 226,230,238,263,264
PTE SAN GLI 264
PTE SAN MAZA 240
PTE SAN NUPA 217
PTE SAN OYATE 233
PTE SAN SINA 249
PTE SAN WASTE 202,226
PTE SAPA WIN 177
PTE TACANKU 24
PTE TALO 151,315
PTE TOKAHE 69,232,292
PTE TOKAHEYA 308
PTE WAKAN 41,117,205,280
PTE WASTE 14,108,130
PTE WASTE WIN 179
PTECELA ... 45,108,118,208,286,292
PTEHE 69
PTEHINCALA . 125,144,287,288,308
PTEHINCALA CINCALA 124
PTEHINCALA HA 107
PTEHINCALA SKA 74,114,123,
.... 278,286

PTEHINCALA WIN 112,115,276,279
PTEHINSA 271
PTESAH NOPA 45
PTESAN 8,11,14,17,20,24,
. 55,63,93,102,111,114,119,121,151,
.... 176,182,255,274,277,284,315
PTESAN GLESKA 36,200
PTESAN HINAPA 14,49,74,75,
.... 103,123,179,213,237,286
PTESAN HINAPA WIN 12
PTESAN HIYAYA 148,312
PTESAN HOKSILA 5,171
PTESAN IYOTAKA 131,294
PTESAN KICI MANI 219
PTESAN KINAPA 236
PTESAN KTE 181,189
PTESAN LUTA 7,12,76,238
PTESAN LUTA WIN 178
PTESAN MANI 125,288
PTESAN MAZA 77
PTESAN NAJIN 31
PTESAN NUPA 53,64,68,227
PTESAN OYATE 71
PTESAN RLA WIN 21,186
PTESAN SAGYE 122,285
PTESAN SAPA 12
PTESAN SINA 87
PTESAN SKA 49
PTESAN SNIA 110
PTESAN TATANKA 127,290
PTESAN WAKPA 139,303
PTESAN WAMBLI 264,272
PTESAN WANBLI .. 103,108,128,290
PTESAN WANYAKA 238
PTESAN WANYANKA 75
PTESAN WASTE 38,63,121,284
PTESAN WAYANKA 19,187
PTESAN WAYANKAPI 23
PTESAN WICAKAGA 53
PTESAN WICAKTE 114,115
PTESAN WICASA 38,202
PTESAN WIN 54,126,185,289
PTESAN WINYAN 21
PTESAN WOKIYAKA 132,295
PTESAN YATAPI 23,59,117,
.... 223,280
PTESAN YUHA 20
PTESAN YUHA MANI 55
PTESANHA SINA 274
PTESAU 184
PTESN NUPA 208
PTEWAN WAKPA 304
PTEWASTE WIN 293
PTEWINYELA HINZI 128
PTEWINYELA OTA 132
PTEWINYELA SA 63,226
PTEYELA AGLI 217
PTEYUHA NAJIN 277
PUCA OYATE 189
PUGH
   Jennie 8,174
   Stanley R 8,174
   William G 8,174
PUKE 77,239
   Rosa 77,239
PULLIAM
   Amos 103,265
   Fannie 229
   James 103,265
   John 103,265
   Lucinda 103,265
   Rena 103,265
   Rosa 229
PULLS IT OUT 152,316
PULLS OUT 101,262
PUMPKIN 18,183
PUMPKIN SEED 39,114,203,278
   Asa 43,206
   Eliza 43,206
   Jackson 207
   James 43,206
   John 43,206
   Joseph 43,206
   Julia 43,206
   Mary 43,206
   Nicholas 39,203
   Robert 43,206
   William 39
   Wm 203
PURE WOMAN 108,291
PURIER, John 224
PUSHES GROUND 65,228
PUTE 303
   Lip 139
PUTEPI, Mark 181
PUTIHIN 205

Index

PUTINHIN.................... 41,84,246,298
PUTINHIN SAPA.................. 131,293
PUTINKIN..................................... 41
PYRDASN TOKAHEYA............ 118
QUICK HAWK 7,172
QUILLED WOMAN 60,224
QUIT... 181
QUITE 16
QUITS THEM 95,257
QUIVER 75,140,238,304
    Agnes 305
    Dennis 305
    Harry 141,305
    James 140,304
    Joseph 294
R SHIELD, Louis 213
RABBIT 24,133,296
    Nellie W 306
RABBIT #2 44,207
RABWICAYA 53,99,217,261
RABYA 277
RABYA MANI 173
RABYAPI 65
RAINBOW 49,214
RAISED ALONE 67,230
RAISING COW 122,285
RAMERO
    Maggie 33
    Susy 33
RANDALL
    Amanda 143,307
    Annie 142,306
    Antoine 142,305
    Antoine, Jr. 306
    Catherine 306
    Charles 142,306
    Dollie 142
    Dolly 306
    Ella 142,306
    Emma 142,143,307
    Eva 141,305
    Frank 143,307
    George 156,320
    James 141,305
    Jessie 142,306
    John 142,306
    Joseph 142,306
    Lucy 142,156,306,320
    Lucy W 143,307
    Maggie 142,306
    Mary 146
    Millie 143,307
    Mollie 146,310
    Nellie 142,306
    Richard 307
    Robert 146,310
    Rosa 320
    Sallie 142,306
    Susie 142,306
    William 142,306
RANDO
    Josephine 24,188
    Mary 24,188
    Silvester 188
    Sylvester 24
    William 24,188
RANHI 22,68,231
RANHI WIN 184,276,292,294
RANHILA 131
RANHIYA 294
RANIE WIN 237
RANRAN WIN 100,121,284
RANTE 44,85,97,153,207,247,
.... 259,317
RANTE GI 199,215
RANTE HOKSILA 18
RANTE ICAGA 182
RANTE LUTA 112,118,275,281
RANTE MAZA 52,68,266
RANTE SA 22
RANTE SI 51
RANTE TIPI 133,296
RANTE WIN 23,74,110,273
RANTE ZI 35,98,259
RAPYA MANI 5,7
RATTLE WOMAN 52,216
RATTLER 21,186
RATTLER HOUSE 124
RATTLING 54,100,128,218,
.... 261,291
RATTLING CHASE 133,296
RATTLING CLOUD ... 34,38,96,198,
.... 202,258
RATTLING HAIL 41,110,205,273
RATTLING HAWK 140,304
RATTLING HOUSE 287

Index

RATTLING IRON 13,178
RATTLING LODGE 96,258
RATTLING ROCK 322
RATTLING WHITE COW 21,186
RATTLING WHITE FACE 96,258
RATTLING WOMAN . 34,88,198,250
RAUTE RLO 17
RE SAPA 76
RE SAPE 238
RE SKA 74,237,275
READ LEAF 98
REAL HAWK 67,230
RED 60,100,222,262
RED BEAR 8,55,114,174,218,278
    Dick 9,174
    Edgar 55,218
    Howard 55,321
    Julia 314
    Maggie 55,218
    Rosa 321
    Silver 54,218
RED BEAVER 126,289
RED BIRD 14,30,33,55,59,68,
.... 94,107,194,197,204,215,219,223,
.... 231,271,320
    Paul 34,197
RED BLANKET 52,95,108,216,
.... 257,272
RED BOY 117,281,295
    George 117,281
RED BRAID 189
RED BREATH BEAR 121,284
RED BREATHING 84,246
RED BULL .. 60,118,125,224,281,288
    Sophia 60,224
RED CANE 23,33,187,197
RED CEDAR 22,112,118,275,
.... 281,314
RED CLAY WOMAN 274
RED CLOUD 9,146,175,310
    Alfred 253
    Charles 90,252
    Jack 90,252
    Mary 9,175
RED COB 128,291
RED COW 63,153,226,317
RED COYOTE 96,258
RED CROW 44,71,208,233

Levi 208
RED DAY 10,34,54,94,95,
.... 198,218,262
    Anna 94,320
RED DEER 20,54,70,184,217,233
RED DIRT 130,293
RED DOG 66,229
RED DOG TRACK 140,304
RED DOOR 260
RED EAGLE 13,18,71,95,118,147,
.... 178,183,234,265,281,311
    Julia 95,265
    Martha 265
    Marthia 95
RED EAGLE #1 257
RED EAGLE HORSE 124
RED EAR 63,118,226,281
RED EAR WOMAN 125
RED EARED HORSE 287
RED EARED WOMAN 288
RED EARS WALKS FAST 100
RED EARTH ... 16,64,78,181,227,241
RED ELK 10,57,91,96,127,
.... 176,220,254,257,289
    Emil 57,220
    George 57
    Millie 96,257
    Peter 57,220
RED ELK WOMAN 118,281
RED EYES 96,257
    Daniel 96,257
    Elmore 96,266
    George 88,250
    Louisa 250
    Louise 89
RED FEATHER 15,53,68,110,
.... 180,217,231,274
    Della B 110,274
RED FINGER NAIL 103,264
RED FISH, Frank 102,263
RED FLUTE 128,291
RED FLY 111,275
RED FOAM 130,293
RED HAIL 62,225
RED HAIR 15,18,93,108,123,
.... 124,180,182,255,272,286
RED HAIRED HORSE 108,271
RED HAT 113,277

Index

RED HAWK 64,299
  Alice...................................74,237
  Austin.................................74,237
  Chas 15,180
  James..................................... 74
  Noah...................................... 74
  Susie...................................... 74
  Thomas 15,180
RED HOOP.......................140,304
  Dora 140,304
  Fannie 140
  Grace...............................140,304
  Ophelia..................................140
RED HORN 33,90,197,252
RED HORN BULL......................125
RED HORNED BULL................288
RED HORSE 13,21,71,83,117,
.. 127,144,178,185,234,245,273,280,
....290,308
  George...............................9,175
  Louise 175
  Lucie 9
  Mary..........................144,204,308
  Susie....................................175
RED HORSE OWNER.......8,153,174,
....317
RED HORSES, Mary..................... 40
RED HOUSE 109
RED HWK
  James...................................237
  Noah.....................................237
  Susie....................................237
RED KETTLE
  Alice..................................142,306
  Charles A 93
  Joseph 93,255
  Mary...................................93,255
  Moses.................................93,255
  Robert 142,306
  Rosa 142,306
RED LEAF 124,154,260,287,318
RED LEG.. 20
RED LODGE 10,66,112,120,
.................................229,276,299
RED NECKLACE 36,200
RED NEST 132,145,295,309
RED ONION............................124,287
RED OTTAR 153

RED OTTER 317
RED OWL 17,76,225,238
  Amos 83,245
  Hattie 83,245
  Henry................................ 83,245
  Jessie 83,245
RED PAINT 129,291
RED PAINTED BOY............. 68,230
RED PINE 60,266
RED PIPE GIRL..................... 63,226
RED PLUME 96,258
RED PORCUPINE................. 17,182
RED PRAIRIE DOG 63,321
RED RABBIT 69,231
  Jonas 91,253
RED RING 58,121,221,284
RED ROCK 19,183,295
  George 44,208
RED ROD............................. 103,264
RED ROOR............................... 98
RED SACK 20,185
  Sallie................................. 20,185
RED SCOUT 132,295
RED SHELL.. 30,68,123,194,230,286
RED SHELL WOMAN........... 66,222
RED SHIRT 18,124
  Alfred 61,224
  Anna 18,183
  Charles............................... 61,224
  Emma 61,224
  Henry................................. 61,224
  John 61,224
  Mary 18,61,183,224
RED SHIRT #2.............................287
RED SOCKS 117,280
RED STAR.... 10,56,112,176,220,276
  David 56,220
  Paul.................................... 56,220
  Sallie.................................. 56,220
  Stella.......................................220
RED TOP 143,307
RED TRACK .. 6,14,114,172,257,277
RED TRACL 95
RED TURKEY 141,305
  Anna 141
  Annie 305
RED WAR BONNET..... 11,44,66,71,
.... 176,208,228,233

Index

RED WATER 144,308
RED WEASEL 12,31,178,195
   Charles 58
   Chas 222
RED WHIRLWIND.....................110
RED WHITE COW 7,12,76,178
RED WILLOW 95,257
RED WOMAN........13,23,55,109,111,
  133,179,187,219,273,275,296
REDDY.....................................21,185
REE WOMAN 46,195,209
RESIST 24,128,291
RESPECTS 144,308
RESPECTS NOTHING 70,233
   George.. 71
RETAINOR 122
RETAP INAJIN 107
RETURN SCOUT.............97,247,308
RETURN WARRIOR...................264
RETURNED 108,272
RETURNED FROM SCOUT ..75,238
RETURNED LAST 200
RETURNED LOST 37
RETURNED WARRIOR..............102
RETURNS FROM SCOUT ...122,285
RETURNS SCOUT 144
REVENGER 52,57,67,77,85,90,
  201,221,240,247,252,265
REYAP EYAYA 119
REYAP ICU 133,208
REYAPA ICU............................... 45
REYNAL, Louise 151,315
RIB MAN 33,241
   Alfred... 33
   Jennie..242
   Thomas 33,242
RIBS 6,172
RICHARD
   Alexander...........................39,320
   Alfred.......44,148,151,312,315,321
   Angelina............................151,315
   Anna.........................40,44,204
   Annie...320
   Baptiste 148,312
   Benjamin..............................40,320
   Chales 204
   Charles 40,156,320
   Daniel......................................44,320

   Dora................................... 152,316
   Edward 40
   Eva..................................... 152,316
   James 15,44,180,315,320
   Jennie........................ 151,315,316
   Joseph................... 39,148,312,320
   Josephine 40,148,312,320
   Julia 7,39,40,173,320
   Louis..................... 151,315,320
   Louis, Jr............................ 152,316
   Louise 44,148,151,156,
   312,315,320
   Lucy................................... 40,320
   Mille 315
   Millie 148,151,312
   Nellie 44,321
   Peter.................................... 148,312
   Samuel................................ 151,315
   Sophia................................ 44,320
   Susanna.............................. 148,312
   Theresa 156
   Thomas 44,320
   Venny 204
RIDER.................................. 107,271
RIDES OVER....................... 115,278
RING BUFFALO 286
RINGING 24
RINGING CRACK............... 108,272
RINGING IRON 51,215
RINGING SHIELD 45,208
RINGING WIND 17,182
RISING SUN........................ 103,264
RIVWE, Nellie W C..................... 304
RLA 54,218
RLA O 255
RLA WIN 52,88,128,250
RLALA................................. 100,261
RLAWIN 21,216,291
RLAYA HINAPA 93
RLAYA WAKUWA 133,296
RLO KIYAPI 115,279
RLO KU 231,239
RLOGECA 132
RLOKIYAPI 132,294
RLOKU 68,76
RLOLA.......................... 38,44,207,208
ROACHER............................ 54,218
ROAD............. 50,60,94,124,129,147,

Index

................214,247,256,287,292,311
  Bessie M B..................254
  Bessie N. B. 92
  Lizzie M B 254
  Lizzie N. B. 92
ROAD BREATH 65
ROAD WOMAN 284
ROAN 6,53,140,172,216,304
ROAN BEAR.....................111,274
ROAN EAGLE 7,173
  Annie.........................173
ROAN HORSE, Anna..............49,213
ROAN WOMAN 63,103,129,
................................156,226,264
ROBINSON, Susan................154,318
ROBYA 194
ROCK 119,282
  Bessie......................30,194
  Charles....................30,194
  John.........................30,194
  Samuel 30,194
ROCK BOY 75,237
  James.....................148,312
ROCK COMES OUT............124,287
ROCK LODGE WOMAN.......75,237
ROCK MAN 9,175
ROCK MAN WHITE HORSE 77,240
ROCK ROMAN...........................275
ROCK WOMAN 18,112,145,
....182,309
ROCKY BEAR 56,220
  George......................57,220
  Lizzie........................56,220
  Susie..........................51,215
  Thomas 56
ROCKY MOUNTAIN............111,275
ROKA 42,126,206,294
ROL KU....................................231
ROLAND
  Annie..........................84,247
  Ben.............................84,247
  Mary...........................84,247
  Nellie..........................84,247
ROMERO
  Emanuel........................208
  Emmanuel....................... 45
  Katie.........................45,208
  Maggie..........................208

  Mary............................33,197
  Philip.......................... 45,208
  Philip, Jr........................ 208
  Susy............................... 197
ROOKS
  Alice........................ 149,313
  Annie............................ 305
  Charles..................... 149,305
  Christina........................ 313
  Clara........................ 149,313
  Cristina.......................... 149
  Delia........................ 149,313
  James....................... 149,313
  Jessie 148,312
  Joseph.................. 148,167,312
  Kate......................... 149,313
  Mabel........................ 148,312
  Maggie..................... 149,313
  Martha 313
  Mathia.......................... 149
  Mollie 148,312
  Nancy 149,313
  Nellie 149,313
  Rosana 313
  Rosanna 149
  William..................... 149,313
ROOT 130,292
ROPE
  Jos B 246
  Sarah B 246
ROPE NECKLACE................. 45,208
  Lizzie......................... 45,209
ROSA 7,55,101
ROSEBUD 107,271
ROTTEN WOMAN 225
ROUGH FEATHER................ 74,236
ROUGH WOOD 146,310
RUFF
  Alice........................ 142,306
  Arthur...................... 142,306
  Edna........................ 142,306
  Emma....................... 142,306
  George...................... 142,306
  Gracie 142,306
  John 142,306
  Lizzie....................... 142,306
  Mary 142,306
  Vina......................... 142,306

Index

William 142,306
RULEAU
    Louis 320
    Nicholas 79,320
RUM BONE 59,223
RUN AT HIM 116
RUNNER, Howard B 249
RUNNING ANTELOPE 151,315
RUNNING BEAR 55,135,218,298
RUNNING EAGLE 126,289
RUNNING ELK 66,229
RUNNING HAWK 107,271,284
RUNNING HORSE 12,14,178
    Chas 10
    Fay 88,250
    Felix 199
    George 90,266
    Lizzie 14,88,250
    Rock 88,250
    Samuel 199
    Wm 35
RUNNING JUMPER 128,291
RUNNING LOPER 109,273
RUNNING SHIELD 49,213
    Anna 213
    Leon 49,213
    Louis 49
    Nellie 213
RUNNING WALKER 51,215
RUNS 36,199
RUNS A GRAY HORSES 228
RUNS A T EDGE
    Jas 256
    Peter 195
RUNS ABOVE 5,171
RUNS AFTER 129,292
RUNS AFTER GREY HORSES ... 65
RUNS AGAINST 116,279
    Francis 65,228
    Jacob 65,228
RUNS AGAINST THEM 123,286
RUNS AHEAD 24,56,220
RUNS ALONE 213
RUNS ALONG T EDGE 242
RUNS ALONG T. EDGE
    Jas 94
    Peter 31
RUNS ALONG THE EDGE 46

Jennie 46
RUNS AMONG THEM 37,114,201,277
RUNS AROUND 85,118,152,
.... 247,281,316
RUNS AT HIM 279
RUNS AT LODGE 127,290
RUNS AWAY 5,102,120,128,
.... 171,264,283,291
RUNS AWAY FROM HIM ... 13,128,
.... 178,290
RUNS AWAY WITH HORSES 134,297
RUNS BETWEEN 13,74,83,
.... 179,237,245
RUNS CLOSE 279
RUNS CLOSE TO EDGE 154,318
    Jos 110
RUNS CLOSE TO LODGE ... 16,120,
.... 131,133,181,283,294,296
    Jos 273
RUNS FIRST 30,194
RUNS FOR CAMP 69,232
RUNS FOR HILL 36,200
RUNS FOR LODGE 124,287
RUNS FOR PLUME 85,247
RUNS IN CENTER 78,240
RUNS LAST 150,314
RUNS ON 95,257
    Nellie 95,257
RUNS OUT AT NIGHT 127,290
RUNS OUT ENEMY 236
RUNS OVER 104,133,265,296
RUNS OVER ENEMY 60
RUNS PRAIRIE 14
RUNS THROUGH 109,285
RUNS THROUGH CAMP 113,276
RUNS WITH 24
RUNS WITH HORSES 66,228
RUNS WITH THEM 126,289
RUNS WOUNDED 126,289
RUPAHU MAZA 135,298
RUPAHU SKA 22
RUPAHU WIN 54,218
RUSHES 88,250
RUSSEL, Susie 209
RUSSELL
    Amelia 193
    Amilia 29
    Andrew 154,318

Index

Ella 29,193
Louisa 29
Louise 193
Nellie 29,193
Ruth 29,193
Susie 46
RUSTLER 15,180
RUTH 39,199
S BEAR
   Annie 309
   Edith 309
   Ellen 309
   Emily 309
   George 309
   John 309
   Lena 309
   Sarah 309
S NAKPA HOKSILA 22
S SOLDIER
   Dinah 171
   Henry 171
   Katie 171
   Mary 171
   Philip 171
   Victoria 171
S TANKA CIQALA 21
SA 60,100
SA APA 124,129,292
SA ICIYA 124
SA YUHA MANI 66,96,258
SA YUHA WANI 228
SAAPA 287
SAGA SKA 217
SAGE 54,218
SAGE BUSH 29,193
SAGYE 55,66,96,121,
  141,144,153,218,228,257,284,305,
  308
SAGYE GI 283
SAGYE LUTA 23,33,187,197,264
SAGYE MAZA 128,291
SAGYE MIWAKAN 66
SAGYE MUVAKA 229
SAGYE SKA 53
SAGYE WAKAN WIN ... 99,261
SAGYE WAMBLI 228
SAGYE WANBLI 65,119,282
SAGYE WASTE 85,247
SAGYE WIN 23,187
SAGYE ZI 120
SAHINYELA 122
SAHINYELA HUNKU 88
SAHIYELA 72,86,235,248,285
SAHIYELA HUNKU 250
SAHIYELA IYA 88,250
SAHIYELA OBCA 252
SAHIYELA ONCA 90
SAHIYELA WAPATA 151,315
SAHIYELA WASTE 75
SAHUMWINLA WINORCA ... 45
SAHUNWANLA 12
SAHUNWILA WINURCA ... 209
SAHUNWIN TANKA 174
SAHUNWINLA 33,177
SAHUNWINLA TANKA ... 7
SAHUWINLA 197
SAH~~X~~YELA WASTE 237
SAKE LUTA 264
SAKE SA 103
SAKE SKA 65
SALIVA 59,223
SALLIE 10,239
SALLY 77,128
SALVIS
   Alexander 11,177
   Alexander, Jr 11
   Alice 11,177
   Charles 11,177
   Frank 11,150,177,314
   Frank, Jr 150
   Frank, Sr 314
   George 150,314
   James, Jr 150
   Julia 11,150,177
   Levi 150,314
   Lillie 314
   Lizzie 150,314
   Lucy 11,177
   Mollie 11,177
   Nancy 150,314
   Oliver 11,183
   Sophia 150,314
   Stacy 11,177
   William 150,314
   Willie 11,177
SAMUEL 92,305

Index

SANBLI SINTE 287
SAND 98,259
SANGMANITU ISNALA 95
SANGUMANITU SICA 201
SANK HINTO 148
SANTE MAZA 180
SANTEE 57,220
SAPA SKA 175
SAPA WICASA 133
SASA 21,185
SASTE 276
SAVES BEAR 65,227
    Ida 65,227
SAVES HIM 77,240
SAVES HIMSELF 89,251
SAVES HIS LIFE 126,289
SAVES LIFE 290
SAVES LIVES 73,236
SAVES THE LIFE 116,279
SAVES THEM 97,258
SAVIOR 119,282
SCABBY FACE, Johnson 120,283
SCABBY LEG 139,303
SCABBY WOMAN.100,121,262,284
SCARE HAWK
    Joseph 50
    Louise 50
    Stephen 50
SCARES 113,277
SCARES AWAY 65,194
SCARES HAWK
    Elizabeth 97,259
    Joseph 214
    Louise 214
    Paul 50,214
    Stephen 214
SCARES HIM 222
SCARES THEM 67
SCARES THEM AWAY ...53,99,217,
..........................261
SCATTERS THEM 121,284
SCILI 42,121,284
SCILI HUNSKA 256
SCILI KOKIPESNI 153,317
SCILI KTE 69,149,232,311,313
SCILI TAHUNSKA 95
SCILI WICAKTE 147
SCORNS HIM 58
SCOUT 7,22,55,66,124,127,
..........................219,287,290
    Joseph 54,218
SCRAPER, Col 147
SCRAPES THE HIDE 115,278
SCRATCHES 74,237
SCU SNI 57
SE KAKSA 248
SEARS
    Clarence 46,209
    Cora 46,209
    John 209
    Leander 46,209
    Lulu 46,209
    Matilda 46,209
    Maud 46,209
    Susan 46,209
    Susie 46,209
    Vincent 46,209
    William 46,209
SECOND GROWTH 94,320
SEEN BY ENEMY 51
SEES HER HORSE 21,185
SEES THE BEAR 38,202
SEES THE HORSES 78,240
SEES THE LODGE 113
SEES WHITE 19
SEES WHITE COW 75,238
SEKA HUNPI 239
SELECT 89,251
SELWIN, Mary 153,317
SENT 42,206
SEPA WIN 293
SEVEN RABBITS 97,258
SEVEN UP 7,173
SHAKE MANZA 215
SHAKE SKA 228
SHAKES HARD 98,260
SHAKING LEGS 93,255
SHANGRA, William Wallace 152
SHANGREAU
    Angeline 5,171
    Antonio 5,171
    Emma 152,316
    Jessie 5
    Jessy 171
    John 151,315
    John, Jr 151,315

Index

Joseph 92
Jules 151,315
Leon 151,315
Louis 92,254
Louisa 254
Louise 92
Lucy 5,171
Martin 92,255
Mary 152,316
Myrtle 171
Nelson 92,254
Parker 92,255
Pearl 92,255
Peter 5,171
Roas 92
Rosa 5,171,254
Sarah 5,171
William 152,315,316
William W 316
Winifred 87
Winnie 152,316
SHANGRU, Winifred 248
SHARP POINTED 123,286
SHAVING BEAR 114,278
SHAWL 12,177
SHE STOPS 101,263
SHELL 9,115,122,148,175,278,285,312
SHELL BOY 60,193,223
   Alice 69,232
   Ida 193
   Oda 29
SHELL CREEK 151,315
SHELL NECKLACE #2 97,258
SHELL OY 29
SHELL WOMAN .. 6,7,8,22,37,55,66, 97,114,123,173,174,186,201,218,229, 259,278,286
SHERMAN
   Emily 92
   George 92
   Lizzie 92
   Mark 92
   Rosa 92
   William 92
SHIELD .... 10,40,58,96,176, ... 204,221,247,258
   Alice 40,204
   Hobert 204

Julia 40,204
Lizzie C 201
Mary 58,222
Robert 146,310
SHIELD WOMAN 32,196
SHIELD, JR 58,221
SHINING GROUND, Nellie 113
SHINING PIPE 63,226
SHINNING GROUND, Nellie 202
SHOES 45
SHOOT FOR 107
SHOOTE IN MORNING 135
SHOOTER
   Charles 113
   Sharles 276
SHOOTS 36
SHOOTS AT DAYLIGHT 236
SHOOTS AT HIM 6,172,265
SHOOTS AT LAST 132,294
SHOOTS AT SIDE 119,282
SHOOTS AT THE 252
SHOOTS AT THEM 90
SHOOTS BACK 113,254
SHOOTS BLANKET 114,277
SHOOTS CLOSE 62,227
SHOOTS DUCKS 98,259
SHOOTS ENEMY 5,6,171,172
SHOOTS FIRST 69,232
SHOOTS FOR THEM 79,241
SHOOTS GHOST 69,232
SHOOTS GOOD 119
SHOOTS HIM 129,272
SHOOTS HIM RIGHT 58,221
SHOOTS IN 12,177
   Wallace 177
SHOOTS IN MORNING 298
SHOOTS IN THE MORNING 274
SHOOTS PLENTY 18,183
SHOOTS THE ENEMU 175
SHOOTS THE ENEMY 9,108
SHOOTS WITH ARROW 134,296
SHORT 45,108,118,208,286,292
SHORT BEAR
   Baby 150,314
   Cecilia 150,314
   Grover 150,313
   Josephine 150
   Nettie 150,314

Index

Silas 150,314
SHORT BULL 15,180,283
   Thomas 134
   Thos 296
SHORT BULL #1 120
SHORT BULL #2 134,296
SHORT HORN, Frank 206
SHORT LEG 38,202
SHORT MAN 21,185
SHORT PINE 96
   James 154
   James, Jr 318
SHORT STEP 44,193
SHORT TREE, Bell 184
SHORT WOMAN 58,116,221,279
SHORT WOOD 19,184
SHOT 54,61,218,224
SHOT AT 73,117,130,235,280
   Charles 30,194
SHOT AT HIM 104,133,296
SHOT BY WHITE MAN 68,231
SHOT CLOSE 8,26,35,72,129,189,
.... 198,231,234,292
SHOT FROM HOUSE 135,298
SHOT HER HORSES 43,100,
.... 145,267,309
SHOT HIM 111
SHOT HIS HORSE 124,130,
.... 206,287,293
SHOT IN THE EYE 41,204
SHOT IN THE FACE, Ida 19
SHOT IN THE MOUTH 291
SHOT IN TWO 117,280
SHOT MANY TIMES 69,231
SHOT THE ENEMY 209
SHOT TO PIECES 46,62,134,
.... 225,242,296
   Charles 49,213
SHOT WHITE HORSE 78
SHOT WHITE HORSES 240
SHOT WITH ARROWS 97,259
SHOULDER 64,227
   Amos 64,227
   Henry 58,222
   James 58,222
   Lucy 64,227
   Mary 64,227
   Paul 64,227

Ruben 64,227
SHOUT AT 42,118,144,281,308
   Emma 42
   Frank 42
   John 42
SHOUT FOR 271
SHOUTED 241
SHOUTED AT 33
SHOUTS AT 22,182
SHOVELS GROUND 111,275
SHOW 176
SHOWS 10
SHOWS HER HORSE 26,189
SHOWS THE STICKS 97,259
SHOWS THE TRACK 66,229
SHOWS WHIP MARKS 260
SHOWS WHITE MARKS 98
SI 34,72,87,199,235,249
SI KAHUNPI 46
SI MAZA 134,296
SI TANKA 57,116,279,321
SI TOKAPATAN 287
SI WANICA 112,275
SICA KUTEPI 121,284
SICA WICAKTE 50
SICAN GU WIN 132
SICANGU WIN 84,247,294
SICAYA ECUN SNI 41
SICAYA KTE 214
SICAYA RPAYA 100,101,319
SICI TAHUNSKA 95
SICIYA 287
SICKLER
   Alice 104,322
   John 46,190
   Lucy 104,322
SIDES 121,284
SIERRO
   Antonia 18,183
   Bennet 183
   Bennett 18
   Cemona 18,183
   Joseph 18,183
   Mary 18,183
   Santac 18
   Santo 183
   Seberina 183
   Seberino 18

Index

Susie 18,183
SIGHT 13
SIGHT OF LODGE 113,277
SIHA SAPA 94,256,282
SIHASAPA KTE 293
SIHASAPA WICAKTE 130
SIHASRPA 119
SIKAHUNPI 76,86
SILA 179
SINA 12,51,177,215
SINA GI 33
SINA GLEGKEGA 276
SINA GLEGLEGA 112
SINA GNUNIPI 283
SINA HARWOKA 294
SINA ICU 17,111,182,274
SINA KARWOKA 36,131,200
SINA KSUPI KOYAKA 174
SINA KUTE 114,277
SINA LUTA ... 52,95,108,216,257,272
SINA MANZA 219
SINA MAZA 55
SINA ON APA 288
SINA ON WAAPA 125
SINA OTA 56,219
SINA ROTA 9
   Louise 9
SINA SAPA 110
SINA SKA 87,144,249,308,309
SINA SKA KOYAKA 52
SINA TO 77,127,239,290
SINA TOPA 128,290
SINA WAKAN 21,34,95,107,121,
.... 185,198,257,271,287
SINA WANBLI 79,109
SINA WIN 12
SINA ZI 197
SINASKA IN 216
SINGING BEAR ... 8,66,132,174,229,
.... 295
SINGING ELK 74,236
SINGLE WOMAN 36,64,199
SINGMANITU GI 254
SINGS AND WALKS 156
SINKAKAN ISNALA 123
SINTE 35,199
SINTE CONALA 58,222
SINTE JATA 148
SINTE MAZA 109,273
SINTE NOPA 32
SINTE NUPA 86,196,249
SINTE SAPA 7,173
SINTE SAPELA 59,223
SINTE SKA 131,294
SINTE TANKA 107
SINTE TOKECA 67,230
SINYE TONKA 271
SIRES
   James 157,233
   Jennie 70,233
   John 157,233
   Josephine 157,233
SIS 24
SISTS IN LODGE 281
SISTS WITH HER 188
SITOKAPA 124
SITS 144,308
SITS HOLY 24
SITS IN LODGE 118
SITS IN SIGHT 17,60,87,182,223,
.... 266
SITS IN THE LODGE 57
SITS POOR 75,237
   Franks 75,238
SITS WITH HER 25
SITTING BEAR 145,309
   John 91,253
   Lucy 91,253
   Mary 91,253
   Victoa 253
   Victoria 91
SITTING BULL 21,186
SITTING EAGLE 57,221,266
   Albert 94,256
SITTING ELK 20,133,296
   Julia 20
SITTING HAWK 129,292
   Levi 129,292
SITTING HOLY 51,215
SITTING MEDICINE 15
   Jessie 15
SITTING ROCK 79,119,282,283
SITTING UP 303
   Cora 139,303
   Homer 139,303
SITTING WEASEL 58,222

Index

SITTING WHITE COW 131,294
SIX FEATHER 51
SIX FEATHERS 321
    John 51,321
SIX MEN 149,313
SIYE SAPA 245
SIYO 59,84,126,130,223,246,
    289,293
SIYO CIQALA 282
SIYO SAPA 83
SIYO WINORALA 67
SIYO WINURCA 230
SIYO WITKO 107,271
SIYOTANKA HO 217
SIYOTANKA LUTA 291
SIYOTANKA SA 128
SIYOTANKA SAPA 127,290,292
SIYOTANKA WASTE 125,288
SIYOTANKA YAJO 217
SIYOTANKA YUHA 49,213
SIYOTAUKA YAJO 54
SKA 79,102,241,263
SKA AGLI 8,110,132,174,238,294
SKA GLI 182
SKA KOYAKA 152,316
SKA SAPA 119,282
SKA WIN 303,318
SKAGLI 17
SKUNK, Nellie 156
SKUNK FOOT 135,298
SKUNKS MOTHER 54,218
SLAVIS, Lillie 150
SLECAHAN 111,275
SLEEK RABBIT 117
SLEEP 83,245
SLEEPER 65,228
SLEEPING BEAR 115,278
    John 13,179
    Last Bear 13
    Mato Ehakela 13
SLEEPS LATE 229
SLEEPS WITH HIM 118,281
SLICK QUIVER 131,294
SLOHAN 133,296
SLOHAN KU 118,281
SLOLYAPI 96,258
SLOW 22,68,69,231
SLOW BEAR 132,295

John 132,295
Luke 9,175
SLOW BULL #1 75,238
SLOW DOG 97,258
    Philip 152,316
    Susie 316
SLOW WOMAN 20,113,129,131,
    184,276,292,294
SLOWLY 131,294
SMALL BACK 43
SMALL EAGLE 23
SMALL WOMAN 58
SMALLEY, James 165
SMALLL BACK 207
SMELLS GOOD 126,289
SMELLS GUN 74,237
SMITH
    Alice 155,319
    Cahlie 274
    Charles 110
    Effie 34,198
    Janette 34,198
    Joseph 34,198
    Joseph, Jr 34,198
    Josephine 24,187
    Julia 155,319
    Raymond 23,187
    Samuel 155,319
    Susie 110,274
SMOKE 76,238
    Wendell 73,236
SMOKE WOMAN 52,115,216,278
SMOKES FOUR TIMES 34,197
SNA WIN 34,186,198
SNAKE EAR RING 44,207
SNAWIN 24
SNIA ROTA 175
SNOW FLIES 122,285
SOLDIER, Julia E S 306
SOLDIER HAWK 124,286
SOMORROW
    Lilly 9
    Sophia 9,266
SOPHIA 66,228
SORE EYES 151,315
SORE FACE 98,266
SOTA 73,76,238
SOTA WIN 52,115,278

Index

SOUND SLEEPER 114,278
SOUNDING TIDE 133
SPARK OLD HORSE 257
SPAYO 19
SPAYOLA 72,183,234
SPAYOLA WICARCA 112,242
SPIDER 139,303
   Albert 41,205
   Mark 41,205
   Nellie 41,205
   Sallie 41,205
SPIDER BACK BONE 74,237
SPIRIT, Ella 111
SPITS, Ella 275
SPOTTED BEAR 65,139,228,303
   Thomas 56,183
   Thos 219
SPOTTED BIRD 22,186
   Fred 186
SPOTTED BLANKET 112,276
SPOTTED COW
   Martha 45
   Rupert 45
   Susie 45
   Tracy 45
   William 45
SPOTTED CROW 97,258
   Edward 84,246
   Fannie 97
   Katie 97
   Martha 209
   Robert 209
   Susie 209
   Tracy 209
   William 209
SPOTTED EAGE
   Amelia 317
   Charles 317
   Felix 317
SPOTTED EAGLE 18,76,97,238
   Amelia 153
   Charles 153
   Clara 97,258
   Felix 153
   Harry 89,252
   Millie 89
   Mollie 97
   Nellie 252
   Sallie 90
   Sally 252
   Susie 90
SPOTTED ELK 98,126,259,289
   James 98
SPOTTED FEATHER 121
SPOTTED HORSE .... 58,98,146, ... 221,259,310
   James 259
   John 91,253
   Robert 98
SPOTTED HORSE #1 123,286
SPOTTED HORSE #2 118,281
SPOTTED HORSE WOMAN 7,67,173,229
SPOTTED HORSES, Mary 70
SPOTTED OWL 60,223
SPOTTED RABBIT 112
SPOTTED SNAKE 87,248
SPOTTED WEASEL 97,259
SPOTTED WHITE COW 36,200
SPREAD FACE 131,294
SQUIRREL 120,283
STABBER
   Crandall 102,264
   Julia 97,259
   Louisa 264
   Louise 102
   Paul 264
   Sallie 102
   Sally 264
   Thomas 38,202
STABBER #1 97,259
STABBER #2 96,258
STABDING CLOUD, Cora 96
STAKED ROAD 62,225
STAMPEDES HORSES, Charles ... 74
STAMPEEDS HORSES, Chas 236
STAND 130
STAND IN SIGHT 69
STAND UP 39,215
STANDING, Cora 258
STANDING BEAR .... 12,59,177,223, ... 309
   Anna 59,222
   Annie 145,177
   Arthur 146,310
   Clarence 78,241

Index

Edith 145
Elizabeth 141
Ellen 145
Ellis 145,309
Emily 145,146,310
Esther 146,310
George 145
Henry 141,305
Henry, Jr 141,305
Jessie 145
John 145
Julia 146,310
Lena 145
Lillie 146,310
Lizzie 146,310
Luther 146,310
Mary 305
Nellie 146,310
Oliver 146,310
Paul F 146,310
Sarah 145
Stephen 146,310
Willard 146,310
STANDING BULL 21,185
STANDING CLOUD 96,258
   Bessie 102
   Charles 102,263
   Robert 95,257
STANDING ELK 38,202
   George 38,202
STANDING HORSE 111,112,
.... 275,276,293
STANDING IN SIGHT 32,196
STANDING PLENTY WOMAN .. 24
STANDING SOLDIER 16
   Dinah 5
   Elk 142
   Henry 5
   Julia 142
   Katie 5
   Mary 5
   Philip 5
   Victoria S 5
STANDING SOLDIER #1 5,171
STANDING SOLDIER #2 181
STANDING VOICE 122
STANDING WHITE COW 31,195
STANDS 119,293

Lizzie 13,179
Peter 282
Samuel 282
Smauel 119
STANDS AND LOOKS 12,31,178,
.... 195
STANDS ASIDE 107,271
STANDS FIRST 32,196
   Alexander 32,196
   Ella 32,196
   Nancy 32,196
STANDS HOLY 61,118,224,281
STANDS I SIGHT, Robert 30,194
STANDS IN FRONT .. 16,97,179,247
STANDS IN SIDE 102
STANDS IN SIGHT 13,68,117,
.... 178,231,232,280
STANDS IN T WOODS 200
STANDS IN THE WOOD 36
STANDS INSIDE 263
STANDS KILLING 218
STANDS LOKING 43
STANDS LOOKING 207
STANDS LOOKING AT HER125,288
STANDS OUTSIDE 117,281
STANDS UP 15,180,186
STANDS WITH HIM 118,281
STAR..52,59,91,139,216,223,254,303
   Anna 14,179
   Edward 14,179
   Lucy 95,257
   Lydia 95,257
   Mary 54,218
   Nellie 95,256
   Paddy 95,256
   Paddy, Jr 257
   Phoebe 95,256
   Ruben 54,218
STAR COMES OUT 114,118,277,
.... 282
STAR EAGLE 98,260
STAR ROAD 57,221
STAR WOMAN 114,278
STAYS IN FRONT 97,259
STAYS ON TOP 140,304
STEAL HORSES 36
STEALS HORSE 296
STEALS HORSES 14,31,128,133,

Index

.... 155,180,195,319
STEALS HORSES #2 200
STEELS HORSE 291
STELLA 56,220
STEPPED 281
STEPS SHORT 109,273
STICKS OUT 93,255
STINKING BEAR 115,278
STINKING HAND 24
STIRK
   Ellen 23,187
   Emma 23,187
   George 23,187
   James 23,187
   Louisa 187
   Louise 23
   Nellie 23,187
   Prudy 23,187
   Richard 23,187
   Tony 23,187
STONE HEART 17,182
STOP HER HORSES 57,221
STOPPING ELK 96,257
STOUT 33,197
STOVER
   Edith 155,319
   Edward 155,319
   George 155,319
   Grace 155,319
   Jennie 155,319
   Laura 155,319
   William 155,319
STRAIGHT FOREHEAD 74,237
STRIKES HIM 133,296
STRIKES PLENTY 96,258
   Jefferson 96
   Lucy 96
   Paulina 96
   Rosa 96
STRIKES RED 124,129,287,292
STRIKES THREE TIMES 52,321
STRIKES WITH BLANKET . 125,288
STRIKES WITH NOSE 29,193
STRINGS UNTIED 125,287
STRIPPED 118
STRONG TALK 10,176
STRONG WOMAN 19,183
STRUCK BY BOW 231

STRUCK BY CROW 69
   Harry 69
STRUCK BY ENEMY 131,294
SUFFERER 16
SUGA 57
SUGAR 33,131,146,197,293,310
SUGMANITU ISNALA 291
SUGMNAITU PETA 219
SUKA HUNKESNI 258
SUKSKA YUHA 241
SUMMERS, Abe 18,183
SUN BEAR 51,215
SUN FLOWER 63,226
SUNDAY 51,61,91,215,253
SUNDSY 224
SUNG SAPA 220
SUNG TAOPI 220
SUNGALI 216
SUNGILA 140
SUNGLESKA CIQALA 119
SUNGMANITU AKICITA ... 143,307
SUNGMANITU CIQALA 78,135,241
SUNGMANITU GI 8,46,50,54,83,
.... 91,92,214,215,218,245,254
SUNGMANITU HALPIYA 99
SUNGMANITU HANSKA 15,46,
.... 135,180,297
SUNGMANITU HINAPA 88,250
SUNGMANITU ISNALA. 91,95,128,
.... 147,153,257,311,317
SUNGMANITU LUTA 258
SUNGMANITU LUTE 96
SUNGMANITU LUZAHAN 141,142,
.... 154,306,307,318
SUNGMANITU MATO. 128,151,315
SUNGMANITU NAKPA.. 9,130,175,
.... 293
SUNGMANITU NAKPA HOKSILA
.... 186
SUNGMANITU NIGE 85
SUNGMANITU OHITIKA 287
SUNGMANITU OTA 22,187
SUNGMANITU PETA 55,103,265
SUNGMANITU SAPA 84,116,127,246,
.... 279,289
SUNGMANITU SICA 38,113,277
SUNGMANITU SKA . 6,7,65,97,101,
.... 171,172,228,258,263

Index

SUNGMANITU TANKA .. 13,53,179, ...217
SUNGMANITU W 37
SUNGMANITU WAKAN 309
SUNGMANITU WAKUWA ..86,110, ...256,274
SUNGMANITU WANJILA 254
SUNGMANITU WANKA 42
SUNGMANITU WANKATUYA201, ...204,206
SUNGMANITY TANJA 53
SUNGMANU 31,221
SUNGMONITU WAUKAT 41
SUNGWAKITA 215
SUNK AGLI 42,53,206
SUNK CIQALA............100
SUNK GLESKA 253,259,286
SUNK GLESKA YUHA 248
SUNK GLIYOHI 96
SUNK GLUHA 234
SUNK GNANI............229
SUNK HEYOHE 246
SUNK HINROTA............ 49
SUNK HINSA OTA 40
SUNK HINSA YUKA 153
SUNK HINTO 35,199,312
SUNK HINTO AGLI 40
SUNK HINZI 54,144,218
SUNK HIWOHI............ 84
SUNK HIYO HI 235
SUNK HIYOHI 72
SUNK ICU 11,71,77,133,146,213
SUNK IYANAJICA 228,236,238
SUNK IYANAJINCA............66,74,76, ...134,152,297
SUNK KARNIGA 86
SUNK KARNIGE............248
SUNK KARNIR AGLI 41,204
SUNK MANI 57,128,133
SUNK MANU 155,195
SUNK MANUSA 75,238
SUNK NAKPO GLI 130
SUNK NAKPOGI............124
SUNK OHITIKA 131
SUNK OLE 41,46,89,202,205
SUNK OTORAN 50
SUNK OTURAN 214
SUNK SAPA .... 13,40,56,115,121, ..135,144,178,187,203,278,284,298, ...308
SUNK SKA .... 24,51,77,128,176, ...234,264
SUNK SKA OTA 132
SUNK SKA TANKA 45,208
SUNK SKA WIN 281
SUNK TACANKU 11,151
SUNK TAINYA MANI 230
SUNK TOKCA 314
SUNK TOKECA 45,150,208
SUNK WAKETA 207
SUNK WATOGLA 140,149
SUNK WICAKU 111
SUNK WICAQU 274
SUNK WITKO 258
SUNK YUHA 118,281
SUNKA 197,202
SUNKA BLOKA 119,282
SUNKA CIQALA .... 57,88,130,220, ...250,262,292
SUNKA GLAKINYAN 108,272
SUNKA GLUHA 119
SUNKA GNASKINYAN 86
SUNKA HANSKA 57,221
SUNKA HETON 132,294
SUNKA HO WASTE 298
SUNKA HOWASTE 108
SUNKA HUNKESNI 97,152,316
SUNKA HUSTE 68,76,231,239
SUNKA ISNA 15,180
SUNKA LUTA 66,229
SUNKA MANI 71,234
SUNKA NAGE TANKA 83
SUNKA NIGE TANKA 245
SUNKA NUPA 85,98,247,259,260
SUNKA OHITIKA 294
SUNKA ONCA 149,313
SUNKA OYATE 257
SUNKA OYE LUTA 140,304
SUNKA PAHA AKAN 59
SUNKA PAHA AKAN NAJI 223
SUNKA SKA 7,173,240
SUNKA WANAGI 54,217
SUNKA WANKATUYA 131,293
SUNKA WASTE 20,185
SUNKA WITKO .... 64,96,119,227, ...248,282

Index

SUNKA YATAPI 73,236
SUNKA YUHA 109,272
SUNKAGLI 16,181
SUNKAHAN WIN 292
SUNKAIYPHI 119
SUNKAKA OPI............................228
SUNKAKAN 25
SUNKAKAN ISNALA..................122
SUNKAKAN WIN 110,274
SUNKAWAKAN...........................188
SUNKAWAKAN NUPA...............145
SUNKAWAKAN WAN................. 78
SUNKAWAKAN WANJILA........ 78
SUNKAWAKAN WANWICAYANKA
....240
SUNKAWAKAN WIN.................. 58
SUNKGLESKA............58,91,98,118,
...................123,146,221,281,310
SUNKGLESKA CIQALA.....119,282
SUNKGLESKA OTA............70,232
SUNKGLESKA WASTE.......127,290
SUNKGLESKA WIN....7,67,173,229
SUNKGLESKA YUHA.............14,86
SUNKGLISKA OTA....................130
SUNKGLIYOHI...........................282
SUNKGLIYOKI............................. 6
SUNKGMANITU WAKUWA...... 94
SUNKGMUNI 67
SUNKHIN SA 108,127,271
SUNKHINSA 9,13,21,71,83,
...........117,144,175,178,245,273,290
SUNKHINSA AGLI......................127
SUNKHINSA YUHA..8,174,308,317
SUNKHINTO 8,19,20,174,184
SUNKHINTO AGLI....................204
SUNKHINTO KNWA.................. 65
SUNKHINTO KUWA..................228
SUNKHINTO NUPA 96,265
SUNKHINTO YUHA............125,288
SUNKHINZI WIN...................60,223
SUNKHIYOHI 258,299
SUNKHIYOHIPI 10
SUNKHUNSA 144
SUNKICU 13,107,126,177,
....................178,271,292,298
SUNKITACAN AGLI 6,172
SUNKITESKA YUHA..................238
SUNKMANI............................... 14
SUNKMANITU GI..................... 174
SUNKMANITU IPIYAKA..........260
SUNKMANO SA.......................200
SUNKMANU... 180,288,291,296,319
SUNKMANU SA.......................36
SUNKMANUSA........................ 125
SUNKMUN................................304
SUNKNAKPO GI 287
SUNKNAKPOGI 293
SUNKNUNI 313
SUNKOKILE 213
SUNKOLE 16,49,89,143,251,
....252,307
SUNKOWA................................8,174
SUNKPA SKA YUHA................. 75
SUNKSAPA................................. 23
SUNKSKA 11,72,103,116,117,
....291,321
SUNKSKA AGLI................33,196
SUNKSKA OPI.............................65
SUNKSKA OTA WIN 295
SUNKSKA TAWA 118
SUNKSKA WICAO............... 78,240
SUNKSKA WIN 8,70,118,174,232
SUNKSKA YUHA......... 20,57,65,78,
....228,321
SUNKTACANKA......................110
SUNKTACANKU................ 176,315
SUNKTERILA 282
SUNKWAKAN WIN 221
SUNKWAKAW WIN 129
SUNSHINE 85,133,247,296
SUNSULA AGLI 215
SUNSULA SKA........................240
SUNSULA YUHA 250
SUNSUNLA AGLI 39
SUNSUNLA SA............................78
SUNSUNLA SAPA.................20,172
SUNSUNLA YUHA 88
SUNTAYA MANI 245
SUNYMANITU SKA 173
SURROUNDED......... 13,16,30,53,56,
76,87,110,115,120,121,122,144,178,
..196,202,217,220,238,248,273,278,
....283,285,308
SURROUNDED IN LODGE 130,293
SURROUNDED IN WOOD 146
SURROUNDED IN WOODS......310

Index

SURROUNDED KILLED 70,232
SUSIA 24
SUSIE 15,51,109,113,
         121,182,215,247,273,277,284
SUSUNI HAUNKA 293
SUSUNI KAUNKA 130
SUSUNI KTE 67,230
SUTA 221
SUTE SNI 62
SUWIAL KUTE 119
SUYOTANKA SAPA 129
SWALLOW 19,35,91,184,199,
.... 225,254
   Amelia 132,295
   Antoine 132,295
   Benjamin 295
   Benjamine 132
   Hattie 155,319
   Ida 132,295
   John 155,319
   Julia 132,295
   Louise 132
   Lucy 132
   May 132,295
   Oliver 132,295
   Susie 295
   Willie 132,295
SWEET BREATH, Myrtle 208
SWEET BUSTLE, Myrtle 45
SWIFT BIRD 9,175
   Marion 9,175
SWIFT CLOUD 87,248
SWIM FOR 276
SWIMMER 11,71,128,177,233,291
   John 71,233
SWIMS FOR 113
SWOLLEN FACE 43,207
SWORD
   Archie 172
   George 6,172
   Jessie 6,172
   Lucy 6,172
T. BEAR, John Alder 51
TA CANTE 218
TA OLE 289
TA OWICALE 126
TA RPAYA 59,223
TA SINA 231

TA TIYOPA 64
TA WASTE 150
TAAINA MAZA WIN 120
TAANPETU 12,17,34,178,182
TAANPETU TO 140,304
TAANPETU WASTE 298
TAANPITU WASTE 198
TACANGLESKA GI 292
TACANGLISKA ZI WIN 130
TACANKU ... 21,51,112,185,276,321
TACANKU OTA 116,279,284
TACANKU OTA WIN 121
TACANKU WASTE 13,21,36,78,
.... 149,185,193,200,313
TACANKU WASTE WIN 29,178
TACANNUPA OTA 214
TACANTE 55
TACANUPA 11,177
TACANUPA OTA 114,277
TACANUPA WAKAN 152,316
TACANUPA WANBLI 177
TACANUPA WASTE 46,209
TACUPA 20,184,185
TAHA SAKA 24
TAHALO 19,183
TAHU MAZA 115,278
TAHU RMI 274
TAHU RNI 110
TAHU WANICA 56,130,219,292
TAHUNI KOKIPESNI 245
TAHUNI OLE SNI 240
TAHUNSKA WASTE 275
TAIL 35,199
   John 199
TAIL WOMAN 72
TAINA WAKAN 257
TAININYA NAJI 231
TAINYA KU 230
TAINYA NAJI 232
TAINYAN 18,183
TAINYAN HINAPA 114,277
TAINYAN HIYAYA 154,318
TAINYAN KTE 73,100,235
TAINYAN KU 67,114,129
TAINYAN KU WIN 189,292
TAINYAN MANI 73
TAINYAN NAJIN 13,32,68,69,
.... 117,178

Index

TAINYAN NAJIN WIN 118
TAINYAN TI 38,93
TAINYAN WAKUWA 12,178
TAINYAN WICAKTE 73
TAINYAN YANKA 17,60,87,223,
.... 266
TAINYAN YANKE WIN 182
TAISTA 101,263
TAKA KUTE 171
TAKEN OFF 45,208
TAKES 76,239
TAKES AWAY 119,133,282,296
TAKES AWAY FROM ENEMY
.... 117,280
TAKES AWAY FROM THEM 134,297
TAKES AWAY TWICE 128,291
TAKES AWAY TWO 85,248
TAKES BLANKET 17,182
TAKES ENEMY 113,125,276,288
TAKES GUN 75,238
TAKES HER OWN 116,284
TAKES HIM IN 114,277
TAKES HORSE 126
TAKES HORSES 13,71,77,146,
.... 178,213,292
TAKES IT HARD 93,255
TAKES OUT AND KILLS 275
TAKES PITY 46,72,235,299
TAKES PITY ON THEM 149,313
TAKES ROBE 111,274
TAKES SHIELD 116,120,279,283
TAKES SPOTTED 52,216
TAKES THE EARTH 119,282
TAKES THE GUN 17,79,107,
.... 182,241,271
TAKES THE HORSE 11,107,177,271
TAKES THE HORSES 133,298
TAKES THINGS 70,233
TAKES WAR BONNET 67,230
TAKOLA WIN 8
TAKOLAKAI 252
TAKOLAKU OTA 174
TAKOLEAKU, Many Friends 8
TAKPE 154
TAKU KTE 16,181
TAKU OLI 266
TAKU YUHA 119
TAKUNI 133,296
TAKUNI KOKIPESNI 83
TAKUNI OHOLASNI 233
TAKUNI OKOLA SNI 70,71
TAKUNI OLE SHI 78
TAKUNI OLE SNI 207,315
TAKUNI OLESNI 43,151
TALKED ABOUT 96,257
TALKS ABOUT 10,43,121,
.... 132,175,207,295
TALKS ABOUT HER 114
TALKS ABOUT HIM 74,89,96,
.... 114,236,251,277
TALKS CHEYENNE 88,250
TALKS HOLY 117,280
TALKS OUTSIDE 64,226
TALKS PITIFUL 65,228
TALKS TO WHITE COW 132,295
TALKS TOO MUCH 44,193
TALKS WITH LIGHTNING .. 98,260
TALL 57,221
TALL GIRL 113,276
TALL WOMAN 17,30,39,54,83,
.... 149,194,203,218,235,245,313
TALL WOMAN #1 182
TALL WOMAN #2 182
TALO 148,312
TALO KAKSA 188
TANATAN 127
TANINYA 196
TANINYA KTE 261
TANINYA MANI 235
TANINYA NAJI 194
TANINYA TI 202
TANINYAN MANI 6
TANINYAN NAJIN 30,280
TANINYAN TI 255
TANINYANWIN 79
TANIYA KTE 235
TANKA MANI IYAYA 132
TANKA NUPA 232
TANKAL KUWA EYAYA 109
TANKAL MANI 294
TANKAL NAJIN 117,281
TANKAL TI 113,277
TANKAL WOGLAKA 64,226
TANKAYA WAKAWA 261
TANKAYA WAKUWA 99
TANYA KTE 213,216

TANYA KU 225
TANYAN HINAPA 9,175
TANYAN HUTE 119
TANYAN ICAGA 221
TANYAN KTE 46,209,283,311
TANYAN KUTEPI 58,221
TANYAN NAJIN WIN 281
TANYAN WIYUKCAN 143,307
TAOPI 21,64,107,141,185,
  227,247,249,271
TAOPI CIQALA 25,83,89,92,
  188,251,254
TAOPI GLI 93,255
TAOPI GLINAPA 255
TAOPI KTE 291
TAOPI OTA 8,21,22,45,54,117,
  174,186,208,280
TAOYANKE WASTE 220
TAOYANKE WASTE WIN 123
TAPANKESKA 17,40
TAPI SAGYE 70,232
TARCA 31,86,195,249,259
TARCA CINCALA 15
TARCA GI 152,316
TARCA HA 30,194
TARCA HINAPA 115,278
TARCA IYANKA 151,315
TARCA LUTA 70,184,217,233
TARCA NITE 111,275
TARCA SA 20,54
TARCA SAPA .. 133,134,284,296,297
TARCA SKA 13,86,179,248
TARCA SUNKALA SAPA 121
TARCA WIN 12,24,59,115,121,
  123,278,284,286
TARCA WION 189
TARCAHA WIKAN 139
TARCAQHA WIKAN 303
TASINA
  68,101,110,134,141,177,262,274,297,
  305
TASINA LUTA 203
TASINA LUTA WIN 39
TASINA MANI 295
TASINA MAZA 132
TASINA MAZA WIN 283
TASINA NUPA 77,240
TASINA OTA 21,114,185

TASINA RLECAHAN 70
TASINA SAPA 274
TASINA WAKAN 17,95,124,201,
  252,284
TASINA WAKAN WIN 90,182
TASINA WAMBLI 273
TASINA WANBLI ... 12,122,177,285
TASINA WANYANKAPI 253
TASINA WASTE 228,277
TASINA WASTE WIN 66
TASINA WAYANKAPI 91
TASINA ZI 73,115,236,278
TASPAN 18,182
TASPAN SAPA 39,203
TASPAU 175
TASUNEK WAKAN 252
TASUNKA CIQALA 320
TASUNKA MAZA 107
TASUNKA OYATE 95
TASUNKA SKA 227
TASUNKAWAKAN 225
TASUNKE 7,19,31,77,94,95,
  108,146,173,183,184,240,256,
  257,272,279,292,310
TASUNKE AGLI 222
TASUNKE AGLIPI 58
TASUNKE CIQALA 20,126,156,
  184,289
TASUNKE EHAKE 307
TASUNKE EHAKELA 24,46,97,
  143,188,259
TASUNKE GLESKA 70,232,289
TASUNKE GLESKA WIN 126
TASUNKE GLIYUNKA 41
TASUNKE HETON 108
TASUNKE HIN SA 221
TASUNKE HIN TO 253
TASUNKE HINAPA 71,95,234,
  257,279
TASUNKE HINROTA 52,213,216
TASUNKE HINSA .. 57,141,144,195,
  204,234,305,308
TASUNKE HINTO WIN 86
TASUNKE HINZI 10,46,88,125,
  175,189,250,287
TASUNKE HIYCHIPI 53
TASUNKE HIYOHI 216
TASUNKE HOTAN 277

Index

TASUNKE HOTON 113
TASUNKE INAJIN 60,224
TASUNKE INYAKA 231
TASUNKE INYANKA 12,199,266
TASUNKE INYANKE 250
TASUNKE IYANKA 10,14,35,68,
.... 88,90
TASUNKE IYANKE 88
TASUNKE IYUNKA 205
TASUNKE KINYELA15,78,180,240,
.... 321
TASUNKE KOKIPAPI 104,107,
.... 113,271
TASUNKE KPAZO 26,189
TASUNKE KU 321
TASUNKE LUTA 31
TASUNKE LUTA WIN 222
TASUNKE LUZA 157
TASUNKE LUZAHAN....6,25,89,99,
.... 135,188,189,251,260
TASUNKE LUZAHAQN 172
TASUNKE MANI 276
TASUNKE MATO 122
TASUNKE MAZA 233
TASUNKE MAZA ..35,45,70,95,102,
124,171,199,208,257,264,271,272,287
Iron Horse 5
TASUNKE NAJIN 111,112,
.... 275,276,293
TASUNKE NUPA 71,95,112,133,
.... 234,257,275,309
TASUNKE OPI11,25,37,38,43,56,66,
111,112,123,124,125,130,134,151,177
,188,195,200,202,206,228,267,274,
... 275,286,287,288,293,297,309,315
TASUNKE OPI WANYANKA....224
TASUNKE OPI WAYANKA........ 61
TASUNKE OPI WIN.................... 145
TASUNKE OTA... 17,22,33,37,42,63,
97,109,110,128,135,183,186,201,205,
226,259,272,274,286,291,298
TASUNKE OTA WIN 58,123
TASUNKE OTAWIN 196,221
TASUNKE OYESPAPI 221
TASUNKE OYUSPAPI 57
TASUNKE SICA 124,296
TASUNKE SICA WIN 133
TASUNKE SKA 41,64,205,281

TASUNKE T NAJIN 30
TASUNKE TAINYAN MANI 67
TASUNKE TANINYA NAJI 194
TASUNKE TOKAHEYA 281
TASUNKE TOKEY HIYAYA 202
TASUNKE TOKEYA H 38
TASUNKE TOKEYA IYAN 118
TASUNKE TOKEYA IYANK 118
TASUNKE TUNUS 213
TASUNKE WAKAN 64,72,77,89,93,
.....96,226,234,240,251,255,257,284
TASUNKE WAKAN WIN 90
TASUNKE WAKITA 43,50,131,
.... 132,151,295,315
TASUNKE WAKUWA 35,40
TASUNKE WAMBLI 7,233
TASUNKE WAMNIOMNI.......... 109
TASUNKE WANAN 121
TASUNKE WANBLI........ 21,71,131,
.... 173,185
TASUNKE WANGLAKA 202
TASUNKE WANICA 102,264
TASUNKE WANJILA.......... 240,286
TASUNKE WANKATUYA .. 77,134,
.... 239,297
TASUNKE WANYANKAPI 261
TASUNKE WASTE30,37,70,71,72,88,
99,100,126,128,135,153,201,207,228,
232,233,235,249,250,261,289,291,
.... 298,314,317
TASUNKE WASTE WIN 43,66,
.... 120,126,150,283
TASUNKE WATAKPE 199
TASUNKE WAYANKA............... 185
TASUNKE WAYANKAPI . 21,25,38,
.... 99,125,186,189,288
TASUNKE WESARCA 257
TASUNKE WICARCA 95,257
TASUNKE WICASA 118
TASUNKE WICOPI 100
TASUNKE WIN 116
TASUNKE WITKO .. 71,139,234,303
TASUNKE WOPOTEPI 67
TASUNKE YUHAPI 72
TASUNKE YUKAN 24,188
TASUNKEAGLI 116
TASUNKEAJAKE 259
TASUNL 18

Index

TASUPKE CIQALA 125
TATA WABLUSKA 127
TATANK WICOTA 178
TATANKA 18,95,118,257
TATANKA CANGLESKA ... 123,286
TATANKA CANTE SICA.... 123,286
TATANKA CATKA.... 76,91,239,254
TATANKA CIQALA 15,31,52,56,66,
.. 107,120,132,133,195,220,228,266,
.... 283,294,295,296
TATANKA GI 100,101,102,
.... 253,262,263
TATANKA GNASKINYAN 101
TATANKA HANSKA
.... 19,71,91,110,143,
.... 198,234,253,273,307
TATANKA HAUSKA 34
TATANKA HE LUTA 125
TATANKA HELUTA 288
TATANKA HOTANIN MANI 274
TATANKA HUNKE SNI 75
TATANKA HUNKESNI 238
TATANKA HUSTE 55,218
TATANKA ISNALA 153,317
TATANKA ISTA 103,264
TATANKA ITE SKA 101,201,262
TATANKA IYOTAKA 21,186
TATANKA KTE 194
TATANKA KTEPI 30
TATANKA LUTA 60,118,125,
.... 224,288
TATANKA MANI 98,259
TATANKA MATO.... 84,196,246,254
TATANKA MAZA.... 42,135,206,297
TATANKA NAJIN 185
TATANKA NATA 96,117,280
TATANKA NUPA 24,69,188,231
TATANKA OHITIKA 124,287
TATANKA OTE SKA 37
TATANKA PAPYA MNI 110
TATANKA PSICA 121,284
TATANKA PTECELA 120,134,
.... 180,283,296
TATANKA PTESELA 15
TATANKA SAPA 39,203
TATANKA SINTE 31
TATANKA SITE 194,195
TATANKA SKA 31,34,195,198

TATANKA SKA KAGA 216
TATANKA SLASLA 107,271
TATANKA TAMAHECA 66,228
TATANKA WACIPI 60,224
TATANKA WAJIN 21
TATANKA WAKA 250
TATANKA WAKAN 53,88,101,
.... 216,263
TATANKA WAKINYAN 85
TATANKA WANAGI 25,189
TATANKA WANBLI 49,50,214
TATANKA WANKATUYA 12
TATANKA WAPAHA 38,202,241
TATANKA WASTE 33,64,197,
.... 209,241
TATANKA WICASA 86,261
TATANKA WICOTI 13
TATANKA WITKO 124,262,287
TATANKAN WAKINYAN 247
TATANKE CIQALA 271
TATANKE LUTA 281
TATASNKA WANKATUYA 177
TATE PEJUTA 72
TATE RMU WIN 182
TATE SINA 38,58,202
TATE SINA WIN 298
TATE WAKAN 235
TATESNA 17
TATESNA WIN 17
TATIYOPA 10,146,176,310
TATIYOPA WAKAN 107,271
TAUNSKE WACARCA 95
TAWA AGLI 22,60,186
TAWA IKI HCE 116
TAWA IKIKCU 284
TAWA KTE 10,57,221
Tawa 176
TAWACIN WASTE 58,70,140,
.... 221,304
TAWAKIN 140,304,305
TAWANBLI 11
TAWANIBLI 195
TAWAPAHA 126,289
TAWASTE 107,271,314
TAWAWBLI 31
TAWICINCALA 38,201
TAWIYAKA WASTE 151,315
TAWUNKE 129

414

Index

TAYAN HINAPA 14
TAYAN KTE ... 15,53,58,120,147,256
TAYAN KU 62
TAZUNKE IYANKE 178
TAZUSKA 216
TE TANI 199
TE WAKAN 208,235
TE WEGNA 256
TEANA KETAN 232
TEGLAKA WASTE 223
TEHAN GLI SNI 130,293
TEHAN RPAYA 66,229
TELLS HER 79,190
TELLS HER NAME 18,182
TELLS HERSELF 112,276
TELLS HIM 124,287
TELLS HIS NAME 33,197
TELLS LIES 92,254
TEN FINGERS 112,275
TENDER 155,319
TERILA 131
TERILAPI 68,127,230,289,294
TERIYA ICU 93,255
TERIYA KTE 110,122,274,285
TERIYA KTE SNI 127,290
TERIYA KU 116,279,304
TERIYA MANI 83,124,287
TERMUGA 19,184
TERMUGA LUTA 111,275
TERRAPIN 102,264
TERROPIN LIGHTS 35,199
TEZI 22,71,75,237
TEZI RIECAHAN 113
TEZI SKA 33,38,39,195,197,202
TEZI TANKA 127,290
TEZI WIN 282
TEZI YURLECAPI 276
THANKFUL 130,293
THAYER, Minnie 104,322
THE HEAD 5,171
THICK BRAID 24,188
THICK BREAD 56,219
THINKING 52,216
THINKS WELL, Julia 143,307
THOMAS 18,183
   Lucy 95,262
   Mary 96,258
   Rosa 96,258

THREE 36,199
THREE BEARS, Thomas 23
THREE STARS 145,309
   Clarence 145,310
   Eva 145,309
   Harry 145,309
   Jennie 145,310
   Jessie 145,309
   Louise 145,310
   Lucy 145,309
   Martha 309
   Paul 145,310
   Sallie 309
   Sally 145
   Sophia 145,310
   Susie 145,309
THREE WOMAN 227
THREE WOMEN 64
THRICE
   Alfred D 91
   Edward D 91
THROAT 51,215
THROWS HER VOICE 19,184
THROWS HIM 32,196
THUNDER 79,241
   Andrew Y 263
   Asa C 240
   Brave Y 263
   Charles F 227
   Columbus C 240
   Earth F 227
   Jennie F 227
   Lizzie P 239
   Louise C 141,305
   Sophia C 240
THUNDER BEAR
   Alice 51,215
   Jno Alder 215
   John 51,215
   Julia 51,215
   Victoria 51,215
THUNDER BEARD 120,283
   Emma 120
   Lizzie 120
THUNDER BULL
   Charlie 85
   Chas 247
   Joseph 85

Index

Shield 85
Susie 85
THUNDER CLUB 122,285
THUNDER ELK 19,133,184,296
THUNDER HAWK ... 40,139,203,303
   Charles 43,206
   Eva 304
   Fannie 42,206
   Joseph 43,206
   Martin 42,206
   Mary 40,197
THUNDER HORSE 49,213
THUNDER NATION 229
THUNDER ROBE 131,294
THUNDER ROCK 227
THUNDER ROPE 54,209
THUNDER TAIL 133,295
THUNDER TRAVELER 20,185
THUNDER WOMAN .... 104,108,265, ... 272
TI EL KTE 117
TI KIYELA 209
TI TANI 35
TI WEGNA 94
TI WICAKTE 115
TIANATAN 69,124,287,290
TIAPA WICAKTE 16
TIAPAWICAKTE 181
TIBBETS
   Ben 85
   Emily 87
   Susie 85
TIBBETTS, Susie 157
TIBBITTS
   Benj 247
   Emily 248
   Susie 247
   Thomas 247
TIBLOKE OTA 120
TIBLOKU 135
TIBLOKU OTA .... 35,78,121,240, ... 284,298
TIBLOPU OTA 199
TICAGLA INYANKA 273
TICAGLA IYANKA 296
TICAGLA KTE 278,280,298
TIGLAKE ... 7,32,93,153,172,173,255
TIGLAKE WASTE 37,59,201
TIGLISNI 34,198
TIKANYELA 133,149
TIKANYELA IYANKA .... 16,110, ... 131,294
TIKANYELA KTE ...... 61,78,96,241, ... 257
TIKANYELA KUWA 119
TIKANYELA WAKUWA ... 109,272, ... 282
TIKANYLA WAKIWA 120
TIKAUYELA IYANKA 283
TIMA NAJI 263
TIMA WAKITA 241
TIMAHEL HIYU OKIHI 64
TIMAHEL MANI 279
TIMAHEL TI 123,286
TIMAHEL WICAKTE 85
TIMAHEL YANKA 118,281
TIMAHEL YOU OKIHISNI 227
TIMBER 90,252
TIMBER BANK 44,207
TINAHEL NAJIN 102
TINAHEL YANKA 57
TINGA 36,134,200
TINGLESKA 180,288
TINOPA 19
TINPSILA TANKA 66,229
TINYATA WOTA 112
TIOKTE 32
TIOLE 238,296
TIONAJINYAPI 130,293
TIOTAWIN 277
TIOWICAKTE 51,196,215
TIPI 30,38,89,194,202,251
TIPI IKCEYA 10
TIPI LUTA .... 10,66,109,112,120, ... 276,299
TIPI MAZA 273
TIPI OTA 149
TIPI RLA 124
TIPI RLA WIN 96
TIPI RLO WIN 287
TIPI SA 229
TIPI SKA 14
TIPI SKA WIN 179
TIPI TANKA 9,175
TIPI WAKAN .... 44,61,70,73,129, ... 224,233

Index

TIPI WAKITA 290
TIPI WANBLI 45,208
TIPI WANKATUYA 116,279
TIPI WASTE 124,288
TIPI WAYANKA 113
TIPI WIN 123
TIPI YUHA 22,187
TIPI ZI 43
TIPI ZI WIN 176
TIRLA 258
TISINA 245
TITAN OPI 135,298
TIWEGNA IYANKA 113,276
TIWICAKTE 22
TIWICARILA 240
TIYATA WOTA 275
TIYOPA 123,134,183,296,299
TIYOPA LUTA 58,98,260
TIYOPA TAWAY 226
TIYOPA WASTE 37,201
TIZI 207
TO OBTAIN 113
TO WAKAN 292
TOAPI WICAKTE 128
TOBACCO 108,122,285
   Adam 108,272
TOBLOKU OTA 77
TOCAGLA IYANKA 181
TOHA OYUSPA 16
TOHICUN 201
TOK HUWA 14
TOK KUTE 5,6,9
TOKA 144,308
TOKA APA 89,251
TOKA APAPI 131,294
TOKA ICU 113,125,276,288
TOKA KAGA 70,177,233
TOKA KAHINRPEYA 60,236
TOKA KICO 61,224
TOKA KINWA 280
TOKA KOKIPA 90,252,290
TOKA KOKIPAPI 14,127
TOKA KTE 13,16,17,25,41,113,
   114,117,128,129,139,148,179,181,
         205,230,277,280,291,304,312
TOKA KTE WIN 189,292
TOKA KU 184
TOKA KUTE 108,172,175,209
TOKA KUWA 52,72,98,216,235,
.... 260
TOKA OLE 67,96,112,127,
.... 230,258,275,290
TOKA OPI 11,73,236
TOKA OYUSPA 31,116,126,
.... 130,259,279,289
TOKA OYUSPE 181,292
TOKA OYUSTA 98
TOKA SLIPA 83,245
TOKA TAKPE 117
TOKA TASUNKE AWICA 75
TOKA TASUNKE AWICAGLI .. 238
TOKA WASTE 68,114,126,230,
.... 277,289
TOKA WAYNKAPI 51
TOKA WICAKI 117,280
TOKA WICAKTA 67
TOKA WICAKTE 67,113,276,277
TOKA WICAKU 19
TOKAHEYA 54,217,238,285
TOKAHEYA WIN 178
TOKAHIYA 247
TOKALA 111,274,304
TOKALA NIGE 247
TOKALA SAPA 61,224
TOKALA WANBLI 30,194
TOKALA WIN 174
TOKANL IGLAKE 229
TOKATA HIYU 290
TOKATAKIYA 84,246
TOKEYA 117,183,280
TOKEYA HINAPA 111,120,179,
.... 275,283
TOKEYA HIYAYA 72,90
TOKEYA IHUNI 89,90,251
TOKEYA INYAKA 220
TOKEYA INYANKA 30,194
TOKEYA KET 109
TOKEYA KIHUNI 109
TOKEYA KTE ... 13,49,67,70,76,112,
..119,133,141,150,179,229,233,239,
240,266,273,275,282,285,295,305,314
TOKEYA KU 76,239
TOKEYA KUTE 69,232
TOKEYA MANI 53,69,99,
.... 119,217,232,282
TOKEYA NAJI 196

417

Index

TOKEYA NAJIN 32
TOKEYA SHUNI 252
TOKEYA WICAKTE 78,122
TOKEYA WIN 13,16
TOKEYA YA 234
TOKICEM 265
TOKICUN 52,57,67,77,85,90,
.... 122,221,240,247,252
TOKUNI OHOLASNI 233
TOLD TO HER 71,233
TONKA WIN 273
TONKAN YANKE WIN 282,283
TONKANWIN 275
TONKAU WIN 309
TONWAN 13,179
TONWEYA 7,22,54,55,66,124,
.... 127,219,287,290
TONWEYA CIQALA 76,101,103,239
TONWEYA GLI. 8,10,75,97,122,144,
.... 174,176,285,308
TONWEYA KTE 22,186
TONWEYA LUTA 295
TONWEYA SA 132
TONWEYA WIN 51,73,321
TONWICA OTA 216
TOP BEAR 98,260
    Fred 102
    Hugh 99,261
    Jessie 102,263
    Red 263
TOPA 113
TOPA CANUPA 34,197
TOPA HUNKA WIN 181
TOPA OYNSPA 195
TOPA WACI CANUPA 16
TOPA WIN 182
TOPLA 276
TOPO KAKSA 24
TORN BELLY 113,276
TOTA WABLUSKA 290
TOUCHES PINE 39,203
TOWAN WIN 109
TOWEYA WIN 235
TOYANKE 286
TOYANKE LUTA 285
TRACK 56,220
TRAVELER 7,173
    Benj 12

Beny 177
TREE LEG 114,277
TRIBE 315
TRIBE EAGLE 40,204
TRIBE HAWK 52,53,216,217
TROUBLE IN FRONT 151,315
TROUBLESOME HAWK 40,204
    Bessie 204
TRUTH 77
TSTA GI 199
TSUNKE NUPA 295
TTANKA 281
TUCUHU 6
TUCUHU WACASA 242
TUCUHU WICASA 33,241
TUCUKU 172
TUGA 73,235
TUNKANYANKE WIN 79
TUNRING HOLY, Henry 321
TUNRS BACK 285
TUNWEYA 218
TUNWEYA CIQALA 264
TUNWEYA CIQQLA 262
TUNWEYA GLI 238,247
TURNING BEAR 116,280
TURNING HAWK
    Charles 249
    Hobart 86,249
    Philamena 249
    Philomena 86
TURNING HOLY, Henry 63
TURNS 38,213
TURNS BACK 65,122,228
TURNS OVER 85,247
TURTLE 125,288
TUWINCU OTA 52
TWAY
    Emma 62,321
    Mary 321
    Nora 62
    Norah 321
    Thomas 62,321
TWEICARILA 78
TWIN 8,14,174,179
    Fred 140,304
    Reuben 140,304
TWINE 95,257
TWISS

Index

Adelia 203
Charles 79,241
Clara 241
Fannie 29,193
Flowrence 241
Frank 29,39,193,203
James 29,193
Jesse 241
Joseph 39,203
Louise 241
Maggie 29,193
Mary 39,203
Nellie 77,239
Rosella 29,193
Stella Dora 242
Thomas 29,193
William 29,242
TWIST
   Emma 103,264
   Henry 103,264
   John 103,264
   Louis 103,264
TWISTED WOOD 18,182
TWO 40,204
TWO ARROWS 64,118,226,281
TWO BEARS 21,185
TWO BLUE HORSES 96,265
TWO BONNET 22
TWO BONNETE 189
TWO BULL
   Anna 231
   Mary 231
TWO BULLS 24,188
   Amos 69,231
   Anna 69
   Charles 232
   Joseph 69,232
   Mary 69
TWO COMES AFTER HER . 130,293
TWO CROW, John 98,260
TWO CROWS 98,260
TWO DOGS 98,259
   Alice 98,260
   Jacob 260
   Jenna 98
   Lizzie 98,260
   Oscar 85,247
TWO EAGLE 22,110,127,186,274

   John 186
TWO EAGLES 290
TWO ELK 46,139,242,304
   Bessie 140,304
   Gerald 140
   James 140,304
   Julia 7,173
   Nellie 140
   Nettie 140,304
   Richard 26,189
   Robert 140,304
   Thomas 140,304
TWO FACE 18,183
TWO FACES 116,279
TWO FEATHER 183
TWO FEATHERS 18,68,231
TWO HILLS 130,293
TWO HORSE 133,295
TWO HORSES 71,112,145,234,
.... 275,309
TWO LANCE, Thomas 49,213
TWO LANCE, JR 49,213
TWO LANCE, SR 49,213
TWO MONTHS 275
TWO MOUTHS 111
TWO NOSTRILS 140,304
TWO STANDS 109,273
TWO STICKS, John 21,185
TWO TAIL, Charles 86
TWO TAILS
   Ada 32,196
   Charles 249
   Thomas 86,249
TWO TWO 60,224
   Alexander 61,224
   Eagle 61,224
   Jennie 61,224
   Joseph 61,224
   Mary 77,240
   Richard 61,224
TWO WAR BONNET 126
TWO WAR BONNETS 289
TWO WHITE COWS
.... 45,53,64,68,208,217,
.... 227,230
TWO WOMAN 22
TYON
   Adelia 134,297

Index

Eliza 134,297
Elizabeth 134,297
Oliver 134,297
Susie 134,297
Thomas 134,297
TYOPA LUTA 221
U T BAGGAGE
   Alice 205
   Susie 205
UNBRAIDED 24
UNDER T. BAGGAGE, Alice 41
UNDER THE BAGGAGE 41,205
UNKAKAPA 79,241
UPIJATA 312
USED ARROW 112,276
USES BOW 14,179
USES HER LANCE 114,277
USES HIS BOW 111,274
VANE WOMAN 23
VLANDRY
   Emma 152,316
   Hattie 152,316
   Jennie 152,316
   Minnie 23,322
   Owen H 152,316
   Robert C 152,316
   Sadie 152,316
   William 152,316
VOICE ABOVE 134,297
VOICE IN SIGHT 31,195
VOICE ON TOP 76,239
W EAGLE 278
WA IWOBLU 122
WA[OSTAN LUTA 277
WAAGI WITKO 230
WABKAL TI 93
WABLISKA ZI 63
WABLUSKA GI 321
WABLUSKA TIYOSLOLA 57,220
WABLUSKA WASTE 250
WABLUSKWASTE 88
WACAKIZE 227
WACAPA 38,96,97,102,
.... 202,258,259,264
WACARPI 52
WACI HIYAYA 93
WACI YA 255
WACICU CIQALA 264

WACIHIN ANATAN 247
WACIHIN WASTE 208
WACINCALA 183
WACINHIN 66
WACINHIN ANATAN 85
WACINHIN LUTA 96,258
WACINHIN MAZA 67,230
WACINHIN SKA 71,234
WACINHIN WASTE 44
WACINKO 64,72,227,229
WACINWAPI 217
WACINYAPI 53,93,255
WACISU WINYAN 260
WAGLE MOCCASIN 221
WAGLEKSUN LUTA 141,305
WAGLURE 91,253,287,312
WAGLYRE 148
WAGMEZA 33
WAGMEZA APE 24
WAGMU 18,183
WAGMU SU . 39,43,114,203,206,278
WAGMY SU 203
WAGNEZA 197
WAGNUKA 79,241
WAGNUNI 53
WAGYE WAKAN 60
WAHA PARPA 115
WAHACANKA 10,58,96,176,
.... 204,221,222,258,310
WAHACANKA CIQALA 126,289
WAHACANKA GI 50,214
WAHACANKA ICU116,120,279,283
WAHACANKA INYAKA 213
WAHACANKA IYANKA 49
WAHACANKA MARPIYA 11
WAHACANKA MAZA 110,298
WAHACANKA SNA 45,208
WAHACANKA TO 12,178
WAHACANKA WAKCUWA 33
WAHACANKA WAKUWA 37
WAHACANKA WANBLI 36
WAHACANKA WARPIYA 10
WAHACANKA WASTE 57,108,
.... 117,122,209,213,280,285
WAHACANKA WICARCA .. 31,196,
.... 198
WAHACANKA WICARCALA 32
WAHACANKA WIN 196

Index

WAHACANKE WICARCA 34
WAHACANKU WASTER 220
WAHACANKUWA 37
WAHACAUKA 40
WAHACAUKA WANBLI 36
WAHACAUKA WICARCA 31
WAHAHA WICAKU 229
WAHANCANKA WAKUWA 201
WAHANCANKA WICARCA 195
WAHAPARPA 278,312
WAHASANKA WAKUWA 197
WAHINKPE NUPA 226
WAHINKPE ON KUTE 296
WAHINKPE OTA 152
WAHINKPE SKA 49,213
WAHINKPE WICAKU 134
WAHINKPELYANAJINCA 121
WAHINYAN GI 263
WAHINYAN WASTE 83
WAHLEN, James 171
WAHORPI LUTA ... 132,145,295,309
WAHOSI GLI 126,289
WAHOSI HI 108
WAHOSIGLI 272
WAHUKEYA WASTE 296
WAHUKEZA 39,113,203,276
WAHUKEZA KICUN 114,277
WAHUKEZA NUPA 49,213
WAHUKEZA SKA 99,261
WAHUKEZA WANBLI 123,286
WAHUKEZA WASTE 49,133
WAHUKEZA WIN 20,316
WAHUKEZA ZI 145,309
WAHUWAPA LUTA 128,291
WAHUWAPA SICA 15,180
WAICU 70,233
WAINYAN WASTE 224
WAIT FOR HIM 116,279
WAJAJA 112,275
WAKACANKA 146
WAKACANKA WASTE 108
WAKAN GLI 17,84,110,182,
.... 246,274
WAKAN HINAPA 13,24,38,40,
.... 109,178,202,204
WAKAN HIYAGA 129
WAKAN HIYAYA 111,272,275
WAKAN HOKSILA 77
WAKAN IYOTAKA 15,24,51
WAKAN IYOTOKA 15
WAKAN KOYAKA 240
WAKAN LECALA 75,238
WAKAN MAHEL WAYANKA
.... 151,315
WAKAN MANI 71,233,240
WAKAN NAHOMNI 63,321
WAKAN NAJI 224
WAKAN NAJIN 61,118,281
WAKAN OTA 123
WAKAN WACI 174
WAKAN WACIPI 8
WAKAN WAGLAKA 117
WAKAN WIN 19,195
WAKANYA YANKA 215
WAKANYAN WASTE 62
WAKAU WIN 175
WAKICAGE WIN 312
WAKIL HINAPA 70,99,233,260
WAKIL NAJI 195,207
WAKIN 144,308
WAKIN ORLATE 41,205
WAKINLA SKA 100,262
WAKINYA 241
WAKINYA CIQALA 259
WAKINYA HANSKA 239
WAKINYA LUZAHAN 220
WAKINYA OYATE 229
WAKINYA PETA 214,227
WAKINYA SKA 197,198
WAKINYA TAMAHE 239
WAKINYA TAMAHECA 239
WAKINYA TASUNKE 213
WAKINYA WAKUWA 227
WAKINYA WANBLI 225
WAKINYA WASTE 225
WAKINYA WITKO 225
WAKINYA YUHA 231
WAKINYAN 79
WAKINYAN CIQALA 97,120,283
WAKINYAN GI .. 98,99,101,260,263
WAKINYAN KOKIPAPI 154
WAKINYAN KTEPI 121
WAKINYAN LUZAHAN 56
WAKINYAN MARPIUYA 276
WAKINYAN MARPIYA 113
WAKINYAN OMANI 20,185

WAKINYAN OPWOGLAKA 260
WAKINYAN PETA 19,50,147,
.... 154,184,311,318
WAKINYAN PTEA 64
WAKINYAN PUTINHIN 120,283
WAKINYAN SINTE 133,295
WAKINYAN SKA 34
WAKINYAN TACANKSA...122,285
WAKINYAN TAMAHECA 76
WAKINYAN TASINA 131,294
WAKINYAN TASUNKE 49
WAKINYAN TONWANPI 98
WAKINYAN WANAGI 122
WAKINYAN WANGI 285
WAKINYAN WASTE 60,246
WAKINYAN WATAKPE 65,141,
.... 240,305
WAKINYAN WATAKPI 77
WAKINYAN WICAKTE 284
WAKINYAN WIKAN 54
WAKINYAN WIKAU 209
WAKINYAN WIN .. 104,108,265,272
WAKINYAN WITKO 62
WAKINYAN YUHA 68
WAKITA 62,225,266
WAKIYA HANSKA 76
WAKPA OINKPA 311
WAKPALA CIQALA 107,271
WAKPAMINALA 275
WAKPAMNILA 108,112,272
WAKSICA KARLECA 265
WAKSICA KERLECA 103
WAKSICA LUTA 130
WAKTE GLI 32,112,276
WAKTEKA 313
WAKUKEZA WIN 152
WAKUN 74
WAKUWA 312,318
WAKUWA KTE 184
WALK HARD, Edward 245
WALK OUT 294
WALKING 20,117,185,280
WALKING DAY 65,228
WALKING DOG 71,234
WALKING ELK 114,119,277,282
WALKING HAIL 123,285
WALKING HOLY 240
WALKING HORSE 276

WALKING RAIN 62,225
WALKING SHAWL 132,295
WALKING WHITE COW 125,288
WALKING WOMAN 89,251
WALKS 85,247
WALKS AHEAD 232
WALKS FAST 99,261
   George 100,261
   Good Bird 261
   Red Ears 261
   Thomas 100
   Thos 267
WALKS FIRST 53,69,217,232
WALKS HARD 124,287
   Edward 83
WALKS HOLY 71,233
WALKS IN CENTER 121,284
WALKS IN LODGE 279
WALKS IN SIGHT 6,73,235
WALKS ON, Susie 45,208
WALKS ON HIM 100,251
WALKS ON ROCK 99,260
WALKS OUT 132
WALKS U GROUND
   Alice 198
   Amos 198
   Jacob 266
   Joshaway 198
WALKS U. GROUND
   Amos 34
   Jacob 52
WALKS UNDER GROUND .. 34,198
   Wm 52,216
WALKS WITH PIPE 76,154,318
WALKS WITH RED... 66,96,228,258
WALKS WITH WHITE COW 55,219
WAMBLI 218,223
WAMBLI CANGLESKA 237
WAMBLI CANTE 248
WAMBLI CIQALA 231,237
WAMBLI CUWIGNAKA 236
WAMBLI GLESKA 238,252,258
WAMBLI GLESKA CIQALA 261
WAMBLI HANPA 221
WAMBLI HETO 234
WAMBLI HETON 248
WAMBLI HINAPA 277,283
WAMBLI HOKSILA 232

Index

WAMBLI IYOTAKA............256,266
WAMBLI KOKIPAPI 9
WAMBLI KOYAKA...............8,232
WAMBLI LUTA 234,257,265,281
WAMBLI NACA.................241,247
WAMBLI NOPA 7
WAMBLI NUPA 274
WAMBLI OGLE 222
WAMBLI OHITIKA 246,256,261
WAMBLI OKITIKA 246
WAMBLI ORANKO 248
WAMBLI OTA....................238,262
WAMBLI OYATE 232
WAMBLI OYE...........................238
WAMBLI PAHA 265
WAMBLI ROTA 7
WAMBLI SAPA.........................223
WAMBLI SI 236
WAMBLI SKA...........................273
WAMBLI SUN.............8,13,261,273
WAMBLI SUN PEJUTS 239
WAMBLI TACANUPA .201,233,235
WAMBLI TASMA 241
WAMBLI TIPI............................238
WAMBLI WAHANCANKA........200
WAMBLI WAKAN..............205,236
WAMBLI WAKUWA..................266
WAMBLI WANKATUYA...........225
WAMBLI WASTE 9,201,276
WAMBLI WATAPKI..................247
WAMBLI WICARPI 260
WAMBLI WICASA 227
WAMBLI WIN............................. 10
WAMBLI WINYA 230
WAMBLI WINYAN 232
WAMBLI YATAPIKA.................274
WAMNI HIYUICIYA 91
WAMNIOMNI 6,14,34,52,55,
.... 113,141,147,172,179,276,309
WAMNIOMNI HINAPA............... 57
WAMNIOMNI HUNKU 44
WAMNIOMNI KOYAKA34,296,308
WAMNIOMNI KOYAKE............134
WAMNIOMNI LUZAHAN 56,100
WAMNIOMNI SA 110
WAMNIOMNI SAPA 53,114,277
WAMNIOMNI SKA..........22,99,186
WAMNIOMNI TASUNKE..........273

WAMNIOMNI TO................. 25,188
WAMNIOMNI WICASA 109
WAMNIONMNI KOYAKA........144
WAMNIYAMNI HUNKU...........208
WAMNIYOMNI 198,217,219
WAMNIYOMNI KOYAKA........197
WAMNIYOMNI LUZAHAN219,262
WAMNIYOMNI SAPA 217
WAMNIYOMNI SKA 261
WAMNIYOMNI WIN 220
WAMNYOMNI SAPA 216
WAN AGLI............................ 77,239
WAN ICARYA 62,225
WAN IYANAJINCA 284
WAN KICUN...................... 112,276
WAN NUP 281
WAN NUPA................................. 64
WAN ON OPI 54,97,134,218
WAN ONOPI 259
WAN OPI 196
WAN OTA 316,317
WAN TAOPI......................... 72,234
WAN WICAQU 297
WANAGI 64,65,227
WANAGI KUTE........................232
WANAGI TOKEYA 37,201
WANAGI WICAKUTE 69
WANAGI WITKO 68
WANAPA GLI............... 146,173,310
WANAPA GLICU 93
WANAPA IYANKA............. 126,289
WANAPIN LUTA................... 36,200
WANARON 8
WANBLI 21,22,25,53,54,59,60,
..107,115,129,185,186,216,217,223,
.... 271,278,292,293
WANBLI CANTE..........................87
WANBLI CEPA 131
WANBLI CINCALA 34,125,197,
....288
WANBLI CIQALA 23,68,75,146,
....310
WANBLI CONICA................. 26,189
WANBLI CUWIGNAKA 74,150,
....314
WANBLI GI................................317
WANBLI GLESKA 18,76,89,90,
.... 97,153,317

Index

WANBLI GLESKA CIQALA 99
WANBLI GLI 153
WANBLI HANPA 58
WANBLI HE 36,200
WANBLI HETON 20,86,185,293
WANBLI HINAPA 34,113,120,198
WANBLI HOKSILA 69,222,293
WANBLI ISNALA 14,179
WANBLI ITE 36,216
WANBLI IYANKA 126
WANBLI IYANKE 289
WANBLI IYOPATAKA 94
WANBLI IYOTAKA 57,221
WANBLI KOKIPA 175
WANBLI KOYAKA .... 36,69,174, ... 188,200
WANBLI LUTA .... 13,18,71,95, ... 118,147,178,183,265,311
WANBLI NAPE 49
WANBLI NAPI 213
WANBLI NUPA. 22,110,127,186,290
WANBLI OGLE 58
WANBLI OHITIKA 84,94,100
WANBLI OHITKA 94
WANBLI ORANKO 87
WANBLI OTA 75,101,144
WANBLI OYATE .. 40,68,69,204,230
WANBLI OYE 75,122,285
WANBLI PAHA 52
WANBLI PSISA 207
WANBLI ROTA 173
WANBLI SAPA 60
WANBLI SICA 117,280
WANBLI SITUPI 32,124,196
WANBLI SKA .... 44,140,154,208, ... 304,318
WANBLI SUN 29,36,87,99, 109,132,143,174,178,200,249,295,307
WANBLI SUN HOYAKA 101
WANBLI SUN KOYAKA 25
WANBLI SUN PEJUTA 76
WANBLI TAHEYA 119,179,282
WANBLI TAKEYA 13
WANBLI TIPI 75
WANBLI TOKAHE 33
WANBLI WAKAN 41,74,205
WANBLI WANKATUYA .... 45,52, ... 62,208,216

WANBLI WASTE ..... 38,46,113,115, .. 122,142,151,152,175,201,278,285, ... 306,315,316
WANBLI WATAKPE 85
WANBLI WICARCA 14,25,188
WANBLI WICASA 22,56,64,219
WANBLI WIN .... 16,20,70, ... 123,176,181,185
WANBLI WINYAN 68
WANBLI WIYAKE 193
WANBLI YATAPI ... 85,110,144,308
WANBLI YUHA 127,129,290,292
WANECA 88
WANGLEGLEGA 87
WANGLI SKA 109
WANGLI TOKEYA 197
WANHAL MATO 102
WANI AKU 213
WANIKIYA 282
WANITA 9,175
WANIYAKA 119
WANIYETU KTE 72,305
WANIYETU OPI 129
WANIYETU TAOPI 292
WANIYETU WAKEWA 284
WANIYETU WAKUWA ..... 109,121, ... 272
WANIYETU WICAKTE . 52,141,266
WANJIGJILA WICAKTE 72,234
WANJILA AGLI .... 68,125,225, ... 231,288
WANJILA ANGLI 62
WANJU .... 20,75,140,141,184, ... 294,304,305
WANJU STOLA 131,294
WANKAL ETONWA 275
WANKAL ETONWAN 111
WANKAL HIYU 66
WANKAL HO 134,297
WANKAL IYANKA 5,171
WANKAL KINYAN 249
WANKAL KIYAN 87
WANKAL KTE 36,154,200,318
WANKAL MATO .... 98,99,102, ... 260,261,263
WANKAL ON 228
WANKAL TI 56,219,318
WANKAL WICASA 93,255

Index

WANKATUYA NACA 45
WANKPAHI 23
WANOPA GLI 7
WANOPI 32
WANTAUYEYA 42
WANTE THEM PLENTY 103
WANTS HIM 85,100,125,262,
....288,321
WANTS IT 43,207
WANTS THEM PLENTY 265
WANTS TO BE A MAN 32,196
WANUPA 118
WANYECA 250
WANYU 238
WAOKA 150
WAOKIYA 214,266
WAOKIYE SNI 282
WAONJICA YUHA 121,218,284
WAONJINCA 123
WAONJINCA HUHA 55
WAONSILA 46,72,149,299,313
WAPAHA 38,39,57,72,73,112,
.. 123,126,202,203,220,221,235,236,
.... 242,275,289
WAPAHA CIQALA 113,276,277
WAPAHA ICU 67,230
WAPAHA LUTA 11,44,66,71,
.... 113,176,208,228,233
WAPAHA NUPA 22,126,189,289
WAPAHA OPI 69,232
WAPAHA SAPA 155,319
WAPAHA WICAKU 66,76,238
WAPARTAPI 68,231
WAPIN ORLATE 41
WAPIYA ITACAN 119,282
WAPIYELA 181
WAPOSTAN 120,283
WAPOSTON 120
WAPOTAPI 134
WAPSAKAPI 10,176
WAQUPI 154
WAR BONNET 39,57,72,73,112,
.... 123,203,220,235,236,242,275
 Conrad 38,202
 Kate 57,221
WAR EAGLE 128,291
WAR HORSE 111,275
WARAPYA 113

WARCA JI 226
WARCA ZI 63
WARD
 Elbridge 152,316
 Mattie 152
 Mattier 316
WARDEN, Oscar 204
WARPA TANKA 29,56,272
WARPATANKA 109
WARPE 49,213
WARPE GI 221
WARPE KASNA 285
WARPE KOYAKA 96,130,152,
.... 257,293,316
WARPE LUTA 260,287
WARPE MATO 37,201
WARPE SA 98,124,154,318
WARPE SNA 69
WARPE SNA WIN 122
WARPE TO 115,278
WARPE WAKAN 33
WARPE ZI 58
WARPIYA SNA WIN 38
WARRIOR 16,95,109,122,
.... 181,249,257,273,285
 Ellen 254
 Ellen C. H. 92
WARRIOR WOMAN 151,315
WASAKA 33,197
WASE SA 129
WASICAU WICAKTE 21
WASICU 250
WASICU CIQALA 103,156
WASICU HO 135,297
WASICU KTE 110,185,274
WASICU MATO 116,127,279,290
WASICU MAZA 178
WASICU OPI 68,231
WASICU OTA 116,279
WASICU PETA 130
WASICU TASUNKE 56,72,83,98,
.... 219,235,245,260
WASICU WAKAN 16
WASICU WANKATUYA 126,289
WASICU WAYANKAPA 173
WASICU WAYANKAPI 7
WASICU WAZA 13
WASICU WIN 224

Index

WASICU WINYAN .... 72,99,117, ... 119,139,217,235,282
WASICU WINYAN WASTE .. 20,185
WASIN WANICA 128,291
WASLIPA 5,171
WASMNIOMNI WICASA 272
WASNA 66,229
WASTE .... 57,73,90,112,221,236, ... 252,275
WASTE AGLI 41,45,205,208
WASTE HER GOOD SEAT 286
WASTE ICELA 214
WASTE ISAGA 58
WASTE KAGA 148,153,154,317,318
WASTE KARNIGA 296
WASTE KOYAKA 236
WASTE KTE 94
WASTE MNA 126,289
WASTE WICKTE 49
WASTELAKAPI 221
WASU .... 43,46,76,94,206, ... 209,239,256,271
Mary 94,256
WASU CUWIGNAKA 75
WASU ISNALA 29,193
WASU KIYAN 133,295
WASU LUTA 62,225
WASU MANI 123,285
WASU MATO 133,296
WASU MAZA 128,291
WASU PETA 90,266
WASU SINA 104
WASU SKA 113,276
WASU SNA 110
WASU SNA WIN 41,205
WASUNKE WASTE 88
WASUSNA WIN 273
WATAGA 64,125
WATAGE 227
WATAGE LUTA 130,293
WATAKPE 69,95,148,232,256
WATANWEYA 206
WATAPE KTE 139
WATAYEYA 10
WATE KOYAKA 74
WATER 19,144,184,308
Maggie 184
WATER COMES OUT 11,176

WATER MAN
  Charles 75
  Joseph 75
  William 238
  Willian 75
WATERMAN, Fannie 77,239
WAWAKPANSNI 15,180
WAWANGANKA 274
WAWAYANKA 110
WAWICASI 229
WAWIYOKIPIYA .. 119,132,282,294
WAWOHIYA 117
WAWOKIYA .... 9,19,41,50,93,98, ... 122,175,204,260,285,298
WAWOKIYE SNI 119
WAWOSLATA 123
WAWOSLATE 286
WAWOYUSPA 62
WAWUCASU 66
WAYAKA OYCESPAPI 320
WAYAKA OYUSPA 94
WAYAKA WASTE WIN 283
WAYAKAWASTE 79
WAYANK HIPE 37
WAYANK HIPI 111,175,274
WAYANK HOPI 201
WAYANK KTE 107,258
WAYANK NAJIN 12,31,43,178
WAYANK NAJINPI 125,288
WAYANKAPI 10,178,304,317
WAYANKNAJIN 271
WAYARTAKA 30,50,214
WAYARTHA 247
WAYATA 129
WAYONK KTE 96
WAYPEZI WIN 16
WAYURLATA 74,237
WAZI 114,115,277,278
WAZI APE 67,230
WAZI EYUTAN 39,203
WAZI KONATKE 214
WAZI KONTKE 50
WAZI LUTA 266
WAZI PTECELA 96,154,318
WAZI SA 60
WAZI WAKATUYA 90
WAZI WANKATUYA 90,252
WAZI ZINTAKLA 31

Index

WAZI ZINTKALA 38,195,201,202
WE EYALASE GLI 296
WE EYALASE KU 133
WEAGLURE 148
WEAR EAGLE FEATHER 25
WEARS EAGLE 36,69,200,232
WEARS EAGLE FEATHER 188
WEARS EAGLE FEATHERS 101
WEARS GOOD 74,236
WEARS GOOD CLOTHES 313
WEARS GOOD CLOTHS 149
WEARS HOLY 240
WEARS LEAF 96,130,152,257,
.... 293,316
WEARS PLENTY 74,236
WEARS SHOE, Jacob 78
WEARS THE BIRD 117,280
WEARS THE CLOUD 141,305
WEARS THE EAGLE 8,174
WEARS WHIRLWIND ... 34,134,144,
.... 197,296,308
WEARS WHITE 152,316
WEARS WHITE ROBE 52,216
WEASEL 9,50,51,55,66,76,
.. 108,124,126,175,214,215,229,239,
.... 272,280,287,289
   Herman S 222
WEASEL BEAR 60,120,223,283
   Mary 147,311
WEASEL BONNET 63,226
WEASEL WOMAN 116,279
WEBBER
   Emma 66,321
   Frank 157,321
   Julia 157,321
WECEGNA 130
WECEGNA INYAN 201
WECEGNA KU 246
WECOTI YUHA 110
WEGNUKE 214
WELLS
   Alma A 155,319
   Mark 155,320
   Patrick F 320
   Philip 155
   Philip F 319
   Philip W 155
   Philip, Jr 319

   Thomas H 155,319
WET MOCCASIN 76,239
WEYUKCAN 216
WHALEN
   James 5
   Jennie 5,171
   Julia 5
   Mary 5,171
   Nellie 5,171
   Richard 5,171
   Rosa 5
WHETSTONE 29,193
   Ida 34,198
   Joseph 141,305
   Nellie 34,214
   Thomas 142
   Thos 306
   William 141,305
WHIRLWIND 6,14,34,52,55,113,
... 147,172,179,198,217,219,276,309
   Cora B 229
   Joseph B 217
   Lucy 141
   Stella F 219
WHIRLWIND BEAR 101,110,130,
.... 263,273,292
WHIRLWIND HORSE 109,273
WHIRLWIND MAN 109,272
WHIRLWIND MOTHER 44,208
WHISTLER 109,116,273,279
   Carolus 146
   Charles 310
   Fannie 146
   Julia 310
   Julian 146
   Newman 146,310
   Sarah 146,310
WHITE 79,241
   Archie 6
   Emma 45,208
   Frank 45,208
   Frank, Jr 45,208
   Jessie 102,263
   Mary 45,208
   Robert 102,263
   Rosa Lee 22,186
   Susie 45,208
   William 55,219

Index

WHITE AROUND HEAD............116
WHITE ARROW......................49,213
WHITE BEAR ...99,115,116,260,278,
....279
    Alice...............................12,177
    Annie..............................99,260
    Jennie.............................12,177
    Lucy.......................................177
    Nellie..................................... 99
    Wm................................12,177
WHITE BEAR CLAW 129
WHITE BEAR CLAWS ...73,236,292
WHITE BEAVER..........9,69,175,232
WHITE BELLY......................38,202
    Frank....................................195
    Jessie..............................39,202
    Louise 39,202
    Willard............................33,197
    William 38
    Wm..202
WHITE BIRD..................21,121,284
    Leon................................21,185
WHITE BLANKET ...87,144,249,308
    Harry...................................144,309
    Kittie 144
WHITE BONE.......................144,308
    Lydia.....................................144
WHITE BOY 16,179
WHITE BULL 31,195
    Clara.....................................195
    Helena 31
    Richard............................31,195
WHITE BULL #2 34,198
WHITE BUTTER FLY............12,177
    Annie..................................... 12
WHITE CALF 74,114,123,278,286
WHITE CANE........................53,217
WHITE CLAY......................133,295
WHITE CLOUD 101,262
WHITE COW 8,11,14,17,24,49,55,
. 63,66,75,102,111,114,119,121,151,
.. 176,182,184,213,219,226,229,238,
..................263,264,274,277,284,315
    Millie.................................93,255
    Red..................................173,238
WHITE COW BLANKET.......87,249
WHITE COW BOY..................5,171
WHITE COW BULL.............127,290

WHITE COW CANE 122,285
WHITE COW CHIEF, Alice... 59,223
WHITE COW COMES OUT
.... 12,49,103,213
WHITE COW EAGLE.. 103,108,128,
.... 264,272,290
WHITE COW GOES OUT 74,236
WHITE COW MAN................ 38,202
WHITE COW OUT... 14,123,179,286
WHITE COW RIVER........... 139,303
    Nellie... 139
WHITE COW ROBE 110,274
WHITE COW TRIBE 71,233
WHITE COW WOMAN ... 21,54,126,
.... 185,217
WHITE COWN WOMAN 289
WHITE COYOTE 65,228
    Martha.......................................65
    Susie..228
WHITE CROW 101,146,310
WHITE CW COMES OUT 264
WHITE DAY 70,96,233,258
WHITE DEER......................... 13,179
    Conrad 86
    Conran 248
    Marget 86
    Margret 248
WHITE DOG 7,173
WHITE DRESS..................... 100,262
    Allen................................... 89,251
WHITE EAGLE 44,109,154,
.... 208,273,318
    Charles..................................... 140
    Chas... 304
WHITE ELK 36,65,124,194,
.... 200,287
    Ellis...37
    Lucy.................................... 36,200
    Maggie................................ 36,200
WHITE EYE LASH 75,238
WHITE EYES 57,101,120,221,
.... 262,283
    Addie................................ 19,184
    Daniel............................... 58,221
    Edith 253
    Ida... 183
    Jacob................................ 91,253
    Jessie 97,258

Index

WHITE FACE 35,45,99,111,
.... 143,199,208,261,274,308
   Ethel 147,311
   George..........................147,311
   John...........................199
   Lucy 147,311
   Mary........................99,261
   Sallie 99
   Sophia 99,261
   Thomas 199
   Thp,As 35
   Winnie........................147,311
WHITE FACE BULL 37,201,262
WHITE FACE FULL....................101
WHITE FACE OWNER................ 21
WHITE FACE WOMAN.......127,290
WHITE FACED WOMAN...........298
WHITE FEATHER.. 100,132,261,295
   Hattie......................100,261
WHITE FINGER NAIL............65,228
WHITE HAIL 113,276
WHITE HAIR............................108
WHITE HAWK 16,78,103,181,
...............................240,265
WHITE HEAD....................125,288
WHITE HORSE....... 11,24,51,77,103,
... 116,117,128,176,240,264,291,321
   John..........................72,234
   Katie.........................72,234
WHITE HORSE OWNER 57,65,
.....................................228,321
WHITE HORSE WOMAN..8,70,118,
.....................................174,232,281
WHITE HOUSE 14,179
WHITE KETTLE....................49,214
WHITE LANCE 99,261
   Frank 99,261
   Julia..........................99,261
WHITE MAGPIE 128,291
WHITE MAN, Kate....................250
WHITE MAN BEAR.............127,290
WHITE MAN VOICE 135,297
WHITE MEDICINE 53,217
WHITE MOUNTAIN 74,237
WHITE MOUSE.....................34,198
   Ella............................34,198
WHITE MULE 78,240
WHITE OWL.............76,118,239,281

   Ida................................ 118,281
WHITE PACKET....................... 100
WHITE PLUME.................. 71,234
WHITE POCKET........................262
WHITE PORCUPINE 100,262
WHITE RABBIT.. 6,142,172,278,306
   Annie................................ 6,172
   Julia.................................. 6,172
   Nellie................................. 142
WHITE ROCK 54,218
WHITE SILVER 115
WHITE TAIL 131,294
WHITE THUNDER 34,197
   Bessie 34,198
   Harrison 198
   Harry 34
WHITE WEASEL 53,217
WHITE WHIRLWIND 22,99,186,261
WHITE WING 23
WHITE WOLF............ 6,101,171,263
   Alice 7,173
   Charles................................. 173
   Herbert............................. 97,258
   John 7,173
   Rosa 263
   Sarah 97,258
   Wm 6,172
WHITE WOMAN ... 53,61,72,99,117,
..119,139,154,217,224,235,260,280,
.... 282,303,318
WI CIQALA.................... 52,108,216
WI HINAPA......................... 103,264
WI ISNA............................. 184,303
WI ITE...................................... 175
WI MATO 51,215
WICA KTERCIN 32
WICAKABLECA........................ 284
WICAKAONKA 125
WICAKARPA........................... 113
WICAKEZA............................. 229
WICAKICAGLUZA 134
WICAKICICUTE......................... 79
WICAKICIGLUZA.................... 297
WICAKICIKUTA 241
WICAKICO........................ 126,172
WICAKICU.............................. 255
WICAKIZA............................... 67
WICAKTE ... 127,133,289,290,

429

Index

..................................296,297
WICAKTE HI..........................94,256
WICAKU................................86,248
WICAKU SNI.........................85,247
WICAKUPI....................................133
WICAKUTE........90,113,218,252,276
WICAPAOSKICA.........................178
WICARPI.................14,54,59,91,139,
..................179,216,218,223,254,303
WICARPI CANKU..................57,221
WICARPI GI..................................283
WICARPI HINAPA........114,118,277,
....282
WICARPI HO WASTE...........57,221
WICARPI LUTA................10,56,112,
....176,220,276
WICARPI OTA......................131,294
WICARPI WAKAN......................274
WICARPI WANBLI..........14,98,144,
......................................146,308,310
WICARPI WANJILA..9,133,175,296
WICARPI WANKATUYA....56,151,
....219
WICARPI WIN......................114,278
WICARPI YAMNI.........145,309,310
WICARPI ZI..................................120
WICARPU LUTA.........................220
WICASA HANSKA...............147,311
WICASA ISNALA..........35,104,128,
....198,265,291
WICASA KTERCIN.....................196
WICASA PTECELA................21,185
WICASA SAKPE....................149,313
WICASA SAPA.............................296
WICASA WAKANL.....................255
WICASA YATAPI.........................279
WICASU YATAPI........................116
WICAYAJIPA....................53,64,266
WICAYAJIPE................................227
WICEGNA........................22,186,296
WICEGNA GLICA.........................84
WICEGNA GLICU.....5,117,122,171,
....189,280,285
WICEGNA HIYU...........................25
WICEGNA HYAYA....................101
WICEGNA IYAGA......................263
WICEGNA IYANKA.......37,114,277
WICINCALA............17,19,34,35,72,
.75,96,97,103,113,125,181,182,199,
........................234,258,259,264,283
Girl..237
WICINCALA HANSKA..............113
WICINCALA KU...........................65
WICINCALA WAKAN...............314
WICINCALA WASTE............88,274
WICINCALA YUSNA............75,237
WICITOKAB NAJI......................247
WICIYELA......14,54,86,175,218,249
WICIYELA WIN.5,14,38,65,98,110,
................123,171,179,228,274,286
WICIYELA WINYAN..........202,259
WICKTE....................................25,299
WICOKANYAN.............................19
WICOKANYAN HIYAYA..........183
WICOKUJE.............................74,237
WICONI...120
WICONI TERILA...................64,227
WICOTI MAZA...........................174
WICOTI YUHA............................274
WICRPI WANKATUYA.............315
WIGMUKE......................................49
WIITE...9
WIKAN....................................95,257
WIKAN ICIYAKASKAPI....125,287
WIKAN MAZA....................144,308
WIKAN NAPIN....................208,209
WIKAN PAPSAKA...........84,98,246
WIKAN WANAPIN.......................45
WIKAN YNSLOHAN..................235
WIKAN YUSLOHAN....................72
WILD, James................................104
WILD HORSE.........140,149,304,313
WILDE, James.............................265
WILLIAM...12
WILLIAMS
  Annie.................................148,312
  Cahrlotte...................................312
  Charlotte...................................148
  Jennie..313
  Lizzie.................................148,312
  Mary..................................148,312
  Maurice.............................148,313
  Minnie.......................................313
  Winnie.......................................148
WILSON
  Edna..298

430

Index

James John 298
Zona 298
WIN WASTE 222
WINARCA TAOPI 256
WINCAKABLECA 121
WINCALA 198
WINCINCALA 119
WINCINCALA HANSKA 276
WINCINCALA WAKAN 150
WINCINCALA WASTE 111,250
WIND BLANKET 58,298
WIND SHAWL 38,202
WING LITTLE CHIEF 99
WING WOMAN 54,218
WINKTE ONASO 131,294
WINOLA 114
WINONA 278
WINORCALA 32,94,101,117,280
WINORCALA CATKA WIN 125,288
WINORCALA CIQALA 110
WINORCALA SICA 5,20,171,184
WINORCALA WAKAN 20,185
WINULA 114,278
WINUNI WIN 220
WINURCALA 196
WINURCALA SICA 264,273
WINYA 215
WINYA CUWEGNAKA 219
WINYA HANSKA 218
WINYA HUSTE 216
WINYA ISNALA 229
WINYA LUTA 219
WINYA PTECELA 221
WINYA PUPUN 225
WINYA TANKA 242
WINYA WAKAN 218
WINYA WASTE 196,217,227
WINYA ZI 238
WINYAN 39
WINYAN CIQALA 9,58,109,
.... 120,175,272,284
WINYAN CIQALA WASTE 109,272
WINYAN CUWIGNAKA 15,55
WINYAN CUWIGNAKE 180
WINYAN GI 75,102,121,284,
.... 297,321
WINYAN HANSKA . 17,30,39,54,68,
. 70,72,83,108,182,194,203,231,232,
.... 235,245,272,313
WINYAN HASKA 149
WINYAN HUNKESNE 113
WINYAN HUNKESNI 20,129,131
WINYAN ISNALA 19,22,66,71,
.... 75,92,186,199,237
WINYAN ISTAGONGA 240
WINYAN KTE 93,116,255,257,
.... 279,315
WINYAN LUTA ... 13,23,55,111,133,
.... 179,187,273,275,296
WINYAN MANI 251
WINYAN MAZA 208
WINYAN NAWIZI 109
WINYAN NITE 150,314
WINYAN NUNI 57
WINYAN NUPA 22
WINYAN OCIN SICA 131,133
WINYAN ORLATE 125,288
WINYAN OTA 108,148,272,312
WINYAN OTA NAJIN 24
WINYAN PTECELA 58,116,279
WINYAN RANRAN 262
WINYAN RCAKA 108,291
WINYAN ROPA 96,102,141,264,281
WINYAN SA 109
WINYAN SAPA 109,155,273,319
WINYAN SICA 5,112,171,276
WINYAN SKA 53,61,154,280
WINYAN SUTA 15,252
WINYAN TANKA 5,11,17,41,68,92,
97,104,114,129,171,177,205,230,254,
258,277
WINYAN TERI 89
WINYAN TIPI 286
WINYAN TOKCA 272
WINYAN TOKECA 109
WINYAN TOPA 17
WINYAN WAKAN 9,55,78,112,
.... 139,151,240,262,276,303,315
WINYAN WAKAU 31
WINYAN WAKIN 103
WINYAN WARANICILA 50
WINYAN WASAKA 19,183
WINYAN WASTE 12,15,21,32,37,
40,43,44,53,59,65,71,72,89,107,108,
..117,118,124,143,186,200,204,206,
..207,233,234,251,258,271,280,287,

Index

..................................305,307
Good Woman..........................234
WINYAN WICAKTE.................151
WINYAN WINURCALA............262
WINYAN YAMNI 64,227
WINYAN ZI 55,76,85,134,237,
....247,263
WIPATA...................................120
WIPATA WIN.....................60,224
WIPATAPI 283
WIPI......................................67,230
WIPI SNI 139
WIPISNI 303
WIRCINCALA............................ 16
WISAKE...............................16,181
WISHED FOR 74
WISHED TO BE A CHIEF 57,221
WITANSNA ON 36
WITANSNAON 64
WITKE KTE..............................185
WITKO...............................134,297
WITKO KTE 21
WITKO WIN 172,221,271,279
WITKO WINLA...........6,58,108,109
WIYAKA..............51,62,87,225,249
WIYAKA GLESKA 121
WIYAKA LUTA 53,110,217,
...................................218,231,274
WIYAKA MATO FEATHER BEAR
....155
WIYAKA NUPA 18,68,183,231
WIYAKA OTA.......................75,237
WIYAKA PEGNAKA..............51,77
WIYAKA PEGNAKE 241
WIYAKA PEYNAKA.................... 51
WIYAKA RAKA......................... 74
WIYAKA RARA........................236
WIYAKA SA............................. 53
WIYAKA SAKPE 51,321
WIYAKA SAPA...................123,286
WIYAKA SKA........100,132,261,295
WIYAKA WANJILA 54,76,90,93,
...................................238,252,255
WIYAKA WASTE 15,127
WIYAKA WICASA 87,249
WIYAKA WIN......................116,280
WIYAKA ZI 107,271
WIYAKASA................................ 15

WIYAKE PEGNAKA........... 215,239
WIYUKCAN................................ 52
WIYUKCAN SNI 63
WIYUNKCA SNI 226
WIYURLOKA 108,272
WIZIPAN 15,180
WKAYANKA KTE 87
WKINYAN GI 101
WNIWANCA............................. 217
WOHITEKA 194
WOHITIKA................................. 30
WOJOSA..................................... 38
WOJUSA................................... 202
WOLF
    Georgiana W........................... 172
    Georgianna W............................. 6
    Johnson B 246
    Josephine F............................ 142
    Samuel................................... 217
    Susie B................................... 246
WOLF BEAR 128
WOLF EARS 9,130,175,293
WOLF SKIN BELT................ 99,260
WOLF SOLDIER 143,307
    Edward 143
    Josephin................................ 143
    Josephone 307
WOLOTA.................................. 119
WOLOTESA.............................. 282
WOMAN 39,215
    Susie Y H 238
WOMAN FACE..................... 9,175
WOMAN IN LIGHT 281
WOMAN IN SIGHT 118
WOMAN LODGE................. 123,286
WOMAN UNDER 125,288
WOMANS BACK................. 150,314
    Lizzie............................... 150,314
WOMANS DRESS 55
    Mary 15
WOMANS' DRESS..................... 219
    Mary 180
WONT GIVE UP 85,247
WOOD 290
WOOD LET 297
WOOD PECKER 79
WOOD WOMAN....................... 227
WOODEN GUN................... 116,279

Index

WOODEN LEG 134
WOODPECKER 241
WOODRUFF
   Julia O S 195
   Julia O. S. 31
WOOLY LEGGINS 265
WOPOTAPI 46,49,62,213,242,296
WOPTURA 83,85,103,140,246,
   248,304
WOPTURE 264
WOQUPI 318
WORDEN, Oscar 40
WORINYA 235,258
WORINYAN 66,73,96
WORKS FOR PEOPLE 134
WORKS PLENTY 148,312
WORLOKAPI SNI 130,293
WOSICA 121,284
WOSICA KUWA 125,287
WOSLA IYOTAKA 139
   Sitting Up 139
WOSLA NAJI 215
WOSLA NAJIN 15,39,180,186
WOSLA YANKA 303
WOUALA WASTE 289
WOUND
   Day B 307
   Ella B 307
WOUNDED 21,64,141,185,227,
   247,249
   Bessie 271
   Morris 271
WOUNDED (MORRIS) 107
WOUNDED ARROW, George 196
WOUNDED ARROWS, Geo 32
WOUNDED BEAR 42,206
   Susie 42,206
   Vina 42,198
WOUNDED BONNET 69,232
WOUNDED BY ENEMY 73,236
WOUNDED CLOSE 58,222
WOUNDED HEAD 101,262
   William 101
WOUNDED HORSE. 11,25,31,37,56,
   66,111,112,123,124,125,134,151,177,
   188,195,200,220,228,274,275,286,
   287,288,297,315
   Paul 151,315

WOUNDED IN WINTER 129,292
WOUNDED MORRIS 271
WOUNDED NOSE 112,276
WOUNDED TWICE 153
WOUNDED WHITE HORSE. 65,228
WOWAPA 133
WOWAPI 134,296,297
WOWAPI YUHA 188
WOWAPI YUKA 25
WOWASI YUHA 234
WOWASR YUHA 71
WPATAPI 225
WUJAKA LUTA 180
WUNGMANITU WAKAN 145
WUNIRCAKA SICA 102
WUWANPI 291
WYE WAKEN 239
WYNSTANPI 199
Y. HAIRED WOMAN, Susie 76
YAJUSKA 53
YAMNI 36,199
YAMNI APA 52,321
YAMNI HIYUICIYA 91
YAMNI IYUCIYA 253
YANKTON 54
   Albert 54,218
   Charles 86,249
   Creighton 54,218
   Dollie 86,249
   Edward 14,175
   Fat 86,249
   Helen 86,249
   John 86,249
   Julia 86,249
YANKTON WOMAN 5,14,38,65,98,
   ..110,123,171,179,202,228,259,274,
   286
YASLO 146
YATA 291
YATES, Angeline 32,196
YAWA 30,194
YEGO, Frank 40
YELLOS HAIR
   Emma 89
   Jessie 89
YELLOW 102,115,263
   Julia 74,236
   Lucy 73,236

Index

YELLOW BEAR 41,135,149,
.... 205,297,313
   James 29,193
YELLOW BIRD 11,101,131,
.... 241,262,293
   Alex 12
   Annie 11
   David 11
   Eddie 11
   Harry 11
   Josephine 11
   Lizzie 11
YELLOW BLANKET 33,73,
.... 197,236
YELLOW BOY 17,182
   Cahrles 17
   Charles 182
   George 17,181
   Grover 16,181
   Jessie 16,181
   Kittie 16,181
   Lucy 16,181
   Mamie 17,182
   Mary 17,182
   Robert 54,218
   Thomas 17,181
YELLOW BUG 63,321
YELLOW BULL
   Emma 100
   Etta 262
   James 102,263
   Jennie 102,253
   Julia 101
   Lizzie 102,263
   Susie 100
   Thomas 102,263
   Wilson 100,262
YELLOW BULL #2 101,263
YELLOW CANE 120,283
YELLOW CEDAR 51,98,215,259
   Adelin 35,199
YELLOW COW 128,291
YELLOW CRANE, Nettie 113,277
YELLOW DEER 152,316
YELLOW EAGLE, Mary 153,317
YELLOW EAR 124,287
YELLOW ELK 60,119,131,213,
.... 282,294

YELLOW EYES 14,38,58,61,63,
.... 101,202,222,224,263,321
YELLOW FEATHER 107,271
YELLOW FEET WOMAN 16
YELLOW GRASS 125,288
YELLOW HAIR .. 10,14,37,51,62,67,
.. 107,110,121,127,128,140,179,201,
...215,225,229,271,273,290,291,304
   Asa 108,272
   Daniel 145,309
YELLOW HAIR WOMAN 61,127,
.... 224,290
YELLOW HAIRED 36,199
YELLOW HAIRED WOMAN 76,89,
.... 238,251
YELLOW HAWK ... 146,150,311,314
   Emma 150,314
   Frank 150,314
   James 150,314
   John 150,319
   Julia 150,314
   Jullia 311
   Susie 314
YELLOW HEAD WOMAN . 110,273
YELLOW HORSE 10,125,144,
.... 175,189,287
   Joseph 46,88,250
   Lillian 10
YELLOW HORSE WOMAN . 60,223
YELLOW HORSES 54,218
YELLOW HOUSE 176
YELLOW KNIFE 39,203
YELLOW LANCE 145,309
YELLOW LEAF 58,221
YELLOW LODGE 43,207
YELLOW RING 234
YELLOW SHIELD
   Grace 50,214
   Henry 50,214
   Lame 50,214
   Millie 50,214
YELLOW SHIRT 77,239
YELLOW SPIDER 115,298
YELLOW SPOTTED 129,292
YELLOW STAR 120,283
YELLOW THUNDER 101,263
   Andrew 101
   Brave 101

Index

Joseph 99,260
Katie...................................99,260
Thomas 98
Thos 260
Wallace 99,260
Wm 99,260
YELLOW WOLF 8,50,174,214
   Albert...................................... 92
   Alex....................................83,245
   Alice...................................54,218
   Charles..................................... 50
   Chas..215
   Julia.....................................91,254
   Lucy 91,254
   Sally 91,254
   Susie... 46
YELLOW WOMAN.......55,75,76,85,
... 102,134,237,238,247,263,297,321
YELLOW WOOD 19,183
YELLOW YELLOW.............108,272
YELLS AT HIM 78,148,241
YELLS FOR HIM......................... 65
YELS AT HIM 312
YESIPI.................................42,206
YESLO..310
YOKATA HIYA.........................127
YOUNG
   Alfred................................154,318
   Amelia...............................154,318
   Edward..............................154,318
   Frank 25,154,188,318
   George...............................154,318
   Henry 154,318
   Ida...318
   Lizzie 154,318
   Louisa 25
   Louise 154,188,318
   Maggie 25,188
   Mary..................................154,318
   Philip.................................154,318
   Victor................................154,318
   Walter 25,188
   William 154,318
YOUNG BAD WOUND........143,307
YOUNG BEAR 119,141,282,305
   Joe... 40
YOUNG BEAR JOE................40,203
YOUNG BULL BEAR 104,265

YOUNG CALF 124,287
YOUNG CUB 56,219
YOUNG DEER, Mary............. 15,180
YOUNG EAGLE....... 34,125,197,288
YOUNG ELK..........................98,260
YOUNG MAN AFRAID....... 107,271
   Geo...................................... 107,271
   Jennie................................... 113,251
   Minnie 107
YOUNG SKUNK 113,276
YOUNG WOLF EARS 22,186
YUHA 6,14
YUHOMNI.................................. 38
YUSE 21
YUSELAKA 185
YUSINEYEWICAYA.................. 67
YUSINIYEYAPI..........................58
YUSINYEYAPI 222
YUSLUTA 101,152,316
YUSLUTAPI.............................262
YUTIMAHEL ICU..................... 181
YUYA KTE................................291
ZEZELA.....................................241
ZI 115,236
ZI AGLI.....................................238
ZICA................................. 120,283
ZINTAKALA 102
ZINTAKALA SAPA...................219
ZINTAKALA WASTE 253
ZINTAKALA ZI 101
ZINTKA TO.... 72,91,93,108,135,176
ZINTKAELA MAZA..................... 11
ZINTKAKA, Herbert J................ 188
ZINTKAKA NACA 99
ZINTKAKA NATA 43
ZINTKAKA NOPIN 26
ZINTKALA............... 12,63,115,123,
...131,173,177,226,263,278,286,294
ZINTKALA CIQALA.... 100,129,292
ZINTKALA GLESKA 22,186
ZINTKALA HINAPA............. 66,228
ZINTKALA HINSMA 7,112,173
ZINTKALA HINSNA.................276
ZINTKALA ISNALA 262
ZINTKALA KOYAKA.......... 117,280
ZINTKALA LUTA14,30,33,34,55,194,
.........197,204,215,219,223,231,271
ZINTKALA MATO 13,178

Index

ZINTKALA MAZA.............20,37,67, 177,185,201,229
ZINTKALA NACA 261
ZINTKALA NANPI 219
ZINTKALA NAP0IN 189
ZINTKALA NAPIN 55
ZINTKALA NATA 207
ZINTKALA OGLE................128,291
ZINTKALA ORANKO 9,175
ZINTKALA OTA 56,220
ZINTKALA PA 99,261
ZINTKALA SA 59,68,94,107
ZINTKALA SAPA 78,193,219,240
ZINTKALA SKA 21,121,185,284
ZINTKALA TO......11,42,55,206,219, 234,253,255,272,298
ZINTKALA WAKAN ...9,10,175,299
ZINTKALA WAMBLI..........258,280
ZINTKALA WANBLI.........16,17,96, 117,171,181,280
ZINTKALA WASTE.......12,55,59,73, 86,100,114,177,219,223,229,235,286
ZINTKALA WICASA.51,71,233,321
ZINTKALA WIMBLI 5
ZINTKALA ZI..............11,12,24,131, 188,262,293
ZINTKALA ZI, Herbert J.............. 24
ZINTKATO 91
ZINYKSLS LUTA.......................320
ZIZILA...241
ZNYA 257
ZNYA AHAKE 195
ZUYA 92,95,249,254
ZUYA CIQALA 9,92,174,254
ZUYA EHAKE............................. 31
ZUYA GLI.............................102,264
ZUYA ISNALA......................40,204
ZUYA ITACAN 281
ZUYA KTE....................................235
ZUYA TASUNKE.................111,275
ZUYA TERILA 71,95,234
ZUYA WANBLI 128,291
ZUYA WASTELAKA..................265
ZUYA WICAKTE 73,271,288
ZUYA WIN 151,315
ZUYA YESA........................109,122
ZUYAHIYAYA KTE...................107
ZUYALA......................181,273,285
ZUYAYA WICAKTE.................. 125
ZUYAYESA 16
ZUZECA GLESKA.....................248
ZUZECA OWIN 44,207

www.ingramcontent.com/pod-product-compliance
Lightning Source LLC
Chambersburg PA
CBHW020237030426
42336CB00010B/518